NEWS WRITING
AND REPORTING

NEWS WRITING AND REPORTING

THE COMPLETE GUIDE FOR TODAY'S JOURNALIST

Second Edition

Chip Scanlan

THE POYNTER INSTITUTE

Richard Craig

SAN JOSÉ STATE UNIVERSITY

New York   Oxford

OXFORD UNIVERSITY PRESS

Oxford University Press is a department of the University of Oxford.
It furthers the University's objective of excellence in research,
scholarship, and education by publishing worldwide.

Oxford   New York
Auckland   Cape Town   Dar es Salaam   Hong Kong   Karachi
Kuala Lumpur   Madrid   Melbourne   Mexico City   Nairobi
New Delhi   Shanghai   Taipei   Toronto

With offices in
Argentina   Austria   Brazil   Chile   Czech Republic   France   Greece
Guatemala   Hungary   Italy   Japan   Poland   Portugal   Singapore
South Korea   Switzerland   Thailand   Turkey   Ukraine   Vietnam

For titles covered by Section 112 of the US Higher Education
Opportunity Act, please visit www.oup.com/us/he for the
latest information about pricing and alternate formats.

Published by Oxford University Press
198 Madison Avenue, New York, New York 10016
http://www.oup.com

Oxford is a registered trademark of Oxford University Press.

Library of Congress Cataloging-in-Publication Data
Scanlan, Christopher.
    News Writing and Reporting: The Complete Guide for Today's Journalist / Christopher "Chip" Scanlan,
The Poynter Institute, Richard Craig, San José State University. — [Second edition].
        pages cm
    Includes bibliographical references and index.
    ISBN 978-0-19-518832-5 (main text : acid-free paper)
1. Reporters and reporting—Problems, exercises, etc. 2. Journalism—Authorship. I. Craig, Richard. II. Title.
    PN4781.N49 2014
    070.4'3—dc23
                                                                    2012047551

Printing number: 9 8 7 6 5 4 3 2 1

Printed in the United States of America
on acid-free paper

CONTENTS IN BRIEF

CONTENTS

CHAPTER 1   **NEWS JUDGMENT 1**

CHAPTER 2   **THE SIX-STEP PROCESS APPROACH TO REPORTING AND WRITING 23**

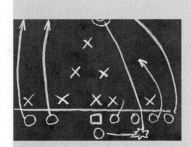

CHAPTER 3   THE COACHING WAY: TAKING CHARGE OF YOUR STORIES 53

CHAPTER 4   STORYTELLING VERSUS SPEED: DEADLINES IN THE 21ST CENTURY 75

CHAPTER 5   THE REPORTER'S TOOLBOX 99

CHAPTER 6   INTERVIEWING 121

CHAPTER 7   RESEARCH 143

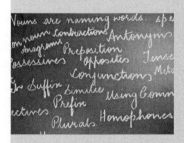

CHAPTER 8   GRAMMAR, LANGUAGE, STYLE: USING ACCURATE WORDS 169

CHAPTER 9 NUMBERS: USING ACCURATE FIGURES 189

CHAPTER 10 LEAD WRITING 217

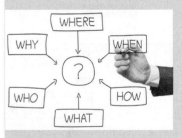

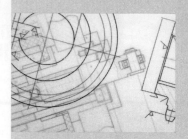

CHAPTER 17 FIRST ASSIGNMENTS 367

CHAPTER 18 BEATS: POLICE, COURTS, SPORTS, BUSINESS, EDUCATION AND MORE 393

CHAPTER 21 GETTING AND KEEPING A JOB 465

LIST OF *CLOSE-UP* ANNOTATED WRITING EXAMPLES

Most chapters in this textbook conclude with one or more examples of annotated journalistic writing. Additional examples can be found on the book's companion Web site. The entire list is shown here as a reference for the reader.

ABOUT THE AUTHORS

Christopher "Chip" Scanlan is a reporting, writing and editing faculty affiliate at The Poynter Institute in St. Petersburg, Florida. He was an award-winning journalist for two decades at newspapers in Connecticut and Delaware, and at the *Providence* (RI) *Journal*, the *St. Petersburg* (FL) *Times*, and Knight Ridder Newspapers' Washington Bureau. From 1994 to 2009, he directed writing programs at Poynter. He is a graduate of Fairfield University and the Columbia Graduate School of Journalism, where he taught as a visiting associate professor in 2009–2010. He has led reporting and writing workshops around the United States and in Europe and Asia. His nonfiction, essays and fiction have appeared in numerous publications. He is co-editor of *America's Best Newspaper Writing*, and edited seven editions of the *Best Newspaper Writing*. He lives in Florida with his wife, Katharine Fair.

Richard Craig is an associate professor at the School of Journalism and Mass Communications at San José State University. He earned a Ph.D. in 1995 from the Institute of Communications Research at the University of Illinois at Urbana-Champaign. He is the author of *Online Journalism: Reporting, Writing and Editing for New Media* (Cengage Learning, 2005). His journalistic work has appeared in *The New York Times*, *Atlanta Journal-Constitution*, *Miami Herald*, *San Jose* (CA) *Mercury News* and many other publications. He lives in California with his wife, Melissa.

PREFACE

If that job advertisement appeals to you, this book is designed to help you join the ranks of thousands of working journalists around the world. *News Writing and Reporting: The Complete Guide for Today's Journalist* furnishes students and instructors with the theoretical underpinnings and practical knowledge needed to master this exciting and challenging field.

To reach that goal, we have distilled the most critical information about the nature and practice of contemporary journalism and presented it in accessible and innovative ways. In each of the book's 21 chapters we explain the concepts that underlie news judgment, the wide range of reporting and writing challenges, including lead writing, interviewing, numeracy, beats, assignments, grammar, research, producing for multiple platforms, as well as ethical dilemmas and diverse coverage that reflects a multicultural world.

To bolster these concepts, the book gives instructors and students a wealth of practical information, drawn from interviews and examples from hundreds of print, broadcast and online journalists and the authors' long-standing experience as professional journalists and journalism instructors. By blending abstract principles with real-world applications, we believe that our approach will give instructors all the pedagogical tools they need to help students master a vital, demanding and exciting field, one that requires critical thinking, creativity and courage.

Journalism, above all, is a craft, one that can be mastered through study, time and practice, practice, practice. Our book aims to demystify the process of reporting and writing. Students will learn how journalists do their jobs—how they think, act and produce newsworthy stories. By applying its content, instructors can teach students how to report, interview, write and revise stories—not just for a grade—but to succeed as a journalist in the real world.

For many students, social media and the Web already dominate the way they communicate and absorb news—in 2010, a survey found that among 18- to 29 year-olds, nearly two-thirds said they got their news from the Internet. By necessity and belatedly, print and broadcast outlets have embraced online journalism and social media, making them critical components of the journalistic toolbox. Accordingly, this book places great emphasis on the marriage of technology and journalism and offers numerous opportunities for instructors to drive home the implications and applications the development demands.

It's no longer enough to know how to write an engaging story or conduct an effective interview. Reporters must now be as familiar with computer databases and search engines as they once were with reverse directory telephone books. Lines that were once clear are now blurred. Newspaper reporters take their own photos and videos and regularly appear on TV in their newsrooms. Broadcast journalists rewrite their scripts for stations' Web sites as their news organizations reach out to their audiences on the Internet.

The comprehensive lessons of this book are necessary for anyone interested in becoming a journalist, no matter whether the news is conveyed by computer, newspaper, radio or television broadcast. News gathering and distribution have changed, and will undoubtedly continue to do so, but at the heart of journalism remain the men and women who consider journalism not just a job but also a calling. They are driven to produce stories that reveal universal truths about the human condition. They ask penetrating questions, listen intently to the answers and apply critical analysis to the information they have collected. They are mindful of ethics and the threats of libel and invasion of privacy. In a free society, they play a vital role, equipping citizens with the knowledge they need: to decide whom to vote for, weigh in on government actions, assess opinion, and figure out which ball game or movie to watch. They recognize their job is to inform but to entertain their audiences as well. They write to serve their audiences, not themselves. And, as many are quick to tell you, they have a lot of fun doing it.

THREE PILLARS OF EXCELLENT JOURNALISM

No matter what the delivery medium, reporters must demonstrate the ability to collect information with speed and accuracy, analyze its significance, and then communicate the news with clarity, vigor and grace. That is this book's essential message for instructors and their students. Its foundation rests on three pillars of excellent journalism.

Process

Journalism, especially news writing, may seem magical or mystifying, especially to a beginner, but it's not magic. It's a process—a series of rational steps, actions and decisions that can be described, learned and repeated to produce consistently excellent work. By making the processes of reporting and writing for print, broadcast and online news transparent, instructors can help students learn not only how to cover a meeting or write a profile, but also what it's like to do these things to make a living, what's challenging and rewarding about such work, how to land a job and succeed in the workplace.

Coaching

Pioneered by the late Donald M. Murray, a Pulitzer Prize-winning journalist and teacher, and spread worldwide by Scanlan and his colleagues at The Poynter Institute, the coaching movement is based on another simple premise: The power to recognize a story's problems and the means to fix them lies with the writer. This doesn't remove instructors from the equation, as their response to student work remains a critical element in teaching. Coaching allows instructors to teach students that by asking good questions about their assignments, beginning journalists can uncover the solutions to challenges faced by every journalist. Just as process reveals how journalists work, coaching gives instructors a valuable approach to help students produce their best work and make them self-reliant and attractive to potential employers.

Storytelling

At a time when consumers of news are bombarded with information, *News Writing and Reporting: The Complete Guide for Today's Journalist* emphasizes the importance of storytelling as an effective means to connect with audiences and as a way for students to realize their own creative potential. Success in journalism requires more than a mastery of basics. Most successful reporters are able not only to get the facts, but also to present information in ways that are clear, accurate and on their best days, unforgettable.

Journalism instructors are the conduits through which experience, insight and teaching excellence produce today's journalists. Throughout years of intense research and writing, we have been guided by our commitment to produce a resource-rich text that we believe is the most complete and most accessible for them to accomplish their demanding and crucial role. We hope you find this to be the case and wish you the best of luck creating a new generation of excellent journalists.

HALLMARK FEATURES

While the job of news reporting focuses on how to write an effective story, there are many other aspects of the work that inform and guide this practice. We've endeavored to bring you a set of chapter features that underscore the basic writing and reporting instruction by providing great examples and advice from practicing journalists. These include:

- **Story examples.** Scores of concrete examples of reporting and writing that deconstruct and reveal journalistic practice, techniques and philosophy.

- **Quotations.** Every chapter includes testimony from professional journalists, educators and media thinkers that amplify the main text, provide historical perspective and deliver informative, inspirational commentary.
- **Journalists at Work.** These are illuminating and entertaining profiles of professional journalists detailing their methods drawn from interviews and analysis.
- **Quick Tips.** Instructors and students are hungry for practical advice needed to accomplish the myriad tasks journalists face. These checklists offer key points, relevant questions and directions related to a given section.
- **The Coaching Way.** This recurring box features concrete, specific advice and questions to help students take ultimate responsibility for their work and guide them toward excellent and ethical journalism.
- **Chapter conclusions.** Each chapter includes several features to help students remember, apply and understand the main ideas just presented. A list of *Key Terms* reminds the students about the most important terminology introduced in the chapter. Three to five critical thinking and practical *Exercises* enable students to apply what they've learned to real-world situations and give the instructor ideas for class discussion and assignments. Each chapter also includes *Readings*, a set of three to five annotated recommended readings that take students deeper into the subject matter.

NEW TO THIS EDITION

This edition of *News Writing and Reporting* has been significantly revised and adapted for today's college reader. The result is what we hope will be a new standard by which this course will be measured. Among the extensive revisions are the following:

- **New organization.** The order of the chapters has been revised to reflect an approach that begins with foundational skills (e.g., news judgment, the process approach to writing, meeting deadlines) before transitioning into chapters focused on specific skills (e.g., interviewing, research, working with numbers) and aspects of writing in a variety of media (e.g., writing leads, story forms, and writing for print, broadcast and online media).
- **Six new chapters.** The book now consists of 21 shorter chapters instead of 15 longer ones, making the material more easily adaptable to the course. Having six more chapters also allowed us to expand certain topics to provide more expert advice and examples on coaching, research, grammar and language, working with statistics, writing obituaries, and the challenges of covering disasters and conflicts.
- **New: Professionals' Roundtable.** Every chapter includes a box comprising transcripts of 64 interviews with industry insiders from print, broadcast and online outlets, journalism professors, and leading authors, using a question-and-answer-format and reflecting opinion and practice on every element of the journalism process.

- **New: Chip's Corner.** This recurring box provides varied and pertinent accounts of journalistic experience provided by co-author Scanlan based on nearly two decades as an award-winning print journalist, online writer and interactive instructor, and 15 years training students and professional journalists at The Poynter Institute, a leading source of continuing education for journalists. This feature also points instructors and students to relevant annotated Web resources, more than 100, spread through every chapter. These will be regularly updated on the companion Web site for the text.
- **New: Ethical Dilemmas**. This recurring box recounts situations that test the journalist's beliefs about the way to behave and to maximize truth telling and minimize harm. Framed as case studies based on the real world, these examples stimulate discussions that challenge one's critical thinking and the limits of journalistic fairness and accuracy.
- **New: Chapter Summary Guides.** Each chapter now concludes with an innovative summary feature that includes the main point of each chapter section plus an interpretive statement to help the student remember key takeaway points.
- **New: Close-Ups.** Stories from print, broadcast and online journalism are deconstructed to show the process of creating exemplary work. These 38 Close-Ups provide real-life examples of journalists' work, explaining and clarifying points that were made in the chapter. Many are included in the book following the chapter with which they are associated. A number of supplementary Close-Ups are also included as part of the complete set provided on the book's companion Web site.
- **New: Convergence Point features.** These annotated links are found in chapter margins and point the student to supplementary Web resources.
- **New: Key Terms and Glossary.** Key terms are highlighted in bold in the chapters. Definitions for each boldfaced terms can easily be found in the Glossary at the end of the book
- **Expanded discussion of journalistic practices across all media.** The book now provides foundational concepts for all media plus expanded discussion and examples for the three major outlets for journalism: print, broadcast and digital or online reporting.

ENSURING STUDENT SUCCESS

Oxford University Press offers instructors and students a comprehensive ancillary package for qualified adopters of *News Writing and Reporting*.

- **Student Workbook**
  - Written by co-author Richard Craig, this idea resource reinforces the lessons found in each chapter of the main text and provides a wealth of additional well-crafted exercises and activities to sharpen the skills your students need to be successful journalists. Our workbook can be packaged for FREE when purchased with the main text.

- **Companion Web site at www.oup.com/us/scanlan**
  - For instructors, this site includes the teaching tools described later, available for immediate download. Contact your local OUP sales representative for access.
  - For students, the companion Web site includes a number of study tools, including self-quizzes, Web links, a blog and Twitter account access to supplementary Close-Ups (see earlier).
- **Instructor's Resource Manual and PowerPoint-based Slides**
  - The Instructor's Resource Manual, written by co-author Richard Craig, available for download on the book's companion site, includes chapter objectives, a detailed chapter outline, lecture suggestions and activities, discussion questions, video resources and Web resources. Available at **www .oup.com/us/scanlan**.
  - **PowerPoint-based Slides**—Each chapter's slide deck includes a succinct chapter outline and incorporates relevant chapter graphics. Available for download at www.oup.com/us/scanlan.

To inquire about instructor resources, please contact your Oxford University Press sales representative at (800) 280-0208.

PACKAGING OPTIONS

Adopters of *News Writing and Reporting* can package *ANY* Oxford University Press book with the text for a 20 percent savings off the total package price. See our many trade and scholarly offerings at **www.oup.com**, then contact your local OUP sales representative to request a package ISBN. In addition, the following items can be packaged with the text for free:

- *Student Workbook*
- *Oxford Pocket World Atlas*, **Sixth Edition:** This full-color atlas is a handy reference for international relations/global politics students.
- **Very Short Introduction Series:** These very brief texts offer succinct introductions to a variety of topics. Titles include *Terrorism* by Townshend, *Globalization*, Second Edition, by Steger, and *Global Warming* by Maslin, among others.

ACKNOWLEDGMENTS

Every book represents more than the work of a single author or two. This edition was made possible by the generous assistance of hundreds of journalists, from beginners to prizewinners, journalism instructors and media thinkers. Specific contributors are listed on page xxx.

It is our privilege to acknowledge their contributions and no exaggeration to say it would not exist without their help. Our thanks to you all and apologies to anyone we inadvertently fail to include. We bear responsibility, of course, for any errors and omissions.

Numerous news organizations and their leaders, and institutions generously allowed us access to their staff, and permissions to reprint examples of their work. They include, but are not limited to: *Al Dia*, Miami; *The Anniston* (AL) *Star* (editor Bob Davis; The *Arkansas Democrat-Gazette* (deputy editor Frank Fellone; *Biloxi* (MS) *Sun Herald*; *Cedar Rapids* (IA) *Gazette*; *Charlotte* (NC) *Observer*; *Cleveland* (OH) *Plain Dealer*; *The Charleston* (WV) *Daily Mail* (editor Nanya Friend); *The Charleston* (SC) *Post and Courier* (editor Bill Hawkins); *The Columbus* (OH) *Dispatch* (editor Ben Marrison); *Dallas Morning News* (editor Bob Mong, Sunday and enterprise editor Thomas Huang); Digital First Media, New York City (director of community engagement and social media Steve Buttry); ESPN.com (editor-in-chief Rob King); The E.W. Scripps Co. (senior director, local operations TV, Scripps Digital Chip Mahaney); *Fort Myers* (FL) *News-Press*; Gannett Co.; *Harrisburg* (PA) *Patriot-News*; Lexington (KY) *Herald-Leader*; *Los Angeles Times*; *Miami Herald* (executive editor Mindy Marques); *Milwaukee Business Journal*; *Milwaukee Journal Sentinel* (senior vice president/editor Marty Kaiser); National Public Radio; *New Orleans Times-Picayune* (editor Jim Amoss); *Newark Star-Ledger* (editor Tom Curran); *Newsday*; *The New York Times*; Omaha (NE) *World Herald*; *Philadelphia Inquirer* (editor Bill Marimow); *Portland* (ME) *Press Herald* (executive editor Cliff Schechtman); *Revista Cálculo*, São Paulo, Brazil; *Roanoke* (VA) *Times* (editor Carole Tarrant, Meg Martin); *The Portland* (OR) *Oregonian* (editor Peter Bhatia); Sarasota Herald-Tribune (executive editor Mike Connelly); *South Florida Sun Sentinel*; *St. Cloud* (MN) *Times* (Rene Kaluza); St. Petersburg Police Department; *The Lance*, Evangel University (adviser Melinda Booze); TBO.com, Tampa, Florida; The Pew Research Center's Project for Excellence in Journalism; *Tacoma* (WA) *News Tribune* (executive editor Karen Peterson); Town of Southampton, Massachusetts; *Tulsa* (OK) *World* (executive editor Joe Worley); University of Houston-Victoria; U.S. Library of Congress; *USA Today*; *The Wall Street Journal*; *The Washington Post* (Peter Perl), *Washington* (DC) *Blade*; WFTS-TV, Tampa (general manager Rich Pegram); *Wichita* (KS) *Eagle* (editor Sherry Chisenhall; and the *Worcester* (MA) *Telegram and Gazette* (editor Leah Lamson).

A special thanks to executives and staff at four news companies who made it possible to use numerous examples of stellar journalism: Anders Gyllenhaal, vice president, news and Washington editor of The McClatchy Company and its predecessor,

Knight Ridder Newspapers; Tom Heslin, editor; Joel Rawson, former editor; Michael Delaney, managing editor/visuals of the *Providence* (RI) *Journal*; Neil Brown, editor of the *Tampa Bay Times*, formerly the *St. Petersburg Times*; Tom Curley, former president of The Associated Press; Cathy Gonzalez; and Gloria Sullivan.

We also thank Professor Lee B. Becker and colleagues at the University of Georgia, Grady College of Journalism and Mass Communication, who allowed us to use statistics from their Annual Survey of Journalism & Mass Communication Graduates.

Thanks also to the American Society of Newspaper Editors and the scores of writers whose award-winning stories and interviews have been celebrated in the *Best Newspaper Writing* for more than three decades.

Our book is illustrated by the superb work of numerous photographers, illustrators, designers and online staffs, especially the staff of The Associated Press, Sigrid Estrada, Sharyn L. Decker, Kathleen Flynn, Ivan Farkas, Gerald Grow, Claire Holt, Kenny Irby, Mike Lang, Delcia López, Jon Marcus, Bruce Moyer, Jim Stem, Javier Torres and Chris Zuppa. Maria Jaimes of The Poynter Institute helped secure many valuable photos.

Oxford University Press is a textbook writer's dream. Thanks to Peter Labella, Danielle Christensen for kickstarting the project, the indefatigable Caitlin Kaufman, Mark Haynes for his support and guidance, our gifted development editor Thom Holmes, who propelled the book in creative new directions and pushed us over the finish line, and production editor Barbara Mathieu.

Richard Craig: First and foremost, I'd like to thank Chip Scanlan for including me in this project. Being invited on board after the process was well under way could have been construed as a hostile takeover, but Chip couldn't have been more supportive. I'm pleased to have been given the opportunity to contribute to this book, and to have my contributions acknowledged as a co-author.

I would like to thank the faculty, staff and students in the School of Journalism and Mass Communications at San José State University for their support and input throughout this process. In particular, I'm grateful to Bob Rucker and Bill Briggs, directors of the school during this period, for understanding the amount of time and effort that goes into putting something like this together and working with me to adjust various duties accordingly.

I'd also like to thank my co-advisers on the *Spartan Daily* student news outlet, Mack Lundstrom, Jan Shaw and Kim Komenich, for their suggestions and support. I'm a far better journalist and teacher because of their influence, and my portion of this book is much richer and better informed because of the impact they've had on my life. My other faculty colleagues at SJSU have also contributed immensely, and I deeply appreciate all they've done for me over the years. I should also include the legendary Dwight Bentel as a great inspiration—a man who cared fiercely for journalism and worked to instill that love for the craft in generation after generation of students at SJSU. I aspire to have a fraction of the impact he had in his 103 years of life.

The Poynter Institute is another source of inspiration, and I'd like to thank all of the faculty and staff there for motivating me to evolve as a teacher, journalist and thinker. All of us who have visited and participated in workshops there owe Poynter a great debt of gratitude for continuing to fight the good fight in spite of the monumental changes in the journalism industry.

Most important, my wife Melissa has been patient beyond all reason as I've holed up for weeks and months at a time working on chapters. With all this writing, she probably sees the back of my head more than the front, but she's supported me all the way. One of these days we'll both have time to enjoy each other's company for more than a day or two at a time.

Chip Scanlan: I'd like to especially express my gratitude to my co-author Richard Craig. He contributed his expertise in the world of digital journalism by writing the Online Writing and Content Production chapter, contributing throughout the book and including important new voices to the conversation about journalism. Richard's willingness to join a project at a late stage and his generous and deft revisions have made this a much stronger book. Would that every collaboration be so successful.

I would like to thank the faculty and staff of The Poynter Institute in St. Petersburg, Florida (http://about.poynter.org/about-us/faculty-staff), which has continued to be my professional home for nearly two decades and is a constant source of inspiration and support. I'm especially grateful to Bobbi Alsina, Trevor Brown, Stephen Buckley, Roy Peter Clark, Aly Colón, Karen B. Dunlap, Rick Edmonds, Gregory Favre, Jill Geisler, Nico Guerrero, Bob Haiman, Kathy Holmes, Maria Jaimes, Christine Martin, Bill Mitchell, Julie Moos, Steve Myers, the late Jim Naughton, Dave Pierson, the late Paul Pohlman, Vidisha Priyanka, Jeff Saffan, Nafi Schwanzer, Omar Schwanzer, David Shedden, Jennette Smith, Maryanne Sobocinski, Roy Taravella, Al Tompkins, Mallary Tenore, Latishia Williams and Keith Woods.

Great thanks also to Jennifer Dronkers, Casey Frechette, Vanessa Goodrum, Vicki Krueger and Leslie Passante of Poynter's News University, who support my interactive learning work with creativity and boundless enthusiasm. A special note of gratitude to newsu.org's creator, Howard Finberg, who let me in on the ground floor.

I owe an enormous debt to the thousands of journalists and students I have worked with and taught at Poynter and in newsrooms around the world. Their lessons are too numerous to count.

I owe my mentors, Melvin Mencher of the Graduate School of Journalism at Columbia University, and the late Donald M. Murray, my dear friend who first taught me the process approach and the coaching way, more than I can say; their fingerprints are all over this book. Special thanks to Dr. Antoinette M. Falk and my chiropractor Dr. Rod Jones.

The faith, love and support of my mother, the late Alice S. Harreys, and my five brothers and sisters and their families have sustained me.

Our daughters, Caitlin, Michaela, and Lianna, her husband Klein Grimes, and Henry, our first grandchild, bring joy and meaning to my life. It is the lucky writer who has a spouse who writes and edits as well as mine. I am a writer today because Kathy Fair believes in me.

MANUSCRIPT REVIEWERS

We have greatly benefited from the perceptive comments and suggestions of the many talented scholars and instructors who reviewed the previous edition of this book and its revised manuscript. Their insight and suggestions contributed immensely to the published work.

Sandra A. Banisky
University of Maryland,
College Park

Robert Berkman
Keuka College

Carolyn S. Carlson
Kennesaw State University

Susan Dawson-O'Brien
Rose State College

Keith Forrest
Atlantic Cape Community College

Kym Fox
Texas State University-San Marcos

Christopher Frear
Sussex County Community College

Bruce Garrison
University of Miami

Victoria Goff
University of Wisconsin-Green Bay

Cheryl Heckler
Miami University

Teresa Heinz Housel
Hope College

Dale M. Jenkins
Virginia Polytechnic Institute &
State University

Valerie Kasper
Saint Leo University

Sharon Kobritz
Husson University

Gordon D. "Mac" McKerral
Western Kentucky University

Marian Meyers
Georgia State University

Matt Nesvisky
Kutztown University of
Pennsylvania

Selene Phillips
University of Louisville

Kathryn Quigley
Rowan University

Jerry Renaud
University of Nebraska-Lincoln

Vicki Rishling
University of Idaho

Leslie Rubinkowski
University of Pittsburgh

Scoobie Ryan
University of Kentucky

Bob Schaller
Texas Tech University

Ivana Segvic-Boudreaux
University of Texas at Arlington

Cathy Stablein
College of DuPage

Carl Sessions Stepp
University of Maryland

Susan Thompson
University of Montevallo

Christine Tracy
Eastern Michigan University

Chris Waddle
Jacksonville State University

Lisa Crawford Watson
California State University
Monterey Bay/*Monterey County
Herald*

Nancy Whitmore
Butler University

Melanie Wilderman
Northwestern Oklahoma State
University

CONTRIBUTORS

The following journalists and journalism educators contributed material to this book.
(Some affiliations and titles may have changed since publication.)

Kevin Acee
San Diego (CA) *Union-Tribune*

Jill Agostino
The New York Times

Dan Ashley
ABC7 News, San Francisco

Cary Aspinwall
Tulsa (OK) *World*

Alana Baranick
Elyria (OH) *Chronicle-Telegram*

The late Craig Basse
St. Petersburg Times

Kevin Benz
News 8, Austin, TX

Howard Berkes
National Public Radio

Sandra Combs-Birdiett
Michigan State University

Erika Bolstad
Miami Herald

Greg Borowski
Milwaukee Journal-Sentinel

Mark Briggs
KING5, Seattle

Trevor Brown
Former dean, Indiana University
School of Journalism

Harold Bubil
Sarasota (FL) *Herald-Tribune*

Stephen Buckley
The Poynter Institute

Jane Briggs Bunting
Michigan State University

Steve Buttry
Digital First Media

Erin Caddell
Former reporter, *The Keene* (NH)
Sentinel

Sheila Callahan
Freelance writer, Warsaw, Poland

Gerald M. Carbone
Freelance author and journalist

Rebecca Catalanello
Former reporter, *Tampa Bay Times*

Aly Colón
NBC News

Paul Conley
Consultant

Lane DeGregory
Tampa Bay Times

Brady Dennis
The Washington Post

Steve Doig
Arizona State University

Karen Brown Dunlap
The Poynter Institute

Lillian R. Dunlap
The Poynter Institute

Richard Dymond
Bradenton (FL) *Herald*

Peter Elbow
Professor emeritus, University of
Massachusetts, Amherst

Wendy Farmer
ABC11TV Raleigh

Samuel Fifer
SNR Denton

Stan Finger
Wichita (KS) *Eagle*

Karin Fischer
The Chronicle of Higher Education

David Folkenflik
National Public Radio

Margalit Fox
The New York Times

Mark Fritz
Author

Ken Fuson
Former reporter, *Des Moines* (IA)
Register

Sara Ganim
CNN

Jill Geisler
The Poynter Institute

Kristen Gelineau
The Associated Press

Elizabeth Gibson
Columbus (OH) *Dispatch*

Dave Greenslit
Worcester (MA) *Telegram
and Gazette*

Frank Greve
Former reporter, Knight Ridder
Newspapers

Joe Grimm
AsktheRecruiter.com

Gerald Grow
Florida A&M University

Bryan Gruley
Former professor, *The Wall Street Journal*

Mark Hamilton
Kwantlen Polytechnic University, Vancouver, BC

Don Hammack
Biloxi (MS) *Sun Herald*

Lee Hancock
Former reporter, *Dallas Morning News*

Eben Harrell
Former reporter, Time, Inc.

Jane Harrigan
Former professor of journalism, University of New Hampshire

Meg Heckman
Nackey S. Loeb School of Communications, Manchester, New Hampshire

Macarena Hernandez
University of Houston-Victoria, Texas

Dennis Hoey
Portland Press Herald

Thomas Huang
Dallas Morning News

Boyd Huppert
KARE-Minneapolis

Jack Hart
Former editor, *The* (Portland OR) *Oregonian*

Brandie Jefferson
The Providence Journal

John Jackson
Former online editor, roanoke.com

Alan Johnson
Columbus (OH) *Dispatch*

David Cay Johnston
Reuters.com

Rene Kaluza
St. Cloud (MN) *Times*

Louise Kiernan
Northwestern University

Peter King
CBS News

Rob King
ESPN.com

Vicki Krueger
News University, The Poynter Institute

Michael Kruse
Tampa Bay Times

Dion Lefler and Jeannine Koranda
The Wichita (KS) *Eagle*

Elizabeth Leland
The Charlotte (NC) *Observer*

Teresa Leonard
Raleigh (NC) *News and Observer*

Scott Libin
Internet Broadcasting, Minneapolis-St. Paul

Sue LoTempio
Buffalo (NY) *News*

Mack Lundstrom
Wired Journalists; faculty, San Jose State University

Macollvie Jean-François
Former reporter, *South Florida Sun-Sentinel*

David Maraniss
The Washington Post

Ann Marimow
The Washington Post

Bill Marimow
The Philadelphia Inquirer

Kevin McGrath
The Wichita (KS) *Eagle*

Michele McLellan
Former editor, *The* (Portland, OR) *Oregonian*

Molly McMillin
The Wichita (KS) *Eagle*

Margo Melnicove
National Public Radio

Victor Merina
www.reznetnews.org/

Philip Meyer
University of North Carolina-Chapel Hill

Karen Miller and Lewis Kamb
Tacoma (WA) *News Tribune*

Arlene Morgan
Columbia University Graduate School of Journalism

Carolyn Mungo
KRIV-Houston

Steve Myers
The Poynter Institute

Naka Nathaniel
The New York Times

Mirta Ojito
The New York Times

Erik Olson
The Centralia (WA) *Chronicle*

Karen Peterson
Tacoma (WA) *News Tribune*

O. Ricardo Pimentel
San Antonio News-Express

Deborah Potter
NewsLab

Amanda Punshon
Kwantlen Polytechnic University,
Vancouver, BC

John Raess
The Associated Press

Martha Raddatz
ABC News

John Raess
The Associated Press

Bertram Rantin
The (Columbia, SC) *State*

Michael Regal
Erie (PA) *Times-News*

Mahawish "Misha" Rezvi
Freelance multimedia journalist,
Pakistan

Maggie Rivas-Rodriguez
University of Texas, Austin

Preston Rudie
WTSP-Tampa

Michaela Saunders
Former reporter, *Omaha* (NE)
World-Herald

John Sawatsky
ESPN

Jan Schaffer
J-Lab: The Institute for Interactive
Journalism

Matt Schudel
The Washington Post

Jeremy Schwartz
Reporting and writing fellow,
The Poynter Institute

John Silcox
Reporting and writing fellow,
The Poynter Institute

Craig Silverman
regretterror.com

Marcio Simões
Revista Cálculo, São Paulo, Brazil

Roger Simon
Politico.com

Joseph A. Slobodzian and John P.
Martin
The Philadelphia (PA) *Inquirer*

Sreenath Sreenivasan
Columbia University Graduate
School of Journalism

Mark Story
Lexington (KY) *Herald-Leader*

Mallary Tenore
The Poynter Institute

Tommy Tomlinson
Former reporter, *The Charlotte*
(NC) *Observer*

Greg Toppo
USA Today

Susan Trausch
Author and former reporter,
The Boston Globe

Doris N. Truong
The Washington Post

Vidisha Priyanka
The Poynter Institute

Chris Vanderveen
KUSA-Denver

David Von Drehle
Time, Inc.

Lori Waldon
WISN 12 Milwaukee

Mike Weinstein
Former editor, *The Charlotte* (NC)
Observer

Roy Wenzl
The Wichita (KS) *Eagle*

Charles Wilson
The Associated Press

Jan Winburn
CNN.com

Keith Woods
National Public Radio

Ben Yagoda
University of Delaware

NEWS JUDGMENT

WHAT IS NEWS? For veteran journalists, news decisions are reflexive. For beginners, developing news judgment—the ability to recognize what makes an event, issue or trend "news"—takes time, experience, and a firm grasp of the qualities that make something newsworthy. In this chapter, we will help you develop the skill of news judgment so you can identify news with speed, confidence and accuracy.

Which of the following quotations from notable journalists best answers the question, "What is news?"

• Verified information that is relevant to public life.—Ellen Hume
• What protrudes from the ordinary.—Walter Lippmann
• The departure from normal.—Leo Rosten
• What I say it is.—David Brinkley

The answer is any or all of these, depending entirely on the context of the event or issue you're covering. Reporters and editors must determine if an event or piece of information is **newsworthy**—interesting or compelling enough to a target audience to justify reporting.

WHAT IS NEWS?

For beginning reporters, learning how to recognize news is the first hurdle that must be cleared. A survey of 200 news writing professors identified the following questions about news as stumbling blocks for their students:

• How do I decide what's news?
• What sources do I use?
• Of the information I collect, what is relevant and what should be highlighted or left out?

Answering these questions requires **news judgment**, which is the ability to recognize and communicate information of interest and importance to an audience. Developing that skill takes time, experience, patience, lots of practice and some mistakes. Once you become practiced at deciding what makes something newsworthy, it will become a reflex action.

So let's get to it:

Consider these two scenarios. Which one is more newsworthy?

1. A motorist pulling out of a parking space at the local mall backed into a parked car, denting the rear fender and breaking a taillight. No one was hurt, and the drivers exchanged information about their insurance companies.

2. Another motorist ran a stop sign at a busy intersection and collided with a school bus carrying the high school band to a concert. Three students were taken to the hospital, one with serious injuries. Police arrested the motorist and charged him with drunk driving.

Later in the chapter, we'll return to this example to explore why the school bus accident is more newsworthy than the fender bender at the mall.

The morning budget meeting at the *Sarasota (FL) Herald-Tribune* draws editors and producers from the newspaper, online site and cable news channel who decide what stories its converged newsroom should cover that day.

THREE BASIC ELEMENTS OF NEWS

News Is Timely

As the word implies, news is "new." It's the vote that just occurred, the game that just ended, the war that just broke out, the verdict just in. Often, it's a fact, event or issue that provides what journalists call the "peg," or reason, to publish or broadcast news right now. It's what you didn't know when you last turned on the television or went online. It's the freshest angle, the latest word, the most recent development.

News Is Important

News matters. As the world becomes more complex, the job of the journalist broadens to include dealing with those complexities, and answering the questions that arise from them. It's not enough to simply report events; reporters have a responsibility to know their audiences well enough to make them understand why this information matters—or should—in their lives. News is important as well because it affects more people than those merely involved in an incident or event.

News Is Interesting

News is anything that makes a reader declare, "OMG!" In essence, reporters are explorers, on the hunt for stories that will be compelling enough to grab readers' attention amid today's constant avalanche of information.

Given the two vehicle accidents mentioned earlier, why was the second accident more newsworthy than the first? The short answer is that it includes the three essential

❝ News is, in effect, what is on a society's mind. Has a bill been passed? Has anyone been hurt? Is a star in love? Through the news, groups of people glance at aspects of the world around them. Which of the infinite number of possible new occurrences these groups are able to see, and which they choose to look at, will help determine their politics and their philosophies. **❞**

—MITCHELL STEPHENS, AUTHOR, *A HISTORY OF NEWS*

When Hurricane Katrina devastated New Orleans in 2005, displaced residents like Angela Perkins begged for help from the government, which was accused of responding too slowly to their desperate needs, a newsworthy development that became a top story.

CONVERGENCE POINT ⚡

Can Journalists Truly Be Objective?

"The Fading Mystique of an Objective Press" takes you behind the scenes to see how news judgments are made, and the flawed reasoning and reliance on dubious newsworthy elements that lie behind many of these journalistic decisions.

Find this link on the companion Web site at **www.oup.com/us/scanlan.**

elements of news. Let's take a closer look at the thinking that a journalist does when considering whether something is news:

1. *Is it timely?* Yes. The news happened today, so readers likely don't know about it unless they witnessed the accident or had friends or family involved.
2. *Is it important?* Yes. An accident at a busy intersection that injured children is a serious incident that a whole community should know about, not merely those who have a personal connection. Drunk driving is a serious social problem.
3. *Is it interesting?* There's nothing unusual about a fender bender in a mall parking lot. On the other hand, school buses are not normally involved in serious accidents. The fact that the students were band members on their way to a concert—an exciting occasion—lends the story an added poignancy.

DEVELOPING NEWS JUDGMENT AND CRITICAL THINKING SKILLS

Using these criteria to determine newsworthiness seems easy enough. Yet the elements of a story that might draw in readers aren't always immediately apparent. A burglary in a Washington, D.C., office building doesn't sound exciting on the surface, but when it's at the national offices of a political party *and* the suspects are connected to the White House, you've got yourself a big story—the Watergate scandal that toppled the presidency of Richard M. Nixon.

Veteran reporters often recognize the makings of a good story by seeking connections and asking smart questions that seek the root causes behind events. While no one expects a student reporter to have finely tuned news instincts right away, basic

QUICK Tips ⏱ INGREDIENTS OF NEWSWORTHINESS

Not everyone agrees on what makes one story more newsworthy than another, but there are certain story elements that tend to attract and maintain audience interest. Any of these factors can make a story draw attention, but if two or more are present, it could easily dominate headlines.

Here are some characteristics that tend to make stories stand out among the rest:

■ The **exceptional**: It's out of the ordinary (a farmer grows a pepper that resembles the president of the United States)

■ **Proximity**: It happens nearby, involves a person or group with local ties (a fire in a neighboring state isn't locally relevant, unless it's particularly devastating or a local resident dies in it)

ESPN.com, the online partner of the successful sports channel, earns much of its success by focusing on celebrity athletes.

■ **Impact**: It affects lots of people (Hurricane Katrina, the terrorist attacks on Sept. 11, 2001)

■ **Prominence**: It involves someone famous (public officials, sports and entertainment figures)

■ **Conflict** (or action): Fights that pit individuals or groups against each other (wars, disasters, political campaigns, residents fighting city hall)

■ **Human interest**: Focuses on the human condition or appeals to emotions (children, animals, hard-luck stories)▼

curiosity often unearths interesting elements in otherwise mundane stories. Is this important to a certain type of people? Why or why not?

Good reporters are often said to have a "nose for news." Thinking effectively and imaginatively about news requires developing "news senses," which help you better understand what makes something newsworthy. They include:

- *Audience.* The reporter knows the **audience**—the core group of readers or viewers—for whom the story is written and what it cares about, whether it's an increase in property taxes or the score of the championship game.
- *Relevance.* News matters to people because it is **relevant**—it is information they need or believe is important, if not vital, to their daily lives.

- *Drama*. News is action. Journalists cover wars, skirmishes, infighting, battles for supremacy and legislation, struggles for civil rights and protection from pollution. The news media are criticized for focusing too much on violent conflicts—crime, war, political intrigues and social unrest. They must also focus attention on lesser-noticed but equally dramatic struggles that go on every day.
- *People*. Names make news. People are the lifeblood of journalism. Sociologist Herbert Gans found that less than 10 percent of all the stories he studied were about abstractions, objects and animals. News is primarily about people, Gans observed, what they say and do.

Once they've built these instincts, reporters don't need to ask, "What's the news?" They know it when they see it.

Dramatic events, such as the terrorist bombings of the World Trade Center in New York City on Sept. 11, 2001, command the attention of journalists who recognize the newsworthiness of tumultuous events. News consumers complain, often rightly, that the media focus too much on negative news, but war, emergencies and disasters compel attention.

News focuses on people and the media are especially attracted to stories about celebrities. A parade of news media satellite trucks lines up outside Neverland Ranch for a memorial service for the late pop singer Michael Jackson in July 2009.

So how do you, a beginning reporter, develop the reflexive skill of the veteran? How do you learn to pick out the relevant, interesting, important information from the mountains of data in your notebook?

The only way to give yourself a head start is to begin thinking critically from the first moment, even if it's something you know nothing about.

Questions are your best tool. Ask yourself:
- What's the news here?
- Why does this story matter to my audience?
- Is it timely?
- Is it important?
- What's the point of the story?
- Why is it worth telling?
- Who does it affect and how?
- What does it say about life, about the world, about the times we live in?

Critical thinking is the act of drawing inferences or conclusions from a body of information, and is vital to reporters. As a journalist, you will be bombarded with messages and points of view by politicians, advertisers, activists and many others—this candidate is the best for the job, my plan for school reform is the smartest, our device is the most state-of-the-art on the market. The list goes on and on. Your job is to help your readers and viewers sort out the conflicting claims and gain a better understanding.

AUDIO, VIDEO AND CITIZEN JOURNALISM

With the Web's limitless capacity, news organizations can enhance their reports with audio and video files, digital photos, interactive animation and outside links to primary sources, including databases and government reports.

For decades, most news reporting was limited to credentialed staffers. Once reporters established journalism as a profession in the first decade or two of the 20th century, there were lines drawn between those who produced news, those who were the subject of news coverage and those who consumed news. With the occasional exception (bystander accounts or film footage) these roles remained unchanged until roughly 2000, when significant numbers of so-called citizen journalists started to emerge.

In the past decade or so, **citizen journalism** has produced numerous examples of newsworthy content that received national and international attention. Major media coverage of the Sept. 11, 2001, terrorist attacks included amateur footage from many sources, as did coverage of the Indian Ocean tsunamis in 2004, Hurricane Katrina in 2005 and camera phone videos of Syrian army shelling of defenseless villagers in 2012. In April 2007, when a student at Virginia Tech killed 32 people and injured many more, the first video reports came from a student's cell phone camera.

CONVERGENCE POINT

Misjudging Newsworthiness

In "News Judgment and Jihad," journalist and author Mark Bowden (*Black Hawk Down*) explains why terrorists love journalism's flawed sense of newsworthiness and how the news media play right into their hands.

Find this link on the companion Web site at **www.oup.com/us/ scanlan.**

66 Too often journalism students are afraid to provide critical analysis. They interpret it as negative and it scares the hell out of them. It's easier to just report the facts, ma'am, steering clear of the kind of analysis that might offend. 99

—DAVID HAYES, JOURNALIST

SEE CLOSE-UP, P. 17: BASIC NEWS STORY

Citizen journalism may broaden a news organization's reach, but it can pose ethical challenges by encouraging overreliance on anonymous sources, links to questionable Web sites or blogs with hidden agendas and unsubstantiated stories. These should be verified by professional journalists to ensure accuracy.

WHERE NEWS COMES FROM, WHERE TO FIND IT

The front page of a newspaper or magazine, a splash screen that introduces a Web site or the lead stories on a television news broadcast give clear signals about some common sources of news:

- Events
- Official records and announcements
- News conferences
- Press releases
- Decisions and other actions by government bodies: courts, police, legislatures from the local to the federal level

But good journalism means moving beyond the traditional sentinel posts for news. Reporters have to go where news is happening—from a suburban neighborhood plagued by a series of daytime burglaries to the housing project where families struggle with poverty and its stigma.

All too often, student journalists think they have gotten the story when they read a tweet or a Facebook post. Others may settle for information from a press release or press conference or an interview with one official. In contrast, the best reporters interview a whole hierarchy of people, from the president to the janitor.

When news happens, packs of journalists descend on the scene, such as this encounter between Denver Broncos quarterback Peyton Manning (18) and New England Patriots quarterback Tom Brady (12) at the end of a game on October 7, 2012, in Foxborough, Massachusetts.

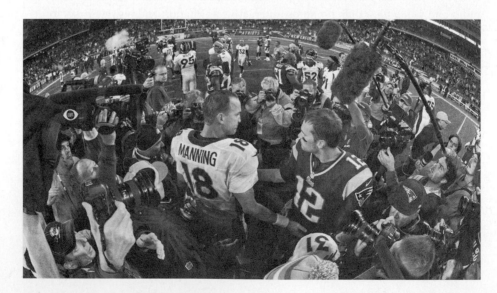

The police department and other public agencies remain major news sources. As a reporter, you will need to monitor your beats: checking the daily police and fire logs, checking the agendas of meetings, keeping track of next actions such as arrests, autopsy reports and impact of decisions for follow-up stories, talking with city officials and police officers, people on the street, kids in playgrounds, parents in the supermarket parking lot, the elderly, minorities, workers, and crime victims. Reporters train a radar screen on their world, sweeping it constantly for the blips that signal a change that people need to know about.

Once you've found the news, how do you connect your audience to it? By asking the questions that place the news in context so your readers understand why they're being told certain information. The best stories relate a specific incident or event to the larger community. They take the extra step to help readers understand what impact a news event or development might have on their lives.

POSITIVE VERSUS NEGATIVE NEWS: STRIKING A BALANCE

"News is never good; it's always bad things," a young North Carolina woman told the *Raleigh* (NC) *News & Observer* when it surveyed community attitudes toward the news media. We all know what she means. But consider this: What if the front page of the paper today reported that 800 flights took off safely from a local airport and landed without incident?

Throughout the Iraq War, journalists were criticized for focusing almost exclusively on violence, death and destruction, while ignoring positive signs of change, including the development of a legislature that included common enemies Sunnis, Shiites and Kurds; rebuilding efforts and sections of Iraq where peace reigned.

One of the essential characteristics of news is that it focuses on the exceptional, the out-of-the-ordinary. That's why "Dog Bites Man" isn't news, but "Man Bites Dog" is. Yes, journalists focus attention on the painful realities of the human condition. But that's also a positive sign. Most things go right, and it's only when they go wrong that the news media sit up and take notice.

Syndicated columnist William Raspberry regularly took his colleagues to task for the steady and unrelenting diet of bad news. He countered that approach with a simple method. Whenever he visited a town he asked for examples of success stories, such as neighborhood crime watches that were working, young people who were succeeding, the performance of excellent teachers. Typically, he found, journalists were hard-pressed to come up with any good news.

But everything is relative, and news—like beauty—is in the eyes of the beholder.

When the Supreme Court upheld a ban on partial-birth abortions in April 2007, it was welcome news for abortion opponents but bad news for those supporting abortion rights. A balanced news story reflects that duality. News is not just a record of society's failures. It must also be a record of its achievements.

SEE CLOSE-UP, P. 19: STRIKING THE BALANCE BETWEEN GOOD AND BAD NEWS

CONVERGENCE POINT ⚡

*News Judgment
and Photos*

The Associated Press
Managing Editors
Association presents a
series of dramatic and
sometimes gruesome
images and asks readers
if they'd publish the
photos and to explain their
decisions.

*Find this link on the
companion Web site at*
**www.oup.com/us/
scanlan.**

Some news organizations strive to counter bad news with positive developments. After a beloved babysitter was found dead in her home, apparently the victim of her estranged husband who was charged with murder, the *Bradenton* (FL) *Herald* wrote about a memorial service celebrating her life.

NEW NEWS: THE IMPACT OF AUDIENCE, CULTURE AND TECHNOLOGY

Knowing Your Audience

Audiences today can choose from a seemingly endless buffet of print, broadcast and online sources for news and information, many of which specialize in areas reflecting the interest of specific groups. The challenge for the 21st-century journalist is how to analyze audiences and to gather and present news and information that will attract and hold the attention of people chronically confronted with increasing choices.

How can—and should—journalists think about audiences? You can think of them the way market researchers do, as audiences identified by their demographics—age, gender, race/ethnicity, income, education, occupation, location. Trevor R. Brown, the former longtime dean of Indiana University's journalism school, advised his students to think of their audiences in light of the varying roles people play in their personal lives:

- As citizens who are part of "we, the people" on the one hand and as individuals with certain unalienable rights on the other, with responsibilities and interests, needs and wants, as they seek to enjoy their liberty and pursue happiness.
- As individuals who are children, siblings, parents, lovers, friends, workers, bosses, volunteers, consumers, fans, gamblers, investors and on and on.

Talk to your friends, neighbors, classmates and others in your community or on your beat. Ask them what stories news organizations miss, what stories need to be told, what stories move and instruct them.

Ethical Dilemmas WHO DESERVES NEWS COVERAGE?

You're a police reporter for a community newspaper. Thumbing through the day's incident reports you come across an arrest for drunken driving. It's rare for your newspaper to report such offenses unless a fatality is involved, and even then it's usually relegated to an inside page, although the paper has been running editorials about the perils of drunk driving. You realize that the person charged is your paper's publisher. Is it news? Do you tell your editor about it? What do you think your paper should do? If the editor decides to publish the story, where should it appear? ▶

"People resent journalists not because we fail to understand, but because they think we don't try," says Judy Bolch, an editor at the *Raleigh News & Observer*. "Instead of news hounds anxious to learn it all, we're seen as lazy know-it-alls. They don't mind if we ask questions; they do object when we assume the answers."

How Audience Affects Content

When Schwinn Bicycle Co. filed for bankruptcy, it was a national story covered by newspapers and television news. In the four examples published Oct. 9, 1992, that follow, each news organization reflects, unconsciously or not, its view of what constitutes news and the audience it wants to reach. News, as these classic examples demonstrate, is in the eye of the reporter and editors, who then transfer that vision to their audience. The numbers in brackets indicate the newsworthy elements of interest to particular audiences, and are keyed to the accompanying discussion that follows each example.

1. Schwinn Bicycle Seeks Chapter 11 as Talks With Banks Break Off

❯EXAMPLE Chicago — Schwinn Bicycle Co. said it [1] filed a voluntary petition for relief under Chapter 11 of the U.S. Bankruptcy Code. [2] The bicycle maker, [3] founded in 1895, [4] said the filing was prompted by a breakdown of negotiations with banks over payment of about $75 million in debts. [5]

—The Wall Street Journal

The Wall Street Journal aims at a national business and financial audience. Attributing the news to the company [1] reflects the need for confidence in the paper's reporting, especially of a development that will affect stocks, markets and investors. The use of legal jargon [2] assumes readers understand the process of bankruptcy. The second sentence describes the business, [3] provides a date that places the story in historical context, and answers a top-of-mind question about cause and financial information. [4–5]

2. Schwinn Files for Chapter 11

❯EXAMPLE Bicycle maker Schwinn, [1] squeezed by competitors and poor management, [2] is rolling [3] into Chapter 11 bankruptcy-court protection. [4]

—USA Today

USA Today attracts a national audience of time-pressed travelers who want their news fast and lively. In 15 words, it identifies and describes the company [1] sums up causes [2] before it uses word-play [3], leading to the most salient information—the bankruptcy. The style [4] blends legalese with a breezy, accessible word choice that makes the story easy to understand.

3. Schwinn Bicycle Files

❯EXAMPLE Under pressure from its creditors, [1] the Schwinn Bicycle Company, [2] America's oldest bicycle manufacturer, [3] said yesterday [4] that it had filed for protection under Chapter 11 of the United States Bankruptcy Code. [5]

—The New York Times

> ❝Who writes the stories matters. . . . When minorities and women and people who have known poverty or misfortune first-hand are authors of news as well as its readers, the social world represented in the news expands and changes.❞
>
> —MICHAEL SCHUDSON, JOURNALISM HISTORIAN

The New York Times views itself as the nation's paper of record. Its approach is more stylish than the *The Wall Street Journal*. It begins with causation [1], identifies the company [2] and describes the business in historical context [3], provides attribution that is a cautious cornerstone of news, as well as a focus on timeliness [4] ending with legalese [5] all contributing to the density of the lead.

4. Schwinn: It Was the Wheel Thing

❯**EXAMPLE** Schwinn Bicycle Co. filed for bankruptcy yesterday, [1] thereby tolling the knell for the era when boys were boys and bikes were bikes [2] and nobody went pedaling around wearing stupid little helmets. [3]

—The Washington Post

> **66** As information explodes, so does confusion. The world, even the community, changes faster and faster, with layer upon layer of social issues, technology, relationships, and stresses. The newspaper can be a translator, making sense of the increasingly complex world. This competitive advantage can be realized as newspapers improve their writing and cultural literacy. On every major story, a reporting and editing point should be: What might a reader see as unclear in this situation? How can this story clarify it? **99**
>
> —FRANK DENTON, *WISCONSIN STATE JOURNAL*

The Washington Post published the story in its feature section, where style, voice and an arch tone places news as information in a social context. It reports the news and date, [1] but the writer is given latitude to add a note of nostalgia [2] tinged with sarcasm about overregulation of what used to be childhood fun. [3] Even the headline pun distinctly sets the story apart from the play-it-straight headlines employed by the three other papers.

News in the Information Age

Everybody's talking these days about how technology is changing the news business. But that's not new. More than 150 years ago, the invention of the telegraph changed the way news was reported, spawning the so-called objective style of reporting that replaced partisan politics with factual coverage of government and business affairs.

What has changed is the public's access to news. In the 1800s you needed a telegraph key, poles and wires, and knowledge of Morse code to get instant access to news. Once the World Wide Web appeared in the early 1990s, a computer and a network connection were all that was needed. Cable and satellite television offer 24-hour channels and even the live (and sometimes raw and unedited) feed of network news operations. More recently, all you need is a smartphone to receive headlines, stories and tweet updates.

"Yesterday's editors decided what was important and made it so," says Doug Clifton, former executive editor of *The Plain Dealer* in Cleveland, Ohio. "Today the consumer is at least an equal arbiter of what is important."

Despite their increased power, consumers will still need someone to filter news and help make it coherent. Even fierce critics of the media such as the late Michael Crichton—the novelist who created *Jurassic Park* and who predicted in 1993 that the media would be a dinosaur, extinct—have seen a role for reporters in the future. "They will give me high-quality information," Crichton said.

Technology changes news, the nature of it, how we get it, how we present it. Whether the task is writing for the newspaper, the television or the computer screen, the process of thinking about news remains the same. The tools the reporter may use to collect and deliver the information will undoubtedly differ. Today's reporters are equipped with smartphones, video cameras and other devices to capture and deliver news electronically. Still, no matter what the tool, the reporter has to figure out what the news is.

PROFESSIONALS' ROUNDTABLE

WHAT'S THE NEWS?

News, a journalist once said, "is what I say it is!" In the 2000s, however, news is no longer defined solely by journalists. This panel reflects on the characteristics of news. Their answers illustrate the impact of technology, audience and a sea change in who defines news and how.

Participants

MAGGIE RIVAS-RODRIGUEZ, associate professor, University of Texas, Austin.

JAN SCHAFFER, director of J-Lab: The Institute for Interactive Journalism

JOEL RAWSON, former executive editor, *Providence* (RI) *Journal*

> ### What is your definition of news?

Rivas-Rodriguez: Journalism should be about informing citizens and residents about issues affecting them, so that they might make informed decisions.

Schaffer: A process of imparting information that can meet any number of benchmarks—not necessarily all at once:

- Surprise or enlighten
- Hold public officials accountable
- Help people navigate their daily work and personal lives
- Give people opportunities to participate in news gathering, analysis, reaction—or in addressing subjects at issue

Rawson: Whatever is going on in an area that interests you. Crime, politics, sports, the Iraq war, quilting, the latest advances in outboard motors.

> ### What makes something newsworthy?

Rawson: Timeliness mostly, but also that which you did not know about previously. The *Toledo* (OH) *Blade* won a Pulitzer for reporting on atrocities committed 35 years earlier in Vietnam.

> ### What is not news?

Schaffer: Parroting quotes because someone important said them. It's not reporting lies just because a high official said them. It's not requiring a conflict or semblance of a conflict before it's decreed to be a "story."

> ### Who decides what's news?

Rawson: The reader or viewer.

> ### Who should decide what's news?

Rivas-Rodriguez: This is where diversity comes in. It's vital to have a pulse on various parts of the community—not just the "leaders," self-appointed, or elected. Journalists should be observing all the time, they're on 24-7. When they go to church or a PTA meeting, they hear something that becomes a big news story.

Schaffer: Pandora's box has opened. Anyone can decide what's news and report it, write it and deliver it as well.

"We now have too much information to rationally deal with on a daily basis," says Beth Agnew in an essay titled "Writing for the Third Millennium." "We need skilled professional help to turn that information into the currency of the next millennium—knowledge."

SUMMARY GUIDE   NEWS JUDGMENT

WHAT IS NEWS?

News is a constantly updatable record of change that has relevance to an audience.

What to Remember →   News has many definitions. To discover its essential meaning takes time, experience and practice. In the age of social media, journalists also participate with their audience in discovering what matters.

THREE BASIC ELEMENTS OF NEWS

The three basic elements that make a worthy news story are timeliness, importance and interest level.

What to Remember →   Journalists must decide if an event, person or issue justifies the effort of reporting and writing based on these criteria. These aren't the only characteristics—they also include the unusual, human interest and conflict—but they are the most crucial.

DEVELOPING NEWS JUDGMENT AND CRITICAL THINKING SKILLS

Thinking effectively and imaginatively about news requires developing "news senses," which help you better understand what makes something newsworthy.

What to Remember →   Critical thinking is the foundation of good news judgment. Journalists must sort through a vast stream of information, messages and points of view. In so doing, the journalist will draw inferences and make conclusions that weigh the validity of sources to provide audiences with accurate stories that make sense of disparate knowledge and viewpoints.

AUDIO, VIDEO AND CITIZEN JOURNALISM

The seemingly limitless availability of Web audio and video resources as well as the contribution of citizen journalists offer today's news organization many ways to supplement and extend the reach of its news stories.

What to Remember → Citizen journalism may broaden a news organization's reach, but it can pose ethical challenges by encouraging overreliance on anonymous or questionable sources. The careful professional journalist must vet such sources to ensure accuracy.

WHERE NEWS COMES FROM, WHERE TO FIND IT

News comes from a multitude of sources, including events, people, releases and decisions made by official bodies.

What to Remember → Official sources remain vital, but the best journalists go to where news is happening and by reaching out to uncommon sources that are rarely tapped. They place their reporting in context, making the sources and impact of news relevant to their audience.

POSITIVE VERSUS NEGATIVE NEWS: STRIKING A BALANCE

There's no doubt that journalists focus on disturbing aspects of human events, whether war or political battles.

What to Remember → News should be more of a record of failures and disasters. It should also highlight achievements and positive developments.

NEW NEWS: THE IMPACT OF AUDIENCE, CULTURE AND TECHNOLOGY

Journalism must reflect the needs of different audiences and the profound impact of a diverse, multicultural society.

What to Remember → Journalists have the responsibility to make sense of information spread by a technological revolution that has transformed the speed and quantity of news delivery. They filter the meaningless and using critical thinking provide not only information but knowledge vital to the workings of a democratic society.

KEY TERMS

audience, p. 5
citizen journalism, p. 7
conflict, p. 5
critical thinking, p. 7

exceptional, p. 5
human interest, p. 5
impact, p. 5
news judgment, p. 2

newsworthy, p. 2
prominence, p. 5
proximity, p. 5
relevant, p. 5

EXERCISES

1. Write a 250- to 500-word essay recounting your personal experience with news. When was the first time you were aware of news, either by reading a newspaper or magazine or by hearing a news, online or radio report? What was your reaction?

2. Write your own definition of news, in no more than 25 words, based on your personal experience as a consumer of news and your personal sense of mission as an aspiring journalist.

3. Examine the front page of your local newspaper (it can be the campus newspaper, a local weekly or daily paper), watch the evening news (record it if you have access to a machine or make a list of the stories) or study an Internet news site. Review the contents, and decide what made the stories newsworthy. Try to figure out where the story originated. In a press release? A news conference? An action by a government body? An emergency? Study the story carefully, and identify the sources of the information contained in it.

4. Make a survey of your news landscape. Identify and itemize all the news sources you're exposed to in a single day from radio, online, television, newspapers and magazines. Which ones are your favorites and why? Which do you consider the most reliable or unreliable? What kind of news are you most interested in?

5. Evaluate the contents of a single newspaper, news or online source, and list the stories under the headings "Bad News" and "Good News." Which side has more stories? Consider the justification for each choice.

READINGS

Adam, G. Stuart, and Clark, Roy Peter. *Journalism: The Democratic Craft.* **New York: Oxford University Press, 2006.**
An anthology of seminal essays that addresses the definition and nature of news and the ways that journalists marshal facts and evidence.

Fuller, Jack. *News Values: Ideas for an Information Age.* **Chicago: University of Chicago Press, 1996.**
A veteran Pulitzer Prize–winning editor offers a challenging prescription for effective journalism in our information saturated society: Journalists must provide stories that make sense of events and issues and present knowledge as well as facts—and, on occasion, even wisdom.

Paul, Richard, and Elder, Linda. *Critical Thinking: Tools for Taking Charge of Your Learning and Your Life.* **Upper Saddle River, NJ: Prentice Hall, 2011.**
A useful introduction to concepts of critical thinking and analysis, this guide will help students strengthen news judgment skills by learning how to think for themselves.

Schudson, Michael. *Discovering the News: A Social History of American Newspapers.* **New York: Basic Books, 1978.**
A prominent media historian examines the changing definitions of news over two centuries. He offers a valuable historical perspective to beginners striving to determine what makes something newsworthy.

Stephens, Mitchell. *A History of News.* **Fort Worth, TX: Harcourt Brace, 1998.**
An authoritative survey that explains how the definition of news has evolved over time to meet social and economic imperatives.

BASIC NEWS STORY

The majority of news stories are written in a familiar format that is based on sound reporting principles, smooth organization and clear and accurate style. The standard form, illustrated as follows, uses the inverted pyramid, which organizes facts in descending order of importance. The information is attributed to named sources. Subject-verb-object sentences, using short words, active verbs and definite objects, are the foundation of the effective news stories.

MIDWAY AIRPORT BACK IN BUSINESS AFTER POWER OUTAGE

By The Associated Press
June 29, 2012

CHICAGO (AP) — Planes are flying again at Chicago's Midway International Airport after a nearly four-hour shutdown caused by a lack of runway lights.

Chicago Aviation Department spokeswoman Karen Pride says a problem with the lighting equipment caused the outage at about 8:30 p.m. Thursday. Pride says 85 flights were canceled or diverted while the airport was closed.

Flights resumed early Friday, and airlines are working to get back on schedule.

The outage didn't affect the terminals, so passengers aboard planes when the runways went dark were returned to the terminals and taken off the planes.

Commonwealth Edison spokeswoman Martha Swaney says the outage wasn't caused by a ComEd power failure, but she says the utility's crews worked with Midway's personnel to help them get their equipment working again.

The opening paragraph, known as the lead, focuses on the most newsworthy elements reflecting the values of news judgment and how they underlie the composition of a basic news story. It addresses the "what," "where," "how" and why," and, in the dateline, "when." It would have been easy to include the day, but it can be addressed later in the story. The lead is a concise 21-word sentence that, like all the sentences in the story, follows the preferred subject-verb-construction. It easily meets the rule that a lead should take no longer than a single breath to read aloud.

The second paragraph immediately presents a credible authoritative source to support the assertion made in the lead. The reporter has obtained a spokeswoman's name, which enhances transparency. The time element missing in the lead is introduced. She elaborates how the shutdown occurred and addresses a likely reader's question: What was the impact? The sizable number of affected planes in a major airport hub amplifies the story's newsworthiness. Notice how each sentence contains a complete thought.

Inverted pyramid stories may also use time as an organizing principle. Chronology makes the stories easier to understand, as the paragraph shows. Readers learn when flights resumed. The clause addresses the question "What next?"

Paragraph four effectively addresses another newsworthy element. For years, passengers have complained about being stranded on runways during storms. The reader learns that this has been avoided. Effective stories anticipate audience questions.

A second source, again named, addresses in the fifth and final paragraph why the outage happened. Journalists may not be able to answer every question in a news story; in this instance, the cause of the malfunction wasn't addressed. Stories should never rely on a single source.

SUMMARY

This is a story that could occur in any community with an airport and could easily be assigned to a new journalist. It is worth studying because of what it reveals about reporting, organization and journalistic style. It illustrates how timeliness, interest and importance dictate newsworthiness.

It's a brief, five-paragraph story that illustrates the qualities of the basic news story and the impact of news judgment. It uses the inverted pyramid form that presents information in descending order of newsworthiness. It is based on two interviews. In the hands of a skilled journalist it could have been completed in 30–60 minutes including interviews and writing. It is accurate, clearly written and supported by facts. Notice the lack of opinion.

It was apparently reported exclusively by telephone, a decision based on the determination by editors of how many resources should be directed to a newsworthy event. It could have been enhanced by on-scene reporting with interviews with passengers affected by the shutdown. The most effective stories put a human face on the news.

STRIKING THE BALANCE BETWEEN GOOD AND BAD NEWS

News consumers and media critics complain that journalists devote too much attention to the negative aspects of life. Journalists counter that criticism by pointing out that bad news—wars, accidents, natural disasters—are news events that merit coverage if society is to be fully informed. Reporting bad news remains a painful but necessary journalistic obligation. But there are countless opportunities to strike a balance. The *Bradenton* (FL) *Herald* accomplished this goal in a story about the aftermath of a murder that focused on the positive by writing about a memorial service celebrating the life of a murder victim and the impact she had on others.

CROWD OF 200 GATHERS IN BRADENTON TO LIGHT CANDLES AND CELEBRATE SLAIN WOMAN

By Richard Dymond — rdymond@bradenton.com
May 19, 2012

MANATEE – All you need to know about Alisa Hartmann you could learn by looking inside her car.

Her older model four-door Honda, still parked in the driveway of her Harvard Avenue home, has two child safety seats in the back even though her children, Dylan, 15, and Bryce, 8, have long outgrown them.

The reason the seats are there is that Alisa, according to many, was one of Manatee County's most dedicated, skilled and passionate babysitters.

"Raise your hands if Alisa was your babysitter," Teresa Kinlaw said, addressing a crowd of approximately 200, many from Bayshore Gardens, who packed the driveway of the Hartmann home for a candlelight vigil and celebration of life Friday.

The lead draws in the reader by summarizing the victim with a significant detail. To create suspense, the reporter holds off answering a question: What was inside Alisa Hartmann's car?

Good stories raise questions and then respond to reader interest by immediately addressing them. The paragraph provides a wealth of factual information—a description of her car, its location—but focuses on the child safety seats. The details are specific. It's not just a car, but "an older model four-door Honda," making it possible for readers to visualize the scene. Good news writing is concrete and specific. It sustains suspense by leaving unanswered the obvious questions, such as why the seats were there even though her two children were too old to need them. News features such as this one employ the tools of narrative such as significant details, setting and drama.

Once again, the reporter answers the question. Effective journalists try hard not to frustrate readers by withholding significant information for too long. At this point the story still does not address the fact that she was murdered. Instead, it describes her as an important figure in the community. This serves as a so-called nut graf, a device used to readers know why they are reading the story.

Smart journalists listen carefully for narrative quotes, which place the reader in the scene, rather than summary quotes spoken to a reporter. This completes the nut graf by placing the quote in context. The reader learns that a large crowd of neighbors has gathered for a candlelit vigil in Hartmann's driveway. That fact returns the reader to the information in the lead, explaining why the reference to her car is significant. The reporter holds off explaining the purpose of the vigil. The time frame introduces chronology, which can help readers process disparate facts.

About 50 hands shot up in honor of Alisa, who ran a daycare from her home, the same place she was found dead Tuesday.

Alisa's husband, Nicholas Hartmann, who many in the crowd said they have known for decades and have held in high regard, was being held without bond at the Manatee County jail Friday and is charged with Alisa's murder.

Funeral plans are still in the works, Kinlaw said.

At 7 p.m. people gathered, cried and hugged. They later lit candles and signed a poster for the family.

One person wrote on the poster, "Never forget your smile. Always loved your contagious laugh! Thank you for your friendship."

"This is the epitome of tragedy," said Jennifer Hogan, who graduated with Alisa at Bayshore High in 1991. "Alisa was nothing short of amazing and Nick was just as great. This has come out of nowhere.

"So many questions," Hogan continued. "Not for one moment would I think Nick would harm his wife. He adored her."

Like many, Hogan said she came to the vigil not to find answers, but to just be with others who loved Alisa.

Many who spoke described a woman with an unforgettable laugh who was devoted to her family, friends and especially the children placed in her care. "The sun rose in 1973 and set in 2012," said lay minister Lavelle Bing, in describing life now for those who were touched by Alisa.

This paragraph serves two purposes: It supports Hartmann's status as a popular babysitter and daycare provider and for the first time reveals the purpose of the vigil. This story clearly follows up on previous reporting of her death. News organizations can find opportunities for positive news in follow-up stories.

Until now, the story has focused on Hartmann's exemplary life. The time has come to report that she was murdered, allegedly by her husband. The paragraph provides information about his status. Note that the reporter is careful to say he has been charged with murder rather than writing he murdered his wife. This makes the story libel-proof and acknowledges the presumption of innocence that the legal system affords criminal suspects. The story also effectively conveys the distress and puzzlement among friends over the man's alleged actions.

Even feature stories weave in newsworthy information. This paragraph addresses a question that may be on readers' minds.

The story resumes a chronological approach, signaled by the specific time of day. Mindful of space requirements, it now summarizes the action. Notice the action verbs that use active tense— "gathered, cried, hugged, lit, signed." These are the engine of effective narrative. They are also economical. Short sentences slow down action to heighten impact.

Journalists look for a variety of documentation in their reporting. The reporter uses the opportunity to record what one person wrote on the poster to provide more details about Alisa Hartmann.

For the first time, the story quotes a source directly. The paragraph addresses an obvious question: Why did the murder occur? Notice how the journalist stays out of the story. Writing "No one knows why the murder occurred" would be hyperbole and express an opinion that has no place in a news story. Opinions are reserved for editorials, commentary and news analyses.

The paragraph uses the same source to repeat the purpose of the gathering and to explain their motives for attending. Too many sources can clutter a story and confuse readers.

This paragraph melds the good and bad news that lie at the heart of this story. The reporter chooses an evocative quote to express the loss felt by the victim's friends.

"I have known Alisa since I was 14," said Heather Coleman, who worked with Kinlaw to organize the vigil. "She was a true friend. If you knew Alisa, you loved Alisa."

Carol Donoho, a remediation para-professional at nearby Bayshore Elementary School, told the crowd that Bayshore Elementary staff have Alisa and her family in their thoughts.

"We all miss Alisa picking up children at the school," Donoho said. "But I especially miss the way she would look at Bryce, her own second-grader, when she would pick him up. They would lock eyes and she just beamed."

Another quote from a friend. Reporters must question whether everything they record deserves a place in their story. Is this quote necessary?

The story draws to an end by setting up the final quote and placing it in context.

The story comes full circle, describing Hartmann's role as a babysitter and her devotion as a mother. The contrast is bittersweet.

SUMMARY

Journalist Richard Dymond displays uncommon skill as a reporter and writer faced with a sensitive assignment. His story demonstrates that even a story about a murder can train its focus on positive aspects of life. Note that his byline includes an email address, which makes it possible for readers to contact him, a practice used by many newspapers.

CHAPTER 2

THE SIX-STEP PROCESS APPROACH TO REPORTING AND WRITING

GOOD WRITING MAY seem mysterious, but it's not magic. The late Donald M. Murray of the University of New Hampshire taught students and professional journalists that it is a process, a series of rational steps, actions and decisions that demystify writing. Fortunately, that process can be observed, understood and—on the best days—repeated. Effective writing benefits from a "process approach" of reporting, focusing, organizing and rewriting information into lively and clear prose. That's true whether it's a deadline-driven hard news story, an editorial, a broadcast script, a blog post, a feature or a profile.

This chapter lifts the veil of mystery that conceals how journalists proceed from idea to revision. It demonstrates how three "C's"—creative work, critical thinking and courage—lead to "A" reporting and writing. It traces bad writing to a "first draft culture" and shows you a radical yet quick and simple way to make journalism not only a search for information but also a quest for meaning.

The process approach to reporting and writing has six steps (see Figure 2-1): (1) idea, (2) focus, (3) collect, (4) order, (5) draft, (6) revise.

Calling something a process does not mean the same as calling it a formula, a recipe that you must slavishly follow. "Mix one part interview with two parts background material to produce one story" is far too simple.

A **process** is a description, rather than a prescription. It describes the way reporters work. The process approach gives reporters and editors a common language to discuss their craft. It furnishes a set of road signs that helps writers figure out where they are, and it offers the direction needed to succeed. Best of all, it provides diagnostic tools that can help writers and editors discover the flaws in their stories and develop solutions to the problems that inevitably surface.

Journalists don't need to be in the newsroom to write stories. Laura Ruane, business reporter for *The News-Press* in Fort Myers, FL, updates her blog at a beachside table.

> **Six Steps of the Process Approach to Reporting and Writing**
> 1. Idea: Generating Story Possibilities
> 2. Focus: Finding the Heart of the Story
> 3. Collect: Reporting the Story
> 4. Order: Mapping the Story
> 5. Draft: Discovering the Story by Writing
> 6. Revise: Rewriting the Story

FIGURE 2-1 The process approach follows six steps—idea, focus, collect, order, draft and revise—that demystify reporting and writing and guide journalists from start to finish as they produce stories.

TABLE 2-1 Where Ideas Come From

- Your publication, broadcast or online site
- Yourself, friends, classmates, family, co-workers, neighbors, children, movies, chat rooms, the Internet, newspapers, television, magazines, books
- News releases
- Your editor

STEP 1. IDEA: CREATIVITY SKILLS FOR TODAY'S JOURNALISTS

Generating story ideas is a perennial challenge for many journalists. Smart journalists maintain a steady supply. The quantity and quality of your ideas will determine your success as a reporter. Editors look to hire reporters who generate their own story ideas. If you don't, you may find yourself saddled with story assignments that you don't want to do, although there are some you may not be able to avoid.

Tools for Thought

If you're having trouble coming up with story ideas, there are several creativity tools that can help you take full advantage of your own private idea generator—your brain.

1. Brainstorming

Brainstorming is simple: Choose a topic and make a list of everything that comes to mind without judging any idea as either good or bad (see Figure 2-2).

Brainstorming can be a solitary exercise or can be done with other reporters and editors.

The key is to suspend critical judgment at first.

Quickly, write down all the ideas and related thoughts that surface on a particular topic. Don't stop to evaluate items. Don't worry if the ideas seem lame; don't cross out or ignore any idea. Don't worry about spelling or punctuation or fill in details. Write in your personal shorthand if that helps.

> **"** The single most important ingredient that a good reporter has is curiosity. And as long as you maintain that curiosity you will be a good reporter. **"**
>
> —BOB SCHIEFFER, ANCHOR, *CBS NEWS*

FIGURE 2-2 Brainstorming is a basic creativity tool that helps journalists generate story ideas. The method is simple: Choose a topic, and make a list of everything that comes to mind without judging any idea. Once the flow of ideas stops, then review, evaluate, discard and organize, clarify and expand. Alternate methods include mapping and branching which are useful for people who think in nonlinear, visual ways.

BRAINSTORMING THE SCHOOL BUDGET STORY

Next week, the School Board meets to vote on the school budget. The superintendent of schools has proposed a $14.1 million budget for the next school year with proposals for 5- and 10-year spending.

Without even looking at the budget, you can brainstorm ideas:

The making of a budget
1. How many people participate?
2. Who participates? Teachers? Principals? Students? Parents?
3. Is it top secret or an open process?
4. When does the process begin?

Mr. Holland's Opus
1. Are there any teachers whose programs are being cut in the budget?
2. Which programs are getting the biggest bite of the budgetary pie: computer science or the arts? Football or girls basketball? Why?

Inflation and the "three R's"
1. What does it cost to run a school in the 21st century?
2. How have school supplies changed—from chalk to computers—and how does that affect the budget?

Choose a topic and make a list of everything that comes to mind. There are no bad ideas in a brainstorming session.

Once the flow of ideas stops, then, and only then, review, evaluate, discard and organize, clarify and expand. Look for the information that surprises you or that connects with other information in an interesting, unexpected way.

2. Mapping

Brainstorming is a linear process. You write down a list of ideas, in no particular order, and see what sticks. But the brain processes ideas in other ways. Some people think in nonlinear fashion. **Mapping**, or mind mapping, is a technique that accommodates that way of thinking.

This time, instead of making a list about a story idea, put the topic or subject in the center of a page. Draw a line out from the center and write the idea at the end. If that idea triggers a new one, draw a new line from that word or return to the center and draw new lines for each idea.

3. Daybook

A **daybook**, or journal, can be a seedbed for ideas. Use it to record your observations, ideas, memories, imaginings, details, snippets from your reading or viewing, overheard conversations and lines of writing that pop into your head but that will evaporate if not recorded. Keep it with you and write down your ideas as they come to you. Once you have an idea, or an assignment, you're ready for the next step: focus.

CHIP'S CORNER

BRAINSTORMING

When Susan Trausch was writing editorials for *The Boston Globe*, on deadline, she didn't turn to her computer keyboard like most journalists. Instead, she picked up a pen and a legal pad. Before she could tell editorial page readers what to think on a given subject, she first had to find out what her own thoughts were. The notes she made in those first moments made sense of the jumbled thoughts in her head. They drove her reporting, planned her structure, formed connections—all in rehearsal for the writing to come. "Then I turn to the screen, and somewhere in that list is a lead," she says.

With her legal pad and pen, Trausch employed a basic creativity tool known as **brainstorming**. It has been seldom used in journalism, I believe, because one of its essential qualities—withholding judgment—is a foreign concept to many reporters and editors. They are often most comfortable in the role of critic or watchdog. If a watchdog doesn't bark, it's not doing its job. Brainstorming can be a solitary exercise or can be done with other reporters and editors. Reporters often complain that the nature of the news they cover is boring. Government meetings, budgetary matters, legislation aren't the stuff that gets their creative juices flowing. Maybe that's why newspapers are so boring. They needn't be. Brainstorming requires you to apply creativity. Brainstorming is simple: You simply choose a topic and make a list of everything that comes to mind and search for the best ideas that have emerged. ▶

STEP 2. FOCUS: FINDING THE HEART OF YOUR STORIES

At a time when readers can get information from a variety of sources, the thinking we do as journalists is the way we transform information into an exceedingly more valuable commodity—knowledge. Journalism remains a challenging and exciting profession because it requires reporters to:

- Think fast and on their feet, think clearly, logically, soberly, and deeply at moments of intense chaos.
- Draw connections between disparate events and developments, to fashion a mosaic from bits of information, details and facts.
- Do so in a matter of minutes.

Effective stories contain a single, dominant message. They are about one thing: fear, loss, triumph, challenge and other universal truths about the human condition. Answering "What's it *really* about?" identifies a **focus**, a theme, that guides the writer through the rest of the process. Don't confuse it with "the" theme, but "a" working hypothesis that may change with reporting, drafting and revision.

How Three C's Can Make You an "A" Writer

Effective news writing calls on three requirements, each based on a principle and a technique.

> ❝The one ingredient that's often left out of the whole process is not the writing or the reporting, but the thinking. . . . Take a few minutes to think about the theme and images before you start writing.❞
>
> —DAVID MARANISS, WRITER-EDITOR, *THE WASHINGTON POST*, AND BEST-SELLING AUTHOR

1. **Creative work**
   - Principle: Lower your standards (at first).
   - Technique: Freewrite.
2. **Critical thinking**
   - Principle: Think hard to raise the bar.
   - Technique: Answer five focusing questions.
3. **Courage**
   - Principle: Journalism takes guts.
   - Technique: Practice counterphobia (do what you fear).

Creative work involves evading the inner critic that dooms so many writers and stories. That fate can be avoided by freewriting.

Freewriting, also known as speed, rapid or stream-of-conscious writing, is easy: Just put your pen to the pad or your fingers to the keyboard, and start writing. As fast as you can. Don't worry about spelling. No crossing out, no deleting. Move, move, move. Setting a time limit is an excellent motivator.

Freewriting often produces surprising insights and prose that, while not perfect, can be polished. Reporters sometimes scribble answers that surprise their colleagues—and themselves—with their raw eloquence. Sometimes answers are elusive, but the questions have to be addressed since those are the questions that readers and viewers bring to the news. The biggest benefit of freewriting is that it demolishes writer's block. Once you start freewriting you need never block again. Just keep those fingers moving.

Don't discard your freewriting. Just because it was easy doesn't mean it's bad. Make it your first (or zero) draft. It may contain your lead or best scene.

Courage. Journalism takes guts: to walk up to complete strangers and persuade them to talk with you; to break through the stonewall of bureaucracy designed to protect officials from criticism; to convince your editor you have a great story that requires more time to finish and merits front-page display, to write despite qualms about inadequacies, and finally, to cope with post-publication criticism.

Journalists must battle these fears. Their most effective tool is **counterphobia**, or doing what you fear. The more you overcome your fears, the faster your anxieties will disappear.

Journalist at Work **LISTENING FOR FOCUS**

Regardless of the media platform—print, broadcast or online—focus remains a critical part of the process. Radio journalist Margo Melnicove learned that lesson the hard way when she produced a story for National Public Radio (NPR) about a nine-year-old jazz pianist prodigy with autism. She had recorded eight hours of sound, yet lacked a focus. She explained why this was so important: "Because if you don't have one, you can't tell what to include or what to leave out. You can't make all the choices you have to make and they won't be intelligent choices. Worse, at the end of the day you will leave the listener, with an unacceptable question—namely, 'what was that story about?'" ▶

Faced with a daunting task—writing a deadline account of President Richard Nixon's funeral—*Washington Post* reporter David Von Drehle did what more of us need to do. He stepped back and asked himself some tough questions.

1. Why does my story matter?
2. What's the point of my story?
3. Why is this story being told?
4. What does it say about life, about the world, about the times we live in?

To these, add a fifth question: What is my story *really* about—in one word?

Writing teacher Peter Elbow says that writing calls on two mutually exclusive skills: creating and criticizing. They flower best, he says, independently of each other. First you create, then you criticize.

That's fine if you have time to go away and think between tasks, but not in a newsroom when you have minutes to find your focus. Here's how journalists can quickly find a focus: Take 20 seconds each to freewrite answers to the first three questions listed above. Take 30 seconds to answer question four because, experience shows, doing so will reap the kind of meaning readers crave in stories.

The last answer consists of one word—that's right, one word—in this case a word that is universal, human, emotional, and that carries with it the scent of a story. Words like longing, corruption, redemption, betrayal, hope. Give yourself just five seconds in order to quiet the internal censor and limit yourself to one word, which is a principal definition of theme. You can—and often may need to—refocus later.

Reporters should ask and answer those questions before they start reporting. They are the questions readers, viewers and listeners want their news to answer, or, at the very least, address. But you may ask: how can I do this when I don't know what the story is about? Most ideas or assignments are self-evident: a fire destroyed a home, an underdog team won a game, gay rights, immigration. Obviously, reporting will uncover the details that flesh out the story and ensure that it's accurate, fair and balanced. Focusing before reporting launches the process by searching first for the universal element of a story, the things you already know about life, the world and the times we live in. Beginning with that knowledge increases the chances that your story will connect with many readers who share the same knowledge about the human condition.

And this method does involve reporting, because it requires interviewing, and writing, drafting by interviewing your first and best resource—yourself—and taps into your knowledge as a human being.

But that's the opposite of how journalists often work. Armed with an idea, they immediately start reporting, and many, if not most, spend as much time reporting as they can. When do they focus, order, draft and revise? The most common answer: as they go along.

The result is a "**first-draft culture,**" one that too often delivers unclear, incomplete and downright boring stories. Reporters turn in first drafts, and editors usually have barely enough time to polish them, correcting for style, spelling and grammar, and to avoid libel before publication. Focusing should be done early, but it must be repeated as events change and your reporting turns up facts and points of view that may shift your theme. Intellectual honesty is the hallmark of an excellent and ethical journalist.

> **❝**It's one thing to be given a topic, but you have to find the idea or the concept within that topic. Once you find that idea or thread, all the other anecdotes, illustrations, and quotes are pearls that hang on this thread. The thread may seem very humble, the pearls may seem very flashy, but it's still the thread that makes the necklace.**❞**
>
> —THOMAS BOSWELL, COLUMNIST, *THE WASHINGTON POST*

Journalist at Work  ROY WENZL

Focus played a key role when *Wichita (KS) Eagle* writer Roy Wenzl produced *The Miracle of Father Kapaun*, an eight-part series about a Korean War Army chaplain who might soon become the first person ever to win the Medal of Honor and be canonized as a Roman Catholic saint. Former POWs all said Kapaun rallied hundreds of starving prisoners not only to survive but to defy the brainwashing Communist camp guards. Though the story was packed with action and heroics, Wenzl knew it would not compel readers until he discovered (and showed) why Kapaun gave his life to save hundreds, and how he persuaded men made selfish from starving to make sacrifices for each other. "All good writers should begin reporting with the question, what's the real story here?" Wenzl says. "It is never enough to describe the actions, but to see and understand the souls beneath the skins." ▼

The best way to avoid "first-draft culture" is to rely on the techniques that produce the Three C's: freewriting, critical thinking and risk taking. The best time to do this is at the beginning of the process, right after you get your assignment. That way, you begin by reporting, but also focusing and drafting, thus launching an information hunt with a meaning quest.

With five questions and just 95 seconds, you will have merged creative work, critical thinking and courage to launch the journey of discovery that every good story becomes. You will also have produced the beginning of your first draft. Don't make a common mistake, thinking that just because you wrote quickly and effortlessly that the product is worthless. When we outrace the critic within, we discover things we never knew we thought, believed or could put into words.

Say, for instance, your assignment is to explore tensions between farmers who want to keep their land and developers who want to build housing tracts on it. After you answer the five focusing questions, you decide your theme is competition. Equipped with your theme, you can employ the classic journalistic paradigm—Who? What? When? Where? Why? and How?—to guide the remaining steps of the process, from reporting and choosing an appropriate structure to discovering your story by drafting and revising it to ensure accuracy, clarity, brevity and grace.

> ❝A good reporter is someone who can ask tough questions in a matter-of-fact way, is fair-minded but not soft, straightforward but not coy, and able to shift gears if the story is not what he or she thought it was.❞
>
> —BOB MONG, EDITOR,
> *THE DALLAS MORNING NEWS*

STEP 3. COLLECT: REPORTING THE STORY

Reporting is the foundation of everything you do as a journalist. It encompasses interviews, observation, reading, analysis, computer-assisted reporting. Reporting can be done in person, over the phone, via email, text messaging, video, over the Internet. It includes the skills of the detective, scientist, the confessor and the analyst. It requires initiative, persistence, patience, empathy, courage, creativity, intelligence and nerve.

The Coaching Way ᴉᴉᴉᴉ FINDING A FOCUS

THE PROBLEM

The reporting is done, but what do all these notes mean? How do I find the *focus* of the story?

SOLUTIONS

Back off. Put aside your notebooks and interview transcripts and reports, the whole pile. What you need to know you will remember. What you forget probably wasn't worth remembering. You're the expert. Take a blank pad or create a new computer file and start interviewing yourself:

- What's the news?
- What's the story?
- What information surprised me the most?
- What will surprise my reader?
- What one thing does my reader need to know?
- What one thing have I learned that I didn't expect to learn?
- What can't be left out of what I have to write?
- What one thing do I need to know more about?
- What can I say in one sentence that tells me the meaning of my story?
- Write a headline for your story.
- Write a title. In six words. (Not seven or eight or four.)
- What one thing, person, place, event, detail, fact, quotation have I found that contains the essential meaning of the subject?
- How will my story help the reader?
- What image sticks in my mind and seems to symbolize the entire subject?

- What person, or face, do I remember from my reporting?
- What is the most important single fact I have learned?
- What is the most significant quotation I heard or read?
- What statistic sticks in my head?
- Tell an editor, a colleague, your roommate about the story, to hear for yourself what you say about it.
- How would the reader describe my story to a friend?
- Draft a lead to reveal the direction and voice of your story.
- Identify the five W's and an H (who, what, when, where, why and how).
    Who is character.
    What is plot.
    When is chronology.
    Where is place.
    Why is motive.
    How is circumstances.
- Draft an end to give yourself a sense of destination.
- Write a theme paragraph (also known as a "nut graf") that tells readers why they are reading the story.
- Freewrite a discovery draft or discovery paragraphs as fast as possible without stopping to revise to reveal the meaning and the voice of the story. Write about any part of the story as long as it reveals tone, mood, voice. Am I sad, joyous, incredulous, detached, outraged? Do I smell freshly-cut grass or locker room sweat?
- Listen to what your voice is telling you about the meaning of the story.

The intensity, rhythm and tone of voice often reveal the meaning.

- Form is meaning. Try different approaches to the story. Is it a narrative, hourglass, nut graf story or one of the other forms presented in Chapter 11?
- Look at the story from different points of view. The fireman on the ladder. The horrified parent watching her child trapped in a house.
- Rehearse the story in your head and on paper to hear what the story means.
- Find a frame that limits your subject to one single dominant meaning. Is your story about police stress or one cop's life-and-death struggle?
- Role-play your reader. Ask tough questions of your story.
- Discover the problem to be solved by the writing of your story. How can I communicate a bond proposal without putting the reader to sleep?
- Find the tension in your story. Who is in conflict? How can they be drawn together or forced apart?
- A revealing detail—a fact, a quote, a statistic, a scene, name, place— may give the story focus. Look for the specific image that controls the vision of the piece.
- Look for the anecdote—the little story that combines character, dialogue, action and place—that reveals the significance of the story and shows rather than tells.
- You work for a news organization. What's new? ▶

Reporting is the act of collecting information but it is also the act of communicating information. The two activities are inextricably linked. You can't do one without having done the other. For now, let's concentrate on the first step: gathering information.

TABLE 2-2   What Reporting Involves

- Observing
- Interviewing
- Taking notes/recording audio, video
- Reading
- Analyzing

Building a Reporting Plan

It always helps to have a **reporting plan** in place before conducting interviews. Remember the answers to the five focusing questions about the competition between farmers and developers? Create a two-column table. In the first column, write the questions you have; in the second column, list every source you can think of: farmers, developers, zoning officials, city council members, neighbors, environment activists and so on.

Here are questions that may arise if your theme is *competition*:

- Who is competing?
- What are they competing for?
- Where is the source of competition?
- When did the competition begin?
- How can this competition be resolved?
- Why does the competition matter?

Start drawing lines connecting questions with sources and vice versa. Lines between the two columns may overlap, and you may see that the same question can be answered by more than one source and that sources can generate questions you haven't considered. Sources who can answer what they are competing over could include farmers and developers, but also zoning officials, who could point you to relevant documents. Reverse the situation and link sources with questions. What do neighbors and environmental activists think of the developers' plan? Instead of beginning reporting with a vague idea of the questions you need answered and the sources you need to contact, you have a specific reporting plan.

Another approach, an **abstraction ladder**, helps you identify reporting activities. The one-word theme is on the top rung, and the concrete world sits on the bottom rung.

Draw a ladder. On the top rung, write your one-word theme, which represents what the story is really about.

The bottom rung is home to the concrete world. With your theme in mind, you start asking the five W's and an H. Who's competing? The farmers and developers?

QUICK Tips ⏱ REPORTING THE STORY

THE PROBLEM

How do I report the story better so I can *collect* the information needed for good writing?

SOLUTIONS

> Seek specific, accurate information. We do not write with words, we write with information: who, what, where, when, why, how and so what.

> Collect more information than you can use so you can select from this inventory when you write.

> Revel in information you do not yet understand because writing is a process of discovering meaning.

> Make quick notes on how people move, how they dress, how they speak, how the place feels, how people react to each other.

> Use all your senses. See, but also hear, smell, touch, taste.

> Role-play. Practice empathetic reporting in which you become for a moment the people in the story.

> Adjust distance. Move in close to an unfamiliar subject, back off from a familiar one.

> Keep and update a checklist of what you know, what you need to know, sources to be interviewed, facts to be checked.

> Write and revise the three to five most obvious questions that must be answered in the story. ▶

When did the competition begin? How are the two sides competing with each other? Where?—which may lead you to city land records. The ladder can also help you identify specific people, places, scenes and quotes to flesh out your story as you match the concrete with the abstract (see Figure 2-3).

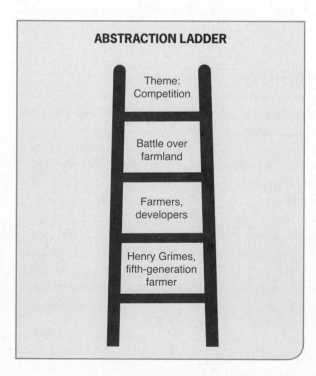

ABSTRACTION LADDER

Theme: Competition

Battle over farmland

Farmers, developers

Henry Grimes, fifth-generation farmer

FIGURE 2-3 An abstraction ladder is a graphical device that aids focusing, reporting, organization, drafting and revision. The story's focus or theme, for example, "Competition" appears on the top rung with this abstraction followed by concrete and identifiable elements. The specific name of the story's subject, a fifth-generation farmer facing the loss of his farm, appears on the lowest rung.

Ethical Dilemmas ! THE ASSIGNMENT VERSUS THE EVIDENCE

Using the three C's, freewriting and five focusing questions approach, you identify a theme. You tell your editor and begin the reporting. It soon becomes clear that the evidence doesn't support the central premise. Your editor is displeased; he's already pitched your story at the afternoon news meeting and clearly wants what you promised earlier in the day. News sources frequently complain that reporters seem to have made up their mind about their stories, and are merely looking for quotes that buttress that theme. You have two choices: (1) begin "quote shopping," to support a theme that's no longer accurate, satisfying your boss, or (2) accept that the story has changed, refocus, and tell your editor you'll keep working, or argue that the story should be dropped. Which approach do you take? ◢

STEP 4. ORDER: MAPPING YOUR STORY

After the thinking, focusing and reporting, the reporter still isn't ready to write. Planning news stories—organizing information into coherent, appropriate structures—is an overlooked activity for too many journalists. The smartest ones plan every step of the process

If your reporting plan or abstraction ladder has generated an abundance of information, you will need a plan to reach your destination without irrelevant detours.

Journalist at Work MATCHING SOURCES WITH QUESTIONS

On a sultry August afternoon, Jeremy Schwartz walked around a St. Petersburg neighborhood that was to be his beat for the next six weeks as a Poynter Institute reporting and writing fellow. This was his first day on the job. His assignment: a shoe-leather tour to learn the area and interview residents about life in their community. Talking with an elderly woman, Jeremy noticed that part of her green lawn was white. The woman told him that boys in the neighborhood had sprayed her lawn with bleach fired from an oversized water gun. It was a problem all over the neighborhood, she said. Jeremy took notes and moved on.

He knew about the toy water guns, known as Super Soakers. In Boston, where he was from, they'd been a problem a few years back; police had mistaken them for real guns. Maybe, he thought, he could do a story about the Super Soaker in St. Pete.

That's how many stories begin, with a seed of information, nourished by a reporter's background and curiosity.

But that's not enough. Reporting takes planning.

It can begin with sources or questions or a combination of both (see Figure 2-4).

If Jeremy wanted, he could draw lines linking questions with sources. He could add new sources and questions to his list and update it. That way, he could keep track of what he knew and what he still needed to know to collect the necessary information for his story. ◢

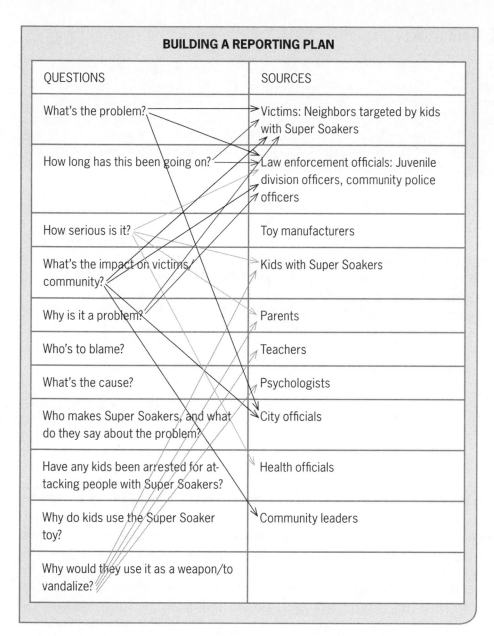

FIGURE 2-4 Building a two-column chart that divides and links necessary questions and sources who can provide crucial information and answers is a valuable way to prepare for reporting.

Some writers make a formal outline. Others jot down a list of the points they want to cover. Another way is to draw a map of your story or a timeline. Where does your story begin? Where does it end? And what belongs in the middle? Don't confuse this map with the brainstorming map you did earlier in the chapter. Think of this planning device as a road map that takes you from a starting point to a destination with clearly marked stops along the way. There is a variety of tried-and-true structures described in Chapter 11, "Story Forms."

QUICK Tips ⏱ MAPPING YOUR STORY

THE PROBLEM

I know what my story's about now. I just don't know where I should put everything. How do I *map* my story?

SOLUTIONS

> Make a list of what you want to say.
> What piece of information should be at the beginning?
> What piece of information should be at the end?
> What belongs in the middle?
> Ask the questions the reader will ask, and put them in the order they will be asked.
> Assign values to quotations.
> Think of "chapters."
> Identify the material in blocks. Organize them in sequence.
> Give the reader information in the lead that makes the reader ask a

question. Answer it with information that sparks a new question. Continue until all the questions are answered.
> Write a headline and subheads for your story.
> Pick a starting point as near to the end as you can. Look for the moment:
   When things change.
   When things will never be the same.
   When we learn lessons.
   When things hang in the balance.
   When you don't know how things will turn out.
> Draft many possible leads—a dozen, two dozen, three dozen—as quickly as possible.
> Write with the clock. Begin at a moment in time. End at a moment in time.

> Seek a natural order for the story: narrative, chronology, pyramid, problem-solution, follow-up, a visit with, a walk-through, a day in the life.
> Draft a lead, list three to five main points and an ending. Consult an editor.
> Draft many endings as quickly as possible. Once you know where you're going, you may see how to get there.
> Diagram the pattern of the story.
> Write an outline.
> Clip the notes on each part of the subject together. Move the piles around until you discover a working order.
> Use timelines.
> Organize your story by the high points. Organize it by scenes. ▸

STEP 5. DRAFT: WRITING YOUR STORY

Next comes the writing. Everything that has come before is preparation. You know your focus. You know what you want to say. You know what you want to include. Now you can set out on the journey.

The writer is ready to draft the story, almost like an artist with a sketchpad. It may start with a line, a paragraph, perhaps even several pages. The writer is discovering the story by writing it. Writers use the draft to teach themselves what they know and don't know about their subject. Some prefer to write the ending first; that way the lead can foreshadow the conclusion.

Too many reporters spend most of their time drafting by focusing on the lead under the mistaken belief that the lead will reveal the story's focus. The problem is that they leave little time to finish drafting and almost no time for revision. Avoid that by finding your focus early. That way, when the time to draft comes, you can ask, "If this story is about competition, what element best exemplifies that for my lead?" It may be a scene, an anecdote or a summary opening. Writers who labor over the lead or the first draft generally resist change because their investment is strong. Writers who freewrite are more willing to follow an editor's advice and jettison parts of their story that don't work.

QUICK Tips 🕐 DRAFTING YOUR STORY

THE PROBLEM

How do I write and keep writing to *draft* the story into publishable shape?

SOLUTIONS

> Write fast without notes. What is remembered probably should be; what is forgotten probably should be. And you can, and should, go back to your notes when the draft is done.
> Write "TK" ("to come") or place a blank underlined space in the text for details that you have forgotten and that can be checked later. Keep writing.
> Write early to discover what you know and what you need to know.
> Select the important points, and take the time to develop them adequately.
> Write with your ear. Listen to what you are saying and how you are saying it. (If stuck, dictate to an audio recorder.)

> When possible, reveal the story to the reader. Show, don't tell. Use scene and anecdote. Let the reader experience the story and discover its meaning.
> Let action or the natural order of the story carry the exposition and description.
> If there is a serious problem in organization that hasn't been solved during the order stage of the process, write a paragraph and leave six spaces between it and the next paragraph. Make a printout, cut apart the paragraphs and play solitaire with them until you find their natural sequence.
> Write the easy parts—the parts you want to write—first.
> If blocked, follow poet William Stafford's advice: Lower your standards. Or heed William Faulkner: "Get it down. Take chances. It may be bad, but that's the only way you can do

anything really good." Writer's block often comes when the writer has set impossible standards.
> Provide the reader with the evidence an intelligent but uninformed person will need to believe the story.
> Vary the documentation. Pick the material and the form of that material (quotation, anecdote, statistic, action, description) that is appropriate for the point being made.
> Answer the questions the reader will ask. The story is a conversation with an individual reader, with only the answers to the reader's questions printed.
> Write down the reasons you're not writing. Define the problems. Devise solutions: more reporting, lower standards, refocus story, new organization.
> Switch writing tools. Turn off the computer, and pick up a pad and pen.
> Take a break. ▸

STEP 6. REVISE: REWRITING THE STORY

Journalism has been called the "first rough draft of history." For many reporters, that seems to absolve them of the need to rewrite. **Revising** is the final but most critical step of the reporting and writing process. It's the last chance to plug holes in your reporting, to verify your facts, to make sure your story is as complete, fair, accurate and clear as it can be.

The writing process isn't a straight line. The idea and focus change during the reporting—the crowd of cars on the side of the road isn't an accident; it's a flea market. The reporter makes another phone call during the drafting. The writer organizes during the reporting by marking up the notes—this quote as a lead, this detail as an ending. Often the writer circles back to re-report, refocus, and reorganize.

QUICK Tips ◔ REWRITING FOR YOUR AUDIENCE

THE PROBLEM

My story is drafted. How do I *clarify* the meaning and keep the story tight and interesting?

SOLUTIONS

> Make a printout of your draft story or script to "see" your story.
> Read your story aloud.
> Read in three stages:
  1. Like a reader/viewer/listener
  2. Like a writer
  3. Like an editor
> Be patient, even on deadline. Take a breath, and read it again.
> Interview yourself. What works? What needs work?

> Find a co-reader, someone who makes you want to keep writing. Avoid destructive types.
> Remember that shorter is better. What can be left out should be left out. A good piece of writing may be judged by the amount of good material that isn't used. Everything left in develops the single dominant meaning of the story.
> Does your story employ the senses: hearing, sight, smell, touch, taste?
> Does your story also have a sense of:
  People?
  Time?
  Place?
  Drama?

> Build in rewriting time. Write early. Print out early. Mark up the copy. Revise again.
> Is there another way to write this story? Try it.
> Do I need more reporting?
> Are all the facts checked?
> Is there anything else I can do to make the story:
  Simple?
  Clear?
  Graceful?
  Accurate?
  Fair?
  Shorter? ▶

SEE CLOSE-UP, P. 43: REPORTING AND WRITING: THE PROCESS APPROACH AT WORK

That aspect of the process—the need to circle back to earlier stages—surprises many student journalists. They think that once they've done their interviews and other reporting, all that's left to do is the writing. But good journalists are never content. They're always trying to find telling quotes, vivid details, clear sentences, a sharper focus, a beginning that captivates, a middle without muddle, and an ending that leaves a lasting impression on the reader.

PROFESSIONALS' ROUNDTABLE

THE PROCESS APPROACH

The process approach to reporting and writing offers multiple advantages. It sharpens focus, guides reporting, aids in drafting and revision, and transforms a nebulous topic into a complete story. A newspaper editor, journalism teacher and a student agree on one point: Focus is the most important step. Their tips:

- Focus your story from the start.
- Constantly check the focus against your reporting to either sharpen or change the story.
- Remember that journalism is hard work, but the process demonstrates that a story is something you can control even on a tight deadline.

Participants

 MARK HAMILTON, journalism instructor, Kwantlen Polytechnic University, Vancouver, British Columbia

 AMANDA PUNSHON, feature writing student, Kwantlen Polytechnic University, Vancouver, British Columbia

 KEVIN MCGRATH, assistant metro editor, *The Wichita* (KS) *Eagle*

> *What's the value of the process approach?*

Hamilton: It provides students with a clear focus on both the real story and the research that's needed. Through drafting quickly and polishing slowly, students can produce better writing.

> *Why is it important that students learn and use a process approach?*

Hamilton: It helps teach them that a journalistic story is something they control. And that while journalism is hard work; there is a way to approach it effectively and (if needs be) quickly.

> *How does the process approach help reporters diagnose problems in a story and correct them?*

McGrath: A process approach saves you a lot of mental pain: You don't "take a look at" brain surgery; you focus your idea on one practitioner or one breakthrough or one really good hospital and what makes it/him/her tick.

Hamilton: It overcomes two common weaknesses in beginning journalists: the inability to identify the real story within the topic or "story idea," and the tendency to over-research and hope there's something in the resulting pile of paper that resembles an interesting piece. Using the draft as exploration also helps them find any holes in the research.

> *What does the process approach provide as reporters work toward deadline?*

McGrath: Comfort: If you have to report or write quickly, you know both where you're going and why.

> *What's the most important step of the process?*

McGrath: Focus.
(Kevin McGrath died Feb. 5, 2013.)

> *What is your opinion of the process approach?*

Punshon: The process approach is a very logical, intuitive way to approach the writing process.

> *Does it help you? If so, how?*

Punshon: It helps me use my time more effectively, so I can spend more time on necessary research and less time trying to figure out exactly what my story is about.

> *What is the biggest advantage of the process approach you're learning this semester?*

Punshon: You'll know almost right away if you are able to do the story you want. If you can't do it, you can usually find another story idea from the work you've done to narrow your topic down—you don't have to start over.

> *Which step of the process do you find the most helpful?*

Punshon: Focus. Narrowing it down before I begin researching keeps me from doing unnecessary work and gives me the time to do deeper research.

SUMMARY GUIDE

THE SIX-STEP PROCESS APPROACH TO REPORTING AND WRITING

STEP 1. IDEA: CREATIVITY SKILLS FOR TODAY'S JOURNALISTS

Generating story ideas is a crucial and challenging first step in producing quality journalism.

What to Remember → A variety of tools exist to overcome the difficulties of coming up with story ideas. Reading, brainstorming, branching and keeping a daybook make production of story ideas a painless and productive process.

STEP 2. FOCUS: FINDING THE HEART OF YOUR STORIES

Good stories require a focus—a single dominant message that captures news and its meaning for audiences and avoids the "first-draft culture" that dominates news writing today.

What to Remember → Discovering with speed and precision what your story is about can be accomplished in just 95 seconds by answering five focusing questions, freewriting and by relying on creativity, critical thinking and courage.

STEP 3. COLLECT: REPORTING THE STORY

Reporting accurate information through interviews, observation and research forms the foundation of all good journalism.

What to Remember → Reporting is not only the collection of information, but the communication of that information with accuracy, precision and clarity. Building a reporting plan and creating an abstraction ladder leads the reporter to credible sources that generate the information necessary for this critical step of the process.

STEP 4. ORDER: MAPPING THE STORY

Effective news stories are clear and well-organized and depend on careful planning.

What to Remember → Whether you make a formal outline, a timeline or a list of key elements, ordering information produces a road map that leads through the final steps of drafting and revising. Think of planning as the step that takes you from a starting point to a destination with clearly marked stops along the way.

STEP 5. DRAFT: WRITING THE STORY

Effective writers use drafting as a way to discover their story by writing it as quickly as possible.

What to Remember →

Writers use the draft to teach themselves what they know and don't know about their subject. Freewriting enables journalists to rapidly produce workable drafts that can be revised with care. Avoid spending too much time on the lead at the expense of the story, especially the ending.

STEP 6. REVISE: REWRITING THE STORY

Revision enables journalists to make sure that their stories are complete, accurate, fair, well-organized, and, above all, clear.

What to Remember →

Effective journalists revise in order to shift focus as stories evolve, plug reporting holes, reorganize, draft new material, polish language and follow rules for style, spelling and grammar. Revision prevents mistakes that can tarnish all the good work accomplished during the entire process.

KEY TERMS

abstraction ladder, p. 32
brainstorming, p. 27
counterphobia, p. 28
daybook, p. 26

first-draft culture, p. 29
focus, p. 27
freewriting, p. 28
mapping, p. 26

process, p. 24
reporting, p. 30
reporting plan, p. 32
revising, p. 37

EXERCISES

1. Describe your current writing process. Use words or a drawing to convey the steps you now take to write, whether it's news stories or term papers.

2. Practice brainstorming. Choose a topic or subject and write down every idea that comes to mind, no matter how good you think it is. Put the subject in the middle of a page and draw lines for each idea, or try the branching approach, where each idea and sub-idea gets its own limb or twig.

3. Freewrite answers in 95 seconds to David Von Drehle's five focusing questions about your story idea to help you develop a focus.

4. Hone your observational skills by writing down everything you can see, smell, hear, touch and taste about a place.

5. Make an outline to organize the information you've collected during your reporting and research. Decide where the story begins and ends.

READINGS

Clark, Roy Peter. *Writing Tools: 50 Essential Strategies for Every Writer.* New York: Little, Brown and Co., 2008.
A prominent writing coach guides writers by using the process approach to improve their writing from generating ideas to effective revision.

Hart, Jack. *A Writer's Coach: An Editor's Guide to Words That Work.* New York: Pantheon, 2006.
Hart, who has edited several Pulitzer Prize–winning stories, distills decades of experience, editing and training into a readable, practical and inspirational journey through the writing process that produces excellent storytelling.

Klauser, Henriette A. *Writing on Both Sides of the Brain: Breakthrough Techniques for People Who Write.* New York: HarperOne, 1987.
A classic handbook for generating quality ideas using brainstorming, branching and other techniques to tap inner creativity.

Murray, Donald M. *Writing to Deadline: The Journalist at Work.* Portsmouth, NH: Heinemann, 2000.
Blending practical theory and real-world examples, the pioneer of the process approach demonstrates how journalists move from ideas and focus through reporting, organizing, drafting and revision to produce excellent journalism.

Scanlan, Christopher, ed. *How I Wrote the Story.* Providence, RI: Providence Journal Co., 1985.
Journalists at a metropolitan newspaper present their stories and discuss the process that lies behind the work of quality beat, features and profile journalism.

Zinsser, William. *Speaking of Journalism: 12 Writers and Editors Talk About Their Work.* New York: Harper Collins, 1994.
A group of top-ranked newspaper and magazine journalists talk about their process, focusing on reporting and writing strategies behind their exceptional stories.

REPORTING AND WRITING: THE PROCESS APPROACH AT WORK

Good writing may seem mysterious, but it's not magic. It is a process, as we've seen, a series of six rational steps, actions and decisions that demystify writing. Effective writing benefits from a process approach of generating ideas, focusing, reporting, organizing, drafting and rewriting information into lively and clear prose. John Silcox, a participant in The Poynter Institute's summer fellowship in reporting and writing, relied on the process approach in the following story. Here's how he did it.

IDEA

Walking his community beat one day, Silcox visited a recreation center where he learned that an aerobics instructor was back at work following a severe car crash that badly injured one of her legs. He decided that this untold story within his community was worth pursuing. Starting out, all he knew was that he wanted to tell the story of her accident and recovery.

FOCUS

In this chapter, you learned how to focus your story immediately to guide your reporting, organizing, drafting and revision. Journalists use many techniques to focus their stories. The chapter suggests freewriting answers to five focus questions. Some journalists focus by writing a lead or a headline. Others craft a nut graf, which sums up the story. Whatever the method, the goal is the same: to help you distill your story into a single dominant message that reports news and tells a story. As you'll see, the focusing, or "front-end work," that Silcox carried out informs and influences all the work that followed. He relied on five focus questions assigned by his instructors to find the essential meaning of his story and to state explicitly why his story is worth writing—and reading.

What's the news?

Aerobic exercise not only keeps you fit but also can speed up the body's healing process.

What's the story?

Campbell Park aerobics instructor Alvina Miller doesn't let a knee injury keep her from exercise.

What's the image that best captures the meaning of the story?

Alvina Miller leading an exercise class wearing a knee support.

What is your story about in six words?

Aerobics can help body heal faster.

So what?

Another benefit of living an active lifestyle.

COLLECT

Silcox set about reporting. He cast a wide net. In addition to in-person interviews with the subject of his story and women who attended her aerobics class and nurses where the aerobics instructor was treated, he located expert sources through Internet research and then conducted telephone interviews with three medical experts in the fields of orthopedics and rehabilitation. He spent time observing her class. Notice that he also interviewed another accident victim with a similar story. Good journalists always look for multiple sources to bolster their focus and provide readers with more relevant examples. Silcox more than met the standard for complete, credible and authoritative reporting that produces excellent journalism.

ORDER

Armed with his focus and reporting, Silcox now moves on to organizing, or mapping, his story. He uses an outline form, using shorthand that connects with the knowledge he's gathered. But even though it looks set in stone, an outline is not the story, simply a vision of it. Study how the structure of John's draft differs from his outline once he begins writing.

    I. Lead
        A. women at aerobics
   II. Introduction of Alvina
        A. aerobics
        B. accident
  III. Nut graf
  IV. Background on Alvina
        A. car wreck
        B. knee injury
        C. rehabilitation
           1. nurses at Bayfront
           2. Dr. Rodriguez
    V. Expertise on issue
        A. Dr. Brown
           1. athletes
           2. smoking
        B. physical therapist
  VI. Countermoves
        A. mitigating factors
        B. lifestyle
 VII. Aerobics class
        A. Alvina at work
        B. encouraging/inspiring women
VIII. Ending

DRAFT: WRITING THE STORY

Silcox has his focus, reporting and his map. Now it's time for him to discover his story by writing it. You'll see that he quickly abandons his original outline, choosing to begin with the accident rather than the aerobics class. He chooses the most dramatic scene available to captivate reader interest. As with any draft, there are awkward spots, style errors or grammatical lapses that should be caught and fixed during revision. Notice how he uses subheads to organize his material. It's an approach that helps the writer keep similar material together rather than ranging all over the landscape.

FIRST DRAFT
John Silcox
Points South Staff Writer

The paramedics on the scene couldn't help but admire her shapely, well-defined legs. Alvina Miller was just worried she might lose one.

The 26-year-old aerobics instructor couldn't bear the thought of not being able to run, as she looked down at the left leg that was severely broken in a car crash that could have killed her.

Since graduating from Florida A&M University in 1995, exercise has been her passion. When not working as a marketing representative for Air Quality Control, chances are she's running laps, lifting weights or doing whatever it takes to slip into her size-three skirts. The accident on April 19 left her with a broken leg above her left knee, but that didn't stop Miller from maintaining her daily exercise regime, even doubling her efforts. Within a couple of months, she was back at Campbell Park leading her faithful flock of women in a chorus of scissors kicks.

Everyone knows that exercise gets rid of the lovehandles, but it can also help you heal faster. Doctors say that a healthy and active lifestyle can speed up recovery and spare injury patients months of painful rehabilitation. Although healthy living is not the only factor in recovery, physical therapists agree that aerobic exercise and proper nutrition can not only keep you fit but also can speed up the body's healing process.

MILLER'S BEST BUD

Miller's story begins with a brown collie named Bud, which she describes as "Lassie with smaller eyes." Technically Bud belongs to Miller's neighbor Mrs. Arlie Jones, but over the years he has become a constant companion, accompanying her on evening runs around Tropicana Field.

Miller was on her way back from the store to give Bud a shampoo on the day of the accident. While making a left hand turn just a block from her house, Bud jumped in front of the wheel and blocked her view. Miller jammed her brakes, but the car's momentum carried her into the oncoming lane, where she smacked into a Toyota Corolla and then rolled her own Grand Am three times before slamming into a stop sign along the curb.

"I didn't feel anything for about three minutes," she said. "I didn't even hear what happened."

Miller crawled out through an open window, with the chivalrous but shaken collie following patiently behind her. Based on the status of the car, the paramedics on the scene presumed she was dead. They were surprised to find Miller alive and well, except for the bone above her left knee, which had broken through the skin. Miller was rushed to Bayfront Hospital. Bud walked home.

Miller suffered a broken leg above her left knee that required a 20 mm stainless steel rod to be inserted into the bone to help the knee heal properly. Miller spent her four-day stay chatting with nurses about nutrition and exercise, swallowing painkillers and doing leg lifts and crunches from her hospital bed. Dr. Jorge Rodriguez, a physician at All Florida Orthopedic Associates, said that it typically takes patients 8 to 12 weeks just to get off crutches. Miller was back in aerobics after two months.

"Before you know it, you'll be running like a gazelle," said Rodriguez, at a recent checkup.

Rodriguez said that because Miller was in such good shape to begin with, she didn't need to develop the muscle strength necessary to begin rehabilitation.

"People who are aerobically fit and in good health are in the best possible position to heal," he said.

HAPPY HEALTHY HEALING

The reason is simple. Exercise strengthens the bones and joints by circulating the blood, according to Dr. Mark D. Brown, professor and chairman for the department of orthopedic and rehabilitation at the University of Miami school of medicine. Doctors have observed for years that athletes with injuries heal faster than unconditioned individuals of the same age. Brown even recalls a conditioned young dancer who fractured her thigh bone and femur and lost one leg below the knee. She was dancing in a recital in New York four months after the accident.

Studies show that heavy smokers, drinkers and people with poor eating habits are slow healers. Even back pain can be exacerbated by smoking. Brown cited studies that show that smokers who undergo spinal fusions have only a 50 percent success rate, compared to 95 percent for nonsmokers.

"In a good happy person, the pain doesn't bother you as much," said Neil Spielholz, a research professor in the division of physical therapy at University of Miami.

But when it comes to bone healing, exercise is not the only thing that makes it or "breaks it." Brown said that family genetics, disease history and age are also important factors in recovery.

"Of course, when you are young, younger people heal much faster than older people," he said. "But it doesn't make any difference how old you are if you are in good health."

Miller stays healthy by sticking to a diet of fruits and vegetables, wheat bread and baked chicken, occasionally splurging for a vanilla milkshake at Dairy Queen or a slice of Grandma's sweet potato pie. But even that demands a penance of push-ups.

LEADER OF THE PACK

Fifteen woman have turned out for Miller's Monday class. Some have even brought their children, who mimic Mom's movements on the leftover blue mats in the back of the room.

Pat Crumb, 47, comes because of her high blood pressure and cholesterol. "441V s down to 200," she beams proudly. Dorothy Daniels, 48, relieves the stress of teaching 25 first-graders at Eisenhower Elementary in Clearwater. Both are inspired by their instructor's determination.

Miller, limping slightly with her left knee wrapped in brown gauze, fires up the women with words of encouragement that get more intense as the night wears on. One flash of her toothy smile is always good for an extra set of sit-ups.

During an intense round of knee-bends, Miller scolds 38-year-old Deborah Wynn for not going down far enough. Wynn's winded reply:

"It's Monday."

REVISION

Stories don't emerge whole with just some fine-tuning. Writing can be pretty messy. It's like refinishing an old, paint-encrusted piece of furniture. You start by laying on stripper that gets it all gunky. You scrape and peel, then you wipe it off and start again. Finally, you start sanding, starting with a coarse grade and then moving on to finer ones, working down, layer by layer, until nothing remains but tiny blemishes.

After consulting with his writing coach, Silcox digs deeper. He conducts additional interviews, finds compelling new details and telling statistics, and, most important, deletes much of what he has drafted, replacing it with new information and more polished prose. Writers usually fall in love with what they have written, but the best ones recognize that the rough draft holds the promise of the final one. Silcox used the track-changes feature on his word-processing software to visualize his revision. With some exceptions, strikeouts indicate the cuts he made, while underlined passages represent revisions and additions. In the following draft, notice how much of the new material came from his notebook and additional reporting. Silcox makes changes that correspond to news writing style.

But revision is more than fiddling with language. The initial idea may change, the structure shifts, what seemed right in the first draft on reconsideration is no longer necessary or must be supplemented with fresh writing. In the published story, which appears at the end of this example, note how Silcox continued to refine his work, even adding a new ending. Good writers never stop revising. By following the process approach, he produced a story that more than lived up to its promise.

FOR ONE AEROBICS INSTRUCTOR, AN ACTIVE LIFESTYLE SAVED MONTHS OF REHABILITATION

By John Silcox
Staff Writer

The paramedics ~~on the scene~~ couldn't help but admire her shapely~~, well defined~~ legs. Alvina Miller was worried she might lose ~~one.~~ one. ~~The 26-year-old aerobics instructor couldn't bear the thought of not being able to run, as~~ As she looked ~~down at the left leg that was~~ at her left leg, severely broken in a car crash that could have killer~~her.~~ her, the 26-year-old aerobics instructor couldn't bear the thought of not being able to run.

"I was afraid they were going to have to amputate," said Miller. "But the paramedics told me, 'They can do anything in hospitals now; don't worry, we'll save your leg.'"

Since graduating from Florida A&M University in 1995, exercise has been her passion. When not ~~working as a marketing representative for Air Quality Control, chances are she's running laps, lifting weights or doing~~ writing letters to customers of Air Quality at 30th Avenue North, she's running laps, lifting weights or whatever it takes to slip into her size ~~3~~ three skirts. Her diet of vegetables, wheat bread and baked chicken is interrupted only by an occasional Dairy Queen vanilla shake or slice of Grandma's sweet potato pie. Afterwards, a penance of pushups.

The accident on April 19 left her with a leg broken above her left knee, but that didn't stop Miller from maintaining her daily exercise regime—even doubling her efforts. Within a couple of months, she was back at Campbell Park, leading her~~faithful~~ flock of women in a chorus of scissors kicks.

Everyone knows that exercise gets rid of~~the love-handles, but it can also help you heal faster. Doctors say that a healthy and~~love handles. Miller now knows it does more. One benefit often ignored is that an active lifestyle can help injuries heal faster. More than 61 million injuries wee reported in the united States in 1994 alone, the fifth-leading cause of death, according to the National Center for Health ~~speed up recovery~~

and spare injury patients ~~months of painful rehabilita-tion. Although~~ Statistics. And although healthy living is not the only factor in recovery, ~~physical therapists agree that aerobic exercise and proper nutrition can not~~ doctors say that Miller's physical condition spared her months of rehabilitation.

~~only keep you fit but can speed up the body's healing process.~~

~~MILLER'S BEST BUD~~

~~Miller's story begins with a brown collie named Bud, which she describes as "Lassie with smaller eyes." Technically Bud belongs to Miller's neighbor Mrs. Arlie Jones, but over the years he has become a constant companion, accompanying her on evening runs around Tropicana Field.~~

~~Miller was on her way back from the store to give Bud a shampoo on the day of the accident. While making a left hand turn just a block from her house, Bud jumped in front of the wheel and blocked her view. Miller jammed her brakes but the car's momentum carried her into the oncoming lane where she smacked into a Toyota Corolla and then rolled her own Grand Am three times before slamming into a stop sign along the curb.~~

~~"I didn't feel anything for about three minutes," she said. "I didn't even hear what happened."~~

~~Miller crawled out through an open window, with the chivalrous but shaken collie following patiently behind her. Based on the status of the car, the paramedics on the scene presumed she was dead. They were surprised to find Miller alive and well, except for the bone above her left knee which had broken through the skin. Miller was rushed to Bayfront hospital. Bud walked home.~~

"People who are aerobically fit and in good health are in the best possible position to ~~Miller suffered a broken leg above her left knee that required a 20 mm stainless stell rod to be inserted into the bone to help the knee heal properly. Miller spent her four day stay chatting with nurses about nutrition and exercise, swallowing painkillers and doing leg lifts and crunches from her hospital bed.~~ heal," said Dr. Jorge Rodriguez, ~~a~~ Miller's physician at All Florida Orthopedic Associates, ~~said that it typically takes patients 8 to 12 weeks~~

~~just to get off crutches. Miller was back in aerobics after two months.~~

~~"Before you know it, you'll be running like a gazelle," said Rodriguez, at a recent checkup.~~

~~Rodriguez said that because Miller was in such good shape to begin with, she didn't need to develop the muscle strength necessary to begin rehabilitation.~~

~~"People who are aerobically fit and in good health are in the best possible position to heal," he said.~~

HAPPY HEALTHY HEALING

~~The reason is simple.~~ Exercise ~~strengthens~~circulates the blood to the bones and ~~joints by circulating the blood, according to~~joints, said Dr. Mark D. Brown, ~~professor and chairman for the department of ortho-pedic and rehabilitation~~chairman of the Department of Orthopedic and Rehabilitation at the University ~~of Miami~~of Miami school of medicine. Better blood supply to the tissue allows for faster healing.

Doctors have ~~observed~~known for years that athletes with injuries heal faster than unconditioned individuals of the same age. Brown recalls ~~a~~conditioned young dancer who fractured her ~~thigh bone and~~femur and lost one leg below the knee. She was dancing in a recital in New York four months after the accident, he said.

Rodriguez said it typically takes patients with Miller's injuries eight to 12 weeks just to get off crutches. She was in aerobics after two months.

MILLER'S BEST BUD

Miller's road to recovery begins with a neighbor's brown collie named Bud, a faithful companion on her evening jogs around Tropicana Field.

Miller, driving with her left leg tucked under her body as she often does, was on her way back from the store to give Bud a shampoo on the day of the accident. While she was making a left turn a block from her house, Bud jumped in front of the wheel and blocked her view. She jammed her brakes, but the Grand Am slid into the oncoming lane and smacked into a Toyota Corolla, rolled three times and slammed into a stop sign. "I didn't feel anything for about three minutes," she said. "I didn't even hear what happened."

Miller crawled out an open window with a shaken collie behind her. The woman in the Toyota was not injured, but based on the looks of Miller's car, the paramedics on the scene presumed she was dead. They were surprised to find Miller alive and well, except for the bone that had broken through the skin behind her left knee. Miller was rushed to Bayfront Medical Center. Bud walked home.

Surgeons inserted a 20 mm stainless steel rod into the bone to help the knee heal properly. She spent her four-day hospital stay chatting with nurses about nutrition and exercise, swallowing painkillers and sweating out leg lifts and crunches in her hospital bed. "Before you know it, you'll be running like a gazelle," said Rodriguez, during a recent checkup.

HAPPY HEALTHY HEALING

Studies show that heavy smokers, drinkers and people with poor eating habits are slow healers. ~~Even back pain can be exacerbated by smoking. Brown cited studies that show that smokers who undergo spinal fusions have only a 50 percent success rate, compared to 95 percent for nonsmokers. In good happy person, the pain doesn't bother you as~~ Brown said elderly patients with poor diets who have hip fractures suffer more infections and complications in healing. But physical therapist Sherie Wynn has seen active senior citizens, because of their endurance and muscle strength, bounce back from hip and knee replacements in six months. Wynn, who works at Bayfront, said people who aren't used to exercise get tired during recovery.

"The body expends so much energy trying to heal that there is nothing left over for functional activities," said Wynn, who compares it with someone being extremely sore after taking up jogging. "Somebody who runs 26 miles a day, if you add an extra mile, they won't feel it very much," she said.

And it helps to have a healthy outlook like Emily Peck.

A speeding car hit Peck as she crossed Fourth Street South at 13th Avenue in St. Petersburg on June 10, leaving her with two broken legs, a broken arm, a pair of cracked ribs and a collapsed lung.

"You just have to think, I'm going to do the best I can and not be beaten by this," said Peck, who was to be certified in scuba diving the weekend after the accident.

~~much," said~~ Mental attitude is a catalyst to healing faster, according to Neil Spielholz, a research professor in the division of physical therapy at the University of Miami. "If you are a happy person, the pain doesn't bother you as much," he said, adding that exercise releases endorphins, opiate-like substances that create a sense of well-being in the body.

Peck, a 34-year-old television producer from Alabama, was out of the hospital faster than expected, and doctors told her that because she was young and healthy she would bounce back quickly.

But when it comes to bone healing, exercise is not the only thing that ~~makes it or "breaks it."~~ "makes it or breaks it." Brown said that family genetics, disease history and age are also important factors in recovery.

~~"Of~~ "Of course when you are young, younger people heal much faster than older ~~people," he said. "But it doesn't~~ people," he said. "But it doesn't make any difference how old you are if you are in good ~~health."~~ health."

~~Miller stays healthy by sticking to a diet of fruits and vegetables, wheat bread and baked chicken—occasionally splurging for a vanilla milkshake at Dairy Queen or a slice of grandma's sweet potato pie. But even that demands a penance of pushups.~~

LEADER OF THE PACK

Fifteen women have turned out for ~~Miller's Monday class. Some have even brought there~~ Miller's aerobics class on a night just 12 weeks after her accident. Some have brought children, who mimic ~~mom's~~ Mom's movements on the blue mats in the back of the ~~room.~~ rec room at Campbell Park.

Pat Crumb, 47, comes because of her high blood pressure and cholesterol. ~~441 down to 200," she beams proudly.~~ "It's down to 200," she beams. Dorothy Daniels, 48, relieves the stress of teaching 25 ~~first graders~~ first-graders at Eisenhower Elementary in Clearwater. ~~Both are inspired by their instructor's determination.~~

Miller, limping slightly with her left knee wrapped in brown gauze, fires up the women with words of ~~encouragement that get more intense as the night wears on.~~ encouragement. ~~One flash of her toothy smile is always good for an extra, set of sit-ups.~~

During an intense round of knee bends, ~~Miller scolds 38-year-old~~she scolds 38-year-old Deborah Wynn for ~~not going down far enough. Wynn's winded reply:~~dogging it. Then Miller laughs to let her know it's all in fun.

~~"Its Monday."~~

One flash of her toothy smile is always good for an extra rep.

PUBLICATION

The published version is quite revealing. Silcox has eliminated large chunks of information that don't support his focus or reorganized them into a clearer shape. He doesn't abide by every change in his revision, keeping some edits and ignoring others. He understands that good journalism depends on collecting an overabundance of information and is unafraid to jettison any that drag down his story. But he weaves in important new information, such as a second example of quick healing in a healthy accident victim. The story is 178 words longer than the first draft, but it reads smoothly. Sentences have been trimmed to quicken the pace. His revision shows attention to clarity and telling details and revealing quotes. He has corrected most, but not all, spelling, grammar and style lapses. ("Since graduating from Florida A&M University in 1995, exercise has been her passion" is a dangling modifier, a word or phrase that modifies a word not clearly stated in the sentence. Exercise did not graduate. A grammatical revision: "Exercise has been Alvina Miller's passion since she graduated from Florida A&M University in 1995.") He uses Alvina Miller's story as a narrative thread that pulls readers along and alternates her account with information that puts the individual case into a larger context. The story is extremely informative, relying as it does on authoritative sources. His revision was thorough. It's worth comparing the first draft and published version to learn how Silcox improved his story in a variety of ways. He could have made more changes, mostly for clarity and pacing, but eventually deadline arrives and revision must cease. He can be proud of his story, which reflects his considerable talents and demonstrates the extraordinary value of the process approach to reporting and writing.

BACK IN STEP

Exercise speeds up the road to recovery, experts say. For one aerobics instructor, an active lifestyle saved months of rehabilitation.

By John Silcox
Points South Staff Writer

The paramedics couldn't help but admire her shapely legs. Alvina Miller was worried she might lose one. As she looked at her left leg, severely broken in a car crash that could have killed her, the 26-year-old aerobics instructor couldn't bear the thought of not being able to run.

"I was afraid they were going to have to amputate," said Miller. "But the paramedics told me, 'They can do anything in hospitals now; don't worry, we'll save your leg.'"

Since graduating from Florida A&M University in 1995, exercise has been her passion. When not writing letters to customers of Air Quality Control at 30th Avenue North, she's running laps, lifting weights or whatever it takes to slip into her size three skirts. Her diet of vegetables, wheat bread and baked chicken is interrupted only by an occasional Dairy Queen vanilla shake or slice of Grandma's sweet potato pie. Afterwards, a penance of push-ups.

The accident on April 19 left her with a leg broken above her left knee, but that didn't stop Miller from maintaining her daily exercise regime—even doubling her efforts. Within a couple of months, she was back at Campbell Park, leading her flock of women in a chorus of scissors kicks.

Everyone knows that exercise gets rid of love handles. Miller now knows it does more. One benefit often ignored is that an active lifestyle can help injuries heal faster. More than 61 million injuries were reported in the United States in 1994 alone, the fifth leading cause of death according to the National Center for Health Statistics. And while healthy living is not the only factor in recovery, doctors say that Miller's physical condition spared her months of rehabilitation.

"People who are aerobically fit and in good health are in the best possible position to heal," said Dr. Jorge Rodriguez, Miller's physician at All Florida Orthopedic Associates.

Exercise circulates the blood to the bones and joints, said Dr. Mark D. Brown, chairman of the Department of Orthopaedics and Rehabilitation at the University of Miami School of Medicine. Better blood supply to the tissue allows for faster healing.

Doctors have known for years that athletes with injuries heal faster than unconditioned individuals of the same age. Brown recalls a young dancer who fractured her femur and lost one leg below the knee. She was dancing in a recital in New York four months after the accident, he said.

Rodriguez said it typically takes patients with Miller's injuries eight to 12 weeks just to get off crutches. She was in aerobics after two months.

Miller's road to recovery begins with a neighbor's brown collie named Bud, a faithful companion on her evening jogs around Tropicana Field.

Miller, driving with her left leg tucked under her body as she often does, was on her way back from the store to give Bud a shampoo on the day of the accident. While she was making a left turn a block from her house, Bud jumped in front of the wheel and blocked her view. She jammed her brakes but the Grand Am slid into the oncoming lane and smacked into a Toyota Corolla, rolled three times and slammed into a stop sign.

"I didn't feel anything for about three minutes," she said. "I didn't even hear what happened."

Miller crawled out an open window with a shaken collie behind her. The woman in the Toyota was not injured, but based on the looks of Miller's car, the paramedics on the scene presumed she was dead. They were surprised to find Miller alive and well, except for the bone that had broken through the skin behind her left knee. Miller was rushed to Bayfront Medical Center. Bud walked home.

Surgeons inserted a 20 mm stainless steel rod into the bone to help the knee heal properly. She spent her four-day hospital stay chatting with nurses about nutrition and exercise, swallowing painkillers and sweating out leg lifts and crunches in her hospital bed. "Before you know it, you'll be running like a gazelle," said Rodriguez, during a recent checkup.

Studies show that heavy smokers, drinkers and people with poor eating habits are slow healers. Brown said elderly patients with poor diets who have hip fractures suffer more infections and complications in healing.

But physical therapist Sherie Wynn has seen active senior citizens, because of their endurance and muscle strength, bounce back from hip and knee replacements in six months. Wynn, who works at Bayfront, said people who aren't used to exercise get tired during recovery.

"The body expends so much energy trying to heal that there is nothing left over for functional activities," said Wynn, who compares it with someone extremely sore after taking up jogging. "Somebody who runs 26 miles a day, if you add an extra mile, they won't feel it very much," she said.

And it helps to have a healthy outlook like Emily Peck.

A speeding car hit Peck as she crossed Fourth Street South at 13th Avenue in St. Petersburg on June 10, leaving her with two broken legs, a broken arm, a pair of cracked ribs and a collapsed lung.

"You just have to think, I'm going to do the best I can and not be beaten by this," said Peck, who was to be certified in scuba diving the weekend after the accident.

Mental attitude is a catalyst to healing faster, according to Neil Spielholz, a research professor in the division of physical therapy at the University of Miami.

"If you are a happy person, the pain doesn't bother you as much," he said, adding that exercise releases endorphins, opiate-like substances that create a sense of well-being in the body.

Peck, a 34-year-old television producer form Alabama, was out of the hospital faster than expected, and doctors told her that because she was young and healthy she would bounce back quickly.

But when it comes to bone healing, exercise is not the only thing that "makes it or breaks it." Brown said that family genetics, disease history and age are also important factors in recovery.

"Of course when you are young, younger people heal much faster than older people," he said. "But it doesn't make any difference how old you are if you are in good health."

Fifteen women have turned out for Miller's aerobics class on a night just 12 weeks after her accident. Some have brought children, who mimic Mom's movements on the blue mats in the back of the rec room at Campbell Park.

Pat Crumb, 47, comes because of her high blood pressure and cholesterol. "It's down to 200," she beams.

Dorothy Daniels, 48, relieves the stress of teaching 25 first-graders at Eisenhower Elementary in Clearwater.

Miller, limping slightly with her left knee wrapped in brown gauze, fires up the women with words of encouragement. During an intense round of knee bends, she scolds 38-year-old Deborah Wynn for dogging it. Then Miller laughs to let her know it's all in fun.

One flash of her toothy smile is always good for an extra rep.

SUMMARY

Too many journalists begin writing as soon as they have done some reporting. If you ask them when they focus, organize, draft and revise, the typical answer is: "As I'm going along." This approach cheats them and their audience of stories that are sharply focused, well-organized, quickly drafted and carefully revised. As a result, journalism is largely a "first-draft culture," one that produces sloppy, haphazard stories that drive audiences away. In this example, a student journalist demonstrates the beneficial influence of taking a process approach to produce an authoritative, engaging story that uses the dramatic experiences of real people to help convey important health information. Fortunately, that process can be observed, understood, and—on the best days—repeated. By carefully managing their time, journalists can use the process to quickly focus, report, organize, draft and revise stories on deadline. Rather than waste time procrastinating, process-savvy journalists can tackle their work using intelligence, critical thinking and creativity. And, as John Silcox shows, they can deliver a story that's timely, informative, interesting and a pleasure to read.

THE COACHING WAY

Taking Charge of Your Stories

BY THE END OF THIS CHAPTER,

you should be able to...

> Learn the basics of coaching

> Identify situations when coaching help tends to be useful

> Learn to work with others as part of the coaching process

> Illustrate the costs and benefits of prescriptive responses ("You should do it this way") and descriptive ones ("What's the point of your story . . . in one word?")

> Grasp the coaches' most effective questions: "What works in your story?" and "What needs work?"

> 66 The author himself is the best judge of his own performance; none has so deeply meditated on the subject; none is so sincerely interested in the event. 99
>
> —EDWARD GIBBON, BRITISH HISTORIAN

IN THE "GOOD old days," grizzled editors snatched up your stories, growled at their incompetence, and rewrote them. Sometimes you wouldn't see the changes until the paper emerged the next day. An editor's job was to fix stories. Since the early 1970s, a new approach, known as "coaching," has emerged.

The idea is this: You know all the problems in your stories, and how to fix them, whether you realize it or not. In an age when news organizations are changing and budgets are shaky, beginning journalists have to work harder to develop on their own. The ability to improve your own work will be a vitally important skill for you in the still-developing world of 21st-century journalism.

In this chapter, you will learn what coaching is, why coach, who can coach, when and where is coaching most useful; discover the tools of a good coach; understand the difference between descriptive and prescriptive responses to story elements; and master the hallmarks of effective coaching.

COACHING BASICS

As a reporter, you'll confront daily challenges that will test your intelligence, energy, courage and sense of what is right and wrong. Although this may sound like pretty tough territory to enter, fortunately, there's good news for you.

You understand all your problems.

You have all the solutions to all those problems.

Yeah, right.

Granted, those are startling statements coming at the beginning of a textbook designed to help teach the craft of news reporting and writing. But this philosophy is the heart of this book. "The Coaching Way," as we'll refer to it, is based on the approach pioneered by the late professor and journalist Donald M. Murray and further developed and spread worldwide by The Poynter Institute, a school for professional and student journalists in St. Petersburg, Florida, and journalists who embraced coaching's power.

Coaching is based on the idea that the power to recognize a story's problems as well as the means to fix them lies within the person reporting and writing the piece. This doesn't mean you won't need teachers, editors, classmates or colleagues to help you master the range of skills needed to report and write the news with power, clarity and grace. These relationships form the heart of the one-on-one coaching that will help you produce your best work. The best writers often say that the more they write, the more they realize how little they know about writing.

What "The Coaching Way" does is place the ultimate responsibility for learning on you. It also recognizes that the person who knows most about the story is the reporter; after all, he or she has done the reporting and writing. Coaching allows you more control over your stories, but in turn it requires active participation rather than sitting back and waiting for others to tell you what to do. The search for answers must begin with you. Coaching can help you achieve success by drawing on two basic journalistic

Effective coaches listen to reporters talk about their work rather than tell them what to do. Lori Waldon, news director, WISN-TV Milwaukee, listens to producer Tanya Simpson discuss a story.

skills: asking good questions and listening to the answers. (As you'll see, these often aren't as easy as they sound.)

What's the news? What's the story? What works in this story? What needs work? Where can you go to find that information? Who can you talk to about this story? Those are the kinds of open-ended questions that good editors and teachers have always used to get the best from their reporters and students. "The Coaching Way" asks you to help yourself and others do the same.

Effective listening requires **empathy**, the ability to identify with another person's point of view and to communicate that understanding. It requires a range of other skills and qualities, too: patience, flexibility, confidence, a willingness to experiment, a keen awareness of another's situation and a genuine desire to help someone else achieve his or her goals.

COACHING OR CODDLING

Newsroom skeptics, usually editors but often jaded reporters, scorn coaching as "coddling" or, uncomfortable with the physical or emotional intimacy that focus on the self-doubt and insecurity journalists often feel, dismiss it as "touchy-feely." However, years of coaching print, broadcast and online journalists have convinced the authors of this textbook that these critics are flat-out wrong. Coaching, which places responsibility on the individual journalist, is demanding and rigorous.

Coaches don't give advice as much as they ask a single question: What do you think? It's not a question journalists hear often, and at first, they balk. Ultimately, you come to understand that a coach asks questions that you must answer.

The qualities of a good coach are described in the obituary of a *New Yorker* magazine editor named Robert Gerdy: "He was generous, he was sensitive, he was tactful, he was modest, he was patient, he was imaginative, he was unfailingly tuned in... He found his own joy in helping people bring their writings to a state of something like perfection."

THE COACHING WAY

Throughout this book, you'll find sections labeled "The Coaching Way," which contain lists of questions, along with tips and techniques designed to help you discover what you may already know about your story, what you may still need to find out, and where or whom to go to for information and guidance. These questions can also be used to help classmates or colleagues diagnose problems in their stories and devise solutions. When working in groups, as is so common in today's online journalism classes, members can work on their assigned tasks and then look over each other's efforts to help them improve their work.

Historical Perspectives: The Origins of Coaching

In the 1970s, newspaper editors began to express increasing concern about the quality of writing. In 1977, Eugene Patterson, president of the American Society of Newspaper Editors, convinced the organization to create an award to recognize better writing. Some newspapers began hiring outside writing experts. At others, editors such as Jack Hart of *The* (Portland) *Oregonian* and Joel Rawson of the *Providence Journal* began conducting writing workshops, distributing copies of excellent writing that participants discussed. One of the most prominent coaches was Donald M. Murray, a Pulitzer Prize winner who created the journalism program at the University of New Hampshire.

"I was invited," Murray recalled years later, "to work with writers at *The Boston Herald* and called myself a 'writing coach.'" The term stuck, and today there are writing coaches working in newsrooms around the world.

How Can I Help? When Coaching Is Needed

You're having trouble getting a source to talk with you. You'd like to improve your interviewing by asking better questions. You have a story idea, but your teacher or editor tells you it's a topic, not a story. You have trouble generating story ideas. Your boss tells you your broadcast stories have too many "experts," also known as "talking heads." She wants more people who are directly affected to tell their stories, not experts spouting opinions. Your stories drag in the middle. You don't know where to begin or to end. You've gathered hours of audio or video and don't know which to use in your online story.

Donald M. Murray

The late Donald Murray, shown here with a journalism student at the University of New Hampshire, believed that an effective coaching session need not be long and that the writer should do most of the talking.

These scenarios demonstrate when a coach can help:

IDEA

Coaches brainstorm ideas and assignments with the journalist. Together, they brainstorm a list of the readers' questions, or what Scanlan's journalism teacher Melvin Mencher labeled "non-negotiable necessities"—the elements that absolutely must be present in a story of this given type—required for fires, council meetings, profiles and similar stories.

FOCUS

Coaches press the journalist to answer, "What's your story really about? In one word?" They suggest the journalist come up with a headline for their blog posts, or news updates. They ask, "What is the dominant message of this story?" Often, your answer will be better than what you think it is. If not, the coach can ask for or suggest an alternative.

COLLECT

Coaches help the journalist develop a reporting plan, linking sources with questions. If the journalist is a newcomer, coaches share their institutional memory. They encourage the journalist to identify the non-negotiable necessities the story needs and where to find them. Coaches suggest ways to report—direct observation, telephone, email—but always encourage the journalist to leave the newsroom if the deadline allows.

"I discovered the obvious—that students had very different writing strengths and problems, and very little awareness of their particular strengths and weaknesses. Individually, in conference, they could be given the kind of attention—coaching—that could help them recognize what worked and needed work in their writing."

—DONALD M. MURRAY, PROFESSOR, UNIVERSITY OF NEW HAMPSHIRE

At *The Charlotte* (NC) *Observer*, editors, such as Michael Weinstein with feature writer Elizabeth Leland, often read stories back to writers so they could hear how the story sounds and make appropriate changes.

ORDER

Coaches make sure the journalist knows the various types of story shapes—inverted pyramid, hourglass, narrative, alternative story forms, such as info boxes, timelines, blog posts, tweets and interactive elements, such as audio, video, photo galleries, shifting content from radio and television to websites.

DRAFT

Coaches help journalists defeat writers' block and procrastination by encouraging them to start with something less polished, to freewrite, print out early and often and mark up the draft and let it lead them toward better ones.

REVISE

Coaches ask journalists two questions:
1. What works?
2. What needs work?
They let the journalists, who know the story better than the coach, diagnose the pluses and challenges raised by the draft. Journalists should write answers to the questions before a teacher or editor reads their story and then make changes so they can present their best effort. For many reasons, writers usually end up asking: "What doesn't work?" Failures can be instructive, but paying attention to successes is a stronger and more positive approach. Remind yourself, "What needs work in my story? (We'll look more at this process later in the chapter.)

"Broadcast coaches do the same kind of story coaching, helping focus, identify sources and resources," says long-time broadcast journalist Jill Geisler, who now heads the leadership and management program at The Poynter Institute. "Make good ethical decisions and discover ways to share the abundance of information we may need to pack into a finite amount of time or space."

"3-2-1. You're on," is a command heard more often as newspaper and online journalists take to the airwaves. Many need "on-air performance coaching." In 1978, Geisler became the country's first female news director of a major market network affiliate, and built an award-winning newsroom culture at WITI in Milwaukee, her hometown. Hers was a teaching newsroom, where coaching and collaboration were as important as ethics and enterprise. But not at first. "I was an inveterate 'fixer' who loved to improve copy by simply re-writing it for people," she says. "It was efficient and ego-stroking for me. It was a total disservice to others."

Then she learned about coaching at a Poynter Institute seminar that transformed her and her newsroom. She made a pledge: "I vowed that when I returned to my newsroom I would sit on my hands when working on stories." Geisler made good on her promise even on tight deadlines when reporters came to her for a look. "If I saw a problem I'd ask, 'May I type?' before touching my keyboard. It was my way of reminding them and myself that the story is first and foremost theirs, and their manager is there to help, not hijack."

Coaches ask journalists how they would solve the problems in the story. Students who embrace the coaching method look at their stories more critically, and are able to make more objective judgments—"I don't think my story backs up the lead." "I'd cut this section. It's not what the story is really about." "I've got lots of misspellings." "My verbs are weak." They spot holes in the story that an editor may have missed and suggest quick ways to fill them with reporting or material they have already collected.

COACHING VERSUS FIXING

In *Coaching Writers: Editors and Reporters Working Together Across Media Platforms*, Roy Peter Clark and Don Fry spell out five important differences between coaching a story and fixing it.

Coaching	Fixing
1. Improves the reporter.	Improves copy.
2. Takes the long view.	Deals with the now.
3. Done over time.	Done now.
4. Corrects tendencies.	Corrects errors.
5. Shares control.	Takes control.

CONVERGENCE POINT ⬇

The Writing Coach in the Broadcast Newsroom

In "The Writing Coach in the Newsroom," veteran newsroom manager Jill Geisler makes the case for the benefits of coaching writers versus simply fixing scripts.

Find this link on the companion Web site at **www.oup.com/us/ scanlan.**

❝ I cannot teach anybody anything, I can only make them think.❞

—SOCRATES, GREEK PHILOSOPHER

These two approaches can also be thought of in another way, as description versus prescription:

1. The coach describes his reaction to the story.
2. The fixer prescribes her reaction.

In many cases, your boss will prescribe how to change the story, based on his or her reaction and experience, and you follow the directions. **Prescription** means telling writers how to fix something or fixing it themselves.

In the best cases, an editor describes how he or she responded to the story, and you make the necessary changes.

Description explains the way a reader's mind processes the story. A reader may be intrigued by a newspaper lead or the splash page of a Web presentation, but then bog down, or become confused. Readers question stories: What is this story about? Why should I read it? Why should I click this audio link or an entire photo gallery? Why should I keep watching, or should I just turn the channel? Those are the kinds of questions a reader and viewer will ask. Coaches are their surrogates.

COACHING TECHNIQUES

There are a number of techniques available for reinforcing and facilitating the act of coaching. These range from using your imagination to get inside the thoughts of the reader ("movies" of a reading), to reading aloud and even taking dictation. These methods all help writers see their work from the inside out, recognizing issues that might not be obvious through traditional techniques. This section explores some of these proven coaching techniques.

1. Let the writer speak first.
2. Listen—often an unnatural act for editors and teachers.
3. Ask open-ended questions (what, how and why?) that encourage the writer to diagnose problems and prescribe solutions.
4. Coaching sessions need not be long, especially when the coach responds to a question with, "What do you think you should do to improve your story?"
5. The coach and the writer each have a printout. The coach reads the story aloud. Often, the writer will begin marking up the copy when problems jump out at them.

A Movie of My Reading

Writing teacher Peter Elbow (*Writing with Power* and *Writing Without Teachers*) says that writers don't need "advice about what changes to make [or] theories of what is good and bad writing," but rather "movies of people's minds while they read your words."

Inspired by that philosophy, one coaching approach involves giving the writer a **"movie reading"**: Rather than the coach prescribing what writers should do, she describes how she processed their stories. To be sure, this is highly subjective—no two

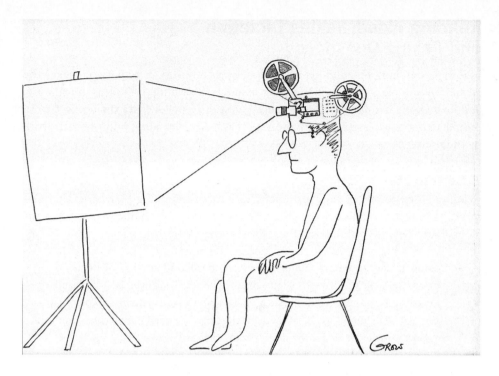

The idea behind a "movie reading" that describes reactions to a draft without prescribing action by the writer is captured in this whimsical cartoon by journalism professor Gerald Grow.

editors/coaches will go through a story in the same way—but it provides a straightforward, sometimes blunt commentary on a knowledgeable person's first reaction to the piece. An effective movie reading should generally consist of constructive commentary—questions and suggestions—but given the spontaneous nature of the task, all manner of comments may pop up.

A typical movie reading sounds like this:

> Hmm. What's this story about? The lead is intriguing. I get a hint of what's going on, and I'll keep reading. When I get to the third graf I slow down. I'm confused. I had to go back and read that sentence twice to make sense of it. Okay, I'm back on track, but now I'm beginning to wonder again what this story is about. What's the point here? I'm getting bogged down in this section. Hmm, that's a funny quote, but who said it? Okay, now I'm completely lost, but I'll keep plugging away. Page two. Oh, I get it, that's what it's about. Gosh, why didn't you tell me that sooner?

Although this is often delivered in conversation, it's more effective when the movie reading appears in the margins of a printout of a story or a splash page or interactive timeline in Flash, or in comments embedded in an electronic version of the story. This approach is especially useful for reporters who come to a coaching session thinking a story is done or those who recognize the story has problems but they have no idea how to solve them. Movie readings aren't vague and useless critiques (e.g., "It just doesn't work for me"). Instead they give journalists a sense of how one reader absorbed their work.

SEE CLOSE-UP, P. 68: MOVIE READING: HOW A COACH RESPONDS TO A WRITER'S WORK

Reading Aloud, Taking Dictation and Asking Questions

Making a coaching session interactive sometimes requires an activity to engage the writer. The simple acts of reading a story aloud, transcribing one's ideas in real time, and addressing a couple of fundamental questions out loud are often effective in jumpstarting a successful coaching session that helps journalists improve their work by themselves.

Read It to Me

Reading stories aloud is standard operating procedure at *The Charlotte* (NC) *Observer*, recipient of many writing prizes. "Not only do I read aloud, my editor reads aloud," said Tommy Tomlinson, an award-winning columnist.

> During the editing process, (editor) Mike Gordon will read through the story and pick out things he wants to talk about, and then he'll call you over to his desk and you just sit there and he reads the story aloud, and it's excruciating—it's excruciating and incredibly powerful at the same time because you immediately see all the places where you're slowing down because he can't read well out loud. So if he's not reading it well, then I'm probably not writing it well. So you go back and try again until you get it to flow a little better.

Here's another helpful technique. During the read aloud, coach and writer make simple check marks (✔) anytime something strikes them as good or needs work. It may be a word, a phrase, a sentence, even a complete paragraph or passage. The checkmarks remind each of a reaction. The reaction may be positive—"Great active verb!", reflect a question, "Will I see the interesting character in the lead again?" or signal difficulty, "That sentence stopped me dead in its tracks. I wonder why?" or disappointment, "I'm never going to see that character in the lead again, am I? Darn, I feel like I've been a victim of bait and switch."

Contrary to expectations, coach and writer display near-total recall of the thoughts or feelings beneath a simple mark on the page. Now the writer can build on the draft's successes—noticing how a period can tighten long sentences, resolving to look for more opportunities—or address its challenges, such as deleting material that doesn't support the story's focus.

Ironically, the better the writer, the more checkmarks dot her story draft.

Take Dictation

Another useful approach in coaching sessions is to ask the writer to answer questions verbally, then simply jot down his or her answers. Writers who find themselves bogged down at the keyboard regain fluency when trying to communicate with their tongues. No deleting, no getting up for a soda, but instead conveying a sure-voiced eloquence and wisdom that needs to be preserved. It's the same principle as finding the lead of a story in what you would tell a friend about it—sometimes it's easier to distill a story into its important elements by talking than by writing.

Journalist at Work **COACHING ONLINE JOURNALISTS**

In online news operations, coaching focuses on multimedia, says Vidisha Priyanka, former audience editor for TBO.com in Tampa, Florida, who coaches colleagues and college students. Coaching sessions range from how to present deadline stories with links to short-term media, such as photo galleries, and long-term ideas, producing interactive environments that engage the reader. She coaches storyboarding, an essential planning tool for Web stories that may include text, audio, video and interactive elements, by showing examples and then brainstorming approaches for the story at hand.

Two Questions That Drive Revision

1. What works?
2. What needs work?

These two questions, raised earlier in the chapter, require reporters to be honest about their stories, which isn't something reporters are always inclined to do. They've worked hard on their pieces, and often arrive at story conferences exhausted, pessimistic and insecure about the quality of their work (although they may mask it with bravado, indifference or defensiveness). By asking these two questions in this order, the revision process remains positive in nature.

A good way to start is for the reporter to freewrite answers to these two questions before a coaching session. Upon arrival, the writer reads these freewritten answers aloud, allowing the coach to make notes as needed. By beginning a session with a discussion of what's working, it gives the writer a confidence boost. If the writer and coach both understand the structure of what's working, they can then focus on the remaining material with a positive point of view.

The second question is where reporters get defensive—though it's phrased as "What needs work?" they often frame it as "What doesn't work?" It's a subtle difference but an important one that reflects the need for optimism as the writer enters the revision stage. More important, it allows the reporter—rather than the coach, editor or teacher—to identify elements that need revision. The conference becomes less a battle of wills than a collaboration between writer and reader (see Figure 3-1).

Engaging the Writer During a Coaching Session

Give a "movie reading."
Take dictation.
Ask two questions:
- What works?
- What needs work?

FIGURE 3-1 There are many ways to conduct an effective coaching session. Here are the three most important ones.

PROFESSIONALS' | COACHING

ROUNDTABLE

Coaching is a revolution in newsroom cultures where reporters normally defer to editors for everything from story assignments to final revisions taken out of the writers' hands. Coaching doesn't mean editors or instructors lose these important responsibilities. But coaching newsrooms give writers more control—and responsibility—as coaches ask good questions and listen to writers describe what works and needs work about their stories. Anyone can coach, three prominent coaches agree, as long as they follow these guidelines:

- Ask lots of open-ended questions.
- Suggest solutions rather than dictate them.
- Study the process of writing and editing to enhance your worth to writers who need help.
- Remember that coaching builds confidence, leverages the writer's strengths and inspires risk taking and collaboration.

Participants

ROY PETER CLARK, writing coach and author

JACK HART, former managing editor and writing coach, *The* (Portland) *Oregonian*, and author of *The Writer's Coach*

JILL GEISLER, 25-year TV news veteran, newsroom coach and author

> *How do you define coaching?*

Geisler: Coaching is the art of helping people discover answers to their challenges.

Clark: Coaching is the human side of editing. It develops a partnership between editor and writer.

> *Why is coaching valuable?*

Hart: We all need someone to lean on.

Geisler: Telling people what to do simply trains them to conform to your way of thinking. Coaching people teaches them to think independently—and find answers and solutions they care about more deeply because they are their own.

> *What advice would you give students who'd like to coach or be coached?*

Hart: Remember that you're there to help writers accomplish what they want to accomplish, not what you want to accomplish.

SUMMARY GUIDE THE COACHING WAY: TAKING CHARGE OF YOUR STORIES

COACHING BASICS

Coaching rests on two basic principles: Writers have the power to grasp a story's problems, and they can come up with solutions to fix the problems.

What to Remember → Coaching doesn't mean journalists don't need teachers, editors or colleagues to help improve their stories. It does, however, place ultimate responsibility on the person reporting and writing the story. No one knows a story better than the journalist producing it.

COACHING OR CODDLING

Coaches challenge writers to bring their stories to the heights of journalistic excellence by teaching them to think for themselves.

What to Remember → Skeptics think coaching means coddling writers by denying them tough criticism of their stories. But coaches are as demanding as the most hard-bitten editor who would rather fix a story than coach writers to take responsibility for improvement themselves.

THE COACHING WAY

Coaching helps journalists discover the strengths and weaknesses of their stories and how to find solutions to produce excellent work.

What to Remember → Coaches guide journalists through the entire process of reporting and writing. They ask penetrating questions and offer practical advice that helps produce work in publishable form, but leave execution of changes to the journalist.

COACHING VERSUS FIXING

There are two types of editors: coaches who collaborate with journalists and fixers who focus on copy.

What to Remember → Fixers seize control and, rather than give journalists the chance to improve their stories, take over and do it themselves. Coaches share control, giving reporters the chance to make changes and master their craft firsthand.

COACHING TECHNIQUES

Three coaching techniques offer the quickest path to writing success: movie readings, reading aloud and asking two challenging questions.

What to Remember → A movie reading describes how you or a reader process a story and provides honest reactions, useful questions and helpful suggestions. Reading drafts aloud provides distance that helps reporters identify reporting holes, organization problems and writing flaws. Asking "What works?" and "What needs work?" about a story drives effective revision.

KEY TERMS

coaching, p. 54
description, p. 60

empathy, p. 55
movie reading, p. 60

prescription, p. 60

EXERCISES

1. Coach yourself by asking what works and what needs work in your story. Stay positive, even if you despair that your entire story is a mess: "Well, I've spelled everything correctly" or "I think my lead works well." Using the six steps of the process approach, consider the strengths of your work and what you think needs improving. Is more reporting needed? Have you written a resonant ending? Work quickly to make changes.

2. Practice coaching with another student. Before you read their story, first ask, "How can I help?" Listen carefully. Take notes. There's a good chance the aspects of the story that trouble them aren't a problem, so say so. "Your lead doesn't stink." Help them with remaining problems by staying positive. "What thoughts do you have about reorganizing some of the sections in your story?"

3. Ask yourself what "non-negotiable necessities" belong in your story. Invite a friend or fellow student to suggest other ideas.

4. Experiment with movie reading. Ask a fellow student to read your draft and tell you what he thought as he read it, or offer to do the same for someone else. Make notes as you go along, including positive comments, such as "Great quote!" but don't be afraid to be honest about problems—"I'm bored here," "This confuses me"—or make suggestions, such as "Wonder if the story begins in the third paragraph?" It's best to do so in writing.

5. Discuss the merits of coaching with your fellow students or colleagues. Debate whether you consider it coddling or helping make each others' work better. What are the best ways to help?

READINGS

Clark, Roy Peter, and Fry, Don. *Coaching Writers: Editors and Reporters Working Together Across Media Platforms.* **New York: Bedford/St. Martin's, 2003.**
Two influential writing coaches updated their classic in the field to include print, broadcast and online writing in the methods of coaching writers and editors to produce their best work.

Hart, Jack. *A Writer's Coach: An Editor's Guide to Words That Work.* **New York: Pantheon, 2006.**
An acclaimed newspaper coach details how he works through the reporting and writing process with journalists and provides a wealth of advice that demonstrates how coaching produces award-winning journalism.

Murray, Donald M. *A Writer in the Newsroom.* **St. Petersburg, FL: The Poynter Institute, 1996.**
One of the first newspaper coaches recalls his early days developing the techniques that have benefited generations of journalists.

Murray, Donald M. *Expecting the Unexpected: Teaching Myself—and Others—to Read and Write.* **Portsmouth, NH: Boynton/Cook, 1989.**
In a series of inspiring and educational essays, Murray provides a handbook for writers, editors, teachers and students who need to coach themselves and others.

MOVIE READING: HOW A COACH RESPONDS TO A WRITER'S WORK

Sheila Callahan, a freelance writer, produced a first draft and final revision of a story about a school program that brings children with reading problems together with dogs trained to listen. Scanlan, her writing coach and author of the running comments in this example, read the story and provided her with a movie of his reading. The technique tells the writer how the coach processed the story. Rather than fix the story by rewriting, the coach provides honest commentary, challenging questions and practical suggestions. The goal is to leave control of the story in the writer's hands. Note: A "nut graf," newsroom shorthand for "nut paragraph," is a device that lets readers know what the story is about.

DOG ON IT
By Sheila Callahan
First Draft

Justin Ortiz sits cross-legged on a bright rug patterned with a United States map in Room 202, Christy Crawford's third grade classroom.

"It's 6 o'clock in the morning," says the 8-year old to Bodhi.

I love this opening! You start with a subject and an action verb in active tense. Good choice. The best stories are about people. Program stories are abstract. While their existence is newsworthy, readers need concrete, specific ways if they are going to be engaged.

A good detail, but what makes it bright? What's the color? Bright blue, red? Good details are precise.

The map is interesting, but distracting. Readers assume every word is chosen with care and may wonder why you mention it. You don't want to slow them down with too much detail. Is this one necessary/relevant?

Subject-verb-construction in this first paragraph is excellent. It should be used as much as possible as readers find the information easy to follow. Great opening! Establishes setting in precise fashion and introduces an important new character. Good reporters take note of things like room numbers and other minor details to enhance reader interest and credibility. They sense the reporter is paying attention. Stories raise expectations, especially at the beginning and they assume people will play a further role in the story. Too many writers introduce characters that disappear after the lead.

Again, specific detail about Justin's age is good, but two issues come up: Who is Bodhi? The question stops me in my tracks. Writers often leave out important information as a way to generate but this may sow confusion and should be used carefully. But I could be wrong about this. Readers may be encouraged to read on to find out the answer. The second is stylistic. "says to Bodhi" is four words long. "tells Bodhi," just two and more active. Consider revising.

"It's time to wake up," he continues.

Actually, it is 2:45 in the afternoon, and Bodhi, a 58-lbs Standard poodle, is awake and at work: helping children improve their literacy.

He's listening to Ortiz read "In the Morning," a children's book.

Six schools and several New York Public Library branches work with 25 certified therapy dogs provided by Brooklyn's Good Dog Foundation.

Students who need practice read aloud to them. The organization assigns the volunteer dog-and-owner teams to schools that request help for children lacking reading confidence.

I really like the way you're using dialogue. These are narrative quotes that put the reader in the scene. You avoid summary quotes, which inject the reporter's presence and break the spell of unfolding action. Is "he continues" necessary? The dialogue is in the same graf so the reader assumes it's an ongoing conversation.

As this is a feature, an informal contraction—"it's—is okay.

GREAT JOB WITH THIS SENTENCE. It's concise, detailed and gets to the heart of the story. You've written a solid anecdotal lead—a little story with characters, action, suspense, and a beginning, middle and end. And you've done it concisely at just under 40 words. Anecdotal lead should be tightly written. Readers are impatient. They want to get on with the story.

It also functions as a nut graf letting readers know what the story is about quickly. "awake and at work" is a great phrase! It makes readers wonder how a dog could be at work. You've got a misspelling. [Note that the coach doesn't identify it. It's the writer's responsibility to find and fix, using a dictionary or style guide.] I also wish I knew earlier that Bodhi was a dog, but this does settle any confusion and if flows well.

Great! Specific detail, not just a children's book, but "In the Morning."

Good. You've extended the nut graf by providing information about the program Justin and Bodhi are part of. You've started with a sharp focus that should guide the decisions you make as you write. It's an ideal location because it answers a reader's obvious question: What's the story about? But written this way I get bogged down in summary narrative about a program. Stories about programs are interesting when they are told through the prism of narrative, focusing on characters in action. You could keep the focus on characters with a simple revision. A suggestion: "Bodhi is one of 25 certified therapy dogs working in six schools and several New York Public Library branches. . . ."

Your reporting has been very specific, but "several" is vague. Can you get the exact number? The more specific the better.

Breaking up the paragraph—"Their mission: to improve children like Justin improve their literacy by reading aloud to them."—would separate the information into two sentences. Remember: a single thought per sentence heightens comprehension.

This way you can build on the nut graf while maintaining reader interest. Give it a shot and see if it works for you.

"I'm a little bit shy," explains Ortiz, a second grader. But with Bodhi, Ortiz doesn't feel foolish if he gets a word wrong. "It's just a dog," he explains.

Students who need practice read aloud to them. The organization assigns the volunteer dog-and-owner teams to schools that request help for children lacking reading confidence.

Suzanne Soehner, an acupuncturist and white poodle's owner says, "Bodhi loves to help kids learn to read."

Children practice reading out loud so that teachers can verify their pronunciation and comprehension.

On the second floor of PS 51, the Bronx New School, children ages 7–10 meet each Tuesday afternoon for reading club. "Having the dogs is a big draw," explains Crawford, especially since reading club competes with basketball, cooking and knitting clubs. "I don't have to beg you to come to reading class. Everybody and their mother wants to come."

"Emotion, fluency, projection" intones Crawford to the group practicing their books to sitting down with Bodhi.

Children who lack confidence often read barely above a whisper and like robots, mostly because they fear getting words wrong. Having a dog present "has a real calming effect," says Crawford.

Nice quotes. Clearly spoken to the reporter but even summary quotes breathe life into a story. I like the way you let us know Justin's grade, another excellent specific. Why are you repeating "explains"? In any case, no need to describe the quote, IMO. It's obvious he's explaining. "Says" or "said" is the default choice for attribution. Also, do you need the second one, anyway? You set it up nicely and "It's just a dog" is a wry punch line that loses it power with another attribution. Repetition is unnecessary. Why clutter it up?

Is this necessary? Do you think you've made it clear already?

Is an article missing in the first sentence? The quote, in this case, trumps attribution. How would it read if you flipped the sentence around, beginning with the quote? Does it matter that she's an acupuncturist? Every word must be selected with ruthless care. How does that detail support the theme?

Gotta be honest. This sentence as written bores me. It's important stuff, but does it deserve its own 14-word paragraph? Could the information be included somewhere else in a condensed version?

Good details, but a bit confusing. Is this the same school where Justin reads to Bodhi? And I've forgotten who Crawford is. Admittedly I have a short attention span. Do you want me to go back and find out and risk losing my interest? What if you flip it to "Children ages 7–10 meet each Tuesday afternoon in Ms. Crawford's classroom on the second floor of PS 51, the Bronx New School" and then pick up with her good quote. Your call.

Again, no need for "explains." Always give readers credit.

Is the last quote necessary? Sounds a bit like hyperbole.

"Intone." A big word. Why not just "tells the group"? Short simple words produce a conversational style appealing to most readers. The rest of the sentence seems overly long. Can you tighten it?

Excellent! I understand and sympathize with these children and appreciate the role the dogs play. One thought: Could you save three words if you dropped "and like robots" and simply describe the whisper?

Struggling readers also get stuck decoding words. One girl in Tuesday's club stumbled on the word "revolution" while reading her book "Young George Washington," but by practicing it repeatedly, she had it nailed when she took her turn reading to Bodhi. "She was fearless," enthused Crawford.

Parents or teachers looking to bring a therapy dog into a school can contact the Good Dog Foundation at 718-788-2988 or www.thegooddogfoundation.org. If you have a certified therapy dog or want to get certified, contact Suzy Nastasi, Director of Training and Program.

If you have a certified therapy dog or want to get certified, "We always need more teams," says Susy Nastasi, Director of Training and Program

Not sure I understand what the first sentence means.

Why don't you name the girl?

Good choice of the verb "stumbled." The sentence runs on, though, at 34 words. Remember the one-breath rule: if you can't say a sentence in one breath it's too long. Consider breaking up the two sentences and see how they read. I like the way you take over and find a great, informal phrase—"she had it nailed." But it takes four words. Could you tighten it, drive it home as a single sentence?

And please, stick with "says." It's clear from the quote that Crawford is pumped.

This is a service story so it's entirely appropriate that you provide contact information at the end. This could also be provided as a stand-alone box so it doesn't distract from your excellent story.

On second reference, the speaker should be identified by last name only and without repeating the title.

GREAT FIRST DRAFT, SHEILA!

Solid reporting, excellent organization and a firm grasp of narrative style. You've made what could be a boring program story come alive.

SUMMARY The coach responds to the entire draft with a running commentary on the writer's choices. There's an emphasis on providing positive feedback while at the same time challenging the writer to consider other options and in some cases offering mini-writing tutorials and suggestions for further reporting, reorganization and revision. The coach makes clear that the decisions are the writer's to make.

FINAL DRAFT

DOG ON IT

By Sheila Callahan

Justin Ortiz sits on a rug in Room 202, Christy Crawford's third grade classroom. "It's 6 o'clock in the morning," the 8-year old tells Bodhi. "It is time to wake up."

> Great! It's detailed, a specific, active scene that draws readers in without any clutter. Dropping "continues" maintains the flow. A simple but effective change.

Actually, it's 2:45 in the afternoon, and Bodhi, a 58-lbs. Standard poodle, is awake and at work: helping children improve their literacy. He's listening to Ortiz read "In the Morning," a children's book.

> I take back what I said about identifying Bodhi in the lead. You get to it quickly, solving the mystery. And you make clear what the story is about from the beginning.

"I'm a little bit shy," explains Ortiz, a second grader. But with Bodhi, Ortiz doesn't feel foolish if he gets a word wrong. "It's just a dog," he explains.

> Great quotes and I like that you add to Justin's description.

Bodhi is one of 25 certified therapy dogs sent by the Good Dog Foundation to work in six schools and four New York Public libraries. Their mission: Help children like Justin improve their literacy by having them read aloud.

> Terrific nut graf. I love the way Bodhi is the centerpiece.
>
> So glad you got the exact number of library branches. Good follow-up reporting.

"Bodhi loves to help kids learn to read," says Suzanne Soehner, his owner.

> Great quote and I'm glad we only learn that she's an owner without superfluous detail about her job.

Building children's reading confidence is the purpose of the program. When schools ask for help, the Brooklyn organization assigns volunteer dog-and-owner teams so students can read to them.

> FANTASTIC! I love the way you keep the story on track, alternating narrative with summary descriptions of the program. You anticipate reader's questions.

On the second floor of PS 51, Bronx New School, children ages 7–10 meet each Tuesday afternoon for reading club. They practice reading out loud and Crawford listens for students' comprehension. Third grader Rachel Osei reads the word "W-I-N-D" and pronounces it "wind" as in "wind the clock." "Does it sound right?" asks Crawford. In this context the proper pronunciation is "wind" as in "there's a fierce 'wind' blowing."

> So glad to be back in the middle of the action. You get across what the teacher looks for. You add another character and convey the teaching method with dialogue. It's a great example of showing rather than telling. Each has its place and you've found the right balance.

Reading club competes with basketball, cooking and knitting clubs, so "having the dog is a big draw," says Crawford. Once the pooch arrives, the children can't wait to get there.

> I really admire the way you've revised this to set up the competition and then explain why dogs win out. Rather than rely on a quote, you feel confident to tell the story in your own words. "Pooch" is a great choice.

Children who lack confidence often read barely above a robotic whisper, mostly because they fear getting words wrong. Having a dog present "has a real calming effect," says Crawford.

> Telling is important. Here you help the reader understand why the read aloud program works. And I like the way you introduced "robotic whisper" with economic power. Crawford's comment punctuates the graf, effective use of a powerful device.

Struggling readers also get stuck trying to decode unfamiliar words. Shanon Santiago stumbles on the word "revolution" while reading "Young George Washington." Santiago keeps practicing, and when her turn to read to Bodhi comes, she nails it. "She was fearless," says Crawford.

Parents or teachers looking to bring a therapy dog into a school can contact the Good Dog Foundation at (718) 788-2988 or www.thegooddogfoundation.org. If you have a certified therapy dog or want to get certification, contact Suzy Nastasi, the foundation's training director.

Nastasi says, "We always need more teams."

What a great kicker to your story. It brings it full circle. This is a great graf. Adding "unfamiliar" helps me understand what "decoding" means. Your first sentence explains a particular difficulty and then you shift directly to a scene that illustrates the problem and solution. You've shown that scenes need not be long. Short sentences, active verbs drive the narrative. And you took over, writing a stronger sentence about Shannon nailing it than the teacher's quote. Keep in mind: if you can say it better than the quote, do so. You're the writer, after all.

I was glad to see "enthused" dropped in favor of "says." It's really all you need. Sorry to keep harping on it, but it's important.

In the end, this is a program story, but one you've brought to life with your characters, scenes and dialogue. It's the appropriate time to use the story to make a pitch for help. Giving the readers specific contact information helps them play a role.

Ending with the quote drives home the point. I'd still argue that this should be in an info box so it doesn't dilute the power of the last scene.

You've described a creative, useful program that deserves support. You've done a wonderful job bringing what could have been a dry story into a lively one!!!!

SUMMARY

The writer has transformed the first draft into a well-organized, smoothly written story that is 402 words long. Even though the final draft is just 62 words shorter, it's remarkable how much material the writer deemed unnecessary or condensed, redrafted and revised to include necessary information without bogging down the narrative. Program stories are a routine part of news coverage. In Callahan's hands, the result is a tightly written story about a program that skillfully focuses on the people affected by it, shown in dramatic action. Coaches encourage, but they often ask tough questions and may make suggestions that the writer is free to accept or reject. In the end, credit always goes to the writer.

The bottom line: Writers don't want to be told what to do. They want to know how a reader reacts so they can make changes that better serve their audience. A movie reading accomplishes these goals, encouraging the writer while advocating for improvement.

Postscript: *The New York Daily News* published Sheila Callahan's story virtually intact. The paper favors short stories. Editors trimmed the seventh paragraph and made a few other minor changes. You can read the story at http://www.nydailynews .com/new-york/education/good-dog-pups-kids-learn-read-article-1.256220.

CHAPTER 4

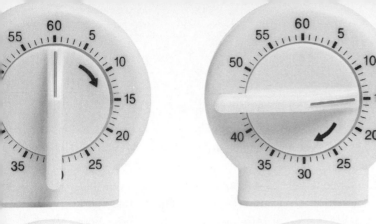

STORYTELLING VERSUS SPEED

Deadlines in the 21st Century

MOST WRITERS WISH they had hours to craft and fine-tune their prose. As a reporter in the 21st century, however, this is seldom a reality. Learning to write effectively with the clock ticking may be the most important challenge that you will face as a journalist. It's especially tough in today's world of instant news, where reporters face continual and multiple deadlines, often for platforms such as multimedia and social media in addition to print and broadcast. Time management is a key skill. In this chapter you will learn—or refresh—ingrained lessons about storytelling that are easy to forget in newsrooms that demand quick information.

ONE SIDE OF THE EQUATION: STORYTELLING

Story. It's a word you'll hear echoing in a newsroom on an average working day. "I've got a great story." "Hey, Malika, great story!" "I'm working on a story about . . ."

But what journalists mean when they say "story" is often something else. We call them stories, but most of them are **articles**—organized collections of information. Many are competent, complete, clear and accurate, and they convey vital material to readers. They may present facts—about an accident, a public meeting, a speech—in clear, logical fashion. But they're not *stories*.

On deadline, you and your readers can be satisfied if your story meets the qualifications of this definition:

> A story features characters rather than sources, communicates experience through the five senses and a few others: a sense of people, sense of place, sense of time and, most important, a sense of drama, has a beginning that grabs a reader's attention, a middle that keeps the reader engaged and an ending that lingers in the reader's mind like the reverberations of a gong.

Let's examine these guidelines more closely:

Writing on deadline is a fact of life for working journalists. Curt Nickish of National Public Radio has just minutes to write his script about an American League Championship game in the media center of Boston's Fenway Park.

1. Features Characters Rather Than Sources

In too many deadline-driven news reports, people are often little more than a name, title, age and address. It takes more effort to zero in on the attributes that distinguish one person from another.

Notice how Anne Hull of the *St. Petersburg Times* put people on the page, not as sources or as talking heads, but as fully rounded **characters**:

>**EXAMPLE** Carl's skin was black-gold, and his eyelashes curled over his eyes, just like Eugene's. His beard needed trimming, and the T-shirt he wore was faded and too small, but there was something proud and impenetrable about him.

A person can be sketched quickly and with powerful effect with a few brush-strokes, as Mitch Albom of the *Detroit Free Press* does with his deadline profile of a football player and convicted rapist: "He is kind of thin for a football player, with a gangly walk, dark hair that falls onto his forehead, a thick neck, crooked teeth, a few pimples."

Sometimes it takes no more than a word or two to create a striking description. In her story about a woman known as Mama Gert, Rebecca Catalanello could have simply written, "Jason Myron, 8." Instead, she wrote, "Jason Myron, a freckle-faced 8-year-old," evoking a child's face.

In each of these cases, the reporter was careful to record details that could give the reader a sense of what made each person unique. To put them in your story, they must be in your notebook.

2. Uses Your Senses to Communicate

Thorough reporting relies on the five senses: hearing, sight, touch, smell and taste.

To tell powerful stories, the writer should add five more:

> A sense of people
> A sense of place
> A sense of time
> A sense of drama

Observing helps place the reader at the scene of an event. Out in the field, Gerald M. Carbone of *the Providence Journal* records sensory details in his notebook. "I will always write down 'Sight,' and I'll look around and see what I'm seeing," he says, "and I'll write down 'Sound,' and then 'Smell' or 'Scent.'" This habit enabled him to report and write an award-winning story about a dramatic mountaintop rescue that provided a sense of place with this evocative passage lifted directly from his notebook.

>**EXAMPLE** Below the treeline, the White Mountains in winter are a vision of heaven. Deep snow gives them the texture of whipping cream. Boulders become soft pillows. Sounds are muted by the snow. Wind in the frosted pines is a whisper, a caress.

By using his senses and rendering them with the power of poetry, Carbone placed the reader in the mountains.

Gerald M. Carbone

3. Has a Beginning That Grabs a Reader's Attention

On March 13, 1964, a young New York City woman named Kitty Genovese was stabbed to death near her home in Queens. The case became a cause célèbre about a callous society because police said a number of witnesses—estimated to be 38, but many people believe that number is too high—didn't respond to her cries for help; only one called the police. *The New York Times* led its brief next-day story with a straight news lead, apparently directly off the police blotter, reporting the stabbing death of a 28-year-old woman, Catherine Genovese, outside her apartment. Screams awoke neighbors, who discovered the body. Nothing out of the ordinary, it seemed.

But the *Herald Tribune* took a different approach.

▶EXAMPLE The neighbors had grandstand seats for the slaying of Kitty Genovese. And yet, when the pretty, diminutive 28-year-old brunette called for help, she called in vain.

One story. Two leads. One reports the news, the other tells a devastating story in 26 words, immediately capturing reader interest with a sense of drama.

4. Has a Middle That Keeps the Reader Engaged

Like a runner who falls flat halfway through a race, reporters too often use the middle of their story as a dumping ground for boring information. But the middle can be a

CHIP'S CORNER

THE RIGHT DETAILS IN THE RIGHT PLACE

When Tony Conigliaro, a much-beloved former Boston Red Sox player, emerged from a four-month-long coma after suffering a heart attack in 1982, I was assigned to cover a hospital press conference about his condition for the *Providence Journal*. I decided to use the middle of my deadline story to convey details about his physical condition that provided a sense of people and time.

▶EXAMPLE Reporters were not allowed to see Conigliaro, who had auditioned for a sportscasting job the day of his heart attack. What they would find in a second-floor hospital, Dr. Kaulbach said, is a 37-year-old man "in extraordinary condition. He is lean, he looks like an athlete, his muscles have not lost their tone."

It is a mirage.

"If you watched him for a while," the doctor said, "you would realize he does not behave like a person who is awake. He's sort of vague, he sort of stares. He is no longer truly comatose, but you cannot say he is conscious."

Conigliaro faces "many months" of physical therapy, and even after that, the doctor said, he could not predict a full recovery or a normal life.

"He will not recover to the point where he will go jogging or do anything that is within the realm of possibility for the average citizen."

The information about Conigliaro's medical condition and the timing of his recovery was important but was too detailed for a lead or an ending because my focus was on the devotion of his family and fans. Rather than slow the reader down, I used the line "It is a mirage," set off as a paragraph, to heighten surprise and maintain the story's interest. ▶

useful spot for a telling anecdote, including a historical perspective or a vivid description of a process or different points of view that enlarges a reader's understanding in a painless way.

Rather than simply listing facts, you can let interviewees explain terms and concepts, providing additional depth in voices other than your own. You can add material that helps to flesh out the items in the lead and lets you and your sources elaborate on the elements that grabbed the reader's attention in the first place.

5. Has an Ending That Lingers in the Reader's Mind

Frequently news stories don't really have endings—they just stop, often with a dull quote. Ideally every story should build to a logical conclusion, and the best stories should have endings that resonate beyond the last word.

Matthew Purdy of *The New York Times* meets that standard in his Oct. 15, 1994, story about the testimony of seven-year-old Johnny Morales, a boy who witnessed his father being murdered. After testifying that he saw the defendant shoot his father, Johnny then left the courtroom, a little boy in a suit sheltered by two women. Purdy's final paragraph conveys an abrupt transition as Johnny leaves the adult world of criminal justice. "The door banged open and Johnny was a boy again. He quickly drew his hand up to his mouth as if it had been hit by the door, let out a big 'Ah,' and broke into a big, toothy smile."

THE OTHER SIDE: GET IT DONE, NOW!

Such attention to storytelling technique seems to run counter to today's trends in journalism, but it doesn't have to. The best newspapers strive to write narratives even on a breaking news story.

Reporter Michael Kruse demonstrated the technique while covering a court hearing when Nicole Batiste, 19, pleaded guilty to aggravated manslaughter of a child. After giving birth in her bathroom, Batiste had hid the baby in a Rubbermaid container. Kruse closes his story with a closely observed moment that captures news and drama.

❯EXAMPLE Batiste went back to her seat and sat in front of her mother and took a pen and a clipboard and signed the plea agreement and then sat still again. She looked tiny and cold and pulled the sleeves of her shirt over her hands. Her mother had a sweater and placed it on the shoulders of her daughter.

—*St. Petersburg Times, Jan. 14, 2007*

But where traditional newspaper writers often had hours to compile facts and interview material and lovingly craft their stories, today few have that luxury. Today's journalists often find themselves writing stories in pieces, sending in quick snippets of information from the site of an event (or posting them to Twitter), then returning to the newsroom to turn those tidbits and any new information into complete stories.

❝❝ Of the many definitions of story, the simplest may be this. It is a piece of writing that makes the reader want to find out what happens next. ❞❞

—BILL BUFORD, FORMER FICTION EDITOR, *THE NEW YORKER*

SEE CLOSE-UP, P. 92: BREAKING NEWS NARRATIVE

If a reporter must stay at the scene, these chunks of information are assembled by an editor and posted as completed stories.

This approach echoes the long-held practices of news services such as Associated Press and Reuters, which have always needed to update information constantly to accommodate different time zones and deadlines. As a result, they developed techniques that got stories done quickly without sacrificing accuracy.

Notable among these is a technique called "reporting by accretion." **Accretion** is the act of adding to something gradually (like the financial term "accrue"); to report by accretion is to submit succeeding portions of a story to your editors as you write them. Editors assemble the pieces into stories for quick transmittal, or if the story is big news, they'll transmit the pieces so that their subscribers can assemble it themselves to suit their own deadlines. A full story created from these pieces is called a **writethrough**. Whether snippets or complete stories, the journalist brings news sense to the task, assessing what is timely, important and interesting.

"With traditional newspaper stories, you can toy around with (a story) all day long, doing the reporting, then piecing it together and writing it fluidly in the last couple of hours of your shift. With accretion, it's built one layer on one layer, writethrough by writethrough. It allows you to see the story as it's building, to see the holes in the story as it's building," says Associated Press bureau chief John Raess.

Another element that adds to the time crunch these days is that many reporters are called upon to post separate Web material in addition to their stories. For example, Kevin Acee of the *San Diego Union-Tribune* has embraced **multimedia** journalism, regularly posting blog and Twitter entries, videos and other online material over and above his traditional writing duties (see Figure 4-1). "I love what I do," Acee says, "but I'm working *constantly* now." His multimedia approach to sports coverage has earned him great recognition, yet he acknowledges that it's had an impact on his writing. "I

Ethical Dilemmas ❗ BLOGGING WITH ANONYMOUS SOURCES

A murder has been reported in your community. You are live-blogging the event from the scene, filing multiple posts as events unfold. The victim is a young mother who was found slain in her home. You have identified the victim, based on information from a police spokesperson. Then a detective tells you that investigators have identified the woman's estranged husband as a suspect and are searching for him. The detective insists that the information can't be attributed to him, but only as a "law enforcement source close to the investigation." It's an important break in the story, and you are under pressure to file timely and important information on tight deadlines. You discover that a broadcast outlet has gone on the air with the information credited to the anonymous source. Your organization has a policy against using anonymous sources, but it's routinely violated. You know that some of your posts go online before they are edited. You write the post but hesitate before hitting send. Should you publish simply because the competition has done so? What if the police are wrong? What is your obligation to the husband, who will be forever identified as a suspect in his estranged wife's death? To their children? To your audience? The clock is ticking. Would you delay until you can consult your editors? Or, mindful of the deadline and competitive pressure, would you send the post anyway, noting that information came from a law enforcement source who demanded anonymity? ▶

FIGURE 4-1 For today's journalists, the world of online news requires additional and often new responsibilities, as demonstrated by *San Diego Union-Tribune* sportswriter Kevin Acee's weekly schedule.

haven't written as many stories that I'm proud of as a writer because of all the things I have to do now."

The challenges that Acee and other journalists face require effective time management skills, especially with multiple deadlines. You can use your time wisely by relying on the process approach and a timer—a watch or the countdown features on most cell phones—which will give you greater control. Make a quick plan and set a time limit: 95 seconds to find your focus (very often, you can plug some of your free-writing directly into the story), 30–60 seconds to sketch a plan, and then divide the time left for reporting, drafting and revision. Set your own deadlines, especially for revision, which is the time to guarantee, accuracy, fairness and clarity. Aim to deliver your story earlier than your editor calls for. Your copy will be better for it, and you'll sweat less.

QUICK Tips ⏱ AN ACCURACY CHECKLIST

■ *Proper names.* Did I check the spelling of a person's name directly with the person? Did I ask the person to spell it back to me? If the primary source isn't available, have I checked with two independent, knowledgeable sources? Have I applied similar scrutiny to other biographical details in my story such as age, family members, job title, educational background? Is all information up-to-date?

■ *Telephone numbers and addresses.* Did I call any telephone number in my story, using the version I have typed into the computer? Have I verified related information such as addresses and locations?

■ *Information about events.* Have I double-checked the date, place and time provided and compared it to what I've typed in my story or listing? Does my editor have the information so he or she can double-check it, too?

■ *Math and numbers.* Have I checked the calculations of my source? Is he or she using the correct method, and is the calculation free of math errors? If I am doing my own calculations, have I used the correct methods and double-checked my math? If I'm not a math whiz, have I run my calculations by a colleague who knows math? Have I provided my original numbers in clear form to my editor and the graphics department for double-checking?

■ *Photos, captions, graphics.* Have I compared the information in my story to that provided in the captions or graphics that will accompany it? Does information match up?

■ *Different versions.* Have I independently verified accounts of such things as historical events and records, legal situations and descriptions of problems with an authoritative source? For example, if I

am quoting an opponent about the impact of a new law, have I looked up the law, and have I checked the opponent's version with legal experts? If there are different versions of the facts, have I done everything I can to resolve them, or does my story at least make clear that some information is in dispute? Does my story assert opinion as fact? Have I taken potentially out-of-date or incorrect information from old clips without verifying it? What additional verification do I need to do?

■ *Assumptions.* Am I relying on assumption or memory that some information in my story is factual? Have I accepted information from a second-hand source as correct? What must I do to verify the information? ▸

Michele McLellan, The (Portland) Oregonian

Journalist at Work THE WEB AND THE TICKING CLOCK

When he took the job of covering the National Football League's San Diego Chargers, Kevin Acee of the *San Diego Union-Tribune* had no idea how much or how quickly that job—and its deadlines—would evolve.

"All I ever wanted to be was a beat writer," says Acee, who has covered the Chargers since 2005. "All I wanted was to write for the newspaper and tell the story of the team."

When he started, during football season Acee's job mainly consisted of doing the work necessary to write a story or two per day about the team, then covering each Sunday's game in depth with details of the action and interviews from the players.

As one of today's most active multimedia journalists, his in-season weekly tasks now include:

- Writing daily stories for the newspaper and its Web site
- Posting Twitter updates and blog entries multiple times per day
- Responding daily to readers' questions in his "Chargers Mailbag"
- Producing and posting "Chargers Report" videos for the paper's Web site once or twice a week
- Participating in a "Chargers Roundtable" video with other sports staffers once a week
- Producing and posting "Acee Advance," a video previewing the upcoming game a day or two before it's played
- Appearing throughout the week in local and national media to discuss the game and his outlet's coverage
- Covering the game itself, including getting quotes from players and coaches, video of which is then posted to the Web site
- Producing and posting "Acee Analysis," a video postgame discussion

"I have multiple deadlines—it's almost like my job never ends," Acee says. "I'm tweeting during a game, perhaps blogging during a game, blogging before a game. Then when a game is done, after doing my fact gathering and all that, I might tweet again. I have at least one video to do, then three or more stories to do by my deadline for the paper. And that's just on game day—all through the week I also tweet, blog, and post videos. I have six, seven, eight deadlines throughout the day." ▶

FOCUSING AND PLANNING ON THE FLY

Reporting is where most reporters spend their time. Few focus or organize, even though those are two of the most important steps of the process.

The search for focus must be relentless. The news storyteller keeps asking, "What is this story about? Why does it matter?"

That's why effective writers recognize that the most important task is finding the central idea. If you're unclear on the central element that will make the story compelling, ask some of the people involved why it matters to them. Find the connective thread that makes these people care about the topic. The human responses to events are often the most compelling elements of a story, and can provide a point of connection with your readers.

Finding your focus will give you a destination. Now you need a map to get there. Whether writing on a laptop at the scene, driving back to the newsroom or editing a broadcast story for airing, you need to **organize** your story to ensure it will be coherent for your audience once it's done.

You should identify the most important points, terms and quotes as soon as you can after gathering your material. Most professional reporters reflexively hunt for the leads to their stories as they gather information, but truly effective ones develop a talent for thinking of story structure on the fly as well. If you begin to see a narrative thread emerge as you report, make sure you jot it down or record it. Circle good quotes in your notebook. If you can already begin to see what your story may look like while you're getting your facts and interviews, you'll go a long way toward being able to produce quality writing on tight deadlines.

The Coaching Way ⚐ STORYTELLING ON DEADLINE

So how does a reporter reconcile the opposing forces of storytelling and speed? A smart way is to develop methods that help you focus your efforts in tight deadline situations. Keep these process terms in mind when reporting on deadline:

- **Idea**. News drives storytelling on deadline (the union's strike vote, the first day of school, a fire at the town's biggest employer). But news storytelling reveals truths that don't emerge in straight-ahead news reports. The reporting of meaningful information and developments is the primary responsibility of the journalist, but the principles of narrative—establishing character and plot, writing with a sense of people, place, drama and time—are the engine of stories that will captivate your audience.
- **Focus**. Critical and creative thinking fuel storytelling. The writer has a

firm grasp of the story's theme—the central meaning—and can express it with economy and verve. A lack of focus leads to lack of clarity, which will cost you readers and viewers.
- **Collect**. Good writing demands excellent reporting. The deadline storyteller must collect the details that convey the sense of story. As noted earlier, a good reporter must be observant—stop and take note of the sights, sounds and smells of a scene.
- **Order**. Even though time is short, planning is vital for an article or story. Effective writers know that a few moments of planning at the outset will save them and their editors time in the final minutes when time is even shorter, pressure is higher and the chance for errors greater. Make a quick list of the high points of the story and organize your thinking before you write.

- **Draft**. Deadline writers can use the draft as a means of discovering the best way to deliver on the promise of their planning. If you're having trouble matching your material to your outline, start out with a "brain dump"—just start typing what you have into chunks, then find the material that fits into the structure you had in mind.
- **Revise**. On deadline, you might assume there is no time to revise. But if you want your stories to stand out, you must always make the effort to **clarify** the meaning, structure and language before you hit the "send" button. That means making time, even when it is short, to cut, refine and reorganize your story to make it clear, accurate, fair and compelling. Hold off, even just for a few seconds, to make sure you've got it right. It won't matter if you make the deadline if your story is wrong. ▼

DRAFTING ON DEADLINE

The writer continues the process of discovery by writing the story. For some, that means transcribing their notes and starting the writing process once that's done. Others start writing by zeroing in on the lead or the ending. Either way, the idea is to generate copy that you can work with and revise.

Notice how Christine Vendel of *The Kansas City Star* got to the heart of her story with this lead on a deadline story about teenagers facing possible criminal charges for Halloween candy thefts. It demonstrates how an article can easily be transformed into a story on a tight deadline with a sharp focus and the most newsworthy elements presented in a compelling lead that drives the point home.

▶**EXAMPLE** Halloween tricks are one thing. But knocking down children to steal their treats may be something else: a felony.

Use the scene—action occurring in a definite place and time—as a building block of narrative. Study how Andale Gross of *The Kansas City Star* opened her story about an inspirational teacher with a precise rendering of a moment in a classroom. Notice how she uses action and her senses to convey what's going on.

> ❝Readers don't just want random snatches of information flying at them from out of the ether. They want information that hangs together, makes sense, has some degree of order to it. They want knowledge rather than facts, perhaps even a little wisdom.❞
>
> —JACK FULLER, AUTHOR, *NEWS VALUES: IDEAS FOR AN INFORMATION AGE*

Mobile technology makes on-the-spot reporting possible. Dan Ashley, ABC 7-TV, San Francisco, uses his cell phone to file a live shot from the scene of an accident on the Bay Bridge.

▶EXAMPLE Eleventh-graders in a Kansas School for the Deaf chemistry class swarmed around a lab table Monday. Time for a lesson in polymers.

Melissa Nix, 17, poured water into a measuring cup containing rock salt. She stirred the mix, scooped out a spoonful and placed the mush in her right palm.

"It feels cold," Melissa said, using sign language.

Teacher Becky Goodwin nodded. "It should feel like the absorbent inside of a baby's diaper," said Goodwin. "We have created a polymer of a different kind. Just like atoms connect, the water and salt connected."

Experiments like that one are common in classes taught by Goodwin, who last weekend was named Kansas Teacher of the Year for 1995.

Even when you think you're finished, good writing requires you step back at least briefly and ask tough questions: Is this clear? Is it accurate? Is it fair? Could I say it better?

Write your story once through and then go back to polish, to reorder, to refine. If your time is limited, it's likely best spent on your ending. That's the last thing readers will experience. Make it memorable.

DEADLINES AND TECHNOLOGY: A TV REPORTER'S STORY

Dan Ashley has been in the news business for more than two decades. But until October 15, 2009, he'd never used a birthday present to file a report.

The veteran anchor and reporter was driving to work at ABC7 in San Francisco when he came to a stop on the Bay Bridge heading into the city. A tractor-trailer full of groceries had overturned on the bridge, bringing traffic to a standstill for hours and rendering him incapable of getting to the station in time for his news broadcast.

"I called into the desk to see what was happening and found out that this truck had flipped," Ashley says, "and I talked to the anchors live on the air about what I was seeing. After I hung up, I remembered that for my birthday my wife had gotten me a new iPhone, which shoots video."

The device wasn't exactly battle-tested—"I had shot my golf swing with it once or twice, but that was it," he says—but Ashley put it right to work. "I jumped out of the car, documented what I saw, talked to some people and then emailed it in to the station for the 5:00 news. It worked out great."

The result went on the air and allowed viewers to see what was happening on the bridge. "It was a terrific way to take advantage of being there, caught unexpectedly in the middle of a news event. This is technology that teenagers have at their fingertips these days and don't even think about, and I was able to use it in a news gathering situation."

CONVERGENCE POINT ↓

Multimedia Tools

Dan Ashley reports from a Bay Bridge accident with his cell phone's video camera, demonstrating vividly how multimedia tools have transformed news gathering and delivery on tight deadlines.

Find this link on the companion Web site at **www.oup.com/us/ scanlan.**

PROFESSIONALS'
PROFESSIONALS' ROUNDTABLE

THE EVOLUTION OF DEADLINES

Many generations of reporters spent their whole working lives aiming for one deadline per day, expending significant time checking facts, contacting sources and developing their stories. In today's age of instant information, however, journalists say they don't often have the time for such reflection. A wire service reporter, a print journalist and a broadcast journalist point out the differences and demands of journalism in the 21st century:

- Journalists must be prepared to deal with multiple deadlines a day.
- Speed increases the chances of errors so extra care must be taken to ensure credibility.
- Journalists reporting across multiple platforms face new demands for speed, clarity and accuracy.

Participants

KEVIN ACEE, San Diego Chargers beat writer, *San Diego Union-Tribune*

DAN ASHLEY, anchor, ABC7 News, San Francisco

JOHN RAESS, Associated Press bureau chief for Northern California, Northern Nevada and Hawaii

> ### What were deadlines like before online news?

Raess: A reporter would come in about 9:00 or 10:00 in the morning and start the first calls of the day, which he or she knew wouldn't come back until lunchtime or sometime in the afternoon. And they would build the story throughout the day and it would culminate with going to their line editor and then to the copy desk and the button would get pushed at 9:30 p.m. So between the time they came in at 10 a.m. and 9:30 at night there was nothing on that story anywhere, probably. That's completely changed now.

Ashley: In the early days, you might work on a deadline that was hours or even days away, utilizing film at the time. Then videotape came along, which meant we could turn around that material faster. Then satellite technology came along which enabled us to go live immediately. That changed our deadlines. So before, when it was a 6:00 deadline we had all day to prepare. Now if something breaks, the deadline becomes immediate. As soon as we can get on the air, we go on the air and that becomes your deadline.

> ### Are there potential pitfalls to today's constant deadlines?

Acee: You don't always have the time to flesh out everything. Let's say I have 10 what I think are facts, but I've only verified six of them. I'm only going to put those six things in my blog right now, and wait until I can get further verification and then update my blog. Five years ago I would have had the time to make 10 more calls to verify the other stuff because it was going in the paper the next day. But the Internet is "now, now, now," so you need to be extra careful.

Raess: Because of the speed that's necessary, it can lead to errors unless you're careful about how you report. That's why the AP has built up a reputation for being so cautious. Errors for us are dreaded because as many as 3 billion people around the world can see our stories. That's billion with a B. Those same 3 billion will have to see the correction, too.

> **Do video skills and experience with multiple deadlines make broadcasters better prepared for today's journalism than print reporters?**

Ashley: I think to some degree that's true, because everyone's now expected to turn their material around much more rapidly than they had in the past. That's always been one of the challenges for print media, to keep up with breaking news as the technology has allowed the other media to bring you information immediately. So I think it has forced print journalists to get a little bit more used to the kinds of deadlines that broadcast journalists have had to deal with since the beginning of the industry.

Raess: TV has had a style of reporting that fit better with the digital platform than print reporting, with the emphasis on speed and video. But I also think for them, the Web has changed things too, because the Web turns them into print reporters as well. They have to spell things right now, which never mattered before, and there's more of a permanent record. In the past, if you made an error in broadcast copy, you could easily correct that in the current broadcast or the next one. Well, now you have to be careful that your material stays accurate all the way through.

SUMMARY GUIDE

STORYTELLING VERSUS SPEED: DEADLINES IN THE 21ST CENTURY

ONE SIDE OF THE EQUATION: STORYTELLING

Articles are organized collections of newsworthy information, but they should not be confused with stories that convey news and experience to audiences.

What to Remember →   Stories feature characters rather than sources, rely on the five senses to communicate experience as well as a sense of people, place, time and drama. They captivate audiences with an enticing beginning, an engaging middle and an ending that lingers.

THE OTHER SIDE: GET IT DONE, NOW!

Today's journalists face multiple deadlines, making the ability to quickly report and write more important than ever.

What to Remember →   With the clock ticking, journalists write stories, post blog entries and tweets, contribute to online packages, interact online with audiences, produce videos and appear on air to report the news. Many file stories in snippets, adding more information as it becomes available before producing a complete version. Accuracy and time management skills are a must.

FOCUSING AND PLANNING ON THE FLY

Even with deadlines looming, journalists must follow two critical steps: quickly discover a focus and develop a plan for organizing their stories.

What to Remember → An effective story first requires a theme, the connective thread that unifies the disparate information journalists have collected. The writing journey also requires a road map, even if only a brief outline, that will keep audiences on track.

DRAFTING ON DEADLINE

Effective writers discover their stories by drafting quickly, leaving adequate time for revision.

What to Remember → Armed with a focus and a plan, writers get to the heart of the story immediately, using scenes, details, quotes, dialogue and anecdotes to craft compelling narratives. Free-writing enables speedy drafting, leaving time for changes that make stories complete, accurate and clear.

DEADLINES AND TECHNOLOGY: A TV REPORTER'S STORY

New tools and technology have transformed news gathering and delivery.

What to Remember → Using a cell phone equipped with email and video capabilities, journalists can report and transmit eyewitness news in near real time. Mobile journalism is the new reality.

KEY TERMS

accretion, p. 80
article, p. 76
characters, p. 77
clarify, p. 84
collect, p. 84

draft, p. 84
focus, p. 84
idea, p. 84
multimedia, p. 80
observing, p. 77

order, p. 84
organize, p. 84
revise, p. 84
story, p. 76
writethrough, p. 80

EXERCISES

1. Compare stories that appeared in one edition of a newspaper, a TV news broadcast and an online news page. Identify which ones are articles and which are stories. Explain your choices. Which do you find most compelling?

2. Select an example of news storytelling. Identify the various sources that went into producing the story and how they contributed to meeting the elements that make up a story rather than an article.

3. Following is a verbatim transcript of a conversation between a reporter and a police desk sergeant.

   a. Based solely on this information, take 20 minutes to write a 300-word blog post that will be posted on your online news site. Begin by answering two questions: What's the news? What's the point?

   b. Take 30 minutes to write a storytelling account. Begin with David Von Drehle's five questions from Chapter 2, freewriting the answers in 95 seconds. After you've finished, your editor says it's not strong enough. She wants it fleshed out. Build a reporting plan. What additional information do you need? Who else do you need to talk with? What documents would bolster the story? What characters, details and quotes would you be looking for? Where would you begin and end the story? What goes in the middle?

POLICE: Westerly Police. Sgt. Johnson.

POLICE REPORTER: Hi, Officer, this is Lois Lane of the *Westerly Journal*. Anything going on today? Any arrests?

POLICE: No, pretty quiet.

REPORTER: How about accidents?

POLICE: Couple fender benders. Nothing serious.

REPORTER: Okay. Well, thanks.

POLICE: Oh yeah, we had that train accident.

REPORTER: What?! There was a train accident?

POLICE: Yeah. Yesterday about noon. You know, the one where the kid got hit.

REPORTER: A kid got hit by a train!

POLICE: Yeah. I guess you could say she got hit. Hold on, let me get the report. Okay, here we go. Yeah, Lani Reynolds, white female, DOB 5-6-97. (Note: The current date is 6-12-2012. She is 15.) Address: 5546 Sylvan Oaks Lane, Westerly.

REPORTER: What time did this happen?

POLICE: 12:10 p.m.

REPORTER: Where?

POLICE: On the trestle just outside town, where the tracks cross over the Westerly River.

REPORTER: Gosh, what happened?

POLICE: Not much of a report. Let's see, the victim was on the trestle when an Amtrak train, the Colonial, en route to New York out of Boston, began to cross the trestle when she heard the train. Didn't have much of a choice, jump into the river 100 feet below or try to dodge the train. So she lay down next to the track. Poor kid, the wheels severed her leg at the knee. Victim transported to Westerly Hospital.

REPORTER: What was she doing on the trestle?

POLICE: No idea. Doesn't say.

REPORTER: Do you know her condition?

POLICE: As of last night she was stable. This is one lucky kid. She'd probably be dead if it wasn't for another kid. Jon Tessie, DOB 9-16-95. (He is 16.) He works over at Toscana's Men Shop on Main Street, was walking back from a delivery when some kids hanging out at the tracks came running and told him what happened. According to our chief, Milton W. Wilson, the kid rushed over and gave her first aid until rescue showed up. Report says he's a Boy Scout. Guess he got his merit badge.

REPORTER: Yeah, I'll say. Wow, what a story. Have you got any more details?

POLICE: No, that's it. Just this incident report. I can't give you anything else. Call back later for more information.

REPORTER: What was your name again?

POLICE: Just say a police spokesman.

REPORTER: Okay. well, thanks a lot.

READINGS

Clark, Roy Peter. *Writing Tools: 50 Essential Strategies for Every Writer.* **New York: Little, Brown and Co., 2008.**
For journalists who want to focus on storytelling, Clark's collection of tips and techniques presents narrative opportunities: ways to reveal character, employ dialogue and nail the details that linger in the reader's mind.

Fryxell, David. *Write Faster, Write Better.* **Cincinnati, OH: Writers Digest Books, 2004.**
A veteran news editor and columnist explodes the myth that good writing must be a product of agony and endless time. He offers tips and techniques to write well while the clock is ticking.

Hart, Jack. *Story Craft: The Complete Guide to Writing Narrative Nonfiction.* **Chicago: University of Chicago Press, 2011.**
Hart draws on the work of Susan Orleans, Tracy Kidder and other celebrated nonfiction writers and his experience editing Pulitzer Prize–winning narratives at *The* (Portland) *Oregonian.* He reveals the theory, structure and practical reporting and writing strategies that produce the best true stories.

Murray, Donald M. *Writing to Deadline: The Journalist at Work.* **Portsmouth, NH: Heinemann, 2000.**
Murray, who cultivated a career meeting tight deadlines, produced this excellent handbook for writers who want to speed up their writing process. Murray knows the difference between articles and stories, and he outlines the approaches that each demands.

BREAKING NEWS NARRATIVE

When a fire devastated a local factory in Milwaukee, Wisconsin on December 6, 2006, journalists at the *Journal-Sentinel* confronted a familiar problem: how to write about a story that has already been extensively covered on TV, radio and social media when your print deadline is a day away. Their solution: to provide their audience with a vivid reconstruction of the tragic events that would present the most complete account of the news. Their tool: a narrative that tells the story behind the news using the techniques largely unavailable to the inverted pyramid with its orderly collection of facts arranged in newsworthy importance. Writer Greg Borowski, working with reports from 27 colleagues, recreated the fire and its aftermath with dramatic scenes and vivid details and quotes, all the while weaving in the pertinent facts. The story demonstrates that breaking news can be written as a compelling story under a tight deadline drawing on the size and skills of a large news organization and the talents of a narrative writer.

A HINT OF TROUBLE, THEN TRAGEDY

3 DEAD, 46 HURT AS EXPLOSION RIPS BUILDINGS TO PIECES AT FALK CORP.

By Greg Borowski of the *Journal Sentinel*
Dec. 7, 2006

As the first shift at Falk Corp. cranked along Wednesday morning, the troubling smell of gas drifted through an annex just off the main production building.

Workers called supervisors and began heading for the doors.

Moments later, at 8:07 a.m., a massive and deadly explosion ripped through the Menomonee Valley factory. It killed three, injured 46 and left a swath of one of the city's oldest companies a charred, smoking skeleton.

The three killed were identified as Curtis J. Lane, 38, Oconomowoc; Thomas M. Letendre, 49, Milwaukee; and Daniel T. Kuster, 35, Mayville.

Police Chief Nannette Hegerty said that had employees not discovered the propane leak and begun evacuating, "the death toll would have been much higher."

The death of Kuster, said his uncle, Tim Izydor, "kills my heart."

Foreshadowing—providing a hint of events to follow—is a valuable device aimed at drawing readers into a story. In two paragraphs, the lead launches a story by recreating the moment just before disaster strikes. It sets the scene, time and uses telling details—the troubling smell of gas, the flight of workers—and active verbs that launch the action and inject suspense and drama at the outset.

The story backs up immediately to report the news and the aftermath of a "massive and deadly explosion." Victims are identified by name, hometown and age. An official spokesman makes the newsworthy observation that the death toll would be higher were it not for fast action by employees. The section ends with a gut-wrenching quote from a relative of one of the dead. "Good quotes up high" is a journalistic mantra because human speech conveys human drama. A quote need not be a complete sentence. The fragment "kills my heart" is tragic poetry.

David Mays, a journeyman machinist, was working inside the annex when the gas smell first became apparent.

"I left," said Mays, 61, who has worked for Falk for 39 years. "But some of them stayed."

The explosion hurled Mays to the ground, reminding him of incoming mortar rounds from his service in Vietnam. It rattled windows and shook houses as far away as Franklin and New Berlin, and filled the gray morning sky near downtown with a chilling spiral of smoke.

The blast shattered the Falk family of workers, and ultimately tested a legion of police, firefighters, emergency personnel and hospital workers.

"We've all been there for over 20 years," said Mays, who later went to the hospital on his own. "We are all like a family."

Journeyman machinist David Sternig, 59, who has worked at Falk for 42 years, was in the southwestern part of the plant when the blast hit. Two of his brothers also work at Falk.

"It was like a bomb went off or a plane crashed," he said.

The light bulbs popped. The room went dark. The whir of machines came to a dead stop.

The room was eerily silent, and the air was filled with gray soot, Sternig said. Huge sections of concrete block were blown out. The annex was leveled.

Dean Sternig, 44, was on his way to see his brother when the blast knocked him from his feet like a bowling pin. Looking up from the shaking ground, he saw huge flames fill the sky.

"I didn't know if it was going to start to rain down on me or not, but I wasn't about to lie there and find out," he said.

He scrambled to his feet and ran into a nearby garage, diving on the ground into a pile of glass shards, cutting his arm in three places.

He got up again and worked his way back to his work station. The mood there was calm. No screaming or yelling.

Injured workers were transported in pairs. He was treated at a hospital and released. Neither of his two brothers was seriously injured.

"I feel real lucky," he said.

With the news and context delivered, the narrative resumes. A character, machinist David Mays, is introduced. His story reveals in vivid detail the powerful impact of the blast and employs a metaphor—his Vietnam War memory of mortar rounds—to help readers grasp the explosion's power. Like a filmmaker, the writer moves from a close-up to a long shot that reveals scope and impact at familiar locations and ends with a chilling but almost lyrical description that paints an apocalyptic scene. The writer knows how to report the news and tell a compelling tale that enables readers to experience the story through narrative power. This account would have been impossible to write without the massive amounts of detailed and dramatic information collected by skilled journalists working under intense deadline pressure.

The story constantly shifts between summary and narrative, pulling out of scenes to explain the effect of the fire on those who battled it and the workers. Mays continues what amounts to a voice-over, commenting on the events, an effective device that helps reader stay connected to a fast-moving event composed of many disparate elements.

Narrative follows news, anticipating reader interest in the how behind the what. This long passage uses two workers to describe what happened when the gas ignited. The story follows a chronological approach, a timeline that keeps the story and readers on track. Notice how the writer uses short sentences with active verbs—"cranked," "ripped," "hurled"—and passive verb forms—"The annex was leveled." These slow down the action for maximum impact and step back to reveal the devastation. Another worker appears and through his eyes and a familiar simile we experience the power of the explosion. The story follows his path as he tries to reach safety. In a single sentence with two detailed clauses, readers watch the terrible scene of his escape. The next sentence summarizes the mood—an eerie sense of calm amid destruction. A quote again punctuates the scene.

'THERE WERE PEOPLE IN THERE'

Falk is classic blue-collar Milwaukee. It is a place where life still runs on eight-hour shifts, where co-workers become friends who bowl together, play on the company softball team, trade deer hunting tales over a post-work beer.

To many people, though, the company passes without notice. Few likely could name its product: giant gears.

From the nearby highway and the viaducts that criss-cross the Menomonee Valley, the complex can fade into the mix of brick and smokestacks in the valley.

On Wednesday, Katie Porter was one of those passers-by, following her normal route from Wauwatosa down Canal St. to her job in the Historic Third Ward. Suddenly, her Saturn Ion was shoved off the side of the road.

"There was a truck or a van next to me, and I thought it had slammed into me," Porter said.

But the truck had come to a stop behind her.

"I saw the building explode outward and then just fall in," she said. "The walls were pushed outward, and the whole thing collapsed."

On S. 27th St., car alarms went off. In the nearby Merrill Park neighborhood, windows were broken and garage door bolts were shaken loose. Some thought it was an earthquake - others a sonic boom or an airplane crashing.

Jill Huffer was driving north across the 27th Street Viaduct, taking her two kids - Calvin, 9, and Casey, 5 - to Hawley Environmental School. It was not their normal route, but Calvin had an early morning appointment at the orthodontist.

"I saw debris flying way into the sky, and then I saw a flash and then a fire blast down on the ground," she said.

She kept driving, and found herself crying as she drove. Calvin asked what was wrong.

"I just kept thinking," Huffer said, "there were people in there."

In the valley below, forklift driver Otha Beamon, 56, was driving a Jeep about 20 feet outside the building.

"All of a sudden, 'Boom!' That was it," Beamon said.

He got out of the Jeep and was knocked down by falling debris. He got up, was knocked down again. Then, he said, "some guy came out of nowhere" and helped him get to safety.

Subheads sprinkled through a long story signal what's to come and are designed to maintain reader interest.

In the first paragraph, the story provides a mini-biography of the plant, its tight-knit workforce and its place in the community. It's noteworthy that the writer puts the information deeper into the story and then uses it to present a different perspective in the two paragraphs that follow.

The action resumes as the story moves outward to several locations. It now presents the dramatic accounts of eyewitnesses whose everyday lives were upended. Their experiences, conveyed with descriptions and amplified by stark quotes, testify to the power of the blast. Through their eyes, the reader watches the building explode and collapse. A single detail-rich paragraph summarizes how the explosion caused havoc far beyond the factory walls.

In a nearby building, 35-year Falk employee Bill Gebhard was working when the blast tossed him into the air.

"Glass was shattering everywhere," he said.

Once he got his bearings, he realized he was looking outside; the building's walls had disappeared.

SOOTY FACES, SHOCK

At the Engine 28 fire station about six blocks north of Falk, the entire building shook and the garage door sucked in, then blew outward - so much that the firefighters could see daylight. Some thought a car struck the station.

It had happened before.

They ran outside. No car. But James Youngblood, a driver for the department, saw smoke rising to the south. An engine and a paramedic unit were sent toward the smoke. South of the freeway they could tell the smoke was coming from a large building in the Falk complex.

They arrived about three minutes, 40 seconds after the blast to a scene of devastation about the size of two football fields. Lt. Frank Alioto, a firefighter for 23 years, called in a second alarm and requested extra paramedics and the department's heavy urban rescue team. Ultimately, it was a five-alarm emergency.

"There were people with blackened, sooty faces. Some bloody. They looked in shock. They were kind of wandering aimlessly," Alioto said.

Some workers were carrying out their Falk co-workers.

A triage site was set up to sort through the severity of injuries. Then the effort turned to fighting the fire.

The Palermo's Pizza plant became a gathering place, with Falk workers signing in when they arrived so they could be accounted for.

While they waited for more direction, Palermo's workers served them pizza and coffee.

"It was pretty quiet," said Liz Bentzler, a quality auditor at the Palermo's plant. "Very surreal."

Falk workers were eventually loaded onto a dozen Milwaukee County Transit System buses and taken to nearby Miller Park. As they arrived at the stadium, some still looked shaken, and they walked in with the assistance of co-workers.

The action shifts back to the site of the explosion and the tale of another worker whose experience demonstrates the power of the blast. Following chronology, the reader sees glass shattering around him. The story's power rests on eyewitness testimony rather than reportorial summary. In cinematic fashion, the scene comes to a close with a chilling coda: "the building's walls had disappeared."

Readers could understandably have stopped there, but the writer wisely shifts gears. The focus shifts to another dramatic location: the fire station just blocks away which also felt the impact, conveyed with the powerful image of the garage sucked in and blown outward. The action stops for a moment as confused firefighters wonder if a car had struck the station. The story maintains its strict focus, unwilling to dwell except for a single evocative sentence: "It had happened before." Fire teams launch in action and the scope of the blast is conveyed with an analogy that uses a familiar comparison to convey the swath of destruction. Analogies and similes are quick and useful ways to help readers understand the unfamiliar by comparing it to something they know. A firefighter's quote describes a horrific scene. The final sentence signals another turning point.

The writer keeps readers engaged by constantly shifting locations where the drama continues to play out. Alternating points of view is another effective device to keep readers interested. "The Palermo's Pizza plant" is an example of the power of names. It needs no description. Surviving workers enter and in a local park tell their stories. Good stories rely on reporters present at the scene so they can see a worried wife beam when she sees her husband talking on a cell phone.

A quote summarizing their feelings brings the scene to a close.

Later, worried families streamed into the stadium looking for loved ones, their faces stricken.

Dena Cahala beamed when she saw her husband, Glen, safe and talking on a cell phone. But her elation was tempered by her husband's fears for co-workers.

"I can't tell you how sad this is," said Glen Cahala, who was in the administrative building. "I just hope everyone is OK. I can't think about what this means for some families."

NO FOUL PLAY SUSPECTED

The building is part of a complex that covers 61 acres, with 1.5 million square feet of buildings. In all, there were about 600 people working at the complex at the time of the explosion. The building that exploded is actually two structures that are connected, said Evan Zeppos, who was handling public relations for Falk late Wednesday. One, called the Annex, was used for storage of component parts used in the manufacturing process. The other, known as the 2-2 building, was used largely as a maintenance facility.

For hours, it was unclear how many people had been in the building when the explosion occurred.

And whether everyone had gotten out.

Law enforcement officials ultimately interviewed some 500 workers and witnesses, trying to sort out the details of what had happened. Hegerty would later say the investigation would take at least a week, but that it "appeared to be a tragic, accidental situation."

No foul play. No crime.

Just tragedy.

Mayor Tom Barrett, who coincidentally had toured the plant the day before, called the blast a "serious tragedy for Falk, for (parent company) Rexnord, for the city of Milwaukee. And I would ask the citizens of Milwaukee to remember the families in their prayers."

Speaking at a news conference at Miller Park, he said investigators did not know how much time had elapsed between the time the propane leak was discovered and the blast.

Barrett said that the city conducted an inspection of the plant on Sept. 14 and found some safety violations.

"They were few and minor, and they were corrected," the mayor said.

The narrative breaks off. For the first time extensive background is provided about the plant, the location of the fire and the numbers of workers on site at the time. Such detailed information would have bogged down the narrative if presented earlier.

Narratives alternate between scenes. They can jump stretches of time as this passage does to report concerns about the number of workers involved, how many survived, the investigation and the possible cause. Although the passage breaks the narrative flow, it sums up a question on everyone's minds: What happened?

Two paragraphs, three sentence fragments, give the answer.

Conceivably, the story could have ended here, but the narrative is not over. There is more news to report, the appearance of the mayor who addresses a critical question about safety at the plant, and testimony from plant workers. A massive fire, rescue and investigative effort is described. To maintain reader interest it's important to return to the narrative as quickly as possible.

Several employees said the plant was very safety conscious. There always seemed to be safety training and drills, they said.

Machinist Robert Long, 46, predicted a quick recovery for Falk, where he has worked for 15 years.

"It will be up and running before you think," Long said.

In briefings through the day, officials laid out what it took to manage the scene. About 125 Milwaukee firefighters were sent to the scene in 34 different vehicles. In addition, 52 Milwaukee police officers arrived, plus 25 detectives. The response also included a host of private ambulances, state and federal officials, and the American Red Cross.

City crews checked nearby bridges for structural damage but did not find any problems. Building inspectors also began visiting homes in nearby neighborhoods, where some windows had been shattered.

By 5 p.m., the search was complete. No one else was missing, although Falk set up a hotline, at (414) 643-2420, for its workers to call to get more information.

> The story does just that, returning to the chronology that spans a day of tragedy. News organizations also provide public service information in times of emergency.

Two hours later, Falk employees gathered at Wisconsin State Fair Park. In a brief, emotional meeting, David Doerr, Falk Corp.'s president, assured workers they would be paid while the company regroups.

"They just told us to hang in there," said Michael Kleczka, a third-shift worker.

A day earlier, the meeting would have been a family reunion.

Wednesday night, it was a family in mourning.

> The story comes to a close 11 hours after it began at a gathering of employees in a location familiar to readers. The worker's quote sets the tone for the two-paragraph ending. In a narrative, the storyteller usually gets the last word. A rule of thumb: If you can say it better than a quote, do so.
> The writer takes it upon himself to sum up what the event means and brings to the story to a sad and resounding conclusion.

Story written by Greg Borowski. ***Staff of the Milwaukee Journal Sentinel*** *reporting from Miller Park, surrounding neighborhoods, area hospitals, Oconomowoc and the paper's main office contributed to today's coverage of the Falk Corp. explosion. They include Rick Barrett, Gina Barton, Thomas Content, Joel Dresang, Darryl Enriquez, Tom Held, Annysa Johnson, Mark Johnson, Mike Johnson, Tom Kertscher, Meg Kissinger, Sheila B. Lalwani, Avrum D. Lank, Jacqueline Loohauis, James B. Nelson, Derrick Nunnally, Georgia Pabst, Amy Rinard, Marie Rohde, Raquel Rutledge, Susanne Rust, Steve Schultze, Linda Spice, Felicia Thomas-Lynn, Dave Umhoefer, Don Walker and Ruth Ward. Helicopter photos were taken from WTMJ Chopper 4.*

> Note the acknowledgments, adding even more credibility to an already strong story.

SUMMARY In the age of blog posts and tweets, news organizations still have the power to tell a long story that captivates reader interest. Journalists writing from an overabundance of information can select the scenes, details and quotes that most effectively convey an experience that engages readers. A day after the Falk Corp. fire, editors and reporters at the *Journal Sentinel* demonstrated that storytelling on deadline is possible and that newspapers with large staffs and space still retain an edge when the goal is to report the news and tell a powerful story. For their efforts, the paper earned the 2007 award for team deadline reporting from the American Society of Newspaper Editors.

THE REPORTER'S TOOLBOX

BY THE END OF THIS CHAPTER,

you should be able to...

> Identify assorted tools of reporting

> Understand the situations in which specific tools work well

> Know the best journalistic uses for various electronic devices

> Grasp the importance of software programs that can help journalists

> Identify the advantages of reporting on the scene of events

> Demonstrate how a reporter's mental approach can affect interviewing and reporting

FOR MANY DECADES a reporter needed nothing more than a pencil and paper to take notes. In some ways that's all some reporters still need. "Even in these days of high-tech weaponry, the writer's most effective research and interviewing tools remain the humble pen and low-tech notebook," says David Fryxell, a veteran editor. There are countless reporters who bring nothing more than an empty notepad, a pen and an open mind to an assignment and produce compelling journalism.

But today's journalist has available an array of other tools to use. Changes in the way news is consumed and delivered have increased the demand for journalists to gather sound, pictures and video, as well as words on paper. Whichever you use, never forget that it's not the tool that matters as much as the way it's used.

PENS, PENCILS AND REPORTER'S NOTEBOOK

A notebook is the reporter's basic tool. It's the repository of everything from quotes and descriptions to directions and phone numbers. Even today beginning journalists should learn to report stories accurately and effectively with nothing more than pen and paper—you never know when batteries will die or wi-fi connections will fail.

Note taking provides the foundation for news stories. Examine your notes for highlights—underline or circle the best quotes, statistics and other facts, and make notes where you might want to pursue something further. Try freewriting the answers to David Von Drehle's focusing questions from Chapter 2, and select possible leads and endings. "Things become pieces as you're reporting, and you think, 'Ah, there's my lead,'" says Mark Fritz, who learned the habit with the Associated Press wire service where he won the Pulitzer Prize for deadline coverage of the 1994 Rwandan massacres. Notations become "a scribble along the side" of his notebook. Or, "I'll circle something, or put an asterisk, or write a little note next to it. I'll underline it three times. I'll write in block letters LEAD."

Reporters who master shorthand can accurately capture every word of an interview without relying on a tape recorder. Thomas French, of the *St. Petersburg* (FL) *Times*, whose notebook is shown here, used his high school shorthand skills on "Angels and Demons," which won the 1998 Pulitzer Prize for feature writing.

David Finkel, a Pulitzer prize–winning staff writer for *The Washington Post*, fills up lots of notebooks on stories.

> I tend to write down everything I see, even if it's something like, "2 rocks off to left- sedimentary??-resemble poodle." My hope is that as the reporting process continues, the significance of my notations will emerge. Usually, that doesn't happen. Out of a 50-page notebook, I'll have five pages of possibly usable quotes, ten pages of other possibly usable notes, and 35 pages of hieroglyphics.

You won't write down every word someone says, but rather you must decide, usually in a split second, what is worth preserving in your notes. You're not taking dictation. You are taking notes selectively.

A word of caution: Don't let your notes get in the way of the writing. Many journalists write without leafing through their notes. Instead of writing an exact quote, they place a marker in the draft, such as "TK," newsroom slang for "to come." You'll likely remember the most important information you've written down, but you should always recheck your notes before you submit your story. Jane Harrigan, former director of the journalism program at the University of New Hampshire, tells her students, "Notes are like Velcro. As you try to skim them, they ensnare you, and pretty soon you can't see the story for the details." Her advice? Repeat this mantra: The story is not in my notes; the story is in my head.

QUICK Tips ⏱ TAKING NOTES QUICKLY

Most people no longer learn the art of taking shorthand, although it used to be a common practice among reporters. Even if you don't know shorthand, you can follow the example of countless reporters by developing your own speedwriting style. "The importance of developing a personal shorthand can't be stressed too much," says journalism teacher Sandra Combs Birdiett. She leads her Wayne State University classes in exercises, reading speeches aloud and playing songs as they struggle to get the words down, and encourages them to practice regularly until they have a workable and efficient shorthand. One quick way is to drop vowels from words and use phonetic spelling. For example, using phonetic spelling and eliminating vowels transforms a sentence such as the following:

▶**EXAMPLE** Because when they go out into the field, they need more tools than we can give. (63 characters)

and transform it into the much shorter:

▶**EXAMPLE** Bcz whn thy go out nto th fld thy nd mor tls thn we cn gv. (44 characters)

Here is a small sample of common speedwriting symbols reporters use:

> w—with
> w/o—without
> &—and
> pox—police
> b & e—breaking and entering
> adw—assault with a deadly weapon
> hrg—hearing
> mtg—meeting

Whatever "briefhand" system you employ, make sure that it enables you to "take detailed, accurate notes, while leaving accurate time for careful listening," as *The Oregonian* of Portland advises its reporters in its accuracy guidelines. Any system should:

1. Clearly indicate what is a direct quote and what is not. Use quotation marks " " for direct quotes and brackets [ ] or parentheses ( ) for indirect quotes or paraphrases.
2. Make clear the source of each fact and quotation in the notes.
3. Include citations to additional sources (such as a reference book, court record or title of a government report quoted) that will help verify the accuracy of questionable items. ▶

THE COMPUTER

For more than a century, journalists used typewriters, first manual then electric, and low-grade paper stock to write their stories. Editors revised stories on the page, usually with a pencil or red pen, then sent it via pneumatic tubes to the linotypists, who used machines that looked like a cross between a typewriter and church organ to make a hot lead plate for each page. Once inked and laid onto the printing press, the process of printing newspapers, a sight often seen in movie montages, began.

That all changed in the 1970s with the development of **word-processing** software and "cold type" printing. With a few keystrokes, the computer allowed journalists to insert words, copy, delete, move entire passages on the screen, count the words and check spelling and grammar. Now *every* laptop is a word processor in addition to handling many other tasks that were once the purview of large, centralized computer systems.

Most of today's journalists take the computer for granted. In newsrooms today, typewriters are museum objects. Computerized word-processing skills are essential for today's reporter. Writing software is loaded with features, but you can get by with the basics: how to create and save a file, cut and paste, format text, check word count, and run spell-check.

NOTE TAKING ON THE SCREEN

A common sight in many newsrooms is a reporter with a telephone headset taking notes as she conducts an interview. It can be an efficient way to increase your note-taking speed, with some cautions.

Be sure to keep your notes organized: Note the source, date and time of your interview. Separate your interviews with line breaks, asterisks or symbols so you don't confuse one person's remarks with another's.

A caution: For many journalists, tethering themselves to keyboards and telephones leads to painful repetitive stress disorders, leaving them unable to type without pain.

There's another hazard, one that poses more danger to journalism. Skype, the popular Voice over Internet Protocol (VoIP) service, removes the limits of time and space, and has prompted some print and broadcast journalists to use it to successfully record audio and video interviews. But stories reported by phone or via the Internet bear the telltale signs of inadequate contact with the people, places and things that make news. As convenient as a telephone or computer may be when a deadline is tight or when sources are too far away to see in person, it also can insulate you from the world you are covering.

Digital devices have replaced the notebook in the age of multimedia journalism. A student journalists interviews a subject using a digital video and audio recorder.

CHIP'S CORNER

TEXT MESSAGING

As students, you're used to sending real-time text messages, with your computer or cell phone. Texting or instant messaging (IM) is a popular way to keep up with family and friends, but journalists also use it to keep in touch with editors and for rapid communication with sources and readers who share the same platform. "IM is exactly the sort of tool a reporter needs," says Paul Conley, who began using instant messages to reach sources in the early 2000s when he was reporting for the financial news service Bloomberg. "It's faster than email. It's transparent (the system tells you whether or not someone is online). And, for reasons that I don't quite understand, sources who hesitate to talk on the phone or exchange emails are willing to chat via IM."

Here's what Conley has learned about using instant messaging as a reporting tool. Pay close attention to his warnings.

- Sources who traditionally have been hard to reach will suddenly become accessible.
- The speed of your reporting will increase rapidly.
- IM is a form of chat. Eloquent conversations are nonexistent. You can use IM effectively to get yes/no answers, figures, dates, story tips and general information. But to get a useable quote, you will often have to ask sources to elaborate.
- IM is an informal medium. Sources don't see talking via IM as an interview. The advantage of that is they will talk more freely than if you get them on the phone. The

disadvantage is that the first time you publish a quote from IM, you're likely to lose a source. Here's my rule. I'd urge you to adopt it. Unlike a phone call, which is on-the-record unless otherwise stated, an IM conversation is not-for-attribution unless otherwise stated. In other words, if you want to pull a quote from an IM chat, tell your source you want to do that.

- IM conversations are filled with icons that denote emotions, such as the widely understood smile symbol :) . There's a reason for this: Rapid typing and use of abbreviations and short phrases make it easy for people to misunderstand IM. In particular, jokes and puns are often read as serious. Learn the icons and use them. ▶

There's no substitute for face-to-face contact. Sometimes deadline pressures make that difficult, but you don't want all your stories to read as if they were reported from a desk, or from press releases and telephone interviews. Stories about neighborhoods need to indicate the reporter walked the area's streets and met with its residents, not just chatted on the phone with so-called community leaders. Broadcast and mobile journalists (**mojos**) have an edge as they have to work in the field to conduct interviews with digital video cameras and audio recorders.

CELL PHONES

While professional journalists got by without them in the past, today's reporters wouldn't dare go anywhere without a cell phone. Most college students probably can't imagine living without one, but the fact is that reporters need them much more. As a tool that enables instant communication with editors and sources from nearly anywhere, they've revolutionized the act of covering breaking news.

Case in point: When TWA Flight 800 exploded on July 17, 1996, over the Atlantic Ocean off Long Island, New York, killing all 229 people on board, editors at *Newsday* told reporter Steve Wick to charter a boat and get out to the crash scene as quickly as possible.

Within a few hours, Wick was in the middle of a surreal scene: "For miles the ocean was covered with debris, seat cushions, insulation, big pieces of metal, a section of a wing, luggage, backpacks. An empty baby bottle floated by. The debris was so thick you could not see the water," he recalled.

In the past, Wick would have had to wait until he returned to shore to file his story. Armed with a cell phone, however, he spent all night dictating what he saw and heard directly to a reporter back in the newsroom, who transformed his descriptions into a story for the next morning's paper. Today he would likely have posted moment-by-moment updates on Twitter.

The cell phone and Twitter give journalists the ability to be eyewitnesses and instantly communicate what they see and hear "as opposed to someone who takes just notes, then goes to a phone, and then calls in notes to rewrite," Wick said. "I just was dictating what I saw. It was literal deadline work, literally as close to the line as you can get. . . . The value was that 600,000 people on Long Island awoke to an eyewitness account the next morning." Wick's on-scene reporting contributed to coverage that won the newspaper a Pulitzer Prize. Sara Ganim, who won the 2012 Pulitzer Prize for her newspaper coverage of the Jerry Sandusky child sex abuse scandal, calls her smartphone "her mobile newsroom." (Ganim has since joined CNN as a correspondent.)

Today's cell phones that can record video can come in quite handy if news is breaking. Jamal Albarghouti, a graduate student at Virginia Tech University, was on his way to meet with an adviser on April 16, 2007, unaware that a fellow student was roaming the campus on a shooting rampage that would become the deadliest school shooting in U.S. history. But when he heard gunfire outside a classroom building and saw armed police, he knew something was terribly wrong. Instinctively, he began

The cell phone is the new media equivalent of the reporter's notebook. When Jamal Albarghouti, a graduate student at Virginia Tech University, heard gunshots on campus, he began recording video on his phone, capturing the sights and sounds of what was the deadliest school shooting in U.S. history. His video became worldwide news.

Virginia Tech School Shooting Caught on Camera phone   Like   Share   More info

recording video of the scene with his cell phone. The sound of gunfire can be heard on the grainy, unsteady footage he captured, crude but captivating coverage that traveled around the world when he uploaded his video to I-Report, a feature of CNN.com that airs user-generated audio and video.

To compete, there's a good chance your news organization will equip you with a video-capable phone, trading off image quality for speedy 24/7 coverage. If not, invest in one yourself to enhance your reporting capabilities.

AUDIO RECORDERS

Many of today's reporters carry audio recorders as part of their basic reporting equipment. Without this tool, "you really can't capture the full emotional breadth of what people are saying to you," says Mitch Albom, the *Detroit Free Press* sports columnist and best-selling author (*Tuesdays With Morrie*). "When you're talking to a grieving family, the way they say things, sometimes even a small little sentence, or the way their voice trails off is very important to re-create the mood and the spirit." Albom offers another practical reason: "I don't trust my penmanship to try to get it down."

That fear of missing something important, especially in an electronic era when radio and television crews are recording news events, prompts many reporters to use the recorder as a backup to their handwritten notes. While for decades reporters used portable tape recorders for this purpose, the new industry standard is the **digital audio recorder**. It provides numerous benefits, most notably that it allows easy use of the material in a podcast on a news Web site.

Many cell phones can double as an audio recorder, but reporters do not rely on these devices as their primary means for recording sound. That's because cell phones were not principally designed for the purpose, although they'll do in a pinch as long as they have a USB output or wireless Web connection. Most phones and MP3 players equipped with recording capabilities come with adapters that allow for transfer of audio files to a computer. The iPad and other tablets offer a variety of dedicated applications that are ideal for on-scene reporting.

Journalists are using mobile devices, such as Apple's iPad, in innovative ways, relying on their audio and digital video recording capabilities that provide unobtrusive multimedia coverage, from routine news to dangerous street protests.

To Record or Not to Record

Multimedia journalism requires the use of digital audio recorders to capture the voices and sounds that tell

Journalists need help managing the flood of social media information to stay on top of the news and connect with sources and other contacts. TweetDeck, a dashboard application that separates tweets and other posts, is one of the most popular ways to manage the onslaught of social media.

Ethical Dilemmas IS THAT HOW IT REALLY HAPPENED?

Electronic tools pose the greatest ethical challenges because of features that make it easy to alter digital photos, videos and audio.

"Photography lost its innocence many years ago," says Dartmouth professor Hany Farid, who regularly studies doctored images. "In as early as the 1930s, shortly after the first commercially available camera was introduced, Stalin had his enemies 'air-brushed' out of photographs. With the advent of high-resolution digital cameras, powerful personal computers and sophisticated photo-editing software, the **manipulation** of digital images is becoming more common."

- In 2012, a *Sacramento* (CA) *Bee* photographer was fired for combining two wildlife photos into one, leading to an investigation of his previous work by a major photography organization.
- A *Los Angeles Times* photographer covering the war in Iraq used Adobe Photoshop to create a composite photo from two similar images. The photographer was fired.
- In 2006, the Reuters news agency withdrew a photo after bloggers reported that it was manipulated to show more smoke and damage to Beirut from an Israeli air strike. To achieve the result, the photographer apparently used Photoshop's "cloning tool" that makes it possible to cut and repeatedly paste parts of an image to create a more dramatic one.
- Audio and video editing software can lead to similar unethical behavior. A Las Vegas TV station added the sounds of gunfire and slot machines to enhance silent surveillance video. "There is no doubt that there were two shots," noted Al Tompkins, co-editor of an ethics guide for broadcast journalists. "There is no doubt about what slot machines and casinos sound like.

But the sounds did not exist on that tape."

These examples illustrate the risks posed at a time when new media tools make it easy to alter reality, whether captured in a photograph, a video, or audio. While these tools enhance the delivery of news in dramatic, informative fashion, journalists must take care to avoid unethical behaviors that such devices make possible. "The power to change someone's comments and leave listeners with the impression that what they heard is what the speaker said is awesome and easily abused," said Jonathan Baer, an associate producer for National Public Radio.

"If it didn't happen that way, don't create the illusion it happened that way," concluded an ethics guide for public radio journalists. ▶

a compelling a story. If another journalist is recording the same interview or press conference, capturing what's said verbatim, you may not want to rely on handwritten notes. But recording equipment isn't required for every interview, especially those conducted by print journalists. Reporters who don't want to use an audio recorder don't have to, although they often feel compelled to justify their choice. Recorders malfunction, the charge wears out, batteries dry up. A truck barrels by, or a humming air conditioner drowns out all sound just as the subject whispers, "Yes, I did it. I embezzled the animal shelter's cash fund." Even if you get all the quotes, the audio still takes forever to transcribe.

Still, there are few technology-averse reporters who don't wish they had a recorder going during some interviews, especially when the pace is fast or the content compelling. It's estimated that even a speedy note-taker can get down only 25 to 30 words a minute, a fraction of the 100 words a minute of a normal conversation. Magazine writer Matt Schudel prefers a notebook, but when he interviewed Southern writer Reynolds Price, "I was glad I had a tape recorder to convey the beauty of his spoken words." Even so, Schudel believes he listens more attentively when he takes notes. "I have to be an active listener. I ask better questions and participate more fully in the conversation."

Even audio recorder fans know better than to put all their notes in one medium, however. Albom notes, "I work with a notepad even with the tape recorder, because I don't trust technology."

> **❝Lately new technology has grabbed everyone's attention. New cameras, faster computers. But it's important to remember they are merely tools. It's eyes and minds and hearts, passion and commitment, that make the most compelling images. Remembering also, it's the people in the pictures and those who view them that are the important ones.❞**
>
> —CAROL GUZY, PHOTOGRAPHER, *THE WASHINGTON POST*

QUICK Tips 🕐 ADVICE FOR REPORTERS TAKING PHOTOS

Kenny Irby

Poynter Institute faculty member Kenny Irby, a photojournalist and former photo editor at *Newsday* in Long Island, New York, provides practical tips for journalists who take photos:

- Train yourself to see the world as photographers do: through the viewfinder of a camera.

- Turn around. Sometimes you get so focused on the action that you don't see how other people and aspects are acting or reacting. Focus on the crowd as well as the players.

- Get as close as you can. Fill the frame up. The closer you get to the photograph, the more pleased you're going to be.

- Get comfortable with verticals. Don't limit your photos to horizontal shots. Picture editors and Web page designers may want variety.

- It's the eye that counts, not the camera. At Poynter, students in our college fellowship programs use disposable cameras, also known as PHD ("Push Here, Dummy") cameras.

- When using a flash, move your subject away from the walls to avoid shadows.

"The ability to make technically excellent photographs is a shallow skill," says Rich Beckman, acclaimed wildlife photographer and professor of visual communication at the University of Miami. "Photographs become important only when you add content and context and point of view." ▼

CHIP'S CORNER

WORKING WITH PHOTOS AND PHOTOJOURNALISTS

Whether or not you take photographs, you will undoubtedly work with photojournalists. Appreciation of their craft is vital. Two of my most important reporting teachers were photographers, Andy Dickerman of *The Providence Journal* and Ricardo Ferro of the *St. Petersburg Times*. From them, I learned how to be assertive without being aggressive, how to climb a tree to a roof to see a story from every possible angle and how to work as a member of a team. They taught me not only a different way to see the world, but also about courage, hard work and passion for excellence.

Unfortunately, many reporters don't think of their photographer colleagues as collaborators in the story process. Every photographer I've ever met remembers the sting of reporters introducing him or her as "my photographer," as if he or she was a servant rather than a collaborator.

Photography is a form of storytelling. "A photograph can be a powerful witness and an eloquent voice for those who have none," says Carol Guzy of *The Washington Post*, who has won journalism's highest awards, including the Pulitzer Prize, for her stunning photography documenting the agonies and triumphs of humanity around the planet. ▼

CONVERGENCE POINT ⋇

Reporting With the iPad

Jim Colgan, a veteran producer and digital editor, describes how he and other journalists use the iPad and other mobile devices to conduct live interviews and take photos in New York City's Times Square and among the protests in Egypt's Tahrir Square. "Like any profession, the quality of the journalism depends more on the journalist than on the tools," he writes. "But if the tools let you capture stories you wouldn't otherwise get and expose you to platforms you wouldn't ordinarily go to, they can greatly improve the quality of the stories you tell."

Find this link on the companion Web site at **www.oup.com/us/ scanlan.**

It can be equally dangerous to trust the human ear. Chip once covered a speech by the late journalist and grammarian Edwin Newman along with a reporter for the local university campus daily. He had a tape recorder. The student reporter, he assumed, did not.

Compare the two versions of the same speech:

Recorded Version

❯**EXAMPLE** People like Edwin Newman because he makes them laugh. He does that by making fun of **"the jargon, the mush, the smog, the dull pompous, boneless, gassy language"** that afflicts the world today.

Unrecorded Version

❯**EXAMPLE** "We have no hope of dealing with things unless we dig ourselves out of **the smog, the bog, the hash and the jargon**. . . ."

The bottom line: Smart reporters learn how to take accurate, detailed notes by hand and use the audio recorder in those instances where a verbatim record is valued, such as press conferences or other events where electronic media are present.

Journalistic lore is rich with stories about reporters whose recorders failed or who couldn't take notes until after they had left the interview. In those cases, the reporters wrote down or dictated into a recorder everything they could remember. Reporters ask whether they can use verbatim quotes reconstructed from memory. Bear in mind that working from memory is one of the most common causes of journalistic inaccuracy.

Technology notwithstanding, you're better off finding something—anything—to write notes on or with if news breaks and you're on the scene. Famously, *Dallas Morning News* reporter Hugh Aynesworth wasn't working on Nov. 22, 1963, when President

Multimedia producers at the *Dallas Morning News* took advantage of archival photos, documents, and audio and video footage to produce a dramatic interactive timeline that allowed readers to re-create the trip President John F. Kennedy took to the city that ended with his assassination on Nov. 22, 1963.

John F. Kennedy was shot and killed in Dallas—he just wanted to see the president in person, after which he planned to mail some bills. When the shots rang out, he had no materials for note taking, but he saw a young child nearby with a jumbo souvenir pencil. He bought the pencil from the child and began taking notes with it on the envelopes he'd intended to mail, enabling him to scoop competitors and earn a spot in American journalistic legend.

SOFTWARE TOOLS

The most common software journalists rely on is word-processing software. But it's not the only one. Software to edit digital photos, sound and video enables journalists to distill and add multimedia elements to their stories online. Other programs create spreadsheets and analyze data to distill vast amounts of information and break important news and support enterprise and investigative reporting. Some software requires so much training that it will probably be handled by online producers and photo staff.

But **digital literacy**, including knowledge of these programs' basics, will make it possible to report across multiple platforms. Audio editing software abounds, including Audacity, Garage Band, and others that are relatively easy to learn. News companies are increasingly providing training in many new media skills. But they are eager to hire those who come equipped with digital audio and video editing experience. Journalism programs at some colleges and universities now require their students to take at least a beginning multimedia course before graduation. Even if this is not required at your school, taking classes that teach you these skills will help you tremendously as you move into the professional ranks.

66 The old adage, 'A good reporter is good anywhere,' is no longer so convincing. We need good reporters who can bring appropriate tools to bear on constantly changing situations. In this environment, journalists who can do more than one thing well will be in demand. Economics and deadline pressures will ensure it. 99

—PHILIP MEYER,
AUTHOR, *THE VANISHING NEWSPAPER: SAVING JOURNALISM IN THE INFORMATION AGE*

THE REPORTER'S MINDSET

CONVERGENCE POINT ⚓

A Guide to Digital Literacy

Mark Briggs, director of digital media at KING 5 Television in Seattle, wrote *Journalism 2.0: How to Survive and Thrive: A Digital Literacy Guide for the Information Age*. This downloadable 128-page all-in-one handbook introduces online tools, skills and, the introduction says, "break[s] down each skill and technology into digestible lessons that will be immediately usable for you in your work."

Find this link on the companion Web site at **www.oup.com/us/scanlan.**

You might not think of a state of mind as a tool to be used in reporting, but it is. Approaching politicians, emergency personnel and all manner of strangers out of the blue and asking them questions takes a special **mindset** in addition to special skills. This, however, is only one element of the mental state reporters must employ to do their jobs well.

Accuracy Above All

Surveys show that the public expects the news media to be accurate, even though people are less confident than they used to be that news organizations get the facts right. Accuracy is a mindset, an attitude. The best reporters die a thousand deaths when they learn a story they wrote includes an error. Everyone makes mistakes, but journalists must take great care to get it right. Otherwise they lose a news organization's greatest asset: **credibility**. Accuracy is the goal; fact-checking is the process.

After tracking errors in *The* (Portland) *Oregonian*, editors concluded that the three most frequent sources of error are the following:

1. Working from memory
2. Making assumptions
3. Dealing with secondhand sources

Some magazines employ fact-checkers. They verify names, titles, ages, addresses and the accuracy of quotations in the story. Newspaper copy editors fill that job, but with staff cutbacks, fact-checking is increasingly a benefit that reporters rarely enjoy. Most professional journalists know they must act as their own fact-checkers. What

New media tools for today's mobile journalist: digital camera, laptop, digital audio recorder and broadband card for wireless access.

An Accuracy Checklist

As part of ASNE's Journalism Credibility Project, the *San Jose Mercury News* asked a group of editors and reporters to use a short checklist every time they put together a story. During an eight-month test in 1999–2000, the group had 10 percent fewer errors than a similar group not using the checklist.

- Have we double-checked all names, titles and places mentioned in this story?
- Are the quotes accurate and properly attributed? Have we fully captured what the person meant?
- If there are phone numbers or Web addresses, have we tried and CQ'd them?
- Is the lead sufficiently supported?
- Is the story fair?
- Were all the stakeholders identified, called and given a chance to talk?
- Who will be annoyed/angry with this story tomorrow? Why? Are we OK with that?
- Did we pick sides?
- Did we make value judgments about outcomes we want?
- Will some people like this story more than they should?
- What's missing from the story?

FIGURE 5-1 Accuracy is the gold standard of effective journalism. Eleven questions developed by the *San Jose* (CA) *Mercury News* helped journalists avoid the most common inaccuracies and provide independent verification in news reporting. "CQ'd" in item three is shorthand inserted into copy to let editors know information has been verified.

news organizations have to sell is credibility, especially now that technology enables anyone to report news electronically. If you get small things wrong, like an address or the spelling of a person's name, you lose the trust of your editors and your audience. Accuracy counts. (see Figure 5-1).

Gulp and Go: Assertiveness in Reporting

Reporting and writing the news demands courage. What surprises many new reporters is the fact that reporting involves meeting strangers and persuading them to tell you things they may not want to tell you. There's only one way they learn that lesson.

Here's how one student journalist, Steve Myers, described his **assertiveness** training:

> I was surprised the most by the fact that I was able to get over my fears of doing the actual reporting. No matter how the writing of the story turned out, in my mind it was secondary to the fact that I knocked on all 18 doors on 56th Avenue S. I felt a little bit like an encyclopedia salesman, but I got over the nausea in the pit of my stomach by the fourth or fifth house.

What may help is knowing that many people are terrified of journalists. Although it may be hard to believe, most people will be more afraid of you and the power you wield as a reporter than you are of them. Consider what J. C. McKinnon, a burly, stern-faced St. Petersburg police officer, told reporting students: "I carry a can of pepper spray, a Glock pistol and 51 rounds of ammunition. But you've got something that can destroy me: a pen and a notepad."

Journalists must demonstrate assertiveness to do their job. At a press conference, reporters crowd around the speaker, knowing they must get close enough to get the facts.

If you're avoiding doing something—making the phone call, knocking on the door, visiting a part of your community you've never been to before—acknowledge that you're anxious and then go do it.

Assertiveness reflects a belief in yourself and your profession. You have the right to ask questions, to approach someone for an interview, to request information. The flip side, of course, means that the person you're asking has the right to say no. Assertiveness also demands empathy. You have to understand that you wield power as a journalist. Your press pass will get you places the general public often can't go.

Don't be afraid. Gulp. And go.

Ten Tools to Make Your Stories Stand Out

Not every journalistic tool is tangible. Some are metaphors for mental skills and attitudes that will help you achieve excellence. Here are ten tools the authors consider essential for every journalist.

1. *A tightrope.* If you're going to be a writer, you need to take risks. Journalists need to be counterphobic—that is, do what they're afraid to do.

    Walk a tightrope every day. Where is the one place in town you've never been because you're afraid to go there? Try a new approach to writing a story. Ask yourself every day, "Have I taken a risk?"

2. *A net.* The best writers cast trawler's nets on stories. They cast them wide and deep. They interview 10 people to get the one quote that sums up the theme. They spend hours mining interviews for the anecdote that reveals the story. They hunt through records and reports, looking for the one specific fact that explains the universal, the detail that captures person or event.

3. *Someone else's shoes.* Empathy—the ability to feel what another person feels, to walk in another's shoes—is the writer's greatest gift, and perhaps most important tool. The late Pulitzer winner Richard Ben Cramer, talking about the reporting he did in the Middle East in the late '70s, said he tried to give readers a sense of what it is like to be living in a situation of terror, of life on the edge: "It's

very hard to know what someone would feel in a situation unless you at least feel something of it yourself."

4. *A loom.* Journalists weave connections for their audiences. We connect the police report at the station house to the red bungalow in the tree-lined neighborhood. We connect city hall with the sewage project. Writing is a process of making connections, of discovering patterns.

5. *A zoom lens.* David Finkel of *The Washington Post* tries "to look at any site that will be the focus of a narrative passage as if I were a photographer. I not only stand near something, I move away. For the long view. I crouch down, I move left and right. I try to view it from every angle possible to see what might be revealed."

6. *Six words.* "Tell your story in six words," is the advice that former AP feature writer, now syndicated columnist Tad Bartimus, gives. By reducing it to the single phrase, reducing it almost to a line of poetry, you can capture the tension of the story. You can capture the entire story. You can do it in three words or, as suggested in Chapter 2, one word, as long as the word or words capture the theme of the story.

   One classic example, perhaps the shortest short story ever written: "For Sale: Baby shoes, never used." Six words.

7. *An accelerator pedal.* "There are some kinds of writing," William Faulkner said, "that you have to do very fast. Like riding a bicycle on a tightrope." Race past your internal censor. Novelist Gail Godwin called it "the watcher at the gates." This is the voice that says, "You're an incompetent. You can't write. You've lost it. You didn't do the reporting. You're an idiot." To trick the watcher at the gates, write as fast as you can, which leaves you more time to revise. And the way you do it is to take off running.

8. *Scissors. Or its electronic equivalent: the delete key.* In *The Elements of Style*, William Strunk Jr. and E. B. White said, "Vigorous writing is concise. A sentence should contain no unnecessary words, a paragraph no unnecessary sentences, for the same reason that a drawing should have no unnecessary lines and a machine no unnecessary parts. This requires not that the writer make all his sentences short, or that he avoid all detail and treat the subject only in outline, but that every word tell." Less is more. How many gallons of maple sap does it take to make a gallon of maple syrup? Forty. Boil away the sap.

9. *A trash can.* Isaac Bashevis, the Nobel Prize–winning writer, once said, "If you see something is no good, throw it away and begin again. A lot of writers have failed because they have too much pity."

   Journalists will have little pity for sources, but feel sorry for the weakest prose because it flows from their keyboard. "Hey!" a reporter will protest, "I spent two hours on that lead. I can't throw it away. Remember Singer: "I say that a wastepaper basket is a writer's best friend. My wastepaper basket is on a steady diet."

10. *A bible. Lowercase "b."* The sacred writing texts you read for guidance or inspiration. Books or stories that you keep nearby when you're getting ready to write and are trying to go to the next level of excellence. When stumped, take

inspiration from writers you admire. Here's a sample of what excellent journalists read for inspiration.

Clockers by Richard Price
The Elements of Style by William Strunk Jr. and E. B. White
The Essays of E. B. White
"On the Pulse of Morning" by Maya Angelou, delivered at President Clinton's inauguration, 1993
There Are No Children Here by Alex Kotlowitz
The Writer's Art by James Kilpatrick
Writers at Work: The Paris Review Interviews, edited by George Plimpton
Writing for Your Readers by Donald M. Murray
Works by:
    Katherine Boo
    Jimmy Breslin
    Willa Cather
    Joan Didion
    David Finkel
    Ernest Hemingway
    Mark Twain
    John Updike
    Tom Wolfe

The Coaching Way ⅲ TOOL SHARPENING

- Study notes you have taken and identify shorthand or speedwriting symbols you already use. Establish your own speedwriting system.
- Read Mark Briggs' *Journalism 2.0: How to Survive and Thrive: A Digital Literacy Guide for the Information Age.* Complete one to three assignments.
- Find an opportunity to use a digital audio recorder or a good quality camera. If your school doesn't provide this equipment, consider purchasing an inexpensive model.

Capture video with your cell phone if it offers that feature. What surprises you about using these tools? What did the experience teach you? What do you need to learn next?

- Be honest: Are you spending too much time at your desk instead of being out in the community or the area covered by your beat? If you're not on deadline, get out of the office right now.
- Be counterphobic: When you realize you're avoiding something on your next story—calling a difficult source, exploring an unfamiliar neighborhood—stop hesitating. Do it.
- Is your story fair? How would you feel if the subject of the story was a family member or a close friend?
- Is your story accurate? Have you checked every name, address, title and fact against your notes, with a credible source or a document? Have you read sections with technical material to someone who is an expert on the subject? ▸

PROFESSIONALS' ROUNDTABLE

TOOLS

Technology has filled the journalistic toolbox with an array of innovative gadgets and software that enable journalists to gather and deliver the news in the 21st century with speed and sophistication. The most effective journalists combine traditional reporting and writing skills with technological savvy that relies on social media, devices and software, say two digital news veterans and a Pulitzer Prize–winning reporter turned TV correspondent.

Their conclusions:

- Gadgets are essential—and cool—but nothing substitutes for reporting and writing skills, curiosity and tenacity.
- Social media is a rich source for story ideas, staying on top of news and marketing your work.
- The Internet is the best and usually free source for using and staying current with technology.

Participants

MARK BRIGGS, interactive director, KING 5 Television, Seattle, and author, *Journalism 2.0: How to Survive and Thrive: A Digital Literacy Guide for the Information Age*

SARA GANIM, correspondent, *CNN*

VIDISHA PRIYANKA, former audience editor, TBO.com, Tampa, Florida

---

> What reporting tools do you use to carry out your daily reporting and writing duties?

Ganim: I use video to add an element to print stories that might not work on ink in the paper. I use photos as inspiration when writing longer, in-depth pieces. I have learned to write tighter and more illustrative by writing broadcast copy. I call my smartphone my mobile newsroom, because it really is essential to how I gather news daily. I can shoot, edit and post video to the Web. I can get photos up almost instantly. And of course the ability to stay connected constantly through social media is invaluable during breaking news.

> What's the journalist's most important tool?

Briggs: Besides their brain? Just kidding. Anything a reporter needs to do to capture news or content can be done on a good smartphone. I hear they can also make phone calls in a pinch.

Ganim: At the end of the day, no gadget can tell you how to report. Those things only help make you better and more efficient. The most important tool is your head. Always try to think outside the box. Don't get discouraged by closed doors, or dial tones. What's another way to get the information? Be inquisitive. Be curious. Be tenacious.

> What multimedia tools and social media do journalists need to succeed in today's new media world?

Priyanka: Storify (storify.com) is very popular as a smart human curator of social media and is becoming a common format to tell a story using social media posts. Facebook and Twitter are popular. Pinterest is catching on. Smartphone video is growing. Explore all of them as they come about; unless you use them, you can't evaluate which one will work for your area of coverage.

> *What social media do you use?*

Ganim: Twitter is a great way to keep things in perspective. Often times, when reporters are in the weeds of a story, they can lose sight of what their readers care about. Twitter has really helped me stay on track. It's also great for live events. I've often gotten ideas from Twitter. I've even had people tweet during a press conference, giving me questions they want answered.

> *What computer software should journalists be able to use?*

Briggs: All journalists should be comfortable with a Web publishing platform like Wordpress, a photo editing tool like Photoshop (or the much cheaper Photoshop Elements), an audio editing program like Audacity (free) and a video editing tool like iMovie or Final Cut.

> *What ways do journalists use social media, and how important are they today?*

Priyanka: Journalists use it to market themselves. It is a starting point for sources. Twitter is being used as a public scanner to get information so leads can be followed and vetted. Story ideas come from social media as journalists get exposed to diverse ideas and people.

> *Where can they get the kind of training they need to take advantage of the multimedia and social media tools available?*

Briggs: Experiment and ask. Everyone I know learned how to use social media by teaching themselves, experimenting with different platforms and tools, then asking others in those communities for tips or explanations.

SUMMARY GUIDE

THE REPORTER'S TOOLBOX

PENS, PENCILS AND REPORTER'S NOTEBOOK

In the age of multimedia news gathering, the paper notebook remains the basic tool to gather information.

What to Remember → The notebook is the first draft, but don't let its contents weigh you down. The story is in your head, not in your notes.

THE COMPUTER

Computers have revolutionized the way journalists report, write, revise and ensure accuracy.

What to Remember → Advances in computing power enable journalists to use spreadsheets, databases and other software to distill, analyze and present large bodies of information in accessible ways.

NOTE TAKING ON THE SCREEN

Taking notes on the screen is a fast method and allows for rapid organization of information discovered during reporting and research.

What to Remember → Good journalists avoid plagiarism and inaccuracy by creating electronic notetaking systems that avoid confusion about the source of information, including quotes, links and reading matter. They know that the best stories are found outside the newsroom and don't stay tethered to the computer or telephone.

CELL PHONES

In the age of mobile journalism, the cell phone enables reporters to keep in touch with editors, report and deliver news on deadline and use social media to connect with audiences.

What to Remember → The cell phone, especially one equipped with still photo and video functions, is an essential reporting tool. Eyewitness coverage and rapid delivery enable reporters to outperform the competition and have allowed citizens to break important stories.

AUDIO RECORDERS

Digital audio recorders ensure accuracy, capture quotes in context and provide multimedia coverage. They are an essential item in the journalistic toolbox.

What to Remember → Smart journalists don't assume an audio recorder does all the work. They use a notebook as a backup for facts, quotes, observations and follow-up questions in case of equipment malfunction.

SOFTWARE TOOLS

Today's journalists rely on software tools that edit digital sound, photos and video for multimedia platforms and that compile and analyze data.

What to Remember → In the age of multimedia journalism, software skills are vital. Competency improves employment chances and career advancement.

THE REPORTER'S MINDSET

> While journalists have unique opportunities to interview citizens and public officials to report the news, that access carries enormous responsibilities for accuracy and fairness.

What to Remember → Good journalists care deeply about getting their stories right. Journalism is mentally and emotionally challenging and requires assertiveness. Counterphobia—doing what you fear—makes journalists more confident and capable of serving the public trust.

KEY TERMS

assertiveness, p. 111
credibility, p. 110
digital audio recorder, p. 105

digital literacy, p. 109
manipulation, p. 106
mindset, p. 110

mojos, p. 103
note taking, p. 100
word processing, p. 102

EXERCISES

1. Make an inventory of your reporting toolbox. If you've just started studying journalism, the list may be short: a notebook, pen, time-sharing on a news lab computer. Study the various tools cited in this chapter, and decide which ones you need to learn more about.

2. Practice note taking by transcribing dialogue from your favorite songs, recorded speeches and television shows. Compare your version with the original. Measure your speed and accuracy. Use your notebook to record observations: the weather, what people wear, what's on display in their offices.

3. Go out on a photo assignment with a photographer and watch how he or she collects visual information and interacts with subjects. Take a digital still or video camera to a campus event and see what it's like to make pictures. If you have access to software tools, edit what you collected.

4. Open a Twitter account and create a Facebook page.

5. Hollywood has long turned to the newsroom for entertainment, but movies can be windows onto the reporting life. Rent the movie *The Front Page* starring Jack Lemmon and Walter Matthau or *His Girl Friday* starring Rosalind Russell and Cary Grant to get a view of what journalism was like during the 1920s. What were the "tools of the trade" back then? What has been lost and gained? Watch *All the President's Men*, which tells the story of how two young reporters broke the Watergate scandal in 1973. How might those journalists have covered the big story with today's multimedia tools and social media?

READINGS

Briggs. Mark. *Journalism Next: A Practical Guide to Digital Reporting and Publishing.* **Washington, DC: CQ Press, 2010.**
Journalism "is about people, not technology," notes Briggs, who ran newspaper Web sites and is director of digital media for KING 5 Television in Seattle. To connect, he provides an essential handbook of the latest software, tools, social media and approaches to reach out to audiences with new technologies.

Fryxell, David. *Write Faster, Write Better.* **Cincinnati, OH: Writers Digest Books, 2004.**
In this technological age, veteran editor and columnist Fryxell maintains his faith in the power of the notebook. He provides guidance on how best to take notes, organize the material and use the notebook to begin writing early in the process.

Tompkins, Al. *Aim for the Heart: Write, Shoot, Report and Produce for TV and Multimedia.* **Washington, DC: CQ Press, 2012.**
Tompkins, an award-winning television journalist, teaches important lessons about the process of producing multimedia journalism, identifies the necessary tools and explains how to use them for maximum impact

INTERVIEWING

INTERVIEWING IS ONE of the most important skills journalists must develop. At the heart of the interviewer's craft is a talent for talking comfortably with people and persuading them to give you information. Effective interviewing makes good reporting and writing possible. Yet many journalists get little or no training in this vital aspect of their job.

Students often worry more about interviewing than any other element of journalism. How do you walk up to strangers and ask them questions? How do you get people—tight-lipped cops, jargon-spouting experts, everyday folks who aren't accustomed to being interviewed—to give you useful answers? In this chapter, you will learn how to overcome these obstacles and become an effective interviewer.

THE ROLE OF THE INTERVIEW

As a reporter, you can learn a lot about a subject, issue or event by doing background research—it's a necessary part of the process. Only through doing interviews, however, can you transform that knowledge into something personal and relevant to readers. By talking to people who are in the middle of the story, you give readers a personal connection to the people and events that make news.

Interviews usually capture the most current information far better than a Google search. Interviews also capture nonverbal information—how a person acts, reacts, the tiniest details about life—essential to reporting the news and telling the stories of our times. As you develop as a reporter, some of your most challenging and satisfying moments will come during interviews.

The notebook remains the most common interviewing tool, but digital recording devices, such as the equipment used here by a student journalist interviewing a local fisherman, have transformed the way journalists capture words and sounds.

Interviewing is a process. It involves three steps that can be analyzed, described and repeated to produce quality journalism.

1. Preparing for the interview
2. Conducting the interview
3. Writing from interviews

PREPARING FOR THE INTERVIEW

> 66 Interviewing is the modest immediate science of gaining trust, then gaining information. 99
>
> —JOHN BRADY, AUTHOR, *THE CRAFT OF INTERVIEWING*

If you want to flop as an interviewer, fail to prepare. Reporters who dash out of the newsroom or pick up the phone to call a source without preparation will find themselves in a painful situation. If you know the subject and have prepared effective questions in advance before you conduct an interview, you'll almost always get something of value out of it.

Focus

Thinking is the most important step before, during and after an interview. Asking "What's my story about?" and "What do I need from my interviews?" keeps you and your story focused. Stay alert at every stage, but the time you take at the beginning of the process is the most crucial.

Regardless of how well you believe you know the story topic, do some background research about it on the Internet, at the library, or in your newsroom's archive until you're comfortable that you know enough to accurately assess what you hear and see. Verify that the material you find is legitimate—there's nothing worse than going into an interview armed with one-sided or inaccurate background information.

Be ready to change your mind during an interview, especially if answers don't match what you think the story is about. Follow the story where it leads. Sources can tell when a reporter is quote-hunting to support a preordained idea rather than genuinely seeking information.

Research

Students always worry about asking "stupid questions." In reporting, there are no stupid questions, unless they are those that demonstrate you have come to the interview unprepared. Interviewing requires humility, not being afraid to ask someone to further explain a point. A source may consider a question obvious, but your responsibility is to your audience, which needs to fully understand. Compile a list of the questions you want to be sure to ask—don't feel limited to these, but have them on hand to ensure you cover the most important subjects. When you arrive at the interview with the background to ask informed questions; you won't waste time (yours or the interviewees'), and you'll get more and better information out of the questions you do ask.

A. J. Liebling, a legendary writer for *The New Yorker*, landed an interview with tight-lipped jockey Willie Shoemaker. He opened with a single question: Why do you ride with one stirrup higher than the other? Impressed by Liebling's knowledge, Shoemaker opened up.

Choosing the Best Interviewing Method

A good reporter—someone who is well informed, motivated and curious—will use whatever tools are at his or her disposal to gather information. While face-to-face interviews recorded with nothing but pen and paper still work, there are many other tools and ways of connecting with sources that can produce useful results.

Face-to-Face

Be there, advises *Washington Post* reporter Brady Dennis. "In person, you have the benefit of using all your senses and encountering people you otherwise might not. Also, people in traumatic situations tend to trust a live human being more than a faceless voice."

Dennis was at the Tiny Tap Tavern the night of its owner's funeral. He gathered evocative quotes and observations that captured the soul of a neighborhood bar and the man who ran it.

Brady Dennis

▶**EXAMPLE** "I've been coming in here, I guess, at least 25, 30 years," said John "Pistol" Schiestl, 55. "It kind of looks like a Mexican jail, but you don't care. It grows on you after a while. What this place has is character."

Friends and family recalled how Mr. Powell ran the place honestly and fairly. He didn't allow cussing, and if a fight ever broke out (which was rare), the brawlers would have to call Mr. Powell, explain themselves and apologize before he'd let them back inside.

They remembered how he posted signs, which still hang from the walls, that read, "If you drink to forget, please pay before you drink," and "Be nice or be gone," and "In God we trust; all others pay cash."

—*St. Petersburg Times, March, 10, 2004*

Observation—hanging out— is just as important as asking questions in an interview. To profile Jamie Thomas, a teenager blind since birth, reporter Brady Dennis and photographer Chris Zuppa of the *St. Petersburg Times* watched from a distance as Jamie played a *Wheel of Fortune* video game with help from his mother Melissa.

Journalist at Work ◢ BRADY DENNIS

Brady Dennis knows that good writing isn't possible without great reporting. His tips on deadline interviewing confirm there's no difference in interviewing for story, whether you're working on a long project or, like Dennis, scrambling to cover nighttime crime in Tampa, Florida. Here are his top three tips for deadline interviewing.

1. Take it slow. Never let them know you're in a hurry. People sense that. If you must leave, escape gently.
2. Listen and learn. Ask a question, and get out of the way. Silence opens the door to hearing dialogue, rare and valuable in breaking stories.
3. Gather detail. Details provide insight and illuminate the subject. The wrong details bog down a story. The right details elevate it. ▼

Telephone

Deadlines and distance often make personal interviews impossible. Enter the telephone—which some reporters consider their most important tool. "Phones connect reporters to sources, to facts, to information and verification," says National Public Radio host Susan Stamberg. In the hands of a curious, sympathetic and professional reporter, the telephone can be an indispensable device for gathering information about people in the news.

The telephone offers the advantage of allowing real-time give-and-take between you and a source. If someone's response gives you an idea for a follow-up question or two, you can ask right away rather than waiting around for your next message from that source, unlike email and other methods discussed in the following sections.

Digital Audio/Video Recording

Web sites often rely on news captured by digital recorders, tools once used exclusively by radio and TV journalists. They require some technical knowledge, but rely on the same journalistic interviewing skills. "A radio reporter has to do what any reporter does," says National Public Radio correspondent Howard Berkes. "Determine who knows what about the subject and how they might help tell the story."

Technology makes it easy to digitally record phone conversations and use segments in podcasts, but you'll need to get permission from interviewees to record phone interviews. Failing to do this is an ethical or legal lapse that can get you into serious trouble.

For video, it's crucial to learn some of the basics of putting together good shots and quality audio. This isn't just for the sake of putting together something that looks good, it's also to avoid making mistakes that distract viewers from the content of your story. Tutorials in the basics of video are beyond the scope of this book, but are readily available online and through most colleges and universities.

Email

Reporters can easily contact sources by email. In recent years, stories commonly include the phrase "interviewed by email." But there are pitfalls.

"Using email interviews may eliminate rounds of phone tag," Kim Hart wrote in *American Journalism Review*, "but skeptics say it also eliminates the candor, spontaneity and natural dialogue that make for engaging conversations and compelling

QUICK Tips ⏺ EMAIL INTERVIEW TIPS

Jonathan Dube, former senior vice president and general Manager for AOL News & Information and an online journalism pioneer, offers valuable advice to email interviewers.

■ Be upfront. Always identify yourself as a reporter.

■ Expiration date. "Email may last forever," Dube points out; it's easily shared with strangers. Keep yours professional always.

■ Fact-check. Treat email as you would any source, subject to verification and critical thinking.

■ Be careful. It's easy to fake an email address. Check your e-sources and online identities. ▼

stories." Since it eliminates the give-and-take quality of in-person or phone interviews, it inhibits your ability to follow up on answers. This is why email is best used to verify details of stories or to set up interviews. Unless you have lots of time to wait for responses, interviewing via email should be used only as a last resort.

Texting, IM and Other Short-Message Technologies

Texting and instant messaging are popular ways for real-time conversations with family, friends and, increasingly, with sources.

"It's faster than email," says business reporter Paul Conley, who uses it to reach sources. "It's transparent (the system tells you whether or not someone is online).

Journalists have turned to text messaging and online chats to conduct interviews for real-time interactions. Steve Myers, managing editor of Poynter Online, interviews political cartoonist Rob Tornoe about his creative process via chat.

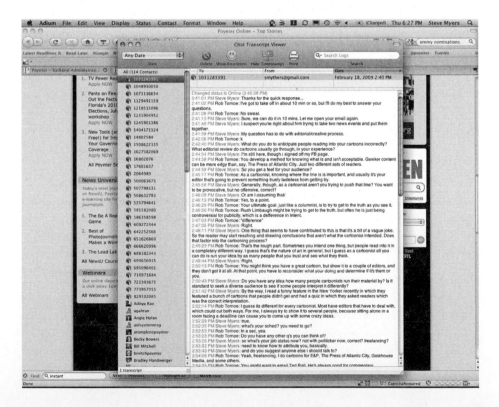

And, for reasons that I don't quite understand, sources who hesitate to talk on the phone or exchange emails are willing to chat via IM."

Text messages, chat and other short-message technologies are also becoming popular tools to enable reporters to contact sources and gather nuggets of information. In today's fast-moving world, sources are often busy people who are more likely to send a quick text message (or a tweet if they use Twitter) via cell phone than they are to sit for an interview.

These technologies are all useful for reporters, but have serious limitations. By their very nature, their information content is limited—160 characters for a text message, 140 characters for a tweet. If you need to ask detailed questions or need in-depth answers, you should look for an interview method that allows for more elaboration on both sides of the conversation.

CONDUCTING THE INTERVIEW

For some beginning reporters, approaching a stranger to ask questions seems terrifying. Students frequently get into journalism because they love to write, but they often have a fear of walking up to people out of the blue and asking questions. Whether they feel that it crosses a social boundary or simply comes across as pushy, it's an issue that some students have trouble conquering.

As a reporter, however, this comes with the territory and must be overcome. Fortunately, with practice it becomes much easier, even to those who are somewhat less gregarious than others.

If this is a problem for you, it helps to remember a couple of things. First, most people love to talk, especially about themselves, and are gratified to be considered an expert worthy of appearing in a news story. Second, being a reporter grants you a special status—it's your job to gather information. Reporters might not wear uniforms like firefighters or police officers, but a news media badge carries with it a social license to ask questions.

If you've done your homework and familiarized yourself with the subject, there's no reason to worry. The more often you do it, the easier it becomes.

Ask Smart Questions

If you've developed a set of questions in advance, use them as the jumping-off point. Ask follow-up questions along the way, but be sure to refer back to those central questions. The best questions are open-ended, or conversation starters. They begin with "How?" "What?" "Where?" "When?" "Why?" They encourage expansive answers that produce an abundance of information needed to produce a complete and accurate story. "Why did you go into journalism?" invites the subject to tell a story you can use in your story.

Second best is the closed-ended question. Ask them when you need a direct answer: Did you embezzle the company's money? Yes, No, No comment. Closed-ended questions put people on the record.

> ❝Somebody once wrote that there's no more seductive sentence in the English language than, 'I want to hear your story.' . . . Often you don't have to do any more than just say that.❞
>
> —MITCH ALBOM, COLUMNIST, DETROIT FREE PRESS

QUICK Tips ⏱ PRACTICE LISTENING AND WRITING

Learn to identify the pauses while following the speaker and to start a new sentence even if you did not complete the previous one. Keep in mind, if you try to "catch up" and write a previous sentence and the speaker already starts another, you'll lose the new sentence.

Use a notebook with pages divided in half. First, write in the left column all the way down and start writing in the right column. This approach will reduce the movement of your arm in half and will help you to write faster.

Don't print letters; write them out in script. It takes more time to print than to write. ▼

The worst are conversation stoppers. These include double-barreled questions and statements masquerading as questions. Double-barreled means asking more than one question at a time. "Why did the campus police use pepper spray on student protesters? Did you give the order?" Double-barreled questions give the subject a choice that allows them to avoid the question they want to ignore and choose the less difficult one. Statements masquerading as questions are easy to spot—there's no question mark at the end. "You don't want students to protest because they give your administration a bad name." They don't provide a question a subject can answer and risk offending the source by sounding like editorializing.

Write out questions in advance to ensure you ask ones that start conversations rather than halt them in their tracks. Stick to the script, and *always* ask one question at a time. You may need to ask follow-up questions for additional information or explanations, but stick to open-ended ones for greatest effect.

If sources talk too fast, or you don't understand the answer, don't be afraid to ask them to slow down or repeat an answer. It's better for everyone concerned to make sure you get it right, especially at key points of an interview. Don't be afraid to say, "That's a really good point. I want to make sure I get it accurately." Or "My audience doesn't have your scientific knowledge. Could you put it in terms the average person could understand?"

Observe

Good interviewers do more than listen. They look around, watch the interviewee deal with people and soak up the whole atmosphere. You can learn quite a bit about people and pick up a lot of incidental story material by seeing their homes or offices, and how they act in those settings.

"I always try to see people at home," says Carol McCabe, who fills her newspaper and magazine feature stories with rich detail gathered during interviews. "I can learn something from where the TV is, whether the set of encyclopedias or bowling trophies is prominently displayed, whether the guy hugs his wife or touches his kids, what clothes he or she wears at home, what's on the refrigerator door."

The value of being there is evident in a Nov. 27, 2011, column by *St. Petersburg Times* outdoors writer Jeff Klinkenberg about the 87-year-old caretaker of the Levy County Quilt Museum.

▶**EXAMPLE** Miss Winnelle led me on a whirlwind tour, stopping at almost every quilt in the museum. They hang from walls and racks or are stacked neatly on tables. Some look like checkerboards; others feature every color in an autumn sunset. One quilt was made recently by a teenager; another, acquired from a Levy County family, goes back to 1857.

"This here one is what I call a feathered square quilt," Miss Winnelle said as I followed. "This quilt here has the double wedding pattern, two rings interlocked. Over here we got a crazy quilt — look at those colors. This quilt on the table tells the story of the Bible. This one with all the watermelons — it's real special   celebrates the agriculture history of this area."

Don't just settle for quotes: Listen for dialogue, those exchanges between people that illuminate character, drive action and propel readers forward.

In a dramatic scene from his 2007 series about life in a city zoo, Pulitzer Prize–winning writer Thomas M. French captured the excited dialogue between a team of researchers as they tracked "Stormy," an endangered manatee with a satellite transmitter fastened to its tail, in a Florida river. Even the transmitter has a voice. Note that French mastered shorthand in high school to enhance his interviewing skills.

▶**EXAMPLE** "Beep . . . beep . . . beep . . . "

On the boats, more joyous yelping.

"Tag up!"

"There he is!"

"See the bubbles?"

Stormy disappears again. The researchers wipe the rain from their faces and smile.

"Are we having fun yet?"

"We're having a lot of fun."

A speedboat roars by, rushing through a part of the river where people are supposed to slow down. Monica watches it pass and hisses.

Finally the research team gets the net around Stormy and takes him toward the shallows, where they wrap him in a sling and carry him onto the banks.

"Let's see if this old boy will hold still," says the vet.

—*St. Petersburg Times*

Don't keep readers waiting for a lively quote, either. Quotes are the breath of any story; they sum up, dramatize and crystallize news. Keep in mind what editors drill into rookies: Good quotes up high. The principle is illustrated in the lead of the *Biloxi* (MS) *Sun Herald*'s Pulitzer Prize–winning story about the 2005 deadly arrival of Hurricane Katrina. A powerful quote that follows the summary lead drives home the storm's impact.

CONVERGENCE POINT ⤋

The Question Man

This is a fascinating profile of John Sawatsky, who has taught interviewing to thousands of journalists. Sawatsky, who trains reporters and anchors at ESPN.com, discusses his theory that interviewing is akin to social science and explains why some questions encourage sources to talk while others make them clam up.

Find this link on the companion Web site at **www.oup.com/us/ scanlan.**

❯EXAMPLE Hurricane Katrina devastated South Mississippi on Monday with a force not seen since Camille 36 years ago, sweeping aside multimillion-dollar casinos, burying the beach highway and killing at least 50 people in Harrison County.

"This," said Biloxi Mayor A.J. Holloway, "is our tsunami."

—*Biloxi Sun Herald, Aug. 30, 2005*

WRITING FROM INTERVIEWS

One of the main reasons interviews add so much to stories is that they add a human touch, a unique phrase or point of view about the subject. As you talk to sources, be alert to evocative quotes and observations that might enrich your story.

Using Quotes Effectively

Some reporters use quotations as a crutch or way to pad their stories, letting sources babble on in ways that baffle readers. If a quote helps explain something in a useful way, use it; if a source is unclear or wordy, don't be afraid to paraphrase the quote. Trim the fat off bloated quotes. Quotations, as Kevin Maney of *USA Today* once said, should occupy a "place of honor" in a story.

The most powerful quotes are short, sometimes just fragments, and convey character and a sense of place and drama. Writing about a 2002 two-car collision that killed two Alabama sisters traveling to visit each other, Jeffrey Gettleman of *The New York Times* used simple quotes that illustrated what the Roman orator Cicero called brevity's "great charm of eloquence."

❯EXAMPLE "They weren't fancy women," said their sister Billie Walker. "They loved good conversation. And sugar biscuits."

Just 11 words, yet they speak volumes about the victims.

Quotes may also be used to drive home a point at the end of a paragraph—as Chip did in a March 1994 Knight Ridder story about the impact on children when parents fail to pay child support.

❯EXAMPLE When friends ask Brian Lesefske what his father does, the teenager has a simple answer: "He runs from the law."

Revising Quotes

People rarely speak in complete sentences. They stumble, stammer, circle around a subject. Consider this hypothetical conversation that follows and how quotes might appear in print. Notice the use of ellipses, three periods that normally mean words have been deleted, but also indicate an unfinished thought. In this case, they signal

Rep. Foghorn's stumbling through an answer about her decision to run for re-election. The reporter edits the quote for clarity.

QUESTION: "Will you run for re-election, Congresswoman?"

ANSWER: Congresswoman: "Um, well, that's a . . . I'm still . . . If the voters want me . . . I mean, that's what it all boils down to, doesn't it? Who am I to say no?"

Answer Quoted in Story

❯EXAMPLE "If the voters want me . . . who am I to say 'No?'" Foghorn said yesterday.

Not every writer or publication uses ellipses. "Even writers who record and transcribe their interviews correct sentence fragments and delete the 'uhs' and 'ahs' and other sounds so common in everyday speech," says James B. Stewart, a best-selling nonfiction author who won a Pulitzer Prize at *The Wall Street Journal*. "The important thing is that the substance of what was said be conveyed accurately."

It's important to do this with care—read over your write-up of the quote and make sure that in the process of making it readable, you haven't introduced or changed anything that could mislead readers about the quote's accuracy. Changing quotes is forbidden. Be especially careful about "cleaning up" quotes to eliminate grammatical errors or colorful language. Reporters frequently do so when interviewing official sources—but rarely, and unfairly, when an ordinary person speaks ungrammatically, a practice that raises ethical questions. You should err on the side of accuracy over perfect grammar—you don't want to drain the quote of the voice of the person quoted.

Staying Faithful to What People Say: Quotation Marks and Ellipses

In 1984, Jeffrey Masson, a psychoanalyst, sued *New Yorker* writer Janet Malcolm. Masson claimed that Malcolm libeled him by quoting several statements he never made. Masson lost his suit, although more than one court agreed that Malcolm apparently made up some of Masson's quotes. In the U.S. Supreme Court's 1991 opinion, Justice Anthony Kennedy established this standard for quote marks, the inverted twins—" "—that indicate a person is speaking:

> In general, quotation marks around a passage indicate to the reader that the passage reproduces the speaker's words verbatim. They inform the reader that he or she is reading the statement of the speaker, not a paraphrase or other indirect interpretation by an author. By providing this information, quotations add authority to the statement and credibility to the author's work. Quotations allow the reader to form his or her own conclusions and to assess the conclusions of the author, instead of relying entirely upon the author's characterization of her subject.

Quotes may be edited using ellipses: three dots . . . that indicate one or more words have been omitted. Some older journalists say they were told to never use them because the average reader wouldn't know that an ellipsis is a punctuation device that alerts a reader that there are words missing from the sentence—words that the writer has left out for space or clarity but whose omission does not alter the meaning. But the standard has changed. The *Associated Press Stylebook*, followed by most news organizations, advises using an ellipsis "to indicate the deletion of one or more words in condensing quotes, texts and documents" and cautions against deleting words that distort the meaning.

"Echo quotes" contain quotations that repeat what has already been written. For example,

>**EXAMPLE** The mayor said he's pleased with the election results, noting that his victory demonstrates his popularity with the voters. "I'm pleased with the results," said Mayor Boggs. "It proves my popularity with the voters."

Readers and listeners don't need a paraphrase *and* a quote to understand. One or the other will suffice. Avoid repetitious quotes by always reading your story aloud as you make final revisions. Reserve quotation marks for words that reveal character, advance the narrative or drive home a controversial point. Use a blend of quotation and paraphrase. Don't use every quote in your notebook to prove you did the interviews. That's not writing; it's dictation.

Using Quotes: Do's and Don'ts

- Do use quotes for emphasis and authority, to breathe life into a story, when someone says something better than you can paraphrase it. For example:

  >**EXAMPLE** No African American has ever been elected to the Pinellas County school board. Waller says his decision to run for school board is part of the struggle for community control of schools. "Black residents must have the power to control their own education," he said.

- Do follow the correct style for quotes:
  Begin a quotation with open quote marks ("), and end a quotation with close quote marks (").
  Periods and commas go inside the close quotation mark. For example:

  >**EXAMPLE** Jason Myron, a freckle-faced 8-year-old, grows pensive at the mention of Mama Gert's name. "She was one of my most favoritest people," he says.

- When quoting dialogue or conversation, use separate paragraphs, with quotation marks at the start and end of each person's quote. Examples:

  >**EXAMPLE** "We paint on the first day?" asked 12-year-old Sharese Bowens.

  "You're going to be exhibiting before you know it," answered art teacher Patsi Aguero.

- Avoid partial quotes to report ordinary expressions. There's no need to say the student government president said she was "going home for the holidays."

- If using a partial quote, put quote marks around only the words the speaker actually said.
- Place attribution and speaker identification at the end of a single-sentence quote. Otherwise break up a longer quote by placing attribution and speaker identification in the middle of a quote for effective pacing. For example:

    ❯**EXAMPLE** "Nobody comes down here. They stop at Fifth," says Thinh Nguyen, owner of the Crab House restaurant on Ninth and Ninth. "When there are games, the whole street is quiet."

- Lead into a quotation with attribution. Example:

    ❯**EXAMPLE** Two blocks to the south, Calvin Baker, owner of the Hogley Wogley Barbecue, says, "There's no extra business on this side. People go to the games and leave. They don't stick around."

- Lead into a quotation with a paraphrase that explains the context of the speaker's comment. Example:

    ❯**EXAMPLE** Berthelot acknowledges there are drugs in the Roser Park area. "See those people?" he says from his cruiser, pointing to a yard full of people huddled around a checkerboard in nearby Campbell Park. "They're selling dope. I know exactly what they're doing, but I have to be able to legally articulate what they're doing. I have to have a legitimate reason to search them."

- Combine physical action with quotes, as in this story about a playground at All Children's Hospital. It not only lets the reader hear the sound of someone talking, but also describes the scene.

    ❯**EXAMPLE** "It's a safe place for Taylor to play," said Gilroy as she gazed at the playground through the hospital waiting room's half-open window blinds. "It's full of appropriate things for her—little cars, toys without small parts, big balls— and toys she uses in physical therapy."

- You can use ellipses to show you have deleted words or sentences from a passage you are quoting.

    ❯**EXAMPLE** "For a parent, bringing a well child to the hospital feels terrible," says David. "Janet was not in pain or sick. Then she was given the chemotherapy. Ten days later she lost her hair. She became sort of lethargic, she lost her appetite . . . she started vomiting."

    Or to show a pause or interruption.

    ❯**EXAMPLE** Sitting in the living room, Bryant and Vaarkova talk about the language barrier. Bryant says, "Sometimes we don't exactly . . ."

    "Understand exactly," Vaarkova says, filling in her host mother's sentence.

- Use single-quote marks to indicate a quote within a quote. Alternate between double quote marks ("") and single quote marks (' ').

CONVERGENCE POINT ⤓

Questions That Start or Stop Interviews

Chip Scanlan examines the vital role of questions that can open doors or act as padlocks during an interview, using examples from presidential press conferences and other media events to illustrate the pitfalls of poor interviewing techniques.

Find this link on the companion Web site at **www.oup.com/us/ scanlan.**

▶**EXAMPLE** Today, Smith gets strength from his religious faith and his music. He writes for everyday people, like his 10-year-old son, Darius. He dreams of becoming the first St. Petersburg rapper to make it big—really big. And when he does, maybe he'll inspire a new rapper in his hometown. "When I do rise," says Smith, "people will say, 'If he can make it, I can make it.'"

—*Source: Stories written by Poynter Institute Summer Reporting and Writing Fellows 1994–2000.*

LEARNING TO LISTEN

This might seem obvious, but it's worth saying anyway: If you're going to conduct effective interviews, you need to learn to listen well. You're not asking questions just to ask them—you're doing it for the purpose of getting answers, or at least obtaining opinion or point of view.

Active listening involves more than simply recording what a source says. It involves thinking about how a response fits in with your understanding of the topic and using that to devise follow-up questions and lines of questioning.

Active Listening Skills

It always helps to be genuinely curious about what your interviewee is going to say—if you don't care, then why waste time with the interview? Genuine curiosity also leads to the body language of good listening, which shows sources that you value their comments.

Make eye contact. People don't trust reporters who won't look them in the eye. Nodding, leaning forward, says you're interested in what your subject says. In both in-person and phone interviews, attentive responses to sources' answers indicate interest.

Empathy

A long-held stereotype about reporters is that they don't care about people, they just care about getting stories. If you can show sources that you have empathy—some understanding of their plight—they're more likely to open up to you.

"Put yourself in the interviewee's place," says Kristin Gilger, associate dean at Arizona State University's journalism school. "People are not afraid of giving you information. They are afraid of looking stupid."

The Power of Silence

The 1976 movie *All the President's Men* focuses on two *Washington Post* reporters investigating corruption in the Nixon White House. At one point, Bob Woodward, played by Robert Redford, is on the phone with a Nixon fundraiser. Woodward asks

BEING HUMAN AS AN INTERVIEWER

Meg Heckman wanted advice. Two survivors from the 9/11 World Trade Center attack were headed home to Maine, where she was a new reporter. How could she get an interview with them, and if she did, what was the best way to handle the encounter?

My advice: Just be a human being. No one owes reporters anything. If journalists in a democracy have the right to ask any question, then everyone else, especially those traumatized by events, is free to say "No comment." Take a moment, I suggested, to imagine what it might be like to be a survivor of the terrorist attacks. How would you feel if a reporter asked you for an interview? How would you want to be treated? Meg's sensitivity was rewarded. The family turned down a network, but she got the interview for her newspaper. ▶

Meg Heckman

how his $25,000 check ended up in the Watergate money trail. It's a dangerous question, and you see Woodward ask it and then remain silent for several agonizing moments, until the man on the other end of the phone finally blurts out incriminating information.

The moral: Ask your questions. Shut your mouth. Wait. People hate silence and rush to fill it. Let them talk.

If there's a central lesson from these examples, it's this—when conducting interviews, keep your cool. Don't rush, don't get flustered, and don't worry about taking a moment to make sure you have your facts straight. As a student, you might not yet have highly developed interview skills, but as long as you know your subject matter, ask effective questions, are willing and allow your curiosity about the subject to guide you, you're well on your way to getting excellent results.

KEEPING CONFIDENCES

In most cases, there should be no doubt who's talking in a story: "A vote on the legislation will take place tomorrow," said Speaker of the House John Boehner.

Whether in your first job, at a school news outlet or even on a class assignment, someday a source may ask you to remain anonymous. **Anonymous sources** are "both toxic and necessary," former *New York Times* ombudsman Clark Hoyt said, used only in national security cases or if a source has reason to fear retribution, such as

> ❝ Sometimes granting anonymity to sources is the only way to acquire publishable information on matters of interest and importance to them. So, if we have confidence in our information, we will print it. ❞
>
> —ROBERT KAISER,
> ASSOCIATE EDITOR,
> *THE WASHINGTON POST*

TABLE 6-1   Anonymous Sources: Pro and Con

PRO	CON
It's the only way to obtain sensitive information.	Information can often be obtained from documents and sources willing to go on the record.
Some sources won't talk unless promised anonymity.	Presenting convincing arguments can persuade a source to go on the record.
The public needs to know important information.	The public needs to know the source to determine the validity and accuracy of the information.

> **"People allowed to say things without having to be responsible for them say things they wouldn't otherwise say. Misinformation, cheap shots—all is possible when no one is accountable."**
>
> —GENEVA OVERHOLSER, FORMER OMBUDSMAN, *THE WASHINGTON POST*

unemployment or prison for going public. Most reporters use unnamed sources only as a last resort, because such agreements come at a price. Using a source anonymously involves agreeing *never* to name that source—if someone gives you information in confidence and you break your word, you've not only reneged on an agreement and put your source in peril, but it's unlikely others will share confidential information with you. Reporters have gone to jail and news organizations have paid hefty court fees to protect anonymous sources.

ESTABLISHING INTERVIEW GROUND RULES

Once you've identified yourself as a reporter, you should operate under the assumption that everything can be used in your story. You may need to educate your sources about this, especially if they have never been interviewed before. Never assume that an interview subject knows the ground rules.

Terms

Here are the agreements between reporter and source, in order of preference:

1. **On the record**. Reporter can use all information, with attribution, in a story. (First choice)
2. **Not for attribution**. Reporter can use information but promises to conceal the source's identity. Sometimes this involves identifying a source by position, not by name ("A senior White House staffer said . . ." or "A person close to the situation said . . ."). Strive to make it clear why you're quoting an anonymous source. A 2013 *New York Times* story included this phrase: "said the official, who requested anonymity because he was not authorized to speak to the news media on this matter."

3. **Off the record.** Information cannot be used in a story, even if the source is not identified. Some reporters take "off the record" to mean that they can use the information, without indicating its source, to gather information from other sources, but the original source must know this. Savvy sources will ask reporters if they can talk "**on background,**" which generally means the information can be published, or, and this is the most detrimental to democracy, officials—even presidents—will give interviews to one or more reporters with the proviso that they not be identified.

Make sure you—and your sources—know the ground rules. When a source wants to go off the record, stop and ask, "What do you mean?" At the end of an interview, a source may say, "But that's off the record." Make clear that retroactive off the record is unacceptable. Often a source has a misguided understanding. If a subject tries to control the ground rules in a way that violates your news organization's principles or that make the interview counterproductive, you should feel free to end the interview. You'll be surprised how often reluctant sources change their tune and agree to talk under the rules you set. Some reporters will let a source go off the record during an interview and then read the quotes back when it's over. Bill Marimow, who won two Pulitzer Prizes exposing police abuses in Philadelphia, used this tactic and found that many sources changed their minds once they'd heard what they were to be quoted as saying. If all else fails, seek the information elsewhere, either in documents or from alternative sources.

Remember that any agreement you make is not between just you and your source but also with your news organization. If you accept confidentiality, be sure you're prepared to accept the consequences. If you have any doubts, check with your editor before making a promise that may be impossible to keep. Checking with your editor or adviser is especially important if a situation like this occurs at a student media outlet. Many college and university outlets prohibit anonymous sources in all but the most extraordinary of circumstances.

CONVERGENCE POINT ⤵

Paying the Price

A list of journalists imprisoned for refusing to reveal their sources demonstrates the risks journalists face when they use anonymous sources and resist efforts to uncover their identities.

Find this link on the companion Web site at **www.oup.com/us/ scanlan.**

Ethical Dilemmas ❗ PROTECTING A SOURCE

It's commencement season and you've been assigned to write a profile of a graduate from a local community college. With the school's help, you identify a likely subject: a middle-aged single mother who had been on welfare for several years, but with help from a government program, has gone back to school and earned her degree. During your interview with her, she is very candid about the struggles she has overcome. At one point, she tells you that in her 20s she was convicted of marijuana possession and served a short jail sentence. But she insists that the episode not be included in the story. Her children don't know about it and she's also worried it might endanger her job prospects. You remind her that the interview was on the record. She begs you to reconsider. A short video has already been produced to accompany your story, and your deadline is tomorrow. You tell her that the information only enhances the obstacles she has overcome, but she is adamant and says she refuses to be part of any story. What's the harm if you omit the information? What if you do so and after the story is published a reader comes forward and criticizes your news outlet for writing a positive story that fails to divulge negative information about the subject? What is your responsibility to the woman? To your audience? ▶

The Coaching Way FINAL POINTERS ON INTERVIEWING

- What are your interviewing strengths: empathy, well-chosen questions, eye for detail? What do you need to work on: preparation, ground rules, listening?
- Ask a question. Remain quiet until the subject breaks the silence.

- What surprised you? What did you learn?
- Read quotes aloud to hear bloated, jargon-filled ones. How can you trim, delete, paraphrase?
- Why are you using every quote in your notepad—to prove you did

the interviews? That's dictation, not writing.
- How can you reserve quotation marks for speech that reveals character, advances the story or drives home a point? ▰

PROFESSIONALS' ROUNDTABLE

EFFECTIVE INTERVIEWING

Experienced journalists recognize that in a good interview, the subject talks more than the questioner. They know that details about a person are as important as what they say. And, as these journalists agree, treating subjects as human beings first, and news sources second, increases the likelihood of an interview's success. Their advice:

- Listen with your ears, your eyes, and your body language.
- Record more than quotes.
- Remember that sources, like journalists, are human, too.

Participants

MIRTA OJITO, former reporter, *The New York Times*

HOWARD BERKES, rural affairs correspondent, National Public Radio

CAROLYN MUNGO, executive news director, WFAA-Dallas

> ### How do you get people to open up?

Ojito: If they are experts, I try to know almost as much as they do about their subject, so it seems we are "chatting." With "regular people," I try to make them feel comfortable. I listen more than I talk and rarely look to my notebook for questions.

Mungo: I am a human first. People have to see that journalists are not just a body behind a microphone. Even if you have five minutes, don't rush, let them know you care.

Berkes: De-emphasizing the gear. Positive body language—eye contact, nodding, no "uh-huh's" or "really?" which distract the listener—will help the subject engage without being distracted. I look like a Martian doing interviews and I've had many people pour out their hearts and souls.

> ### What kinds of things go into your notebook?

Ojito: The time of day, number of steps, food in the refrigerator, bitten nails. The surprising, heart-stopping quotes.

Mungo: I ask basic facts before the camera is set up, so by the time the recorded interview starts, I can maintain eye contact. The questions I ask on camera are real-life sound bites: emotion, not facts.

> *What do your stories teach you about interviewing?*

Derkes: All had something meaningful to say. The goal of any interview is to draw out of people a unique perspective. That requires patience, establishing rapport and focused attention. Probe gently when appropriate. Burrow in mercilessly when public figures are being obscure.

> *What mistakes do beginning reporters make? How can they avoid them?*

Mungo: Beginning reporters often think "if I sound big and important and serious, people will deem me as credible." It's amazing anyone talks to a reporter and a photographer with a huge camera and a live truck. The last thing we need to do is barge in with our reporter banner blazoned on our foreheads. Go in softly.

SUMMARY GUIDE INTERVIEWING

THE ROLE OF THE INTERVIEW

Interviews capture the most current information available about an event, person or issue.

What to Remember → Interviewing is a challenging and rewarding journalistic skill that connects audiences with the news. Interviewers record what people say and take note of nonverbal information about their subjects.

PREPARING FOR THE INTERVIEW

Interviewing is a process that requires three steps: preparing, conducting and writing.

What to Remember → Effective interviewing begins with background research and careful preparation of questions. Journalists search for the dominant message to obtain information that proves or disproves their hypothesis to ensure accuracy and fairness. They rely on interviews to support their story and bring the people, events and issues into sharp focus.

CONDUCTING THE INTERVIEW

Beginning journalists often fear the prospect of approaching a stranger to ask questions, but they soon learn that most people love to talk.

What to Remember → Journalists don't hesitate to ask for confirmation of facts or for answers that they can use to communicate to their audiences. The most effective questions are open-ended, which encourage conversation. Closed-end questions confirm facts. Observation is central to interviewing.

WRITING FROM INTERVIEWS

Journalists depend on quotes drawn from interviews that add personality, uncommon phrases and points of view to write accurate and compelling stories.

What to Remember → Quotes bring life to a story. They shouldn't be a crutch that absolve journalists of the responsibility to paraphrase bureaucratese and bloated information. Quotes can be edited, using ellipses that show where material is omitted, for clarity. Journalists always check their notes to ensure accuracy and context.

LEARNING TO LISTEN

Journalists listen actively during interviews, understanding that silence is a powerful tool that encourages subjects to talk.

What to Remember → Good journalists are curious and sincerely interested in what people have to say, but they're not afraid to stop to make sure they have correctly understood. They treat people as human beings first, and interviewing subjects second. They ask smart questions, shut up and listen.

KEEPING CONFIDENCES

Journalists increasingly rely on anonymous sources, but anonymous sources can have ulterior motives or force journalists to protect them to gain information that should be on the record, eroding public trust in the news media.

What to Remember → The source of information should be made clear by transparent attribution. When someone asks to remain anonymous, determine whether the costs outweigh the benefits and if you can get the information elsewhere.

ESTABLISHING GROUND RULES

Journalists should operate under the assumption that all information they obtain during interviews is "on the record," meaning what subjects say and their identities will be reported.

What to Remember →

Journalists set ground rules at the start of an interview. They recognize that rules governing attribution may vary and make sure their sources understand them. News organizations often establish their own guidelines for sourcing and attribution. Journalists don't make promises they may not be able to keep.

KEY TERMS

active listening, p. 134
anonymous sources, p. 135

not for attribution, p. 136
off the record, p. 137

on background, p. 137
on the record, p. 136

EXERCISES

1. Identify an interview subject who you think might be difficult or reluctant to talk with you—the quietest person in one of your classes, a teacher known as a taskmaster, a campus police official. Do background research to learn as much as you can about your subject. By yourself or with a colleague or editor, consider the problems. Prepare questions in advance. Conduct the interview and write about the experience. What surprised you? What did you learn? What do you need to learn next?

2. Diagnose your interviewing style. What are your strengths: empathy, note taking, good eye for detail? What do you need to work on: setting ground rules, listening more closely, relying on open-ended questions, preparing more thoroughly?

3. Record one of your interviews. Transcribe the questions verbatim. How many are open-ended conversation starters? How many are conversation stoppers? How many are double- or triple-barreled? How many are statements masquerading as questions? Transcribe the answers. Compare the length of the questions with the length of the responses.

4. Ask a dozen classmates, relatives and friends to define these terms: "on the record," "off the record," "not for attribution" and "background." Compare their answers. What are the differences and similarities? Discuss how your findings will affect how you set ground rules for interviews.

5. Study how writers use quotations in their print, multimedia and broadcast stories. Where do the quotes appear? How long are the quotes? Which ones drag down the story, which move it along and reveal character? Compare them with quotes in your stories.

READINGS

Adams, Sally. *Interviewing for Journalists.* New York: Routledge, 2001.
A practical guide for journalists who want to improve their interviewing skills. It clearly explains the types of questions—good and bad—and offers a wealth of advice on the power of listening, taking notes, using quotes and interviewing everyone from celebrities to vulnerable people.

Biagi, Shirley. *Interviews That Work: A Practical Guide for Journalists.* Belmont, CA: Wadsworth, 1992.
A useful handbook that can teach beginning interviewers how to obtain interviews, plan them, craft and pose effective questions and how to cope with the challenges when the subject is reluctant to talk.

Brady, John J. *Interviewer's Handbook: A Guerrilla Guide: Techniques & Tactics for Reporters and Writers.* Waukesha, WI: Kalmbach, 2004.
An accomplished interviewer details the best ways to get the most out of interviews. Full of revealing examples, insights into the power of listening, guidance on interviewing guidelines, a list of ready-made questions and effective ways to interview celebrities, politicians and citizens caught up in the news of the day.

Kern, Jonathan. *Sound Reporting: The NPR Guide to Audio Journalism and Production.* Chicago: University of Chicago Press, 2008.
National Public Radio is famous for its incisive and entertaining interviews. Studded with examples from NPR's accomplished reporters and anchors, this handbook details techniques and tips for radio interviewing and traces the journey from booking interviews to editing and going on air.

Reardon, Nancy, and Flynn, Tom. *On Camera: How to Report, Anchor & Interview.* Waltham, MA: Focal Press, 2006.
Learning to conduct television interviews in a studio or in the field is the subject of this readable, authoritative guide. The authors' practical advice can also be applied for video interviews produced for multimedia reports.

Stein, M. L., and Paterno, Susan F. *Talk Straight, Listen Carefully: The Art of Interviewing.* Hoboken, NJ: Wiley-Blackwell, 2001.
Print and broadcast journalists alike can profit from this examination of interviewing challenges and solutions. Bolstered by examples of professional journalists who reveal their techniques for obtaining high-quality information for news stories, profiles and features, the book sheds light on the ethical dilemmas that often arise during interviews.

CHAPTER 7

RESEARCH

BY THE END OF THIS CHAPTER,

you should be able to...

> Understand the differences between reporting and research

> Grasp the crucial role of public records and know where to find them

> Use private records (letters, diaries, photographs) to enhance stories

> Use the Freedom of Information Act to pry records from reluctant bureaucracies

> Develop a broader view of records to include multimedia documents

> Understand and counter pitfalls of Internet reporting

> Value collaboration with news researchers

> Appreciate the power of computer-assisted and database reporting

> 66 Knowledge is of two kinds. We know a subject ourselves, or we know where we can find information upon it. 99
>
> —SAMUEL JOHNSON, ENGLISH WRITER

144

TOO MANY NEWS stories rest on shaky foundations. A prime offender: the **single-source story**, one that goes no further than a telephone call, a press release or conversation with a public information officer. Such stories ignore a vast array of information sources, leading to errors, gaps and unanswered questions, and a loss of public trust.

In this chapter you will widen the reach of your reporting by learning the power of research; the importance of records (public and private), where to find and how to obtain them; the importance of news researchers; the explosive growth of online records; and the ways reporters use computers to create a bedrock of verifiable information that produces knowledgeable, accurate and compelling journalism.

"REPORTING ON STEROIDS"

Reporting involves on-scene information gathering, capturing observations and human voices that provide timely information and fresh perspectives. This material can come from anyone: from hurricane victims to FEMA officials to people on the street who witnessed or took part in an event of interest. Such information may also be collected by telephone, email, as well as news releases and face-to-face interviews.

Journalism students at Virginia Tech did extraordinary reporting on April 16, 2007, when a student opened fire on classmates, faculty and staff, killing 32 and wounding 26 others. With the professional news media kept behind police tape, the students interviewed fellow students about their experiences and the horrors, such as hearing cell phones ringing in body bags. Using their training, instincts and a desire to share their classmates' experiences, these students distinguished themselves as spot news reporters.

News stories, however, usually require some **research** on the subject to write a more complete story. Even on deadline, research takes reporting a step further than simply providing on-scene observations. To provide a detailed look at a topic often involves using records, information located in computerized databases, newspaper archives, and other sources of data that can be valuable sources, and, in some cases, using computers to analyze the data.

"Research is reporting on steroids," says Arizona State journalism professor Steve Doig. He's a pioneer of using public records to break news, including computer analysis that showed shoddy construction and weakened building codes contributed to the devastation of Hurricane Andrew. His work was cited when his newspaper, the *Miami Herald,* won the 1993 Pulitzer Gold Medal for Public Service.

"Traditionally," Doig says, "'reporting' has been shoe-leather work that focused on interviewing sources and looking at documents. 'Research' is all that and more, including acquiring public data and analyzing it for patterns of interest, or conducting public opinion surveys."

Numbers show racial divide

Here is a look at how blacks in Northeast Ohio compare in several demographic categories with whites in the region and to all Americans, based on U.S. Census Bureau estimates for 2006.

	NE Ohio blacks	NE Ohio whites	All U.S. population
JOBS/INCOME			
Median family income	$34,588	$63,803	$58,526
Unemployed (2006)	10%	4%	4%
LIVING IN POVERTY			
All categories	27%	9%	13%
Families in poverty	23%	7%	10%
Mothers with children and no husband present	44%	30%	37%
HOME OWNERSHIP			
Own home	43%	77%	67%
Rent	57%	23%	33%
Median home value	$97,700	$154,200	$182,200
EDUCATIONAL ATTAINMENT			
Did not complete high school or equivalent	21%	12%	16%
HS graduate, but did not graduate from college	65%	61%	57%
Bachelor's degree or higher	14%	27%	27%
FAMILY STRUCTURE			
Mothers with children, no husband present	20%	6%	7%
Share of births in last year to unmarried mothers	75%	25%	33%
Grandparents raising grandchildren	55%	38%	41%
HEALTH			
Deaths before age 65 (per 100,000 residents)	395	266	254

NOTE: Census data includes Ashtabula, Cuyahoga, Geauga, Lake, Lorain, Medina, Portage and Summit counties.
SOURCE: Plain Dealer analysis of U.S. Census Bureau data

DAVE DAVIS, RICH EXNER AND KEN MARSHALL | THE PLAIN DEALER

Visual display of research aids reader comprehension. Graphic artists at the *Cleveland* (OH) *Plain Dealer* helped reporters display their findings in this chart depicting the racial divide in income, health, poverty, homeownership and other demographic categories based on U.S. Census figures.

A "DOCUMENTS STATE OF MIND"

"**Public records** document practically every human activity," Ronald P. Lovell observes in *Reporting Public Affairs: Problems and Solutions*. "They follow us from birth to death, from school graduation to retirement. They shadow our movements in business, politics and crime. They capture on paper the transfer of wealth, whether it be a motor home or a 5,000-acre ranch. They remember those who pollute the air and water, those who run fire-trap hotels, those who cheat employees out of wages."

" Whenever you're working on a story, you ought to be thinking about what documents can help you. "

—LOUISE KIERNAN, FORMER SENIOR EDITOR, *CHICAGO TRIBUNE*

THE IMPORTANCE OF PUBLIC RECORDS

Records can prove or disprove a politician's assertion, turn up a nugget of detail, bring a character to life, or buttress a conclusion.

Records can also bring about change, as I learned when I covered the local public housing authority for *The Providence* (RI) *Journal*.

The people who lived in the public housing projects complained bitterly about inadequate maintenance. The authority's members didn't meet at the projects, where its members might get a glimpse of living conditions. Instead, they gathered at local restaurants. At the authority offices, I asked to see expense vouchers. I spent an afternoon sifting through restaurant checks, copying down dollar amounts and even jotting down the eggplant Parmesan and other entrees authority officials dined on, totaling $3,000 in recent months. "The restaurant tabs," the subsequent story said, "were paid from authority funds, the majority of which are derived from rents paid by low-income tenants at the city's 14 public housing projects and from federal subsidies." After it appeared, the authority's members decided to forgo their dinner meetings and meet instead at the housing projects they were supposed to oversee. ▶

CONVERGENCE POINT ⚡

A Template for Freedom of Information Requests

"Submitting a FOIA request to a federal agency is not difficult, but a complete, well-written request may help you avoid delays and further correspondence with a government agency," the Reporters Committee for Freedom of the Press says.

RCFP provides an online form to create a FOIA act request letter (see Figure 7-1). It leads you through pertinent information needed, suggests available options such as the appropriate federal agency and lists agency addresses.

Find this link on the companion Web site at **www.oup.com/us/ scanlan.**

To be a good researcher, you need to develop what famed investigative reporters Donald L. Barlett and James B. Steele called a "**documents state of mind**." You must assume that somewhere a record exists. As you gain more experience, you'll come to know which databases and resources are likely to be your best bets in given situations.

CRACKING THE GOVERNMENT SEAL: USING THE FREEDOM OF INFORMATION ACT

In a participatory democracy, it should be a given that citizens have unfettered access to records that reveal how their governments, federal, state and local, operate. To ensure that right, in 1966, President Lyndon B. Johnson signed into law the federal **Freedom of Information Act (FOIA)**, pronounced "Foy-Yah." Every state has similar laws governing **open access** and **open government**.

Freedom of information has led to important stories:

- FBI harassment of civil rights leaders
- Surveillance of authors, scientists and composers
- Environmental impact studies
- Salaries of public employees
- Sanitary conditions in food processing plants (Source: Reporters Committee for Freedom of the Press)

Given the importance of such stories, public records should be a snap to obtain. Unfortunately, that's not always the case, as the Reporters Committee for Freedom of

QUICK Tips ⏻ PUBLIC RECORDS: WHERE TO FIND THEM AND WHAT YOU'LL FIND

> Newspapers:
Facts, obituaries, birth notices, legal notices.

> Telephone directories:
Name, address, phone number, spouse's name.

➤ Courthouse:
Lawsuits, marriage and divorce records, criminal records, wills, guardianships, property records.

> Local government records:
Financial disclosure reports revealing business holdings,

savings and debts of elected officials. Campaign finance reports show who contributed to political candidates.

> State government records:
Department of Professional Regulation: Information about qualifications and disciplinary history of doctors, lawyers, engineers, nurses, real estate agents and other licensed professionals.

> Federal records:
Internal Revenue Service: Individual tax records are private,

but private foundations and tax-exempt organizations must file forms that list income, expenses and salaries of highest-paid employees.
Federal Aviation Administration: Airline inspection records, pilot records. ▼

Source: Jeff Good, Frank Marquardt.

the Press concludes in its "Open Government Guide." "Some public officials in state and local governments work hard to achieve and enforce open government laws. . . . But . . . Hardly a day goes by when we don't hear that a state or local government is trying to restrict access to records that have traditionally been public."

Since the terrorist attacks on Sept. 11, 2001, "Information that was once made public as a matter of routine now requires a formal, written request and, once requested, more and more information is withheld on national security grounds," says Matthew Purdy, investigations editor for *The New York Times.*

With government walling off its records from the public and the journalists who seek them to inform their audiences, journalists need to learn how to file Freedom of Information requests. Government officials often don't make it easy, but you can improve your chances by following FOIA laws' strict requirements.

Don't imagine public officials will drop everything to process your request. Check with agency officials regularly. You must be patient and persistent, and "tend your FOIAs, like a gardener would lavish attention on his plants," as award-winning journalist Katherine Boo puts it. Journalists tell horror stories about waiting months— even years—for records, and of copying fees that can reach hundreds of thousands of dollars. At times like that, your news organization may send in lawyers to wage the battle.

SEARCH ENGINES

Search engines, such as Google, Yahoo! or Bing, allow you to search the World Wide Web for information. You're probably already quite familiar with this, but you're

CONVERGENCE POINT ⟲

What Search Engines Can Track Down

After the worst biological attacks in U.S. history, the FBI created a Web site centered on its investigation into the deadly 2001 anthrax poisonings. An example of how to locate a wealth of documentary evidence, the site includes official statements and correspondence and details on the investigation, forensic analysis and search warrants.

Find this link on the companion Web site at **www.oup.com/us/scanlan.**

FIGURE 7-1 Freedom of Information laws provide access to public records, but federal and state governments generally require official requests. The Reporters Committee for Freedom of the Press makes the task easier with an online FOIA template.

Agency Head [or Freedom of Information Act Officer]
Name of Agency
Address of Agency
City, State, Zip Code

Re: Illinois Freedom of Information Act Request

Dear _____:

This is a request for information under the Illinois Freedom of Information Act, 5 ILCS 140.

I request that a copy of the following documents [**or documents containing the following information**] be provided to me: [**be as specific as you can in identifying the documents or information you are seeking**].

[**Option:**] I would like to inspect these records in person. [**Option:**] I would like to obtain copies of these records.

[**If you request copies of the records, you should consider adding the following text:**] I understand that the Act permits a public body to charge a reasonable copying fee not to exceed the actual cost of reproduction and not including the costs of any search or review of the records. 5 ILCS 140/6. [**Option:**] I am willing to pay fees for this request up to a maximum of **$_____**. If you estimate that the fees will exceed this limit, please inform me first. [**Option:**] I request a waiver of all fees for this request. Disclosure of the requested information to me is in the public interest because it is likely to contribute significantly to public understanding of the operations or activities of the government and is not primarily in my commercial interest. [**Include a specific explanation of why your request is in the public interest.**]

I look forward to hearing from you in writing within seven working days, as required by the Act. 5 ILCS 140(3).

Sincerely,

Name
Address
City, State, Zip Code
[**Optional:**] Telephone number and e-mail

probably not accustomed to using such engines to their full potential, to gain access to public information that can be vital to your stories.

Many public agencies routinely post important records online—no FOIA required. As an example, the Federal Bureau of Investigation maintains a Web site devoted to its investigation of five deaths from anthrax poisonings that began seven days after the Sept. 11, 2001, terrorist attacks. It includes background information, press conference transcripts, photos of letters containing anthrax, and search warrants loaded

KEN BURKE, CPA
CLERK OF THE CIRCUIT COURT
PINELLAS COUNTY, FLORIDA

Mortgage Foreclosure Sale - Fct V

Return to Previous Page Records Main Menu

Foreclosure sale scheduled for:	Location:
02/13/2012	Clearwater/St.Petersburg/Online

All of the following cases are scheduled for a foreclosure sale on the above date, if conducted, title and disbursement due date is: **02/24/2012**

10 Case(s), 08009159CI to 11003684CI Next Page New Search

Link To	Case NO.	Loc.	Cnt*	Judg. Amt.	Purchaser	Purchase Amt.	Title Date	Comments
	08009159CI	OnLine		$ 118,752.96				
	08009336CI	OnLine		$ 180,149.25				
	08010891CI	OnLine		$ 503,828.78				
	08018683CI	OnLine		$ 107,235.83				
	09005710CI	OnLine		$ 229,120.46				
	09012171CI	OnLine		$ 445,338.19				
	10012183CI	OnLine		$ 106,139.90				
	10016226CI	OnLine		$ 140,649.96				
	11003024CI	OnLine		$ 29,462.54				
	11003684CI	OnLine		$ 24,140.09				

Mortgage Foreclosure Sale Locations: Clearwater St. Petersburg
Cnt*=Case Judgment Count

Government records are increasingly available to journalists and the public, such as this calendar of upcoming foreclosure actions posted by a county court clerk's office in Pinellas County, Florida.

with specific details, in one case, seeking a judge's approval to search a mail account screen name—jimmyflathead@yahoo.com—used by a prime suspect.

When you type words into a search engine, you're creating a "query" or "keyword search." You can save lots of time and weed out unneeded results if you think carefully about terms specific to your subject. If you're searching for a specific phrase, be sure to include quotes around it, or else you'll come up with many results that simply include those individual words or combinations of them. One way to test the effectiveness of search engines is to look for something you know about—a musical group, a favorite sport, a hobby. Familiarity with the subject matter will help you evaluate the value of the information located by different search engines. Experiment regularly to find the best ones—you shouldn't just assume the most popular engine is the best for your purposes.

QUICK Tips MAJOR WEB SITES FOR RESEARCH ON SPECIFIC SUBJECT AREAS

Authoritative sources on specific topics of news interest can be easily found online. These include:

HEALTH CARE

- American Medical Association, http://www.ama-assn.org/
- American Cancer Society, http://www.cancer.org/
- Centers for Disease Control and Prevention, http://www.cdc.gov/
- National Institutes of Health, http://www.nih.gov/

ENTERTAINMENT

- The Entertainment Software Association, http://www.theesa.com/
- The Recording Academy, http://www.grammy.com/

REFERENCE

- *Encyclopedia Britannica*, http://britannica.com
- Google Scholar, http://scholar.google.com/
- *Merriam-Webster Online Dictionary*, http://www.merriam-webster.com
- Oxford Dictionaries Online, http://english.oxforddictionaries.com

MULTIMEDIA SOURCES: ADD NEW DIMENSIONS WITH AUDIO AND VIDEO

CONVERGENCE POINT ✻

Footnoting the News Online

Dallas Morning News reporter Lee Hancock shares with readers the documents and other evidence supporting her investigative series about the financial exploitation of an elderly woman by using interactive footnotes with the online version of the story.

Find this link on the companion Web site at **www.oup.com/us/ scanlan.**

Lee Hancock

When reporters see the word "**document**," they may think of court papers and other public records, on paper or in digital format. Anyone familiar with the Internet recognizes that the definition of a document now includes still and video images, audio, and interactive elements.

In recent years, news organizations have begun to take full advantage of these technologies. In August 2006, the *Dallas Morning News* published "Mary Ellen's Will: The Battle for 4949 Swiss," a four-part series that focused on a case of financial exploitation of the elderly. Reporter Lee Hancock interviewed 50-plus sources, but didn't stop there. Her research turned up probate court documents, depositions, family photos, videos of a Christmas party and a chilling scene when a lawyer representing an apparently ill and confused elderly woman watched as she signed over power of attorney to two men who had befriended her. All were included as interactive hyperlinks, a kind of electronic footnote that allowed readers to view the documents supporting Hancock's findings.

In the predigital past, reporters seeking documents often had to go to where the documents were stored, such as a courthouse or agency. Retrieving the information meant persuading record keepers to provide the records, paying for photocopies or relying on tedious and time-consuming note taking. Today, digital publishing of e-books, records and documents using **Portable Document Format (PDF)** has revolutionized document retrieval, creating exact copies of documents that are stored online and made publicly available by linking to them.

PDFs also make publication possible during natural disasters. When Hurricane Katrina flooded the offices of the *New Orleans Times-Picayune* in August 2005, the paper was able to publish without interruption by posting PDFs of the paper's digital pages online.

Creating professionally crafted digital documents that contained all the elements of a print publication was a major step away from traditional publishing. Another major step toward revolutionizing the concept of documents came from something originally referred to as "online communities" that provided ways for people with similar interests to share information. These evolved into discussion forums, chat rooms and other interactive formats. Reporters routinely rely on them as handy sources for information and story ideas from people passionate and knowledgeable about specific topics. The key element: Anyone interested could contribute to the discussion. Information was no longer something handed down by officials and other "experts"—it was something that could emerge from conversations among everyday people.

In the 2000s, these types of media came fully into the mainstream. The explosion of personal **blogs** gave Web users with no programming or publishing experience the chance to start online conversations of their own, and in some cases to gain

⁴**Judge Robert E. Price's view** on the narrow scope of temporary guardianships comes from his bench comments in probate case #02-272-P2, during the Jan. 31, 2005, temporary guardianship hearing, p. 7, 18, 29. Information on Mrs. Bendtsen's mental state comes from Baylor University Medical Center records, Jan. 12-21, 2005, pp. 231-233, 234-240, 281, 371, 375, 379, 381, 383, 385, 387. Information on her continued confusion also comes from Ashley Court at Turtle Creek records, Jan. 21-31, 2005. There, nurses' notes made near-daily references to Mrs. Bendtsen being mentally altered. On Jan. 25, Mrs. Bendtsen asked the man who served her with her daughter's guardianship lawsuit to take her home.

Medical records

The Internet gives journalists the opportunity to show audiences the depth of their research, enhancing credibility. The online version of "Mary Ellen's Will," an investigative series about elderly abuse, featured electronic footnotes to video, public records and other documents collected by *Dallas Morning News* reporter Lee Hancock.

followings and subscribers. Reporters often started blogs and solicited input from readers who might have information about a given story topic, or who might have story ideas of their own. When working on stories, reporters could seek out bloggers who showed expert knowledge about a subject.

In some instances, users interested in building online libraries of knowledge about specific kinds of information created **wikis**, sites where users could add or modify information about a topic. In effect, wikis allow users to arrive at their own definitions and provide their own details. By bringing users into the heart of the information gathering process, wikis created a true democratization of information.

The culmination of this process has been the rise of social media. Sites such as Facebook, Twitter, LinkedIn and thousands of others have revolutionized the business of information, giving anyone with a computer, tablet or smartphone a voice that can reach the farthest corners of the world. Reporters who subsisted on a trickle of information for years suddenly are navigating an ocean of facts, opinions, conjectures and silliness, with the task of deciding what's accurate, notable and newsworthy. The best reporters use their instincts and training when sifting through all this material, mixing curiosity with a healthy skepticism that leads them to look harder than ever for verification of facts.

CONVERGENCE POINT ⬇

Using Interactivity to Connect Readers With the Faces Behind the News

After a deadly train collision in 2008, the Los Angeles Times created an interactive database so its readers could view photos, biographical information and tributes from friends and family of the 25 victims.

Find this link on the companion Web site at **www.oup.com/us/scanlan.**

WIKIPEDIA: POWER AND PITFALLS OF THE INTERNET'S ENCYCLOPEDIA

The most prominent wiki in existence is **Wikipedia**, the well-known online encyclopedia. The site is certainly popular with students, and reporters will often consult it as a first research step.

Jimmy Wales and Larry Sanger created it in 2001 to accomplish a lofty goal: to collect and summarize all human knowledge in every major language on the Internet. Its thousands of contributors and users can correct mistakes and edit entries, which is both a blessing and a curse. Bear in mind Wikipedia's Five Pillars that set forth its fundamental principles:

1. Wikipedia is an encyclopedia.
2. It is written from a neutral point of view.
3. It is free content that anyone can edit, use, modify and distribute.
4. Editors should interact with each other in a respectful and civil manner.
5. It does not have firm rules.

For more information about Wikipedia's oversight policy, regulations and guides, visit http://en.wikipedia.org/wiki/Wikipedia:About.

Wikipedia opens up great possibilities for sharing expert knowledge, but it also clears the way to spreading incorrect information. Check the text against primary sources cited in footnotes or find independent documentation. In the worst cases, Wikipedia has presented hoaxes as fact.

In May, 2005, this item appeared about John L. Seigenthaler, a well-respected former newspaper editor:

❯EXAMPLE John Seigenthaler Sr. was the assistant to Attorney General Robert Kennedy in the early 1960's. For a brief time, he was thought to have been directly involved in the Kennedy assassinations of both John, and his brother, Bobby. Nothing was ever proven.

One problem: It was a hoax.

The only truth in the article: Seigenthaler wrote in an op-ed article in *USA Today*, "I was Robert Kennedy's administrative assistant in the early 1960s. I also was his pallbearer."

Seigenthaler damned Wikipedia as "a flawed and irresponsible research tool." Journalists "shouldn't be using it to check any information that goes into the newspaper," *New York Times* business editor Larry Ingrassia wrote his staff.

While most entries are never falsified, reporters can never be sure that the material is valid. This is why, at most, Wikipedia should be seen as a jumping-off point, a place to begin finding information that must be verified later. Not every subject, person or issue, especially involving local news stories, can be found on Wikipedia or through a search engine. Never assume that knowledge or information doesn't exist simply because you can't find it online. This is the time to reach out to a news researcher, to visit the library, town hall or even better a human being who could be the best primary source.

> ❝ Good journalists have always known that they shouldn't trust what anyone tells them until they check the information. ❞
>
> —BRANT HOUSTON, PROFESSOR OF INVESTIGATIVE AND ENTERPRISE JOURNALISM, UNIVERSITY OF ILLINOIS AT URBANA-CHAMPAIGN

WHY LIBRARIANS STILL MATTER

In the Internet era, sometimes it's easy for beginning reporters to forget that there's a big building full of information resources right there on campus. It's true that the Internet is a library that is open 24 hours a day, needs no library card and features no "Shhh" signs. But the wise reporter knows it's not the only research source.

When you start working on a story, always check in with a librarian or news researcher. Many university libraries have subject-specific **reference librarians**, experts in given fields who can save you huge amounts of time and point you to resources you never knew existed. Many newsrooms have news researchers on staff. An information professional can perform all kinds of useful functions for a reporter—he or she can refer you to books and newspaper and magazine articles that provide crucial background; quickly locate public records; help you avoid useless avenues of research; and, in a moment's time, locate the fact that will make your stories accurate and compelling.

"Not having a researcher would be likened to trying to play softball without a catcher, or field hockey without a goalie," says Theresa Collington Moore, hired in 2002 as a researcher at WTSP-TV in Tampa, Florida.

Going to your university library and making friends with some of the librarians would be a wise investment of your time. This is sometimes done as part of journalism courses, but whether it's on your own or as part of a class, it's something you should pursue vigorously. Librarians are often some of your best resources, and they often enjoy helping reporters. Whether on the college or professional level, these are relationships worth cultivating.

DEFLATING URBAN LEGENDS AND ONLINE HOAXES

Did you know that terrorists have poisoned one in five cans of Coca-Cola with anthrax and arsenic?

Just so you know: If an oncoming car's lights aren't on, don't flash yours—if it's a gang member, they'll shoot you.

Chewing gum takes seven years to pass through the human digestive system.

If you believed any of these, you've been had by an **online hoax**, or "**urban legend**."

There's nothing new about inaccurate gossip, but the Internet has taken it to new heights.

"Thanks to the Internet and the 'send' button, almost any piece of information, no matter how outrageous, has been finding its way into thousands of mailboxes around the world. And, in some cases, into press reports," observed Sreenath Sreenivisan, a Columbia Journalism School professor who regularly warns journalists about online hoaxes. It's your responsibility to track down the truth; fortunately there are several

CONVERGENCE POINT

Online Help From the Nation's Librarians

The Librarians' Internet Index: Web Sites You Can Trust provides journalists with a vast amount of information, allowing them to tunnel into newspapers and magazines, background material and exceptional special collections created by libraries around the United States.

Find this link on the companion Web site at **www.oup.com/us/ scanlan.**

CONVERGENCE POINT

Debunking Hoaxes and Urban Legends

Snopes.com tests the accuracy of "urban legends, folklore, myths, rumors and misinformation." Regularly updated, the site helps journalists avoid being fooled, misleading their audiences, and embarrassing themselves and their news organizations.

Find this link on the companion Web site at **www.oup.com/us/ scanlan.**

Sreenath Sreenivasan

Web sites that track hoaxes and should be consulted. Don't stop there. The Web is dotted with seemingly mundane errors—incorrect dates for wars, birthdays, name spellings and out-of-date job titles. Don't rely on someone else's reporting; it's lazy and puts you at risk of repeating a mistake.

PRIVATE RECORDS: INTIMATE RESEARCH

Public records provide detail, authority, libel protection and the occasional smoking gun that often makes for powerful journalism.

But there's another, less obvious record type that smart reporters use to add unforgettable ingredients to their stories. You won't find them in a government filing cabinet or database or discover them with a Freedom of Information request.

These are **private records**, the documentation that people create and keep about their own lives or others', the kind buried in a box in the attic, hanging on the refrigerator door or found inside a photo album or yearbook.

Among them: baby books, high school and college yearbooks, playbills for student productions, diaries, journals, letters, photos, videos, teacher evaluations. Private records can strengthen your reporting and bring a new level of intimacy and depth to your stories, shedding light on a person's character or a time in history.

"People record their lives in all sorts of ways and often what they write or is written about them is more true than what they tell you," says former *Chicago Tribune* reporter Louise Kiernan, who has used letters, emails and photos to bring characters in her news stories to life.

One of her *Tribune* colleagues relied on teacher evaluations to profile a dying professor, the students' comments opening a window into their teacher's character. In its Pulitzer Prize–winning deadline coverage of the Sept. 11, 2001, terrorist attacks in New York City, the *Wall Street Journal* described a survivor limping into a shoe store to buy comfortable footwear after climbing down 92 floors to escape one of

The Coaching Way ꕯꕯꕯ RESEARCH SKILLS

- What do you do to avoid "single-source stories"?
- When is the best time to approach a newsroom librarian/researcher?
- Are you familiar with the public records law in your state? (Hint: http://www.rcfp.org/ogg/index .php)

- Identify three private records that reveal something about you. Ask a friend to do the same. How might you use this information in a profile?
- How do you verify information found in Wikipedia?
- Have you found out whether there are PDF files or multimedia

document types available to include with your online story?
- How do you determine if a piece of information that seems too good to be true isn't a hoax?
- Have you learned the basics of using a spreadsheet? ▸

the burning Twin Towers. "Mrs. Murray tried on three pairs of shoes before choosing black sneakers for $43." The source, revealed in an accompanying footnote: the woman's credit card receipt.

Look beyond traditional ways to document your stories in vivid detail. Your best protection is a document for every assertion you make, whether it's carefully taken notes or a public or private record.

> **❝ If you see something in a database that's really cool, it's probably an error. ❞**
>
> —JENNIFER LAFLEUR, DIRECTOR, COMPUTER-ASSISTED REPORTING, PROPUBLICA

COMPUTER-ASSISTED REPORTING: PRECISION JOURNALISM

Journalists began thinking like social scientists in the early 1960s when Philip Meyer of Knight Newspapers carried out a survey to analyze the 43 deaths in the Detroit riots to discover their root causes. Five decades later, with the advent of desktop computers, "reporters and editors gloried in a newfound sense of power," says veteran database editor Griff Palmer of *The New York Times*.

The desktop revolution has fueled an explosion of **computer-assisted reporting (CAR)**—that is, "using computers to collect and analyze data using spreadsheets, statistical software and newsroom math," says Steve Doig. This includes calculating simple percentages, percentage change, rates and averages.

We're not just talking about using Google here. Journalists use statistical and mapping software to discover relationships in a database, such as real estate sales grouped by sale price, location, year of transaction, or between two or more databases to identify school bus drivers with criminal records. These databases may already exist, or they may be assembled by reporters and news researchers, relying on their organization's already digitized information or public databases.

For more than a decade, newsrooms have been building **database archives**, notes Bruce Garrison, a journalism professor the University of Miami. For instance, newspapers have long published event calendars. Many have now turned them into

Ethical Dilemmas ❗ TRANSPARENCY VERSUS PRIVACY

You're part of a computer-assisted reporting team that is following the lead of many newspapers by assembling an online searchable directory that discloses salaries of state workers by name. You're proud of the project because it provides greater transparency and public accountability. But when you mention it to a relative who works for the state, he hits the roof. What about my right to privacy, he asks. What about my family's safety and the threat of identity theft if anybody can see how much I'm worth? How do I know if the figures are accurate? They're just numbers without any context. You point out that the database doesn't provide addresses, Social Security or telephone numbers and other personal information. Even so, you're troubled by his questions. How would you justify your work to him, to your audience? What, if any, changes in the database and the reporting based on it would you suggest? Where do your allegiances lie? ▶

interactive features online, such as the searchable calendar on indystar.com, the *Indianapolis Star* Web site, or restaurant reviews on the *South Florida Sun-Sentinel*.

Since the late 2000s, newspapers around the country have provided their online readers with searchable directories of up to four years of data about salaries paid to state workers. Information is indexed by name and position, and includes details such as overtime, retirement payouts and extra pay. Salaries at public universities in the United States are available on the Web site of *Collegiate Times*, the Virginia Tech student newspaper. The information is contained in digital public records, usually maintained by several agencies that the news organizations have merged into one public database. Journalists have an ethical responsibility to verify, as much as possible, the data they collect and the results of their analysis of such digitized information.

Many CAR journalists have learned to do their own programming. Adrian Holloway created chicagocrime.org, an interactive database that can pinpoint crimes by type, location and more. "Each weekday, my computer program goes to the Chicago Police Department's Web site and gathers all crimes reported in Chicago," he told *Online Journalism Review*. The data is then overlaid, or "mashed up," with Google Maps, to link a crime with its exact location.

The explosion of applications designed for mobile devices keeps reporters connected with research resources on the go. With the mobile phone an essential part of the reporter's toolbox, journalists increasingly rely on social media apps, such as Twitter and Facebook, as well as news aggregators such as Google News, and those created by news organizations for their mobile phones to track the news. Skype makes online interviews possible, while mapping software guides them to the scene of the news.

REAPING THE REWARDS: TURNING RESEARCH INTO COMPELLING STORIES

You've gathered and analyzed the data, and developed conclusions, just like a social scientist. Now you have to make sense of your findings in ways that your audience, which may lack your statistical or programming knowledge, will easily grasp.

"Resist the temptation to include everything you've found just because you found it or because you want to prove to your editor or reader how hard you've worked," says the *Chicago Tribune*'s Louise Kiernan, now a journalism professor at Northwestern University's Medill School of Journalism. "Ruthlessly discard the interesting but irrelevant. When you describe or attribute information from your research, keep your writing simple, short and clear."

The more you work on research, the easier it is to get lost in numbers and the harder it is to write. Use the five focusing questions from Chapter 2 to determine your working theme, and freewrite drafts without looking at your notes and data.

Journalist at Work | NAILING DOWN EVERY FACT

Louise Kiernan's epic narrative "Howling Window Signals Skyscraper's Fatal Flaw" was a Pulitzer Prize finalist in 2001 for explanatory reporting. Pulitzer judges called it a "moving and humane portrait of a young mother killed by a falling skyscraper window, its effect on her three-year-old daughter, and the negligence of the company involved." (That same year, she was also part of a team that won the Pulitzer for a portrait of the nation's chaotic air traffic control system.) Kiernan believes that all stories should combine the elements of narrative, investigation and explanation, each bolstered by exhaustive documentation. She describes the research behind a single passage: the 75-word lead of her 4,200-word story.

http://articles.chicagotribune.com/2000-07-16/news/0007160340_1_window-29th-floor-cracked

Kiernan says:

Virtually the entire opening sequence of this story is based upon police reports and other government documents I obtained through the Freedom of Information Act, as well as documents given to me by confidential sources and interviews I conducted with the people whose names I found in those documents.

For example, one police report describes a witness to the accident saying he saw "a 'black blur' strike a woman in the head." I tracked down this witness and others and the description of what happened when the glass struck Ana Flores comes from what they told police at the time and what they told me later.

One interesting note: Given that the accident occurred on a busy street during lunch hour, it would have been extremely difficult to reconstruct without the names of the people who saw it. In the reports I received from the Chicago Police Department, the names of the witnesses had been redacted. But I had requested documents from the city's building department, too, and whoever handled the request there gave me the same police reports with the names intact. The lesson? Ask for documents from any agency which might be involved in your story. You never know what you might get.

To describe the window and the building, I used the very detailed information contained in the police and building department reports, documents from an internal investigation of the accident and photographs taken at the scene. Several physics professors and glass experts explained to me what would have happened to the window as thermal stress acted upon it, until a piece ultimately broke away. And I reviewed with those experts the descriptions people gave me of the accident to make sure it could have occurred the way they remembered. I also checked witness' memories of the weather against records for that day.

As I look through the documents, I'm struck by what descriptive, strong language people used when they talked about what happened and how much that helped me write the story. When the story mentions the window was "humming," that term comes directly from a witness account. So does the description of it "howling." It was a construction worker who noticed that Ana's daughter kept "a step or two" ahead of her mother. If the story carries any power, it comes from these details, these nuggets of gold buried in stacks of paperwork. That's why this story, more than any other, taught me the power of documents." ▼

Otherwise, you'll not only get tangled in them, but you'll write like a researcher, not the storyteller that heavily researched stories need if audiences are going to comprehend your findings. (You can—and should—always go back and check what you've written.)

And remember, you're a journalist, not a prosecutor. If you want to write stories that read like indictments, go to law school.

"You still have to make it plain," says former investigative reporter Lee Hancock of the *Dallas Morning News*. "Like you'd tell your mama."

SEE CLOSE-UP, P. 163: USING RESEARCH TO DOCUMENT A STORY

THE POWER OF RESEARCH

Research is more than running a few Google searches. It's knowing how to search court records, using desktop computers to sift through thousands of records and develop solid evidence, and tapping the skills of news researchers to mine specialized databases. Three specialists in the use of research offer this advice:

- Learn how to use public databases.
- The more exciting the findings, the more checking is required.
- Don't go it alone. News researchers are knowledgeable collaborators.

Participants

LOUISE KIERNAN, former senior editor, *Chicago Tribune*

STEVE DOIG, journalism professor, Arizona State University

TERESA LEONARD, director of news research, *Raleigh (NC) News & Observer*

> ### What basic research skills do journalists need?

Doig: Going beyond simple Google searches. How to find and use such important public databases as property tax records or court dockets.

Kiernan: How to file a Freedom of Information Act (FOIA) request.

> ### What kind of public records have you used in your work? Private records?

Kiernan: Public: Autopsy reports; civil and criminal court records; military records; building inspection reports; police reports; land records.

Private: Journals, letters, email, voicemail. Think of MySpace and Facebook pages as documents.

> ### How do you make a computer-assisted story well written?

Doig: A good CAR story is about the people who are affected, so you need plenty of traditional reporting to get their voices into the story. If lots of numbers are needed for understanding of the issue, put them in sidebar charts or graphics.

> ### What's a news researcher's role?

Leonard: To help the reporter get his/her job done, in whatever form that takes. Looking up a phone number or running a criminal check. Finding sources to interview, databases or public records that produce a key direction for the story, or articles and essays that help a reporter become familiar with a topic to begin reporting.

> ### Why do we need news/librarians researchers when reporters can use Wikipedia or Google?

Leonard: Wikipedia and Google are often our starting point. The expertise of a researcher is to know where (and whether) to go from there.

Because of the way Wikipedia is produced, we always independently confirm what we find there. Google directs us to a bunch of other sources, some good, some bad. Our job: to determine which are which.

SUMMARY GUIDE RESEARCH

"REPORTING ON STEROIDS"

Most journalism relies on reporters gathering information on the scene, but research produces stories that are generally more accurate and complete.

What to Remember → Journalists bolster their live reporting with research into public records, archives, databases and computer-assisted analysis of data. Research can aid reporters on deadline and long-term reporting projects.

A "DOCUMENTS STATE OF MIND"

Public documents record nearly all human activities, from birth and death to those who take advantage of consumers and pollute the environment.

What to Remember → Smart journalists develop a "documents state of mind," operating under the assumption that somewhere a record exists, either in print or on a database, that will enhance a story's accuracy and impact.

CRACKING THE GOVERNMENT SEAL: USING THE FREEDOM OF INFORMATION ACT

State and federal Freedom of Information Act (FOIA) laws are supposed to give journalists and citizens unfettered access to records that show how government operates.

What to Remember → Government officials often try to foil journalistic access to public records. Journalists must learn the requirements of FOIA laws, meet their strict requirements and closely monitor the progress of requests.

SEARCH ENGINES

Search engines enable journalists to scour the World Wide Web for information that can enhance the quality of stories.

What to Remember → Many public agencies routinely post important records online—no FOIA required. These can include background information, transcripts, photos, even search warrants. Savvy journalists master the ways that search engines can be used for maximum impact.

MULTIMEDIA SOURCES: ADD NEW DIMENSIONS WITH AUDIO AND VIDEO

The definition of documents has expanded beyond records on paper to digitized information, photos, audio, video and other multimedia features.

What to Remember → Journalists routinely search for multimedia information in their online searches. They provide links and electronic footnotes to records that enhance credibility and provide new ways of experiencing the news.

WIKIPEDIA: POWER AND PITFALLS OF THE INTERNET'S ENCYCLOPEDIA

Wikipedia, the vast and constantly updated Internet encyclopedia, has revolutionized the collection and distribution of knowledge but not without serious pitfalls that journalists should recognize.

What to Remember → Erroneous information can erase a story's accuracy and credibility. Journalists don't rely on Wikipedia entries as the last word without verifying their authenticity, especially if they are not supported by primary documents.

WHY LIBRARIANS STILL MATTER

Journalists who depend exclusively on search engines ignore one of the most valuable sources of information: librarians and reference specialists who can do much of the work for them with speed and reliability.

What to Remember → Librarians can find untapped resources and help journalists evaluate their credibility. Smart journalists get to know librarians and news researchers and check with them before going online.

DEFLATING URBAN LEGENDS AND ONLINE HOAXES

Urban legends and hoaxes abound on the Internet, but their veracity can easily be determined online.

What to Remember → If a story seems too good to be true, it probably isn't. Just because you find something online, hear about it from your friends or read about it, don't assume it's true. Check it out before you put it into your story.

PRIVATE RECORDS: INTIMATE RESEARCH

Public records make for powerful, authoritative journalism but there's another category—private records—that can make a story unforgettable.

What to Remember → People create or leave behind intimate information about their lives in school yearbooks, diaries, letters and social media entries. These are revealing jewels that can shed light on someone's life and add depth and power to your stories.

COMPUTER-ASSISTED REPORTING: PRECISION JOURNALISM

The advent of desktop and personal computers has made it possible for journalists to bring the power of social science to their work.

What to Remember → The journalist's job is to tell stories that lie behind numbers. Always put a human face on computer-assisted reporting to make your stories accessible and linger in the mind of your audiences.

REAPING THE REWARDS: TURNING RESEARCH INTO COMPELLING STORIES

Once journalists have gathered and analyzed data and developed conclusions, they must communicate their findings in ways that audiences will easily grasp.

What to Remember → The more you work on research, the easier it is to get lost in numbers. Journalists use a focus to determine a working hypothesis, and draw on narrative skills to make data-rich stories comprehensible to their audiences. They populate their stories with people whose experiences reveal the human reality behind the numbers.

KEY TERMS

blog, p. 150
computer-assisted reporting (CAR), p. 155
database archives, p. 155
document, p. 150
documents state of mind, p. 146
Freedom of Information Act (FOIA), p. 146

online hoax, p. 153
open access, p. 146
open government, p. 146
Portable Document Format (PDF), p. 150
private records, p. 154
public records, p. 145
reference librarians, p. 153

research, p. 144
search engines, p. 147
single-source story, p. 144
urban legend, p. 153
wiki, p. 151
Wikipedia, p. 152

EXERCISES

1. Using search engines and library research, trace the history of the tape recorder. Who was the individual who brought back the technology to America after World War II? Who is credited with the invention of the wire recorder? What was the earliest use of the tape recorder to gather news. (Hint: it involves a dirigible.) Write a 250-word essay describing your findings with your sources at the end.

2. Find a transcript and video of the president's latest news conference.

3. Pranksters attached a license plate stolen from a police speed camera van to their car. As a result, police ended up issuing tickets to themselves. True or false?

4. Find the assessed value of your school president's home. Discuss the ethics of carrying out such a search.

5. Think of private records that reveal intimate and revealing details about your life.

6. Introduce yourself to your campus or local librarian and ask for help locating the April 1972 edition of *Reader's Digest*.

READINGS

Gaines, William C. *Investigative Journalism: Proven Strategies for Reporting the Story.* **Washington, DC: CQ Press, 2007.**
Using real-life case studies, this two-time Pulitzer Prize–winning investigative journalist shows how to obtain and analyze public documents and databases, investigate public and private institutions that affect citizens and take advantage of Freedom of Information laws.

Houston, Brant, and Investigative Reporters and Editors, Inc. *The Investigative Reporter's Handbook: A Guide to Documents, Databases and Techniques.* **Boston: Bedford/St. Martin's, 2009.**
The go-to guide for news research, this classic handbook teaches how to investigate government agencies, businesses, hospitals and other institutions; create, obtain and analyze paper and electronic documentation; and, most important, develop a "documents state of mind."

Kovach, Bill, and Rosenstiel, Tom. *Blur: How to Know What's True in the Age of Information Overload.* **New York: Bloomsbury USA, 2011.**
The age of Google and Wikipedia has transformed how journalists find information. Two media critics describe the pitfalls posed by the search engine culture and provide specific examples on how the best journalists cut through the clutter of an information-saturated culture to find the truth.

Meyer, Philip. *Precision Journalism: A Reporter's Introduction to Social Science Methods.* **Lanham, MD: Rowman & Littlefield, 2002.**
Meyer pioneered the use of social sciences to produce investigative stories about government, police abuse and politics. In this classic text, he offers a statistics primer and teaches journalists how to use databases and analyze the information to provide accurate statistical analysis to bolster their findings.

USING RESEARCH TO DOCUMENT A STORY

Most news stories are written based on interviews conducted via telephone or social media and on-scene reporting. Many can be buttressed by research by using public records and other documentary sources. The result: stories based on a solid foundation of evidence that provide the credibility that news consumers demand. In the following examples from "Mary Ellen's Will: The Battle for 4949 Swiss," Lee Hancock, an investigative reporter for the *Dallas Morning News*, demonstrates the abundance and variety of records available to journalists.

The four-part 2006 narrative series exposes a trend of exploitation of the elderly by focusing on the machinations of two men—Mark McKay and Justin Burgess—intent on acquiring ownership of a faded Dallas mansion from an elderly one-time socialite named Mary Ellen Bendtsen in the final months of her life. Bendtsen called them "the boys." They were opposed by Mrs. Bendtsen's daughter, Frances Ann Giron.

The story is ripe for a libel suit, so Hancock is careful to document her story with a wide range of public and private records. In many stories, research is often limited to broad descriptions, such as "public records show," but in "Mary Ellen's Will" the reporter opens the vault of her research by taking advantage of online technology. She employed hyperlinked footnotes throughout that link to pop-up text boxes listing detailed descriptions of her sources, allowing the writer to keep the storyline free of cumbersome attribution while showing readers the underlying evidence. (The footnotes appeared at the end of each installment in the newspaper.)

Hancock and her editor, Mark Miller, described the approach in a 2006 *Nieman Reports* article. "Once the idea of using footnotes took hold, we realized that they offered more than just a vehicle for attribution—as they'd been used by other newspapers. They could allow us to provide contextual information and let readers dig deeper into topics of particular interest," using PDF files of original source documents to these pop-up footnotes. "Those would allow readers to explore investigative reports, transcripts, medical records, police reports, wills, deeds and other historic documents that had been amassed in the reporting of the story. This added a level of transparency that would leave no doubt about the depth of reporting that went into a story that we wanted to read like good fiction."

The series opens an uncommon window into the enormous capacities of journalistic research and shows a clear and ingenious path for journalists interested in using records. Following are excerpts from the four-part series and the verbatim source material.

MARY ELLEN'S WILL: THE BATTLE FOR 4949 SWISS

By Lee Hancock

Dallas Morning News, Special Report 2006

PART 1

The mansion at 4949 Swiss Avenue sags like an aging diva. Rusty screens cover dark windows. A beam props up the porch roof, obscuring a once-grand entrance.

If you talked your way inside before the courts started auctioning things for the legal bills, you'd stop in that doorway and stare at the sweeping staircase, trying to place it in some old movie.

Once your eyes adjusted, there'd be more to gawk at: gilded candelabras, faded sprays of plastic flowers, a pair of grand pianos reflected in a mirror bigger than a garage door. The last occupant, Mary Ellen Bendtsen, liked to say her home was built around that mirror, the biggest in any house in Texas.

You'd see her, too, in oversized glamour shots hazy with dust from collapsing ceilings. Those portraits dominated everything. In every one, she was a platinum-blond ingénue.

Forty-nine forty-nine Swiss Avenue was like a forgotten movie set, the kind with too many sad endings. Almost anyone who knows its story will tell you it's straight out of Sunset Boulevard. And Mrs. Bendtsen — she was Norma Desmond, that old movie's faded star.[1]

So Mrs. Bendtsen's sister, Ann McClamrock, by then a working divorcee, paid the $7,500 down payment for the mansion, just as she'd helped cover expenses when the Bendtsens had their only child, Frances Ann. The place needed repairs even then, so her parents got it for $17,500. . . .[6]

Mr. McCay had a way of wanting old people's things — and getting them.

He bought an elderly couple's M-streets home in 1992 after doting on them several years.

Some people questioned how little Mr. McCay paid.[17]

State elder abuse investigators also heard of the business by 1997, as they examined Mr. McCay's ties to another childless couple in their 90s in the M streets. Mr. McCay befriended the couple and soon was a constant presence.

The story begins using traditional information collected by journalists based on interviews and direct observation.

Footnote 1: The opening scene is based on several visits by the reporter to the house, including an extensive walk-through before a court-ordered auction of many of Mary Ellen Bendtsen's furnishings. The description of Mrs. Bendtsen is based on interviews with friends, relatives and others familiar with her.

The well-researched story goes beyond interviews to make its case. Here the reporter reveals the source of information about the property from records easily available in courthouses and, increasingly, online.

Footnote 6. Interviews with Mrs. McClamrock, Dallas County property records.

The story introduces antiques dealer Mark McCay, who developed a friendship with Mrs. Bendtsen and eventually convinced her to leave him the mansion. The story documents, in 25 detailed footnotes, how McCay did this at least once before under questionable circumstances. It illustrates the wealth of records available to journalists from public agencies. These include:

- Multiple Texas Adult Protective Services case files. (Electronic links to original documents are also included in the footnotes.)
- Dallas County Probate Court records.
- Sworn testimony in a lawsuit deposition.
- Deposition taken in Bankruptcy Court for the Northern District of Texas.

[Texas Adult Protective Services] APS investigators did conclude that Mr. McCay neglected the man and his Alzheimer's-afflicted wife, and exploited and abused the man, verbally and emotionally, as he, too, slipped into dementia.[24]

Confidential APS reports include witness accounts of Mr. McCay moving into the couple's home and berating the old man to sign papers that would put about $300,000 in assets into a trust Mr. McCay would control.[25]

A sitter described hearing Mr. McCay scream at the man that his family only wanted his money and would put him away.[26]

Another caretaker described the man weeping over his checkbook, asking if she trusted Mr. McCay.[27]

Mr. McCay told an investigator that he was honoring the couple's wish to avoid a nursing home. Anyone who suggested otherwise, he said, had ulterior motives. The investigator wrote that Mr. McCay appeared to be lying and might also be preying on other old people.

Challenged, Mr. McCay "said that I was against him," an investigator wrote.[28]

APS closed its inquiry after advising a nephew of the man to hire a lawyer and create a guardianship.[29] The nephew, a Carrollton accountant, says he bowed out because his uncle resisted help and seemed to enjoy Mr. McCay's company.[30] Sitters later told of being instructed not to let the nephew call or visit after Mr. McCay took control.[31]

Mr. McCay inherited the man's estate when he died in 1999, though his widow was still alive, bedridden and dependent on a feeding tube.

By early 2000, Mrs. Bendtsen was dependent on the kindness of others.

Her eyesight was so bad that in the fall she quit driving her 1982 Cadillac Fleetwood Brougham.[33]

PART 2

On a rainy Wednesday in mid-January 2005, Mrs. Bendtsen fell down the steps of 4949 Swiss while checking her mail. She gashed her forehead but managed to get back inside. A friend alerted her family, and by nightfall, she was in Baylor University Medical Center's neurological intensive care unit. Stitches covered her left eyebrow, and a small brain hemorrhage worried doctors.[24]

The key to avoiding libel penalties is to document every fact, however minor. Libel cases often center on minor errors.

Footnote 33. Texas Department of Transportation vehicle registration records show Mrs. Bendtsen's car registration expired and was not renewed after September 2001.

The story shifts when Mrs. Bendtsen is hospitalized. Footnotes reveal two new sources.
- Baylor University Medical Center records, Jan. 12–21, 2005, pp. 231–240, 245–247, 371–387.
- Ashley Court at Turtle Creek skilled nursing home medical records, pp. 41, 96.

Over the next few days, doctors noted that she was "clearly not able to return home," and she seemed to realize that, too. She signed power-of-attorney papers on Jan. 14 so Mrs. Giron could pay bills and make decisions.[25]

She was badly confused, thought it was 1960 and was often so agitated that she had to be restrained. She was so wobbly that doctors feared she would fall again and said she needed four weeks of inpatient physical therapy.[26] So Mrs. Giron decided to spend Jan. 18 checking out rehab facilities in Plano.

PART 3

Mark McCay and Justin Burgess walked into Room 1117 at Baylor University Medical Center, legal papers in hand. It was Tuesday morning, Jan. 18, 2005.[1]

Frail and disoriented, Mary Ellen Bendtsen was alone in the claustrophobic room, its antiseptic blandness relieved only by wilting roses at her bedside and a panoramic view of Fair Park.

She had gotten her start as a Depression-era model, and the two antique dealers — business and once romantic partners — usually made a point of fussing over how she'd posed for one of Fair Park's famous art-deco statues.

But Mrs. Bendtsen couldn't sit up to join her visitors in taking it all in: the gleaming buildings, the Star of Texas Ferris wheel, the gilt tower near the Cotton Bowl catching the early morning light.[2]

The 88-year-old was strapped to her hospital bed with a cloth-restraint "Posey vest."

She'd been confined that way for nearly a week. She didn't seem to register the nurses' warnings that she was too unsteady to get up without help. Six days before, she had tumbled down the porch of her Swiss Avenue mansion, leaving her with a gash over one eyebrow and a tiny, but troubling, brain hemorrhage. The nurses feared she might fall again.[3]

After Mrs. Bendtsen was admitted to Baylor, her doctors quickly diagnosed her with dementia. They

Two footnotes display how an effective story relies on public records and direct observation by a reporter. The last entry demonstrates how far a good reporter goes to substantiate every fact.

Footnote 1. Baylor University Medical Center patient records for Mary Ellen Bendtsen, Jan. 12–21, 2005, pp. 237, 327–330.

Footnote 2. The description of Mrs. Bendtsen's room is based on the reporter's visit to the 11th floor of Baylor's Roberts hospital wing and Room 1117, as well as archival weather condition reports from Feb. 18, 2005.

Research points journalists to telling details—"a cloth-restraint Posey vest"—that demonstrate their mastery of the subject. Journalists faced with an overabundance of information painstakingly mine records for ways to summarize action in dramatic fashion.

Footnote 3. Baylor medical records, pp. 231–233, 267–280; 371, 375, 379, 381, 383, 385, 387.

Research enables journalists to describe technical information in ways that readers can easily comprehend.

Footnote 6. Baylor medical reports. On Jan. 15, 2005, a doctor noted that Mrs. Bendtsen had failed an "MMS" or mini-mental status exam, commonly used to screen patients for dementia and other mental deficits, p. 232. Other doctors' and nurses' notes recorded daily observations that Mrs. Bendtsen was confused, seemed forgetful and sometimes couldn't understand where she was.

were waiting that day for a full psychiatric evaluation, believing she might be too impaired to care for herself. But any diagnosis was a medical opinion, not a legal finding. She was vulnerable to whomever got to her first and managed to sway her most. No matter how muddled her mind might be, anything she agreed to — particularly anything she signed — could be hard to undo.[6]

PART 4

A hospital staffer allowed Ms. Tidwell to bring a digital video camera into the emergency room. She, the lawyer, the two men and the sitter gathered around Mrs. Bendtsen's bed.[23]

As monitors blinked and beeped, the lawyer took the old woman's hand.

"Do you want Frances Ann to have any of your money?"

Mrs. Bendtsen's sunken eyes barely opened. Her face was pale and gaunt, her mouth twisted. Her blonde, bobbed hair was matted, '40s-starlet curls limp. In a frail, strained voice, she said, "No."

"Do you want Frances Ann to have your house at Swiss Avenue?"

"I want it for myself," she slurred.

Mr. Olsen paused and rephrased himself.

Who should have the mansion?

"I want — I want to keep it — keep it for myself."

"Right. But if — but just in case you — when you die, who do you want the house to go to?" Mr. Olsen persisted.

"To — the boys," she said.

She looked spent. Prompted, she pointed a shaky finger to the men at the foot of her bed. "Justin and Mark," she said. The camera panned to the anxious looking men.

Putting his briefcase on Mrs. Bendtsen's stomach for a writing surface, the lawyer handed her a pen. Guided, Mrs. Bendtsen scrawled her signature sideways on the last page of the will.[24]

The battle for 4949 Swiss draws to a close. Mark McKay and his business partner arrive in Mrs. Bendtsen's hospital room after she suffered a massive stroke, hospital records showed. She was alone with the two men, their lawyer and a friend of Mary Ellen, Dixie Tidwell.

Hancock sets down the scene that follows, complete with dialogue and vivid description, because she obtained access to an unimpeachable source.

Footnote 23. Videotaped will signing at Baylor emergency room.

Note. The video was posted on the Web site created for the series.

SUMMARY

"Mary Ellen's Will" is documented with 133 footnotes in all. In addition to those cited here, Hancock used city, police and fire records, interviews with more than 50 people, *Dallas Morning News* archives, repeated visits to 4949 Swiss, letters, affidavits, and investigator and social worker reports amounting to thousands of documents reviewed. Her tenacity, curiosity and commitment to the truth is a model of investigative journalism. Two lessons underscore her efforts: Journalists should assume that for every fact, a document exists; and the best journalists are ceaseless in their determination to find them.

Postscript: In August 2005, Probate Court Judge Joe Loving, assigned to hear the will contest, threw out the emergency room will that had left the two men Mrs. Bendtsen's five-twelfths share of the mansion. The ruling made Mrs. Frances Ann Giron (Bendtsen's daughter) sole executor and heir of her mother's estate.

On Feb. 24, 2006, a Dallas County grand jury indicted McCay, Burgess and Olsen for attempted theft of over $200,000, by unduly influencing Mrs. Bendtsen to sign a will giving the two men her home when they knew she was incapacitated. In June 2012, a Dallas County jury convicted McCay of attempted theft of more than $200,000, a felony. He faces up to 20 years in prison. The trials of Burgess and Olsen, who lost his license to practice law, were set for later dates.

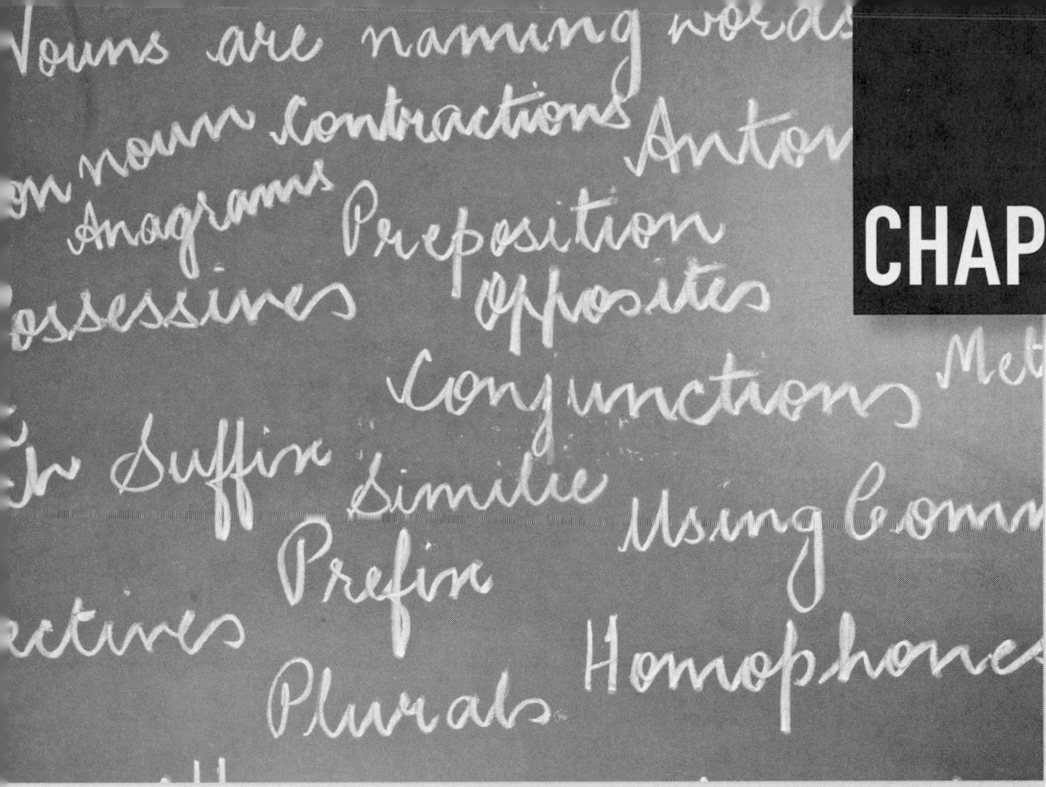

GRAMMAR, LANGUAGE, STYLE

Using Accurate Words

169

JOURNALISTS FACE MANY challenges, but writing is probably the most difficult—they must write clearly and accurately, often under deadline pressure. News writing calls for a command of grammar, usage, spelling, word choice and punctuation—a constellation of skills that combine to produce a journalistic style that is clear, conversational and fair.

In this chapter you will learn the essentials of news writing style, from crafting sentences and paragraphs to the importance of avoiding writing's worst sins: jargon, clichés, and "sloppy copy" that ignore the demands of the *Associated Press Stylebook* and emerging online style resources that govern precision and consistency in news stories.

WHY SPELLING, GRAMMAR AND STYLE MATTER

Sooner or later—whether in an internship, a fellowship or your first job—you're going to work in a professional newsroom for the first time. You might be a confident person by nature, but joining a group of newsroom veterans when you're still wet behind the ears can be an intimidating prospect. Whether your first assignment is covering a fire, doing man-on-the-street interviews or compiling an events calendar, you'll want to make a good first impression.

Copy editors are the "last line of defense" between the newsroom and audiences, flagging typos, factual errors and stylistic lapses.

o accelerate	o exhilarate	o pharaoh (*pharoah*)
o accidentally (*accidently*)	o existence (*existance*)	o pigeon (*pidgeon*)
o accommodate	o Fahrenheit	o pistachio (*pistacchio*)
o accordion (*accordian*)	o fiery (*firey*)	o plagiarize
o accumulate	o flabbergast (*flabberghast*)	o playwright
o acquaintance (*acquaintence, aquaintance*)	o flotation (*floatation*)	o plenitude (*plentitude*)
	o frustum (*frustrum*)	o poinsettia (*pointsettia*)
o acquire (*aquire*)	o gauge	o precede
o acquit (*aquit*)	o genius (*genious; see "ingenious"*)	o presumptuous (*presumptious*)
o aficionado	o grammar (*grammer*)	o proceed
o a lot (*alot*)	o gross	o pronunciation (*pronounciation*)
o amateur	o guttural	o propagate
o anoint	o handkerchief (*hankerchief*)	o privilege (*priviledge*)
o apology	o harass (*harrass*)	o puerile
o argument (*arguement*)	o horrific	o pursue (*persue*)
o atheist	o hypocrisy	o putrefy
o a while (*awhile*)	o imitate	o questionnaire (*questionaire*)
o axle (*axel*)	o immediately	o raspberry
o barbecue (*barbeque*)	o inadvertent (*inadvertant*)	o receipt
o believable (*believeable*)	o incidentally (*incidently*)	o receive
o believe	o incredible	o recommend
o broccoli (*brocolli*)	o independent	o refrigerator (*refridgerator*)
o camouflage	o indispensable (*indispensible*)	o renowned
o cantaloupe	o ingenious (*ingenius; see "genius"*)	o rhythm
o carburetor	o inoculate (*innoculate*)	o ridiculous
o Caribbean	o irascible	o sacrilegious
o cartilage	o irresistible (*irresistable*)	o sandal
o cemetery (*cemetary*)	o its (*it's*)	o savvy
o chauvinism (*chauvanism*)	o judgment (*judgement*)	o seize (*sieze*)
o chili	o led (*lead*)	o sensible (*sensable*)
o chocolaty (*chocolatey*)	o liaison	o separate
o coliseum, also colosseum	o lieutenant	o septuagenarian (*septagenarian*)

You'd like your editors to think they've made a good decision in hiring you, especially when they see your first stories. Maybe they'll be impressed by your writing skills and/or your reporting instincts. One thing's for sure, however—if your copy contains mistakes, whether in grammar, spelling or style, their first impression will be approximately the following: "Great. How much hand-holding am I going to have to do with this person?"

Turn in a story with misspellings and your editor will think you are ignorant or too lazy to open a dictionary or style guide. Publish a story with misspelled words, grammatical mistakes or punctuation errors and your readers will assume illiterates run the paper. Your publication has probably selected one dictionary as its source for spelling words that aren't included in the *Associated Press Stylebook*. When in doubt, consult it.

Perhaps you think knowing when to use "that" versus "which" or "affect" versus "effect" is the copy editor's job. **Copy desks** are staffed with trained editors whose job it is to ferret out mistakes before stories are submitted for typesetting, broadcast or online. Copy editors are considered "the last line of defense," committed to blocking mistakes before news reaches audiences.

First and foremost, your job is to turn in copy that is well reported and factual, but also as clean as you can make it. If editors have to worry about fixing your grammar or style mistakes, it takes away from the time they'll need to devote to making sure the story is accurate, fair, libel-proof and well written. Mistakes erode the credibility of any news organization—why should our audience trust our stories when we can't get the little things right?

CONVERGENCE POINT ⭐

100 Most Often Misspelled Words in English

Most writers stumble when it comes to spelling some words correctly. Yourdictionary.com has assembled a list of the 100 words most commonly misspelled, from "acceptable" to "weird." The site also provides helpful ways to remember correct spellings.

Find this link on the companion Web site at **www.oup.com/us/scanlan.**

> **❝I learned to really go over my copy better, even in a rush, to catch all the major copy errors. I also learned that editors don't take too kindly to reporters who cannot edit their own copy before sending it to them. The better a reporter is in the grammar, punctuation, spelling, accuracy and style departments, more likely an editor won't mind reading the copy. This could aid editors in making the piece better by not needing to correct so many simple copy mistakes.❞**
>
> —CHRIS HALL,
> REPORTING FELLOW, THE
> POYNTER INSTITUTE

Submitting stories with accurate spelling, grammar and style shows respect for editors and others who will work with your copy. "Dirty" copy implies that this obligation is somehow beneath you and that you think someone else should clean it up. Wouldn't you rather be a shining example of someone who doesn't need to be "babysat" in his/her first job? The cleaner your copy, the more likely you'll be the rare individual who walks in the door ready to impress the veterans.

THE HALLMARKS OF EFFECTIVE NEWS WRITING

To readers, the best news stories can seem like they came together on their own. The facts, quotes and transitions flow together so effortlessly that they almost seem to have emerged whole from nature. Unfortunately, as any veteran reporter can tell you, it takes a lot of hard work to make news stories read so easily. Effective news writing reflects five qualities: It is conversational, simple, concrete, specific and direct.

Effective News Writing Is Conversational

Good writers choose everyday words over obscure and complicated ones. They avoid language they think will make them look smart, but, in fact, make their stories difficult to understand.

Poor news writing sounds different from the way people normally talk to each other. It's journalese, a style distinguished by jargon, figurative rather than literal language, clichés, hyperbole and sensationalism.

▶**EXAMPLE** Negotiators yesterday, in an *eleventh-hour decision* following *marathon* talks, *hammered out* an agreement on a key wage provision they earlier had rejected.

Does the journalist really mean that the decision occurred at 11 p.m., the talks took place during a footrace of 26 miles and 385 yards, and that the agreement was "shaped, formed, or ornamented by a metalworker's hammer"?

QUICK Tips ◓ ALTERNATIVES TO COMPLICATED WORD AND PHRASES

- "Resigned" instead of "tendered his resignation"

- "Met" instead of "held a meeting with"

- "Near" instead of "in the vicinity/ close proximity"

- "Use" instead of "utilize"

- "End" instead of "cease/finalize"

- "Make" instead of "fabricate"

- "Before" instead of "prior to"

- "Now" instead of "at this point in time"

- "If" instead of "in the event that"

- "Affect" instead of "impact" ▶

Of course not, but journalists often choose clichés and overinflated language that they absorb from politicians, bureaucrats and professions, such as law or medicine, and regrettably, from bad news writing. It should only take a moment to shorten a redundant **phrase**, or rewrite a word, like these published examples that you'd never say to your mom.

- Don't use "eschew" when you could use "avoid."
    "Mr. Obama has considerable latitude to eschew [avoid] symbolic gestures in choosing subordinates."
- Don't use "affluent" when you could use "wealthy."
    "Some Affluent [Wealthy] Families Pick Public Schools for Children"
- Don't use "opt" when you could use "choose."
    "Many Washington-area parents who could afford private schools are opting [choosing] to keep their kids in the public school system."

> **Never use a 50-cent word when a 10-cent word will do.**
>
> —MARK TWAIN,
> AUTHOR, HUMORIST

Effective News Writing Is Simple

Smart news writers use short words, active verbs, short **sentences** and short paragraphs, making it possible to absorb the information with ease and speed.

News sources often speak or write in completely opposite fashion. It's the journalist's job to streamline bloated language into **simple sentences**, rephrase incomprehensible clichés and jargon—to be society's translator.

Here's an example:

EXAMPLE The couple took the vows of marriage half a decade ago, and entered gainful employment with Ned giving aid and assistance to the family-operated manufacturing enterprise in the town of Bristol, while Debby, his better half, worked as an educator in the community of Warren, accepting inconsistent assignments as an teacher those cases when full-time educators were incapable of working.

Here's the same example simplified:

EXAMPLE They had been married five years. Ned helped run the family manufacturing business in Bristol. Debby was a substitute teacher in Warren.

Campus officials are often just as bad as public officials in using insider terminology and other bloated language. If you're interviewing someone who uses a lot of jargon, do not be afraid to ask him or her for an explanation in plain language. If you can't understand what he or she is trying to get across, neither will your readers or viewers.

Effective News Writing Is Concrete

Good writing names people, places and things, making them easy to understand. A house on Elm Street. A child named Henry. A dog called Charlie. These differ from abstractions, such as "housing," "offspring," or "canine," that are concepts not associated with anything specific.

Concrete writing draws its strength from words that can be understood with our senses. "Currency," defined as "something that is in circulation as a medium of exchange," is abstract. A 20-dollar bill is concrete.

Don't get caught in the trap of trying to make your writing somehow seem more "official" or "dignified" by using indistinct terms. A good way to approach issues like this is to ask whether the term you're using would leave a question in the reader's mind. A "campus housing unit" could mean many things, but a "dorm room" is clear.

Effective News Writing Is Specific

Good writing focuses on the **specific**: what makes people, places and things distinctive.

Generations of *Miami Herald* reporters learned the power of specifics from a legendary reporter and editor. "The Gene Miller rule," as it was called, held, "Don't just tell readers it's ice cream; tell them the flavor of ice cream."

The rule was in effect the Miami morning a deranged man hijacked a school bus carrying disabled schoolchildren. "We had a problem here that newspapers have more and more these days," said *Herald* senior writer Martin Merzer. "This thing happened at 8:30, 9 o'clock in the morning. We couldn't get it in the paper for another 24 hours. All the local TV stations were already on it full-time. . . . Local news was on it, it was on CNN live, and we still had 24 hours to go."

It's a common problem. Editors and reporters know that by the time readers pick up the morning paper or turn on the evening broadcast, they have probably already heard the top stories of the day, from the radio, cable television or an online news source. Even if blog posts and Twitter feeds keep the story updated, the daily newspaper must still produce a riveting account that draws in readers. When that happens, the decision is made: Journalists must take a different approach.

Merzer and his editors agreed. There was no sense in writing a hard news lead— Police shot and killed a man who hijacked a bus and held 13 disabled children hostage Tuesday morning after a tense low-speed chase through rush hour traffic. "No one's going to read into the third paragraph because they figure they know that." The *Herald's* only hope, Merzer said, was "to try to tell it better, in more detail, so that people who think they know a lot about this story figure out real soon that there's more to know, and we're going to tell it to them. I figured our best contribution would be to tell the story in a different fashion with compelling detail."

Drawing on the reporting from more than a dozen colleagues, Merzer focused on carefully researched specifics to signal that the *Herald* indeed had a lot more to say about the story in a vivid, edgy reconstruction that would have made the late Gene Miller proud.

▶**EXAMPLE** A waiter fond of poet Ralph Waldo Emerson attends morning prayers at his church, steps across the street and hijacks a school bus. Owing $15,639.39 in back taxes, wielding what he says is a bomb, Catalino Sang shields himself with disabled children.

Follow my orders, he says, or I will kill the kids. "No problem, I will," says driver Alicia Chapman, crafty and calm. "But please don't hurt the children."

The saga of Dade County school bus No. CX-17, bound for Blue Lakes Elementary, begins.

—*Miami Herald, Nov. 3, 1995*

As a beginning writer, it's important to get in the habit of looking for details like these in the process of your reporting. Get the name of the dog, the ice cream, the flower, the song. You might not immediately know that you're going to use them, but they're there if you need them later. Attention to detail is the trait of a good reporter.

Effective News Writing Is Direct

Good writing gets right to the point; it is **direct**. It avoids unnecessary and pointless anecdotal leads, front-loaded **dependent clauses** and journalese that conceal the message and, like an overdue flight, delay the reader.

Here's a proposed amendment to the Florida constitution on the 2008 ballot:

▶EXAMPLE◀ Inasmuch as marriage is the legal union of only one man and one woman as husband and wife, no other legal union that is treated as marriage or the substantial equivalent thereof shall be valid or recognized.

Strip away the legalese, the mind-numbing repetitions—"shall be valid or recognized"—and gobbledygook boils down to a simple, concise and clear sentence:

▶EXAMPLE◀ If approved, the amendment would change the constitution to ban gay marriage in the state of Florida.

X-RAY READING WRITING NEWS: THE BASICS

A standard news article, that appeared in *The Roanoke Times* on Jan. 11, 2009, demonstrates the grammar of journalism that news writers must follow.

> RICHMOND — When Virginia lawmakers return to the Capitol this week to start the 2009 General Assembly session, they can leave their wish lists at home.

The lead answers: Who? Where? When? Why? and What? It injects a note of suspense: What are the wish lists, and why can the lawmakers leave them at home? The words are short and conversational.

> "As far as bold new programs that cost money, not going to happen," said Del. Morgan Griffith, R-Salem, the majority leader in the House of Delegates.

The second paragraph follows the cardinal rule "Good quotes up high." The writer leaves the quote, which is ungrammatical but direct, untouched.

> "The central problem is that amid the faltering economy, state revenue growth has been far weaker than lawmakers anticipated when they adopted a spending plan last year.

News stories cry out for this type of important context, known as a "nut graf." Reporters often resist, fearful of editorializing, or worried they lack the authority to make sweeping statements without attribution.

> "Kaine last month asked lawmakers to slash . . ."

The story continues for 21 paragraphs, using chronology for clarity, alternating examples, quotes, and contrasting views about proposed budget cuts and their impact on proposed legislation.

> "Ware . . . introduced a bill that would allow for early voting beginning 19 days before election day at sites set up by localities. He said he also supports no-excuse absentee voting.

The writer is clear and direct and uses two sentences to separate different ideas, making them easier to grasp.

> "We really need to look at election laws a little bit and bring them up to date," Ware said. "There's no reason to require people to give you an excuse for absentee voting."

The story circles back to the theme with a legislator's wish, and ends with a pithy quote, known as a "kicker" that supports his argument and brings the account to a satisfying close.

GRAMMAR: THE RULES OF THE ROAD

Grammar is defined as the "science of using words correctly." The building blocks of good grammar revolve around the eight parts of speech: noun, pronoun, verb, preposition, adjective, adverb, conjunction and interjection. Parts of speech are the foundation of clear, precise, powerful and accurate prose. The examples for each term are in italics.

- Term: **Noun**
    Definition: describes a person, place or thing.
    Examples: *Barack Obama* won the presidency. *Alaska* is Sarah Palin's home state. *iPhones* are very popular.
- Term: **Pronoun**
    Definition: General noun that replaces a specific noun ("he" instead of "Tom").
    Examples: *He* won. *It* is home to the Iditarod. *They* are very popular.
- Term: **Verb**
    Definition: shows action or states of being.
    Examples: Barack Obama *campaigned in the South*. Alaska *is* the home state of Sarah Palin. iPhones *sold out* the first week.

Ethical Dilemmas ! CLEANING UP BUTCHERED GRAMMAR

You're a general assignment reporter. For a story about a neighborhood crime watch, you interview the police chief and several residents. The police chief is known for his bad grammar, but there's a tradition among police reporters, who need access to him, to clean up his grammar so he doesn't sound ignorant.

He tells you, "Without the help of residents, we ain't got a chance to win the war against drugs."

The head of the neighborhood watch tells you, "the system is broke, and we the one's who's gotta to fix it, ain't no doubt about it."

What do you do about the ungrammatical errors uttered by the chief and the neighborhood leader? Explain the reasoning behind your decision. ▸

- Term: **Preposition**
  Definition: links nouns, pronouns and phrases to other words in a sentence.
  Examples: Barack Obama campaigned *for* president. Alaska became the 49th state *in* 1959. iPhones combine a phone *with* a music player.
- Term: **Adjective**
  Definition: describes a person, place or thing.
  Examples: *President* Barack Obama. *Frozen* Alaska. iPhones are *pricey* gadgets.
- Term: **Adverb**
  Definition: modifies verbs, adjectives, clauses and sentences (but not nouns). It conveys manner, emotion or mood and generally ends in "ly."
  Examples: Barack Obama *only just* overcame Hillary Clinton in the presidential primaries. Alaskans are *exceedingly* proud of Sarah Palin. iPhones sold *well* the week Apple introduced the product.
- Term: **Conjunction**
  Definition: binds words or groups of words; "but" and "and" are common examples
  Examples: Obama campaigned *for* president, *but* refused to use public financing funds. Alaska and Texas are red states, *and* their voters wouldn't have it any other way. iPhones are expensive, *yet* consumers are willing to pay the price.
- Term: **Interjection**
  Definition: reveals emotion and often ends with an exclamation mark or a period.
  Examples: *Yes We Can! Brrr. iPhones rock!*

STYLEBOOKS: PRINT AND ONLINE

In 1953, the Associated Press published its first **stylebook**. In the years since, it's become known as "the journalist's bible." "Far more than a collection of rules," former AP president Tom Curley said, the book is "part dictionary, part encyclopedia, part textbook." The most recent version includes sections on sports, business and American media law.

> ❝At the most basic level, a style guide is my map for abbreviations and other punctuation, correct names and titles, preferred style for capitalizing words, layout and design formats, and other details.❞
> —VICKI KRUEGER, EDITOR, NEWS UNIVERSITY

The *Associated Press Stylebook*, which sets forth style, grammar and usage rules, is a newsroom "bible" that copy editors and journalists rely on to ensure consistency and accuracy.

The *AP Stylebook* is the first stop to find answers about spelling, style and usage because it provides consistency and avoids confusion. In recent years, *Wired* magazine and Yahoo! have produced style guides for online writing and usage. For spelling, style and usage questions not covered by AP, consult *Webster's New World College Dictionary*, Fourth Edition, published by Wiley.

GRAMMAR'S DIRTY DOZEN: COMMON MISTAKES WRITERS MAKE

CONVERGENCE POINT ⚹

Online Style

Yahoo! makes its *Style Guide: The Ultimate Sourcebook for Writing, Editing, and Creating Content for the Digital World* available online. As online style guides often differ from print and broadcast rules, it's a valuable resource in the age of Internet journalism.

Find this link on the companion Web site at **www.oup.com/us/ scanlan.**

There are many ways to comply with and violate the rules of grammar, language, usage and style. Here are the most common:

- *Dangling modifiers.* "Location is key with modifiers—those words or phrases that describe something in your sentence," Vicki Krueger says in "Cleaning Your Copy," an online course offered by NewsU. "Put them in the wrong spot and the sentence is unclear, worse, inaccurate, and sometimes even comical." A **dangling modifier** connects to a word different from the one the writer apparently meant, as in this famous example from Groucho Marx in the film *Animal Crackers*.

  "One morning I shot an elephant in my pajamas. How he got into my pajamas I don't know."

  Groucho could have said, "One morning, while dressed in my pajamas, I shot an elephant." (Of course, we'd lose the joke.)

- *Dangling participles.* These are the "ing" and "ed" forms of verbs—such as whispering, shooting, rolled—that often start a sentence and quickly lose their way. Writers can easily correct **dangling participles** by using the classic

Web writing shares traditional style rules with print and broadcast, but there is enough of a difference that Yahoo! developed its own style guide for a new generation of online writers.

The Yahoo! Style Guide

Learn how to write and edit for a global audience through best practices from Yahoo!

Attract more readers; give them the gold-standard editorial experience on your site. "The Yahoo! Style Guide" shows you how.

EDITING 101

Best Practices for Online Copy

The smallest details of your content can influence a reader's perception of your website's reliability. Consistency in capitalization and the visual treatment of words—how you use such elements as quotation marks, boldface, and italics—contributes to your content's readability and speeds comprehension. And it does one more thing that's less tangible but very important: It gives the people visiting your site the understanding that your website takes itself seriously.

Punctuate Proficiently

Modern writing tends to be lightly punctuated. When, how, and where you use a mark is crucial for conveying a clear message, especially online, where readers scan. In this section, find guidelines for using each mark competently.

Apostrophes (')	Ellipsis points (. . .)	Question marks (?)
Colons (:)	Exclamation points (!)	Quotation marks (" ")
Commas (,)	Hyphens (-)	Semicolons (;)
Dashes (- and —)	Periods (.)	

subject-verb-object (S-V-O) structure that produces clear and accurate sentences, or revise them to meet that standard.

> Example: Chased along the dark streets, sheriff's deputies arrested the suspect.
>
> Error: The deputies weren't chased.
>
> Revision: Sheriff's deputies arrested the suspect after a chase through the dark streets.

Participles modify words that come from verbs.

> Example: Jogging along in the forest, the bear came out of nowhere, terrifying me.
>
> Error: The bear wasn't jogging.
>
> Revision: As I was jogging along in the forest, the bear came out of nowhere, terrifying me.

- *Subject/verb agreement.* With **subject/verb agreement**, the verbs and nouns in a sentence agree in number with each other (singular to singular, plural to plural). To find out if your grammar is correct, take this step.

  > Identify the subject and verb.
  >
  > Incorrect: CEO John Moneybags and his secretary (plural subjects) is skipping town (singular verb) to the Cayman Islands with the company's pension funds.
  >
  > Correct: CEO John Moneybags and his secretary (plural subjects) are skipping town (compound verb) to the Cayman Islands with the company's pension funds.

- *Lie/lay.* "Lie" means "to recline," and doesn't require a direct object. "She lies on the bed." "Lay" is an action verb meaning "to put or set down," as in, "He lay his books on the desk."

  > Lie/lay tip: "Lay" requires a direct object, in this case, "books." To make it even more challenging, the past tense of "lie" is "lay." It's best, then, to memorize these verbs' tenses, along with the direct object rule. "You lie in the sun," and "a chicken lays an egg."

- *It's/its.* "It's" is a contraction, which requires an apostrophe (') to fill in for the missing "i" in "It is" or "has" in "It has."

  > Examples: It's the first day of school.
  >
  > It's been an exhausting first day of school.

  "Its" is a possessive pronoun, which never needs an apostrophe.

  > Example: The bank lost its assets.

  To make sure you're using the correct form, substitute "it is" or "it has."

- *Passive and active voice.* English has two voices: active and passive. **Active voice** is a grammatical choice that uses the subject-verb-object structure ("The city council passed an ordinance . . .") to make sentences more direct, less awkward and clear.

  Passive voice is writing in which the subject is acted upon rather than acting. It lengthens the sentence, robs it of energy and clarity. The best way to transform passive voice into active voice is to delete the linking verb and identify the **subject** by asking who performed the action of the verb.

An example of passive voice: "A tougher date rape law was passed Friday by the Senate."

To convert to active voice, change "was passed" to "passed."

Identify the subject. Who passed the tougher date rape law? The Senate.

Revision in active voice: "The Senate passed a tougher date rape law on Friday."

The biggest difference between active and passive voice is the absence of the agent, or doer. "The village was burned." (It doesn't say who burned it.) Passive voice may reflect insufficient reporting. Sometimes passive voice is acceptable.

Note: *Action verbs* are sometimes confused with active voice. Action verbs describe an action. Look for the most vivid action verbs, the kind that trigger a picture in the reader's mind—crushed, kissed, fell.

- *That/which.* "That" is used when a clause provides necessary information for the sentence.

    Example: The controversial monument that turned neighbors and friends into enemies will be completed in 2013.

    "Which" is used when a clause provides incidental or unnecessary information for a sentence. It is set off with commas.

    Example: The controversial monument, which turned neighbors and friends into enemies, will be completed in 2013.

- *Who/whom/that.* "Who" and "whom" refer to people. Students (and some professional reporters) often have difficulty determining when each should be used. "Who" is a *subject* pronoun—one that refers to the subject of a sentence. "Whom" is an *object* pronoun—one referring to an object in the sentence. Subjects perform actions; objects receive actions.

    Examples: "Police continue to search for the murderer *who* has killed eight victims so far." (The murderer performed an action.)

    "To *whom* do you report?" (You perform the action of reporting; the object of that action is the one to whom you report.)

    A common way of determining the right choice is to restate the sentence as a question (if it isn't one already). If the answer contains *he*, *she* or *we* (subjects), use "who." If the answer contains *him*, *her* or *us* (objects), use "whom." Using the foregoing examples: Who is the murderer? (He is.) To whom do you report? (To him.)

    That and *which* refer to animals or things.

    Examples: Police will continue the search with K-9 dogs *that* have a sense of smell estimated to be one million times greater than humans.

    Police will continue to search with K-9 dogs, which have a sense of smell estimated to be one million times greater than humans, at first light tomorrow.

- *Comma.* A punctuation mark that divides parts of sentences and three items in a list.

    Rule: Don't use a comma if a word or phrase in the sentence is essential. If they're not essential, separate them from the rest of the sentence with commas.

CONVERGENCE POINT ⭤

A Primer on Cleaning Your Copy

This free, self-directed interactive course by Vicki Krueger, a veteran copy editor and editor of News University, The Poynter Institute's online training site, teaches writers and editors grammar basics, spelling, punctuation rules and AP style. Four sections demonstrate how to avoid the most common mistakes, followed by a "Copy Quotient Test" that tests your ability to produce clean copy.

Find this link on the companion Web site at **www.oup.com/us/ scanlan.**

Examples: The winning candidate's chief aides, *Bill Jackson and Susan Fernandez*, are expected to hold top staff positions after the election. (There are just two aides, so the readers need to know who they are.)

The candidate's many campaign staffers hope they will earn staff jobs if their candidate wins the election. (There is more than one staffer so their names aren't essential. A comma isn't needed.)

- *Colon.* A punctuation mark that draws attention to a list, explanation, quotation or additional information.

  Example: The town's new reduced budget claimed several victims: high school arts programs, repaving projects, electronic voting machines and raises for city workers.

- *Semicolon.* A punctuation mark used to join independent clauses rather than separate them into two sentences.

  Examples: Budget negotiations lasted until dawn without agreement; council members agreed to meet again after a few hours' sleep.

  His survivors include a son, Peter Mosley of Sarasota, Fla.; two daughters, Tamra Perry of San Francisco, and Michaela Lewis of Boston; and his beloved pet dog, Astro.

Uses a comma to join two independent clauses when a semicolon or period should be employed to avoid a run-on sentence.

- *Run-on sentences and the comma splice.* Inexperienced writers often compose sentences that contain multiple independent clauses and thus run uncomfortably long (**run-on sentences**). One example of this mistake: trying to combine two sentences with a comma (**comma splice**) to join two independent clauses when a semicolon or period should be employed to avoid a run-on sentence.

  Example: The Ronald McDonald House provided a place for parents of terminally ill patients to rest and take showers, it's supported by donations from the hospital's annual telethon.

  A way to avoid this problem—simply set off the two independent clauses using a period: The Ronald McDonald House provided a place for parents of terminally ill patients to rest and take showers. It's supported by donations from the hospital's annual telethon.

THE PITFALLS OF JARGON AND CLICHÉS

Jargon is the specialized vocabulary, acronyms ("ICE" for Immigrant and Customs Enforcement), shorthand ("B&E" for breaking and entering) and code words that professionals and other groups use with each other. (Even journalists do it: "nut graf," "tease," "toss.")

Avoid jargon. This is where your dictionary and thesaurus come in. Look for synonyms that are easier to understand. Bureaucrats may use terms such as "revenue" and "expenditures"; keep it simple with "income" and "spending." Doctors may talk with each other about "lateral epicondylitis"; let your readers know it's a case of "tennis elbow."

Clichés are overworked phrases, expressions or ideas that have been used so much they have robbed them of their power and originality.

Examples:

> Never expected. "When Lianna left for work yesterday, she never expected her front tire was flat. Also, "It never occurred to him . . ." or, "Little did he know . . ." ". . . takes no holidays." Fill in the blank: Death, fire, murder, accidents, tragedy. "First, the good news." "This is a story about . . ."

To dodge clichés, ask yourself if you've read or heard the phrase. If so, come up with a more original one. Turn a cliché around. A business story about computer sales used "win hearts and minds," an idea that came into currency during the Vietnam War *six* decades ago.

A revision that plays on the phrase is an easy solution: "win the hearts, minds and modems . . ."

CONVERGENCE POINT ⚡

Testing Your Punctuation and Grammar Prowess

Become a word usage star. Wordista's quiz tests spelling and grammar skills, a fun way to reinforce this chapter's lessons. It presents sentences that may or may not contain an error. Type in the correct usage, and the next question bumps up the level of difficulty. Miss, and game over. Fix 10 sentences to win, and earn a certificate you can print out and hang over your desk.

Find this link on the companion Web site at **www.oup.com/us/ scanlan.**

The Coaching Way ⁙ GRAMMAR: YOURS AND INTERVIEWEES'

- Make a list of the words you regularly misspell and their correct spelling, and post it where you can see it as you write and edit. Bookmark the list of commonly misspelled words on http://yourdictionary.com.
- Do you have a dictionary and your news organization's stylebook on your desk, or bookmarked? How do you use these resources?

- If a source is spouting techno speak or professional jargon, interrupt politely and say, "My readers don't have your scientific [or economic or medical or legal] knowledge and training. Could you put it in terms a layperson could easily understand?" What kind of responses do you get?
- Build a collection of grammar books and online resources. For this chapter, recommended

resources include *The Associated Press Stylebook* (latest edition); *Sin and Syntax: How to Craft Wickedly Effective Prose* by Constance Hale; *Lapsing Into a Comma: A Curmudgeon's Guide to the Many Things That Can Go Wrong in Print—and How to Avoid Them* by Bill Walsh, *The Elements of Style* by William Strunk and E. B. White and *Cleaning Your Copy* by Vicki Krueger. ◢

ROUNDTABLE

THE IMPORTANCE OF CLEAN COPY

Copy editors don't expect reporters to know all the fine points of grammar, language and style. They have little use, however, for stories riddled with misspellings, basic grammatical errors and stylebook lapses. They appreciate reporters who study their edited stories to learn from the changes.

Two editors and a grammarian discuss pet peeves, the importance of clean copy and how to achieve it.

- Keep a list of your frequent mistakes. Correct them before you hit "send."
- Read your stories aloud, listening for grammar, usage and style problems.
- Read widely to see how other writers deal with these issues.

Participants

DORIS N. TRUONG, copy editor, *The Washington Post*

VICKI KRUEGER, editor, News University (http://newsu.org)

BEN YAGODA, author, *When You Catch an Adjective, Kill It: The Parts of Speech, for Better and/or Worse*

> *How important is it for reporters to have a firm grasp on grammar, language and style?*

Truong: Anyone who is a writer ought to have a solid foundation in expressing herself clearly . . . knowing how words should flow is of utmost importance.

> *What are the most important things that students need to know about parts of speech?*

Yagoda: A sense of prepositions—because an abundance of them is an indication of flabbiness in writing. A general sense of the parts of speech helps you recognize what the linguists call "functional shifting"—when a word changes its part, as in "My bad" or "I friended her on Facebook." I don't consider functional shifting good or bad per se—but as with all nonstandard usages, you should be aware that you're doing it when you're doing it.

> *What common problems do you see?*

Krueger: Muddy writing (imprecise word choice or word order) and inconsistent style (capitalization, abbreviation and so on).

Yagoda: Comma splices, dangling modifiers, parallelism issues, excessive passive voice.

> *Aren't these the sorts of things for copy editors to deal with?*

Krueger: If I have to spend precious time on deadline, fixing problems with style, grammar and syntax, I don't get the chance to sell your story (with a fabulous headline) and help you tell it in the best possible way.

Truong: Reporters shouldn't consider it a bother to learn to be clear, concise writers. News organizations aren't in the business of publishing stream-of-consciousness musings. We're here to offer insights into the news of the day, sometimes in unexpected ways, but always with an eye toward serving the reader.

> *What usage pet peeves get under your skin?*

Yagoda: When people say "five-year anniversary" instead of "fifth anniversary," and "arguably" as an underhanded

way of saying, "This is what I think and now I don't need to support it!"

Truong: What's frustrating is when the same fix is made with the same reporter time and again, and the reason for the change doesn't sink in. I appreciate when reporters take the time to notice the edits that are made after they hand in a story and when they try to empathize with the copy desk.

SUMMARY GUIDE | GRAMMAR, LANGUAGE, STYLE: USING ACCURATE WORDS

WHY SPELLING, GRAMMAR AND STYLE MATTER

Editors and audiences expect journalists to display a clear knowledge of spelling, grammar and style.

What to Remember → Stories that are riddled with such mistakes will damage your credibility and possibly your career advancement. Keep a stylebook and dictionary close at hand when you write. Editors will have more time to improve your work instead of cleaning up after you.

THE HALLMARKS OF EFFECTIVE NEWS WRITING

Effective news writing reflects five hallmarks: It is conversational, simple, concrete, specific and direct.

What to Remember → Good writers choose everyday words over obscure and complicated ones. They rely on active verbs, short words, sentences and paragraphs, and specific details. They name people, places and things that readers can understand using their senses.

GRAMMAR: THE RULES OF THE ROAD

Eight parts of speech form the foundation of good grammar: noun, pronoun, verb, preposition, adjective, adverb, conjunction and interjection.

What to Remember → Effective writers understand the science of using words correctly. Journalists must know the definitions of these terms and how effective writers employ them to produce stories that are accurate, communicate clearly and display a firm grasp of style.

STYLEBOOKS: PRINT AND ONLINE

Stylebooks, available in print and online, teach correct abbreviation, punctuation, capitalization and the many other rules that newsrooms follow for publication.

What to Remember → Most newsrooms adhere to the *Associated Press Stylebook*. Online news organizations offer their own guides for Web writing. The writer's other important tool is a dictionary, which provides correct spellings, definitions and alternative word choices as well as valuable lessons in usage.

GRAMMAR'S DIRTY DOZEN: COMMON MISTAKES WRITERS MAKE

There are a dozen grammatical pitfalls that trip up many reporters, and journalists must understand how to dodge them.

What to Remember → Effective writers are alert to the dangers of dangling modifiers and participles; subject/verb agreement; "lie" versus "lay"; "its" and "it's"; the difference between passive and active voice; "that" and "which"; "who," "whom" and "that"; using the comma, colon and semicolon; avoiding run-on sentences and the comma splice.

THE PITFALLS OF JARGON AND CLICHÉS

People in law enforcement, health care and other specialties traffic in jargon—shorthand terms and abbreviations that speed up their communications but mystify readers.

What to Remember → Journalists have the duty to avoid or translate jargon so audiences understand what's really being said. Clichés come quickly to mind when writing, but these phrases, expressions and ideas are the product of laziness and lack of originality. Don't assume you're the first one to ever use a familiar turn of words.

KEY TERMS

EXERCISES

1. Assemble a style bookshelf. It should include the *Associated Press Stylebook*, "the bible of style" for most news organizations, a dictionary, thesaurus and one or more of the grammar guides listed in the this chapter. Study them. Don't expect to memorize everything they contain, but familiarize yourself with their layout and look for examples of problems that frequently crop up in your stories.

2. Make a list of the words you commonly misspell. Use the auto-correct function of your word processing software to avoid the problem, or simply make a list and keep it close by when you write. Use spellcheck, but remember that it's not infallible.

3. Search online for grammar exercises. Purdue University Online Writing Lab (http://owl.english.purdue .edu/exercises/2/) offers a wealth of exercises that will test your knowledge and provides correct answers to enhance your skills.

4. Develop an accuracy protocol that you rely on before you submit your work: spellcheck, check what you've written against the notes, research and documents you've collected during your reporting and verify ages, names, titles, addresses, links and telephone numbers.

5. Make friends with the copy desk. Ask a copy editor or your teacher to show you the mistakes that frequently appear in your copy. If you're unclear about what's wrong, ask them to explain.

6. Read widely, not just newspapers and web sites, but magazines and books. Study the punctuation, spelling, grammar and style rules they follow.

READINGS

Barr, Chris, et al. *The Yahoo! Style Guide: The Ultimate Sourcebook for Writing, Editing, and Creating Content for the Digital World*. **New York: St. Martin's Griffin, 2010.**
Tailored to Web writing, the Yahoo! Style Guide (in print and online at styleguide.yahoo.com) is a rich source of guidance on subjects ranging from online readability to writing for international audiences.

Clark, Roy Peter. *The Glamour of Grammar: A Guide to the Magic and Mystery of Practical English*. **New York: Little. Brown and Company, 2010.**
Clark, an influential writing coach who holds a doctorate in English literature, helps writers produce stores that use correct grammar, from parts of speech to punctuation and stylistic pitfalls. Written in a lively style and full of examples from newswriting and other genres, the book makes this challenging subject a series of painless lessons.

Christian, Darrell, Jacobsen, Sally and Minthorn, David. *The Associated Press Stylebook and Briefing on Media Law.* **New York: Basic Books, 2011.**
The AP delivers news to 130 nations and 1 billion people worldwide. Its stylebook is considered the journalists' "bible" by most newsrooms and contains more than 3,000 entries which explain rules on grammar, spelling, punctuation, capitalization, abbreviation, writing for social media and the use of numbers that journalism follow for consistency.

Sagolla, Dom. *140 Characters: A Style Guide for the Short Form.* **Hoboken, NJ: John Wiley & Sons, 2009.**
One of the creators of Twitter dispenses informed and practical advice on the best ways to communicate with the micro-writing forms of social media that increasingly dominate the way news is reported and written.

Yagoda, Ben. *When You Catch an Adjective, Kill It: The Parts of Speech, for Better and/or Worse.* **New York: Broadway, 2007.**
Author and journalism professor Yagoda has written an entertaining and helpful book about a subject—parts of speech—that normally might put you to sleep. He lays down the grammatical rules of the road, but isn't afraid to preach taking detours that make for accurate, clear and fresh prose.

CHAPTER 9

NUMBERS

Using Accurate Figures

Roger Simon

MANY JOURNALISM MAJORS and professional journalists maintain that they chose journalism because they "don't do math," and had found refuge in a profession where words reigned supreme.

Surprise! Reporters need math skills to do their job of informing the public. As a professional reporter or editor, numbers will stream across your desk and in-box every day—in polls and press releases, company balance sheets and municipal budgets and reports from government agencies, and advocacy groups. The need to understand numbers is not restricted to financial analysis. Mathematical information and insight can enlighten the reporting of nearly every topic in the news.

In this chapter, you will link practical concepts and formulas with writing skills to counter your "math phobia," and get to the real story while making numbers easy for your audience to grasp.

WHY MATH MATTERS

Roger Simon was never very good at math, but this didn't prevent him from becoming a journalist. After all, he was a good writer. But there was one problem, he recalled in a column written decades after his rookie days. "I found I needed math all the time."

- For police stories, he needed arithmetic:

    "If the gunman entered the bank at 4:17 p.m., and the hostages were not released until 1:02 a.m., how long were they held captive?"

- For property tax stories, he needed to know how to calculate percentages.

    "If the average county tax bill was $3,334.47 last year, and this year it's $4,567.29, by what percentage did it increase?"

"Slowly and painfully, I had to learn in real life what I had not learned in school," said Simon, who became an award-winning columnist and best-selling author, and is now chief political columnist for Politico.com, a Web site devoted to national politics and elections.

There's a name for his ailment: innumeracy, defined by mathematician John Allen Paulos as "an inability to deal comfortably with fundamental notions of number and chance."

Had Simon been illiterate, there's no way he could be a journalist. Being math-challenged didn't matter. Newsrooms are full of innumerates.

MAKING NEWS WITH NUMBERS

Erik Olson, government reporter for *The Chronicle* in Centralia, Washington, crunches numbers on his beat with "a regular calculator, conveniently located on the dashboard of my new Mac computer, and my pencil and paper."

RECOMMENDED COUNTYWIDE TAXES AND MILLAGE RATES BASED ON JUNE 1ST ROLL

	FY 2006 (Millions)	FY 2007 (Millions)	$ Increase (Millions)	
General Fund	793.1	870.6	77.5	
General Capital Outlay	41.1	41.1	0.0	
General Obligation Debt Service	64.8	66.6	1.8	
Total	899.0	978.3	79.3	8.8%
Millage Rate	6.7830	6.2038	----------	(8.5%)

To demonstrate the accuracy of numbers in her stories, *Miami Herald* reporter Erika Bolstad provided her editors with her handwritten math calculations for a budget story.

Olson faced a puzzle on his beat one day. An independent citizens' salary commission recommended increases in wages for county officials. But there were holes in their report. It provided percent increases along with officials' current salaries, but left out how the changes would affect their future pay. "That left it to me," Olson said, "to crunch the numbers." Armed only with the desktop calculator on his computer, Olson got his results in just three steps:

1. First he converted the percentage increase—8.02 percent for the sheriff, 5.52 percent for prosecutor—into a decimal by dividing the percentage by 100.
2. Then he multiplied the percentage increase by the current salary—the sheriff's $71,644, the prosecutor's $99,552—to determine the amount of the increase.
3. Finally, he added the amount of the dollar increase to the original salary figure. The results:

The sheriff's salary increased to $77,399.

The prosecutor's pay jumped to $105,047.

The median household income in the county, Olson said, is "roughly $40,000."

County commissioners rejected the pay hikes.

> **❝Journalists need math skills to make sense of numbers the way they need language skills to make sense of words.❞**
>
> —DEBORAH POTTER, DIRECTOR, NEWSLAB, A WASHINGTON DC GROUP DEVOTED TO IMPROVING LOCAL TV NEWS

BASIC MATH SKILLS

As Erik Olson's story demonstrates, good journalism often rests on math skills, ranging from the arithmetic you learned as a child to statistics and other advanced formulas that stump adults. Here are the fundamental skills you must master:

Deborah Potter

QUICK Tips ⏱ MATH FOR JOURNALISTS: REQUIRED SKILLS

- Basic working knowledge of arithmetic

- Familiarity with statistics

- Ability to calculate percentages, ratios, rates of change and other relationships between numbers

- Ability to translate numbers into terms that readers and viewers can understand

- Knowing the difference between median, mean and mode averages

- Understanding of margin of error in polling

- Basic understanding of probability theory

- Understanding of graphs and other pictorial representations of numbers ▼

—*The Poynter Institute*

Average. An average is a way to summarize a set of numbers with a single number: teacher salaries, batting averages or, most familiar to students, grade point averages. These are generally the simplest calculations among those you'll need to perform regularly.

There are three types of averages: the mean, the median and the mode. The purpose of all averages is to indicate a central tendency in a given set of values. Most people, including journalists, confuse the three types of averages and when to use them.

- **Mean**. The sum of a set of numbers divided by the number of terms in the set. The mean is usually the figure that people refer to as "the average."

  Formula: Mean = Sum of terms/Number of terms

  When to use: When the distribution of values, from low to high, is fairly even across the entire range; otherwise the mean will be skewed by outlying numbers or errors that are biased toward a minority of values in the set.

  Problem: In her first semester of college, Caitlin received one A, four B's and two C's. (An A equals four grade points, a B three grade points, a C two grade points.) What was her grade point average?

  Solution:
  1. Add up the grades (sum of the terms).
     $$4 + 3 + 3 + 3 + 3 + 2 + 2 = 20$$
  2. Divide that total by the number of terms in the set.
     $$20/7 = 2.86$$
  3. Caitlin's GPA is 2.86.

  But the mean can mislead, especially when one of the numbers in the set is significantly larger or smaller. That's where the median comes in.

- **Median**. When individual values are put in order by size, the median is equal to the middle value. The median is also known as the middle number or the midpoint. When the total set consists of an even number of values and there is literally no given middle value, the median is calculated as the mean of the two middle values.

  Formula: Set terms in a line in order of size and select the middle number.

  When to use: When the set of numbers includes extreme cases, an inconsistent number of values at the high and low ends of the range or possible errors, the median is the more informative, more accurate and fairer type of average.

Problem: At HyperNews, an online news site, the president makes $200,000 a year, the managing editor makes $55,000, the programmer makes $50,000, the ad sales representative makes $45,000, a reporter and a graphic artist make $35,000 each, and the office receptionist makes $20,000. What's the average salary? If you calculate the mean (the most common choice), the answer is $63,000. But try telling the programmer, ad rep, reporter or receptionist that the average salary at HyperNews is $63,000, and they'll choke on their lattes. That's because the salaries at Hypernews aren't distributed equally—the president makes significantly more than the other employees—which makes the mean unrepresentative.

Solution:

1. Set terms in a line in order of size.

    $20,000; $35,000; $35,000; $45,000; $50,000; $55,000; $200,000

2. Select the middle number.

    $45,000

The median salary average is $45,000.

Here is a case for which you need to find a median from an even set of numbers.

Problem: Burglaries in Pleasantville for each of the first six months of the year were 8, 10, 12, 35, 70, 45. What was the median number of burglaries committed?

Solution:

1. Set out the numbers in a line, by order of size.

    8, 10, 12, 35, 45, 70

2. Add the two middle numbers.

    $12 + 35 = 47$

3. Divide the result by 2.

    $47/2 = 23.5$

The median number of burglaries during the first six months of the year is 23.5.

- **Mode**. The number that appears most often in a set of numbers. The mode is valuable when seeking the most commonly occurring value in a set of information, for example, how many houses sold for the same price in a given community, how many yes or no votes a bill received in Congress or the results of a constitutional referendum.

    Formula: Count each time a value appears and select the value that appears most often.

    When to use: When seeking the most common value in a set of values.

    Problem: The city council is reviewing construction bids for a new police station. Which value represents the mode in this bidding process?

    Firm A: $10 million

    Firms B, C and D: $12.5 million

    Firms E and F: $13 million

    Firm G: $14 million

Solution:
1. Count each time a number appears.
   $10 million once
   $12.5 million three times
   $13 million twice
   $14 million once
2. Select number that appears most often.
   $12.5 million.
The most common construction bid is $12.5 million.

PERCENTAGES, RATES, PERCENTS, PER CAPITA

Somewhat more complex than averages, percentages, rates and percents can mislead journalists or enable them to find the real story behind the numbers.

- **Percentage.** Calculating percentages is the most common math problem journalists encounter, whatever their assignment. What percentage of the school budget went to teacher salaries? What percentage of convicted arsonists went to prison or got probation? What percentage of the vote went to Republicans or Democrats?

  A percentage is the rate or amount of a given item in each hundred. This value is expressed as a portion of 100 in units of 1/100ths. It is primarily a way of expressing a number as a fraction of 100, when 100 equals the whole.

  Formula: Divide the number you want to find the percentage of by the whole. Then multiply the result, known as the quotient, by 100.

  When to use: When finding the significance of a given value in relation to the whole.

  Problem: The $1.2 million school budget includes $700,000 in teachers' salaries. What percentage of the school budget goes to teacher salaries?

  Solution:
  1. Divide the number you want to find the percentage of by the whole.
     $700,000/$1,200,000 = 0.5833
  2. Multiply the result, known as the quotient, by 100.
     0.5833 × 100 = 58.3 percent

  Fifty-eight percent of the school budget goes to teacher salaries.

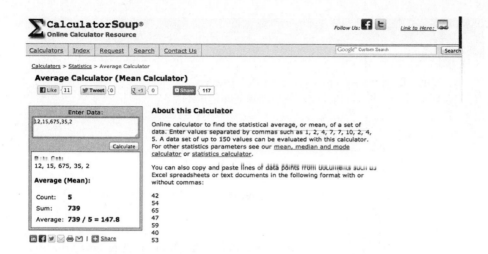

Journalists can turn to the Internet to solve math problems, such as computing averages, that often turn up in their reporting.

- **Rate**. Rate is a ratio, or comparison, of two measurements, usually involving two different units of measure. Typically, a rate measures an individual unit value (e.g., length, mass, or type of event) against a quantity (e.g., time or numeric value): miles per hour, heartbeats per minute, false positive diagnoses per 100 cases or jet engine failures per 1,000 flights.

  Formula: Divide the part by the whole.

  When to Use: When you need to explain the scope or frequency of an occurrence.

  Problem: Motor vehicle deaths on Tyrone Boulevard totaled 48 this year. On U.S. 41 during the same period, 60 people died. Which highway is more dangerous? At first glance, the obvious answer is U.S. 41, with 12 more deaths than Tyrone Boulevard—until you determine the rate by comparing total deaths to a whole, in this case, deaths per highway mile.

  Solution:

  1. Determine length of each highway.

     Tyrone Boulevard is 12 miles long.

     U.S. 41 is 40 miles long.

  2. Divide number of highway deaths by highway mile.

     48 deaths/12 miles = 4 deaths per mile

     60 deaths/40 miles = 1.5 deaths per mile

  Measured by deaths per mile, Tyrone Boulevard is the most dangerous road.

- **Percent**. Percents, the rate per 100 of something, enable you to convey how one value differs from another. Real estate taxes went up from the previous year. By what percent? Crime is down or up from the year before. By what percent? These can vary in complexity, as we'll discuss here.

  Problem: Population in Fairweather County totaled 220,000 in 1997. In 2007, it totaled 355,000. By what percent did it increase?

  Solution:

  1. Subtract old value from new value to find out absolute number of increase or decrease.

     355,000 (2007 pop.) - 220,000 (1997 pop.) = 135,000

CONVERGENCE POINT

Online Calculators

It's one thing to be able to perform basic mathematical functions in your head or with a standard calculator, but for more complex functions it's a good idea to get some help. Fortunately, there are online resources that make this process much easier.

- 3-way percent calculator

- Inflation calculator

- Every conceivable calculator—more than 24,000 at last count

Find this link on the companion Web site at **www.oup.com/us/ scanlan.**

Calculating percent changes can be challenging, but an online calculator makes the math easy.

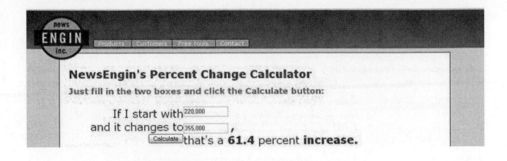

2. Divide absolute number of increase or decrease by old value.
   135,000/220,000 = 0.6136
3. Multiply by 100.
   0.6136 × 100 = 61 rounded off (Rounding off means shortening the least significant digit or digits of a number and changing the remaining number to be as near as possible to the original one. Round down if the number is closest to the lower digit/s . Round up if the number is closer to the highest digit/s. The figure 36.6 can be rounded up to 37 while 36.1 can be rounded down to 36. The process makes numbers easier to process.
4. Add "percent."
   61 percent

The population in Fairweather County increased by 61 percent between 1997 and 2007.

Changing Decimals to Percents and Vice Versa

Many math problems rely on the ability to change a decimal to a percent or to change a fraction into a decimal.

To change a decimal into a percentage, there are two options:
   1. Move the decimal point two places to the right.
      Example: 0.53 = 53 percent
   2. Multiply the decimal by 100
      0.53 × 100 = 53 percent

To change a percent to a decimal, there are two options:
   1. Move the decimal point two places to the left.
      Example: 53 percent = 0.53
   2. Divide the percentage by 100.
      53/100 = 0.53

As Erik Olson's pay raise story shows, sometimes a math problem involves a missing number.

   Problem: The budget for the girls volleyball team is $4,800. The school board cut the budget by 20 percent. How much did the board cut?

   Formula: Percent × Whole = Part

   Solution: Change percent to decimal: 20 percent = 0.20
      Multiple decimal by whole: 0.20 × 4,800 = 960

The board cut the team budget by $960.

- **Per-capita rate**. Per capita is the rate per person of population. This term is commonly used by reporters covering a particular beat, city, neighborhood or other distinct area for a local news outlet.

  Formula: Divide the value (crimes, heart attacks) by total population. To discover the rates per 100, a more understandable comparison, multiply by 100.

  When to use: When you want to compare two or more populations using a common statistic (e.g., murder rate in different cities, sales of ice cream in Japan versus Bolivia)

  Problem: In a neighborhood of 1,000 persons, 20 speeding tickets were issued in one month. What is the per-capita rate?

  Solution:
  1. Divide the value by total population.

     20/1,000 = 0.02 per capita rate
  2. Multiply rate by 100.

     $0.02 \times 100 = 2$

  Two speeding tickets were handed out for every 100 neighborhood residents.

ADVANCED MATH SKILLS

Even reporters who consider themselves fairly conversant in math can become intimidated at the notion of "number crunching"—handling large batches of numbers using sophisticated techniques of analysis. For those of us who are dubious about anything beyond 2 + 2, the idea of having to analyze numbers can be terrifying. Fortunately, a basic understanding of some concepts can help a reporter greatly, and today's computer software can translate that basic knowledge into data that can add new dimensions to stories.

Statistics

To put it simply, statistics transform large amounts of information into smaller quantities that are easier to grasp. Statistics are used for a variety of purposes. For journalists, just two matter: statistics as a *descriptive tool* and as a method for *testing inferences*. **Descriptive statistics** include the following:

- **Nominal measurements**. A statistical method that sorts things into categories, such as the number of men and women in a class, and expresses them as whole numbers or percentages and counts them, often to powerful effect. For example, between March 1993 and Sept. 2004, more than 1,000 military personnel had died in the first Iraq War, the Associated Press reported: "The youngest was just 18. The oldest was 59. More than half had not seen their 30th birthdays . . . 97 percent were men; two dozen were women. While more than 600 were white, others were black, Hispanic, Asian and American Indian—including the first Indian woman killed in combat while fighting for the U.S. military."

Ethical Dilemmas REPORTING A DUBIOUS STATISTIC

A news release from a coalition of church groups in your community calls for the Federal Communications Commission to take action against television stations for broadcasting children's shows that depict acts of violence. To support its cause, the coalition says the American Psychological Association found that "the average child watches 8,000 televised murders and 100,000 acts of violence before finishing elementary school." It's a specific, startling and, you believe, newsworthy statistic. But you wonder about its accuracy. You do an Internet search and find the exact statement repeated countless times on the Web, but can't find the source of the statistic. You're on a tight deadline. Do you repeat what the group says in its release? What do you need to know before you are comfortable using the figures? ▶

CONVERGENCE POINT ⚡

Statistics for Journalists

Robert Niles makes statistics an easy-to-understand tool for journalists trying to make sense of numbers. His site reinforces the basics—averages, per capita and rates—but also makes clear the intricacies of standard deviation, normal distribution and confidence interval. He provides an indispensable guide to data analysis that ensures that your stories aren't tripped up by faulty data.

Find this link on the companion Web site at **www.oup.com/us/ scanlan.**

❝ **The next time you hear someone say, 'everything's going up,' adjust for inflation.** ❞

—NEILL A. BOROWSKI, EXECUTIVE EDITOR, *THE PRESS OF ATLANTIC CITY* (NJ)

- **Ordinal measurement** ranks things—for example, good, better, best; first, second, third—along some relevant dimension.
- **Interval measurement** determines by how much things differ from each other, such as height in inches.

Inferential statistics go beyond merely reporting how much or how many of something there might be. This field lets journalists try to provide measurable parallels and correlations between numbers and the real-world conditions that might cause or reflect them. For example, we might assume there's a link between rising unemployment and a rising crime rate, but is there a way to statistically support such a link? By measuring the extent to which two things vary together, we can find evidence to suggest causation, and can even make predictions based on past events.

The most common methods of analyzing potential parallels are the **t-test**, which examines probability distribution, the **ANOVA**, an analysis of the variance between groups of numbers, and the **regression analysis**, which examines the relationship between dependent and independent variables.

If this all sounds like a foreign language to you, don't worry about it for now, but make a strong effort to learn more about these terms to enhance your skills. Such statistical techniques are important to journalists because they help "sort out the phenomena which seem to require explanation from those that have a good likelihood of being due to nothing more than chance," says veteran journalist and computer-assisted reporting (CAR) expert Philip Meyer.

Vital Statistics

"**Vital statistics** are the statistics of life, health, disease and death, the statistics of much that we hold dear and much that we fear," Victor Cohn and Lewis Cope write in *News and Numbers: A Writer's Guide to Statistics*. Such statistics are usually expressed as rates—basically, the amount of one thing over time or in relation to a unit of something else.

There are four types of vital statistics that you should understand, especially if your story concerns health, science or medicine.

1. **Incidence.** The number or ratio of people in a certain population who are affected by an event or calamity during a certain period of time.

2. **Prevalence**. The proportion of persons who have a disease in a given period of time. It includes new cases and existing cases.
3. **Morbidity**. The number or ratio of a disease or all illnesses in a given population.
4. **Mortality**. The number or ratio of deaths during a certain time in a given population.

Standard Deviation

The **standard deviation**—that determines how much numbers vary around the average—is a useful measurement that can help you find stories behind the numbers. Why, for example, are one school's test scores higher than another's? At first glance, you might assume one group of children is smarter, but further reporting could discover that the school with higher scores has a larger percentage of gifted students.

Adjusting for Inflation

Adjusting for **inflation** (an increase in the price of goods and services) is important in stories where you compare the current monetary value of something to what it was worth a certain number of years ago. When discussing everything from salaries to property values to consumer

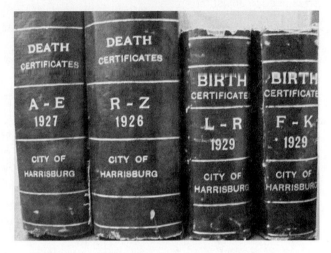

Vital statistics chronicle births, deaths, marriages and other milestones of society and can often be found online. Before the Internet, most vital statistics were collected in thick volumes—they still exist in some jurisdictions—such as this shelf of birth and death statistics in Harrisburg, PA, from the late 1920s.

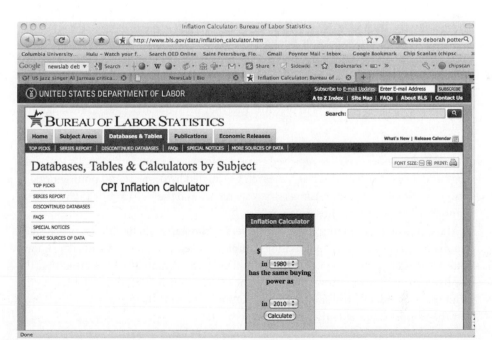

Failure to adjust for inflation renders many stories inaccurate. The U.S. Bureau of Labor Statistics provides online access to the Consumer Price Index and a calculator to accurately compare the current worth of goods and services to the same amount years ago.

CONVERGENCE POINT ⭥

CPI Inflation Calculator

To provide relevant comparisons, journalists often need to adjust the cost of goods and services for inflation using the Consumer Price Index. The Bureau of Labor Statistics provides a handy online calculator to help in computing these figures, enabling comparisons between costs for every year from 1913.

Find this link on the companion Web site at **www.oup.com/us/ scanlan.**

prices, you'll need to remember that a dollar's buying power today does not equate to what it was worth in previous years.

Formula: In the United States, adjusting for inflation requires access to the Consumer Price Index (CPI) for the years in question. If you're looking at price differences between one year and the next, it's a fairly easy calculation—if the CPI jumps 2 percent from one year to the next, you can adjust for inflation by adding 2 percent to what money spent last year would equal this year. Across many years, however, this becomes more difficult.

The Bureau of Labor Statistics, which keeps this data, provides an online inflation calculator that shows the value of current dollars in an earlier year and to calculate the current value of dollar amounts from years ago. This is an enormously handy tool for journalists, and often reveals some fairly staggering figures. For example, adjusting for inflation, to purchase what a dollar would buy in 1913 (the first year covered by the calculator) would cost $23 in 2012. A house that cost $35,000 in 1960 would in 2012 cost in excess of $269,000.

You can see why this would be so important in fairly representing assorted figures across decades and how failing to adjust for inflation can cause embarrassing errors.

In July 2011, Reuters reported the following: "Gold prices hit a record high of $1,622.89 an ounce on Wednesday, as stalled U.S. budget talks fueled fears of a default and drove investors to seek haven in bullion." The only problem: The story did not take inflation into account, says Phillip Blanchard, a former copy editor writing for the Donald W. Reynolds National Center for Business Journalism Web site. "Gold sold for about $850 an ounce in January 1980," Blanchard noted. "That's more than $2,400 in 2011 dollars. No record [was set]. You have to adjust for inflation." His advice: "Be wary of 'record' claims. Check them out."

POLLS AND SURVEYS

Polls are usually short questionnaires, often with only a handful of questions posed as multiple choice. Surveys are generally longer, probe in depth, using a range of question types. Both seek numbers to provide information about attitudes, knowledge and behavior.

It's important to recognize that there's a difference between the professional surveys whose numbers you see reported in news stories and less formal polls found on blogs and other Web sites. Survey research conducted by professional polling organizations, political campaigns, university researchers and the like usually involves large numbers of respondents chosen at random.

Margin of error (or "sampling error") refers to the statistical likelihood of accuracy of polls or surveys based on population samples. By selecting respondents at random, pollsters can use mathematical probability theory to estimate the likelihood that the results accurately reflect the opinion of the population in question. The larger the group of respondents, the smaller the sampling error and the greater the likelihood that the sample represents the population as a whole.

The Coaching Way ᛁᛁᛁ DOING THE MATH

1. Have you added these questions, from mathematician John Allen Paulos, to the traditional five W's, an H and SW?
   - How many?
   - How far?
   - How likely?
   - What percentage?
   - What rate?
2. Have you looked for the reality behind the numbers: how budget cuts affect university staff, city workers, school arts programs, hospital patients?

3. Have you considered how graphics and other pictorial representations can better convey the power of numbers in visual fashion?
4. When's the last time you brushed up on your math skills? Why not choose from online training resources listed in this chapter?
5. Do you look for analogies and metaphors to make numbers come alive in readers' minds?
6. Have you remembered that numbers can numb and followed writing coach Bill Blundell's rule:

"Try not to let two paragraphs with numbers bump against each other"?
7. Identify math experts in your newsroom, on your beat or in local schools that can backstop your math. Ask for tutoring help or get them to check the numbers and analysis in your stories to ensure accuracy.
8. Inventory your math problems that crop up regularly, such as inability to calculate percentage changes, and focus on mastering them. ▼

On the other hand, most online polls don't randomize users—people decide on their own whether or not to respond—which means mathematical probability sampling can't be used to determine the likely validity of their results. These are called self-sampled surveys because the respondents volunteer to respond—select themselves—on their own.

This doesn't mean online polls have no value, just that they're nonscientific—there's no way to statistically measure whether their results are valid. When people can choose whether or not to respond, most often the results skew toward the extremes—people who care passionately about the topic on one side or another will vote—while most others will simply skip it. This is why most online polls are for entertainment value only and shouldn't be treated the same way by journalists (or anyone else, for that matter) as scientific polls. It's important to make this distinction evident in your stories.

A statistically significant survey, says Philip Meyer, a pioneer in teaching math to journalists, has three characteristics:

1. The population surveyed must be clearly defined in advance.
2. Every member of the population must have a known probability of being included in the sample.
3. Everyone must be asked the same questions, and answers must be recorded in the same way.

As a reporter, you should approach all polling data with a wary eye. Many polls, especially national ones, under-represent the opinions of minorities and the poor. Ask who was polled, and how. In many cases, voters who don't have a landline phone won't be included. And make sure if you write about a survey that you share this kind of information with your audience.

CONVERGENCE POINT ⸕

Understanding Survey Error

The Roper Center for Public Opinion Research boasts archives dating back to the 1930s, when polling was in its infancy. It provides learning resources to make journalists and citizens more knowledgeable about the role and methods of polling, including frequently asked questions that will enhance your ability to write with authority and clarity about polls that dominate public discourse.

Find this link on the companion Web site at **www.oup.com/us/ scanlan.**

REPORTING ON BUDGETS

One of the most important things journalists report on is how government spends public money. But news organizations often shortchange the public with reporting that is superficial and uninformed.

To offset that limitation, reporters and editors at *The* (Portland) *Oregonian* are encouraged to consider the following topics in every story:

- Dollar amount of current year's budget.
- Dollar amount of proposed or new budget.
- Percentage change (increase or decrease) new budget represents.
- Impact of changes on individuals—teachers, CEO's, average-income taxpayers.
- Winners and losers in budget process—who wanted what, who got what?
- Sources who will counterbalance what government officials say about their own budgets.

Reporters don't like writing about budgets. For many, says Dave Herzog, a former investigative reporter at *The Providence Journal*, it's on a par with going to the dentist: It's something we know we have to do, we don't like doing it, and it's pretty painful while we are doing it.

First, change your definition of a budget from a stack of computer printouts littered with unintelligible numbers. It's an operating plan, Herzog says. It sets out the vision of the school or town. You learn what your political leaders value. What do they spend money on? A budget is a very political document.

Budgets may be filled with dry numbers, but there are powerful stories lurking behind those numbers. *Journal* reporters looked at the expense account vouchers of school committee members in one suburb. Their story reported that committee members put in for babysitting fees and donations made at funerals.

Budgets typically make news when they are presented, argued over and voted on. After that, reporters ignore them. Herzog advises reporters to go out and see what impact the budget is having. When a reporter toured a high school, he learned that students had to do their dissections on rotten frogs because the school did not have money for fresh ones. That image did a better job than a number would to convey the school's funding woes.

And remember: Not all math is complicated. Some important calculations can be figured out using the tools we all learned in elementary school. For example, you can use long division to determine how much your community spends for education for each child in town. If the school budget is $4 million, and there are 2,000 kids of school age, the per-capita spending rate is determined by dividing the budget by the number of children: $4,000,000/2,000 = $2,000 per child.

There's more to a budget than rows of numbers. Herzog advises reporters to supplement their knowledge by studying other budget-related documents.

- *Annual report.* This is the official feel-good document put out by the town, describing the good things that are happening.
- *Audited financial statement.* This will tell you what is really happening financially in the town. It will say if there are any deficits, pending litigation or

retirement account problems and will include the management letter. The latter describes problems the auditors have found, and often makes recommendations that are repeated year after year.

- *Bond official statement.* Whenever a town needs to borrow money for a big capital project, it floats a bond, and it needs to prepare this document. It includes demographics and the financial condition of the town to help investors in deciding whether to invest in the bonds.
- *Watchdog group report.* In Rhode Island, the Public Expenditure Council Reports analyze property tax rates in all municipalities in the state, equalizes them and then makes comparisons. Check to see if there is a counterpart in your state.
- *Credit report.* Moody's and Standard & Poor both prepare reports on the financial condition of a town. They can be extremely helpful. A good textbook on municipal finance will also be helpful.

SEE CLOSE-UP, P. 213: BUDGET STORY

Tips for Reporting About Budgets

Reporter Dave Herzog offers reporters advice for reporting and writing more effectively about budgets:

- Break out of the mindset that a budget is a dry collection of numbers that you report on a couple of times during the financial season. Remember that it is a document that charts your town's plan for the coming year and reflects the political values of the people who put it together.
- Approach the budget and town financial reporting as a cycle that unfolds during the year. As you do the event-driven stories, keep an eye open for possible enterprise stories.
- Look at the bottom lines. If spending is greater than income, your town will run a deficit.
- Look for stories you can do before the budget is released. For example, you can analyze the budgets from the past 5 or 10 years and discover trends that are important to readers.
- Always adjust for inflation when looking at budgets over time. This will save you from making the embarrassing mistake of writing that spending has doubled in your town. The best way to adjust for inflation is by using the Consumer Price Index. In the example that follows, you can see that what looks like a 50 percent rise over the past decade really is a 5.7 percent rise. (Find the Consumer Price Index online at http://www.bls.gov/data/inflation_calculator.htm.

     1988 spending: $1,000,000
     1988 adjusted: $1,418,624
     1998 spending: $1,500,000
     CPI 1988: 119.2
     CPI 1998: 169.1
     Real difference: $81,376
     Real change: 5.7%

- Put your budget-day stories into context by telling readers whether taxes will go up and by how much. Illustrate by showing what would happen to the tax bill of a "typical" property.
- Make budget-day stories meaningful for readers by telling them what services they're going to be getting or losing. Find out who the winners and losers are.
- Get wish lists from department heads and check to see whether their priorities got into the budget. If not, what are the implications?
- Pick one interesting or unusual part of the budget and write about it some time during the budget cycle. Tell readers something they didn't know before.
- Look at independent audits. These documents cast a cold eye on a town's spending and show what really happened in a fiscal year. Look for deficits in all the funds—not just the general fund.
- Check whether the budgeters are moving functions into enterprise funds. These funds are supposed to pay for themselves and cover government functions that you can measure. An example: providing water service.
- Read the management letters in the audits. There's where you will find criticism of the town's policies and practices.
- Read credit reports and bond official statements. The bond official statements will report, in gory detail, the financial condition of the town and possible risks

QUICK Tips ⏱ BACKSTOPPING NUMBERS IN YOUR STORIES

Use statistical methods as safe-guards, advises Brant Houston of Investigative Reporters and Editors. "They should not make journalists leap to conclusions, but they should prompt journalists to question the veracity of their perceptions and assumptions or those of the people the journalists are covering."

Get help. Copy editors are often the most numerate people in the newsroom. Ask a high school or college math teacher for help. Often knowledgeable sources will be glad to check the accuracy of your computations. After all, it's often in their interest that numbers in a story are correct. Kelly Ryan, who covered city hall for the *St. Petersburg Times*, says a top city budget official was willing to spend time to help clear up any

confusion over budgetary matters, even late at night when Ryan was on deadline.

Questions to ask when dealing with data:

■ Where did the data come from?

■ Have the data been peer reviewed?

■ How were the data collected?

And a warning: Be skeptical when dealing with comparisons. "If you're going to use a number, you'd better know where it comes from, how reliable it is and whether it means what it seems to mean. The garbage-in, garbage-out problem has been with us a long time," says *Newsweek*'s economics columnist Robert Samuelson.

If you're having trouble with numbers in your reporting or writing, mathematician Paulos suggests these techniques:

■ Use smaller numbers.

■ Collect information relevant to the problem.

■ Work backward from the solution.

■ Draw pictures and diagrams. "I can't think without a picture," says Greg Martin, a college teacher who specializes in training math teachers.

■ Compare the problem or parts of the problem to problems you do understand. ▟

to investors. The credit reports, available from ratings agencies (Moody's and Standard & Poor), do a nice job of outlining a town's finances in clear terms.

- Learn how to use a spreadsheet and use it to analyze your budgets.
- Get reports from the state's expenditure council or any other agency that monitors municipal finances and taxation.
- If your town has big year-end surpluses, ask why. Officials may say it's from conservative fiscal practices. It may actually be because they're intentionally asking for money in the budget and not spending it.
- Look to see if the town is setting aside money for legal fees and settlements. If that's happening, the town may be planning to close a lawsuit by settling with a plaintiff.
- Find out whether municipal contracts are set to expire. If the town is negotiating contracts, what effect will these contracts have on the budget (and vice versa)?

Remember that the budget is a living document that has application year-round. Keep it on your desk and refer to it often.

WRITING WITH NUMBERS

Numbers are not just a tool for analysis. Once you've figured out the numbers for your story, the next step is to be able to use them clearly in your writing.

"No matter how rigorous your analysis, numbers aren't a story," says Jeff South, former database editor for the *Austin American-Statesman* who now teaches at Virginia Commonwealth University. "Words, not data, make a story. Your analysis will shape the story; it might be the foundation for the story. But you must tell the story in a way that connects with people who don't know a spreadsheet from a cookie sheet. And that means, ironically, telling the story almost as if it didn't involve computer analysis."

Mathematics is a precise science and requires semantic as well as numerical precision. Even experienced journalists get sloppy when writing about numbers. At *The New York Times*, reporters have been known to use the word "shortfall"—which means the quantity or extent by which something falls short—to mean shortage, decline, unpaid bill, difference, unmet budget, request, debt, remainder and deficit. Avoid jargon. Bureaucrats may use terms such as "revenue" and "expenditures"; keep it simple with "income" and "spending."

In the book *A Mathematician Reads the Newspaper*, John Allen Paulos points out how descriptions of relationships between numbers vary according to the intentions of the person using them. Want to make something appear small? Stress its volume. Want the same object to appear huge? Describe its size in a linear measure. Take four million nickels. Sounds like a lot. But they would fit easily into a cubical box measuring six feet on each side. Doesn't sound too big, does it? But stack those same four million nickels on top of one another, and you'd have a tower that stretched from sea level to the top of Mount Everest.

Paulos offers another example, one with greater relevance to journalists: the number of people affected by an illness, accident or other misfortune. Want to make it seem like a huge problem? Use the number of people affected nationally. So if 1 out of 100,000 people suffers from some illness, that's 2,500 people around the country, a figure that could cause alarm, especially if the news reports include heart breaking stories about individual victims. Want the problem to appear small? Report the incidence rate. Say that there would be just one victim in a crowd that could fill not one but two jam-packed sports stadiums, and the problem seems minuscule.

Tools for Writing With Numbers

Comparison shopping: "When you do use a figure in a story, put it in context by comparing it to something else. A number has little significance on its own; its true meaning comes from its *relative* value," says Paul Hemp, author of *Ten Practical Tips for Business and Economic Reporting in Developing Economies*.

When you use a statistic, compare it to another time, such as an earlier year, or another place, to something people can relate to. That's what this Associated Press writer did in a story about transportation fatalities by comparing the previous year's transportation fatalities with the population of three communities familiar in three major regions of the country:

▶**EXAMPLE** WASHINGTON (AP) — Travel in America claimed the lives of more than 44,000 people last year—roughly the population of Wilkes-Barre, Pa., Palatine, Ill., or Covina, Calif.

Round off and substitute. Economists and financial experts need exact numbers. Readers don't. If 33 percent of the drivers in fatal crashes had alcohol in their blood, it will be clearer if you say, "One in three drivers had been drinking."

Think visually. Make quantities visible in the mind's eye. In an article about the excavation of World War II planes that crashed in the marshes and swamps of the Netherlands, author Les Daly used this vivid picture to convey the enormity of the 7,000 crashes: "To put it another way, the crash of 7,000 aircraft would mean that every square mile of the state of New Jersey would have shaken to the impact of a downed plane."

Use analogies. A poet's tool can help readers grasp abstract numbers. Analogies explain the unfamiliar by comparing it to something familiar. AP Science writer Seth Bronstein used the device to explain how much money a CEO's multimillion salary represents by relating it to other salaries.

Top CEO pay equals 3,489 years for typical worker.

▶**EXAMPLE** David Simon of Simon Property received a pay package worth more than $137 million for last year, and the typical CEO took home $9.6 million, according to an analysis by The Associated Press.

Here are some ways to think about just how much money those salaries represent.

Simon's $137 million is almost entirely in stock awards that could eventually be worth $132 million. The company said it wanted to make sure Simon wasn't lured to another company.

How long it takes others to make that much: A minimum wage worker—paid $7.25 per hour, as some workers at Simon malls are—would have to work one month shy of 9,096 years to make what Simon made last year. A person making the national median salary, $39,312 by AP calculations, would have to work 3,489 years.

By the hour: Assuming Simon worked a 60-hour week, his pay was $43,963.64 per hour, or $732.73 per minute. To put that in perspective, the minimum-wage worker would have to labor for nearly three years to make what Simon earns in an hour. The average U.S. worker makes slightly less in one year than Simon makes in an hour.

Compared with America's CEO: Simon makes about 342 times the $400,000 annual salary of President Barack Obama. In fact, if you add the salaries of Obama, Vice President Joe Biden, the Cabinet, the Supreme Court justices, all the members of the Senate and House of Representatives and all 50 governors, it is less than $110 million, so Simon makes well more than government's top 600 leaders. In the past 100 years, U.S. taxpayers have paid a total of $80.6 million, adjusted for inflation, to presidents from Woodrow Wilson to Obama.

—The Associated Press, May 25, 2012

PROFESSIONALS' ROUNDTABLE | ADDING IT ALL UP

"I don't do math." That excuse from innumerate journalists is no longer acceptable. Math skills are mandatory to survive and thrive in our data-rich world. If you're math-challenged, conversations with three journalists who "do math" offer comforting solutions: Curing math phobia is not so difficult if you keep these ideas in mind.

- Numbers provide perspective and meaning.
- A beat or story without numbers is the exception.
- For many stories, elementary school arithmetic is enough. Formulas and online resources can teach advanced skills.
- Ask for backup. Common sense, critical thinking, a calculator and copy editors can save you from embarrassing errors.

Participants

DAVID CAY JOHNSTON, columnist, Reuters.com

ERIKA BOLSTAD, staff writer, *Miami Herald*

CRAIG SILVERMAN, founder, regrettheerror.com

> *How important are math skills in the daily work of journalism?*

Bolstad: Cops reporters need to understand how crime statistics are collected and calculated to write intelligent crime rate stories. Health care reporters need to understand statistics behind the studies they write about. Political reporters have to write about polls and election statistics. Sports reporters have to have common sense statistical know-how. Schools reporters need to be experts in how standardized tests are compiled.

> *Why are math skills important for journalists?*

Johnston: Numbers allow us to give perspective to news; we all understand that the crash of a single engine plane with only its pilot aboard is not generally as big a story as a jetliner with 200 aboard. Not much math required there.

But what if the mayor announces on deadline that property taxes will have to rise next year by 2.67 percent and says only that the average homeowner paid $136.70 last year? Can you figure out how much the average bill will rise?

> *What math skills should a journalist working today command?*

Johnston: Grammar school arithmetic for starters—addition, subtraction, multiplication and, especially, division. Divide by 100 and you can do percentages, which allows comparisons of scale, as in the property tax example above. Learn to use a spreadsheet, which may seem daunting but is actually quite simple.

> *Your site, Regret the Error, at http://www.poynter.org/category/latest-news/regret-the-error/, tracks math mistakes among other journalistic gaffes. Are journalists simply sloppy, or lacking certain math skills that corrections reveal?*

Silverman: They lack the ability to critically analyze numerical data. There are a lot of organizations that regularly produce specious data—studies, stats etc.—which they think they can get into the newspaper. Journalists always clamor for hard numbers, but I don't think we're well equipped to look at it with a critical eye. People try to take advantage of this; often they succeed.

> *What are the most common math mistakes?*

Johnston: Mixing up M's and B's and T's (million, billion, trillion). Decimal points: is it $10 per or 10 cents per? Inverting digits (786 entered as 768). Not calculating the base correctly (this year's sales minus last year's and then difference divided into last year, NOT this year, to get change). Assuming the numbers in an official announcement are right. They are often rich with math errors.

> *Do you use experts to backstop a numbers-heavy story?*

Bolstad: One of my colleagues is really good at statistics. I often have him double-check my figures. On budget stories, my editor generally asks me to walk her through the steps that I used to get to my results. Our copy desk is good at double-checking these numbers—and I have had late-night calls asking me to show how I arrived at my numbers. (And correcting me!)

SUMMARY GUIDE

NUMBERS:
USING ACCURATE FIGURES

WHY MATH MATTERS

Many journalists are uncomfortable with fundamental notions of number and chance. To succeed, they must battle this innumeracy to cope with the constant challenge of using math effectively in their stories.

What to Remember → Beginning journalists soon realize that math matters in journalism. Effective journalists master the fundamentals of math and statistics to succeed in a numbers-driven world.

MAKING NEWS WITH NUMBERS

Numbers dominate the news, generating stories of importance and interest to audiences about property taxes, tuition, sports, finance and the economy.

What to Remember → Numbers routinely appear in news stories. Journalists must be prepared to meet this challenge by learning, or re-learning, the gamut of math skills the job demands.

BASIC MATH SKILLS

The math skills journalists must possess include basic arithmetic, the difference between mean, median and mode averages, and an understanding of statistics and polls.

What to Remember → A math-savvy journalist armed only with raw data and an online calculator can influence public policy. Journalists grasp the power of pictorial representation, and always ask if a graphic gets the point across more effectively than words.

PERCENTAGES, RATES, PERCENTS, PER CAPITA

Journalists rely on definitions, tried-and-true calculation formulas and the knowledge of when and how to use percentages, percents, rates per capita, fractions and the conversion of decimals to percents in news stories.

What to Remember → Understanding the relationship of numbers is a crucial journalistic skill. You've already learned arithmetic and other basic math skills as a child. They may have become rusty through disuse, so a refresher may be necessary.

ADVANCED MATH SKILLS

Statistics are vital in news writing because they transform large amounts of information into smaller, easy-to-understand quantities.

What to Remember → Statistics measure a wide range of human activities that readers care about. They have two purposes: to describe and to test. Understanding standard deviation and how to adjust for inflation avoids inaccurate and embarrassing errors.

POLLS AND SURVEYS

Polls use numbers to measure attitudes, knowledge and behavior, but they should always be viewed with caution.

What to Remember → Even professional polls can deceive since many under-represent the opinions of minorities and the poor. Always report the way the poll was taken and understand the importance of margin of error. Polls may be taken to prove something that may not be accurate, whether it's a political candidate's chances or a scientific theory.

REPORTING ON BUDGETS

Journalists play a vital role in communicating how government spends public money, but news organizations often shortchange the public with superficial and uninformed reporting.

What to Remember → Budgets may be filled with dry numbers, but there are powerful stories lurking behind the data. Smart journalists supplement their knowledge by studying budget-related documents such as annual reports and audits.

WRITING WITH NUMBERS

Effective journalists know how to make figures accessible to audiences and use writing skills to transform numbers into vivid and clear prose.

What to Remember → Skilled journalists know that behind every number is a human being, and they strive to find illustrative examples. They recognize the importance of rounding off and the power of analogies and metaphors to convey statistical information in accurate and compelling fashion.

KEY TERMS

ANOVA, p. 198
average, p. 192
descriptive statistics, p. 197
incidence, p. 198
inferential statistics, p. 198
inflation, p. 199
interval measurement, p. 198
mean, p. 192

median, p. 192
mode, p. 193
morbidity, p. 199
mortality, p. 199
nominal measurements, p. 197
ordinal measurements, p. 198
per-capita rate, p. 197
percent, p. 195

percentage, p. 194
prevalence, p. 199
rate, p. 195
regression analysis, p. 198
standard deviation, p. 199
t-test, p. 198
vital statistics, p. 198

EXERCISES

1. Study a newspaper, news broadcast or online news page and identify which stories include numbers. What math skills did the journalists employ?

2. Identify your common math mistakes. Using the material in this chapter, reacquaint yourself with the rules and formulas that will enable you to avoid them. Learn the ones you don't understand. Keep them all close at hand.

3. Find a math expert in your newsroom or classroom. Ask him/her to verify the numbers in your stories and the ways you generated them.

4. Compute the mean, median and mode averages of the grades you earned in a semester.

5. What percentage of your day do you spend reading news? Increase your reading time. A week later, recalculate the percentage.

6. As a reporter for *The Wall Street Journal*, William Blundell tried to avoid letting two paragraphs with numbers "bump into each other." Look for examples of numbers in the news and see how rarely or closely journalists follow this rule. Assess their readability. Follow his guideline in your stories.

READINGS

Cohn, Victor, and Cope, Lewis. *News & Numbers: A Guide to Reporting Statistical Claims and Controversies in Health and Other Fields.* **Hoboken, NJ: Wiley-Blackwell, 2001.**
The authors examine common uses of numbers in the news, including polls and polling, reporting on disease outbreaks and using the Internet for help. They provide dozens of humbling examples that show how journalists routinely distort numbers out of ignorance and will help you avoid those errors.

Paulos, John Allen. *Innumeracy: Mathematical Illiteracy and Its Consequences.* **New York: Hill and Wang, 1988.**
Paulos is a mathematician and magazine columnist who has made addressing society's inability to cope with numbers a personal crusade. His illuminating book includes examples of innumeracy and journalistic errors, explains the difference between probability and coincidence, highlights the dangers of pseudoscience and explains statistics in readable fashion.

Paulos, John Allen. *A Mathematician Reads the Newspaper.* **New York: Basic Books, 1995.**
Paulos goes after journalistic innumeracy using news stories as case studies to explore journalists' numerical gaffes, including their effects on news gathering, and the dubious conclusions that news organizations routinely make. His findings can help beginning journalists develop habits to avoid these traps.

Meyer, Philip. *Precision Journalism: A Reporter's Introduction to Social Science Methods.* **Lanham, MD: Rowman & Littlefield, 2002.**
In this classic, Meyer provides a sometimes challenging statistics primer that should be required reading for every reporter and editor. He teaches journalists how to use databases and analyze the information to provide accurate statistical analysis to bolster their stories.

Tufte, Edward R. *The Visual Display of Quantitative Information.* **Cheshire, CT: Graphics Press, 1990.**
Tufte is a pioneer in the use of graphics to display numerical information for those who more easily process numbers through imagery. With stunning examples, he provides inspiration for journalists who seek alternative ways to connect audiences with numbers in the news.

Wickham, Kathleen. *Math Tools for Journalists.* **Portland, OR: Marion Street Press, 2002.**
Wickham, a journalism professor, provides a handbook of basic and advanced math that journalists encounter in their daily work. Readable writing, reliable formulas and practical examples make this a must for every journalist's desk.

BUDGET STORY

Budgets reveal how the government spends public money. They also show how expenditures affect the lives of ordinary citizens. Good journalists report the numbers, but they never fail to address how budgets impact government-financed programs, such as schools, sports and arts programs. The following story, which appeared in the *Columbus* (OH) *Dispatch*, is a good example of the way that journalists meet both these responsibilities.

KIDS' ARTS PROGRAMS A VICTIM OF BUDGET CUTS

By Elizabeth Gibson
The Columbus Dispatch, May 4, 2011

The Greater Columbus Arts Council has temporarily suspended some after-school arts programs as well as community arts grants because of funding cuts by Franklin County.

The county is the biggest contributor to the council's arts-in-education programs. But with worries about potential state cuts to local-government funds, the county commissioners decided yesterday to give the council $300,000, a 33 percent reduction from last year.

"I'd like to see it restored," Commissioner Paula Brooks said. "These are strong programs that keep kids off the streets."

The council decided to use the money for a program that helps schools book professional artists and performers to expose children to the arts as well as for after-school arts programs for children and teenagers. But the council ended after-school programs for 5- to 11-year-olds a month early this spring, and it's uncertain whether there will be money for summer youth activities, said Tim Katz, the community arts-education director. At the least, the council plans to have the program back by fall, although maybe with fewer hours.

A summary lead reports a timely, interesting and important newsworthy element: government-sponsored programs lose out in the wake of county budget cuts. It focuses on a specific that readers can relate to rather than beginning with abstract figures.

The story is an inverted pyramid, which uses facts as an organizational model in descending order of newsworthiness and audience interest. Budget numbers come into play now as the story reports the cause of the cuts. The commission's decision is news, but the reporter delivers the news first and then explains the context. In general, moving from the specific to the general makes it easier for audiences to process information. She provides a specific figure and uses a percent reduction to make the impact clearer. Math-savvy journalists always strive to give readers as much information as possible so they can make sense of abstract figures. If the commission cut the budget by 33 percent last year, how much was the budget before the cuts?

It's always important to use a quote early in the story. It introduces a human element that engages readers and presents a point of view about the story. The quotes are brief, which moves the story along.

The time has come for further explanations. The journalist relies on the Five W's and an H to answer relevant questions: *how* the remaining money will be spent, *who* will be affected by the budget cut, *when* the changes took place and *what* are the prospects for summer youth activities. *Why* has been addressed in the second paragraph. The story covers another important question: What next? The reporter attributes the question of impact to a named source, enhancing its credibility. The final sentence reinforces the news that after-school programs will be hurt in the fall. An effective story always presents information that supports the focus, in this case, the impact of budget cuts on after-school programs.

"We hope we can find other funding because these programs really provide something for the most-challenged neighborhoods in the county, where there tends to be the higher crime rates and lower incomes," he said.

Columbus provides the majority of the arts council's $5.3 million budget. But most of the Columbus money supports the city's premier arts groups, such as BalletMet, the Columbus Museum of Art and the Wexner Center for the Arts.

The county money goes exclusively to arts-in-education programs, accounting for nearly two-thirds of the $662,000 spent on arts-in-education last year.

The council estimated that Artists-in-Schools touches 90,000 students with more than 500 events a year, and about 550 youths participate in after-school activities meant to develop artistic skills in addition to teaching self-expression.

The county money also typically includes about $60,000 for 50 community grants that often provide performers for neighborhood events or pay for public works of art. Last year's recipients included the Dublin Arts Council, the New Albany Symphonic Orchestra, the Upper Arlington Cultural Arts Commission and the Grandview Heights Public Library.

There won't be county money for grants this year. But the council still wants to give at least $20,000 in grants, using $10,000 saved from previous years and $10,000 from the council's reserve funds, Katz said.

Drawing from reserves isn't a long-term solution, but he said it at least will keep the program alive until new donors can be found.

Lauren Emond, Upper Arlington's arts coordinator, said local arts groups already have been dealing with cuts. Upper Arlington downsized its cultural-arts division, so it relied on an arts council grant to help pay for the city's first exhibit of 2011.

"I've seen how much GCAC has helped all the small organizations do more with less recently," Emond said. "Maybe they're going to have to start doing less with less."

The reporter gives the source an opportunity to amplify his comments and provide justification for the programs' funding. The quote is valuable because it explains why the programs are important in poorer neighborhoods with higher crime rates. It addresses the critical question, So what? Journalists look for wide-ranging consequences. It's a rather long quote—32 words—but it provides crucial information. Could it be paraphrased in a way that contains some of the speaker's words? Such an approach is useful to make it easier for readers to process the information.

Budget stories are about numbers, but the reporter wisely alternates between the abstract and the concrete. Figures are followed by the names of the specific arts groups supported, organizations that may be familiar to readers.

The story effectively parcels out information in ways that help readers understand the process, the data and the impact.

The second paragraph dives deeper into the numbers, contrasting how much the city of Columbus spends for the arts compared to what the county allocates for arts-in-education programs, which is the focus of the story. In budget stories, comparisons are especially effective.

These paragraphs provide crucial information that lies at the heart of the story: the numbers of students whose lives are touched by the programs that have been cut and community grants that support arts funding. The story is careful to list the names of the groups affected, yet another way to link the budgetary decision to specific organizations and connect with readers who may be familiar with them.

The story provides still more information about the impact of the cuts and the possibility that some of the damage may be eased. Some hope remains. Some sources and readers might complain that this information, which offsets some of the damage caused by the budget cuts, should have appeared higher in the story. But the impact is relatively negligible and less newsworthy, justifying its placement.

The story concludes with a source familiar with the impact of budget cuts.

The quote helps readers understand the value of county funding and, again, supports the story's focus by concluding with a comment that hints at the future impact of reduced funding.

SUMMARY

Budget stories are a challenge to report and write. The journalist must balance between presenting abstract information with specific real-world examples that illustrate what the figures mean. Elizabeth Gibson's story does a good job addressing that balance. As mentioned earlier, numbers can be numbing. Gibson limits the amount of numbers in her 475-word story to just a dozen figures, ranging from dollar amounts and percentages to the numbers of those affected. Readers come away with the knowledge about a governmental decision, the money involved and, most important, how the action will affect the lives of citizens—in this case, children whose lives are enriched by arts-in-education programs. Budget stories are usually written on tight deadlines and often rely on public officials and representatives of affected organizations. A budget story that strives to find people whose lives are affected by the way government spends public money provides readers with anecdotal information that puts a human face on numbers. What other sources could this story include to achieve this goal?

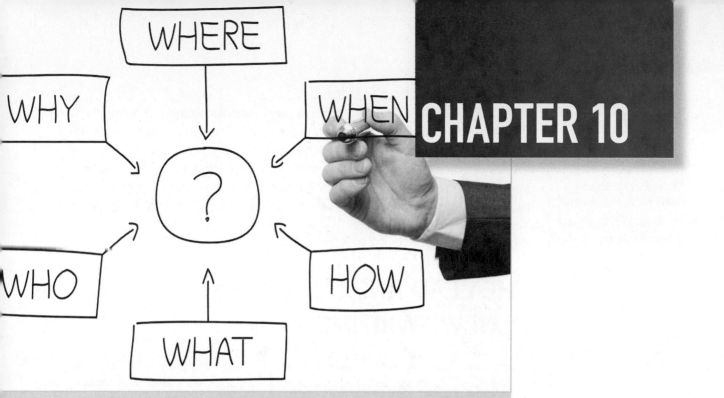

LEAD WRITING

WHETHER ONLINE, IN broadcast or in print, journalists have just moments to grab someone's attention. That's where the lead—newsroom jargon for the beginning of a story—comes in. An effective lead makes a promise to the reader or listener: I have something important, something interesting, to tell you. Lead writing requires critical thinking to distill the material you've collected into its most newsworthy elements, and also creativity to transform that understanding into a single compelling paragraph.

THE LEAD AND ITS ROLE IN NEWS WRITING

When journalists talk about beginnings of stories they use the word "lead," also spelled "lede." Although leads appear at the top of stories, they form their foundation. They are the writer's best and often the only chance at grabbing attention. An eye-catching headline ("USA ATTACKED") or vivid photograph (the iconic images of the World Trade Center collapsing on Sept. 11, 2001) can serve the same purpose.

When the subject is leads, there's no shortage of opinions about their role, their preferred length, the rules they should follow or break. But no one disagrees about this enduring fact of lead writing: It takes effort and experience to write an irresistible one that keeps the reader wanting more.

HOW FIVE W'S, AN H AND SW CREATE COMPELLING LEADS

> **❝**Every story must have a beginning . . . Why is no mystery. Based on the lead, a reader makes a critical decision: Shall I go on?**❞**
>
> —RENE J. CAPPON, AUTHOR, *THE WORD: AN ASSOCIATED PRESS GUIDE TO GOOD NEWS WRITING*

Who?
What?
When?
Where?
Why?
How?
So what?

More than a hundred years ago, Theodore Dreiser, a young reporter, later an acclaimed novelist, learned the importance of five questions from his editor, who had spotted them on a sign posted at a rival's newsroom.

"Over there in the *Tribune* office they have a sign which reads, 'Who or what? How? When? Where?'" he told the rookie. "All those things have to be answered in the first paragraph, do you hear?—not in the last paragraph or the middle paragraph or anywhere but in the first paragraph."

Add "Why?" and "So what?" to the list and you have tools to boil down the answers to those seven questions into an effective lead.

Who?

News is the record of human activity, what people say and do. "Who?" focuses attention on:

- those involved;
- those closest to the action;
- major players; and
- supporters, opponents, victims.

What?

News is about actions, reactions, evidence and intangibles like revenge, loyalty, power, weakness. "What?" takes into account:

- events;
- situations;
- issues;
- impacts;
- arguments; and
- themes.

When?

Timeliness is an essential element of news reporting. "When" helps discover a story's:

- beginning;
- end;
- chronology; and
- key moments.

Where?

News happens in specific places. "Where?" takes your audience to:

- scenes;
- locations;
- settings; and
- the world.

Why?

News explains why events, issues, and trends are significant. "Why" determines:

- causes;
- reasons; and
- attitudes, beliefs.

How?

In a complex society, reporters help people understand how things work. "How" conveys the way news:

- happens;
- develops;
- succeeds/fails; and
- concludes.

So What?

Five W's and an H may still not be enough when people are already overloaded with competing information and distractions. You have to make them understand why your story matters. Asking "So what?" enables you write a lead that honors that need. It enables you to write an informed lead that addresses the impact of news.

An example:

> The news: The school board's proposed budget cuts eliminate arts programs.
> The question: "So what?"
> An answer: "Hundreds of budding musicians, dancers, and actors will lose the chance to practice their art at a time when studies show children in arts classes perform better overall."

66 My leads are there to get you in and to keep you hooked to the story so that you can't go away. 99

—MITCH ALBOM, COLUMNIST, *DETROIT FREE PRESS*

DECONSTRUCTING LEADS

Here are two examples of leads that reflect the various way reporters employ five W's, an H and SW in an information-packed paragraph:

Story 1

Gunmen Make Getaway on City Bus

▶EXAMPLE NEW YORK — Heavily armed gunmen ambushed a payroll delivery and got away with $50,000 after spraying a quiet street with bullets, critically wounding a moonlighting off-duty detective and a retired police officer.

—The Associated Press

WHO?

- Heavily armed gunmen
- Moonlighting off-duty detective
- Retired police officer

WHAT?

- Ambushed payroll delivery
- Critically wounding

WHERE?

- Quiet New York City street

WHEN?

- Not in lead

WHY?

- $50,000

HOW?

- Spraying with bullets

SO WHAT?

- Violence can happen even in on a quiet street.
    Analysis: Aimed at a nationwide audience, this wire service story focuses on the event and players (cops, robbers). Characterizes place ("quiet") but doesn't give precise location.
    Length: 30 words
    Grade: A. Vivid, clear, economical

Story 2

Two Guards Delivering Cash Are Ambushed in Queens

◢EXAMPLE◣ NEW YORK — A frenzied crossfire broke the morning calm of a quiet Queens neighborhood Friday as masked robbers ambushed the two guards of a payroll shipment, leaving the security men—a retired police officer and an off-duty detective—bleeding on the sidewalk with more than a dozen bullet wounds, the authorities said.

—The New York Times

WHO?

- Masked robbers
- Two guards, retired police officer and off-duty detective, bleeding on sidewalk
- Authorities

WHAT?

- Ambush
- Frenzied crossfire

WHERE?

- Quiet Queens, New York, neighborhood sidewalk

WHEN?

- Friday morning

WHY?

- Payroll shipment

HOW?

- Dozen bullet wounds

SO WHAT?

- Even in morning calm, violence can erupt.
  Highlights: Aimed at metropolitan audience, this lead is detailed but gives general description of location (Queens).
  Length: 50 words
  Grade: B-minus. Detail rich but too long

> 66 There is no one way to do leads. . . . Leads need to be both creative and functional, but creativity should not undermine functionality, and functionality should not undermine creativity. 99
>
> —JACQUI BANASZYNSKI, JOURNALISM PROFESSOR, UNIVERSITY OF MISSOURI

Jacqui Banaszynski

DEVELOPING YOUR LEAD FROM A FOCUS

Many new reporters mistakenly believe they will discover the theme of their story by writing a lead. As a result, they waste precious time honing the first paragraph that could be used to report, organize, draft and, most important, revise.

Strong leads emerge from a focus, not the other way around. Speed is the key. Use the questions described in Chapter 2. Give yourself 95 seconds to freewrite answers to five questions to find your theme:

- Why does it matter?
- What's the point?
- Why is the story being told?
- What does this story say about life, about the world, and the times we live in?
- What's the story about—in one word?

This may seem like busywork, but without it, it's likely you will agonize over, and misjudge, how the story should open. Your answers will produce the single dominant message that effective stories demand from the first paragraph to the last. Combined with the five W's, an H and SW, they produce leads that deliver news and meaning.

Once you've identified the news elements and the story's focus, you are ready to write your lead. Use the answers as raw material for your lead. It will speed up drafting and leave you time to revise.

Be patient. It takes years to develop the confidence and expertise to write a lead that sums up notebooks full of information into a single paragraph. Eventually the approaches in this chapter will become second nature, an ingrained habit that produces journalists who are up to the challenge of writing effective, compelling and insightful leads such as this one by an Associated Press writer in 2012.

>EXAMPLE BEIRUT (AP) — A weekend massacre of more than 100 people emerged as a potential turning point in the Syrian crisis Monday, galvanizing even staunch ally Russia to take an unusually hard line against President Bashar Assad's government.

FINDING THE TENSION

News organizations are criticized, often justifiably, for their preoccupation with conflict, when opponents attack each other. Tension, when forces compete, is not the same. Introducing tension in a lead can raise questions and inject suspense that hooks readers. Has your reporting turned up anything that illustrates the tensions in a story? Use it in your lead.

In the following example, Poynter Institute summer fellow Steve Myers used the natural tension between two kinds of objects in the canal behind a waterside community.

>EXAMPLE BROADWATER — On any given morning, residents can look out over their backyard docks and see dolphins, tarpon and manatees swimming in the channels that lead out to Boca Ciega Bay. If it's high tide, they can also see floating aluminum cans, plastic bags and yard clippings.

Because dolphins, tarpon and manatees don't mix well with floating garbage, the reader understandably wants to know what is bringing them together. Myers could have written a lead that told readers about the problem: Broadwater residents are complaining about yard clippings and litter collecting in the canals behind their homes. Instead, he found the tension and followed the classic "show, don't tell" rule, which allowed readers to visualize the problem and compelled them to read on to learn more about it.

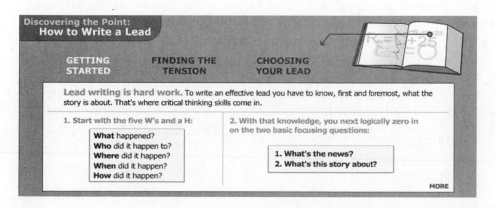

Discovering the Point:
How to Write a Lead

| GETTING STARTED | FINDING THE TENSION | CHOOSING YOUR LEAD |

Lead writing is hard work. To write an effective lead you have to know, first and foremost, what the story is about. That's where critical thinking skills come in.

1. Start with the five W's and a H:

What happened?
Who did it happen to?
Where did it happen?
When did it happen?
How did it happen?

2. With that knowledge, you next logically zero in on the two basic focusing questions:

1. What's the news?
2. What's this story about?

MORE

Lead writing takes practice. The Lead Lab on The Poynter Institute News University Web site is an interactive course that deconstructs lead types, shows examples and offers exercises to enhance the skill of starting out strong.

Journalist at Work MARK FRITZ

While other reporters got their facts from embassy officials about massacres in the African nation of Rwanda in 1994, Associated Press reporter Mark Fritz looked for stories among the victims.

The stories that won him multiple awards, including the Pulitzer Prize, drew much of their impact from leads that opened readers' eyes to unforgettable horror. His story about a village littered with corpses opened with a chilling observation:

▶EXAMPLE KARUBAMBA, Rwanda (AP) — Nobody lives here any more.

Not the expectant mothers huddled outside the maternity clinic, not the families squeezed into the church, not the man who lies rotting in a schoolroom beneath a chalkboard map of Africa.

Everybody here is dead.

But Fritz leaves one critical question unanswered: So What? Why does this story matter?

He answers it using a device that follows many news leads: the so-called nut graf, one or several paragraphs that tell the reader what the story is about. It's called the nut graf because, like a nut, it contains the "kernel," or essential theme, of the story.

▶EXAMPLE Karubamba is just one breathtakingly awful example of the mayhem that has made little Rwanda the world's most ghastly killing ground.

A tragic portrait of genocide's pain. Tearful children fleeing wholesale slaughter in 1994 by warring factions in Rwanda plead to be let across a bridge into neighboring Zaire.

When the nut graf became popular as a story device and a story form in the 1970s (you'll learn more about nut grafs in Chapter 11), many reporters and editors believed that it had to include a phrase that indicated the source of the conclusion—"officials say" or "neighbors and friends of the victim agreed." But today many news organizations permit reporters to draw a conclusion when it is based on their reporting and expertise. Thus, Mark Fritz delivers his interpretation of the Rwandan massacre in the nut graf without crediting a source because he is the source: He was there. Attribution in most other cases is usually necessary.

Mark Fritz on leads:

How would you define your lead?
The hook, the thing that makes readers interested in reading the story. Hit them with the news, the peg. Why are you writing this story? What's it all about?

Are there methods that guide you as you write?
Things become pieces as you're reporting them, and you think, "Ah, there's my lead." I'll scribble along the side and I'll circle something, or put an asterisk, or write a little note next to it. I'll underline it three times. I'll write in block letters "LEAD."

I'm one of the people who believes that if you get the lead right—maybe leading with an anecdote and then your nut graph—the rest just flows. If I don't have that lead, I'll just start throwing notes up on the screen, stuff I know is going to go in the story, and look at it and just wait for lightning to strike.

Your advice to aspiring reporters?
Don't bury your lead.

Put away your notes and try to write the story without consulting them, and sometimes the rudimentary framework will come together. ▸

CHIP'S CORNER

CLICHÉD LEADS AND HOW TO AVOID THEM

Clichés are a common pitfall. Often the first to come to mind, these worn-out phrases might seem like time-savers on deadline, but they drain the energy from what could be a compelling story. As a rookie reporter, I began a fatal fire story on Thanksgiving with "Death takes no holidays." At the time I thought it was original; years later a Google search taught me how many other things "take no holidays":

hunger, fashion, murder, envy, sin, fact checking and Satan. Whenever an editor flagged a cliché in my copy my excuse was, "But I've never used it!"

It never worked. Strive to write stories that are fresh from beginning to end. Here are other clichéd leads to watch for:

"It was the best of times, it was the worst of times." Charles Dickens said it first.

"First the good news." Lazy. Just report the news, don't categorize it. "'Tis the season.'" There's always a season for everything. "Just what is tofu?" Leads don't ask questions, they answer them. ▼

THE TWO TYPES OF LEADS

Leads are often divided into two opposing types, which vary by name: direct versus delayed; hard versus soft; news versus features. It's often easier to understand them by the way they respond to a reader's interest. Each type includes several subtypes.

1. "Report the news"
   - Summary lead
   - Analysis
2. "Tell me a story"
   - Anecdotal
   - Narrative
   - Significant detail
   - Round-up
   - Emblem leads

Summary Leads

The ability to sum up a story in a single paragraph is one of journalism's most basic skills (see Figure 10-1). The **summary lead** generally answers seven questions: Who? What? Where? When? Why? How? and So what? Not all may be answered in the lead.

▶EXAMPLE BEIJING, China — Blind Chinese legal activist Chen Guangcheng, whose daring escape to the American embassy in Beijing last month sparked a diplomatic crisis, left China for the United States Saturday afternoon.

—*McClatchy Newspapers, May 19, 2012*

CONVERGENCE POINT

The Evolution of the Summary News Lead

Media historians disagree about the appearance of the summary lead that characterizes most news reporting. While some think it came into existence during the Civil War with the invention of the telegraph, others argue that it arrived later, during the Progressive Era (1880–1910) "as an outgrowth of the rise of science and education . . . in turn-of-the-century American society."

Find this link on the companion Web site at **www.oup.com/us/scanlan.**

FIGURE 10-1

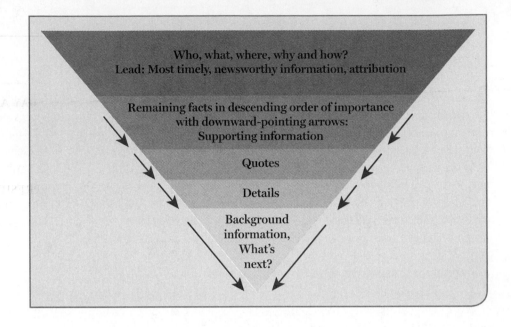

The best summary leads also answer "How?" "Why" and "So what?"

▶**EXAMPLE** WASHINGTON — The U.S. unemployment rate remains above 8 percent, and every politician extols the importance of job creation. Yet each month thousands of manufacturing jobs are there for the taking—but companies are unable to hire sufficiently skilled workers.

—McClatchy Newspapers, May 29, 2012

Analysis Leads

Increasingly, readers are looking for news stories that put the events, issues and trends into perspective. **Analysis leads** call on the ability to draw conclusions based on study, knowledge and confidence that enable the reporter, rather than the newsmaker, to identify the news and convey its significance.

▶**EXAMPLE** WASHINGTON — Public opinion about gay marriage has changed so rapidly that President Barack Obama's historic embrace of it may pose as many political risks to Republicans as to the president and his fellow Democrats.

—The Charlotte (NC) Observer, May 8, 2012

Anecdotal Leads

Of all the leads employed by news writers, one stands out as the least understood. Anything other than a summary lead is often called an **anecdotal lead**. In fact, as *Oregonian* editor Jack Hart notes, the anecdotal lead "takes the form of a short narrative

❝The lead is more important because you will never get to the end if you don't have a good lead.❞

—DANIEL HENNINGER,
DEPUTY EDITORIAL
PAGE EDITOR, *THE WALL
STREET JOURNAL*

X-RAY READING BROADCAST STORY LEAD

Here's an example of a summary lead in broadcast news written by Preston Rudie, a reporter for WTSP-Tampa.

> PRESIDENT BUSH MADE A BRIEF VISIT TO THE BAY AREA TODAY.

The lead answers: Who? What? Where? and When? Broadcast scripts are always written in ALL CAPS.

> AFTER AIR FORCE ONE TOUCHED DOWN THE PRESIDENT APPEARED AT A PRIVATE 25-THOUSAND DOLLAR A PLATE FUNDRAISER.

Dollar signs are written out.

The 60-word lead reports a presidential visit, always newsworthy, adding an eye-raising entry fee to an exorbitant fundraiser. As the anchor reads the reporter-written lead, video of the president leaving Air Force One appears on the studio's rear monitor, sharpening the focus.

> BUT NOT EVERYONE WHO WANTED TO SEE THE PRESIDENT TODAY HAD TO PAY THOUSANDS OF DOLLARS.
> IT ONLY COST THEM A BIT OF TIME.

The writer added the hook: How do you get to see the president by just spending time? Intrigued now, viewers will want to watch the rest of the package to learn more.

---

with a beginning, middle and end." Anecdotal leads often are scenes that feature characters, dialogue and action. "The end is particularly important," says Hart. "It's analogous to the punch line in a joke—it wraps up the story with a flourish." In his "Lexicon of Leads," a collection of various lead types included in his book *A Writer's Coach: An Editor's Guide to Words That Work*, he provides this example from a story by Kathleen Merryman in *The* (Tacoma, WA) *News Tribune*.

❯EXAMPLE Anthropologist Richard Leakey likes to tell about the day in 1950 when he was a 6-year-old whining for his parents' attention. Louis and Mary Leakey were digging for ancient bones on the shores of Lake Victoria, but their little boy wanted to play. He wanted lunch. He wanted his mother to cuddle him. He wanted something to do. "Go find your own bone," said his exasperated father, waving Richard off toward scraps of fossils lying around the site. What the little boy found was the jawbone—the best ever unearthed—of an extinct giant pig. As he worked away at it with the dental picks and brushes that served for toys in the paleontologists' camp, he experienced for the first time the passion of discovery.

As a child, Richard Leakey made his first important archaeological find, and he continues that impressive record as a leading paleoanthropologist to this day. He appears here with prehistoric skulls found in northern Kenya that he says provide solid evidence for human evolution.

Narrative Leads

Narrative leads put "central characters into a scene and begin telling the story that pits those characters against some kind of complication," Hart says. In 34 words, Chip began this *St. Petersburg* (FL) *Times* story about a housing project basketball team, complete with characters, setting and suspense.

❯EXAMPLE❯ Through the rush hour gridlock of weary commuters headed home, a vanload of noisy boys inches along U.S. 19. It's a Friday evening, and the Jordan Park Midgets are bound, they hope, for glory.

Tommy Tomlinson of *The Charlotte* (NC) *Observer* launched his heart-stopping narrative about Michael Kelley, horribly burned in a freak accident as an army paratrooper, who must pass a grueling obstacle course to reach his goal of becoming a police officer.

❯EXAMPLE❯ Nine years of healing. Six months of training.

It comes down to this cold October morning, and a stopwatch set at zero. Michael Kelley throws open the car door and takes off running. His shoes leave tracks in the cold, wet grass. His duty belt sags on his hip. The orange cone is a hundred yards away. To him it looks like half a mile. Behind him, in trainer Bobby Buening's hand, the stopwatch spins. Michael aced the firearms tests. He's solid with the books. Through six months of training he has proved he can do everything else it takes to be a Charlotte-Mecklenburg police officer.

Now he must conquer the obstacle course. He has to run, drag, climb, crash, push, bend and crawl through a course built to weed out those who lack the strength or speed or will.

And he has to do it in seven minutes and 20 seconds.

He rounds the orange cone now, heading back toward the rest of the course. From a hundred yards away he could be anyone. But with each step closer something new is revealed. The skin is seared. The feet won't flex. Pieces are missing. Two fingers. An ear. Nine years ago, Michael Kelley was swallowed by fire. He went through 37 operations. He crawled through his house until he could walk. And every day he inched closer to the man he used to be.

He has seven minutes and 20 seconds to make it all the way back.

—*The Charlotte Observer, Nov. 10, 2003*

Significant Detail Leads

A **significant detail lead** uses a detail to tell a larger story about a news event, or introduce tension.

▶EXAMPLE◀ WASHINGTON — In an Information Age first, the White House on Wednesday gave reporters its hefty 1,300-page health-care reform plan on a pair of computer disks weighing less than two ounces.

—*Knight Ridder*

▶EXAMPLE◀ FBI agent Jerry Spurgers knelt on the floor of 13-year-old Kacie Woody's bedroom, holding two crumpled pieces of paper that might reveal the identity of Kacie's kidnapper.

—*Arkansas Democrat-Gazette, Dec. 16, 2003*

Round-up Leads

Stories that report trends and multiple events often rely on **round-up leads** or **wrap leads**.

▶EXAMPLE◀ Tacoma Fire Department units responded to a pair of fires on Saturday evening, one at a commercial facility at the Port of Tacoma and the other at an East Side residence.

—*The (Tacoma, WA) News Tribune, May 20, 2012*

A variation of this type is a **gallery lead**, which assembles anecdotes and examples to demonstrate a trend, exemplified by this *Miami Herald* lead about growing numbers of employees choosing to work at home.

> ▶**EXAMPLE** When Sergio Piazza rolls out of bed in the morning, he can be at work in under 10 seconds. He sleeps just feet from his desk in a live-work loft at the edge of Wynwood. That allows the Italian jewelry company's South Florida representative to clock in without ever getting into a car, 24 hours a day.
>
> Attorney Lawrence Blacke lives with his wife in an apartment directly above his law office and mortgage title company in Fort Lauderdale's North Beach area. "I have zero commuting expenses," he says. "So I'm not as concerned when I see the increases in gasoline prices, because it doesn't affect me every day. Of course, it affects me when I'm traveling on business. But on a day-to-day basis, it doesn't impact me directly."
>
> Jami Baker has to go a little farther. The marketing associate lives two doors down from her office, on the 39th floor of a Brickell Avenue condominium. "Sometimes," she says, "the longest part of my commute is the elevator ride."
>
> —*The Miami Herald, May 20, 2012*

Emblem Leads

An **emblem lead** uses a single instance or individual to illustrate a larger issue by putting a human face on a social problem or trend, as in this story about preteen dieters.

> ▶**EXAMPLE** Worried about her weight, Sarah swore off dessert and cut back on meal portions. Eventually, she began skipping breakfast and was just nibbling at lunch and dinner. Within six months, she dropped 13 pounds.
>
> A weight-loss success story? Not at all. Sarah is only 10 years old. Her diet cost her 20 percent of her weight.
>
> —*Knight Ridder*

The Coaching Way ⁖⁙ THINKING ABOUT LEADS

- What do you want to do: report the news or tell a story? Why and how will that affect your lead?
- What does your audience need to know FIRST?
- How will timeliness affect the lead you write?
- Launch a lead search. Comb newspapers, online sites, television and radio news stations for good leads and assess their effectiveness. Copy them out and study why they work. (Make sure you write the byline first so you won't someday confuse another journalist's lead with your own.)
- Have you read your lead aloud? If you stumble, feel bored or feel confused, start revising.
- Does your lead sound like something you'd tell a friend?
- Do your leads follow the "one breath" rule?
- Is your lead accurate? Clear? Fair?
- Are you spending most of your time on your lead? Remember: You can revise it later, and you may discover a better lead. Move on. ▶

CHOOSING THE RIGHT LEAD

How do you decide which is the right lead? It depends on three conditions:

- *Time*: Did the story just happen? Are you the first to report it, or will most people in your audience already know about it from another news source? Is the time element crucial?
- *Audience needs*: Will your readers get the news first from you? If they already know the news, would they be better served with a lead that anticipates their knowledge?
- *Exclusivity*: Are you the only news organization that has the story? Scoops once counted for a lot more in the days when several newspapers published in a city. Now the competition is from television and online sources. But there may be stories only you have, and you might want to tell the reader this is an exclusive.

Exploding the Myths of Lead Writing

Lead writing may be the writing activity most shrouded in myth—long-standing, often unspoken rules that govern the way journalists write and edit the news.

There are often good reasons for these old rules. Remember: Every editor is also a reader and can pinpoint problems in your lead that confuse your audience. Most of these rules apply to the summary lead, which is a more rigid form. Storytelling leads can take more chances. Beginning reporters may do better being asked to stick to some rules. As your news judgment and writing skills grow, so will the confidence that allows you to write leads that set their own standards of excellence.

There are rules, of course: Leads must be accurate, logical, fair and syntactically correct. Few would disagree that a news lead should contain the most newsworthy elements. But successful leads are ones that make you want to keep on reading, which is the lead's most important function. You'll find that the best ones often seem not to follow rules, but rather to defy them, break them, or make new rules. The central myth about the lead is that there are strict rules governing its construction, rules that can never be broken. Among the reigning myths that you will undoubtedly confront:

- *Leads must never begin with a quote.* A good guideline, but had Saul Pett of the Associated Press followed it, his readers would have been cheated of this revealing, in more than one way, opening to a 1963 profile of Dorothy Parker, the legendary tart-tongued writer of the 1930s:

  "Are you married, my dear?"

  "Yes, I am."

  "Then you won't mind zipping me up."

  Zipped up, Dorothy Parker turned to face her interviewer, and the world.

- *Leads must always contain attribution.* Although it's important to let readers know where information in a story comes from, slavish allegiance to the principle can bog down readers with unnecessary clutter. But attribution must come quickly to support the lead's contention as in this example.

QUICK Tips ⏺ MAKE YOUR LEADS SHINE

- *Accuracy.* Clever, strong and clear leads can contain errors. Double-check the facts.

- *Breath test.* If your lead takes more than one breath to read aloud, start cutting.

- *Delete key.* Count the words. Trim by 10 percent.

- *Read aloud.* Do you stumble, feel bored or feel confused? So will your readers. Rewrite.

- *"To be" diet.* Get rid of variations on the verb "to be" wherever possible. Passive verb forms rob leads of energy. Replace "is planning," "are hoping" with "plan," "hope." ▼

CONVERGENCE POINT ⤓

*Avoid Clichés
Like the Plague*

Writing coach Dick Thien provides an inventory of clichéd leads and "overworked formulas" that journalists should keep in mind when beginning their stories.

Find this link on the companion Web site at **www.oup.com/us/ scanlan.**

❯**EXAMPLE** NEW YORK — Billionaire Warren Buffett is dipping into the ketchup business as part of $23.3 billion deal to buy the Heinz ketchup company, uniting a legend of American investing with a mainstay of grocery store shelves.

—*Associated Press, Feb. 14, 2013*

- *A good lead is never more than three or four lines long.* "Keep it short" is always a good prescription for the news writer, but readers would have been cheated of an insight into the voyeuristic role of the audience at freak shows had David Finkel heeded it in his profile of T. J. Albert Jackson, a carnival performer billed as "the world's biggest man."

❯**EXAMPLE** COCOA — Behold the fat man. Go ahead. Everybody does. He doesn't mind, honestly. That's how he makes his living. Walk right up to him. Stand there and look. Stand there and look. Stand there and gape. Gape at the layers of fat, the astonishing girth, the incredible bulk. Imagine him in a bathtub. Or better, on a bike. Or better yet, on one of those flimsy antique chairs. Boom! If you're lucky, maybe he'll lift his shirt. If you're real lucky, maybe he'll rub his belly. Don't be shy. Ask him a question.

—*St. Petersburg (FL) Times, Nov. 10, 1985*

QUICK Tips ⏺ DODGING CLICHÉS

Mitch Broder, a columnist for Gannett Suburban Newspapers, recommended three steps to weed out clichéd leads.

- *Boycott generics.* Every story could start with a quote. Or a word. Or an "Ah." But very few stories, if any, should.

- *Cliché watch.*"—takes no holidays" leads sprout everywhere. Keep a cliché collection and consult it before you hit send.

- *Try again.* Don't be satisfied with the first lead that comes to mind. "When something is the first thing that pops into your head," Broder says, "yours is probably not the first head it popped into." ▼

- *A lead must sum up the story in a paragraph.* Readers won't wait, proponents of this rule insist. They want the entire story, compressed like sardines in a can, in the lead. But if your lead is dramatic and suspenseful, readers will want—need—to know what will happen and keep reading, as in the case of this story about a traumatic childbirth.

  ➤**EXAMPLE** In the labor room at Kent County Memorial Hospital, Jackie Rushton rose from the stretcher, her face pale and smeared with tears. A nurse pressed the fetal pulse detector against her abdomen, a taut mound stretched by seven months of pregnancy. The detector was blue, the size and shape of a pocket flashlight with earphones attached, and Jackie Rushton's eyes fixed on the nurse who strained to hear the bird-like beating of her baby's heart.

  "Here's the heartbeat," the nurse said after several moments of silence. "It's 126, and it's fine."

  If there's a heartbeat, why isn't she giving me the earphones so I can listen? Jackie thought. That's what the doctor always does when I have my check-ups. First he listens, and then he says, "Here's the heartbeat. Listen." She didn't say, "Here's the heartbeat. Listen."

  I've lost the baby. The baby's gone.

  —*The Providence (RI) Evening Bulletin, March 25, 1981*

REVISING YOUR LEADS

Even in your earliest journalism classes, some leads will fly off your fingers and appear instantly on your computer screen. But most are the product of hard work, of cutting and moving, adding and deleting, asking tough questions, searching for the right word. Don't assume that once you've written a lead, you have a lead, whether it seems to work or not. Think instead of leads like a piece of clay that you can play with and refine.

QUICK Tips ◓ DANGEROUS LEADS

■ *Question leads.* Some editors simply ban question leads, reasoning that readers want answers, not questions. But let's concede that a lead in the form of a question occasionally works, for all the right reasons. Nevertheless, question leads often fail because they seldom perform the basic function of a lead—stating the central theme that organizes and explains the entire story. Furthermore, they can be irritating. Readers probably do resent frivolous questions when what they really want is news. Question leads seldom represent the best solution.

■ *Quote leads.* Quote leads, as discussed earlier, are also banned in some newsrooms. The rationale is similar to the rationale used for banning question leads: The chance that a quote is the best way to express a story's theme is awfully slim. Use them cautiously. Here is an example that succeeds:

▶**EXAMPLE** Michael H. Walsh calls it "teaching the elephant to dance." That's his term for making the enormous, historic Union Pacific Railroad Co. competitive and profitable in the 20th century.

■ *Topic leads.* Topic leads probably should be banned. The point of a news story is to tell us what happened, what the outcome was. In the case of a meeting story, for example, the important thing is not that the meeting took place, but rather the consequence of the meeting. What was the key decision? Why is that important? Where do we go from here? In other words, topic leads should be restricted to information. An ineffective topic lead:

▶**EXAMPLE** Supporters and defenders of a new prison in town argued their case yesterday before the city council.

■ A more appropriate topic lead would be:

▶**EXAMPLE** The prospect of tripling this town's population with a 3,000-inmate prison was the subject of a hot debate Tuesday.

—*Jack Hart,*
The (Portland) Oregonian ▼

LEAD WRITING

ROUNDTABLE

An effective lead grabs attention and delivers on its promise. Among the tips from television and wire services reporters and an online editor:

- Write with an audience in mind.
- Keep alert to possible leads as you report.
- Put your notes aside to discover your lead by writing it.
- Study good lead writers in your newsroom.

Participants

PRESTON RUDIE, reporter, WTSP, Tampa

JILL AGOSTINO, assistant national editor, *The New York Times*

KRISTEN GELINEAU, Associated Press, Sydney, Australia

> ### *How important is the lead for a broadcast story? An online story?*

Rudie: It is your hook. Lose someone in your lead, they will tune out.

Agostino: As important for a story in print. The difference is that in an online story the writer might include "this afternoon" or "earlier today" that lets the reader know that this has happened recently.

> ### *What's the ideal lead length?*

Rudie: Most television leads should be 15 to maybe 20 seconds in length.

Agostino: Online news leads, the same as in the paper, should be a couple of paragraphs or so.

> ### *What advice do you give reporters struggling to write a lead?*

Agostino: Think as the reader: what do people clicking to the site need to know and what are they looking for immediately?

Gelineau: In an urgent series, the five W's and How go first, followed immediately by the context.

Rudie: Think like a producer. Do you want to include a graphic, or video, in your lead? Using video can usually better focus your story.

> ### *How much time do you have to write a breaking news lead?*

Gelineau: About one minute to put out the NewsAlert—one sentence long. After that a 130-word story written in a hybrid style of print and broadcast, then switch back to print style and put out an urgent lead—a few paragraphs with the essential information and an editor's note that the story will be updated quickly.

The process up until this point should take NO longer than five minutes.

> ### *What does it take to develop that expertise?*

Gelineau: Watch, listen and ask a lot of questions during slow news moments. Do a few practice runs on your own time. You'll get the hang of it (eventually).

SUMMARY GUIDE LEAD WRITING

THE LEAD AND ITS ROLE IN NEWS WRITING

The lead is the top of a news story; leads are the journalist's first and perhaps the last way of grabbing a reader's attention.

What to Remember →

Opinions about leads—their role, length and whether they should follow certain rules—abound. Learning to write an enticing lead takes time, thought and lots of practice.

HOW FIVE W'S, AN H AND SW CREATE COMPELLING LEADS

Effective leads answer one or more of seven questions: Who? What? When? Where? Why? How? and So what?

What to Remember →

Leads report the most newsworthy elements: people, action, place, timeliness, causes, explanations, and relevance. These are the factors that best respond to the interest of news audiences.

DECONSTRUCTING LEADS

Deconstructing leads shows how combinations of newsworthy elements are highlighted or omitted depending on the way writers and editors view information.

What to Remember →

Leads can vary widely, affecting length, pace, density and quality. There is no one way to write a lead.

DEVELOP YOUR LEAD FROM A FOCUS

Journalists often waste time trying to discover their story's theme by writing the lead when their effort is best spent discovering its focus by answering key questions about the action, rationale and relevance to audiences.

What to Remember →

Taking 95 seconds to answer the five focusing questions listed in Chapter 2 helps the journalists discover a theme leaves time for the rest of the process of reporting, organizing, drafting and revising a story that is ready for publication. The entire story—not just the lead—must shine, or audience interest will flag.

FINDING THE TENSION

Introducing tension in a lead raises questions and injects suspense that grabs an audience's interest and attention.

What to Remember → Consumers fault the news media for focusing on conflict. Tension, by contrast, occurs when forces compete. Look for natural tension when you report.

THE TWO TYPES OF LEADS

While leads have many names, it's best to distinguish a lead by the two ways it responds to reader interest.

What to Remember → "Report the news" leads directly summarize news events or analyze a situation. "Tell me a story" leads draw in readers with anecdotes, scenes, significant details and examples that round up a series of events or a person emblematic of an issue or trend.

CHOOSING THE RIGHT LEAD

Three conditions drive lead choices: timeliness, the needs of your audience and exclusivity of newsworthy information.

What to Remember → Journalists select the most appropriate lead once they've settled on a focus. Leads must be accurate, logical, fair and syntactically correct.

REVISING YOUR LEADS

While some leads instantly come to mind, most are the product of careful revision.

What to Remember → Leads can always be sharpened to guarantee accuracy, readability and avoid wordiness. A good lead should take one breath to read and avoids "to be" verb constructions to heighten the action.

KEY TERMS

analysis lead, p. 226
anecdotal lead, p. 226
emblem lead, p. 230

gallery lead, p. 230
narrative lead, p. 228
round-up lead, p. 229

significant detail lead, p. 229
summary lead, p. 225
wrap leads, p. 229

EXERCISES

1. Study a recent newspaper, online news source or news broadcast and identify the types of leads being used. Compare how many "report the news" and how many "tell a story." Discuss the reasons you believe lie behind the choices.

2. Examine a national story and compare the various approaches used by different news organizations. Which do you think are more effective and why?

3. Is your cliché meter running when you write leads? Must police dodge a "hail of bullets"? Study your work and the stories you read for clichés. Think harder. Revise to make them more original.

4. Look at the last 10 leads you wrote and put a label on them. Choose alternative approaches and rewrite them. What additional reporting do you need to do?

5. Collect favorite leads. Copy them into your computer or your daybook. (Make sure you include the source and byline so you avoid the risk of plagiarism.) Deconstruct them: What did the writer include, leave out?

6. Pick a major story and collect as many leads as possible. Compare and contrast the different approaches. Discuss which is more successful and why. Write your own version.

READINGS

Blundell, William E. *The Art and Craft of Feature Writing: Based on The Wall Street Journal Guide.* **New York: Plume, 1988.**
After two decades as an award-winning writer and editor, Blundell became the writing coach for one of the nation's best-written newspapers. In this well-regarded handbook, he presents a valuable framework, bolstered by published stories, for reporting and writing leads that distill a subject with vivid scenes and anecdotes that make for compelling openings.

Cappon, Rene J. *The Word: An Associated Press Guide to Good News Writing.* **Lawrenceville, NJ: Peterson's, 1999.**
Drawing from a long career with the international wire service, Cappon devotes an entire chapter of advice on lead writing. He focuses on the pitfalls of burying the news, the value of writing visually and the importance of timelessness.

Hart, Jack. *A Writer's Coach: An Editor's Guide to Words That Work.* **New York: Pantheon, 2006.**
Veteran editor Jack Hart introduces his "Lexicon of Leads," an illuminating discussion of the various leads available to journalists and examples that illustrate how they differ and which to choose.

Murray, Donald M. *Writing to Deadline: The Journalist at Work.* **Portsmouth, NH: Heinemann, 2000.**
After a lengthy career as a working reporter, columnist and coach, Murray introduces writers to the multiple ways to begin a story, the thinking that goes into making choices and real-world examples that demonstrate this crucial element of the journalist's craft.

Tompkins, Al. *Aim for the Heart: Write, Shoot, Report and Produce for TV and Multimedia.* **Washington, DC: CQ Press, 2012.**
Writing the broadcast lead challenges journalists to write short and enticing openings. With decades of professional experience and a long career training broadcast journalists, Tompkins outlines the various approaches and concepts, and includes interviews with working journalists that demystify the process of lead writing for broadcast and online.

STORY FORMS

BY THE END OF THIS CHAPTER,

you should be able to...

> Demonstrate familiarity and fluency with the structural elements of traditional and new story forms, including the following:

> > Inverted pyramid

> > Hourglass

> > Nut graf

> > Five boxes

> > Short-short stories

> > Long-form narratives

> > Serial narratives

> > Alternative story forms

> Choose the most suitable form for your stories

NEWS STORIES NEED a shape and structure, in the same way a building needs a frame and our bodies a skeleton. Effective news writers, like architects, know that form follows content. Today's journalists must be familiar with, and able to write, stories in a variety of forms suitable for the news and information they need to deliver and the platform in which it is to appear.

In this chapter you will learn traditional story forms widely employed by news writers, story shapes used since humans began telling stories and new approaches that respond to readers' changing needs.

SHAPING THE NEWS

Faced with deadline's ticking clock, journalists often turn to **traditional story forms**, and the formulas that shape how news is reported. It's vital that journalists understand and are able to use all the forms at their disposal. Some are old, the offspring of social changes, economics and technology dating back nearly two centuries. Some are new, reflecting the news industry's efforts to meet audience demand for quick and easy-to-digest news. One is timeless, born when early humans told stories by firelight, yet relevant to this day. As a novice journalist, you need to have each of these in your toolbox.

Planning is the first step in organization of a story form. News artists at *USA Today* based a NASCAR graphic on this storyboard that sketched their approach for the final product.

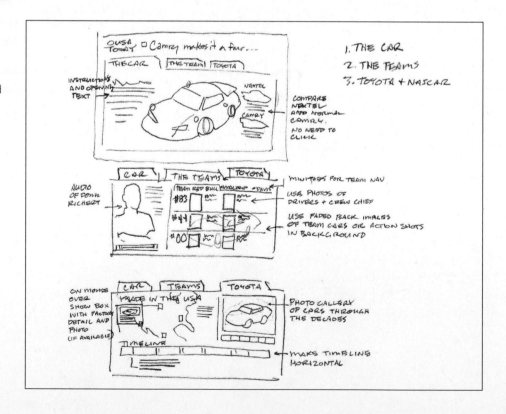

INVERTED PYRAMID:
NEWS FROM THE TOP DOWN

The **inverted pyramid** puts the most newsworthy information at the top using a summary lead (see Figure 11-1). The remaining information follows in order of newsworthy importance, with the least crucial facts at the bottom. Its purpose: to furnish the news fast and let audiences decide how much they want to read.

To do so, reporters must sum up in a single, concise paragraph that answers the question, "What's new?" and provides as many responses to the five W's, an H and SW questions that determine newsworthiness. It's the most basic form to report news.

"The inverted pyramid organizes stories not around ideas or chronologies but around facts," journalism historian Mitchell Stephens writes in *A History of News.* "It weighs and shuffles the various pieces of information, focusing with remarkable single-mindedness on their relative news value."

Developed in the mid- to late 1800s to take advantage of new communications technology—the telegraph—the inverted pyramid is a widely used, yet somewhat controversial, story form. Despite regular calls for its demise, the inverted pyramid remains a standby and has even found a new home on the World Wide Web, where readers are seemingly always in a hurry.

Why inverted? Turning the pyramid on end broadens the top to accommodate as many newsworthy facts as possible in the summary lead. Succeeding paragraphs follow in descending order of importance, signified by the narrowing to the pyramid's tip. If pressed for space, editors can trim the story from the bottom up, removing background (known as B-copy) or material that isn't as critical as the opening three paragraphs.

Historical Perspectives:
Birth of the Inverted Pyramid

Newspaper stories in the mid-1800s were slow-paced (some might say long-winded). That changed when Samuel Morse patented an electrical telegraph in 1837. With

> 66 "Design informs even the simplest structure, whether of brick and steel or of prose. You raise a pup tent from one sort of vision, a cathedral from another. 99
>
> —WILLIAM STRUNK AND E. B. WHITE, AUTHORS, *THE ELEMENTS OF STYLE*

SEE CLOSE-UP, P. 259: INVERTED PYRAMID STORY

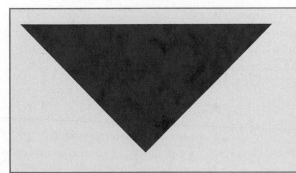

The information is presented to the reader in descending levels of importance.

Traditional wire service style. Useful for breaking news. Editors can cut from the bottom.

FIGURE 11-1 The inverted pyramid presents the most newsworthy information in descending levels of importance and relevance. It is organized by facts and is useful for breaking and online news.

News about the assassination of President Abraham Lincoln at Ford's Theater in Washington DC on April 15, 1865, helped introduce the inverted pyramid form, an approach that persists nearly 150 years later.

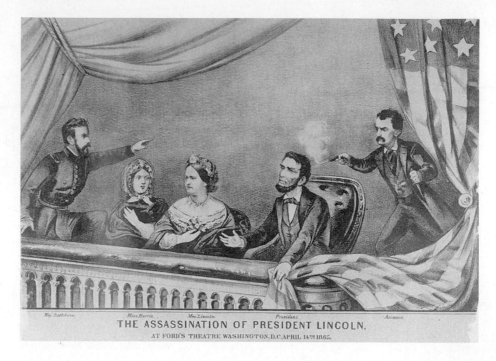

THE ASSASSINATION OF PRESIDENT LINCOLN.
AT FORD'S THEATRE WASHINGTON, D.C. APRIL 14TH 1865.

information now transmitted in bursts of Morse code, a new, concise form emerged that arranged facts by their newsworthiness. Historian David Mindich traces its birth to Abraham Lincoln's assassination on April 15, 1865. As Lincoln lay dying, war secretary Edwin Stanton telegraphed a message to the commanding general in New York City. Many editors chose his account for their front pages.

▶EXAMPLE This evening at about 9:30 p.m. at Ford's Theatre, the President, while sitting in his private box with Mrs. Lincoln, Mrs. Harris and Major Rathburn, was shot by an assassin, who suddenly entered the box and approached behind the President.

The assassin then leaped upon the stage, brandishing a large dagger or knife, and made his escape in the rear of the theatre.

The pistol ball entered the back of the President's head and penetrated nearly through the head. The wound is mortal.

Stanton got right to the point, a tradition that holds today. "On or about April 15, 1865," Mindich declared, "the character of news writing changed." Other historians date the summary lead later, during the Progressive Era (1880–1910), arguing that it was an "outgrowth of science and education. . . ."

Pros and Cons

Journalists have long had a love-hate relationship with the inverted pyramid.

Its supporters consider it essential, especially for breaking news and when time and space are at a premium. Critics say the inverted pyramid, just like the telegraph, has outlived its usefulness and been replaced by more effective forms. The pyramid starts out deceptively strong, weakens quickly and peters out at the end—a surefire way to turn off readers. Some call it "anti-story."

Despite the criticism, the pyramid survives, and thrives. Its quick summary of events makes it one of the most recognizable shapes in communications today, in newspapers, radio and television, Web sites, even press releases.

Its biggest flaw lies not in the form, but with journalists, teachers and editors who believe the inverted pyramid is the only shape available to news writers, an attitude this chapter seeks to change by introducing other forms.

THE HOURGLASS: SERVING NEWS AND READERS

The **hourglass** is a hybrid form that combines the strengths of two forms: the news value of the inverted pyramid and the storytelling power of narrative (see Figure 11-2). It has three parts:

SEE CLOSE-UP AT WWW .OUP.COM/US/SCANLAN: HOURGLASS STORY

Top. A four- to five-paragraph summary lead that condenses the most newsworthy information.

Turn. A brief transition paragraph that shifts the story from a report to a story. It attributes the source of the information to come—"according to police," "supporters and critics agree," "eyewitnesses described the event this way."

Narrative. An expanded version of the story reported in the top, using chronology details, dialogue and scenes.

The hourglass "respects traditional news values, considers the needs of the reader, takes advantage of narrative, and spurs the writer to new levels of reporting," according to writing coach Roy Peter Clark, who coined the term.

The hourglass can be used for all kinds of stories: crime, business, government and meetings. It's best suited for dramatic stories that can be told in chronological fashion.

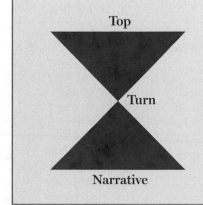

The important information appears high in the story. Then the story turns in the middle, and events are retold chronologically.

An important form, not new, but more relevant than ever. Combines news reporting and narrative. Excellent for police stories and other dramatic events.

FIGURE 11-2 Most newsworthy information appears at the top of the hourglass form. The story then turns in the middle, leading to a narrative that retells the story chronologically. It combines news reporting and narrative and is ideal for police stories and other dramatic events.

THE NUT GRAF: GIVING READERS A REASON TO CARE

SEE CLOSE-UP AT WWW.OUP.COM/US/ SCANLAN: NUT GRAF

Journalistic story forms, like many creative ideas, are often linked with the places where they originated. The inverted pyramid, popularized by newspaper wire services, is often referred to as an "AP" or "wire service" story. *The Wall Street Journal* is home to a form best known as the **nut graf** story, also known as a "news feature" (see Figure 11-3). (The spelling of "graf" is traditional journalistic shorthand for "paragraph.")

This form includes anecdotal leads that hook the reader, followed by alternating sections that amplify and illustrate the story's thesis. But its chief hallmark is a context section—"nut graf" in newsroom lingo—that generally appears in the fourth to sixth paragraph. Newspapers and magazines around the world publish stories following this form that emphasizes explanation and understanding over raw information.

The nut graf tells the reader what the writer is up to; it delivers a promise of the story's content and message. It's called the nut graf because, like a nut, it contains the "kernel," or essential theme, of the story. At *The Philadelphia Inquirer*, reporters and editors called it the "You may have wondered why we invited you to this party" section.

The nut graf has several purposes:

- It tells readers why they should care.
- It explains the lead and its connection to the rest of the story.
- It tells readers why the story is timely.
- It includes attribution and hints at supporting material that will help readers see why the story is important.

As the name implies, most nut grafs are a single paragraph long and immediately follow the lead, but it's not uncommon for them to run several paragraphs long.

> ❝ **Prose is architecture, not interior decoration.** ❞
>
> —ERNEST HEMINGWAY, NEWSPAPER REPORTER, NOVELIST

FIGURE 11-3 Nut graf stories include anecdotal leads that hook the reader, followed by alternating sections that amplify and illustrate the story's thesis. Its chief hallmark is a "nut graf" in the fourth to sixth paragraph that delivers a promise of the story's content and theme. Newspapers and magazines rely on the form for stories that emphasize explanation.

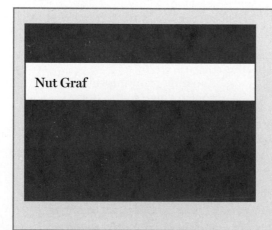

Nut Graf

The lead is an anecdote or scene or portrait. The news value is communicated in the third or fourth graph. The rest of the story delivers the promise in the nut graf.

Wall Street Journal style. Excellent for news analysis or trend stories. Forces writer to consider the most interesting information and the essential news value.

EXAMPLE CAIRO — Support for Egypt's Islamist political parties has plummeted ahead of this country's presidential election next week, a Gallup survey released Friday has found, while early returns showed the candidate of the Muslim Brotherhood, thought to be Egypt's dominant political group, running third among Egyptians voting overseas.

Both the poll and the early election results are the first authoritative measure of the state of Egyptian politics just days before the country's first truly contested presidential election. Taken together, they suggest the grip that the Muslim Brotherhood has seemed have had on Egypt's political system has loosened, giving liberals and Christians hope of avoiding an Islamist sweep of the new government

—*McClatchy Newspapers, May 18, 2012*

In this example, the nut graf, the second paragraph of the story, has done its job: giving readers enough information early on to see where the story is heading so they can decide whether they want to keep reading.

> 66 Readers love stories, and they'll read stories, from beginning to end, and they'll react to stories. Not articles, not text. What narrative does so well is invite people to come along for a ride. 99
>
> —MARIA CARRILLO, NARRATIVE EDITOR, *THE VIRGINIAN-PILOT*

FIVE BOXES: HOW READERS PROCESS STORIES

Good writing comes from an overabundance of information. But crowded notebooks and computer files of notes pose a challenge: where to put it all. Here is a way, suggested by Pat Farnan, a *St. Petersburg* (FL) *Times* editor, to quickly organize and write a story using **five boxes** (see Figure 11-4).

SEE CLOSE-UP AT WWW.OUP.COM/US/ SCANLAN: FIVE BOXES

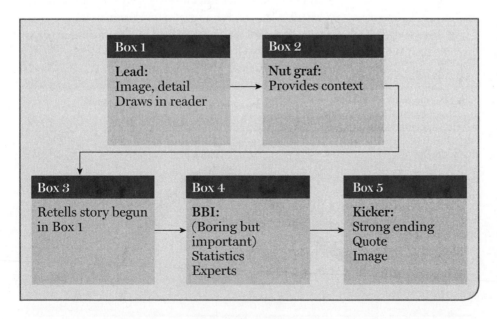

FIGURE 11-4 The five boxes form divides information into separate categories: lead, nut graf, resumption of story launched in lead, boring but important information (BBI) and kicker ending. It's an efficient and graceful way to organize news and narrative, especially on deadline.

1. *Lead.* The first box contains a scene, anecdote, image or detail to grab the reader's attention. It can be a single paragraph or several.
2. *Nut graf.* One or more paragraphs that sum up the story and provide the reader with context and attribution.
3. *Resuming the story begun in the lead.* Almost a second lead, which signals the readers that the story which hooked them continues. Length can vary.
4. *BBI.* Shorthand for "boring but important," the **BBI** box contains less compelling but valuable history, expert testimony, statistics that bolster the nut graf.
5. *Kicker.* A "**kicker**"—a resonant quote, image, observation that ends the story— helps to amplify the story's subject and theme.

Five boxes can be organized on paper or computer screen with bulleted lists or shorthand suggestions. Armed with this rudimentary outline, you can flesh out your story. It breaks the story into components that can be developed and refined.

THE NARRATIVE: THE WAY WE TELL STORIES

The narrative is a timeless story form, the kind we read or were told to as children (see Figure 11-5). Narratives feature plots (beginning, middle and end), characters, settings, dialogue, details, a theme, complication, climax and resolution.

Storytellers don't give away the story in the first paragraph the way news writers do. They set up a situation, using suspense or the introduction of a compelling character to keep the reader turning pages. Rather than put the least important information at the end the way an inverted pyramid writer might, the storyteller waits until the end to give the reader a "big payoff"—a surprise, a twist, a consummation.

Narrative writers rely on four literary devices, described by narrative journalism pioneer Tom Wolfe in *The New Journalism*:

1. **Scenes**, or dramatic narrative, that show subjects in action.

FIGURE 11-5 The narrative form follows a curved line that connects the beginning of a story to the end with an arc that includes exposition, complication/conflict, climax and resolution. The oldest story form and one best suited for features, profiles and human interest stories.

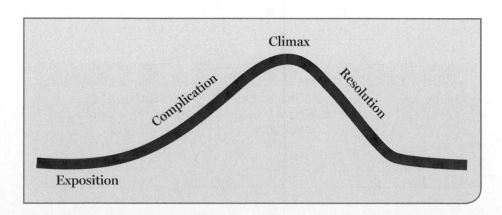

2. **Status details**, such as the way people dress, talk, gesture, the car they drive, how they furnish their home or decorate their office. Through these, Wolfe says, "people express their position in the world or what they think it is or what they hope it to be." Journalists must take care to verify such details: An expensive wristwatch might not signal personal wealth, but a gift from a wealthy relative.

3. **Dialogue**. Dialogue between characters, rather than quotes to a reporter "involves the reader . . . establishes and defines character more completely than any other single device."

4. **Third-person point of view**, which presents scenes through the eyes of a particular character gives the "feeling of being inside the character's mind and experiencing the emotional reality of the scene as he experiences it." Responding to criticism of journalistic mind reading, Wolfe said point of view writing is possible by interviewing a story subject "about his thoughts and emotions."

SEE CLOSE-UP AT WWW.OUP.COM/US/ SCANLAN: NARRATIVE

SERIAL NARRATIVE: "TO BE CONTINUED . . ."

Newspapers have been home to serial narratives since a young reporter for London's *Morning Chronicle* named Charles Dickens published the first one in 1836. A **serial narrative** is "any story, whether told with words, visual images or drawings, that is broken up into segments and is revealed gradually," says Tom French, who has written several award-winning serial narratives for the *St. Petersburg Times*.

A successful serial depends on several elements. The most important is what French calls "the engine," usually an unanswered question that drives the story—and the reader—forward. In *The Wizard of Oz*, the engine is whether Dorothy will get home to Kansas. In mysteries, it's "whodunit."

Other key ingredients, according to French and Jan Winburn, who has edited serial narratives at *The Baltimore Sun* and *Atlanta Journal-Constitution*, include:

-   **Stakeholder**. A key character with something important at stake.
-   **Gold mine source**. A willing source with a great memory; court records, a diary, a trunk of letters.
-   **Narrative arc**. The curved line that connects the beginning of the story to the end. In *Romeo and Juliet*, it is a boy and girl from feuding families falling in love, their deaths showing their families the cost of such hatred. In *Angels and Demons*, Tom French tracks a murder from the crime to the killer's conviction.
-   **Switchbacks**. Surprising reversals of fortune and other plot twists that shock the reader.
-   **Cliffhanger**. A dramatic point at which to conclude a chapter, encouraging the reader to come back tomorrow.

In recent years, serial narrative subjects have shifted from reconstructions of events and long-term immersion to live reporting, such as criminal trials, chronicled in daily installments.

CONVERGENCE POINT ⟋

News Storytelling

Created by Ben Montgomery, a journalist passionate about narrative nonfiction, this site regularly posts examples of long form writing, interviews and commentary that explore how journalists use stories to tell the news of our time.

Find this link on the companion Web site at **www.oup.com/us/ scanlan.**

CONVERGENCE POINT ⚜

*Serial Narratives:
Example and Serials
on Deadline*

"Black Hawk Down: An
American War Story"
is an original 29-part
Philadelphia Inquirer series
by Mark Bowden, featuring
multimedia elements that
Dickens could never have
imagined, that led to the
best-selling book and
movie.

   Serial narratives can
consume weeks and
months of reporting and
writing time. In "The
Verdict in the 112th
Paragraph," Pulitzer
Prize–winning serialist
Tom French explains how
daily deadlines require
exhaustive reporting and
mastery of the form.

*Find this link on the
companion Web site at*
**www.oup.com/us/
scanlan.**

SHORT-SHORT STORIES: WRITING FOR A TIME-PRESSED AUDIENCE

In many newsrooms during the last few decades, narrative meant two things: lots of words and lots of time to report and write them. **Long-form narratives**—cathedrals of prose—remain popular, but talented reporters have demonstrated that short-short stories—"pup tent" narratives—can be produced with tighter limits on length and time. (The Internet age has brought us even shorter forms, which we'll get to in a moment.) **Short-short stories**, relying on the long-form techniques, provide an alternative to "just the facts" inverted pyramid stories long used to report crimes and accidents. They evoke emotions, telescope moments in time and present unforgettable characters with empathy and insight. In the finest hands, these elliptical stories break the mold.

In 2005, *St. Petersburg Times* reporter Brady Dennis won the prestigious Ernie Pyle Award for human interest stories with "300 Words," a series limited to that length and produced about once a month while Dennis worked as a night police reporter.

"It doesn't take 3,000 words to put together a beginning, middle and end," Dennis told the *Charlotte* (NC) *Observer*'s Michael Weinstein. "A good story is a good story, no matter the length. And sometimes the shorter ones turn out [to be] more powerful than the windy ones."

Working with photographer Chris Zuppa, Dennis focused on rodeo clown Ashley "Stretch" McClellan, 24, in the moments before he enters the ring to protect riders who have been thrown by bulls. That information is contained in the picture caption. Notice what else Dennis leaves out and what he keeps in his story and how these choices leave a lasting impression.

❯**EXAMPLE** Inside the locker room, the drifter drifts to sleep.

He pays no attention to the country music blaring outside, or the bulls pacing restlessly, or the bullriders swaggering in too-tight Wranglers.

They call him Stretch, a wild man, a bullfighter, the American kind, who paints his face clown-like and dresses in red and throws himself willingly into the path of angry beasts who have just bucked cowboys to the ground.

When he was 14, the road called, and Stretch answered. He ran away from home and landed at an Oklahoma rodeo and has lived a hundred lifetimes since.

He's slept at truck stops, on the shoulder of highways, in the dirt beside livestock. He's drunk his share of Jack Daniels. He's been tattooed a half-dozen times in a half-dozen cities, dipped enough Copenhagen to roof a house with the tin cans. He's been arrested for fighting. He found a girlfriend in Utah named Kasey.

He's stared down a thousand bulls in a thousand nowhere towns from Tennessee to Texas, Montana to Mississippi. The bulls have knocked out his front teeth and broken his arms, ribs, ankles, tailbone, collarbone and kneecap. They've given him more concussions and stitches and joy than he can measure.

"I live kind of different," Stretch says, smiling toothlessly.

Back in Kansas, the family never understood. His dad's a lawyer, his sister a dentist. His brothers turned out normal, too.

But Stretch, well, he lives kind of different. He owns two bags of clothes and probably won't ever own much else, except this: "I'll have a lot of good stories."

And maybe that's enough.

Maybe, unlike so many people, he has found the place he belongs, in the ring with the other untamed souls, kicking up dust and mud.

The drifter opens his eyes.

Showtime.

—*St. Petersburg Times*

CONVERGENCE POINT 🌿

The Story Behind a Short-short Story

Ben Montgomery, a reporter for the *St. Petersburg Times*, dissects one of Brady Dennis' short-short stories that won the Ernie Pyle Award for Human Interest Writing.

 Dennis tells the story of the reporting and writing behind his prize-winning story "After the Sky Fell."

Find this link on the companion Web site at **www.oup.com/us/scanlan.**

USING STORY FORMS ONLINE

Narratives and serial narratives appear in static form in newspapers: columns of type, accentuated by headlines and subheadings and accompanied by photos and graphics. The World Wide Web is a dynamic medium that accommodates companion multimedia elements that enhance standard news stories. Among them: photo galleries, sound and video presentations, interactive maps, tours and timelines, such as those featured in "Black Hawk Down: An American War Story."

Electronic footnotes, which buttress a story's credibility, can link to supporting documents and trigger pop-up boxes that display character profiles, transcripts, public records and links to stories from the paper's archive. While newspapers provide limited space for letters to the editor, Web readers can chat in real time with journalists and each other. (Story tips can emerge from such interaction, too.)

Beyond this, today's technology has added new formats into which writers place their prose. Given the nonlinear nature of most online information, many outlets encourage their writers to write in "**chunks**"—small blocks of information that are quickly and easily read by users who hopscotch through different sites.

Two additional online forms seem to guide writers in opposing directions. Blogs (short for Web logs) are generally used by professional journalists to update news or to report material of interest that may not merit a fully reported article. Sometimes writers also use them to post the full text of interviews, as opposed to the portions used in a print story. Since the chief hallmark of news blogs is informality, and there's no physical restriction to their length, individual posts can run very long. They are most effective when restricted to two or three paragraphs.

Another new format, however, has significant restrictions in length. Many journalists now use Twitter, the online service designed primarily for mobile phones, to post brief comments and updates. While short-short stories might be limited to 300

CONVERGENCE POINT ⤲

Online Investigative Serial Narrative

Investigative reporter Lee Hancock of the *Dallas Morning News* exposed financial exploitation of the elderly in a four-chapter serial narrative that included compelling audio, video, PDF documents and other supporting evidence included in hyperlinked footnotes.

Find this link on the companion Web site at **www.oup.com/us/ scanlan.**

words, a Twitter post ("tweet") can contain no more than 140 characters. Writers and citizen journalists must convey the relevant information in one medium-length sentence or phrase. This makes Twitter mostly useful for quick updates like a 2013 Boston Marathon bombing tweet. They often include links to full stories. While forms remain largely the same across media platforms, the Web offers a multiplicity of ways writers can report the news.

▶**EXAMPLE** Mother Jones @MotherJones

> Reports: Boston Marathon bombing suspect Dzhokar Tsarnaev arraigned in hospital bed, complaints against him sealed http://bit.ly/117eL2A

ALTERNATIVE STORY FORMS

The *Raleigh* (NC) *News & Observer* could have chosen a traditional story form, such as the inverted pyramid, when the chancellor of the University of North Carolina gave his annual state of the university speech. They took a different path: **alternative story forms**.

"Instead of appearing in standard paragraph form, the report is broken into small chunks of information," executive editor John Drescher told readers on "The Editors' Blog," which shares information about the *N&O*'s reporting. Such forms range from question-and-answer format, graphics or charts, stories so short they don't jump to another page, and, in the chancellor's case, bulleted information introduced with a small headline or "**subhead**."

▶**EXAMPLE** CHAPEL HILL — UNC-Chapel Hill Chancellor James Moeser delivered his State of the University speech Wednesday.

The speech is the chancellor's annual accounting of campus priorities and accomplishments. About 400 people attended the event in the student union.

Some of the Chancellor's Top Goals
  · Improve graduation rates.
  · Pump up UNC-CH's research prowess.
  · Recruit top faculty.
  · Emphasize global education for students.

The emergence of alternative story forms, or ASFs, reflects an effort to respond to readers, Drescher wrote, "who tell us they want the news faster, and this is one way to do that." ASFs are ideal for graduations, festivals, speeches and other periodic events. Andy Bechtel, a former copy editor at the Raleigh paper who teaches journalism at UNC-Chapel Hill, itemizes benefits of the ASF. They:
  • "inform readers, providing not only quick facts but also deep context";
  • "provide information in 'bite sizes' that are easier to digest (and) add up to something nutritious";

Alternative story forms report the news with small chunks of information and graphics, presented in question-and-answer format, charts and bulleted information introduced with a small headline or "subhead." Ideal for speeches, mini-profiles and to explain difficult concepts.

Journalist at Work THE LONG AND SHORT OF IT

Ken Fuson, a former reporter at the *Des Moines (IA) Register*, is a master of story forms. Among his achievements: a 290-word single paragraph weather story, an award-winning six-part serial narrative about a high school production of "West Side Story," and a weekly series of short stories about life's firsts. His philosophy:

Selecting a form: *"It's the most important decision a writer makes. It forces you to ask, "How can I best tell this story?" That requires you to think deeply about what the story is about, and the needs of readers."*

A form's demand: *"Short-form writing puts a tremendous amount of pressure on the ending. There has to be a payoff if people are going to remember it."*

Serial narrative: *"When I've failed, it's invariably because I haven't limited the number of characters. You must decide, 'Who has the most at stake?' and focus on them."*

Getting facts: *"Envision what a story might look like before you head out. But you have to do the reporting to find out if it will work. Many times, I've discovered a better approach for a story - or even a better story - by doing the reporting."*

Favorite form: *"I really enjoy trying to apply the tools of narrative writing—scene-setting, dialogue, etc.—on shorter daily stories. I like showing that narrative writing is not limited to 12-part Pulitzer nominees."* ▼

- "educate readers and bolster our role as watchdogs over government and other powerful institutions";
- "offer variety and surprise the reader"; and
- "bring visual pizzazz to a page."

ASFs are gaining in popularity online, where storytelling often works best in chunks that readers can click through at their own pace.

CHOOSING THE BEST STORY FORM

Some story forms lend themselves to certain topics. Here are some examples:

STORY FORM	STORY TYPE
Inverted pyramid	Breaking news: police and crime news, accidents, meeting coverage, elections, sports events.
Hourglass	Breaking news: stories with strong news value and dramatic appeal that can best be told with a chronological narrative.
Nut graf	News analysis, news features, profiles, trend stories.
Narrative	Dramatic events that rely on characterizations, rising action, climax and resolution. Profiles and investigative series.
Five boxes	News features, trend stories, profiles, breaking news.
Serial narratives	Dramatic and suspenseful stories that lend themselves to unfolding in gradual installments. Live coverage of an ongoing story.
Short-short	Breaking news. Crimes, accidents, verdicts, profiles.
Blog posts, tweets	Breaking news. Seeking story ideas, news tips and other reader input.
Alternative story forms	Periodic stories: speeches, graduations, festivals, meeting stories, election results, profiles.

CONVERGENCE POINT ⤵

*Choose the Right
Story Structure*

"The right structure depends on you and the story. As you report and discover the story, seek the best way to tell it. Consider alternatives," says writing coach and online editor Steve Buttry. He advises strong reporting, collaboration with editors and planning a structure as key ways to find the best way to tell a story.

Find this link on the companion Web site at **www.oup.com/us/ scanlan.**

QUICK Tips HOW TO KNOW WHICH STORY FORM TO USE

- The purpose of the story helps determine the form to use.

- Are you trying to convey information (e.g., inverted pyramid form), or are you trying to create an experience for the reader (e.g., the narrative form)?

- Read other examples widely to get ideas. ▼

The Coaching Way ⁞⁞⁞⁞ SHAPING THE NEWS

To write an inverted pyramid, list everything you think belongs in your story. Arrange the list by newsworthiness, with the most important in your lead and the rest in descending order of importance.

Does your story have news and the elements of narrative: characters, scenes, dialogue, a beginning, middle and end told in chronological narrative? If so, try using the hourglass form.

If you have those elements, along with a question that serves as the engine, switchbacks, and cliffhangers that can sustain installments instead of a single story, try writing a serial narrative.

Stuck on a story? Try the "five boxes" approach. "Even if you just completely scramble it later on," Rick Bragg says, "at least it got you going."

The next time you cover a speech, festival or graduation, consider alternative story forms: Q&A format, bulleted lists, subheadings, graphics, charts.

Telegraph a story in a blog post of two or three paragraphs that focus on newsworthiness, or tweet the news in 140 characters. ▼

PROFESSIONALS' ROUNDTABLE

SHAPING STORIES

Choosing the right story form is like choosing the right container for a present. You wouldn't use a huge box for a ring, nor would you choose a story form that doesn't reflect the contents. Reporters and editors base their decisions on these beliefs:
- Reporting dictates form.
- Reader needs matter most.
- Story forms depend on where you work.
- Forms don't mean formulaic.

Participants

 JAN WINBURN, CNN, former special projects editor, *Atlanta Journal-Constitution*

 BRYAN GRULEY, former Chicago bureau chief, *Wall Street Journal*

 MARCIO SIMÕES, editor, *Revista Cálculo*, São Paulo, Brazil

> ### What factors determine which story form to use?

Winburn: The purpose of your story helps determine what form to use. Are you trying to communicate information to the reader, or are you trying to create an experience for the reader?

In the first case, you may want to use an inverted pyramid. If you are attempting to give the reader an experience, the narrative form might be an option.

Gruley: As always, what you have in your notebooks determines what you're going to write.

> ### What about critics who say story forms make for formulaic writing?

Simões: A car always has wheels and nobody talks about formulaic cars. We must make ourselves understood by readers. That's why we use well-known story forms.

> ### How much influence does your news organization have on your choice of story form?

Gruley: We want to keep the reader reading by continually giving him new, interesting information that seeks to answer the story's central question. Chronological story telling is usually the simplest, clearest, most natural way to tell a story.

> ### What advice would you give beginning journalists struggling with structures for their stories?

Winburn: Read widely—especially magazines, print and online. They have long used story forms that newspapers have been slow to adopt. This will open your eyes to more ways to approach stories. Form a group intent on studying pieces by accomplished writers who are taking some risks with form.

SUMMARY GUIDE | STORY FORMS

SHAPING THE NEWS

Journalists rely on established story forms and must be familiar with all the forms at their disposal.

What to Remember → Story forms continue to evolve. From the most traditional to emerging ones designed for online audiences, they shape how news is best conveyed to consumers. Like architects, news writers understand that form follows content.

INVERTED PYRAMID: NEWS FROM THE TOP DOWN

The inverted pyramid is organized around facts and places the most newsworthy information at the top, and the remaining information follows in order of importance, with the least important at the bottom.

What to Remember →
> The aim of the inverted pyramid is to furnish the news fast and let readers decide how much they want to read. Despite its critics, it remains the go-to shape for breaking news stories in print, broadcast and online.

THE HOURGLASS: SERVING NEWS AND READERS

> The hourglass combines two story forms: inverted pyramid and narrative.

What to Remember →
> The hourglass consists of a top, which includes the most newsworthy elements; a turn, or transition; followed by the narrative, usually a chronological account employing scenes, anecdotes, dialogue and details. It can be used for routine stories, but is best reserved for dramatic events.

THE NUT GRAF: GIVING READERS A REASON TO CARE

> The nut graf form usually begins with a scene, followed by a one to three paragraphs that explain what the story is about and alternating sections of supporting material in support of the focus.

What to Remember →
> Nut graf stories are useful for issue stories and profiles. The name derives from its central device, short for nut paragraph, that contains the kernel of a story that provides context and a rationale to continue reading.

FIVE BOXES: HOW READERS PROCESS STORIES

> The five boxes form provides containers that organize facts, details, quotes and anecdotes into a structure that mirrors how readers process information, making for a satisfying reading experience.

What to Remember →
> The five boxes include a lead with a scene or anecdote that hooks readers, a nut graf that justifies the story, a resumption of the narrative, a section for statistics, history and other background information and a resonant ending that brings all the pieces together.

THE NARRATIVE: THE WAY WE TELL STORIES

> The narrative is a timeless form that employs plots with a beginning, middle and end; characters; settings; a theme, complication, climax and resolution.

What to Remember →
> Four elements provide the narrative's enduring hold on readers: scenes, dialogue, details and third-person point of view. Rather than give away the story in the lead, the narrative delays resolution until the end to build suspense and keep readers engaged.

SERIAL NARRATIVE: "TO BE CONTINUED . . ."

Serial narratives break stories up into dramatic segments and unfold gradually, usually in installments.

What to Remember → Successful serials need an "engine," usually an unanswered question that drives readers forward. Other ingredients include a major character with something important at stake; a "gold mine source" with access to documents, reliable memories and a wealth of facts and details; a narrative arc; plot twists; and cliffhangers—dramatic endings that leave a reader hanging and wanting to read more.

SHORT-SHORT STORIES: WRITING FOR A TIME-PRESSED AUDIENCE

Short-short stories are brief narratives that provide an alternative to inverted pyramid stories long used to report crimes and accidents on deadline.

What to Remember → Short-shorts tell the story with characters, dialogue, action and vivid details. They demonstrate that powerful storytelling need not depend on lots of time and words.

USING STORY FORMS ONLINE

Technology has added a variety of new online story forms to the journalist's tool kit.

What to Remember → Journalists now communicate with short, easy-to-read blocks of information, brief blog posts that telegraph information with the inverted pyramid, and 140-character tweets. Online storytelling encompasses audio, video and interactive footnotes that provide supporting evidence.

ALTERNATIVE STORY FORMS

Alternative story forms combine text and graphics to create charts, lists and fact boxes that compress reporting into easy-to-digest presentations.

What to Remember → News organizations have turned to alternative story forms to meet the needs of readers who want their news fast. These forms are best used with routine, recurring stories such as fairs, graduations, speeches, and profiles.

CHOOSING THE BEST STORY FORM

Selection of a story form depends on the information to be presented, timeliness, news value and audience interest.

What to Remember → Story form selection depends on the effects the journalists want to produce, whether to report the news or tell a story. Smart news writers consider more than one option before settling on a story form tailored to their reporting and their audiences' needs and interests.

KEY TERMS

alternative story forms, p. 250
BBI, p. 246
chunks, p. 249
cliffhanger, p. 247
dialogue, p. 247
five boxes, p. 245
gold mine source, p. 247
hourglass, p. 243
inverted pyramid, p. 241

kicker, p. 246
long form narratives, p. 248
narrative, p. 243
narrative arc, p. 247
nut graf, p. 244
scenes, p. 246
serial narratives, p. 247
short-short stories, p. 248
stakeholder, p. 247

status details, p. 247
subhead, p. 250
switchbacks, p. 247
third person point of view, p. 247
top, p. 243
traditional story form, p. 240
turn, p. 243

EXERCISES

1. Study 10 news stories and determine what form they follow: inverted pyramid, hourglass, nut graf, narrative, five boxes, short-short, serial narrative, alternative story form. Explain your choices and the reporting and writing demands behind the selection of story form.

2. Rewrite an inverted pyramid into an hourglass story. If you need to do additional reporting, identify what else you need.

3. Find an inverted pyramid story and rewrite it into a short-short. What are the reporting and writing challenges behind such a transformation?

4. Determine whether one of your stories needs a nut graf. Follow the advice of writing coach Jack Hart: "Try putting yourself in the reader's place. Forget what you know about the story, read the first three paragraphs and ask yourself what the entire story's about. If you can't answer with reasonable accuracy, you need a nut paragraph."

5. Break up the reporting elements of one of your stories into five boxes by selecting the paragraphs or sections that make up the lead, the nut graf, resumption of the narrative, the boring but important information and the kicker.

6. After you've reported a story, decide what elements would work most effectively as an alternative story form. If it's a profile, write a bio box or "fast facts" list. Select an issue or process and distill it into a series of bullet points.

READINGS

Blundell, William E. *The Art and Craft of Feature Writing: Based on The Wall Street Journal Guide.* New York: Plume, 1988. *The Wall Street Journal* pioneered the use of the nut graf as a narrative device to tell feature stories. Blundell, a master of the craft, shares the strategies and techniques, including anecdotal leads, scenes and the connective tissue of the nut graf, all designed to inform readers and make them care about a subject.

Murray, Donald M. *Writing to Deadline: The Journalist at Work.* Portsmouth, NH: Heinemann. 2000. Murray examines story forms by drawing on a wide range of stories from *The Boston Globe*, where he was a longtime writing coach, and his varied career as a prolific newspaper reporter, columnist and magazine writer. He details the reporting demands and organizing techniques required for the inverted pyramid, nut graf, profiles and feature stories.

Sagolla, Dom. *140 Characters: A Style Guide for the Short Form.* Hoboken, NJ: John Wiley & Sons, 2009. Sagolla, one of the creators of Twitter, explains what makes tweets and blog posts effective and why social media influences how journalists communicate with their audiences. His guide provides practical advice and examples that demonstrate why micro-writing forms that rely on bursts of information have revolutionized the way news and information is delivered.

Scanlan, Christopher, ed. *How I Wrote the Story.* Providence, RI: Providence Journal Co., 1985. Story forms in all their variety are on display in this collection, which features the work of journalists at the *Providence Journal,* a newspaper known for its path-breaking approaches to writing. The writers discuss the hows and whys behind their decisions to write using different story shapes.

Stern, Jerome. *Micro Fiction: An Anthology of Fifty Really Short Stories.* New York: W. W. Norton & Company, 1996. This collection of short stories, some no longer than 250 words, offers inspiration for journalists seeking to serve time-pressed readers by telling stories in tight spaces. While they are fiction, the examples are rich with ideas and approaches for journalists who want to excel at writing the short-short news story.

Stewart, James B. *Follow the Story: How to Write Successful Nonfiction.* New York: Simon and Schuster, 1998. Stewart, who won a Pulitzer Prize at *The Wall Street Journal,* where he also edited page-one stories, writes for *The New Yorker* and is a best-selling nonfiction author. His book is a revelatory exploration of the many ways stories can be told for newspapers and magazines, bolstered by numerous examples and his firm grasp of the organizational principles that go into choosing the best way to tell a story.

INVERTED PYRAMID STORY

The inverted pyramid is the oldest, most common story form employed by news organizations to deliver news. In writing such stories, journalists rely on the three most important ingredients of news: timeliness, importance and the interest level of their audience. Such stories, as the following example demonstrates, follow an orderly procession of facts, quotes, context and background.

HILLTOP RESIDENTS SHARE SEX-OFFENDER CONCERNS WITH TACOMA COUNCIL

Karen Miller and Lewis Kamb; Staff Writers
***Tacoma News Tribune*, July 10, 2012**

Hilltop neighbors urged the Tacoma City Council at its meeting Tuesday to help prevent a rumored halfway house for sex offenders from moving into South Grant Street.

The house in question, in the 1600 block of South Grant Street near Stanley Elementary and Al Davies Boys & Girls Club, is owned and being renovated by Richard Garrett. Neighbors claim Garrett plans to house level 2 and 3 sex offenders—a claim Garrett disputes.

About 20 people spoke out at Tuesday's meeting. Jeanne Peterson of the Hilltop Action Coalition told the council the neighborhood is tired of being a haven for sex offenders. She said 17 houses on Hilltop already house multiple sex offenders.

The lead of an inverted pyramid story summarizes the most newsworthy elements. This lead distills the news of an event—a protest against the location of a halfway house for sex offenders at a public meeting. Note the use of the qualifier "rumored." The reporters are careful to base the story on what is known and unknown. The lead follows a subject-verb-object format that makes it easy for readers to process the information. They also use an action verb in active tense, which imbues the sentence with energy. The lead is a brief 27-word sentence that meets the one-breath rule. The style makes it easy for readers to absorb the information.

An inverted pyramid story raises and answers question in the order that readers expect. In this case, it immediately gives a specific location, enhanced by providing familiar landmarks, and identifies the property owner. This paragraph is information rich and provides a balanced account. The neighbors' complaints are followed by a refutations from the owner. The paragraph includes information about the types of sex offenders, but could have explained what the categories represent to readers unfamiliar with the bureaucratic language.

Scope is an essential element of complete news stories. This paragraph lists the number of protesters and how many locations in the neighborhood already house sex offenders. It supports the lead by including the reason behind neighborhood protests and provides necessary context. Most important, it provides attribution from a named source and identifies her as a community leader. In the first three paragraphs, the story has already answered six of the eight questions journalists must address: What? Where? When? Who? Why? and So what? Unlike narratives, which emphasize chronology, drama and suspense, the inverted pyramid delivers news and information quickly. Timeliness, reporting and the needs of audiences determine which form to choose.

"There's a point where we have to draw a line in the sand," Peterson said.

Many people asked why there wasn't a city ordinance prohibiting sex-offender housing close to schools.

"Nothing stays in the Hilltop," said Renee Walker, who lives across the street from Garrett's property. "Eventually, (offenders) will make their way to your house."

City officials say that they are restricted under state law from regulating where anyone—including sex offenders—can or cannot live.

Garrett, a former convict who now works as a prison minister, has insisted he never planned to house sex offenders. He said he has thought about possibly renting the home to veterans or ex-cons who have participated in his prison ministry.

Adrian Johnson, a DOC regional housing director for Pierce County, said Tuesday that he met with Garrett last month to discuss a possible group-home plan.

Quotes breathe life and inject human voices into stories. They belong high up in the story and usually punctuate the most newsworthy element. The quote is colorful and to the point, illustrating the frustration of concerned neighbors.

A second newsworthy element is introduced: concern about the lack of a city ordinance barring housing of sex offenders close to schools. Including this in the lead would produce unnecessary and confusing clutter. Journalists rely on a sharp focus to help them make such decisions. Rather than quote a single individual, the reporters use "many people" to convey the scope. Inverted pyramid stories are economical and use ways to present more than one piece of information in a sentence. At the same time, the writers follow the rule that a sentence should be limited to one thought.

Quotes also provide action, which let readers experience a story through their senses. Journalists should avoid giving opinions. Here the reporters use the quote to include another example of neighborhood concerns rather than offering their own point of view.

Effective news stories depend on sources that readers can trust. The reporters back up the assertion about the lack of a city ordinance blocking the location of halfway houses that appeared two paragraphs earlier. They provide an authoritative source, city officials, who explain the challenge that neighbors opposed to the halfway house face. Credible, authoritative sources are a mainstay of effective journalism.

Journalists must strive for balance and fairness in their stories by including as many relevant points of view as possible. In this story, neighbors are pitted against the property owner. Here the story rightly presents his explanation about the use of the property and his insistence that he never intended to house sex offenders. The source is clearly identified with a clause that describes his occupation and relevant background as an ex-offender. The verb "has insisted" suggests that Garrett didn't appear at the public meeting and is based on background, perhaps derived from previous stories about the issue. Could an argument be made that for fairness sake, Garrett's comments belong higher up in the story?

Good journalists don't limit their reporting to a live event. Instead they seek additional information that provides further context and background. The reporter uses an acronym—DOC—that may not be familiar to readers. Don't make assumptions about reader knowledge.

"He had not mentioned making use of that residence for sex offenders when I met with him. And in fact, I told him it would not work," Johnson said. "Because our officers would not approve the placement due to the proximity to the elementary school and the Boys & Girls Club."

Before the council took public comment, Council-woman Lauren Walker addressed the crowd, telling the Hilltop neighbors that the city will continue to monitor the property as Garrett renovates it.

Quotes are necessary to amplify summary paragraphs like the one earlier. They provide further context and give readers additional information. It's unclear whether the official's statement undercuts Garrett's contention that he never planned to house sex offenders, but it does make clear that such a move would not be approved. Identifying the location of an elementary school and a Boys & Girls Club helps readers visualize the threat neighbors feel a halfway house for sex offenders would pose. Many quotes can be paraphrased, but this one is clear, detailed and to the point. It's a good choice.

The story ends in a useful way, addressing a seventh crucial question "What's next?" It concludes the story with information that engages readers who want to know about future developments. Quotes are the default choice for most stories, but they are often unnecessary and irrelevant tags that add little more than emotion. The reporters have taken control by summarizing an important point. It brings the story to a satisfying close.

SUMMARY

Critics of the inverted pyramid say it's outdated, unnatural, boring, artless and a factor in the declining readership that newspapers have been grappling with for decades. But its top-down model survives because it remains an effective way to present an orderly series of facts based on a sharp focus. In just 335 words, reporters Karen Miller and Lewis Kamb describe an event, put an issue in context and provide countervailing points of view and necessary background. They use quotes to convey information and enliven their story. The organization and clear writing make for quick reading and easy comprehension. Inverted pyramid stories require a firm grasp of newsworthiness, strong organization, attention to style and the different ways journalists document stories. The form is the default choice for online news stories for audiences who want the news conveyed as briefly as possible. By presenting the information in descending order of importance, readers are free to stop reading as soon as their information needs are met. The inverted pyramid is a challenging and essential form but one that can be mastered with experience.

CHAPTER 12

WRITING FOR PRINT

BY THE END OF THIS CHAPTER,

you should be able to...

> Understand the anatomy and workflow of a newspaper

> Distinguish between and write different classes of stories

> Expand your grasp of newspaper's reporting process and writing forms

> Assess newspapers' role in a multimedia and multiplatform world

LONG BEFORE THE Web, before radio, before television, the sole source of news and information was the newspaper. Millions of people still buy them, millions more read them, even though the Internet and television have eclipsed the newspaper as the primary source of news. Newspapers also remain a vital source of jobs, despite staff layoffs, buyouts and declining advertising and circulation revenues.

In this chapter, you will learn the essentials of writing for print, a brief history of newspapers, the twin sides of the industry that make them possible, the role newspapers play in a new media world and the story types and reporting and writing skills required to succeed as a print journalist.

WRITING FOR NEWSPAPERS

Writing for newspapers requires familiarity with newspaper format, style and presentation. That comes from reading, careful study and practice, a requirement many student journalists and even professionals ignore. In the authors' years of contact with students who say they want to write for newspapers, the disturbing reality, we found, is that few of them actually read a newspaper.

In chapter 2, we reviewed the process of reporting and writing news stories by following the six-step approach: idea, focus, report, organize, draft and revise. Two factors influence writing for print: time and space. The time a reporter has to produce a story depends on the deadline, which is determined by production timetables, news

There's no doubt that news consumers are fast moving from print to online sources, yet nearly one in four Americans said they read a newspaper every day in 2012, the Pew Research Center reported. A student reads *The Lance*, the campus weekly at Evangel University in Springfield, MO.

gathering conditions and editors' decisions. Available space determines story length and story placement.

Study a newspaper and you will see a variety of story forms and shapes, and graphic elements described in previous chapters: inverted pyramid, hourglass, narratives, briefs, photographs and informational graphics.

Now it's time to become familiar with the newspaper—as a public service, a profit-making business, and an organization—and to look closely at the product itself so you understand the various journalistic roles this media offers.

BEHIND THE PAGE: WHO DOES WHAT

Newspaper companies are divided into two parts: editorial and business (see Figure 12-1).

The first, made up of editors, reporters, and other journalists, fills space allotted for news and information, called the "**news hole**."

The second, comprising the advertising and circulation sales forces, generates revenue for the business. The advertising group sells **ad space** in the newspaper, ranging from full-page display ads, such as those promoting supermarket specials, and classified ads to individual spots and promotions distributed to every available space on the printed page not devoted to editorial content. The circulation group sells newspapers

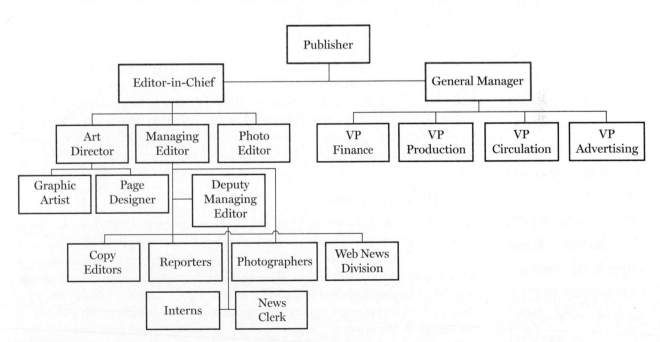

FIGURE 12-1 An organizational chart of a newspaper that shows the separation of duties and responsibilities between the editorial and business sides of the enterprise. The setup may vary depending on the size and approach of an individual news organization.

on the street and subscriptions to individuals and commercial interests, ranging from a corner newsstand to a hotel chain. Each side has a hierarchy—an organizational structure organized by levels of authority, job specialization and groups. These two groups generally stay completely separate, both functionally and geographically. Depending on the size of the newspaper, the two departments, and their affiliates, may occupy separate floors or spread out on a single floor.

The News Side

The top news manager, generally known as **editor-in-chief** or executive editor, shares dual responsibilities, overseeing publication of the paper and representing the editorial department as a member of the senior management team. Some editors play a major role in editing major stories, while others maintain a hands-off policy, leaving the job to subordinates.

Below the editor is a collection of news managers who oversee the processes of newsgathering and writing, editing and design. Their titles reflect authority and/or responsibilities, and are often abbreviated in newsroom talk. They include **managing editor** (ME), assistant and deputy managing editor (AME, DME), photo editor or director of photography (DP), city editor, and assorted other managing or deputy editors in charge of copy, design, investigations, online and other areas.

Reporters and photojournalists are at the heart of any news operation. Their titles reflect responsibilities, specialties or seniority: staff reporter, staff writer, database reporter, police reporter, courts reporter, senior writer, investigative reporter. Also in the information mix are **copy editors**, photographers, photo editors, **paginators**/page designers and graphic artists (sometimes now called "visual journalists") who make final edits on stories or create the look of the newspaper.

Beginning journalists often get their first professional experience as **interns**, working in news roles for a limited period of time. Depending on performance, this job can lead to a full-time position, often as a **news clerk**—someone who can capably perform many different newsroom tasks as needed—or promotion to staff reporter. This is why it's so important for new journalists to be versatile—getting your first job may depend on how easily you can be plugged into different roles.

The Business Side

The business side of a newspaper starts with the **publisher** or chief executive officer (CEO), the newspaper's chief management figure, who oversees the budget, editorial pages and business departments. The paper's top editor reports to the publisher, as will a senior vice president or general manager. At the next management tier there are generally vice presidents overseeing advertising, circulation, production and finances. Most of these management figures won't spend much time mingling with journalists, but they're all important in the process of getting the newspaper produced.

As a reporter, it can be easy to overlook the business side of your newspaper. But ads and subscriptions provide the revenue streams that underwrite the expense of news gathering and delivery. Bringing in dollars is a responsibility that reporters have

> ❝Newspapers are likely to remain our most powerful engines of discovery for many years to come. . . . It is hard to envisage a better device for displaying the news than the familiar paper product—swiftly scanned, easily clipped, a very tangible form of budget constraint . . . only newspapers will be able to meet the enormous fixed cost of maintaining a staff of expert editors and reporters who work together to perform what they like to call 'the daily miracle': the hashing-out of a reasonably coherent answer to the question every morning: What's going on out there?❞
>
> —DAVID MARSH, FORMER ECONOMICS REPORTER, *BOSTON GLOBE* AND *FORBES*

long disdained: "They" are after money; "we" are after stories. At the best papers, a philosophical wall divides the editorial side from the business side to prevent ad managers from pitching stories favorable to their customers and to protect the newsroom from complaints from aggrieved subjects and sources. It's important to keep the two sides separate to ensure journalistic credibility, but it's also important to remember that each side of the operation cannot exist without the other. News stories are literally printed on the same sheets sold for advertising.

From the 1990s to the present day, newspapers—especially those in publicly traded companies such as Gannett and McClatchy Co.—have seen profit margins shrink, and felt pressure from their Wall Street overlords. As they began searching for new ways to generate revenue, the wall began to crumble.

As newspapers face growing economic challenges, it's time for reporters to better understand what goes on behind the "wall." Journalists need to understand the business side of their newspaper, just as they would dissect the anatomy of their beat, whether it's a city council or the White House. This doesn't mean that journalists should become part of the sales force. Rather, it gives them information they need to understand the business pressures, and if possible, offer ideas that might generate revenue without compromising their roles as journalists.

CONVERGENCE POINT

An Interactive History of News

The Web site of the Newseum, located in Washington, DC, provides a rich multimedia exploration of the news and journalism. Among its highlights: news stories, "this day in news history" exhibits, videos, interviews and more than 800 front pages posted every day.

Find this link on the companion Web site at **www.oup.com/us/ scanlan.**

CHIP'S CORNER

NEWSPAPERS PAST AND PRESENT

When I became a newspaper reporter in 1972, I thought I was just getting my first job after college. Little did I know that the *Milford Citizen*, a small daily newspaper in a New Haven suburb, belonged to a long line of publications that began in America three centuries ago.

Nor was I aware that I had become part of an evolutionary process that would unfold in the next 35 years as I worked as a newspaper reporter and later as a journalism teacher. Perhaps it's understandable that journalists who produce "the first draft of history" don't have time to consider their own profession's background. But as students it's important that you have a grasp of what came before you entered journalism.

The newspaper business began in this country with "Publick Occurrences Both Forreign and Domestick." Its publication presaged a continuing struggle between newspapers and the government over freedom of the press guaranteed in the First Amendment to the Constitution. Benjamin Harris published just one edition, on September 25, 1690, before the British colonial government shut it down, arrested the publisher and ordered all copies to be destroyed.

Until the 1830s, news consisted largely of information of interest to the wealthy and powerful. "Most newspapers were little more than excuses for espousing a political position, for listing the arrival and departure of ships,

for familiar essays and useful advice, or for commercial or legal announcements," historian Daniel Boorstin observed.

The definition of news changed with the 1833 appearance of *The Sun* in New York City. It cost a penny, was aimed at the working class filling the cities and looked beyond political and shipping news. As journalism scholar Leon Sigal said, *The Sun* chose "to sample the rich variety of everyday social life in the city—crimes, accidents, the occasions of high and low society." News became a commercial product, and story types, such as the human interest story, developed as a marketing tool to sell newspapers. ▼

Journalist at Work A NEWSPAPER REPORTER'S LIFE

Michaela Saunders

Michaela Saunders' professional newspaper career began when she was 14 and earned $20 from her hometown paper for a review of the Disney movie *Pocahontas*. But two other experiences set her on the journalism path even earlier: Mrs. Blue, her fourth grade teacher, praised her writing, and Saunders, who is Native American, remembers watching reporters interview her father about University of North Dakota student opposition to public schools using "Fighting Sioux" as a mascot.

From then, she worked on school papers through college, summer camps, internships and training programs, and journalism dominated her life. Her full-time career began in 2003 when the *Omaha World Herald* hired her as an education reporter.

Her beat included the 47,000-student Omaha Public Schools, two suburban districts, youth and family issues, and major projects.

She regularly put in nine to 10 hours a day (her favorite days "are out of the office, not attached to my phone"). She produced a mix of breaking news, enterprise stories and briefs for the paper's morning and afternoon editions. Her paper was pumping up its online operation, but Saunders' convergence experience was limited to posting breaking news and contributing audio interviews. "I'm still a newspaper reporter," Saunders said, but she tried to train herself to think in terms of multimedia options. Her views on the career path she chose:

Why did you pick print journalism?
Print provided the best opportunity to give a full picture of the story . . . the best and most effective public service.

What's the best part of your job?
I'm shy, so I've always appreciated how liberating it is to be able to talk to people—and ask questions—that I would never ask without this job. And, I am passionate about the role of journalism in our society, in democracy.

And the worst?
The hours are bad, there's not enough feedback and often I feel underappreciated. But worse than that is the struggle, the pang even, of understanding how the business side of things can influence coverage. From the size of the news hole to challenges of the business community as subject. Omaha is a big small town and the paper's relationship with the community reflects that.

What story are you most proud of?
A narrative about a high school senior who suffered a brain injury, then came back to graduate with his class.

Your advice to aspiring reporters?
If you're not passionate about it, keep looking for your passion. Journalism takes a lot out of you and if you don't feel it in your bones it will wear you out. ▶

ON THE PAGE

Newspaper writing demands solid, accurate reporting and clear, compelling writing. Here are some categories of news that reporters starting out should learn how to cover:

- **Breaking news**. Breaking news refers to a current, ongoing and dramatic event, such as a fire, an important vote or a natural disaster. In response, editors dispatch one or more reporters, depending on the story's magnitude. Unlike broadcast stations and online sites that can update stories in real time, newspapers often have to wait several hours to publish the story, requiring editors and reporters to devise ways to provide fresh information on a story that readers may think they know well. Updates are written for newspapers' Web sites, but print stories must stand alone and provide depth and context.

- **Trend stories**. Newspapers try to step back from breaking news and provide context, background, the how and why of social developments ranging from a crime wave to eating disorders among young women and men.

- **News analyses**. Reporters with knowledge in specialized areas, such as politics, government or science, step back to interpret complex trends or developments for readers. These appear in news pages and are usually labeled "news analysis."

- **Editorials**. Editorials are opinion pieces that usually express the collective view of the publisher and editorial writers who comprise an editorial board. Nearly always unsigned, editorials are written in the third person plural— "We believe the president's decision on . . ." They appear on a separate editorial page, often accompanied by a political cartoon, produced either by a staff cartoonist or, more likely, by a syndicated one. The editorial page usually includes letters to the editor. The opposite page, known as "the op-ed," provides space for opinion columns, often written by political reporters, local experts and syndicated columnists, that attempt to provide a range of viewpoints.

- **Local and community coverage**. Newspapers furnish readers with news and information about their community, from the state to the neighborhood level. The city or suburban editor guides this coverage, with many stories generated from the bottom up by beat reporters who are sometimes grouped into law enforcement, education and subject-area teams.

X-RAY READING LOCALIZING A TREND

Here is how a newspaper links a national trend—a health warning about peanut allergies—to a local audience, with a story timed to the start of the new school year with details that inform and likely spark controversy.

> **OXFORD CITY SCHOOLS JOIN NUT-FREE TREND**
> Fearing the rare, yet potentially fatal dangers linked to peanut allergies, Oxford City schools are now nut-free—no peanut butter, no peanut brittle, no foods cooked with peanut oil. The new rule commands attention from the classroom to the cafeteria to even the teachers' lounge.
> —*The Anniston (Ala.) Star, Aug. 13, 2008*

Notice how two sentences of a summary lead telescope the news.

- **National and international coverage**. National and major metropolitan papers employ national and foreign editors who supervise correspondents scattered around the globe, although budgets have cut into their ranks in recent years. Smaller papers rely on wire services, such as Reuters and the Associated Press, to get national and foreign stories.
- **Enterprise/investigative projects**. "It's only a matter of time before South Louisiana takes a direct hit from a major hurricane. Billions have been spent to protect us, but we grow more vulnerable every day." That prediction appeared in "Washing Away," a five-part series published in the *New Orleans Times-Picayune* in 2002. Three years later, the forecast came true when Hurricane Katrina hit the north-central Gulf Coast, causing more than 1,830 deaths and widespread destruction. New Orleans was hit hardest, when storm surges breached levees, flooding 80 percent of the city and neighboring communities for weeks. "Washing Away" is enterprise and investigative reporting at its best. Enterprise means looking beyond breaking news to find larger contexts and employ different ways to tell stories and alert readers to issues that lie beneath the surface of press releases, news conferences, the police blotter and commission agendas. Investigative reporting refers to the methods and techniques used to uncover such hidden stories, including computer-assisted reporting, time-consuming requests for and poring over reams of documents to find evidence for a hypothesis, multiple interviews that seek facts, opinions, faces behind the story and secret histories not to be found in a database.
- **Feature writing**. Feature writing focuses on individuals and their stories. It can usually be found in lifestyle sections, food and fashion sections and other so-called service journalism, although strong features may get front-page play. The stories are frequently long and told through narratives and serial narratives. Feature writers often take risks. One such story is "The Old White Oak of Matthews." *Charlotte* (NC) *Observer* reporter Elizabeth Leland chose the style of a children's book to tell, in 10 chapters, the story of a 129-year-old tree and the struggle to save it from development.
- **Criticism**. Newspapers offer readers news about art and popular culture. Even small papers have a TV reporter or a writer specializing in art and popular culture. Their stories also appear in lifestyle pages.

NEW ROLES FOR REPORTERS AND EDITORS

Newspaper reporters and editors must reconcile themselves to seismic changes in news gathering and delivery. This requires taking on new roles, filing news stories, photos, audio and video to the paper's Web site during the day; appearing on radio and television to discuss their stories and then compiling a story with a fresh take for the newspapers; and deciding how much to write for the newspaper, a painful development for journalists who still measure their success by the number of column inches their stories consume.

The Financial Times, a British international business newspaper, has imposed a no-jump rule: no matter what page, including the front page; wherever the story begins it must end there without jumping to another page. "What is new and important to relate is compressed into the shortest possible space, along with just enough background material to make sense of it," said David Marsh, a veteran business writer. (*USA Today* has abided by a no-jump from the front page since its inception in 1982, with one exception: One cover story per section may jump inside.) Given the impatience of news audiences online and off, brevity has become a necessity.

The technological changes that permit near real-time publication of news online have caused newspapers to do what would have been unthinkable before the World Wide Web appeared in 1994: reveal their stories to the competition before they appear in the newspaper. "As recently as 2005, newspapers would hoard their breaking stories, investigative projects, and big features until the last minute," press critic Jack Shafer wrote in Slate.com. "But no more—newspapers now play nice with their Web siblings, seeing in Web success their own success and the future of their franchise."

CONVERGENCE POINT ⚓

Old News Is Bad News

Media critic Jack Shafer describes the historical time shift that has changed the way we consume news.

Find this link on the companion Web site at **www.oup.com/us/ scanlan.**

SURVIVING IN A CHANGING WORLD

After much resistance and delay, newspaper companies have come to accept the need for an online presence to maintain their audiences. They've created web sites, hired Web-savvy staffs to post news from the daily paper and produce original content with multimedia elements, such as interactive photo galleries, links to full texts of documents, and audio and video. On the positive side, these changes make economic sense. "Online editions are adding readers and advertising revenues at a healthy pace," industry analyst Rick Edmonds observed in the Pew Research Center for Excellence in Journalism's annual "State of the News Media 2007" report. Better still, "when online and print readers are combined, the audience for what newspapers produce is higher than ever."

Not everyone shares Edmonds' view.

"Let's finally come out and say: Newspapers are dead," Michael S. Malone wrote in his ABCNews.com column "Silicon Insider" in 2005. "They will never come back. By the end of this decade, the newspaper industry will suffer the same death rate—90-plus percent—that every other industry experiences when run over by a technology revolution."

Even with radio, television and online news available 24/7, 365 days of the year, the reports of newspapers' death, as humorist Mark Twain responded when an inaccurate report of his demise appeared, are likely "exaggerated."

There's no doubt newspapers face hard times. The 2012 "State of the News Media" report concludes: "The newspaper industry enters 2012 neither dying nor assured of a stable future."

66 There's still a place for appointment media—a home-delivered newspaper on the porch each morning or an evening newscast while making dinner. But it is a smaller place. 99

—TOM CURLEY, FORMER
PRESIDENT AND CEO,
ASSOCIATED PRESS

Among the symptoms:

- Daily newspaper circulation figures, the average number of copies distributed in a day, continue to decline. "though at a rate perhaps only half as bad as the worst of the last decade—under 5% rather than the peak of nearly 10%."
- Advertising, the lifeblood of the industry, was down by $2.1 billion in 2011 from the previous year and expected to continue falling.
- Sliding earnings. Major newspapers are operating at a loss or break even. Stock prices, after a modest rally in 2010, fell by about 25% in 2011. Wall Street, whose investors support the print industry, "remains lukewarm."
- Newspapers are under attack from online operations that provide news and information, much of it for free. Why buy a newspaper when you can read Google or Yahoo! news from around the world, or pick up a free newspaper?

But the news is not all bad.

- On an average day, about 50 million people still buy a newspaper, the 2007 State of the News Media reported, although, admittedly, those numbers continue to show a steady decline. When the number of newspapers shared with non-buyers is factored in—what the industry calls the "pass-along" rate—that figure doubles.
- Daily newspapers continue to close, but their extinction is overrated. In 2009, daily newspapers numbered nearly 1,400, shrinking from about 1,600 since 1990. While dailies suffer, weekly newspapers—about 8,000 in the United States, estimates journalism professor Judy Miller—fill the gap.

Another myth: There are no jobs in print journalism. To be sure, staff cuts have cost thousands of newsroom jobs in recent years, but the American Society of Newspaper editors still counted 41,600 journalists in 2010, its latest survey, up slightly from the previous year.

The byline used to be the only way newspapers identified individuals who reported and wrote the news. Now tag lines with email addresses give readers a way to respond instantly to reporters and social media connects them with journalists instantly. Some reporters feel overwhelmed by the flood of emails and tweets. Others greet the development with enthusiasm. Among the rewards: story ideas, corrections, accessibility to new sources, sounding boards, instantaneous communication and immediate response. In today's interactive news environment, actively using email, blogging and tweeting have become necessary skills for newspaper reporters.

Today, news companies are producing new products that reflect changing demographics and the industry's desperate attempt to build new markets at a time of sliding revenues. They fall into two groups:

1. Ethnic and immigrant publications that serve growing numbers of Latino readers and other ethnic and immigrant populations—for example, *Al Dia,* a Spanish-language newspaper in Dallas, and *Sho-Ban News,* which serves the Shoshone–Bannock Tribe.
2. Free dailies—such as *AM New York, tbt* in St. Petersburg, Florida, and *East Bay Daily News* in Berkeley, California—aimed at younger readers. Their strategies include shorter stories, emphasizing photos and other visual elements, and focusing on consumer news, entertainment and sports.

CONVERGENCE POINT ⚉

The State of the News Media

The Pew Research Center's Project for Excellence in Journalism produces this annual report on the status of the news media, including trends and data on all the major sectors of journalism, including newspapers, radio and television and online news.

Find this link on the companion Web site at **www.oup.com/us/ scanlan.**

Faced with dwindling readership, news companies are reaching out to ethnic and immigrant populations with newspapers tailored to those communities, such as *Al Dia*, the Spanish-language daily in Dallas, TX.

QUICK Tips ⊙ JOB GROWTH IN PRINT JOURNALISM

Print journalism is in the dumps, but there are opportunities in new and growing markets:

■ Publications servicing ethnic and immigrant populations

■ Free dailies aimed at young, urban readers ▼

The Coaching Way ⅲⅰ WORKING FOR A NEWSPAPER

- Have you visited every department of your local or college newspaper? Take a tour and get to know the players who get your story in the newspaper.
- If you're a reporter for your college paper, ask to spend a day or two working as a copy editor so you can understand the pressures—stories filed late, length problems, misspellings and math mistakes that should be double-checked before filing—facing those forced to grapple with your subpar story on deadline.
- Look at the front page of any newspaper and identify all the elements on it, from masthead to briefs and classified ads.

- Have you studied journalism history? To see where your profession came from, read *A History of Newspapers* by Mitchell Stephens, and *The Press in America: An Interpretative History of the Mass Media* by Michael and Edwin Emery. Visit the Newseum online (http://www.newseum.org), or in person in Washington DC. ▼

ROUNDTABLE

WRITING FOR NEWSPAPERS

If newspapers aren't dead, many observers consider them terminally ill. But a media analyst and two generations of newspaper journalists see a brighter future. The how and why they cite include:

- Even as newspapers cede breaking news to the Web, there remains a hunger for enterprising reporting and writing found in newspapers.
- Newspapers remain the home for those passionate about reporting and writing, and committed to public service.
- Newspaper reporters must embrace multimedia, blogs, chats and other online ways to reach readers.

Participants

BILL MARIMOW,
editor-in-chief, *The Philadelphia Inquirer*

RICK EDMONDS,
media business
analyst, The Poynter
Institute

ANN MARIMOW,
staff writer, *The Washington Post*

> *What future do you see for print journalism?*

Bill Marimow: Bright. Data, including the circulation of our newspapers, readership and page views online, proves that the demand for what we report is robust and vibrant.

Edmonds: I don't buy into the dinosaur/dying industry stuff. There will be more of a premium than ever on enterprising reporting and well-told stories.

Ann Marimow: Strong. Most of my friends in their 30s do not look for a newspaper on their doorstep but they still want to be informed and depend on the Web sites of their major hometown or national papers.

> *What would you tell a young person who asks about the wisdom of getting a job in newspapers?*

Bill Marimow: It's a job in which one can make a profound and important difference in a community, nation and world. Learn all the tools of the trade—from the traditional reporter's notebook to the video camera to the art of audio.

Ann Marimow: If reporting and writing is really your passion and you can't imagine doing anything else, pursue it.

> *What do print journalists need to survive and thrive in the new world of multiplatform journalism?*

Edmonds: Reporting basics—the arts of finding things out and the practice of balance and skepticism—is the most basic building block. Go the extra mile in gathering a mix of perspective and context.

Bill Marimow: The skills of a multimedia reporter: write for the newspaper and the Web, conduct interviews that can be transformed into online video, give interviews on radio and television and take photos themselves.

Ann Marimow: Learn to talk about your stories on the radio, television and to interact and engage with readers through blogs, online chats, video and emails.

> *Why did you become a print journalist?*

Bill Marimow: Once I discovered my work could improve the lives of the people I wrote about, I found great fulfillment in the public service component of our profession.

Ann Marimow: An innate nosiness, a love of sharing stories and learning something new every day. Holding elected officials accountable, telling readers why public policy decisions are being made, how their tax dollars are being spent and giving them the information they need to make decisions about their communities.

Edmonds: On a good day, the right story can make a difference, even if it's just giving readers something worth thinking about.

SUMMARY GUIDE   WRITING FOR PRINT

WRITING FOR NEWSPAPERS

To write effectively for newspapers, journalists must be familiar with newspaper format, style and presentation.

What to Remember →   Newspaper stories vary by form, length and purpose. News-gathering conditions, deadlines and production timetables dictate how much time the journalist has to report and write a story, sometimes several, a day, including blog posts, tweets and other social media.

BEHIND THE PAGE: WHO DOES WHAT

Newspaper companies are split in two parts: editorial, responsible for writing and editing news for publication, and business, which provides the funds from advertising and circulation sales needed to support the enterprise.

What to Remember →   Smart journalists understand a newspaper's organizational structure. Editors, led by an editor-in-chief, and reporters, visual journalists and online staffs generate news content. A publisher and other executives oversee the budget, editorial pages and business departments, advertising and circulation. A philosophical wall divides editorial from the business side to prevent conflicts of interest.

ON THE PAGE

Newspaper coverage spans a range of news types and forms that report news and tell stories to serve the public interest.

What to Remember → Among the many categories of newspaper coverage are: breaking stories; updates for a newspaper's Web site; trend stories; editorials; investigative reports; feature stories that illuminate trends; criticism of popular culture; and special sections devoted to crime, politics, government, culture and sports. News services and correspondents report national and foreign news.

NEW ROLES FOR REPORTERS AND EDITORS

In the age of new media, print journalists have taken on new roles writing for the newspaper and contributing to the paper's Web sites.

What to Remember → Editors and reporters have always collaborated to produce a newspaper's daily report for the next day's edition. Today, they divide their duties between producing print stories and filing to the Web site, sometimes posting stories in advance of publication, appearing on radio and television and then compiling a complete story with a fresh take for the newspaper.

SURVIVING IN A CHANGING WORLD

Newspapers, faced with declining circulation and advertising revenues, have finally embraced the Internet as a critical component of news delivery.

What to Remember → While few dispute that the industry is ailing, reports of its demise are exaggerated. With about 200 million subscribers and readers, newspapers are here to stay for the foreseeable future. Layoffs and cutbacks on publication days offer dire warnings at a growing number of metropolitan papers, but smaller dailies and weekly newspapers remain a vital presence in print journalism.

KEY TERMS

ad space, p. 265

breaking news, p. 268

community coverage, p. 269

copy editor, p. 266

criticism, p. 270

editorials, p. 269

editor-in-chief p. 266

enterprise/investigative projects, p. 270

feature writing, p. 270

intern, p. 266

international coverage, p. 270

local coverage, p. 269

managing editor, p. 266

national coverage, p. 270

news analyses, p. 269

news clerk, p. 266

news hole, p. 265

paginator, p. 266

publisher, p. 266

trend stories, p. 269

EXERCISES

1. Study a daily edition of a newspaper to discover what kinds of articles and stories it reports and where reporters go for information. Choose your favorite examples and explain why these stand out.

2. Compare similar stories covered by newspapers, radio and television and online news sites. Discuss the pluses and minuses of the coverage produced by different media platforms.

3. Arrange a tour of a newspaper to see how the different departments contribute to publication.

4. Shadow a newspaper reporter or copy editor for a day, observing how the person reports, writes or edits stories. Stay alert to the way online duties have expanded the traditional job role. Ask how he or she got into journalism, why he or she chose newspapering and to describe the challenges, risks and rewards of the job. Write a 500-word profile that includes answers to three questions: What surprised you? What did you learn? What do you need to learn next?

5. In 300 words, explain why print journalism is important and describe the reasons that a journalism student might want to choose a career in newspapers and magazines.

READINGS

Kovach, Bill, and Rosenstiel, Tom. *The Elements of Journalism: What Newspeople Should Know and the Public Should Expect.* **New York: Three Rivers Press, 2007.**
Two former-journalists-turned-media-critics explore the importance of newspapers and the challenges they face in an evolving media landscape. The authors also offer an essential reporting primer with a focus on the journalism of verification that produces accurate stories readers crave and a democratic society depends on.

Meyer, Philip. *The Vanishing Newspaper: Saving Journalism in the Information Age.* **Columbia: University of Missouri, 2006.**
At a time when newspapers are under assault from changing economic patterns, the Internet, staff shortages and declining readership, Meyer, a journalism professor, dissects the root causes of the industry's problems. His most important point, and perhaps the saving grace for newspapers, connects profitability with journalistic excellence.

Schudson, Michael. *Discovering the News: A Social History of American Newspapers.* **New York: Basic Books, 1978.**
Contemporary newspapers are viewed through the historical prism of shifts in print reporting influenced by social, political and economic forces. Its treatment of the evolution of objectivity and the use of literary realism in news writing make this an entertaining and essential text.

Talese, Gay. *The Kingdom and the Power.* **New York: Ivy Books, 1992.**
Written in 1969, this narrative history of *The New York Times* remains one of the most riveting accounts of newspaper journalism in print today. Talese tells colorful and insightful stories about the workings of one of the world's greatest newspapers. It's a must-read for anyone drawn to the craft, adventure and calling of print journalism.

Zinsser, William. *Speaking of Journalism: 12 Writers and Editors Talk About Their Work.* **New York: HarperCollins, 1994.**
A collection of top-ranked newspaper and magazine journalists reveal the secrets of their trade in a series of interviews that bring alive the rigors and rewards of print journalism.

ONLINE WRITING AND CONTENT PRODUCTION

BY THE END
OF THIS
CHAPTER,

you should be able to...

> Understand the anatomy
  and workflow of a news
  Web site, including
  staff hierarchy and job
  responsibilities, from
  producer to editor

> Recognize and adjust
  to the realities of
  online journalism,
  including the 24/7
  nature of continuous
  news, changing roles of
  journalists in the online
  environment and skills
  needed for electronic
  journalism

> Be familiar with the new
  tools and skills required
  for all journalists

66 Perhaps not since the
invention of the telegraph
or printing press have we
seen such changes. They
are changes that will not
only impact on how we
practice journalism, but
the way we think about our
democracy as well. 99

—KINSEY WILSON,
EXECUTIVE VICE
PRESIDENT AND CHIEF
CONTENT OFFICER,
NATIONAL PUBLIC RADIO

280

AFTER YEARS OF baby steps, online journalism is growing up, although it's still a rapidly developing adolescent. It's the rare print or broadcast newsroom without a multimedia Web site, although their depth and quality may vary. There is also a growing number of online-only news sites. The implications are inescapable; beginning journalists entering today's news industry must master new ways to gather, distill and present news and information using new media technologies. Some skills are so specialized that the average reporter won't need to learn them. But at the very least you should become familiar enough with multimedia tools to recognize their value.

In this chapter, you will learn in depth about the ways that new media have transformed the work of reporters, what leading practitioners have to say about the present and future of journalism, and how to fit into this new world.

THE NECESSITY OF ADAPTATION

Online journalism has transformed how news is gathered and delivered. It's caused seismic changes that contribute to sober economic realities—declining newspaper circulation and television viewership, and the drop in advertising dollars that make journalism possible. These pose threats to the economic health and perhaps the very survival of the news industry as it's existed in years past.

The news business, and the technology that drives much of its changing landscape, is rapidly evolving. Devices and applications not yet created likely will make today's high-tech software and equipment old news. To survive and thrive in the age of new media, journalists, and their organizations, must be ready and willing to adapt.

ONLINE NEWS ORGANIZATIONS: A HIERARCHY OF CHANGE

At this point, it's challenging to outline a typical organization like those well established in TV and newspaper operations. Nonetheless, it's helpful for beginning journalists to get a sense of the nature of online news operations (see Figure 13-1).

Both "old" and "new" platforms share two central attributes: a news side that produces news and information, known as "content," and a business side working to provide revenues that generate profit and support news gathering. When it comes to titles, job descriptions, duties and staffing size, things are not so clear—job titles are fluid and reflect the evolving nature of online news.

Newsrooms vary widely in their organization to support digital operations. Some are integrating digital duties throughout the newsroom and have few digital specialists.

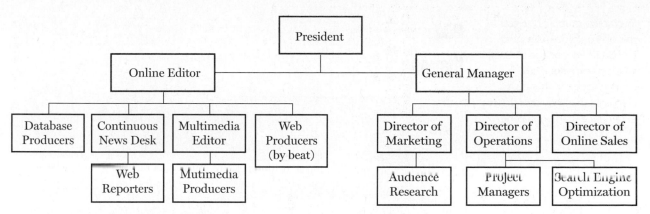

FIGURE 13-1 An organizational chart of a typical online news operation tracks the duties and responsibilities of journalists who produce the news and the business side whose work supports the enterprise. The setup may vary depending on the size and approach of an individual news organization.

Some are taking a digital-first approach that focuses the newsroom primarily on producing digital content, with a smaller team responsible for print production.

News Side (Online Content Team)

The news side of an online operation usually begins with the **online editor** (at some outlets, a **director of content**). As with a newspaper's editor-in-chief, this position usually requires two sets of responsibilities—in this case, leading every aspect of news production and working as a liaison with the print newsroom, if there is one. Given the constantly changing nature of online news, this editor must be vigilant about motivating reporters, visual and online journalists and others to keep updating their skills and learning how to use new storytelling tools.

Positions in online newsrooms are somewhat less standardized below the level of the online editor, but certain types of editors are common. Many outlets have a **continuous news desk**, a team of editors and Web producers that constantly updates the site with new developments. Some have a breaking news team that provides unfolding coverage of big breaking stories such as crimes, storms and disasters and more routine coverage such as traffic stories that are important as they are happening but aren't big enough stories to merit mention on an evening newscast or morning newspaper.

A **multimedia** or **online presentations editor** takes charge of production of digital packages that blend photos, video, audio and other interactive elements. In conjunction with this, some larger outlets have full-time **multimedia producers**, who create and display original content for Web pages using audio, video and other online tools. It's not uncommon for larger outlets to have **Web producers** assigned to different subjects, such as sports, local news or entertainment. **Database producers** can use existing content, everything from movie reviews to digitized public records, to create databases that enable users to search for information.

Interactive graphics, such as this one on global warming by *USA Today*, engage readers who can experience the news through multimedia elements that provide a richer experience than print alone.

While some online sites use print and broadcast newsroom staffs to provide all their material, many have their own Web reporters, photojournalists and copy editors to produce online-only content. Rather than simply "**repurposing**" print material—copying it from print to online—these journalists create material designed specifically for the online medium, to take advantage of its strengths.

Some newsrooms, whether they have a separate online staff or not, are adding community engagement editors or social media editors who are responsible for such duties as hosting live chats, interacting with the community on social networking sites and developing local blog networks. Another position in some newsrooms would be a curator or aggregation editor, who provides news roundups linking to content from other sources.

Business Side (Online Leadership Team)

This facet of the online operation usually starts with a **general manager** (or **director of digital media**), who is responsible for all non-news content on the site, including software, content management systems, databases and/or personnel. There is also usually a **director of operations**, who is responsible for hardware and software issues, and various **project managers**, who work with reporters and editors on special projects.

An **online sales manager** (or director of advertising) handles ads, but other tasks bear less resemblance to traditional news operations. News sites usually employ **marketing directors** to promote Web site content through promotions, social media and agreements with other sites. A **search engine optimization (SEO) analyst** makes the site compatible for major search engines so that the stories and news content show higher up in keyword searches. **Audience analysts** monitor site traffic and user habits to maximize advertising and marketing efforts.

> **"If you haven't started to think beyond telling stories with photos and text, you're walking into the tar pits."**
>
> —JIM RAY, MULTIMEDIA PRODUCER, MSNBC.COM

CONVERGENCE

Online news makes "**convergence**" or "converged journalism" possible. By sharing skills, techniques and technologies, once-competitive print, broadcast and online staffs become partners on the Internet, joining forces to stem declining circulation, audience share and revenue losses.

Before that, journalists learned the professional skills of their chosen medium, assuming their work would appear either in a newspaper or a radio or TV newscast. By 2003, a nationwide study found that convergence had taken hold. Roughly 8 in 10 newspapers and nine in 10 TV stations partnered to share "content and/or staff with another media platform." Meanwhile, nine in 10 of university journalism programs included, or had begun to add, "cross platform training into their coursework."

There remains debate over whether convergence is desirable. Some in the professional and academic ranks see convergence as an excuse to cut budgets in the name of progress, resulting less in innovation than in journalists becoming jacks-of-all-trades but masters of none. Others hold a brighter view, seeing it as an opportunity for journalists from different platforms to cross-pollinate, creating material that tells stories in new and uniquely engaging ways.

One way or the other, journalism teachers and newsroom leaders made it clear that changing roles shouldn't alter the need for the basics of reporting and writing—news judgment, media law and ethics, and a strong liberal arts background, the study found.

THE ABCs OF ONLINE JOURNALISM

At a time when anyone with a computer and a phone line or network connection can publish online, trained journalists are needed more than ever.

To succeed in online publication, journalists must know how to gather, verify, summarize, synthesize, analyze and deliver news and information with clarity and precision.

"The fundamentals still apply," says Michael Rogers, former futurist at *The New York Times*. "It all begins with writers, reporters and editors who can recognize and tell a good story. If you don't have those folks on your side, it doesn't make any difference how good the widgets are."

With these fundamental skills, journalists provide high-value news and information that is the product of critical thinking, news judgment and ethical decision making, which ensures that news stories are:

- Accurate
- Accessible
- Authoritative
- Concise
- Balanced
- Fair

CONVERGENCE POINT ☀

Practical Guidance, News and Online Trends

Since 2000, Jonathan Dube, a print journalist who switched to online news and has led digital operations at AOL.com, ABCNews.com and CBC News and headed the Online News Association, has provided up-to-date news and practical guidance about the online field. His is a go-to site for newbies and veterans who want to master multimedia skills, and read the best of Web news reporting.

Find this link on the companion Web site at **www.oup.com/us/ scanlan.**

NEW ROLES FOR JOURNALISTS AND THE SKILLS THEY NEED TO FILL THEM

Broadcast reporters are accustomed to using sound, images and voice-over narration, described in script form. Now they have to learn how to "develop and rewrite their broadcast scripts to Web-friendly copy," says Wendy Farmer, executive producer of ABC11.com, in Raleigh–Durham, NC.

That means, according to Farmer, that reporters at her station, in addition to producing broadcast stories, now must jettison video or images from their scripts and write a story in AP-style format. "This allows visitors a way to understand the facts and background of the story leading up to the most recent developments," Farmer said. The online story also lets reporters go beyond their scripts to include audio, video and other information that doesn't fit into the typical 30- to 90-second broadcast story.

Newspaper reporters accustomed to carrying nothing more than a notepad and pen have added still and video cameras, as well as digital audio recorders, to their toolbox. Laptop computers equipped with wireless cards have spawned a new kind of mobile journalist—some call them mojos—capable of filing stories and updates directly from the field. News photographers are expected to return with video as well as traditional still imagery.

Web Technologies for Journalists

Employers are looking for new journalists capable of electronic news gathering and editing, as well as providing news and information for newspapers and broadcast stations. Technologies a reporter should know include:

- **Audio slideshows** that merge photos and sound with inexpensive and easy-to-use software like SoundSlides.
- **Blogs**. Short for Web logs, blogs are Web sites that feature mostly short entries, written informally, in reverse chronological order, with links to other blogs or online resources. Embraced by news organizations, journalism blogs range from beat coverage to breaking news. On latimes.com, Jill Leovy's "The Homicide Report" reports on the nearly 1,100 homicides per year in Los Angeles County. *The Roanoke Times* created a breaking news blog when a Virginia Tech student opened fire on students and teachers, killing 32 and injuring 17 before killing himself in April 2007.

    Blogging may become an acceptable alternative for stories where video or audio recordings are banned. In May 2007 a judge in Riverside, California, wouldn't permit cameras during a high-profile case, but did allow live blogging from the courtroom by a *Press Enterprise* reporter.
- **Podcasts**. Conceived in 2005, these are a marriage of old media (broadcasting) and new (webcasting). In the same way that bloggers can dispense with printing presses and transmission towers, podcasters don't need a recording studio or a radio station to store recorded audio that can be played anytime. Think of it as TiVo for the ear.

CONVERGENCE POINT ✄

Five Steps to Multimedia Storytelling

Learn the basics of multimedia storytelling in this free, self-directed course from The Poynter Institute's News University. Jane Stevens, director of online strategies at the digital pioneer World Company in Lawrence, Kansas, guides you through the process: from mapping your story before you begin reporting to identifying elements in a multimedia story and knowing when to use audio, video graphics and other online tools.

Find this link on the companion Web site at **www.oup.com/us/ scanlan.**

- **Media sharing networks**, such as videos on YouTube and photographs on Flickr or Instagram. They connect audiences through social networks and digital communities to share digital information.
- **Social networking sites**—Facebook, MySpace, Twitter and so on—that can be sources of news. "Journalists can't just share news anymore, they need to engage users with news," points out Ellyn Angelotti, who teaches digital trends and social media at The Poynter Institute.
- **Mashups** that merge information from two or more sources, such as a site that combines public records and mapping software.

The Importance of Collaboration

In traditional journalism, stories are either self-generated or assigned. Invisible walls often stand between newsroom departments, separating photo and news art from metro and city desks. Perhaps a photographer is involved, but all too often the reporter is a one-person band.

Collaboration is a hallmark of new media: Brainstorming involves everyone on the team from writer and producer to programmer and designer. To succeed, online journalists must tear down those walls that separate colleagues with different skill sets.

Ethical Dilemmas ! WHEN COMMENTS TURN SOUR

Imagine you're a reporter for a local news outlet that has a well-trafficked Web site. One of the reasons you were hired five years ago was your experience in blogging and online publishing at your university. You've always loved the idea that your stories were the beginning of a conversation between you and your readers, and came into the job believing that online reader comments could be helpful to you as a reporter.

In reality, however, you've found that comments are more often an annoyance than a blessing.

You do sometimes get interesting insights from people who are genuinely knowledgeable about the given subject, and occasionally you've gotten useful story ideas out of them.

Sadly, this is the exception rather than the rule. You've come to expect that regardless of what you report, certain people will write comments along the lines of "You suck!" or "Why don't you get a real job?" or "My uncle at the landfill knows more about city government than you." Others will derail the discussion and snipe back and forth at one another over subjects at best tangentially related to the story topic. Still others will use the forum to push their own unrelated ideas or products, or simply to get attention.

Your supervisor is considering either having an intern filter reader comments or eliminating them altogether. Your initial response to these plans was negative—you're all about freedom of information, so cutting off

or watering down comments seems like something from the last century. It seems like an old-school attempt at controlling information, completely out of step with the realities of the digital age. It might even cost you some readers.

The more you think about it, however, the more you keep asking yourself, "What do these comments really add to our stories? Do the handful of useful comments justify sifting through all the junk? Would the core of our readership object to moderation or elimination of these forums, or might they even welcome it?"

What decision would you make in these circumstances? How would you justify it to commenters? To other readers? ▶

QUICK Tips ◔ **CHECKLIST: STORYBOARDING AN ONLINE PACKAGE**

1. Define elements of a story.
2. Identify the media.
3. Storyboard the concept—chart elements to visualize sequence.
4. Identify your resources.
5. Decide what questions you want to answer. Organize and focus the story.

6. Figure out which medium will work best for each component.
7. Check for holes.
8. Use the appropriate equipment.

What do you need to include in a story?

1. Head
2. Nut graf
3. Key players
4. Main event

5. Process of how something works
6. Pros and cons
7. Background—the story so far
8. Other issues—time, people and so on ▸

Source: Vidisha Priyanka, former news and special projects producer, TBO.com, Tampa

Writing for Online Publication Is Different—and the Same

Some old-school journalists and journalism teachers hear the word "online" and run for the hills. Their biggest fear is that Web writing is vastly different from the broadcast scripts or newspaper stories that have become second nature.

It doesn't have to be. Indeed, the writing rules that have governed their work for years, decades even, remain the same. The best writing is concise; tight writing means the brain has less information to process. Keeping your writing short relies on short words, short sentences, short paragraphs.

The best writing is lively. Action verbs and concrete nouns accomplish that goal.

Storyboarding

Storyboarding, like outlining stories, is a critical step in planning online packages. In some respects, it resembles the "five boxes" approach to story planning described in Chapter 11: identifying story elements and deciding where they best appear.

STORY FORMS AND ELEMENTS

Despite criticism that the inverted pyramid is outdated and antithetical to storytelling, it is the story form of choice for online news. "On the Web, the inverted pyramid becomes even more important since we know from several studies that users don't scroll, so they will very frequently be left to read only the top part of an article," argues Jakob Nielsen, a Web usability consultant. The form, which sums up the news story in a single paragraph, is ideal for busy readers. Still, it hasn't eclipsed online narratives. Enhanced with multimedia and interactivity, these long-form stories still attract readership.

The Bulletin

On July 2, 2007, president George W. Bush commuted the prison sentence of I. Lewis Libby Jr., vice president Dick Cheney's chief of staff, after his conviction for perjury and obstructing justice surrounding the outing of a CIA agent. Within minutes, the NYTimes.com home page displayed a single line: "Breaking News 5:55 p.m. ET: Bush commutes prison term of I. Lewis Libby, Jr."

That six-word sentence is a brief, stand-alone unit of breaking news, known as a **bulletin**. A brief summary of breaking news, it features:

1. Subject-verb-object
2. Strong active verbs
3. Brief length (five to nine words long)

Bulletins aren't new, by a long shot. For nearly two centuries, wire services, such as the Associated Press, have relied on the bulletin to convey news of significant interest as soon as it happens. Before the Internet, newspapers printed "extra editions," and radio and television stations broke into regular programming to issue bulletins—a delivery method that, except for cable TV news, is no longer economically feasible. The bulletin is ideally suited for online news; once the news is confirmed, a reporter, Web producer or editor can quickly craft a brief sentence, usually told in present continuous tense ("commutes") and relying on the subject-verb-object sentence structure.

Web Headlines

Web headlines play the same role as their print counterparts and teasers do on television: catch the attention of a reader or viewer.

But that's where the similarity ends.

Traditional headlines or teasers are usually presented in a context—a photograph, story, a snippet of video, or narration—that makes the subject of the story clear.

➤EXAMPLE Earth's carbon dioxide levels hit 'troubling milestone' in Arctic

—*Anchorage (AK) Daily News, June 1, 2012*

CONVERGENCE POINT ⚹

Multimedia Reporting: Covering Breaking News

When Hurricane Katrina came ashore in the Gulf of Mexico in 2005, six online news organizations set a new standard for online journalism. This free, self-directed course shows you how each organization coped with one of the deadliest hurricanes in U.S. history. They dispatched video journalists on boats to gather news in the flooded streets of New Orleans, created multimedia packages, and employed blogs and social media for breaking news and to connect citizens, victims and loved ones desperate for information.

Find this link on the companion Web site at **www.oup.com/us/ scanlan.**

QUICK Tips ⏱ WEB HEADLINES

Features:

- Often stand-alone items

- Meaning must be made clear and literal: no puns or wordplay as some readers around the world won't get the joke ("Young Baptists Are Going Green")

- Rely on keywords written with search engines in mind

- May be longer than print headlines (e.g., print: "A New Life Informed by the Old"; online: "Starbucks Gives Jolt to Child Soldier's African memoir")

- Subject-verb-object

- Strong active verbs

- Brevity: varies, but use of keywords can make Web headlines longer than their print counterparts ▸

Source: Erik Lukens and Mike Castelvecchi, latimes.com

More than a century before online blurbs and news alerts notified readers of breaking news, newspapers relied on bold print headlines and newsboys, like this one selling an edition of *The Washington, (DC) Evening Star* heralding the America's entry into World War I in 1917, to deliver important developments.

CONVERGENCE POINT ⋇

Newspapers Search for Web Headline Magic

This article from CNET.com describes the dilemma confronting traditional print media as they search to find readers when they post news online. "Pithy, witty and provocative headlines—the pride of many an editor—are often useless and even counterproductive in getting the Web page ranked high in search engines. A low ranking means limited exposure and fewer readers." The solution: search engine optimization (SEO), the science of using popular keywords in headlines to boost online traffic.

Find this link on the companion Web site at **www.oup.com/us/ scanlan.**

Online headlines are usually stand-alone items, unlike in a newspaper where the headline tops a story. They have changed long-embraced guidelines for traditional news presentation, replacing them with new rules.

Blurbs/Summaries

A **blurb**, known as a "**summary**" in some newsrooms, provides a brief introduction to an online story. It is designed to get people to read more by clicking on the headline above it, which is hyperlinked to the story.

Their use is widespread, according to Poynter's 2003 Eyetrack study, "Online News Behavior in the Age of Multimedia." "The vast majority of news Web sites' homepages," the study found, "use a combination of headlines and accompanying blurbs to entice site visitors to click through to stories."

"Identifying which stories get summaries [relies] on news judgment," says Jill Agostino, assistant national editor of *The New York Times*. "Generally, the stories we deem most important are the ones that get summaries."

Typically, blurbs are limited to 15 to 30 words. They shouldn't simply be drawn from the first paragraph of the story; otherwise they risk irritating time-pressed readers looking for fresh information with every click.

QUICK Tips ⏱ WRITING BLURBS

A blurb is a one- to two-sentence story summary that appears below a Web headline, designed to motivate the reader to keep reading. Its features:

■ Reserved for the most important stories

■ Accurately reflects the story

■ Fifteen to 30 words long ▐

Headline

▶EXAMPLE Amid the chaos of a hurricane, cellphones may be useless

Blurb

▶EXAMPLE In today's world of iPhones and social media, the next big storm could leave South Floridians powerless and isolated.

—Miami Herald, June 1, 2012

Links

Hypertext is the heart of online news. The key to hypertext is the link that sends readers traveling through cyberspace with the click of a mouse to another page of text, a video or audio clip, or an animation that allows you to plot the course of a hurricane or to calculate your tax bill.

Linking tip: When creating links, avoid "click here," "here are," "here is," which point to content. Instead use words that describe content ("a new study," "the city budget").

Other elements of online stories include:

- *Photo galleries.* Also known as slideshows, these are online arrangements of photos with captions or supporting audio.
- With programs like SoundSlides, photographers, producers and even reporters can assemble photos, natural sound or voice-over narration.

INTERACTIVE TIMELINE

The trail and trials of Charles Samuel

May 28, 2010

Charles Samuel, who pleaded guilty Friday to the murder of 17-year old Lily Burk, has a criminal record that dates back more than 30 years. This interactive timeline traces his history using court, jail and prison records, as well as other law enforcement sources. Samuel, 50, pleaded guilty to killing Burk, a Los Angeles high school student, in a deal that spared him the death penalty in exchange for a sentence of life without possibility of parole. Click icons on timeline for more information.

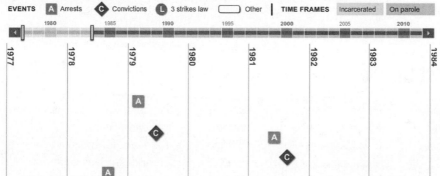

News sites provide journalists with the opportunity to create interactive timelines that help readers understand complex topics. A good example is this graphic depiction by the *Los Angeles Times* that lets readers track the history of a career criminal convicted of murder, using court, jail and prison records.

Eden Valley motorcyclist airlifted after crash
EDEN VALLEY — An Eden Valley man was injured Monday after he lost control of his motorcycle, Stearns County Sheriff John Sanner said. More

Blurbs are short (15- to 30-word) summaries that appear below the headline of an online news. Their goal: provide just enough information to induce readers to click through to the entire account.

CONVERGENCE POINT ↓

Online Journalism Resources

The pre-eminent *Online Journalism Review* keeps readers abreast of developments in the field and maintains informative blogs focusing on digital news and leadership.

The Online News Association is a professional organization for online journalists. Its site features behind-the-story accounts, award-winning work worth studying and information about new applications and software essential to online journalism.

Find this link on the companion Web site at **www.oup.com/us/ scanlan.**

QUICK Tips ⏻ VIDEO CONVERGENCE BASIC PHOTOGRAPHY

Print journalists need training to gather and edit video for their newspapers' Web sites. At Gannett newspapers, they get video convergence training from the company's broadcast journalists who provide these tips.

> Use tripod whenever possible.
> Compose shot before hitting record button.
> Count to 10 so shots are long enough.

> Put camera at different angles.
> Look for strong foreground.
> Shoot wide, medium, tight.
> Shoot in a sequence of shots and/or events.
> Always monitor audio.
> Think about editing as you shoot.
> Zoom:
   with your feet
   with action (someone walking toward you, zoom out)
   to get emotion
   to reveal/surprise
> Make a visual story by looking for a beginning, middle and ending shot. ▼

Source: Lane Michaelson, vice president and news executive, Gannett Broadcast

---

- *Interactive elements.* Games, polls, quizzes, Flash-driven multimedia, video and audio.
- *Timelines and maps.* These provide interactive ways to connect with information.
- *User-generated content.* Comments, message boards, blog entries and tweets to and from your audience.
- *Live chats.* News organizations increasingly host online conversations, using message boards and moderated discussions, and conducting interviews using Skype's Voice over Internet Protocol (VoIP).

The growing presence of the Internet in people's lives has flooded the Web with photos, videos and podcasts, including easy-to-use interfaces, such as YouTube for video, Flickr for photos and CNN's iReport that solicits stories and images. Anyone with a cell phone camera can report news; BBC.com featured videos from passengers on other flights when a plane crashed at the Madrid-Barajas Airport on August 20, 2008. It's reached a point where some news organizations have appointed a "user-generated content manager."

*SEE CLOSE-UP,
P. 296: BLOG POST*

The Coaching Way 👥 ONLINE WRITING

- Are you open to learning new online skills regardless of the platform—print, TV, radio—you have chosen for yourself?
- Try teaming up on an online project. Bring your own set of skills and interests and invite others with different ones to collaborate.

- How might evolving news technologies, as *NPR's* Kinsey Wilson predicts, change the way we think about democracy?
- Have you compared online story versions with those in newspapers or broadcast? Can you identify the aspects that make them different? Judge and explain their newsworthiness.
- Set a goal for yourself to learn a new skill, such as capturing audio or video or multimedia editing. Keep track of what surprised you, what you learned and what you need to learn next. ▼

Journalist at Work A MOJO'S WORK IS NEVER DONE

Macollvie Jean-Francois

Macollvie Jean-Francois's reporting day begins at 5:30 a.m. even before she showers and dresses for work. She checks her pager for stories that broke during the night, and calls police departments in and around Ft. Lauderdale, Florida. Jean-Francois, a reporter for the *South Florida Sun-Sentinel*, is one of a new and growing breed of reporters—mobile journalists, mojos

for short. Her assignment: get to the scene of breaking news events and feed news to the paper's Web sites for the thousands of users who check the Web between 6 a.m. and 11 a.m.—a window of high usage when thousands of people check the Web at home or work.

Jean-Francois checks her gear: reporter's notebook, pen and pencil (useful in rainy weather), and hi-tech gear—Sanyo high-definition video camera, laptop with wireless card, extra batteries and power and computer connection cords. Her camera captures video, still images and audio. Her wireless laptop enables her to file bulletins and updates directly to Web producers who post them on http://www.sun-sentinel.com/.

Her job isn't over. In addition to filing updates, she must now write a story for the next day's paper.

Mojos are popping up all over as news organizations respond to

demand for up-to-the-minute bulletins, summaries and blurbs for Web readers, and traditional news stories. Chances are you will one day describe yourself as a mojo. If so, Jean-Francois's job tips will come in handy:

- Equipment check: You don't want to turn on your camera or cell phone and realize you forgot to charge it.
- Go straight to the scene: That's where your sources will be.
- Stay focused. Keep asking what the story is really about.
- Tell multimedia staff what you've gathered so they can decide what to do with it.
- Use sources' access to media. Bystanders may have taken video or still images with cell phones. Ask for it.
- Spell-check before you hit send. Some information may go online without editing. ◢

PROFESSIONALS' ROUNDTABLE

THREE VIEWS ON ONLINE WRITING

It is true that online news can involve some very different ways of conceptualizing, formatting and telling a story. This has led some critics to worry about the quality of online news becoming watered down and unreliable. According to three professionals, however, changing technologies don't alter the ground rules for online journalism.

Participants

WENDY FARMER,
executive producer,
ABC11TV, Raleigh

EBEN HARRELL,
former reporter,
Time.com

JILL AGOSTINO,
assistant national
editor, *The New York Times*

> ### *What guidelines govern online writing?*

Farmer: While it's important to get the story up fast it's more important to get the story correct.

Agostino: Make sense, be grammatically correct and accurately reflect the story.

> ### *What's the biggest difference between print or broadcast stories and those on the Web?*

Harrell: Length. According to my online editor, research has shown that readers rarely read more than 650–750 words. Even for complicated stories, 750 is the upper limit.

Farmer: It's certainly harder than writing on-air scripts. Many people expect in-depth scripts and if the reporter on the story doesn't provide that kind of information, it's up to the online producer to find some supplemental information.

> ### *How do you decide which stories merit a "blurb," or summary, on the NYTimes.com homepage?*

Agostino: News judgments. Generally, the stories we deem most important are the ones that get summaries . . . of 25–30 words.

> ### *Who writes the blurb?*

Agostino: Generally, whoever is producing the section that night or the homepage producer writes them. I will sometimes weigh in and fiddle with them a little bit at night, and (other news editors) do the same during the day.

SUMMARY GUIDE

ONLINE WRITING AND CONTENT PRODUCTION

THE NECESSITY OF ADAPTATION

Online journalism has revolutionized how journalism is gathered and delivered to audiences.

What to Remember → The evolution of the news business and technological innovations have altered the communications landscape. Journalists must adapt to these seismic changes if they are to survive their impact.

ONLINE NEWS ORGANIZATIONS: A HIERARCHY OF CHANGE

Online organizations mirror newspaper and broadcast outlets but differ in important ways to meet new demands of news gathering and delivery.

What to Remember → Online content teams work closely with their traditional counterparts, or operate independently. Roles in the online news organization include a 24/7 news desk of editors and producers who update news developments continuously; a multimedia team; database producers; online content reporters; Web producers and visual journalists to create original content; online leadership teams take charge of content management systems and technical support, advertising and marketing and search engine optimization.

CONVERGENCE

Converged journalism makes once-competitive news organizations and staffs partners on the Internet.

What to Remember → Critics see convergence as a budget-cutting exercise that dilutes the contributions of specialists across media platforms. Supporters value cross-pollination of expertise making original and audience-friendly content possible. Convergence doesn't dismiss the need for news judgment, basic reporting and writing skills and a firm grounding in media law and ethics.

THE ABCS OF ONLINE JOURNALISM

Online journalists need to know how to gather and verify news and information, summarize, analyze and deliver it with speed, clarity and precision.

What to Remember → Now that Internet access makes it possible for anyone to publish online, trained, professional journalists are needed more than ever. As with any media platform, online news must be accurate, accessible, authoritative, concise, ethical and fair.

NEW ROLES FOR JOURNALISTS AND THE SKILLS NEEDED TO FILL THEM

Online journalism has created new roles for journalists, who must develop new skills to meet the challenges of this new form.

What to Remember → Print reporters write broadcast scripts to accompany their stories and appear on camera to report and discuss the news. Broadcast journalists rewrite their scripts for online publication. Smartphones, audio recorders and video cameras enable mobile journalists (mojos) at news scenes to be ready to transmit. New technologies demand expertise to produce audio and video packages, slideshows, blogs and podcasts, and to use social media tools. Collaboration is key to online success.

STORY FORMS AND ELEMENTS

The inverted pyramid is the dominant story form for online news, but journalists must master new forms.

What to Remember → Timelines, maps, hyperlinks, bulletins, summaries, blurbs and stand-alone Web headlines are new forms journalists must master. Journalists moderate reader interaction with chats, tweets and other social media. You're not expected to possess every skill, but familiarity is a must.

KEY TERMS

audience analyst, p. 282
audio slideshow, p. 284
blog, p. 284
blurb, p. 288
bulletin, p. 287
continuous news desk, p. 281
convergence, p. 283
database producer, p. 281
director of content, p. 281
director of digital media, p. 282

director of operations, p. 282
general manager, p. 282
marketing director, p. 282
mashup, p. 285
media sharing network, p. 285
multimedia editor, p. 281
multimedia producer, p. 281
online editor, p. 281
online presentations editor, p. 281
online sales manager, p. 282

podcast, p. 284
project manager, p. 282
repurposing, p. 282
search engine optimization analyst, SEO, p. 282
social networking site, p. 285
summary, p. 288
Web producer, p. 281

EXERCISES

1. Go to the Online News Association's awards page (http://journalists.org/awards). Select three award-winning stories from this year or a previous year, and discuss how their authors use different media—text, photos, video, graphics, and so on—to serve different elements of the story.

2. Buy a print copy of your local newspaper, and then look at its Web version. Find examples of stories that (a) are identical in both platforms, (b) have small differences between versions, and (c) whose online versions contain lots of additional content. Discuss why you believe certain stories have additional content and others don't.

3. Go to any major online news outlet's front page. Find a link to a story that isn't the lead story or otherwise featured on the home page. Note the exact wording of the link text, then click on the link and note the wording of the story's headline. How do they differ? Would they lead you to different assumptions? Do this for three different stories and write up your observations.

READINGS

Craig, Richard. *Online Journalism: Reporting, Writing, and Editing for New Media.* Belmont, CA: Wadsworth Publishing, 2005.
Guides reporters and editors in conceptualizing story ideas and reporting strategies for the online medium. Uses interviews with reporters and editors in the online news industry to help novice journalists understand the nature of this ever-evolving field.

King, Elliot. *Free for All: The Internet's Transformation of Journalism.* Evanston, IL: Northwestern University Press, 2010.
A veteran of the early online news business, King examines how online news evolved as the computer transformed communications. The book explains how today's standards have evolved and directions they may go in the future.

Briggs, Mark. *Journalism Next: A Practical Guide to Digital Reporting and Publishing.* Washington, DC: CQ Press, 2009.
A veteran-print-journalist-turned-digital-media-director discusses how best to use the latest platforms, software and tools, and provides ideas on how journalists can use technology to make the most of their reporting.

Foust, James C. *Online Journalism: Principles and Practices of News for the Web,* 3rd ed. Scottsdale, AZ: Holcomb Hathaway, 2011.
Shows beginning reporters how to work traditional news values into online environments, stressing that online material should be a vital part of story creation.

Sagolla, Dom. *140 Characters: A Style Guide for the Short Form.* Hoboken, NJ: John Wiley & Sons, 2009.
One of the creators of Twitter dispenses informed and practical advice on the best ways to communicate with the micro-writing forms of social media that increasingly dominate the way news is reported and written.

BLOG POST

A blog post is an entry in a blog or Internet forum. Journalists report and write blog posts that are published on news Web sites. They are the online version of news briefs that appear in newspapers and are broadcast on TV and radio. Blog posts are the way that most crime, accident, fire and other public emergency news is covered. But they are often the first reports of a major story and are frequently updated, sometimes in a form known as "liveblogging." For the most part they are brief, stand alone and frequently are the only coverage of an event. They are often rewritten from news releases or telephone interviews with spokespersons from agencies, business and other entities.

TEEN CRITICALLY INJURED IN PROVIDENCE HOUSE FIRE

By Brandie Jefferson
Providence Journal website, http://www.projo.com
12:34 PM Tue, Sep 09, 2008

PROVIDENCE — A 17-year-old girl was critically injured early this morning in a fire in the bedroom of her home at 127 Merino St., Providence, fire officials said.

Police say Edith Vargas was taken out of the burning, second-floor bedroom by her father, according to Providence Battalion Chief Daniel Crowley.

She suffered burns over 85 percent of her body, including first-, second- and third-degree burns, he said.

Blog posts are written using the inverted pyramid form, which presents information in descending order of importance. The lead summarizes the news and seeks to address the questions readers have: Who? What? When? Where? Why? How? So what? and What next? Given space limitations and the imperatives of timeliness, importance and interest, the lead may not answer all the questions. This lead answers almost all with specific detail and, most important, attributes the information to official sources. Attribution generally comes last. The source of the news is not as important as the event in terms of placement.

The second paragraph amplifies the lead using newsworthiness as its guide. The victim is identified by name as is the specific location of the fire. It introduces a dramatic detail—the girl's rescue by her father—and identifies a credible source by name and title.

Good journalists try to anticipate their audience's questions. The extent of the victim's injuries will be paramount in their minds. Again, note the attribution. There is no need to use the source's name and title when the source appears in the preceding paragraph.

Vargas may have been asleep when the fire started. She was taken to Rhode Island Hospital and is listed in critical condition as of noon according to a hospital spokeswoman.

The fire, called in at about 1:30 a.m., appears to have started in the bedroom and didn't spread much beyond the room, Providence Fire Marshal Anthony DiGuilisaid.

There were seven people in the house, DiGuilio said. The others were not hurt.

The fire marshal's office is investigating, but, DiGiulio said, the fire appears to have been an accident.

News audiences are intensely interested in how things happen, and they expect journalists to provide explanations. The paragraph suggests that the victim may have been asleep when the fire started. No attribution is offered for this statement, but it can be safely assumed that fire officials, identified in the lead as the primary source, provided the information. A second source gives information on the victim's condition at a local hospital. The journalist takes pains to note the timing of the report since a medical condition may change. (In this case, the victim later died of her injuries.) It's not uncommon for spokespersons to be unidentified. In many cases, their organizations do not allow their names to be used. But it's always important to ask for their name to enhance the story's credibility.

Every story type must include non-negotiable necessities—information that must be provided to produce a complete, accurate report. Not all carry the same weight and reflect the inverted pyramid's weighing of facts according to their importance. This paragraph answers an obvious question about the scope and extent of the fire. A third source is identified by name and title. Even under deadline pressure, blog posts demand thorough reporting.

This question answers another important question: Did the fire injure others? The information is attributed. On second reference, only the last name of the source is needed.

The story ends by answering a question—what next?—that many journalists ignore. But audiences care about the future of news events. It also describes the fire as an apparent accident. Could this information have appeared earlier, and if so, how would it benefit readers?

SUMMARY ▶ Online news sites have come to rely on blog posts as a speedy way to deliver breaking news. Sadly, many are devoid of much substantive information, a condition that can be attributed to the demand for content and the limited time journalists have to produce them. Reporters are often expected to furnish at least several posts on their beat a day in addition to their other duties. Brandie Jefferson's post is a good example of a well-written example that is thoroughly reported, uncommonly complete and detailed. Its accuracy draws strength from named sources. The inverted pyramid structure and the post's brevity—156 words in seven paragraphs—make for quick scanning that research shows is the hallmark of quality consumer online news. Blogs may be reprinted as news briefs in a newspaper's later edition. Follow-up reports may also appear using the news blog.

BROADCAST WRITING

BY THE END OF THIS CHAPTER,

you should be able to...

> Recognize the most important rules for broadcast success

> Learn who does what in a broadcast newsroom

> Understand the structure, format and style of radio and television news scripts

> Grasp the importance of teases and tags

> Master visual and audio aspects of broadcast journalism

> Write to sound

> Write to video

Scott Libin

300

EVEN IN TODAY'S Web-wired world, traditional broadcast media still thrive. Television remains America's most popular source of news. Radio broadcasts are heard in cars, online and through iPods and cell phones. But in recent years, in the face of dwindling audiences, broadcast and print and online news organizations have decided that partnership is wiser than competition. Print reporters appear on TV news shows, increasingly gather audio and video for their own news organizations' Web sites while broadcast journalists translate their scripts for online audiences. As the lines between media blur, journalists need skills for each platform, and students who graduate with broadcast training will have a huge advantage in getting jobs.

In this chapter, you will learn the basics of broadcast journalism: gathering, distilling and presenting stories written to be heard and/or seen, a distinction that affects every stage of the reporting and writing of TV and radio news.

BROADCAST NEWS: WHAT IT TAKES

Scott Libin is vice president of news and content solutions at Internet Broadcasting and prior to that was the news director at WCCO-TV in Minneapolis. More than two decades of broadcast journalism make him ideally suited to sum up the essential lessons of TV news.

- *Choose stories—not subjects, events or issues.* Don't do "the plant-closing story." Do a story about the closing's impact on one affected family. Don't try to jam more than one story into a single package.

- *Produce for the viewer—not the boss, the competition, contest judges, even yourself.* Your concerns and interests might be different from your audience's.

- *Fight formulas.* Not every newscast must have a certain number of packages, every package a certain number of sound bites. Viewers watch for information. Provide it in any way that works best for them.

- *Control the "drive for live."* A reporter standing in a dark parking lot in front of a locked building does nothing to enhance storytelling. Don't write or edit just for a few seconds live on camera. Make live matter with references to current conditions: time, weather, traffic, light.

- *Use sound with real bite—to convey emotion, opinion or perspective—not factual information.* Say it yourself if you can do so more clearly. Use a sound bite if it carries impact you can't capture in your own words.

- *Overcome overwriting.* Complement what you have on video; don't compete with it. Use short, declarative sentences, strong nouns, active verbs. Avoid loaded language and subjective or judgmental approaches in favor of more objective, descriptive language.

- *Recognize the power of pictures.* Don't make viewers choose between what they see and what they hear; they can't pay full attention to either. If they're equally compelling, go to the video.

- *Rethink, don't reinforce, stereotypes.* Find new experts. Talk to people of color, other minorities and those with disabilities—even on stories that aren't about "their" issues. Introduce viewers to people they might not otherwise meet. Get some new voices into your work, on the air and off.
- *Be clear.* Don't be a mindless conduit. Translate. What does it mean? If you don't know, find out. Don't leave it to your viewers. It's your job. Never raise a question you don't answer, or at least acknowledge.
- *Be conversational.* Say nothing on the air you would not say in real life. Avoid jargon. Resist clichés—especially "journalese," such as "the 47-year-old local man." "Jones is 47. He lives in Des Moines" is the way people speak.
- *Be credible.* Address obvious gaps in information or odd elements in your stories. Anticipate your viewers' reactions to what they see and hear.

THE BROADCAST NEWSROOM: WHO DOES WHAT

Commercial news stations, like newspapers and online news, are divided into two parts: news and business (see Figure 14-1).

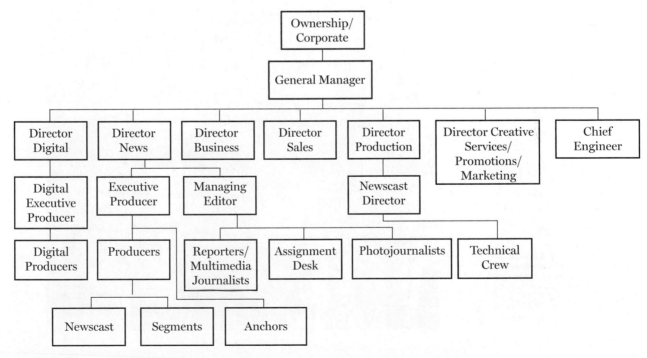

FIGURE 14-1 An organizational chart of a typical broadcast news operation that shows the separation of duties and responsibilities between the editorial and business sides of the enterprise. The setup may vary depending on the size and approach of an individual news organization.

The News Side

There's much more to TV news than an anchor reading stories. The **news director** is the television counterpart to a newspaper's top editor, overseeing news gathering and production, personnel, story selection, ethical decision making and on-air performance. The managing editor runs the assignment desk and coordinates reporters and camera crews. The **newscast director** presides over the technical functions of the control room as the live broadcast is produced. Producers fall into three main groups—**newscast producers**, **field** or **segment producers** and Web producers. **Anchors** are the face of the station, delivering the news, introducing stories and narrating video. Reporters, producers, and photojournalists gather the raw materials for news stories, and then work with editors to assemble everything into the stories that appear on air. Many other assorted editors and producers are required to create the polished, final news show. In many newsrooms, a single person (often called a multimedia journalist) will report, write, shoot and edit his or her own story, from start to finish.

Although reporters can stay on the sidelines watching events unfold, television journalists must get as close to the action as possible. A protester screams in front of NBC cameraman Rodney Batten, in light shirt to the left, during the arrival ceremony for Chinese President Hu Jintao on the South Lawn of the White House in May 2006.

The Business Side

The management of a TV news operation begins with a general manager, the station's top executive, who supervises all station operations and enforces standards. Generally a **controller** or **business manager** handles the finances and a sales manager oversees a staff selling and managing commercial time and digital advertising. A **chief engineer** is in charge of keeping the station on the air and handling other technology issues, while the **production manager** handles non-news programming and commercials. Other management figures handle everything from elements of production to marketing to community relations.

WORKING FAST

Broadcast news has always been a business where time is of the essence. But now, in an age of 24-hour cable news and technology that allows for quick editing and near-instant upload of story material, the need to work faster has never been greater.

The average TV reporter juggles several deadlines: producing a live stand-up for the noon broadcast, updating for the early afternoon news, tweeting and posting items to the Web site, and producing a complete package for the evening or late night newscasts. Radio journalists have to write several versions of the same story to keep the news fresh, or the pieces shorter. Having continuous, multiple deadlines is a reality of the job, and broadcast journalists need skills to work fast.

This doesn't just mean rushing through each task. Effectively working quickly involves managing your time efficiently—today's media environment simply doesn't allow for much downtime. Reporters and editors need to organize and prioritize their

In television news, the control room, such as this one for SNN News 6, the cable channel of the *Sarasota* (FL) *Herald-Tribune*, is the hub where the newscast director and producers guide the broadcast.

work, and learn to complete it with as little wasted effort as possible. You can keep lists of story ideas and ready-to-dial sources on your cell phone. Know tomorrow's tasks today. Break one job into several doable tasks: research, set up interviews, report, write, edit. Use your phone timer and alarm to keep you on track and use your time most effectively. Control your time and you control your life.

INTERVIEWING FOR BROADCAST

If your journalism experience has been limited to writing stories for a school newspaper or Web site, moving to video can be a little scary. The best way to work past this is to simply focus on the task at hand, and to work on several techniques that make for good work on camera. Several of these are discussed later, but first and foremost you should concentrate on something you've presumably done before—interviewing.

Conducting an effective television or radio interview calls on the same skills and techniques outlined in the interviewing chapter. Ask good questions. Listen to the answers. Be a human being, not just a reporter out to snag a gotcha quote or **sound bite** (a short audio clip taken from a longer interview).

You should also be aware that some of the elements of video and audio reporting that can make novice reporters nervous can have the same effect on interviewees. The tools of broadcast journalism—video camera, digital audio recorder, microphones and, on occasion, lights—can intimidate a subject.

"When you think about it, it's amazing anyone talks to a reporter and a photographer with a huge camera and a live truck," says Carolyn Mungo, executive news director at WFAA Dallas and a reporter for two decades. "It's very intimidating."

A reporter can overcome that psychological obstacle, Mungo says, with eye contact and casual conversation as the photojournalist sets up the equipment. Get the facts before the camera rolls so you can focus on the emotions. **Pre-interviews**, conducted before the camera or audio recorder is rolling, identify the best sources, or characters, for the story. **Advance planning** involves finding locations conducive to clear recording, vivid imagery and sound, putting subjects at ease, and identifying questions most likely to gather facts for narration and solicit subjective responses.

WRITING FOR BROADCAST: STYLE, FORMAT AND EXAMPLES

Broadcast news is written to be heard and seen, rather than merely read. That is the essential difference between broadcast and print journalism, and it affects every stage of the reporting and writing. The print journalist relies on words. The broadcast journalist also has sound and moving pictures to tell stories.

Broadcast writing features hallmarks—short sentences, active verbs, conversational style written for the ear—that serve all news writers, no matter what their medium. Like all types of writing, effective broadcast journalism can be described, studied and repeated.

"Great broadcast writing is like poetry," says Deborah Potter, executive director of Washington DC's NewsLab, created to improve local news. "It's written for the ear. It has rhythm and sound."

She points to this sentence from a World War II script by Edward R. Murrow, the famed radio and television journalist considered one of the medium's finest writers.

> The blackout stretches from Birmingham to Bethlehem, but tonight, over Britain, the skies are clear.

Say that sentence aloud, the way it's meant to be read. What makes it work?

"Simple words, alliteration, sentence structure, a crisp ending," says Potter. As a young journalist, she wrote for Charles Osgood, CBS Radio commentator and host of the *Sunday Morning* television show. He taught her: "Bloated words and phrases don't **penetrate**. Well-chosen, well-ordered ones do." That's because such ideas must be "penetrating," must play to the audience's senses and emotions.

That quality "counts even more in radio and television than in print because consuming broadcast news is a secondary activity," she says. "Listeners and viewers are frequently involved in other activities—they may be driving in traffic, fixing dinner or taking a shower while the news plays on. So writers must compete for attention and avoid errors and language that can further distract the audience."

Consider the arresting opening of the story, deconstructed below, about the return home of a fallen Marine by Chris Vanderveen of 9NEWS in Denver:

"If the shoes are shined, if the uniforms are pressed . . ."

Two parallel clauses, voiced over shots of Marines ensuring that their uniforms are spotless, is a good example of the type of short, crisp and clear style of broadcast writing.

TEASES AND TAGS: STARTING AND ENDING STRONG

Broadcast stories have a beginning, middle and end, with a special focus on the start and finish.

Beginnings are known as **lead-ins**, or **teases**, to attract the viewer's attention. They should hook the viewer and signal why they should care.

Like the first paragraph of a newspaper story, the TV lead-in sums up the story, provides attribution and, as in this example, concludes by introducing the reporter and promising relevant information to the station's audience.

▶**EXAMPLE** Now to a new twist on identity theft, one we're hearing is easily overlooked. Police and prosecutors are now targeting little-known Houston businesses that make fake IDs and drivers licenses. Investigators reveal the beginning of this crackdown with 11 News reporter Jason Whitely who explains why a flood of fake IDs can end up costing you.

Edward R. Murrow

❝This instrument [TV] can teach, it can illuminate; yes, and it can even inspire. But it can do so only to the extent that humans are determined to use it to those ends. Otherwise it is merely wires and lights in a box. There is a great and perhaps decisive battle to be fought against ignorance, intolerance and indifference. This weapon of television could be useful.❞

—EDWARD R. MURROW, BROADCAST JOURNALIST

Watch out for these lead-in traps:

1. Don't beat people over the head—"Now, a story you'll want to see."
2. Don't bait the hook with promises the script can't deliver.

Two examples of honest and alluring teases:

❯EXAMPLE❮ He's just 13 years old. And charged with murder. But police say he didn't act alone.

❯EXAMPLE❮ Today: another arrest. As cops try to close the case on a killing in Clarksville.

Broadcast writers call their ending a "**tag**," or "close." It sums up the story. It shouldn't be "an overflow valve for material that didn't fit the script," NewsLab's Potter says. "It is the final punch line, and it needs to be focused and tight. You can add background and context here—so you can stay focused on your characters in the package. It's the last thing people will experience, so it's what they will remember most." For example:

❯EXAMPLE❮ The state attorney will decide if Aaron will be charged as an adult and if both men are to face the death penalty for the crime.

TV WRITING: THE PACKAGE

In TV news, a complete story is called a **package** because it's told on digital video with audio and video clips, plus graphics, animation and video effects. A package is usually divided into three parts:

1. *Lead-in*. The introduction read by the anchor. The reporter, most familiar with the story, typically writes the lead that sets up the story.

News anchors rely on the teleprompter, a device that scrolls an electronic version of the script just below camera level making it possible for the reader to look directly at the audience.

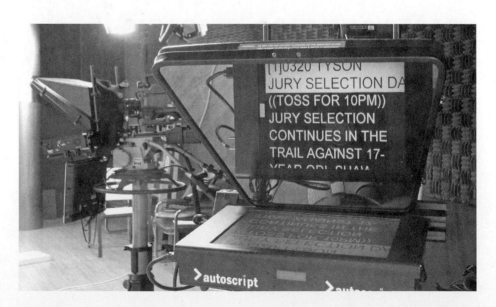

QUICK Tips 🕐 SCRIPT BASICS: TV AND RADIO

Like those in other media, broadcast stories have their own format, influenced by the technology used to gather and present information. Each television and radio newsroom will have its own distinctive hallmarks, which you will learn when you begin work.

In general, scripts are written what's known as a **"split page"** format, in two columns. The left column contains information about what is shown on screen, such as graphics, audio and video, which guides technical and production personnel. The right column contains the **narration**— the words spoken by the reporter,

anchor or sources whose comments have been prerecorded. (This is often abbreviated **VO/SOT**, for voice-over/ sound on tape.)

Other script basics include:

> *Length*. Most broadcast stories range in length from 15–30 seconds for a brief to one minute and 30 seconds (1:30) for a package.
> *Attribution*. In broadcast news, attribution usually comes first. "Mayor Jones told voters . . ." Otherwise the statement may sound like the reporter's opinion.
> *Punctuation and spelling*. Nothing in a script should be difficult to

read. Names should be spelled out phonetically or with hyphens. For example:

▶EXAMPLE Tonight, several children and a Y-M-C-A counselor are nursing wounds from yellow jacket stings they received during a field trip. Some youngsters were stung a dozen times.

In the past, spelling wasn't as important in broadcast news. But convergence has changed that. Television scripts that are rewritten in story form for a station's Web site have to be spelled and punctuated correctly. ▶

2. *Package.* The portion of the story narrated by the reporter. The package can be interspersed with live shots from the scene or in the newsroom.
3. *Tag.* The end of the story. May be read by the anchor or the reporter, although the reporter usually writes it.

News scripts are written in ALL CAPS so that they are easier to read, except for words spoken by persons interviewed, which appear in lowercase.

SEE CLOSE-UP, P. 319: TV NEWS SCRIPT

WRITING FOR VIDEO

Think of television news, and moving images likely come to mind, especially in a field where "Film at 11" was for decades a promotional clarion cry designed to attract viewers.

What often goes unnoticed is the craft, and sometimes the artistry, of the broadcast journalist who must write a companion narrative in words.

Video storytellers choose their words—and sound bites—carefully. They don't think that the "words, pictures and sound should 'match' on TV," as Al Tompkins of The Poynter Institute writes in *Aim for the Heart: A Guide for TV Reporters*. Tompkins calls that the "say dog, see dog" mistake that happens when the writer tells viewers what they're seeing, instead of telling them about what they see. Give the viewer credit. For example, they can see the dog on the screen, so tell them something about the dog—his name, the time he saved a child's life. "Words should explain the pictures," Tompkins says.

Ethical Dilemmas ❗ THE REAL THING?

You're preparing a news package about the drowning of a teenager in your community at a popular swimming hole. You've interviewed her parents, friends and classmates. But you're looking for dramatic footage to convey the drama of the story. There's no video of the search for her body, so you contact the fire chief who led the search effort and tell him your problem. Sensing an opportunity for good publicity, he agrees to launch the boat used to retrieve the body and show a diver in the water. You record the action and include it in your story with a voiceover describing the search. Should your story say the scene was staged? Or do you argue that's there no reason to do so since it merely shows what rescuers already did? What arguments would you make in support of either decision? Can staging ever be justified? What is your responsibility to the victim's family and your audience? ▼

An example: When a fire hose showering the dust of a demolition caused a rainbow, KARE-TV reporter Boyd Huppert did not write what people could see on the screen. Instead he let the viewers experience the "what" on screen. Huppert let words—a neighbor's and his own—to tell them "what about that."

▶EXAMPLE◀ HUPPERT: Yet, out of the dust, the mist, and the sun came a symbol.

NEIGHBOR NUMBER FIVE: Did you see the rainbow? Yeah.

HUPPERT: A sign of hope.

Print Versus Broadcast: A Technological Edge

When newspaper reporters and broadcast journalists cover the same story, TV news has a production and technological edge, one that sets the medium apart from others. As the following stories demonstrate, both rely on the same sources and report the same facts. But the newspaper story was published the day after the TV news story aired. (The TV news story was transcribed from the broadcast version with production details interspersed.) The print story includes background information not included in the broadcast version. What the newspaper doesn't have is video of the beating, including a production graphic that zeroes in on the suspect allegedly kicking the victim. Print versus Broadcast. It's the difference between reading a story and seeing it.

Newspaper Story

By Marissa Lang, Times Staff Writer

▶EXAMPLE◀ TAMPA — The fourth man accused of violently mugging Army Sgt. Johnny Aparicio in a May 13 attack that was caught on camera and triggered an outpouring of national sympathy turned himself in Tuesday.

Brandon J. Miller, 18, of Tampa was the last of four teens accused in the attack to be arrested.

> ❝ You tell a compelling, worthy story with words and sounds, the same way you tell it with images. You capture emotion. You get close to your subject. You approach things from a new angle with a curious mind and a sensitive heart. ❞
>
> —EILEEN AND J. CARL GANTER, MULTIMEDIA JOURNALISTS

When deputies booked him into the Orient Road Jail on Tuesday afternoon, Miller "was uncooperative" and "showed no remorse," officials said.

Tampa police had issued a warrant for Miller's arrest on Friday after they identified him as one of the men who stole Aparicio's cellphone and wallet after repeatedly punching and kicking the soldier about 3 a.m. May 13.

Police have also charged Geroshe Lewis, Lerome Howard and Jared Richardson in the aggravated battery and robbery case. Miller will face similar charges, police said.

Aparicio was new to the area when he was attacked. He had been assigned to MacDill Air Force Base about three weeks before the attack, which happened after his car broke down on Iowa Avenue. The robbery was caught on surveillance video near Renellie Drive.

Last week, the sergeant told the *Tampa Bay Times* that he was grateful for the outpouring of support. He has since physically recovered.

—*Tampa Bay Times, May 30, 2012*

Television News Story

▶**EXAMPLE** [Anchor intro]

New developments tonight in the beating attack on a MacDill soldier . . . a major one. Tampa police say the fourth suspect has turned himself in. Chris Martinez is following this development and joins us live in Tampa. Chris.

[Take to live shot of reporter. Name of reporter appears on screen.]

Well, Jamison, that fourth suspect is Brandon Jakob Miller and right now he's being booked into the county jail which is where he turned himself in a little earlier ago this afternoon. Now police tell us this 18-year-old is so far

[Roll video to surveillance video of beating and mug shot of suspect. Reporter continues voice under]

not cooperating with any of their detectives tonight. They say he is not showing any sort of remorse at all.

[Show mug shot full screen. Reporter voice under]

Miller is now the fourth and final arrest in the case of this vicious attack caught on camera at Iowa Avenue and Renellie St. in south Tampa.

[Take to surveillance video]

Police believe Miller is the man seen in that surveillance video delivering the final two blows to MacDill based soldier Johnny Aparicio.

[Production graphic illuminates one part of the video showing a man kicking soldier twice]

This is not Miller's first arrest.

[Take reporter full up]

Far from it in fact. He was arrested just a few weeks before that attack on that soldier over in Clearwater on weapons charges and just a few weeks earlier than that he was picked up in Atlanta for shoplifting.

We're live in Tampa. I'm Chris Martinez for ABC Action News.

—*WFTS ABC Action News, May 29, 2012*

CONVERGENCE POINT ⟋

Advice for Radio Storytellers

Explore a wealth of links to sites providing advice to radio storytellers with an emphasis on interviewing, technology, exceptional stories and an interview with Ira Glass, acclaimed creator of *This American Life*.

Find this link on the companion Web site at **www.oup.com/us/scanlan.**

WRITING FOR AUDIO

Television news relies on two senses—sight and hearing—while radio journalists have just hearing to attract and inform listeners. Sound can be a powerful and intimate way to report news and tell rich stories.

Radio journalists use a digital audio recorder, microphone and headphones to record "**actualities**," comments that print reporters call quotes. Their gear also picks up natural or ambient sound (environmental sounds usually abbreviated as "**natsound**") such as the chorus of conversation in a crowded diner. Coupled with narrative written by the reporter, sounds can turn listeners "into witnesses of your story," says Howard Berkes of National Public Radio.

Howard Berkes, a reporter for National Public Radio, uses a boom microphone and digital audio recorder to interview Ron Barnes of Coastal Electric Power Co. in Mississippi after Hurricane Katrina hit the region in 2005.

Effective radio writing follows the same principles of every news medium:

- Find the heart of the story.
- Use conversational style.
- Think in scenes.
- "Show, don't tell."
- Make every word count.

Radio reporters face the challenge of tight time limits. Peter King of CBS News Radio usually has less than 30 seconds to tell a story. Generally that means sentences that take five to six seconds to read. "If it seems awkward and long when you say it aloud, it probably sounds that way to the listener," King said in an interview with Poynter's Al Tompkins. "Long sentences can be exhausting to read—and hear. I try to keep each sentence focused on a single thought, and keep it simple."

An example from a story about drought in Florida:

King begins with a sentence fragment in his own words.

▶EXAMPLE KING: Some parts of Lake Okeechobee are so dry . . .

King relies on **microbites**—sound bites no longer than a few seconds—to finish a sentence or thought. Here King uses a two-second microbite to complete the sentence, this time in the source's words.

▶EXAMPLE ACTUALITY: There is not a drop of water anywhere.

It takes just five seconds to read the 18-word sentence that sets up his tag.

▶EXAMPLE KING: Kim Day was looking at what used to be a boaters' canal that surrounded the J&S Fish Camp.

He gives the source the last word.

CONVERGENCE POINT ☀

*Telling Stories
With Sound*

Everyone interested in radio storytelling will benefit from this free, self-directed course. It covers the process of planning, working in the field and producing in the studio. You will learn how to choose the right gear, use microphones effectively, harness the power of ambient sound and write compelling radio narratives.

Find this link on the companion Web site at **www.oup.com/us/ scanlan.**

Journalist at Work SHIFTING FROM PRINT TO RADIO

David Folkenflik

David Folkenflik spent more than a decade as an award-winning newspaper reporter. In 2004, he took a job as a National Public Radio correspondent, covering media and the arts. Making the shift from print to radio has taught him to:

- "Cast aside my ignorance of (and relative lack of interest in) technology to recognize its importance in conveying the stories I want to tell."
- "Think very consciously about sound. Avoid the noises—leaf blowers, computers—that interfere with your ability to hear people's voices and yet . . . capture the clatter and chatter that make up the soundtrack of real life."
- "Honor the way people speak, to let their cadences unspool and thoughts unpack, more than I did for written articles."
- "Economize. You have to tell complex stories more tightly—but without losing any of the sophistication or vital context."
- "Leverage material online with expanded excerpts of interviews and links."
- "Be willing to collaborate." ▼

▶**EXAMPLE◀** ACTUALITY: There's just nothing there but grass now.

A typical radio story breaks down into two parts: half recorded audio, half narration written and spoken by the reporter. "For us, sound is what it's all about," says Margo Melnicove, a veteran radio journalist. "We're oral storytellers first and foremost."

To tell their stories, they must find the ideal blend of actualities, natural sound and narrative. Actualities and natsound must be **logged**, or transcribed verbatim, to create the skeleton of the story. Narration, or **voice-overs**, comes next, serving as the glue linking sound bites and natsound.

Stories may begin with narration, but many radio writers prefer natsound to establish a scene, followed by narration that helps listeners understand what they are listening to. Ira Glass, who created the acclaimed radio show *This American Life*, advises students to build stories by alternating sound bites with ambient sounds.

ON-CAMERA PREPARATION/ PERFORMANCE TIPS

Appearing on camera is the most obvious and significant difference between newspapers and television. Print reporters must merely write their stories; broadcast reporters must deliver them before a camera and an unseen audience.

Appearing on camera requires professional clothing (jacket and tie for men; pantsuit, dress or business suit for women) and makeup to avoid faces appearing shiny under studio lights. In some major markets, stations hire consultants to ensure positive on-air appearance and provide vocal training, hair and clothing tips, and other assistance. A more modest approach is found in the accompanying Quick Tips given to reporters at the *South Florida Sun-Sentinel* to ease their transition to television news reporting.

The Coaching Way ⅲⅰ BROADCAST QUALITY

- Aim to focus your story in three words in response to the question "Who did what?" Examples: "America rescued Iraq," "America destroyed Iraq," "FEMA failed New Orleans," "Cabbie delivers baby."
- Check your equipment before heading to your assignment.

- Don't forget: Get your microphone up close. Rule of thumb: about a fist away—that's about four inches from the speaker's mouth.
- Revise your writing by going over it backward. Take your script, cover up the tag and work back, paragraph by paragraph. You may find

that your story actually ended long before you finished writing.
- Surprise the viewer, not the producer.
- Remember that preparation is the key to good on-camera performance. ▶

QUICK Tips ⏱ PREPARATION

- Avoid open-ended questions ("Tell me about your story . . .").

- Be prepared for anything—expect the unexpected. Find out what will be said about the story prior to your Q&A.

- Warm up (10–20 minutes prior to your appearance; review your notes).

- Relax—especially your upper body (concentrate on your shoulders and stomach muscles).

- Take a few deep breaths (in through your nose, out through your mouth).

- Sit with good posture—it'll help your breathing and make you look more confident.

- Focus on the camera, not on the activity near it or around you.

- Be conversational.

- Be brief and direct with your answers.

- "Humanize" your answers ("How does your story affect the viewers?").

- Avoid fact overload.

- Avoid "legal" or "officialese" ("Officials say the alleged perpetrator was apprehended . . ." when "suspect was caught" conveys the same information).

- If you don't know the answer to a question, say so.

- Take care choosing clothing; solid colors are best.

- Avoid white clothing, thin stripes and checks (all unfriendly to the camera).

- Provide analysis and observation, not opinion.

- Be the "expert"—you have the information viewers need.

- Afterward, get feedback from your peers.

- Practice. ▶

PROFESSIONALS'

ROUNDTABLE

SOUND ADVICE

The power of listening. Respect for their audience. Knowing when to let sound and pictures tell the story. Grace under pressure. These concepts and talents guide the best broadcast journalists.

Participants

LORI WALDON, news director, WISN 12 News, Milwaukee

JENNIFER PIFER BIXLER, senior producer, CNN

BOYD HUPPERT, reporter, KARE 11 TV, Minneapolis

> **What are the most important qualities of a broadcast journalist?**

Waldon: Really care about their viewers and think of them first and foremost when crafting their stories and doing their news gathering.

Pifer: The most informative and profound moments happen when you shut up and just listen to the person you are interviewing.

> **What's the single most important lesson you've learned as a broadcast journalist?**

Waldon: Viewers are much much smarter than we often give them credit for. They want more than car chases, homicides and celebrity gossip.

Pifer: I tend to get burned when I think I have all the answers. When reporting a story, you should ask, "Is there another side to this story?"

Huppert: In visual storytelling there is power in the discovery of little natural moments that linger with viewers long after the newscast has ended.

> **How would you describe what you do?**

Pifer: I am like a quilt maker. On my best days, I take pieces of information, sound and pictures and sew them together into a story that resonates with our viewers.

Huppert: I look for common truths and character traits that will connect the people in my stories with the viewers who are watching them.

> **Is there a journalistic quote you live by or a broadcast figure you look to as a symbol of excellence?**

Pifer: A news director I worked for early in my career used to say, "Trust no one, assume nothing." It sounds harsh, but it's true. The best producers tend to be highly organized, a little paranoid and always thinking two steps ahead.

Huppert: Charles Kuralt and his "On the Road" segments for the CBS Evening News. Kuralt's stories didn't just touch your heart; they got inside it and stayed there.

> **Why did you become a broadcast journalist?**

Waldon: I love the power and immediacy of television. I also hoped in some small way that I could leave an imprint on the industry—even if it's teaching and guiding others to be brave enough to challenge traditional images.

Pifer: During college, I worked at the local NPR station. The news director gave me a shot at producing the local cut-ins for *All Things Considered*. Eventually, he let me go out into the field and report. I was hooked.

SUMMARY GUIDE
BROADCAST WRITING

BROADCAST NEWS: WHAT IT TAKES

Broadcast news draws its strength from the same principles as other news platforms: choosing stories that focus on people rather than abstract subjects and producing for audiences rather than sources.

What to Remember → Broadcast writers make sure their stories reflect the concerns and interests of their audience. They resist formulaic approaches and pick the best ways to tell uncommon stories. They seek fresh sources and stories in under-reported communities.

THE BROADCAST NEWSROOM: WHO DOES WHAT

Like newspapers and online news, commercial news outlets divide their operations into two parts: news and business.

What to Remember → The news director is the top news executive in a broadcast newsroom. A managing editor coordinates anchors, reporters, producers and camera crews, while the newscast director oversees live broadcasts. A general manager oversees the business side, with other managers responsible for selling commercial time, marketing and public relations.

WORKING FAST

Minutes, even seconds, have always mattered in broadcast news, but cable news, technological advances and the Internet have made the need to work fast even greater.

What to Remember → Radio and television journalists routinely produce live stories, updating them for later broadcasts and Web sites and turning around a complete package for later in the day. Continuous and multiple daily deadlines are a challenging reality.

INTERVIEWING FOR BROADCAST

Interviewing is the foundation of broadcast news reporting and requires journalists to ask good questions and listen to the answers.

What to Remember → Broadcast technology may intimidate interview subjects. Pre-interviews, casual conversation and eye contact relax interviewees. Effective interviews focus on emotions, not facts.

WRITING FOR BROADCAST: STYLE, FORMAT AND EXAMPLES

Broadcast news relies on the eye and ear as stories add sound and video to narrated words.

What to Remember → Effective broadcast writing uses short sentences, active verbs and a conversational style. Writers must compete for viewer's attention and choose their words and video with great care.

TEASES AND TAGS: STARTING AND ENDING STRONG

The beginning and end of broadcast stories are the most crucial elements in effective broadcast writing.

What to Remember →

Lead-ins or teases sum up the story, provide attribution, introduce the reporter and promise relevant and interesting information. Deliver on the promise. The tag concludes the story. Like the punch line of a joke, it's the last thing viewers remember. It should be focused and tightly written, not a grab bag for extraneous information.

SCRIPT BASICS: TV AND RADIO

The format of broadcast scripts reflects the technology used to gather and present information.

What to Remember →

News scripts are split into two columns written by the reporter or producer. The left column displays production info about graphics, video and audio. The right column includes words spoken by the reporter, anchor or interview subjects. With broadcast news appearing online, correct punctuation and spelling is required.

TV WRITING: THE PACKAGE

A complete TV news story, told with audio and video clips, narration, graphics and animation, is called a package.

What to Remember →

The package is divided into three parts: the lead-in; the package, which includes audio, video and other multimedia features narrated by the reporter; and the tag. Broadcast stories are short: 10–30 seconds for a brief to one minute and 30 seconds for a package.

WRITING FOR VIDEO

Video storytellers carefully choose their words—and sound bites—knowing that words should explain the pictures, not merely repeat what's on screen.

What to Remember →

Images and sound capture emotions. Narrative is the thread that links these powerful tools. Let viewers watch what's on the screen. Tell them something else about the image.

WRITING FOR AUDIO

Radio listeners rely on just one sense—hearing—to absorb news.

What to Remember →

> Sound is a compelling tool to report news and tell stories. A typical story is split into an ideal blend of recorded audio and narration written and spoken by the reporter. Radio journalists follow the rules of effective writing: focus, conversational style, "show, don't tell," and carefully chosen words.

ON-CAMERA PREPARATION/PERFORMANCE TIPS

> Broadcast journalists who appear on camera or radio to present the news personally, must conform to certain rules for appearance and delivery.

What to Remember →

> On air, relax, be conversational and direct, and avoid journalese or bureaucratic mumbo jumbo. Be ready for anything to happen. TV news appearances require professional dress and even makeup. Looking good may be a plus, but the best advice for on air performance is to be a human being.

KEY TERMS

actuality, p. 310
advance planning, p. 304
anchor, p. 302
business manager, p. 303
chief engineer, p. 303
controller, p. 303
field producer, p. 302
lead-in, p. 305
log, p. 312

microbite, p. 311
narration, p. 307
natsound, p. 310
news director, p. 302
newscast director, p. 302
newscast producer, p. 302
package, p. 306
penetrate, p. 305
pre-interview, p. 304

production manager, p. 303
segment producer, p. 302
sound bite, p. 304
split page, p. 307
tag, p. 306
tease, p. 305
VO/SOT, p. 307
voice-over, p. 312

EXERCISES

1. Using the interview notes with a police spokesman about the girl hit by a rushing train in Chapter 4, write a TV script for a 30-second broadcast news story. What additional reporting, including audio, video and graphics, would you need to broaden it into a 1:30 package?

2. Write three news lead-ins and tags for the story.

3. Arrange to shadow a broadcast journalist for a day. Find out why he/she chose TV or radio news, the best part of the job, the worst part, and what it takes to excel in the field. Write a 500-word story about your day, ending with answers to these questions: What surprised me? What did I learn? What do I need to learn next?

4. Watch a national TV news broadcast and listen to a radio newscast. Compare the length of stories. How did the reporting elements vary? What news judgments went into selecting the story lineup? What worked and why? What needed work and why?

5. Compare a national story in print, online, radio and television. Identify the major differences in content and presentation. Compare the advantages/disadvantages of meeting audience needs. Which did you prefer and why?

READINGS

Block, Mervin. *Writing Broadcast News, Shorter, Sharper, Stronger: A Professional Handbook.* **Boulder, CO: Taylor Trade Publishing, 2004.**
A veteran television news writer and writing coach shares tips of the trade, a "dozen deadly don'ts," techniques for writing effective lead-ins, tags and voice-overs, while emphasizing clarity, brevity and other hallmarks of broadcast newswriting excellence.

Kern, Jonathan. *Sound Reporting: The NPR Guide to Audio Journalism and Production.* **Chicago: University of Chicago Press, 2008.**
National Public Radio is famous for its incisive and entertaining interviews and stories. Studded with examples from NPR's accomplished reporters and anchors, it guides radio news hopefuls through the entire process: news gathering, interviews, technology, editing sound and putting your work on the air.

Reardon, Nancy, and Flynn, Tom. *On Camera: How to Report, Anchor & Interview.* **Waltham, MA: Focal Press, 2006.**
Learning to conduct television interviews in a studio or in the field is the subject of this readable, authoritative guide. The authors' practical advice can also be applied for video interviews produced for multimedia reports.

Tompkins, Al. *Aim for the Heart: Write, Shoot, Report and Produce for TV and Multimedia.* **Washington, DC: CQ Press, 2012.**
With decades of professional experience and a long career training broadcast journalists, Tompkins distills the secrets of successful broadcast news with illuminating examples, tips and techniques for the novice and professional alike.

TV NEWS SCRIPT

Broadcast writing communicates news and experience through sight and sound by merging video, audio and narration written by the journalist. It requires collaboration with photojournalists, producers and production personnel to get stories on air. Broadcast writers choose stories over subjects and issues; they resist formulaic approaches and listen for sound bites that convey emotion, opinion or perspective rather than factual information. They say it themselves if they can communicate more clearly. At its best, broadcast journalism is an art as well as a skill, as the following example, a deadline TV story about a fallen Marine returning home from Afghanistan, by Chris Vanderveen of Denver's 9NEWS, shows. The description of the video was taken from the broadcast story. The analysis was provided with assistance from Al Tompkins, broadcast group leader at the Poynter Institute and author of *Aim for the Heart: Write, Shoot, Report and Produce for TV and Multimedia*. His comments appear in the second column.

Note on technical terms:

NATS is shorthand for natural or ambient sound, environmental noises that can include background voices, machinery, music, and so on.

SOT means "sound on tape," also known as voice-over (VO). A news anchor or reporter reads narration as video or audio is played.

COVER means to use play video over the reporter's audio track.

Numbers next to NATS or SOT (SOT: 4:09) indicate the location of audio recorded by the journalist, either on the scene or when logging in the script by listening and watching the raw footage.

These directions are used for production personnel who are responsible for transforming the written script into a format that merges written narration, video, quotes and other audio.

Formatting: Narration is written in ALL CAPS. Quotes, or sound bites, appear in lowercase.

Normally, a script is written in two-column format. The left column displays what viewers see and hear via graphics, audio and video. They guide technical and production workers. The right column includes words spoken by the reporter, anchor, or interview subjects, abbreviated VO/SOT for voice-over/sound on tape. In this case, these elements appear in the left column. The descriptions in the right column are taken from the broadcast version.

Vanderveen writes his scripts in one column. "I tend to not use a lot of editor instructions on paper," he says, "as I like to hash a lot of that out before we go to edit."

"WELCOME HOME"
9NEWS, Denver March 23, 2011

NATS: OF OUTSIDE

SOT: 4:09 (COVER with shots of getting set up)

"they deserve the honor — they deserve the recognition — they deserve the dignity . . ."

IF THE SHOES ARE SHINED, IF THE UNIFORMS ARE PRESSED,

NATS: 25:34 (COVER WITH BEST INTRODUCTORY SHOT OF HER TALKING TO FOLKS)

"They're gonna give me a ten minute . . ."

"We need to have someone opening the door."

THEN BARBARA ATWELL,

NATS: 25:38

"That's the best I got . . ."

MUST BE READY TO GO.

SOT: 22:10

"it's a big responsibility — I love it . . ."

The story opens with video of six Marines in full dress uniforms marching toward the camera.

An unidentified woman's voice is heard over the video, a quote known as a "sound bite."

Additional video of soldiers in uniform standing at attention. The video then cuts to a close-up of the sun glinting off a brilliantly shined shoe worn by a Marine wearing midnight blue trousers with a so-called scarlet blood stripe down the outer seam. The images are underscored by the reporter's narration.

The viewer hears the same woman's voice saying "Are you ready?" interspersed with a close-up of a Marine's white gloves.

A woman appears in close-up, wearing glasses and an oversized white blouse directing with an outstretched finger. The sound bites play over the video.

Another close-up of a Marine walking on an airport tarmac.

This bite did not survive the editing process and is not included in the broadcast.

Al Tompkins: The story open sets tension. The viewer has a few seconds to ask, "What's happening here?" The open gives us the feeling that we are on the inside, that we have been given special access to a way of seeing this story that the public doesn't usually get to see. The video, which darts between close-ups and long shot, tells a compelling story without sound bites. A writer runs a risk in this setup. The viewer may begin to drift away wondering if there is a point to this story or whether it is just a reporter and photographer getting artsy. Remember: Tell stories for the living more than for the newsroom.

Barbara Atwell appears in profile, speaking to the reporter.

Tompkins: Chris Vanderveen is wisely choosing to allow the character to deliver the best lines. Chris could have said "she loves her job" but allows her to say it instead. It is more authentic when SHE says it. Remember to write "objective copy" and use "subjective sound." In other words, the reporter delivers the facts while the character delivers the emotions that can come only from the person herself.

AS BUCKLEY'S CHIEF OF PROTOCOL, IT'S HER JOB, TO *MAKE* SURE, EVERY DIGNITARY FEELS WELCOME.

SOT: 22:20 (COVER)

"People tell you pay attention to details — I pay attention to the tiniest of details."

NATS: 24:20

"They're in the DV Lounge — the door is closed . . ."

ON THIS DAY —

NATS: 31:20

"Whenever you're ready sir."

ON A TARMAC THAT HAS WELCOMED PRESI-DENTS AND FIRST LADIES,

NATS OF PLANE ARRIVING

IT IS CLEAR — THIS PLANE — IS NOT AIR FORCE ONE.

SOT: 6:14

"it's a tradition — we have to take care of them until the job is done . . ."

YET IF YOU CAME TO BUCKLEY AIR FORCE BASE RIGHT AROUND NOON, YOU SAW, THE ARRIVAL OF A DIGNITARY — NONETHELESS.

Over narration, a rapid succession of images to illustrate an association of ideas, known as a montage: close-ups of dress white caps, a rear shot of three Marines standing in formation, a Marine straightening his white glove, a sergeant's shoulder patch—three gold chevrons atop crossed rifles on a scarlet background.

Maxwell's voice is heard over these images that illustrate the minute details that underlie this important mission.

Tompkins: The middle of the story is usually when the reporter steps back to provide context, as Chris does here. This story is as old as storytelling, as old as war. So Chris Vanderveen has the burden of putting a new frame on an old story. It would be tempting to begin the story with an arriving casket and tearful bystanders. But Chris didn't choose "casket comes home" as a story focus. Instead the story is "Atwell honors soldier," so the story revolves around Barbara Atwell, not around the casket and not around the Buckley Air Force Base.

The bite also did not survive the editing process.

Maxwell speaks over video showing her speaking to two officers in dress uniforms inside an aircraft hangar.

A wide shot of a Marine Corps formation and a group of civilians flanking a hearse on the tarmac. Narration underscores the video.

The sound of a jet approaching.

A long shot of a charter jet arriving on a runway. A close-up of a woman stroking a man's back. They are dressed in civilian clothes. Another close-up of two anxious women followed by a young woman dabbing her eyes with a handkerchief.

Maxwell speaks over the images.

A shot of the plane door opening with Marines in the foreground. Cut to another shot of mourning relatives and friends. The video appears over the reporter's narration, written in ALL CAPS.

Tompkins: This is the big moment, the big reveal of the story. Notice that in narrative stories, stories that are not breaking news, the biggest surprise, the most emotional moment usually comes three-fourths of the way through the story. Movies and songs are like that too. The opening sets tension, the middle provides context, then the big explosion of action goes right here.

SOT: 3:42 (COVER WITH SHOT OF CASKET GETTING OFF PLANE)

"We on our end — need to bring them home . . ."

SOT: 18:51

"It is absolutely one of the most difficult things I have ever done . . ."

COL. TRENT PICKERING WANTS CHRISTOPHER MEIS' FAMILY TO LEAVE WITH ONE DISTINCT FEELING.

SOT: 17:50

"How much their son is appreciated — that he won't be forgotten . . ."

ATWELL JUST WANTS THEM TO BE ABLE TO SAY — WELCOME HOME.

SOT: 3:32 (COVER)

"it means their son has paid the ultimate price . . ."

SOT: 4:56

"This is really hard — it takes a lot to hold your emotions in when you really want to be with the families shedding a tear . . ."

NATS of silence of them bringing him to hearse

CHRISTOPHER MEIS.

WAS 20 YEARS OLD.

A COLORADO NATIVE.

A SON.

A MARINE.

SOT: 5:58 (COVER)

"We have to take care of our own . . ."

A flag-draped coffin emerges from the plane.

Maxwell speaks over the video.

Close-up of an air force officer, speaking to the reporter, followed by another shot of the fallen Marine's family.

An extended (four-second) shot that lingers on a man, woman and a teenage boy, accompanied by a Marine, approaching the coffin on the tarmac. A man and woman, apparently the Marine's parents, stand by the coffin and then rest their heads on it. The woman sobs. Cut to video of a military photographer capturing the scene.

Pickering speaks over the images.

Notice how attribution is artfully presented, coming after the sound bite.

Close-up of Atwell.

This bite did not survive editing.

Shot of Atwell standing at attention, holding back tears. Her voice is heard over the scene.

Tompkins: This is a perfect use of a subjective sound bite. It would not be appropriate for the reporter to steal this line, the only person who can say this with true emotion is the character herself.

A montage underscored by the reporter's narration: beribboned Marines slowly saluting the coffin, carrying the casket to a waiting hearse, a line of service members saluting.

Tompkins: Chris is sending a message by the order he selects. The message would be different if he put "20 years old" at the end. That might have telegraphed the message "what a waste of a human life."

If Chris had put "A Colorado native" at the end the story, it would have taken on a tone of "it's even worse that one of our own from our own state died."

Chris chooses to end the sequence with "A Marine." It implies that connection is critical to understanding who was lost when Christopher Meis died.

This bite did not survive the editing process.

HE WAS NOT A PRESIDENT — NOT A VICE PRESIDENT — BUT THE MOMENT HIS HEARSE LEFT THE AIRFIELD — HUNDREDS — MAYBE A THOUSAND ON THE BASE — SPONTANEOUSLY LEFT WORK — IF JUST FOR A FEW MINUTES — IN ORDER TO SAY — YOU'RE HOME. JUST HOW ATWELL ENVISIONED IT.

SOT: 6:29 (COVER)

"I want them to say that this was the way they expected him to be brought home . . ."

Chris Vanderveen NINE NEWS.

An image of Marines in formation is reflected in the highly polished door of the hearse emblazoned with the Marine Corps seal.

Shots of civilians lining the highway as the hearse passes by in a procession of vehicles. The reporter's narration is heard over the video. The last line of the narration did not appear in the broadcast version, a choice that makes the line "You're home," even more powerful.

A montage of Marines and airmen and civilians lining the sidewalk and saluting as the hearse passes them. A civilian stands alone, an American flag waving in the breeze behind him. The hearse passing bystanders is the story's final image.

Atwell has the last word.

Tompkins: The story comes around to the beginning, with Atwell's voice. Narrative stories often return "full circle" to give reason that we chose to open the story as we did.

With this phrase, known as a "sign-off," broadcast journalists signal that the story is over. They identify themselves and their news station by name. It serves the same function as a newspaper byline, except that broadcast sign-offs appear at the end of the story. Reports from the field often identify the location of the story.

SUMMARY   Effective broadcast writers have an advantage over print journalists because they add video and audio that helps audiences experience stories directly through their senses. "Fallen Marine," by award-winning TV journalist Chris Vanderveen, illustrates the power of video storytelling that relies on a blend of different visual perspectives and montages as well as recognition that video, narration and sound bites play different roles. Great broadcast journalists give their audiences credit to fill in gaps and don't need these elements to match. An eye for visuals, an ear for human voices, the ability to find a sharp focus, a writing style that is conversational, informal and direct, and artful editing typify best practices. To watch the complete broadcast story, visit http://www.9news.com/rss/story.aspx?storyid=189194.

DIVERSITY

325

BY THE END OF THIS CHAPTER,

you should be able to...

> Understand the importance that diversity plays in producing excellent journalism

> Master and use the five W's of diversity coverage

> Recognize and avoid stereotypes and other clichés of vision

> Connect with diverse communities

> Report and write effectively about groups that lie outside of the mainstream of society

> Equip yourself with tips and techniques to reverse the trend of bias in racial and ethnic identification in the news

66 "We have to remember that diversity isn't just about numbers, it's about making our news reports better. Diverse staffs lead to better journalism. 99

—DAVID ZEECK, FORMER PRESIDENT, AMERICAN SOCIETY OF NEWSPAPER EDITORS

326

THE CORE OF reporting involves learning your way around new situations and unfamiliar people, on the fly, so you can understand their stories and gain the trust of your sources. Yet American journalism as a whole has been dominated by points of view that reflect a narrow slice of society. The resulting stories often fall prey to stereotyping and can fail to reflect realities of race, gender, age, ethnicity, disability and sexual orientation.

This chapter reveals ways to improve your research, reporting and ability to move within any community, using all your senses, asking effective questions and using precise language to tell accurate untold stories. Its central aim: to help you broaden knowledge of your communities and beats and report and write with precision, fairness and sensitivity.

MAKING THE CASE FOR CULTURAL COMPETENCE

"The increasing **cultural diversity** of the United States, coupled with global interdependence, presents journalists today with a need to become culturally competent," according to Keith Woods and Aly Colón, who specialize in diversity training for journalists and news organizations.

Historical and demographic changes, they argued in a 2002 report for The Poynter Institute, have made cultural competence a core journalistic skill:

- Immigration to the United States is unmatched since the beginning of the 20th century.
- New immigrants represent cultural, religious, ethnic and racial groups far more varied than previous waves of newcomers.
- Global economics require journalists who understand and can communicate across barriers of language and customs.
- Besides the growing numbers of new citizens, there are significant existing segments of society—Latinos, Native Americans, African-Americans, Asian-Americans, disabled Americans and gay and lesbian Americans—that receive different treatment from the news media than the mainstream.

"Once seemingly invisible to the white population," Woods and Colón observed, "these cultural groups occupy increasingly significant and visible places in the American mosaic" (see Figure 15-1).

Cultural competence makes it possible for journalists to look beyond themselves to recognize the "Other," that is, those different from them. Such expertise makes it possible for journalists to know, for example, the differences between a Cuban American, a Puerto Rican, a Dominican and a Mexican American; or the role of a mosque, the temple for followers of Islam, one of the fastest growing religions in America. Connecting with multicultural communities is crucial if the news is to reflect the reality of the world.

CONDITIONS *of* DIFFERENCE

An exercise in diversity awareness from The Poynter Institute

Your Name: _____

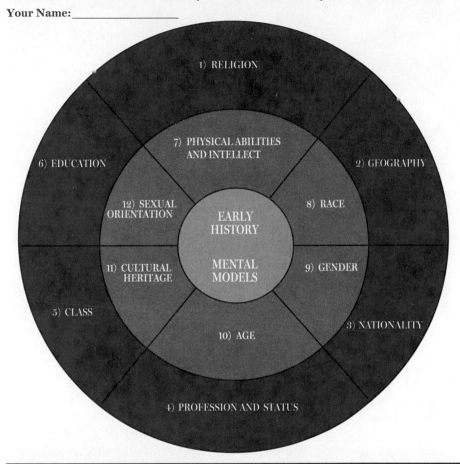

1) RELIGION

7) PHYSICAL ABILITIES AND INTELLECT

6) EDUCATION

2) GEOGRAPHY

12) SEXUAL ORIENTATION

EARLY HISTORY

8) RACE

MENTAL MODELS

11) CULTURAL HERITAGE

9) GENDER

5) CLASS

3) NATIONALITY

10) AGE

4) PROFESSION AND STATUS

About the Wheel

Conditions of Difference are components that shape the human experience. As journalists we must become smarter about differences and learn to understand and accept them as they are. This wheel can help you explore issues of difference in several important ways:

• The difference wheel illustrates 12 basic conditions of difference we have in the United States for codifying people and their experiences.

The inner core, "early history/mental models" is the individual's core experiences that formulate an individual's thinking.

The outer circles, change with some frequency,

but categorize the individual nonetheless.

Under each section of the wheel, write specifics about yourself or the person you are interviewing.

• The difference wheel is an effective interviewing exercise that allows journalists to see some personal and revealing areas of understanding. When used during an interview, it could afford more insightful and meaningful reporting.

• The difference wheel can help focus our attention on under covered communities and groups that exist in ostensibly homogeneous-groups.

Poynter.

Developed by Kenny Irby, Senior Faculty / Visual Journalism & Diversity Programs
Source: Marilyn Loden, Implementing Diversity, 1996, McGraw-Hill Publishing, Burr Ridge, IL.

FIGURE 15-1 Diversity reaches far beyond race, color or creed. Kenny Irby of The Poynter Institute created a "diversity wheel" to demonstrate 12 conditions of difference that separate and unite human beings. It's a useful tool for interviewing.

CONVERGENCE POINT ⚛

Eight Steps Toward Multicultural Competence

To get the stories you want, your goal, says journalism professor Ruth Seymour, "is to minimize the discomfort strangers might feel" when you encounter those who are different from you. She identifies eight issues—physical closeness, saying hello, facial expressions, showing respect, touch, talking style, gifts and food, gender and age roles—explains them and provides specific examples. Seymour's advice can serve journalists well in every interview, not just those that cross cultures.

Find this link on the companion Web site at **www.oup.com/us/scanlan.**

Worshippers gather for prayer during Eid-al-Fitr morning services marking the end of the Muslim holy month of Ramadan at Toyota Park on Sept. 10, 2010, in Bridgeview, IL. An American flag adorns the stage.

❝The news industry needs journalists of color to better reflect the diverse communities that it covers . . . and (to) keep in mind that America is changing. It is becoming multicultural, multiracial and multiethnic. The 21st century will bring an America where diversity will be the norm and a way of life.❞

—KAREN LINCOLN MICHEL, PAST PRESIDENT, NATIVE AMERICAN JOURNALISTS ASSOCIATION

Karen Lincoln Michel

HOW CAN REPORTERS SEE PEOPLE AS PEOPLE?

Sometimes it takes someone else to make reporters aware of the blinders they wear. But there are other ways they can learn to see people as individuals, rather than stereotypes, and that enable them to produce journalism unclouded by bias and prejudice. Among them:

- *Research*. They read books that broaden their understanding. For Michael Dobie, a sports reporter at *Newsday*, a pivotal text he read for his award-winning series about race and high school sports was *Why Are All the Black Kids Sitting Together in the Cafeteria?* by psychologist Beverly Daniel Tatum.

- *Immersion*. "As a reporter, you have to spend a lot of time in these communities. You have to check in with people every day or every couple of days. Because just in the normal course of conversations it's amazing what will come out," said Copley News reporter S. Lynne Walker. Over a period of seven months she returned again and again to Beardstown, Illinois, a predominantly white community whose face changed when Mexican and African immigrants migrated there in the 1990s, drawn by work at a pork slaughterhouse. Walker, fluent in Spanish, wrote a series of articles focused on the racism of locals, success stories

CHIP'S CORNER

WHY DIVERSITY MATTERS TO JOURNALISTS

For more than a year, I shared a cubicle in the news features department of the *St. Petersburg* (FL) *Times* with a reporter named Diane Mason. We compared leads and story ideas and traded family stories and newsroom gossip. One day, she taught me the value of diversity.

I had been working on the first installment of a series on ethics. "Choices" asked readers and a panel of experts to consider a range of ethical dilemmas in the fields of law, medicine, business and journalism. First we published the case studies, based on real-life examples, and asked our readers to respond. We ran follow-up stories that would report their answers and comments from relevant experts. The first installment focused on medical ethics. I told Diane about the doctors and medical school professors I was considering

for my panel of experts. Her reply threw me for a loop.

"What?" she said. "There aren't any women doctors? There aren't any black doctors? No Hispanic doctors?"

My list of sources, read so proudly, consisted exclusively of middle-aged white men. Until Diane's question and the heated discussion that followed, it hadn't even occurred to me that anything was wrong. If communication is not so much what's said, but what's heard, then what was the message that my story would convey? That men and whites are the only experts on medicine and ethics? That women and people of color don't have the qualifications? If the news media holds up a mirror to society, didn't my sources present an incomplete picture? To be honest, I didn't really want to hear any of this. I'd already done a lot of work, and it would have been a lot simpler to

dismiss my colleague's questions as just another example of politically correct thinking. But I knew she was right, that my reporting was incomplete. The mistake might have been understandable if committed by an inexperienced journalist, but I'm embarrassed to say I'd been a reporter for 15 years and was still blinded by unthinking stereotypes and unacknowledged prejudice. Chastened, I went back to work and found that, with a little extra effort, I could find a wider range of sources—women and people of color—whose inclusion made the series richer and more reflective of social and cultural reality.

The failure that Mason helped me avoid stemmed from cultural incompetence, blinkers that focused my attention on who I was—a middle-aged white man—at the expense of others different from me. ▶

among new arrivals and the pain of undocumented immigrants who had to sacrifice their true identities—"living with a lie"—to support their families.

Walker put Beardstown in context: "It was part of the new American Midwest, where brown faces and Spanish are woven into daily life." Such reporters visit off deadline, knowing that diverse communities resent the news media showing up only to report crime and other trouble. That's why Anne Hull of *The Washington Post* went to a baby shower and a bakery as she reported a story about a Muslim family in Paterson, New Jersey.

- *Listening and observing before asking questions.* What are "effective questions" to help a reporter understand a new situation? Reporting on race in high school sports for *Newsday*, Michael Dobie said, "I thought it was very crucial that I go into this with as few preconceptions as possible. I wanted to make sure my questions were not motivated at all by what I expected to find."

Ethical Dilemmas CHALLENGE DISCRIMINATION OR REMAIN SILENT

You're assigned to cover a charity golf tournament at an exclusive country club, an event which features white, black and Latino athletes. You find out that the club has a whites-only membership policy, although the issue hasn't been raised by any of the celebrity golfers nor has there been any public criticism raised. You are presented with two choices: report the tournament without reference to the exclusionary policy, focusing on it solely as a charity event, or include the fact that the players of color wouldn't be allowed to join the club, and seek comments from club officials and local activists who fight against discrimination. Which approach do you take? How would you justify your decision? What is your ethical responsibility—to the charity organizers, the country club, the players and the public? ▼

TALKING ACROSS DIFFERENCES

CONVERGENCE POINT ⚘

"Diversity at Work" Blog

A team of multicultural journalists contributes daily posts to this blog, which offers "fresh ways to encourage and enhance journalistic storytelling from different perspectives." Recent posts include advice on interviewing, a report on immigrants when you don't speak their language, an updated entry on racial identification style in the *Associated Press Stylebook* and the media's use of "illegal" or "undocumented" to identify immigrants.

Find this link on the companion Web site at **www.oup.com/us/ scanlan.**

In 1993, the *New Orleans Times-Picayune* published a six-part series, "Together Apart/The Myth of Race." It exposed racial discrimination in the city and included a candid exploration of the paper, which "had a long history of supporting slavery before the Civil War and backing segregation through the 1950s into the 1960s," wrote Jack Nelson, an acclaimed former investigative reporter for the *Los Angeles Times*. "No other newspaper had ever taken such a searing look at its own role in perpetuating segregation and white supremacy."

But when the idea for the series was first presented to the newsroom, white and black journalists balked. "Oh, my God, we were so far apart we couldn't even talk about it!" recalled project editor Kristin Gilger. "The distrust! I ended the meeting as quickly as I could."

Keith Woods, the black city editor who had proposed the series, persuaded the publisher to invest $30,000 in diversity training for the biracial project staff. The sessions were often painful. Paula Devlin, a white copy editor, recalled the reaction when Stephen Casmier, an African-American reporter, said he would "pay a million dollars to have skin that was white." She continued:

"The mouths of all the whites in the room dropped, but the other blacks nodded their heads up and down. It made me ashamed of my skin. My life changed. My husband's life changed. Race is everything in this country, I'm much more aware of it now."

According to Woods, who later taught diversity and ethics at The Poynter Institute before joining National Public Radio as vice president of diversity, the experience taught him five lessons:

1. *Be honest.* Cross-difference conversations pass through filters that interpret, analyze and sometimes bend the message. You build trust when you're clear about what you mean.
2. *Seek clarification before confusion and conflict.* Ask questions before reacting. "What do you mean?" "Can you explain that a little more?"

3. *Challenge with passion, not poison.* When conversations hit rough spots, let the other person know you care deeply to get past misunderstandings.
4. *Be willing to change your point of view.* You don't always have to change your mind. Just make sure it's possible.
5. *Stay in the room.* When conversations turn painful, the easiest thing is to stop talking. Have faith that there is gain on the other side of the pain.

USING PRECISION TO AVOID EUPHEMISMS, STEREOTYPES AND CLICHÉS OF VISION

Keith Woods

Stereotypes are generalizations about a person or group of persons. **Clichés of vision** are ways of looking at the world that, consciously or unconsciously, assume that certain stereotypes are correct. Reporters can unwittingly structure their whole reporting process—choice of story angle, choice of interviewees, focus of research—so that it confirms their limited knowledge or beliefs about the subject. This can exclude worthwhile voices and points of view, and lead groups within society to conclude that journalism doesn't speak for them.

In conversation, stereotypes rely on **code words**—euphemisms that substitute an inoffensive word or phrase for offensive ones. Welfare mom. Black or Hispanic ghettos. White. Liberal. Conservative. They are often shorthand for mindless, negative assumptions. Lazy baby-makers living off the public's tax dollars. Criminals. Victims of a system that they used to rule. Tree-hugging, antibusiness bleeding hearts. Uncaring biased protectors of the status quo.

Although code words often reflect ignorance or **prejudice**, when used by journalists they are usually the product of laziness—a linguistic easy out. But you may counter such bad habits with the hard work of reporting, precise writing and context.

In his series about the role race plays in high school sports, *Newsday* reporter Michael Dobie described the damage stereotypes can cause. Dobie wrote with empathy about the isolation of minority athletes, male and female, who excelled equally well at academics and rode "an emotional seesaw—camaraderie on teams, loneliness in classrooms."

One of his stories captured the impact of stereotypes in the high schools he visited:

❯EXAMPLE Sports can bring kids together. It can also pull them apart by feeding the misconception that race predetermines what athletes can and cannot do.

Blacks are good in basketball. White men can't jump.

Such phrases often are uttered without second thought—or any thought. . . . These labels can hurt in unexpected ways. Stereotypes create expectations. Expectations create pressure.

❝As a lesbian, I can assure you that while I walk with privilege as white and middle class, I experience my share of discrimination and oppression. As a lesbian journalist—working in broadcast—I, for many years, feared coming out in my newsroom. I wondered if I'd be demoted, shunned aside in the kinds of assignments, reduced in airtime or even fired.❞

—KAREN LOUISE BOOTIIE, FORMER PRESIDENT, NATIONAL LESBIAN AND GAY JOURNALISTS ASSOCIATION

Journalist at Work THE FIVE W'S OF DIVERSITY COVERAGE

Aly Colón

In the mid-1990s, Aly Colón had one of the most unusual jobs in journalism: diversity reporter/coach at *The Seattle Times*. His new job, as he made clear in an interview with *Editor and Publisher*, was not "a minority affairs beat or any other kind of reporting slot intended to concentrate responsibility for coverage in one person." As coach, Colón roamed the newsroom, encouraging reporters and editors to look for diversity in the paper's coverage. As reporter, Colón produced stories that revealed important, but neglected, aspects of his community. Among them:

- When wheelchair athletes came to Seattle for a National Veterans Wheelchair Games, he recruited one of the athletes to grade the city's accessibility for the disabled.
- What might have been a routine crime story about a shooting at a Vietnamese nightclub that left two dead and several wounded became an exploration of the clash of cultures and the criminal justice system. "There were language problems," Colón wrote. "Confusion about names. Many of the young Vietnamese didn't understand the police or trust them." The investigation, as one police official put it, "ended up being a hell of a mess."
- For a piece titled "Speechless in Seattle," he helped readers understand the social realities faced by minorities. Colón, a native of Puerto Rico, retraced his steps through Seattle speaking only Spanish. "The reactions surprised me," he wrote. "Sometimes, after getting over their initial shock, people attempted linguistic and physical contortions to help me understand what they thought I needed. Other times, their quick, cool dismissal made me feel lost, unimportant, almost invisible."

In Seattle, and later as a teacher, Colón encouraged journalists to discover diversity in news by answering five W's of diversity to help others tell untold stories in their communities:

1. Who's missing from the story?
2. What's the context for the story?
3. Where can we go for more information?
4. When do we use racial or ethnic identification?
5. Why are we including or excluding certain information? ▶

> **❝Clichés of language are significant misdemeanors, but clichés of vision are felonies. . . . We too often leave the city room knowing what we'll find, and then, of course, we'll find it.❞**
>
> —DONALD M. MURRAY, AUTHOR, *WRITING FOR YOUR READERS*

In 1995, San Francisco Mayor Frank Jordan declared that a pregnant, unmarried African-American woman on welfare who died saving her children from a fire in her apartment was the "real hero." The public reacted to the mayor's comment "with letters, calls, faxes, all bubbling with pure white hatred and self-righteous indignation," Peter N. King, a Los Angeles Times columnist, wrote. He quoted one such response: "Where do you get the idea of Nina Davis as a hero? Her act of saving three of her seven illegitimate kids may be taken as a small token of repayment for all those tens of thousands of $$$$$ society, the federal government and California taxpayers have put forward." As talk shows trumpeted this view, King decided he had to write about the case. Using his training as a reporter, he first went to two places: the housing projects where the story happened and Nina Davis' funeral.

In an interview in *Best Newspaper Writing*, King explained why: "It would be one thing to sit in there and say, 'What a bunch of yahoos, criticizing this poor woman—who, all she did was save her children—simply because she was on welfare has therefore forfeited her right to basic human dignity,'" King said. "It's another thing to go out there and see the lie of it all with your own eyes. When you see with your own eyes the reality of their dismal situation, then I think it not only informs the art, but it powers it."

It's tempting to fall back on familiar assumptions about types of people. It's easy and often won't warrant a second glance from an editor or reader. It takes much more effort to find out the details and contexts of a situation, as well as the different sides that people might reasonably take on an issue. Presenting a complex situation in ways that readers can understand is difficult, but this hard work often results in stories that are not only more accurate, but richer and more insightful.

AVOIDING BIAS IN RACIAL/ ETHNIC IDENTIFICATION

"The use of **racial identifiers** in the media was for decades a means of singling out those who were not white," says Keith Woods, vice president of diversity for National Public Radio. "The practice helped form and fuel stereotypes and continues today to push a wedge between people."

When police first identified the man who killed 32 students and teachers at Virginia Tech in April 2007 as an "Asian man," news reporters repeated the term.

"The story was made racial," said Associated Press reporter Dionne Walker, who wrote an article about complaints from Asian professors and journalists that the killer's race was not relevant and fed stereotypes about Asians.

"I could imagine 'Asian man' being used as short hand, intentionally or unintentionally. For outsider." Tom Huang, a *Dallas Morning News* editor, observed. "Intruder. Alien. Alienated. Scheming. Inscrutable. Serious. Calm. Watch out for them. You can't trust them. That is the danger of racial identifiers."

"The inherent flaw in **stereotypical stories** is that they are one-dimensional," says Sue LoTempio, assistant managing editor for readership at the *Buffalo News* and an evangelist for more accurate stories about the disabled. "Stories that are inspirational or medical allow the media to believe we've covered disability, when we haven't."

GUIDELINES FOR RACIAL IDENTIFIERS IN NEWS STORIES

Racial and ethnic identification remains a sensitive topic in many newsrooms. Journalists can handle this delicate material better, Woods says, if they examine every racial reference in a story before publication or broadcast, and ask these questions:

- *Is it relevant?* Race is relevant when the story is about race. Just because people in conflict are of different races does not mean that is the source of their dispute. A story about interracial dating, however, is a story about race.

CONVERGENCE POINT

All Aly Colón Wants Is an Accent

In Spanish, a missing accent mark can mean the difference between "shame" and "rock or group." In this article, Laura Wides-Muñoz reports on the inaccuracy of stories that omit accent marks in Latino names and steps by Anglo news organizations to honor the accurate identification of a person.

Find this link on the companion Web site at **www.oup.com/us/ scanlan.**

QUICK Tips ◔ BETTER DIVERSITY NEWS REPORTING

News organizations often fail to recognize the differences between people. Diversity trainer Lillian R. Dunlap uses the following list to teach professionals, students and teachers how to better report stories involving women and members of America's ethnic minorities:

■ Identify race only when necessary to understanding the story.

■ Include minorities as sources in stories not focused on traditionally minority issues.

■ Avoid direct or implied stereotypes of women and minorities (women and minorities are not always victims or criminals).

■ Provide context for people and ideas in the story. (This may mean interviewing people in their offices instead of on the street or asking for a family photo instead of using the mug shot police provide.)

■ Avoid using euphemisms such as "inner city" or "bad part of town" to describe places where ethnic minority members live or "escape" from.

■ Identify people in photos by correct name and title.

■ Consider a variety of perspectives. (Avoid exclusively making minority members the problem and majority members the solution.)

■ Acknowledge only "leaders" who have been chosen or elected by "followers."

■ Make technical preparation to photograph nonwhites. Pay attention to such issues as lighting to get as detailed and clear an image as possible.

■ Provide context for understanding data and graphics about women and minorities.

■ Resist making race an issue simply because minorities are part of a particular story.

■ Avoid making gender an issue simply because women are in the story. Use relevant documents and human sources for stories.

■ Show the variety and diversity within ethnic groups and women. ▸

- *Have I explained the relevance?* Journalists too frequently assume readers will know the significance of race in stories. The result is radically different interpretations.
- *Is it free of codes, not just racial but political and economic as well?* "Inner city," "blue collar," "conservative," "suburban," "middle class" are often used as **euphemisms**—shortcuts that can perpetuate stereotypes in subtle ways.
- *Take "inner city," for example.* Immigrants have always flocked to cities seeking jobs and to live with their countrymen, where they lived amid poverty, health and sanitation problems and crime. "Inner city" became code in the mid-20th century for "black," sociologists say, when middle-class whites fled the cities for the suburbs to avoid living among blacks and what whites perceived to be urban decay and a rising crime rate. The term persists, but code words may deceive. Gentrification has improved the state of many cities where middle- and upper-class neighborhoods have emerged. The term is often inaccurate, derogatory and mindless. To many readers and viewers, "the inner city" of Washington DC, which is predominantly black, may conjure images of drug dealing and

gun violence. But the neighborhood is also the location of the White House. "Rednecks" is a word first used to refer to farmer's sunburns. Proudly embraced by some white Southerners and comedians, it is also a code word for poor, ill-educated, racists. Be alert to code words. Be precise.

- *Are racial, ethnic and other identifiers used evenly?* If the race of a person charging discrimination is important, then so is the race of the person being charged.
- *Who can I ask for help?* If you're inexperienced about races and cultures, get smart by asking someone who knows more about your subject, just as you would if the subject were science or municipal budgets.

CONNECTING WITH DIVERSE COMMUNITIES

The 2010 Census counted more than 100 self-reported ancestries for Americans. Here are ways to connect with these **diverse communities**, recommended by diversity expert Aly Colón:

- *Specialists.* Contact local diversity and/or race relations specialists at universities, institutes, consulting firms and companies known for diversity efforts.
- *Organizations.* Contact local organizations that represent diverse groups: Hispanic Chamber of Commerce, African American Coalition, health and disability advocates.
- *Publications and broadcast outlets.* Subscribe to newspapers, magazines, newsletters focused on race, ethnicity, sexual orientation, disabilities, and so on, and meet with their publishers, editors or reporters. Check with television, radio and cable stations owned by, or oriented toward, diverse groups.
- *List.* Create a "Rainbow Rolodex," of sources in diverse communities. Meet them for coffee, tea, breakfast or lunch, in their communities.
- *Visits.* Leave your comfort zone. Eat at ethnic restaurants, or diners with a white clientele. Shop at ethnic stores. Meet the owner. Respect the reporter's credo: There is no such thing as a stupid question.

As an experiment, *Dallas Morning News* editor Tom Huang searched Google for "Vietnamese in Dallas" and "Ethiopians in Dallas." He soon found Web sites for a Vietnamese Professionals Society, a Mutual Assistance Association for Ethiopians and several ethnic churches and student associations in both communities. His discovery of Web sites serving diverse groups convinced him that "the digital world can help the reader deepen his understanding of his own community—and build connections within that community." They can also help readers and journalists understand other communities by seeing how multicultural stories can be told with audio, video, photos and interactive graphics. Says Huang: "We need to take advantage of that."

CONVERGENCE POINT ⟟

Handling Race and Ethnicity

"The question of whether and how to include racial and ethnic descriptions in news stories is one of the most debated and least understood topics of journalism," explains the introduction to this free online course. You will examine your own assumptions about race and ethnicity, deconstruct stories where race or ethnicity may or may not play a part and learn how to deal with the issue with greater confidence.

Find this link on the companion Web site at **www.oup.com/us/ scanlan.**

TELLING UNTOLD STORIES: REPORTING AND WRITING ACROSS CULTURES

At the *San Jose Mercury News*, a sports writer found that a mostly Asian suburb couldn't field a football team because few Asian-Americans play the game. "But the tennis and badminton teams were hell on wheels. Those revelations captured a changing America in a powerful way," said David Yarnold, the paper's editor at the time.

That story fits a definition of what diversity specialists refer to as **untold stories**: "compelling stories about different communities that often go unnoticed and ignored."

Good reporting makes it possible for news organizations to share stories that draw their strength from the fact that they haven't been told before.

"Reporting across cultures and writing about differences can be daunting," says Victor Merina, a former investigative reporter for the *Los Angeles Times* who works with young Native American journalists. But it's well worth the effort, he says, "because untold stories reveal not only the differences but also the similarities between groups and communities."

The danger in reporting about groups and communities is that we may fall into the trap of myths, stereotypes and assumptions. Such well-meaning but naive approaches to covering communities usually fall into one of the following categories:

- **"Zoo stories,"** which treat communities like exotic animals on display
- **"Gee whiz stories,"** which marvel at the accomplishments of one group or another as if in astonished amazement
- **"Conflict-only stories,"** which portray a group only when there is tension and violence and/or celebrity involved
- **"Festival and heritage month stories"**—such as Cinco de Mayo, Chinese New Year, and Black History Month—which are the only positive or nuanced coverage of a community's untold stories

John Donvan, correspondent for ABC's *Nightline*, finds his way into untold stories by focusing on what he calls his "blind spots: the things I could not know because no one can know everything."

A blind spot surfaced when an Asian-American TV journalist pitched a story to *Nightline*'s executive producer. The news media, he said, was fostering a "**yellow scare**" in their coverage of Wen Ho Lee, a government scientist accused of selling government secrets to China.

Donvan researched the story, but couldn't find evidence of a racist backlash in any of the stories about Lee, a nationalized citizen born in Taiwan. It wasn't until he began interviewing Asian-Americans that he saw the story his blind spot was missing. The community was reading the Lee stories and "feeling a sense of foreboding . . . of dread. . . . Asian-Americans were reading the Wen Ho Lee coverage, and it was

CONVERGENCE POINT ⋇

The Diversity Style Guide

"The News Watch Diversity Style Guide," produced in 2002 and continually updated, provides an alphabetized list of terms drawn from diverse news associations and mainstream style guides. From "1.5 generation. Bilingual, bicultural Korean Americans who were born in Korea and then immigrated to the United States as children" to "Zebra. Avoid. Derogatory term for a person of mixed race," it's an important resource for journalists who want to increase their multicultural knowledge and avoid code words and stereotypes in their stories.

Find this link on the companion Web site at **www.oup.com/us/ scanlan.**

scaring them," Donvan said in an interview for *The Authentic Voice: The Best Reporting on Race and Ethnicity*.

The stories, he found, had rekindled painful memories of discrimination against Asian-Americans in the country's history. In World War II, the government, fueled by sensationalistic news stories, feared that Japanese-Americans might be spies or saboteurs and forced 110,000 of them into internment camps until the war ended. Many lost their homes, land and businesses. (In 1988, President Ronald Reagan signed a federal law that formally apologized, blaming the internments on "race prejudice, war hysteria and a failure of political leadership," and paid $20,000 to each surviving detainee, totaling $1.2 billion.)

Donvan finally saw why the Wen Ho Lee story rattled Asian-Americans across the country and told the story of their painful past. "It wasn't the media coverage per se, which at the time seemed mostly responsible and accurate. Rather, it was the history of a long-established pattern of Asian-Americans being considered unreliable." In the Lee case, federal prosecutors dropped all but one of the 58 charges against Lee, and was forced to pay him $1.64 million for invasion of privacy. Five major news organizations had to contribute $750,000 for refusing to identify their sources for their stories.

"The morning after the *Nightline* program was broadcast, a black colleague came by my office to discuss the show." Donvan recalls his co-worker saying, "Wow, I just never saw it—what Asian-Americans have to go through. . . . I just never saw it before."

SEE CLOSE-UP AT WWW .OUP.COM/US/SCANLAN: WRITING ABOUT DIVERSITY

The Coaching Way ⁙ DIVERSITY

- Practice empathy. If you're white, practice the skill of truly considering what it's like to be a member of another group. If you're African-American, Native American, Asian-American, do the same. If you're heterosexual, consider how a gay or lesbian might react to the news you're writing about.
- Have you traced the origins of your attitudes toward people who are different than you?

- Are you alert to "**tokenism**" in your stories, so you can avoid letting one minority represent an entire group?
- If you're white, have you asked a colleague of color, ethnicity or sexual orientation different from yours, to check your story for **insensitivity** or **bias**?
- If challenged, how would you defend it? Would you be willing to revise?

- During the writing, do you ask yourself: Am I perpetuating stereotypes, code words and other clichés of vision?
- Do you have a "Rainbow Rolodex," a contact list that enables you to find diverse sources that reflect a range of experiences and viewpoints? ▸

PROFESSIONALS' ROUNDTABLE

FINDING DIVERSITY

In today's multicultural societies, journalism should reflect the diversity of those communities. That raises a challenge since we all carry biases, assumptions and fears about people different from us. Reporters who confront these attitudes can tell untold stories that connect with all of their readers, viewers and listeners. Reporters and editors dedicated to improving diversity in the news and newsroom recommend these steps:
- Be honest about your own prejudices or ignorance.
- Work hard to approach every story with an open mind.
- Go to sources closest to the action, whether it's a disabled person, persons of color or members of ethnic or religious groups.

Participants

SUE LOTEMPIO, assistant managing editor for readership, *Buffalo News*

O. RICARDO PIMENTEL, editorial page editor, *San Antonio News-Express*

VICTOR MERINA, special projects reporter and editor, Reznet News (http://www.reznetnews.org/)

> *Why is it important for news organizations to consider diversity when covering their communities?*

LoTempio: Newsrooms must reflect the communities they serve. Diversity in the newsroom means more voices will be heard, more perspectives will be represented, fewer assumptions (which are usually wrong) will be made.

Pimentel: There is the practical reason. They are the fastest growing part of the market in many communities and in the nation. If we're going to continue having readers, it makes little sense to not include on our pages the folks who look like them and represent their views, their voices. And then there's the Journalism with the capital "J" reason. Covering our community means covering all its parts.

> *What are ways journalists can beef up their "Rainbow Rolodex"?*

Merina: Look beyond the elected leaders, community spokespersons and usual names you quote. Spend time at local listening posts and find those people that others really listen to and what hot issues fan those conversations.

> *What's the single best advice you'd give young journalists who want to reflect diversity in their stories?*

Pimentel: Step out of your comfort zone. Realize that it's usually not racism that causes narrow journalism but simple ignorance. We write with comfort about people we know, often people who look like us. Address your own ignorance.

LoTempio: We assume that we check our biases at the newsroom door, but the truth is, we don't. You need to take a close look inside yourself and be honest about your biases, your fears, and your assumptions. Once you recognize them, then you can actively work on setting them aside and approaching your stories with an open mind and wide-open eyes.

Merina: Don't be afraid of reporting on a different culture because you think you don't know enough or are afraid of making a cultural gaffe. You will learn and, if you make a mistake, you will recover. Take that risk.

SUMMARY GUIDE   DIVERSITY

MAKING THE CASE FOR CULTURAL COMPETENCE

Cultural competence—the ability to reflect increasing cultural diversity—is as important a skill as reporting and writing.

What to Remember → Culturally competent journalists look beyond themselves to recognize those different from them. They are sensitive to cultural differences that influence their reporting and writing, and tell stories that reflect a multicultural society.

HOW CAN REPORTERS SEE PEOPLE AS PEOPLE?

There are a variety of ways that journalists can learn to see beyond stereotypes in their reporting and writing.

What to Remember → Research and immersing yourself in a subject or community enables you to put multicultural stories in context. Listening and observation help you to avoid preconceptions that lie beneath prejudice and inaccurate judgments.

TALKING ACROSS DIFFERENCES

Journalists who encounter unfamiliar people, groups and situations can meet the challenge of talking across differences by focusing on five approaches that enhance understanding.

What to Remember → Being honest about your attitudes, knowledge and feelings builds trust. "What do you mean?" questions seek clarification and bypass confusion and conflict. Challenge with passion, not poison. You don't have to change your mind, but leave open the possibility of a different point of view. Resist the impulse to stop talking.

USING PRECISION TO AVOID EUPHEMISMS, STEREOTYPES AND CLICHÉS OF VISION

Stereotypes, which make generalizations about people or communities, predispose journalists to find what they think they will find when encountering those different from them.

What to Remember → Stereotypes are clichés of vision and, like clichés of language, they are lazy and mindless. They rely on hurtful and inaccurate code words or euphemisms that substitute an inoffensive word or phrase for offensive ones.

AVOIDING BIAS IN RACIAL/ETHNIC IDENTIFICATION

Racial and ethnic identifiers are often inaccurate and fuel hurtful and stereotypes that divide people and communities.

What to Remember → Journalists often make stories racial by repeating mistaken and irrelevant descriptions made by officials. They telegraph mistrust through shorthand that is one-dimensional and mislead audiences in potentially explosive stories.

GUIDELINES FOR RACIAL IDENTIFIERS IN NEWS STORIES

To counter biased racial and ethnic identifiers, journalists should question the assumptions behind them.

What to Remember → Effective journalists ask five questions about racial or ethnic identification. Is it relevant? Is my story about race or something else? Have I explained why a racial or ethnic identifier is relevant and significant? Does my story rely on code words that can perpetuate stereotypes? Have I used identifiers equally?

CONNECTING WITH DIVERSE COMMUNITIES

With Americans dividing themselves into more than 100 self-reported ancestries, effective journalists learn creative ways to connect with diverse communities.

What to Remember → Good journalists visit diverse groups in their communities, churches and social clubs. They consult publications and broadcast outlets that focus on race, ethnicity, sexual orientation, disabilities and other conditions of difference. They develop a "Rainbow Rolodex" of diverse sources available on and off deadline and search Web sites maintained by diverse communities.

TELLING UNTOLD STORIES: REPORTING AND WRITING ACROSS CULTURES

Good reporting and writing introduces audiences to compelling stories about communities that often go unnoticed and ignored.

What to Remember → Sharing untold stories can be daunting, but they expose important similarities between groups as well as differences. Journalists keep an eye out for "blind spots," assumptions fueled by insufficient reporting that get in the way of finding the true story.

KEY TERMS

bias, p. 337
clichés of vision, p. 331
code words, p. 331
conflict-only stories, p. 336
cultural competence, p. 326
cultural diversity, p. 326
diverse communities, p. 335
euphemisms, p. 334

festival and heritage month
   stories, p. 336
gee whiz stories, p. 336
insensitivity, p. 337
multicultural, p. 328
multiethnic, p. 328
multiracial, p. 328
prejudice, p. 331

racial identifiers, p. 333
stereotypes, p. 331
stereotypical stories, p. 333
tokenism, p. 337
untold stories, p. 336
yellow scare, p. 336
zoo stories, p. 336

EXERCISES

1. Study print, broadcast and online stories for use of "code words." What are the underlying messages behind them? How can people, groups or events be more accurately described?

2. Do a content audit measuring how often and in what ways people of color and women are portrayed in pictures and print in the newspapers, newscasts and online news sites that you frequent. Itemize the differences—the times a Chinese-American laundry owner or black criminal appears compared to a white soccer mom or male executive, for instance. Discuss the impact of such differences on audiences. Search for an untold story that you can report, write or produce.

3. Write a 500-word essay titled "When I Was 'the Other'" that explores a time in your life when you felt like a minority.

4. Search for diverse communities on the Internet that are located in your area. Select one or two and visit them on their home ground. Search for an untold story that you can report, write or produce.

5. What are your "blind spots"—what assumptions do you have about different races, ethnic groups, gays or people with disabilities? Interview an expert and an individual within the community to seek a more complete understanding.

READINGS

Clark, Roy Peter, and Campbell, Cole, eds. *The Values and Craft of American Journalism: Essays from The Poynter Institute.* Gainesville, FL: University Press of Florida, 2002.
This thought-provoking collection devotes essays to racial identification in the news and effective ways to reflect diversity in news stories.

González, Juan, and Torres, Joseph. *News for All the People: The Epic Story of Race and the American Media.* New York: Verso, 2011.
Spanning America's first colonial newspapers to the Internet age, this is a compelling history of the American media with special focus on media outlets owned and controlled by people of color, and how they were suppressed—sometimes violently—by mainstream political, corporate and media leaders.

Morgan, Arlene Notoro, Pifer, Alice Irene, and Woods, Keith. *The Authentic Voice: The Best Reporting on Race and Ethnicity.* **New York: Columbia University Press, 2006.**
A collection of outstanding print and broadcast stories and interviews provide a multimedia backdrop to address the challenges and rewards of reporting in a multicultural world. A companion DVD includes seven television stories and 14 interviews that explore diversity in the news and the different ways journalists treat the subject.

Wilson, Clint C. II, and Gutierrez, Felix. *Race, Multiculturalism and the Media.* **Thousand Oaks, CA: Sage Publications, 1995.**
A historical overview focusing on the relationship between mainstream media and the four largest racial groups in the United States: Hispanics, Asian-Americans, African-Americans and Native Americans. Using examples from newspapers, broadcast news, magazines, advertising and film, the authors argue that while the word "minority" has lost its meaning, unequal treatment of the four groups endures in the news and culture.

LIBEL, PRIVACY, ETHICS

BY THE END OF THIS CHAPTER,

you should be able to...

> Understand essentials of media law

> Understand and master a process for ethical decision making

> Understand and avoid invasion of privacy, including "hidden" audio and video recording

> Define, recognize and prevent plagiarism and fabrication

JOURNALISM IS A profession dedicated to seeking out and reporting the truth, yet it continues to be plagued by high-profile scandals about its ethical lapses. The result is a steady erosion of public confidence and trust.

Legal and ethical issues can arise at college and university news outlets, not just at major Web sites, TV stations and newspapers. Sensitivity to potential legal and ethical pitfalls and a process for avoiding them will help you deal with problems that could surface in your career, whether tomorrow or five years from now.

In this chapter, you will familiarize yourself with media law, including on-line libel, and a decision-making process that will enable you to dodge ethical minefields. The idea isn't to transform you into an instant legal expert—it's to familiarize you with some of the most important basic elements of media law and ethics.

THE TWO SIDES OF DEFAMATION: LIBEL AND SLANDER

> 66 Libel can crop up anywhere—in a report of a confession, in a restaurant review, in a [headline] over a photo caption. . . . The best defense, of course, is that the statement that prompted the suit is true. There is no libel, no matter how harmful the statement is, if it's accurate. 99
>
> —CHARLES DELAFUENTE, METRO DESK COPY EDITOR, *THE NEW YORK TIMES*

The first amendment to the United States Constitution is part of the Bill of Rights, added out of concern that the Constitution lacked adequate guarantees for civil liberties. It prohibits the making of any law that diminishes freedom of the press. It reads as follows:

> Congress shall make no law respecting an establishment of religion, or prohibiting the free exercise thereof; or abridging the freedom of speech, or of the press . . .

Reporting the news in any medium provides a public service: to report and discuss matters of public interest. That right is protected by the First Amendment and supported by the United States Supreme Court. In a landmark 1964 ruling, *The New York Times v. Sullivan*, the Court expressed its support for "a profound national commitment to the principle that debate on public issues should be uninhibited, robust, and wide-open."

But freedom of the press isn't bulletproof. Journalists are still vulnerable to legal action from sources or subjects who complain stories have defamed them—that is, damaged their reputation.

Defamation can occur in two ways: orally, known as **slander**, and in writing or other fixed forms, referred to as **libel**.

Libel is the publication or airing of false statements that expose someone to public hatred, contempt or ridicule in writing or pictures. Slander can cause the same result by speaking such statements.

UNDERSTANDING THE ELEMENTS OF LIBEL

Even though newsrooms have editors, news directors and lawyers whose job is to protect news organizations from defamation charges, that doesn't absolve the reporter from knowing the basics. Libel laws vary from state to state, but some general principles apply. Much of the information in this section is drawn from the First Amendment Handbook published by the Reporters Committee for Freedom of the Press and Samuel Fifer, a prominent media lawyer who focuses on legal issues surrounding old and new media.

At the heart of libel law is the conflict between two important interests: **freedom of speech** and the **importance of reputation**. In America we cherish both, and so courts have over the years established rules that govern libel actions. In the last half-century

---

Journalist at Work DODGING THE LIBEL BULLET

Frank Greve

It was a test that investigative reporter Frank Greve had been waiting for all his journalistic life. A stranger appeared at his door and delivered a libel suit filed by the subject of a story Greve had written; he wanted $150 million in **damages**.

After "20 months of acute professional anxiety," countless hours with lawyers poring over the story and the notes, reporting, thought processes and writing that produced it, and an unnerving **deposition**, a three-judge court of appeals decided in Greve's favor. Greve still savors the judges' conclusion: "The truth may sting, but it is the truth nonetheless."

Greve's advice to those who may face the same test:

- To the most obvious question, whether to keep notes or destroy them, there's no right answer. Sometimes they help, sometimes not. Whatever you decide, be consistent.
- The tougher the story, the more generous a reporter should be in allowing its target to have his or her say.
- Reporting findings is more useful to readers than reporting conclusions. Distinguishing between **findings** and **conclusions** is libel insurance.

It's much safer to report that "Event A happened, then Events B and C happened" than it is to say "Events A and B caused Event C."

- Check all numbers. Check them again. Then get someone else to check them.
- After a person you're investigating declines to comment, but well before you publish, send him or her a list of the questions you'd intended to ask. It may not yield an interview or new information, but it's impressive evidence of a reporter's intent to be fair. Follow up with a phone call and report the person's response to the effort.
- Do some reporting on your source's motives. Does this person have a reason to provide misleading information?
- Listen to your inner voice that asks incessantly: Is what I'm writing fair? ▼

the courts have placed the burden of proof on the plaintiff (the person complaining of defamation). The challenge is daunting because to win a libel case, plaintiffs must prove that the news story meets three conditions. Libel occurs when

1. a false and defamatory statement about an identifiable person
2. is published to a third party
3. causing injury to the subject's reputation.

Publishing a false statement of fact that is capable of being proven true or false meets the first element of libel. Reporting that someone was convicted of murder is not libelous if it can be proven with a court document. However, satire, parody, insults and opinion—"I think Paris Hilton is a total loser"—are not considered defamation, because they are not capable of being proven true or false. An editorial or commentary can be libelous if it contains false assertions of fact to support that opinion, however.

Someone reading or hearing the story must be able to reasonably identify the person being defamed. That doesn't mean that the story must actually name the person. Saying that the high school football coach in a small town molested students would identify him or her.

Publication occurs when information is negligently or intentionally communicated by any mass medium—the Internet, TV broadcasts, newspapers, magazines, books, radio—to someone other than the person defamed.

A libelous statement must harm the reputation of a person in the eyes of some other reasonable person. A Texas legislator who won a libel suit against a television station testified that, after the station's defamatory broadcast, strangers in the local mall asked him why he wasn't in jail. The plaintiff must prove that the statement is false and substantially so. If your story reports that the mayor embezzled $25,000, but the actual figure was $30,000, the case would be dismissed because the sting of the statement is not substantially different from the truth.

Nobody's perfect, and judges recognize human frailty by tolerating a margin of error in news reports. Plaintiffs must prove negligence before a news organization can be held liable for defamation. Carelessness can be forgiven, but ignoring obvious ways of substantiation, such as failure to check public records or to interview the subject of a defamatory report, could be considered reckless disregard for the truth and may support a plaintiff's argument.

THE NEW YORK TIMES V. SULLIVAN: A JOURNALISTIC SHIELD

It was an ordinary transaction: A committee bought a newspaper advertisement supporting its cause. But that simple act in March 1960 led to the most important protection journalists have in their effort to report the news.

The New York Times published the ad from civil rights activists protesting police brutality and retaliation against peaceful protests of segregation in the South. L. B.

Sullivan, a city commissioner in Montgomery, Ala., claimed the ad libeled him, even though it did not name him. In 1964, the U.S. Supreme Court ruled that the **First Amendment** protects the publication of all statements about the conduct of public officials. Such statements are protected even if they are false, unless the plaintiff can prove the statements were made with **actual malice**. "Actual malice" means that the reporter knew that the story was false, or should have known it was false, but published it anyway. Later, the court expanded the decision to include so-called **public figures** such as celebrities.

Private figures have an easier time of it in a libel case. They have to prove only that the journalist was negligent and did not take the ordinary care a reporter should take in reporting and writing. Bottom line: the First Amendment is a powerful shield, but it doesn't mean journalists can break laws to get a story.

TARGETING JOURNALISTIC CONDUCT

The First Amendment provides journalists strong protection against libel suits when they write tough but accurate stories. But the legal system doesn't shield journalists if they break laws—such as trespassing, fraud or theft—that apply to every other citizen.

Most lawsuits against news organizations still focus on libel and defamation—alleged harm caused by what was published or broadcast. In the last two decades, however, the emphasis has shifted from the product to the process—how the story was reported. Judges and juries have made it clear that reportorial conduct—how reporters gather information for a story—is as important, legally speaking, as the story itself.

Case in point: In 1998, Michael Gallagher, a respected investigative reporter for the *Cincinnati Enquirer*, co-authored a hard-hitting, 18-page series accusing Chiquita Brands International, the world's largest banana producer, of bribery in Colombia, pesticide practices that endangered workers' health and the use of Chiquita ships to smuggle cocaine. To bolster his case based on a year of reporting in the United States, Europe and Central America, Michael Gallagher said the evidence included information from 2,000 voice mail messages left for Chiquita executives.

The problem: Gallagher had stolen the voice mails with the help of a company lawyer.

Within days, the series began to implode. Two months after it was published, the *Cincinnati Enquirer* published an extraordinary apology to Chiquita Brands for three days on the front page of its newspaper and online site. It renounced the series and said it had fired Gallagher, and paid Chiquita Brands a multimillion dollar settlement, even before Chiquita Brands filed, as expected, a libel suit.

Instead, the company sued Gallagher for defamation, trespass, civil conspiracy, fraud, and violation of laws prohibiting the interception of private telephone communications. Chiquita eventually dropped its lawsuit against the *Enquirer*, which is owned by Gannett, the nation's largest newspaper company. But reporter Gallagher wasn't off the hook.

A local prosecutor stepped in and lodged criminal charges. Three months after the series ran, his career in tatters, Gallagher pleaded guilty to unlawful interception of wire transmission and unauthorized access to communication, both felonies. He faced up to 2½ years in prison and a $7,500 fine. After Gallagher agreed to cooperate with authorities in their case against the company lawyer, a judge sentenced the 40-year-old reporter to five years of probation and 200 hours of community service.

News media lawyers saw the case as an alarming example of a new wave of legal attacks against journalism. Chiquita Brands lawyers recognized that public figures or companies find it difficult to prove actual malice—an essential element of libel. Instead, they went after what they considered criminal conduct by journalists.

Media lawyers had already seen this new approach in action and weren't happy about it. Jane Kirtley, of the respected Reporters Committee for the Freedom of the Press, had decried the tactic as "an end-run around" the First Amendment.

Six years earlier, in 1992, ABC's newsmagazine show, *PrimeTime Live* broadcast a 27-minute **exposé** that accused the Food Lion supermarket chain of unsanitary practices including dosing old chicken with barbecue sauce, wiping out sell-by dates on dairy items with nail polish remover and putting spoiled fish on sale by disguising the smell with bleach. Among its evidence: grainy footage taken inside Food Lion stores with lipstick tube–sized cameras worn in wigs by two ABC producers who went undercover as store employees.

The problem: the producers—the broadcast equivalent of newspaper reporters—lied on their job applications and résumés to get the jobs. Food Lion didn't file a libel suit, either. It sued ABC for fraud, trespassing and breach of loyalty because the producers had video recorded areas off-limits to customers. The chain's lawyers also complained that *PrimeTime* didn't use undercover footage that showed workers saying they threw out outdated food as company policy dictated. In January 1997, a North Carolina jury awarded Food Lion $5.5 million in damages. The judge later reduced that to $316,000. Eventually, an appeals court threw out the fraud claim. Because that was the basis for all but $2 of the damage awarded, Food Lion ended up getting just that—two bucks.

David Westin, president of ABC News, predicted that the Food Lion outcome should help blunt an "important and dangerous shift" that sidestepped First Amendment protections against libel and defamation by "trying to get around through the back door, attacking the process we used to get" information for investigative stories.

Other observers, including jurors and a prominent media ethicist, remained disturbed by the spotlight on *PrimeTime*'s reporting methods. "Deception and hidden cameras should be used only as a reporting tool of last resort, after all other approaches to obtaining the same vital information have been exhausted or appropriately ruled out," wrote ethicist Bob Steele of The Poynter Institute. "And, news organizations that choose to use deception and hidden cameras have an obligation to assure their work meets the highest professional standards."

Two years after the Food Lion story, a Virginia jury found *PrimeTime* guilty of defaming an appliance repair shop in a hidden-camera story. ABC got off lightly. The jury awarded $1 in damages. But not before the jury took an unusual step, issuing a warning to ABC News. Marc Gunther reported in *American Journalism Review*, "Take another look at 'PrimeTime's' goals and objectives. Be sure that the kind of reporting coming from this show is what you, as an outstanding news organization, want to put your name to."

The jury's message is worth consideration by every news organization and individual journalists. One example of unethical behavior by the news media damages credibility and contributes to a loss of trust for all those who strive to deliver excellent and ethical journalism.

Hidden cameras and undercover reporting have led to stories that have exposed bribery and other crimes by public officials and horrific conditions that put the vulnerable, such as elderly patients in nursing homes, at risk.

But journalists have a duty to first explore every other approach to gather information that informs the public about these kinds of abuses.

Ethical Dilemmas ❗ REPORTING VERSUS BLOGGING

A privilege most college students take for granted can create an ethical minefield for a professional reporter. Today people with computers or smartphones can use social media to post their opinions about anything they like. But should journalists, who are expected to remain fair and accurate, be allowed to express opinions in their personal blogs?

There have been numerous examples in recent years of reporters and editors who have been disciplined or fired for posting opinions on their personal blogs. In some cases, they were open about their affiliations with news organizations, while in others they used pseudonyms but were discovered by their employers. Most notably, Chez Pazienza, a senior producer at CNN, was fired after the company found he had maintained a personal blog for a year and a half that offered opinions on politics and the media.

Many news outlets today have policies that address the posting of opinions on outside Web sites. *The New York Times'* policy, for example, says, "Staff members who write blogs should generally avoid topics they cover professionally; failure to do so would invite a confusion of roles." It insists that such sites must be independently produced and free of advertising that might create conflicts of interest and that material on blogs must not be "shrill or intolerant," that it "may include photos or video but not offensive images," and "must avoid taking stands on divisive public issues." Guidelines like these are becoming common throughout professional news organizations.

One of the ironies about these restrictions is that most news outlets today encourage their reporters to write blogs—official blogs on the outlets' own sites. Reporters often use these to provide quick updates to readers before they've written full stories, to offer material that didn't make it into the completed stories, or simply to make brief comments about what they're doing as they go about their work. Such sanctioned blogs are frequently very popular among readers, and valued greatly by their employers.

Some argue that journalism at its heart is based on the free flow of information, on an unfettered exchange of ideas, whether they're unpopular, controversial or even offensive. Yet policies such as these clearly demonstrate organizations' aversion to controversy or to the appearance of bias.

As a new reporter, you may have to decide: Do I want to forfeit a certain amount of the freedom to express my opinions online in return for the opportunity to make a living reporting the news? Is this something I could or should negotiate with a prospective employer? Or do I take the risk of possibly alienating my bosses by posting my opinions anonymously? ◢

Samuel Fifer

"In the Food Lion case, "Gunther wrote in *AJR*, "*PrimeTime*'s . . . producers . . . could have purchased food at Food Lion and had it tested at a laboratory for contamination, the most effective way of proving that the public's health was at risk. Neither was done or even considered, court documents show."

The bottom line: Before you even think of doing anything that could be construed as reportorial misconduct, always make sure you consult with your editor—and your own conscience. Otherwise, like *Cincinnati Enquirer* reporter Michael Gallagher, whose work exposing possible crimes by Chiquita Brands was tarnished by his own illegal conduct, you could be left twisting in the wind.

ONLINE LIBEL: THE NEW FRONTIER

"Welcome to the new world of New Media," media lawyer Samuel Fifer tells journalists. "Inside awaits new opportunities and new liabilities."

More than five decades ago, the case of *The New York Times v. Sullivan* was a watershed event in the history of press freedom. For the first time, the nation's highest court gave the press an extra measure of protection against public officials suing for libel. But how, legal observers wonder, will that precedent survive on the Internet, where anyone has the potential to be a publisher, blogger and news user posting online comments that take aim at public officials, corporations and individuals?

Online **flaming**, or posting hostile or insulting messages on Web sites, carries the risk of libel suits. That's what happened to David Milum, of Georgia, who used his blog to attack Rafe Banks, a lawyer who represented him in a drunken-driving case until Milum fired him. When Banks refused to refund a $3,000 fee, the disgruntled client used his online outlet to accuse Banks of bribing judges for drug dealers. Banks sued, and in 2006, Milum became the first blogger to lose a libel suit, costing him $50,000.

Bloggers and their fans appreciate blogs' commentary and responses written in an informal, opinionated form. But, as Milum learned, bloggers are not immune from legal actions. "Their informal and subjective nature inherently disregards mechanics that should be used to reduce the legal risks of online content," Fifer points out. Even professional journalists with blogs, Facebook and Twitter accounts, while free to reveal opinions and biases, face the risk of publishing content that is potentially defamatory. To protect themselves and their organizations, journalists writing online need to keep these elements in mind:

- Editing and screening policy—how often is content updated?
- Managing a news source that is "always on"—unchecked information can sneak in during quick updates at any hour.
- Reporting breaking news as it breaks—need to verify information while news is still developing.
- Thriving on sound bites that may leave out important information—must provide context.
- Online writing is global and permanent—mistakes can be visible forever.

RISKS OF WHISTLE-BLOWING: THE ETHICS OF WIKILEAKS

WikiLeaks, an online international group that makes public leaked documents alleging government and corporate misconduct, has made headlines since 2006 when it began publishing, sometimes in conjunction with mainstream media, explosive confidential information provided by insiders known as whistle-blowers.

The group's exposés—on questionable spending in the Afghanistan War, corruption in Kenya and a 2007 airstrike in Baghdad that killed 11 (including two journalists) and seriously wounded two children—have exposed government and corporate corruption and questionable military and intelligence practices. But its activities have also raised concerns that some of the unfiltered information published online and in newspapers in the United States and Europe endangered sensitive diplomatic negotiations, put innocent people at risk and invaded their privacy.

WikiLeaks' history of revealing confidential information has come under criticism. Officials complained that it published a U.S. Army report on devices to prevent improvised explosive devices (IEDs) responsible for killing hundreds of American soldiers in Iraq and Afghanistan, and the Social Security numbers of soldiers, which put soldiers at risk.

Julian Assange, WikiLeaks founder, conceded in a 2010 *New Yorker* interview that the group "might get blood on our hands." Acknowledging that some leaks could pose harm to innocent people—"collateral damage," he called it—he told the interviewer he couldn't weigh the importance of every detail in every document.

The whistle-blowers who furnished many of these documents are part of a long and valued tradition of government and corporate insiders who believe, often correctly, that their only option to correct abuses is to leak confidential material to the media, hoping exposure will bring about needed changes. Such stories "tell truth to power," but journalists have the ethical responsibility to "minimize harm and maximize truthtelling," says Bob Steele, a journalism ethicist. "Collateral damage" sounds benign, but unintended consequences can be devastating and raise the troubling possibility that news organizations that work with whistle-blowers could someday have blood on their hands. It begs a question—how do journalists balance the public's right to know with an individual's right to safety and privacy?—that merits serious consideration.

PRIVACY: GUIDELINES FOR REPORTERS

Samuel Warren and Louis Brandeis were upset. The media had been writing scandalous stories about the private lives of their friends. New technology and competitive pressures meant that people were losing their right to be left alone. "Instantaneous

CONVERGENCE POINT

The New York Times' *Policy on Personal Blogs*

Check out the full text of *The New York Times'* policy on personal Web sites and blogs that appear on the newspaper's official Web sites.

Find this link on the companion Web site at **www.oup.com/us/ scanlan.**

photographs and newspaper enterprise have invaded the sacred precincts of private and domestic life," the two lawyers complained in a law review article, "and numerous mechanical devices threaten to make good the prediction that what is whispered in the closet shall be proclaimed from the housetops.'"

That's how bad things had become in the '90s. Not the 1990s, the decade of President Bill Clinton, Gennifer Flowers and Monica Lewinsky, Linda Tripp and Kenneth Starr. The 1890s.

The article that Warren and Brandeis wrote more than a century ago proposed a new kind of legal theory that would allow people to sue the media for invading their privacy. **Privacy**, essentially, is the right to be left alone. The legal right to privacy is not nearly as clear as the legal right to reputation. As a result, it's harder to assess.

Essentially, journalists have sometimes crossed the line into invasion of privacy by:

- **Trespassing** or otherwise intruding on people, physically or otherwise, in a place where they have a reasonable expectation of privacy. Journalists are free to interview or photograph people in public places, but a press pass isn't a license to trespass on private property or climb a tree to see over a fence, photograph inside of a house or hack someone's emails. Just because supermarket tabloids, paparazzi or celebrity-gossip sites and TV shows do it doesn't mean that you should.

- Publishing truthful but embarrassing private facts. In one case, a reporter was held liable when a woman who had been in a car accident sued because the reporter disclosed she was living with a man who wasn't her husband. The defense to a private facts claim is that the information is newsworthy. The court said that the fact of her living arrangement wasn't pertinent to the story.

- Publishing a story that places people in a **false light** by printing or showing them acting in an inaccurate way that reasonable people could consider offensive. "It isn't defamatory to say that someone is rich under most circumstances," Jane Kirtley, former executive director of the Reporters Committee for Freedom of the Press, noted. "But if you said it about Mother Theresa, while she was still alive, that might be false light." This claim has been rejected by many courts.

- Appropriating a person's name or likeness for trade purposes. This involves using a person's name or image to promote a product or service without their consent. Because news coverage provides information rather than promotion this doesn't usually apply to journalists.

Remember: **Consent** is a defense to most types of invasion of privacy. If a person waives the right to privacy by giving consent, then there can be no invasion of privacy. However, the reporter should be sure that the subject has not only consented to be interviewed, but also agreed to the publishing or airing of the interview or photographs. When minors or incompetent people are involved, the consent of a parent or guardian may be necessary. Consent can be revoked by the subject. Invasion of privacy is also measured by the method by which the information is gathered and whether the content is vital, accurate information and doesn't violate a community's standards of decency. As with other legal issues in this chapter, this applies to both student reporters and professionals, so you should be aware of privacy concerns even on college campuses.

QUICK Tips ⏱ GUIDELINES FOR RESPECTING PRIVACY

1. Consent
   - Is the subject an adult?
   - If not, do you have parental consent?
   - Is the person mentally or emotionally disabled and unable to give consent? Have you obtained valid consent from a guardian or other responsible party?
   - Is the subject currently a private or public figure?

2. Method
   - Is it a public place?
   - If it is a private place, do you have permission to be on the premises and permission to interview or photograph?
   - Was the information contained in a public record?

3. Content
   - Would this offend community standards of decency?
   - Have the facts been embellished with information of questionable accuracy?
   - Is the information vital to the story? ▼

Source: The Reporters Committee for Freedom of the Press

Recording Phone Calls

Secretly recording phone calls has been "standard practice" in many newsrooms, Tom Goldstein writes in *The News at Any Cost*, a comprehensive account of ethical practices in American journalism.

Depending on the law of the state in which you are working, or calling, and on the policy of your news organization, a call may be recorded without informing the other party. According to the Reporters Committee, 37 states and the District of Columbia permit people to record a conversation to which they are a party without informing the other party that they are doing so. Federal laws allow recording with the consent of one party. These laws are referred to as "one-party consent" laws, and as long as you are a party to the conversation, it is legal for you to record it.

Thirteen states require, under most circumstances, the consent of all parties to a conversation. Those states are California, Connecticut, Delaware, Florida, Illinois, Maryland, Massachusetts, Michigan, Montana, Nevada, New Hampshire, Pennsylvania and Washington. Be aware that you will sometimes hear these referred to as "two-party consent" laws. If there are two or more people involved in the conversation, all must consent to the taping.

Given the differences by state, the Reporters Committee advises caution when making an interstate call.

A case in point: Linda Tripp taped her phone calls with Monica Lewinsky, the White House intern at the center of the 1998 impeachment of President Clinton. Even though Lewinsky lived in the District of Columbia, which, like federal law, permits one-party consent, Tripp lived in Maryland, a two-party consent state. A Maryland grand jury indicted Tripp, but the charges were later dismissed.

Broadcasters and the Phone Rule

Federal law also governs recording for broadcast, a relevant issue in the age of podcasts and other broadcasts. Under Federal Communications Commission rules, a

CONVERGENCE POINT ⚿

Recording Laws

The Reporters Committee for Freedom of the Press offers "'Can We Tape?': A Practical Guide to Taping Conversations in the 50 States and the District of Columbia."

Find this link on the companion Web site at **www.oup.com/us/ scanlan.**

CHIP'S CORNER

ABOUT RECORDING TELEPHONE INTERVIEWS

Legal or not, is recording phone calls ethical? I've recorded my telephone interviews for years. I don't take shorthand, and there are times I want a verbatim record of a conversation, especially if the subject is unfamiliar or the story sensitive. There's no doubt it heightens the accuracy of my story, and not only because the quotes are accurate. Recording means I have the full context of an interview. Many, if not most, complaints about misquotes, I believe, stem from a person's remarks being taken out of context. I regret to say that as a young reporter, I often didn't inform the people I was interviewing that my tape recorder was on. I confess I was afraid that if I told

them, they would refuse to let me tape and that my poor note-taking skills would lead me to make a mistake. I was also worried that they might hang up or clam up or just become overly cautious. But I never felt good about it and always worried that the person on the other end would ask, "Are you recording?" I didn't know anything about laws governing recording of conversations, but that's no excuse. It was a relief when I went to work in Florida, a "two-party state" where it was against the law to record without telling the other person. What I found was that people didn't care, especially after I told them the reasons: I don't take good notes, and I want to make sure

my story is accurate. I now believe that, regardless of the law, you should never record a conversation without informing the other person and obtaining his or her consent on tape.

As in most situations involving ethics, the decision of whether to record secretly will probably be up to you, especially in a state where one-party consent is the law. In many newsrooms no one will be peeking over your shoulder or questioning the way you gather news. Always check with your newsroom supervisor about your news organization's policy about recording telephone conversations. In any case, besides any legal barriers, it's unethical to record without permission. ◢

person being interviewed for broadcast must give consent before recording can begin. This is particularly true if the recording is to be broadcast simultaneously, for example, on a live radio broadcast. Anyone who broadcasts a telephone conversation without notifying the other party involved in the conversation may be fined or chastised by the FCC.

The fine is up to $25,000 for a single offense and no more than $250,000 for continuing violations. In 2010, two stations were fined $4,000 and $16,000, respectively, for violating the rules.

Hidden Cameras

As anyone who watches network television newsmagazines such as ABC's *20/20* or NBC's *Dateline* knows, hidden cameras have become a staple of modern investigative reporting.

"The best of hidden camera reporting has exposed systemic racial discrimination, critical weaknesses in airport security, gross incompetence by law enforcement officers, and abhorrent patient care in nursing homes and hospitals," Bob Steele, the Poynter Institute's ethics director, wrote in *Communicator*, a publication of the Radio and Television News Directors Association. "Unfortunately, those moments are outweighed by the glut of hidden camera stories focusing on small-scale consumer problems, 'gotcha' pieces and weak investigative reports that don't justify deception."

Hidden cameras aren't new. In 1928, a *New York Daily News* photographer secretly snapped a picture of a woman being executed in the electric chair. States don't allow any cameras at executions, and some states have made use of hidden cameras illegal. Today's hidden cameras shoot video and are tiny. The TV producers who taped the Food Lion video concealed their cameras in wigs. The network also chose to tape in a state, North Carolina, where hidden cameras are not prohibited by law.

But as the Reporters Committee points out in *A Practical Guide to Taping Conversations*, "The use of hidden cameras or other forms of surreptitious filming can leave journalists vulnerable to a variety of legal charges, such as trespass and intrusion."

ETHICAL DECISION MAKING: SIDESTEPPING MINEFIELDS AND PITFALLS

Is it proper for reporters to pretend to be what they are not to get a story—posing as bar owners, for instance, and using hidden cameras to expose graft and corruption involving city officials? Should a television station broadcast details of an adoption because the child is the daughter of a convicted murderer and the man who wants to adopt her is the prosecutor who sent the child's mother to prison? If a newspaper has a policy against using unnamed sources, would it be ethical to abandon it in the case of a major story, especially if a competitor that has no such restrictions is scoring major scoops?

Ethical decision making is a craft and a skill. Good ethical decision making often means choosing alternatives that allow you to minimize harm and maximize **truth telling**. Practice front-end ethics by thinking ahead about possible conflicts inherent to the subject you're covering. Where are the potential potholes? What are the potential land mines? Ask yourself: What do readers need to know, and when do they need to know it?

"Journalists travel through moral minefields," Bob Steele and Paul Pohlman of The Poynter Institute have written. "Intense deadlines and competitive fervor weigh on reporters and photojournalists. ... Complex issues, convoluted information, and contradictory facts cloud logic, erode common sense and undermine good intentions. Yet many journalists admit to being unprepared and uncomfortable about making the ethical decisions that will improve their chances for getting through the mine field."

The results can be troubling and harmful for journalists and the public we serve. There have been many examples of unethical behavior by journalists in recent years.

In spring 2003, journalism was beset by an unprecedented ethical scandal when Jayson Blair, a young reporter for *The New York Times*, was unmasked as a serial fabricator and plagiarist, caught stealing material from other newspapers' stories and

Jayson Blair (left), a reporter for *The New York Times* who was a serial plagiarist and fabricator, left a trail of victims, including readers, the credibility of newspapers and journalists everywhere, and the top two editors who were forced to resign. His ethical transgressions were discovered after he plagiarized passages from a story written in 2003 by Macarena Hernández, a reporter at the *San Antonio* (TX) *Express News*.

QUICK Tips ⏱ DOING ETHICS: ASK GOOD QUESTIONS

■ What do I know? What do I need to know?

■ What is my journalistic purpose?

■ What are my ethical concerns?

■ What organizational policies and professional guidelines should I consider?

■ How can I include other people, with different perspectives and diverse ideas, in the decision-making process?

■ Who are the stakeholders—those affected by my decision? What are their motivations? Which are legitimate?

■ What if the roles were reversed? How would I feel if I were in the shoes of one of the stakeholders?

■ What are the possible consequences of my actions? Short term? Long term?

■ What are my alternatives to maximize my truth-telling responsibility and minimize harm?

■ Can I clearly and fully justify my thinking and my decision? To my colleagues? To the stakeholders? To the public? ▰

—*Bob Steele, The Poynter Institute*

making things up. It not only cost Blair his job, but led to the downfall of the *Times'* two top editors. For a profession whose credibility has always been suspect, the Blair scandal revealed ethical fault lines that threaten this vital component of democracy. The key to ethical decision making is to ask several key questions before you proceed (see Quick Tips on p. 356).

FABRICATION: "THE LEGEND ON THE LICENSE"

▶**EXAMPLE** Ian Restil, a 15-year-old computer hacker who looks like an adolescent version of Bill Gates, is throwing a tantrum. "I want more money. I want a Miata. I want a trip to Disney World. I want X-Man comic [book] number one. I want a lifetime subscription to Playboy, and throw in Penthouse. Show me the money! Show me the money!" Over and over again, the boy, who is wearing a frayed Cal Ripken Jr. T-shirt, is shouting his demands. Across the table, executives from a California software firm called Jukt Micronics are listening—and trying ever so delicately to oblige. "Excuse me, sir," one of the suits says, tentatively, to the pimply teen-ager. "Excuse me. Pardon me for interrupting you, sir. We can arrange more money for you."

—*The New Republic*, May 18, 1998

Great lead, huh?

It's vivid, rich with details—powerful dialogue.

It was written by Stephen Glass, who crafted the riveting scene of the youthful hacker Ian Restil's demands from executives at Jukt Micronics, in an article titled "Hack Heaven" published on May 18, 1998, in *The New Republic* magazine.

There's just one problem. It never happened. When the article first came out, it struck a skeptical chord among staffers at Forbes Digital Tool, the Web site for *Fortune* magazine. When they couldn't find any trace of the characters, companies or government agencies mentioned in Glass' article, they contacted *The New Republic*, which launched its own probe.

"Hack Heaven," the *New Republic*'s editors said later in a note to the magazine's readers, "was not the product of keen observation or intrepid reporting. The entire article was made up out of whole cloth."

When it's discovered, **fabrication** usually costs the writer his or her job and, in some cases, including that of Stephen Glass, a journalism career. In 1981, Janet Cooke, a young reporter for *The Washington Post*, was awarded the Pulitzer Prize for her graphic story "Jimmy's World," which explored the life of an 8-year-old heroin addict. The paper was forced to return the prize when it was discovered that Cooke had invented the child, along with various facts on her own résumé. Not the first example of fabrication in the history of journalism, the incident still sparked a firestorm of criticism and soul-searching in the newspaper business. It also ended the career of a promising young writer.

CONVERGENCE POINT ↘

Footnoting the News

Providing documentation for stories helps defend against libel accusations. The *Dallas Morning News* took advantage of hyperlinks to create electronic footnotes of public and private records, including video, and demonstrate to readers how reporter Lee Hancock buttressed her series with unassailable evidence about the financial exploitation of an elderly woman.

Find this link on the companion Web site at **www.oup.com/us/ scanlan.**

All journalists pay a price if readers wonder whether or not a story is real.

In a 1980 essay, John Hersey, the reporter and novelist—his nonfiction classic *Hiroshima* is a skillful example of narrative reconstruction—drew an obvious but important distinction between journalism and fiction. "There is one sacred rule of journalism," Hersey said. "The writer must not invent. The legend on the license must read: NONE OF THIS WAS MADE UP."

Journalists who want to invent characters, dialogue or scenes can always write screenplays, short stories, novels or compelling poetry. Those who choose journalism must always remember—and live by—what Hersey called "the legend on the license." When they ignore it, they betray their news organizations, their readers, every other journalist and anyone who admires the power of journalism to inform, educate and inspire. If you choose journalism, remember: Don't make things up.

WHERE CREDIT IS DUE: AVOIDING PLAGIARISM

As a college student you should already be aware of the seriousness of plagiarizing someone's work. You know the penalty—a failing grade, possible expulsion. In journalism, the rules are similarly strict.

Plagiarism is taking someone else's words or ideas and passing them off as your own. The first plagiarists stole not words but rather human beings. Using a net, called a "plaga," they were thieves who made off with another's child or slave. Now the word means the theft of someone's writing.

One of the clearest definitions of journalistic dishonesty is the one that puts journalism students on notice at Northwestern University's Medill School of Journalism:

> The profession of journalism values the gathering of accurate information from a variety of sources and the presenting of such information in a way that clearly indicates its sources. The most profound transgressions of journalistic standards are fabricating information or sources, or representing the words or pictures of others as one's own. The profession traditionally responds to such transgressions with dispatch and severity.
>
> The following conduct violates the school's code of academic integrity:
>
> · *Fabrication.* Fabrication consists of the intentional falsification or invention of information, data, quotations, or sources in an academic exercise or in a journalistic presentation. Fabrication also includes, but is not limited to, misattributing information or presenting information in an assignment that was not gathered in accordance with the course syllabus or other course outline.
>
> · *Plagiarism.* Plagiarism consists of intentionally or knowingly representing the words or ideas of another person as one's own. Plagiarism includes, but is not limited to, the knowing or intentional failure to attribute language

or ideas to their original source, in the manner required by the academic discipline (such as by quotation marks, attribution in the text, and footnote citations in an academic exercise) or in the manner required by journalism practice (such as by quotation marks and attribution in a journalistic presentation).

It's easier than ever to plagiarize. Before computers and scanners, you had to copy someone's words—by hand or with a typewriter. Now you can lift text verbatim by using the copy and paste functions of your Web browsing and word-processing software. (Plagiarism detection software makes it also possible for teachers and editors to reveal word theft.) If you're not careful when you're taking notes, you may find yourself accused of plagiarism. Like many writers caught using others' words, you will claim the defense of carelessness or sloppy note taking. Even so, you may get fired or, if you're lucky, suspended.

Plagiarism doesn't mean lifting entire stories. Michael Kramer of *Time* and his editors apologized after the writer took just a single sentence from a *Los Angeles Times*

CONVERGENCE POINT

Plagiarism: The Damage Done

Washington Post ombudsman Patrick B. Pexton explores the lingering effects after *Post* reporter Sari Horwitz, a three-time Pulitzer Prize winner, plagiarized twice from another newspaper in 2011.

Find this link on the companion Web site at **www.oup.com/us/scanlan.**

QUICK Tips 🕐 AVOIDING PLAGIARISM

- *Avoid what Marilyn Randall calls "note-book syndrome."* By this, she means words copied from other sources that make their way, unattributed, into your copy. Write your first draft without notes. Remember the story is in your head, not in your notes. Make a note where you want to insert a quote. Check and recheck your notes to make sure the quotes are accurate.

- *Give credit.* Thomas Mallon, author of *Stolen Words*, an engaging history of plagiarism, says writers should follow a general rule: "If you think you should attribute it, then attribute it."

- *The only way you can use a quote from another publication is if you attribute it.* ("The mayor is crazy," Smith told the *Daily Blatt*.) The need for attribution should be enough to

make you realize you should do the interview yourself, unless that is impossible. ("The mayor is crazy," Smith told the *Daily Blatt* the day before he disappeared.)

- *Consider using a text box or online links.* In some magazines, readers are directed to source materials for the story if they wish to pursue the subject further.

- *Always identify the sources of your information as you are gathering it* and use quote marks and *ALL CAPS when you transcribe source material.* For example, *Miami Herald*, Feb. 19. 2013: "BUT IN A SIGN OF THE POLITICALLY FRAGILE TALKS OVER IMMIGRATION REFORM, RUBIO REACTED WITH A MEASURE OF FURY SATURDAY WHEN THE PROPOSALS WERE FIRST REPORTED BY USA TODAY."

- *Note your sources.* For instance, jot down the book title, author, page number; address of a Web page (you'd be wise, given how often links expire, to make a printout).

- *Manage your time wisely.* Plagiarism is a desperate act. Writers behind on a deadline, exhausted, anxious, may delude themselves into believing that what they're doing is nothing more than a shortcut. When in doubt, check with your editor.

The bottom line: *Be honest about where you got your information.* Don't steal. Honor instead. Writers belong to a community whose ancestors reach back to early humans. Why not pay homage to the writers and thinkers who influenced you? ▶

article. Five paragraphs from *The Boston Globe*, slightly rewritten and reorganized, tripped up respected *New York Times* reporter Fox Butterfield.

The next time you paraphrase something for a news story you are writing, remember what Judy Hunter, a teacher at Grinnell College in Iowa, tells first-year students:

> In a bad paraphrase, you merely substitute words, borrowing the sentence structure or the organization directly from the source. In a good paraphrase you offer your reader a wholesale revision, a new way of seeing the text you are paraphrasing. You summarize, you reconstruct, you tell your reader about what the source has said, but you do so entirely in your own words, your own voice, your own sentence structure, your own organization. As this definition reveals, paraphrase is a very difficult art.

The Coaching Way 𝒊𝒊𝒊𝒊 ETHICAL JOURNALISM

- Have you familiarized yourself with the media laws governing libel, slander and invasion of privacy in your state?
- Have you attributed the information in your story to reliable sources who are willing to be identified by name?
- Do you rely on public records, transcripts, court papers and other "privileged" information as evidence for your story?
- If you're wondering whether an action is ethical or not—naming a juvenile, using a hidden camera—have you identified the journalistic purpose you're trying to achieve?
- Have you identified all of the stakeholders—the people who could be affected by your decisions? What is the potential harm? How does it contrast with the journalistic mission to tell the truth?
- When you're editing video or audio and are tempted to move the images and sound for dramatic reason, how can you justify misleading your audience?
- If you had to explain your decisions to the public, what would you say?
- Have you examined the methods you use to avoid plagiarism?
- Have you considered the types of pressure that might lead you to steal another's work or fabricate a quote, a detail, a person? Are you willing to tell your superior if you feel this pressure? ▼

PROFESSIONALS' ROUNDTABLE

DOING THE RIGHT THING

Journalists regularly face legal and ethical challenges on the job. Solid work habits and a human approach can keep you out of trouble, say two editors and a journalist-turned-lawyer/professor. Their advice:

- Seeking truth matters. Causing unnecessary harm does too.
- Know the law.
- Ask for help.
- Be prepared to explain your actions.

Participants

THOMAS HUANG, assistant managing editor for Sunday and Enterprise, *Dallas Morning News*

JOHN JACKSON, former online editor, Roanoke.com

JANE BRIGGS BUNTING, director, School for Journalism, Michigan State University

> *What are the fundamental guiding principles for ethical journalists?*

Huang: Follow Bob Steele's prescription to "seek truth and report it as fully as possible. Act independently. Minimize harm."

Jackson: Integrity, fairness, truth, consistency and empathy.

> *What are the best ways to avoid legal problems?*

Briggs Bunting: Always try to figure out . . . why someone is telling you (or leaking to you) certain information. Never take short cuts in reporting. Never rely on someone else's reporting without confirming the info separately. For libel, it's important to fact check like crazy and make the one, two or three extra calls ALWAYS. Go the extra mile to ensure accuracy. Use public records where possible.

> *How do legal issues, such as libel, slander, privacy invasion, differ from ethical dilemmas?*

Briggs Bunting: Some stories may be legally defensible but ethically wrong. The reverse is true, as well.

> *What's the most challenging ethical dilemma you've faced as an online journalist? How did you resolve it?*

Jackson: In some instances, message boards have become a forum for personal attacks. I've resolved such problems by enforcing the terms and conditions that every reader agrees to to submit a comment. There's clear language that comments considered hurtful, false or objectionable will be removed and continued abuse by a user will result in a ban from all discussions.

> *How can aspiring journalists cope with ethical dilemmas?*

Huang: Don't just go with your gut reaction. Take a little time to think through all the issues. How would you explain your decision if the public found out about it?

Jackson: It's OK to ask for help. The ones who tend to get in trouble . . . are those who don't ask questions or fail to seek help and advice from others.

SUMMARY GUIDE LIBEL, PRIVACY, ETHICS

THE TWO SIDES OF DEFAMATION: LIBEL AND SLANDER

The First Amendment protects the right of news organizations to report and discuss matters of public interest but doesn't leave journalists immune from legal action by sources of subjects who complain stories have damaged their reputations.

What to Remember → Defamation can occur in two ways: orally, known as slander, and in writing or other media, referred to as libel. Libel is the publication or airing of false statements that expose someone to public hatred, contempt or ridicule in writing or pictures. Slander can cause the same result by speaking such statements.

UNDERSTANDING THE ELEMENTS OF LIBEL

At the heart of libel law is the conflict between two important interests: freedom of speech and the importance of reputation.

What to Remember → Courts have over the years established rules that govern libel actions. To prove libel, a plaintiff must show three things: a false and defamatory statement about an identifiable person is published to a third party causing injury to the subject's reputation. Opinion, satire, and parody are not considered libelous.

THE NEW YORK TIMES V. SULLIVAN: A JOURNALISTIC SHIELD

A 1964 U.S. Supreme Court decision led to the most important protection journalists have as they report the news.

What to Remember → The Court ruled against an Alabama city commissioner who said a *New York Times* advertisement protesting civil rights abuses in the South libeled him. The justices ruled that the First Amendment protects the publication of all statements about the conduct of public officials, even if they are false, unless the news organization knew the statements were false and published anyway.

TARGETING JOURNALISTIC CONDUCT

The First Amendment is a powerful journalistic shield, but it doesn't protect reporters who behave illegally to get stories.

What to Remember → Most lawsuits against news organizations still focus on libel and defamation, but in recent years, the emphasis has shifted from the product to the process—how the story was reported. Faced with cases of journalistic misrepresentation and theft, judges and juries have made it clear that how reporters gather information for a story is as important as the story itself.

ONLINE LIBEL: THE NEW FRONTIER

Online journalism offers a wealth of opportunities, but risks just as great as those faced by print and broadcast journalism.

What to Remember → Bloggers have lost lawsuits against people who are the subject of hostile or insulting messages if they meet the conditions of libel. Defamatory statements can live on the Internet forever. Information, especially breaking news, should be verified before it goes online.

RISKS OF WHISTLE-BLOWING: THE ETHICS OF WIKILEAKS

WikiLeaks, an online international group, has made headlines since 2006 when it began publishing, sometimes with mainstream media, leaked and explosive information provided by insiders known as whistle-blowers.

What to Remember → The group's exposés have provided great service. But its activities have also raised concerns about information that may damage private individuals. In the Internet age, online whistle-blowers and their media partners may cross an ethical line that separates minimizing harm and maximizing truth telling.

PRIVACY: GUIDELINES FOR REPORTERS

Privacy is the right to be left alone, and people who feel their privacy has been invaded have the right to sue news organizations.

What to Remember → Journalists invade someone's privacy when they trespass, publish true but embarrassing private facts or put subjects in an inaccurate and offensive "false light." The way news is gathered may constitute invasion of privacy. Obtaining consent protects against legal action.

ETHICAL DECISION MAKING: SIDESTEPPING MINEFIELDS AND PITFALLS

Good ethical decision making means choosing alternatives that enable journalists to minimize harm and maximize truth telling.

What to Remember → Ethical decision making is a craft and a skill that must be mastered because ethical journalism is excellent journalism. Ethical journalists ask tough questions about their journalistic purpose, ethical concerns and alternatives, ensuring that all those affected by your decision are taken into account.

FABRICATION: "THE LEGEND ON THE LICENSE"

Making up stories, interviews or people in news stories undermines journalistic credibility and is the fastest way to lose a job.

What to Remember → Journalists caught fabricating often claim they were under deadline or competitive pressure. Many are unable to explain their actions. Follow the cardinal rule of journalism: Don't make anything up.

WHERE CREDIT IS DUE: AVOIDING PLAGIARISM

Plagiarism is the use of someone else's words without authorization or attribution and usually results in the plagiarist's firing.

What to Remember → Lifting a single quote or line from another story is plagiarism. While electronic technology has made it easier than ever to plagiarize, software makes it possible to trip up word thieves. The best antidotes: Carefully note your sources, paraphrase and always credit the work of others.

KEY TERMS

actual malice, p. 347
conclusions, p. 345
consent, p. 352
damages, p. 345
defamation, p. 344
deposition, p. 345
exposé, p. 348
fabrication, p. 357

false light, p. 352
findings, p. 345
First Amendment, p. 347
flaming, p. 350
freedom of speech, p. 345
importance of reputation, p. 345
libel, p. 344
plagiarism, p. 358

privacy, p. 352
public figure, p. 347
publication, p. 346
slander, p. 344
trespassing, p. 352
truth telling, p. 355

EXERCISES

1. *Absence of Malice* is a 1981 film, starring Sally Field and Paul Newman, about a businessman who is the innocent subject of a criminal investigation. But it's the power and ethics of the news media that are on trial in this compelling movie. Watch the film, and write a 500-word essay describing your reactions to it as a reporter and consumer of news.

2. In Dec. 2011, a blogger named Crystal Cox lost a $2.5 million defamation case for publishing blog posts accusing real estate agent Kevin Padrick of tax fraud. Google the case, and weigh the arguments for and against Cox. Discuss the ramifications for journalist bloggers.

3. Visit the Web site of the Reporters Committee for Freedom of the Press and read "The Privacy Paradox" at http://www.rcfp.org/rcfp/orders/docs/PRIVPARADOX.pdf. Write a 250-word essay explaining how you as a journalist can justify disclosing information that people might want to keep private.

4. Watch *Shattered Glass*, the 2003 film that told the story of magazine writer Stephen Glass, who was outed as a serial fabricator. What were the tensions that led to Glass making up characters and stories? Write a 250-word essay that explores his motives and whether what he did can ever be justified.

5. Make an inventory of the steps you can take to avoid plagiarism.

READINGS

Black, Jay, Steele, Bob, and Barney, Ralph. *Doing Ethics in Journalism: A Handbook With Case Studies*, 3rd ed. **Boston: Allyn and Bacon, 1998.**
The authors are ethicists who focus on the critical connection between excellent and ethical journalism. The book explores cases of positive ethical decision making and those that show how unethical practices derail solid journalistic effort. It focuses on minefields journalists must dodge when reporting the news in ways that skirt the law and intrude on privacy. Expert commentary and analysis accompany each case study, ranging from highly publicized to little-known examples, and the book provides guidelines to help journalists make ethical decisions.

Brown, Fred. *Journalism Ethics: A Casebook of Professional Conduct for News Media.* **Portland, OR: Marion Street Press, 2011.**
Drawing on the Society of Professional Journalist's code of ethics, this guide takes a cross-platform approach to help students navigate ethical dilemmas encountered in their daily reporting. It uses real-world case studies to help students isolate ethical dilemmas and strategies to avoid pitfalls that erode journalistic credibility.

Bugeja, Michael. *Living Ethics Across Media Platforms.* **New York: Oxford University Press, 2008.**
An indispensable guide to ethics in the wired world of today's journalism. Blending discussions with real-life examples of cross-media-platform journalism, the book confronts the temptation of digital manipulation, the demands for disclosure and avoiding online hoaxes, and provides a solid ethical framework to handle these challenges.

Lewis, Anthony. *Make No Law: The Sullivan Case and the First Amendment.* **New York: Vintage, 1992.**
The late columnist and lawyer Anthony Lewis of *The New York Times* reconstructs the story behind the libel suit that pitted *The New York Times* against a Montgomery, Alabama, city official and redefined what journalists can print and say.

Mallon, Thomas. *Stolen Words: The Classic Book on Plagiarism.* **Boston: Marine, 2001.**
Mallon has written an exhaustive survey of plagiarism tracing word theft from 17th-century authors to contemporary writers. While acknowledging a long history of writers imitating others, he clearly delineates between homage and stealing. Journalists, like many plagiarists, are often repeat offenders, leading to discovery of this literary crime. He explores the psychology of plagiarism and the reluctance publishers show in holding them accountable.

CHAPTER 17

FIRST ASSIGNMENTS

367

THE DAY HAS finally come. It's your first day at work in a newsroom. Chances are good that your first assignment will be one of several types covered in this chapter: covering a meeting or festival, reporting an accident or a fire in your community, writing a profile or covering a speech.

This chapter describes such stories, detailing the basic information used to compile them and how to produce accurate and excellent journalism. In this chapter, you will learn the importance of non-negotiable necessities that every story must contain to satisfy readers, viewers and listeners. Most important, however, you'll see the sets of attitudes and behaviors—including planning and a sense of wonder—that will make your first story and every one after a success.

PREPPING FOR YOUR FIRST ASSIGNMENTS

You're probably nervous as you get ready for your first assignment, whether you're writing for the student paper, interning at a local TV station or starting your first professional news job. All sorts of doubts, questions and worries assail you. As uncomfortable as this may be, your concerns demonstrate that you care about getting it right. Increase your chances by keeping these guidelines in mind.

- *Let the five W's, an H, SW and WN guide your reporting and writing.* You've heard it before, but the basic journalistic paradigm—Who? What? Where? When? Why? and How?—as well as So what? and What next?—will get you through almost any news story, whatever the assignment. Chapter 2 introduced you to this concept. Here are specific examples showing how they are used in first assignments.

  1. *Who* are the people involved in the story: victims, rescuers, speakers, opposing sides? Identify the people.
  2. *What* is the story about: a car crash, a picket line, a contentious public hearing? Describe the event.
  3. *Where* did the story occur: a sun-dappled park, a crowded intersection, a mobile home community, outside a small factory? Establish the place.
  4. *When* did the story occur: the last day of school, 5 a.m., the dead of night, at the height of rush hour? Give the time.
  5. *How* did the story happen: a driver lost control on a curve, children were playing with matches, management and labor were unable to agree about wages and the workers went out on strike? Explain the circumstances.
  6. *Why* did the story happen: speeding, carelessness, to raise funds, to celebrate a holiday? Explore the cause.
  7. *So what?* An accident holds up traffic, a festival brings a community closer together, a strike affects customers? Assess the impact.
  8. *What next?* Criminal charges, hospital treatment, funerals, a new traffic light, higher prices? Look ahead.

- *Practice humility.* Don't be afraid to admit your ignorance. It's better to look stupid when you're reporting than it is to see your faults when your story appears. People may criticize you for not knowing something, but they can't criticize you for trying to learn and wanting to get smarter.
- *Look with fresh eyes.* A good reporter is forever astonished at the obvious. Bring a sense of wonder to your first story and every story after that; your work will have energy and excitement that captivates readers.
- *Know the turf.* For every story you work on, there are specific sets of rules, jargon and procedures that govern fields of knowledge or activity from courts to sports. Become familiar with them so you can translate and make these domains meaningful to the public.
- *Include **non-negotiable necessities**.* These, defined by journalism professor Melvin Mencher, are facts, details and other information that must be included for a story to be complete and to answer the reader's questions. As you'll see, these vary by story type. In general, always write down all names, ages, figures, time and place of the interview, as well as verbatim quotes or paraphrases.

> ❝ When you cover breaking news, your deadline is as soon as you can verify the information and file a bulletin. . . . [C]all or e-mail a brief of three or four paragraphs with basic facts for the web. ❞
>
> —STEVE BUTTRY, DIRECTOR OF COMMUNITY ENGAGEMENT AND SOCIAL MEDIA, DIGITAL FIRST MEDIA

NEWS RELEASE STORIES

Although you will often encounter people who don't want to have anything to do with you or your news organization, there are many others who want your attention. To get it, they will inundate your desk and in-box with **news releases**: announcements of events, promotions, new products, services, developments and other activities that they hope will be treated as news. These are commonly among a new reporter's first assignments.

News releases are the way companies, advocacy groups, institutions and others interested in news media attention make their case for coverage. Journalists should always do follow-up reporting before writing a story based on a release.

USA Sevens Rugby Breaks Attendance Records with 64,551 Fans During 2012 Event at Sam Boyd Stadium in Las Vegas

Largest American Crowd Ever for Live Rugby Event

LAS VEGAS, Feb. 14, 2012 /PRNewswire/ -- The sport of rugby and city of Las Vegas are proving to be a perfect match after the 2012 USA Sevens international rugby tournament broke all previous attendance records in its third year at Sam Boyd Stadium.

The three-day tally of 64,551 rugby fans was a significant increase in attendance from the 2011 USA Sevens. A crowd of 30,323 on Saturday, Feb. 11 was the largest crowd to ever attend a live rugby match in the United States. Attendance was 10,611 on Friday, Feb. 10 and 23,617 for the semifinals and finals matches on Sunday, Feb. 12.

"We brought USA Sevens to Las Vegas because there was a feeling this city was the perfect international backdrop for our diverse fan base," said A. Jon Prusmack, owner and CEO of USA Sevens LLC. "Ten years ago, when we took over operations of the tournament, we had a vision to grow rugby in the United States. This weekend's record-breaking attendance figures prove that vision has become a reality."

Those who made the trip to Sam Boyd Stadium for USA Sevens were given the chance to enjoy 45 rugby matches during the three-day competition as 16 international teams battled for points in the HSBC Sevens World Series. After a thrilling championship match, which came down to the final play, the team from Samoa emerged as the champions with a 26-19 victory over New Zealand.

Additional activities for attendees at Sam Boyd Stadium included the three-day fan festival outside of the stadium, the USA Sevens

A news release (a.k.a. "press release") is a document, usually printed, but increasingly offered in video or electronic format, that provides information from a company or other organization interested in getting news coverage of the subject presented in the release. You may receive an **email release** or a **video news release**, which is the video version of a printed news release and is distributed to television newsrooms nationwide without cost, to be used either in full or in edited form. (News outlets should disclose the source of the information.) New media technology has created an updated version, as online news columnist Steve Outing predicted in early 1999: "Increasingly, reporters will see news releases that contain add-on components: photos (including high-resolution shots suitable for publication); audio clips; video clips; PowerPoint slide shows; and spreadsheets." Outing was right, but publicity has evolved past much of what he foresaw. For large events, these days detailed Web sites are often created specifically to disseminate media information, including downloadable audio, video, photos and biographies of the people and institutions involved.

News releases are generally written in inverted pyramid style, with what the person writing the release considers the most important information in the lead. Your job is to read the entire release and use your own news judgment to determine what is most important to your audience.

Again, ask the basic questions—What's the news? What's the point?

Don't ever write up a news release without also calling up the originator of the release to verify that it is genuine and accurate. Always do additional reporting, for balance and context, before you write a story based on a news release. Your job as a journalist is to evaluate information and events that others want to promote, not to serve as the promoters' assistant. Reporters always supplement the information in a news release with information they get through interviews, either by phone, email or direct observation. NEVER submit a release verbatim.

Consider this comparison between the beginnings of a news release and a news story on the same subject.

News Release

First Engine Celebration Held at New West Virginia Toyota Plant

▶EXAMPLE◀ BUFFALO, W. Va., Dec. 11 — Less than three years after announcing the building of a new Toyota engine plant in Buffalo, W. Va., today a ceremony was held commemorating production of the first four-cylinder engine built at Toyota Motor Manufacturing, West Virginia, Inc. (TMMWV). Dr. Shoichiro Toyoda, chairman of the Board of Directors of Toyota Motor Corporation (TMC), Akira Takahashi, executive vice president of TMC, Sen. Jay Rockefeller (D-WV), West Virginia Gov. Cecil Underwood and other officials joined TMMWV President Tomoya Toriumi in a ceremonial tightening of bolts on the first engine produced by TMMWV's team members.

Observations

1. Notice the density of the lead's two sentences. The first is 39 words; the second, 53 words. Total of the two combined: 92 words. They violate the one-breath rule.

2. Notice the abbreviations ("TMMWV"). If they're not commonly understood—CIA, FBI—avoid them.

3. In the first sentence, the passive "was held" is used. Active is always better, such as "Toyota Motor Manufacturing held a ceremony . . ."

4. Having five names in the lead boggles the mind—it's too much to process, and we may not know who these people are and why they matter.

5. Who is the intended reader—company officials or the public?

Resulting News Story

▶**EXAMPLE** BUFFALO — Sen. Jay Rockefeller, D-W.Va., and Gov. Cecil Underwood joined Toyota Chairman Shoichiro Toyoda and other dignitaries this morning in a ceremonial bolt-tightening of the first engine produced at Toyota's new factory here.

"The day is fast approaching when these engines will be installed in Corollas that will be driven all over North America," Toyoda said.

"Yes! It's something to be proud of. Your energy and enthusiasm will be the spark that gets the motors running.

"Soon, when I drive a car with an engine made here, I will say to my colleagues, 'Listen! Can you hear the beating pulse of West Virginia?'"

—Charleston (WV) Daily Mail, Dec. 11, 1998

Observations

1. The first paragraph is 32 words long, much tighter than in the news release.
2. In the first sentence, "joined" is an active verb—it tightens action and cuts one verb.
3. Three names make the lead easier to process.
4. Notice how the writer uses economy and colorful language: bolt-tightening (one hyphenated word) versus tightening of bolts (three words).
5. The lead reports the news and uses lively comments from the Toyota chairman, not simply a dry retelling of the event.
6. It's written for readers.

Toyota's public relations staff prepared the news release, while the news story was written by George Hohmann, business editor for the *Charleston* (WV) *Daily Mail*. Hohmann attended the event, provided background information and kept his eyes open. He ended his story this way:

▶**EXAMPLE** Although the plant is still under construction, Toyota did everything possible to present the best impression. Less than two hours before the event, employees of Lawns Unlimited, Teays Valley, were working feverishly in a heavy fog, placing ferns in a planter at the main gate.

That's the kind of detail that a public relations person probably wouldn't point out, but the smart reporter gets to the scene early and sees as an emblematic detail supporting the story's theme. News releases rarely include the kind of human touches that bring news alive. That's the reporter's obligation.

ACCIDENT STORIES

Accidents—at home, on roads and highways, everywhere people live, work, play and travel—kill an estimated 120,000 Americans a year and cause more than 26 million disabling injuries, according to the National Safety Council. The annual price tag in lost wages and productivity, property damage, and medical care totals more than $680 billion.

There are nearly 11 million motor vehicle accidents every year in America, killing nearly 34,000 people. In a society where cars are the principal means of transportation, motor vehicle accidents are news, but most news outlets usually limit coverage to accidents that are fatal, affect large numbers of people or involve unusual circumstances.

What makes a traffic accident newsworthy? Readers may drive by what looks like a terrible collision and wonder why they don't see anything about it in the next day's paper, TV news show or online news site. The answer lies in the numbers: There are just too many accidents occurring daily to write about every one. Depending on the size of the community, news organizations generally use the following criteria to determine which accidents are story material:

1. Fatal accidents
2. Multiple vehicle collisions resulting in severe injuries
3. School bus accidents even when no injuries result
4. Accidents that severely tie up traffic

News organizations generally don't cover accidents that end with minor vehicle damage and no injuries (unless a celebrity or prominent figure is involved). That's why the example in Chapter 1, of the single-car crash with no injuries, had little news value while the school bus accident involving the high school band that resulted in three injuries and the arrest of a drunken motorist would surely have been reported in the news.

SEE CLOSE-UP,
P. 390: ACCIDENT STORY In cities and communities, many motor vehicle accidents, even fatal ones, rate little more than a few paragraphs in a metro brief. In some cases, coverage is limited to a photograph and caption, or a few seconds of airtime.

QUICK Tips ⏱ ACCIDENT STORY NECESSITIES

■ *Who*: Drivers, passengers, dead, injured.

■ *What*: Accident type—motor vehicle, airplane, boat.

■ *When, Where*: Day, time, location, proximity to major landmark.

■ *How, Why*: Cause. Circumstances (weather, rush hour, speeding, alcohol, drugs), seat belt usage.

■ *So what?* Impact on traffic, road or bridge closure.

■ *What next?* Deaths, medical condition of any injured. Arrests. Highway repairs. ▶

QUICK Tips ⏲ CRIME STORY NECESSITIES

- *Who?* Suspects, victims, witnesses, neighbors, crime watch members, police officers, investigators, rescuers, heroes. Names, ages, addresses, relationships.

- *What?* Crime type. Property losses. Deaths and injuries. Impact on neighbors and residents. Police response: patrol cars, rescue vehicles, coroner vans, police command units. Search for suspects.

- *When? Where?* Time crime occurred and discovered. When police responded. Scene of crime: vehicle, home, street, bank, convenience store. Address, neighborhood. Scope of search for suspects.

- *How? Why?* Armed robbery. Arson. Drive-by shooting. Car theft and chase. Assault, murder. Robbery, alcohol-related, domestic violence, revenge. Cause may be undetermined pending investigation.

- *So what?* Impact on victims, survivors, children, street, neighborhood, community. Is this part of a pattern of crime? Actions by law enforcement. What precautions can readers and viewers take to reduce the risk of this happening to them?

- *What next?* Treatment of injured. Removal of those fatally injured. Arrests. Investigation. News conference and updates. ▶

CRIME STORIES

In 2010, more than 10 million crimes were reported in the United States including 1.2 million violent crimes and 9 million property crimes, according to the Federal Bureau of Investigation. Police reporters, whose work is described in greater detail in the next chapter, are responsible for most crime coverage, but beginning journalists, especially at smaller news outlets, report crime in their communities from trespassing, thefts and drug abuse violations to assault and murder. Many crimes, such as burglaries and larceny, are limited to a paragraph or two in a blog post or a "Police Blotter" feature.

Major crimes, especially sensational ones such as bank robberies and murders, draw intense interest. Regardless of the crimes' severity, journalists must produce accurate and complete stories, usually under daily deadline pressure, about incidents affecting neighborhoods and entire communities. By their nature, crimes are dramatic events and journalists must collect extensive information to report and tell stories about the human and social effect of these offenses. Follow-up and feature stories are common with this assignment. Journalists must develop sources among police officials and neighborhood groups and understand the laws, rules and procedures that govern how crime is covered.

FIRE STORIES

More than 3,600 Americans die each year in fires, and more than 17,000 are injured. An overwhelming number of the 1.3 million fires in the nation occur in the home,

Firefighters in Linden, NJ, clean up after a building fire in 2008.

the U.S. Fire Administration reports. America's fire death rate is one of the highest per capita in the industrialized world. Firefighters pay a high price for this terrible fire record as well: Roughly 100 die in the line of duty each year. The 2001 terrorist attack on the World Trade Center killed 343 firefighters and paramedics, the worst single loss of its kind in history.

Thousands of fires break out in America every day: car fires, kitchen fires, forest fires, house fires, apartment fires, restaurant fires. Direct property losses due to fire approach and often exceed $11 billion a year. Most of these deaths and losses can be

QUICK Tips ▶ FIRE STORY NECESSITIES

■ *Who?* Occupants and owner of structure. Numbers, names, ages of fatal and injured victims. Number of firefighters and injuries. Eyewitnesses (ideally, the person who discovered the fire), citizen rescuers, heroes, suspects (if available).

■ *What?* Fire type: single-family home, mobile home, commercial building, apartment house, building under construction, grass fire, forest fire. Construction type: brick, wood frame. Fire equipment (ladder trucks, pumpers, rescue vehicles) responding. Damage estimate. Property insured.

■ *When? Where?* Time fire discovered. Fire department response. Day, time, address, neighborhood. Where fire broke out.

■ *How? Why?* Accident. Arson. Inattentive workman. Faulty electrical wiring, wood-burning stove, kerosene heater.

■ *So what?* Impact on families, residents, construction, neighborhood blight. Was the fire preventable?

■ *What next?* Treatment of injured. Rebuilding or demolition. Arson investigation. Arrests. Court action. ▶

prevented. Generally speaking, the news value of a fire story is governed by the number of deaths and injuries, property damage and visibility.

Like police officers, firefighters have a job to do at the scene. The journalist who recognizes and respects that is going to have an easier time getting the information needed to report the news. Don't go barging past fire lines. Ask for the officer in charge. Ask when information might be available. (Your contacts list should have numbers for public information officials and other sources.) While the firefighters are occupied, keep yourself busy interviewing victims, if possible, and witnesses, recording quotes and facts. Before you leave, make sure you've got all the facts you need to write your story or file a live update. Back in the newsroom you may need to make a follow-up call about the fire causes and status of victims, arrests and investigations.

SEE CLOSE-UP AT WWW.OUP.COM/US/ SCANLAN: FIRE STORY

COMMUNITY EVENT STORIES

Nearly every weekend, festivals, fairs, art and craft shows and a variety of other events sprout up in communities across America. While reporters might not always find these assignments inspiring, such events are important to lots of people in the community.

Journalists are sometimes quick to dismiss such stories as fluff, but Ariel Sabar, a reporter for the *Providence* (RI) *Journal*, is more insightful about the professional challenge. "In some ways I dread these assignments," Sabar says. "The thought that always crosses my mind is 'What on earth am I going to find here that readers will care about?'"

To counter that attitude and bring new dimensions to these assignments, a group of newsroom writing coaches assembled this list of tips and story ideas that goes beyond routine coverage of festivals and fairs:

- Begin reporting the story before you go, just as you would for any other news feature. By calling the art show coordinator, the dog show director and so on, you can find in advance the "story within the story" that makes your work stand out. As Ann Portal, assistant metro editor of the *Statesman Journal* in Salem, Oregon, says: "It rarely works to show up and hope to stumble across a good human interest feature. But if that happens, at least find a focus. It's not enough to interview a handful of visitors about what they think of the stock car race or the new historical exhibit."
- Talk to organizers, but remember that they usually aren't the story. Also remember that they have their own agendas, and that your job is to report the news, not to act as their public relations agent.
- Be wary of crowd estimates; they're usually inaccurate. Make your own rough count.
- Don't treat it as a boring event. That shows up in your writing.
- Write about people different from you. Reflect the diversity of the event in ethnicity, race, background, disability, sex and age.

Ethical Dilemmas ! WHAT SHOULD YOU REPORT?

The organizers of an arts and crafts show tell you that nearly 1,000 people attended their event. You spent several hours there and, by a rough count, estimated the number at 200 at most.

You ask the organizers about the discrepancy. They tell you that continued funding for the show depends on sizable attendance and beg you to use their figure. Your options include giving in to the organizers because you don't want to be responsible for the show's fate, reporting your estimate or providing both. What do you decide to report? How would you justify your decision to your audience? ▶

> 66 Don't try to tell the history of Cinco de Mayo, or cover the entire Earth Day story, in what will probably be a short story anyway. . . . Find one fifth-grader at Earth Day who is nagging her parents about recycling. 99
>
> —BILL DEDMAN,
> INVESTIGATIVE REPORTER,
> NBC NEWS

- Have a sense of humor but not sarcasm. Have fun but don't make fun of people. Make sure you understand the role the event plays in the culture of organizers and attendees.
- Collaborate with photojournalists. Get their cell phone numbers ahead of time so you can contact them if you're at different areas, but try to go together. Give them a good idea of whom you may write about. If that changes, let them know. Listen to their ideas.
- Brainstorm on what you can do differently. Look at past stories, talk with editors, colleagues, readers and especially photographers who've covered the same event over and over. "It's important to have a diverse group of staff members at the brainstorming," says Candace Page, an editor at the *Burlington* (VT) *Free Press.* "A 20-year-old's interest in Lollapalooza or the county fair is very different from a 60-year-old's."
- Cover the news: malfunctioning rides, injuries, heat stroke, fights and other disturbances, crowd size. Check with organizers and police afterward to see whether there's news that you missed.
- Choose a piece of the event, or a person, and write about that, not the whole thing. Take the approach of describing the overall pie by focusing on a single slice. Adell Crowe of *USA Today* says, "Take a piece of the event and tell a story rather than describing the strawberry queen, the sno-cones and quoting the kids."
- Have a structure, a theme, to your story, not just a collection of anecdotes.
- Don't overload your story with quotes and extraneous people. Stick with your focus.
- Do the math. Use numbers that provide perspective. For example, that fairgoers consumed 12,300 hot dogs, 8,427 sno-cones and 6,000 gallons of soda isn't as clear as reporting that the average fairgoer consumed six hot dogs and two gallons of soft drinks.

*SEE CLOSE-UP AT WWW
.OUP.COM/US/SCANLAN:
COMMUNITY EVENT STORY*

SPEECHES AND NEWS CONFERENCES

Public speakers often make news. One of your first stories will most likely be a speech. You'll be assigned to cover speeches at the local Rotary or Kiwanis club or for other

Beginning reporters are often assigned to news conferences where announcements and decisions are made, scientific findings are presented and newsworthy individuals make statements. Here a Florida county medical examiner reports the findings of an autopsy of Terri Schiavo whose highly publicized "right-to-die" case made national headlines in June 2005.

civic groups, campaign speeches during election races, and lectures by visiting educators and authors. You may be assigned to cover a news conference: for instance, doctors at a local hospital meet the news media to report on the condition of a prominent person, a group of children injured in a school bus crash, or factory workers injured by toxic chemicals.

Generally, the speech story focuses on three items:, the speaker, the speech, and the setting.

Beginners often start speech stories by confusing the fact that someone gave a speech with news. They will write a lead like this:

❯EXAMPLE Secretary of State Condoleezza Rice gave a speech about the political problems in the Middle East . . .

It's not news that someone gave a speech. Your job is to decide the newsworthiness of what a person said and convey that.

Avoid turning a speech story into a list:

❯EXAMPLE Rice then talked about the peace effort in Lebanon. She then told the audience about the problems in reaching peace. Then she . . .

It bears repeating that an effective story, no matter what the topic, has a single dominant message. Your job as the reporter is to listen carefully, analyze what you've heard, decide on the focus of your story and then assemble the material you've collected (in a speech story, that means the speaker's remarks and delivery, audience reaction and necessary background) into a coherent account.

News conferences (some are still referred to as "press conferences," a throwback to the days when newspapers dominated the media) are similar to speeches in that

SEE CLOSE-UP AT WWW .OUP.COM/US/SCANLAN: NEWS CONFERENCE STORY

QUICK Tips ◷ COVERING SPEECHES AND NEWS CONFERENCES

Speeches and news conferences pose specific challenges for beginning reporters. Here are some guidelines to make these assignments a success:

■ *Do some background research.* Read previous stories to learn about the issues and people involved. If another reporter covered the beat before you, ask him or her for a briefing.

■ *Get there early.* Get the lay of the land and a copy of the agenda and an advance copy of the speech or background materials.

■ *Know the players.* It's your job to know who the speakers are, their affiliations, including titles and correct spellings of names and organizations and their positions, whether it's a politician, community activists, corporate spokespeople or individual citizens.

■ *Find a good listening and watching post.* Make sure you can hear the speaker(s) and see the reaction of the crowd.

■ *Count the audience members.* If a speech draws only a handful of citizens, or if a news conference about a controversial coach has the media standing in the aisles, that's newsworthy.

■ *Keep asking: What's the news? What's the point?* Don't leave without knowing the answer to this question: What else do I need to know to write this story?

■ *Organize in your notebook.* Highlight strong quotes, possible leads and endings.

■ *Humanize the story.* People are the essential ingredient of any story, but reporters often forget this when they're writing a speech or news conference story.

■ *Meet and greet.* Always speak to the speakers or officials, if possible, before and after the event so you can clear up any questions or misconceptions you might have. Solicit reaction from audience members.

■ *Remember your role.* If a speaker or organizer requests to talk "off the record," you need to object. You may be a guest of an organization, but you can make the argument that it will be difficult to keep a speech before a group of people a secret.

■ *Report, don't take dictation.* Bear in mind that you won't need the entire text of what is said to write a story, just selected quotes, so don't waste your time writing down every quote or transcribing everything from a recording. ▼

they're usually held by officials or other newsmakers to announce something to the media. As with speeches, the speaker, the setting and the information released can all be important parts of the story, but from a reporter's point of view the event is very different. News conferences are interactive—that is, they allow you to engage with the speaker. They should generally be approached like interviews. The best reporters will learn as much as they can about the speaker and the subject beforehand and are prepared when they're called upon to ask questions.

Novice reporters should be aware that there are common procedures for news conferences. Despite what you might see at times on TV, simply blurting out questions at ear-splitting volume is rarely effective. Reporters generally wait to be called upon by the speaker or by a moderator, and may get to ask only a single question if the event is well attended. Arrive early enough to get a spot close to the speaker. Speak clearly and loudly enough to be heard. Always identify yourself and your news organization before you ask a question.

SEE CLOSE-UP AT WWW.OUP.COM/US/ SCANLAN: SPEECH STORY

Smart reporters will have some possible questions in mind when they arrive at the event, but will listen to the speaker's answers to others' questions and formulate new ones along the way. Remember the interviewing lessons in Chapter 6. Think hard about the answers you're looking for, and tailor your questions accordingly. If you want to confirm a fact, use a closed-ended question: "Are you opposed to abortions in cases of incest or rape?" If you want an expansive response, craft an open-ended question: "How would you justify going to war against Iran?" Avoid statements masquerading as questions; they often sound like editorializing. Your job is to seek information, not show off your knowledge or opinions.

It's not uncommon for another reporter to ask a question you had in mind before you get the chance to do it, but rather than getting upset about it, simply record the speaker's answer and move on to another question. Remember, the purpose is to get worthwhile information to use in your story—it's not a competition between you and other reporters to get your questions answered. If you have a follow-up question or want to ask about an unrelated matter, wait until the news conference is over and approach the speaker for a private conversation.

CONVERGENCE POINT ⤵

Covering Meetings: A Tip Sheet

John Sweeney, an editor and writing coach at the *Wilmington* (DE) *News Journal,* assembled a comprehensive list of reporting and writing tips to help you produce successful stories about meetings and hearings.

Find this link on the companion Web site at **www.oup.com/us/ scanlan.**

MEETINGS AND HEARINGS STORIES

As a reporter, you will spend a lot of time at public meetings and hearings. These events are the principal way public business is done in a democracy. Open to the public and the news media, meetings are the forums where civic decisions—affecting everyone from an individual looking for a zoning change to corporations proposing large-scale building or development projects—are discussed, debated and voted on. Hearings are organized to hear testimony from experts, concerned citizens and opposing sides on an issue. Community groups may also convene meetings to discuss issues such as neighborhood crime.

SEE CLOSE-UP AT WWW .OUP.COM/US/SCANLAN: PUBLIC HEARING STORY

Streaming video has enabled public agencies to make meetings available to citizens via the Internet. The town of Southampton, MA, made a 2010 meeting of the Board of Selectmen available on its Web site. While such videos are available for review, journalists should always cover such events live.

QUICK Tips ⏱ COVERING MEETINGS AND HEARINGS

■ *Background*. Before the meeting, use archives and databases to report and write background information you can put in your story. Governments generate reams of documents. Read everything you can.

■ *Pre-report*. Determine what will be the key issues and talk to the main sources beforehand, and weave those into your story. Before the event, visit the neighborhood that will be affected by a zoning change. To do a complete job, you need to be where the action is, not just where it's being talked about.

■ *History*. Remember a key lesson about government: Every issue, every person, has a history. Learn what lies behind the rhetoric.

■ *Note taking*. Note times, dates, use initials to identify speakers. Go back and fill in as soon as you can, or else you may find you can't use a good quote because you can't decipher it a week after the meeting when you may need it for a follow-up story.

■ *Keeping track*. How long do meetings last? When did pivotal moments occur? How often do officials speak, argue, doze?

■ *Technology*. Come digitally prepared. Reporters frequently file blog posts and tweet as the meeting or hearing is going on. Digital video and audio recorders enable you to produce a multimedia report and a verbatim record of the event.

■ *Learning the geography*. Know where the public officials and staff can be found before the meeting and afterward. Get contact information for important sources.

■ *Following up*. You may have follow-up questions or need to clarify something that was said or decided. Hand out your business cards to officials and witnesses. Ask for theirs.

■ *Math*. Numbers dominate at these events. Check your figures with another reporter, editor or an informed source.

■ *Dress*. Wear professional attire—jacket and tie for men, pantsuit, skirt and top or dress for women. If you want to be treated as an adult, don't dress like a kid.

■ *Creature comforts*. Meetings and hearings can go on for hours without a break and long into the night. Bring gum, power bars or candy to ward off distracting hunger pangs. Get a good night's sleep the night before.

■ *Focus*. Never stop asking yourself: What's the news? Why does it matter? How would I describe what happened to my friends, to my parents? ▶

Here's a sampling of the kinds of public meetings and hearings you may be assigned to cover:

- School board
- Planning and zoning commission
- City or town council
- Housing authority
- State legislature

Public officials meet to discuss policies and transact business, including taking votes, approving the spending of public money and deciding on personnel matters or how property owners use their land, homes or businesses.

In addition, the meetings of private groups also make news. Reporters attend meetings of neighborhood groups, companies and business organizations.

Journalist at Work JOURNALISTIC RIGHTS UNDER OPEN MEETING LAWS

The First Amendment of the U.S. Constitution protects a journalist's right to publish information about the government without interference. But it doesn't always guarantee access to that information or to the meetings, hearings and other sessions where government officials make the decisions that affect the public.

The people's right to know is protected, however, by state and federal laws, known as **open meeting or "sunshine" laws**, that require public officials to conduct public business in the open. Because those regulations vary, reporters need to know the laws governing open meetings in their communities. The Reporters Committee for Freedom of the Press, a nonprofit group that provides free legal help to reporters and news organizations, publishes "Open Meeting Guide," a complete reference to open meetings and open records statutes and cases in all 50 states and the District

of Columbia. Laws vary from state to state, but, according to the Reporters Committee, essential elements of open meetings laws generally include the following:

• Public agencies, such as city councils and planning and zoning commissions, must give advance notice of all meetings, even emergency ones, and publish or post agendas in advance, listing items to be discussed.

• Agencies must keep minutes and/or transcripts of all meetings, even the ones they can legally close to the public. Some agencies also record their meetings, and those audio and video recordings are available for review.

• Every state allows agencies to conduct certain discussions out of the public eye in closed meetings, which they usually refer to as **executive sessions**. (They usually can't take formal action, such as vote,

unless they are in public session.) The following kinds of discussions may be held in secret:

1. Personnel matters, such as hiring, firing or disciplining an employee
2. Collective bargaining sessions, with a teachers union, for instance
3. Discussions with agency attorneys about a pending or imminent lawsuit
4. Discussions about buying or selling public property

If a meeting is closed in violation of open meetings law, you are within your rights to lodge a complaint to the officials holding the meeting. Be prepared to do so. The public and news media may complain to the courts. Inform your editor or news director if a public agency violates the public's right to see not just what decisions it makes, but also how and why. ▶

Middletown Zoning Board of Review

- Info About This Entity
- All Meetings

Contact Information
Contact Person:
John Kane
Phone:
401-847-5769
Email:
✉ buildingofficial at ci.middletown.ri.us
Meeting Information
Date: December 14, 2004
Time: 07:00 PM
Location:
Town Hall, 350 East Main Rd., Middletown, RI 02842
Filed on:
December 14, 2004 at 10:09 AM
Agenda
- Agenda filed on December 14, 2004 at 10:09 AM 🗎

Meeting Minutes
- No minutes on file for this meeting. Please contact this entity using the information above.

Record shows meeting held 7 hours 51 minutes after agenda was filed with the Secretary of State - State Law Requires 48 hours notice.

State laws govern the conduct of public meetings. This graphic, posted by the Ocean State Librarian, clearly shows that the Middletown, RI, Zoning Board of Review violated the rule stipulating 48 hours' notice before a public meeting is held.

(Continued)

Journalist at Work  CONTINUED

When officials wrongfully exclude the public from meetings and courtrooms, journalists should be prepared to object. Media lawyers prepared these cards for the *Dayton* (OH) *Business Journal* reporters to lodge their protests on the record.

ACCESS TO PUBLIC MEETINGS
Specific Reasons for Executive Session

The specific reasons for executive session are to discuss:
- personnel matters;
- purchase or sale of property;
- pending or imminent court action;
- collective bargaining;
- security arrangements and matters required by federal / state law to be kept confidential.

FROST BROWN TODD LLC

Richard M. Goehler   513-651-6711
Bonnie Sohngen /   513-651-6814
  Practice Group Coordinator

DAYTON BUSINESS JOURNAL
ACCESS TO COURTROOMS

I am a reporter / photographer for the Dayton Business Journal and on behalf of the Newspaper and the public, I object to closure of this courtroom. Prior decisions of the United States Supreme Court, including *Press Enterprise v. Superior Court*, have established a First Amendment right of public access to courtroom proceedings. The State Constitution provides a similar right of public access. I wish to state this objection on the record and I request an opportunity for our attorneys to be heard on this issue before and such closure takes place.

REQUESTS FOR PUBLIC RECORDS

Under the Public Records Law, an individual has a right to prompt inspection of public records during regular business hours and, upon request, copies of those records within a reasonable amount of time. It is the burden of the public agency attempting to withhold any such record to clearly specify the exemption for withholding which is being relied upon. The Public Records Law recognizes the following exemptions: medical records, trial preparation records, confidential law enforcement investigatory records, attorney-client privileged information, trade secret information and federal tax return information.

ACCESS TO PUBLIC MEETINGS

I am a reporter / photographer for the Dayton Business Journal and I object to closure of this public meeting. Under the Sunshine Law, meetings of public bodies are to remain open to the public unless a specific reason for an executive session is identified by motion request-ing the executive session, seconded and voted on by roll call before adjournment into the executive session. I wish to state this objection on the record and I request an opportunity for our attorneys to be heard on this issue before adjournment into executive session takes place.

PROFILES

People, as you learned in Chapter 1, make news. Profiles are the chief way news organizations introduce newsworthy subjects to their audiences. Whether you are a general assignment reporter or cover a beat, writing profiles will be a regular assignment throughout your journalism career.

There are two types of profiles: person-in-the news and feature. The first profiles someone whose activities, community role or involvement in a news event makes them newsworthy. Among the possibilities: political candidates, award winners, artists, entrepreneurs, volunteers, teachers, retiring educators. Such profiles are long on biographical information and quotes from the subject, but they should include other points of view and place the person in his or her environment. A nut graf is usually needed to let readers know the person is newsworthy. These are usually reported and written in a day to a length of about 500 words.

Feature profiles are more ambitious. They treat a subject in greater depth. Often the subjects are similar to person-in-the-news profiles, but extraordinary profiles reveal also the lives of ordinary people who normally wouldn't make the news. These stories take a more comprehensive approach, not only providing biographical information but showing the person in ways that reveal their character in action. Length varies, from 750 words to several thousand words, and they may take several days to report and write.

Whichever type, a profile is not a résumé, a simple catalog of a person's education, job history or sports career. The goal of a profile is to "find out who someone is," and present that information in a compelling way, says Jan Winburn, senior editor for CNN Digital, who has edited scores of compelling profiles. The goal is to distill a person's life and personality in ways that synthesize rather than recite.

To illustrate the point, Winburn conveyed her own life in a series of bullet points during a News University webinar on the subject.

- Editor who loves writers, avoids meetings and lives to tell a story
- Proud mother of a budding meteorologist
- Obsessed with gardening
- Shaped by Midwest upbringing, A-plus parents, brother's death, husband's stroke, daughter's adoption

To build such a list means extensive reporting and insight. Try creating a similar list for yourself, a relative or close friend. The key to a good profile is finding the focus: what sets this person apart, and what features must be highlighted.

Profiles may be structured in several ways: a day-in-the life or a depiction of a pivotal moment, such as the story of a burn victim facing a grueling obstacle course that will make or break his dreams of being a police officer, an approach introduced in Chapter 10. Lane Gregory, a Pulitzer Prize-winning feature writer for the *St. Petersburg* (FL) *Times*, followed a transplant recipient as he made his rounds in a local hospital boosting the spirits of transplant patients by playing the piano.

The best profiles show people in action, going about their lives in ways that make them special. A profile may center on more than one person. Scanlan wrote a profile

QUICK Tips ⏱ REPORTING AND WRITING PROFILES

■ *Ideas.* Person-in-the-news profiles are frequently dictated by news developments and are usually assigned by editors. Feature profiles require creativity as the journalist seeks subjects. Readers often provide tips about interesting people. But look for subjects in news stories whose lives are worth exploring. Identify a trend and find someone who exemplifies it, explaining the larger issue by focusing on an individual's story: a diabetic child, a woman campaigning for a political candidate. On your beat, ask sources about people whose stories are worth telling.

■ *Reporting.* Excellent profiles rely on extraordinary reporting. The basics include: name, age, address, work history, education, achievements and other biographical information. Flesh these out with physical description, where they work, live, play and pray. Multiple sources are a must. One-source profiles are lazy and sometimes untrustworthy. Seek out comments from relatives, friends, fans, critics. Be on the lookout for revealing anecdotes, details, vignettes. Listen for dialogue or stray comments, not just bland quotes. Be there. Hang out long enough to report scenes that show the subject in action in ways that support the focus. Fact-check ruthlessly. "Memories may be hazy," Winburn says, "and egos come into play."

■ *Interviews.* Ask open-ended questions. What makes you different from others in your position? What is a sacred place you visit at times of crisis? What would you want your epitaph to say? How did your childhood shape your adult life? Greatest influences? Biggest triumphs, failures? Ask other sources for their strongest memories of the person. Seek multiple points of view.

■ *Structure.* Choose a form that best illustrates the person's essence. Narratives show subjects in action. Tommy Tomlinson, who won an American Society of Newspaper Editors feature writing award, profiled a mathematician by tracing his groundbreaking discovery from its genesis to solution.

■ *Writing.* Action, setting and observations rather than static quotes reveal character. Weave background information in between scenes. Describe pivotal moments. Use anecdotes that tell a little story with a scene, dialogue, place, conflict. Select the most telling details: the way a person moves, dresses, treats others, responds to events. Open with your subject doing something. Choose a resonant ending: a moment, an encounter, a killer quote. Study masters of the form: Gay Talese, Lillian Hellman, Susan Orlean for keys to scene setting, characterization and structure that will make your profiles stand out. ▸

The Coaching Way 👥 FIRST ASSIGNMENTS

• Whether your assignment is a festival, speech, news conference or other community event, focus your reporting and writing on an element that reflects the whole story, rather than jamming a story with details from every corner.

• Don't be afraid to take a risk with your leads, especially on perennial stories that have been written umpteen times.

• Have you asked a colleague to read your story, before you turn it in, and tell you any questions she has?

• Have you told your editor you want to try something different with this story? Don't spring it on him.

• Are you prepared to file an online bulletin as soon as something newsworthy happens?

• Have you done your homework— about the meeting agenda, the background of the parade or festival, and so on—before you head out of the newsroom?

• Do you make an effort to write about people who are different than you? ▸

about a couple's struggle to give their blind child a normal life, structured around a single day that took the boy from the breakfast table, where he found his toast by feeling the heat, to school, where he worked with a tutor and a Braille typewriter, and a triumphant moment in a YMCA pool, where he dove in and touched the bottom.

Profiles communicate lessons about the human condition. They are stories that readers can see themselves and their own lives in ways that touch and connect them to strangers.

PROFESSIONALS' ROUNDTABLE

DOING IT RIGHT THE FIRST TIME

Preparation is the key to first assignment success. Bone up on your community, current issues in the news and your news organization—before you walk into the newsroom for the first time or head out on your first story. Be ready to hit the ground running, and get to the scene as fast as you can. First impressions matter, two editors and a top reporter agree. Their advice:

1. Take time to learn geography, what's news, the kinds of stories the news outlet produces—before your first day on the job.
2. Leave the phone and email behind, and hit the street.
3. Report for storytelling, not just facts. Find characters, emotion, drama, a story line.

Participants

STEPHEN BUCKLEY, former foreign correspondent, *The Washington Post*, and dean, The Poynter Institute

RENE KALUZA, enterprise editor/ training editor, *St. Cloud* (MN) *Times*

MIKE CONNELLY, executive editor, *Sarasota* (FL) *Herald-Tribune*

> **What's the most important step of any first assignment (fire, accident, meeting, profile, community event)?**

Connelly: Odds are that your first job will be in a new town and maybe even a new state. Spend a day or two driving around to learn the community. One of my first impressions of you will be based on how fast you get out the door and get to the scene. A preparation mentality—doing what it takes to be ready for the unexpected—separates great reporters from good ones.

Buckley: Asking crucial questions early and often: What time did the accident happen? How many people were injured/killed? How did the accident unfold? Why is this important? What do we not know?

Kaluza: If it's not breaking news, but an event or meeting, gather information ahead of time. It's hard to recognize what's new if you don't know what it was before.

> *What common mistakes do beginners make on their first assignments?*

Connelly: Doing a story by telephone or email. They produce flat, one-dimensional stories.

Kaluza: They stop reporting when they have "a" story. They find themselves with "a" source instead of "the best" sources. Their story's quotes come from the guy who wandered by instead of the guy who called the fire department or alerted the neighbors or saved the toddler.

> *How can they avoid them?*

Buckley: Getting to the scene first and staying longer than everyone else. Avoid over-reliance on officials by talking to people at the heart of stories. Include context by checking archives and public records.

> *What advice would you give a reporter heading out to his or her first assignment?*

Connelly: Create a situation where your energy is devoted to finding interesting, startling facts and telling them well. You will be amazed by the results. Make deadline.

Kaluza: Interview for emotion. What word(s) would you use to describe your reaction? What was your first thought? New reporters tend to interview for facts, but their stories will be better if they interview for storytelling by finding characters, emotion, drama, a story line or plot.

SUMMARY GUIDE FIRST ASSIGNMENTS

PREPPING FOR YOUR FIRST ASSIGNMENTS

First assignments are challenging—and sometimes nerve wracking—for the beginning journalist, but relying on professional habits can keep pressure under control.

What to Remember → Journalists use the 5W's, an H, SW and WN to guide their reporting and writing. They cultivate a sense of wonder and bring fresh eyes to every assignment. They familiarize themselves with rules, jargon and procedure and memorize non-negotiable necessities.

NEWS RELEASE STORIES

News releases announce events, new products and services, promotions and other activities and developments that their organizers want to publicize in the news media.

What to Remember → Releases are judged on their newsworthiness, and not every release should become a story. They are usually written in inverted pyramid style. Journalists never repeat releases verbatim and should always seek additional comments and information to put the news in context.

ACCIDENT STORIES

Accidents, which kill an estimated 120,000 Americans and cause millions of disabling injuries a year, receive regular coverage from the media.

What to Remember → Most news outlets limit stories to major accidents and crashes, but even routine accidents occupy journalists' time. Stick to the basic facts, but look for opportunities to humanize these distressing events.

CRIME STORIES

Millions of crimes occur every year, from minor offenses to major crimes, and they represent a routine assignment for journalists, especially at small outlets that don't have police reporters.

What to Remember → No matter how severe, crime stories must be accurate and complete. Crime victims include neighbors and communities. Good journalists broaden the reach of their reporting to present a complete picture of the offenses and their impact.

FIRE STORIES

Fires of all types kill 3,600 Americans and injure tens of thousands more a year, making the nation's fire rate one of the highest per capita in the industrialized world and their coverage a regular feature of news reporting.

What to Remember → Deaths, injuries, property damage and related crimes govern a fire's newsworthiness. Focus on witnesses, victims and others at the scene. Always follow up to make sure your story is accurate and complete.

COMMUNITY EVENT STORIES

Much of the beginning journalist's time is spent covering community events, such as festivals and fairs.

What to Remember → Community events matter to audiences, and effective stories reflect what happened and why it matters. Wise journalists do advance reporting, stay alert to find the story within the story and look for ways to highlight diversity.

SPEECHES AND NEWS CONFERENCES

Speeches and news conferences make news, and beginning journalists should be prepared to produce newsworthy, compelling stories about them.

What to Remember → Such stories focus on the speaker, the speech and the setting, but just because someone says something doesn't make it news. Journalists determine the news, analyze the content and impact and find a focus that unifies reporting. They pay attention to background information and audience reaction and balance powerful quotes with careful paraphrasing.

MEETINGS AND HEARINGS STORIES

Public meetings and hearings bring together officials and the public to discuss, debate and vote on matters of vital interest in a democratic society.

What to Remember → Smart reporters come prepared to these assignments with necessary background, including advance interviews with officials and those affected by public policy. They seek to put a human face on the issues discussed. Public meeting and hearing stories must answer two questions: What happened? Why does it matter?

PROFILES

Profiles are the chief way news organizations introduce newsworthy subjects to their audiences.

What to Remember → There are two types of profiles. Person-in-the news profiles focus on someone whose activities, role or newsworthiness merits coverage. Longer ambitious features profile famous persons and ordinary people living extraordinary lives. The best profiles require extensive reporting and show subjects in action.

KEY TERMS

email release, p. 370

executive session, p. 381

news release, p. 369

non-negotiable necessities, p. 368

open meeting or "sunshine" laws, p. 381

video news release, p. 370

EXERCISES

1. Attend a meeting—student government, public hearing or county commission. Tweet developments as they happen. Write and update a series of blog posts. Write a 300-word article or 30-second broadcast script. What are the most newsworthy elements? Who else do you need to talk with? Where else do you need to go to produce a complete, accurate and fair account?

2. Using the interview notes in Chapter 4 between the reporter and police spokesman concerning the train crash that severed a girl's leg, write a 250-word inverted pyramid story. What additional reporting do you need to write an hourglass, five boxes, short-short or narrative?

3. Consult the Quick Tips checklist "Fire Story Necessities." Compare a print, an online and a broadcast fire story and determine which of the required questions have been addressed. Which platforms provided the most complete and compelling story? Which take greater advantage of multimedia elements?

4. Go to a festival, fair or campus social event. Estimate the size of the crowd. Compare your figure with that provided by the event organizers. How do they differ? Which is the most accurate and why?

5. Research the open meetings laws in your state. What public meetings should be open to the public and press? What, if any, accommodations has the law made for online meetings, including audio, video, email and Internet chat?

READINGS

Killenberg, George M. *Public Affairs Reporting Now: News of, by and for the People.* Waltham, MA: Focal Press, 2007.
The author focuses on everyday life and the events and issues that journalists must address. Gossip may seem to triumph in news coverage, but it doesn't satisfy the need for solid information about the appearance of a new superstore, quality of neighborhood schools or a crime wave. The book offers a range of best practices for reporting news of interest to the public that serve the common good.

Lauterer, Jock. *Community Journalism: Relentlessly Local.* Chapel Hill, NC: University of North Carolina Press, 2006.
Community journalism is the lifeblood of the news industry. The author, a passionate believer in its importance, explains its critical role in a democracy and offers a wealth of practical reporting, writing and editing advice. The book includes a collection of examples of online community journalism.

Scanlan, Christopher, ed. *How I Wrote the Story.* Providence, RI: Providence Journal Co., 1985.
With local bureaus scattered around the state, reporters at a metropolitan newspaper routinely cover the kinds of assignments described in this chapter. Their stories on accidents, crimes, festivals and public meetings reflect the reporting and writing skills of excellent community stories, and behind-the-story accounts describe the decisions and approaches to make routine stories stand out.

Selditch, Dianne, ed. *My First Year as a Journalist: Real-World Stories From American Newspaper and Magazine Journalists.* New York: Walker & Co., 1995.
The author has collected 22 inspirational stories from successful journalists describing their rookie years on the job. They reveal the learning curve journalists must climb, the mistakes that taught them important lessons about their craft and the risks and rewards of a life in journalism starting at the bottom.

ACCIDENT STORY

Motor vehicle accidents, which number 11 million and kill an estimated 43,000 people every year, are news and form an important part of the daily report produced by print, broadcast and online news organizations. They occur so frequently that most merit little or no coverage at all, unless death occurs, an arrest is made, the crash seriously affects traffic or involves unusual circumstances such as a school bus accident. A list of non-negotiable necessities, identified in this chapter, govern the reporting and writing of motor vehicle accident stories under deadline pressure, as the following example demonstrates.

POLICE ARREST DRIVER IN FATAL KELLOGG CRASH

By Stan Finger
The Wichita Eagle, July 2, 2012

WICHITA — Police said Monday they have arrested a 23-year-old man after a one-car crash on Kellogg near the central business district that killed his passenger Friday night.

Witnesses said the man was driving erratically and at speeds as high as 90 mph in the eastbound lanes of Kellogg at about 10:40 p.m., Lt. Joe Schroeder said Monday. The man's black 2005 Scion was weaving in and out of traffic when he attempted to move to the center lane from the left lane.

Another car was merging into that lane from the right lane, prompting the Scion driver to over-correct and strike the concrete divider separating east- and westbound traffic, Schroeder said. The impact knocked the Scion onto its side, then the car struck the barrier again and rolled over.

Jerodd H. Moffett, 27, a passenger in the car, was ejected onto the pavement. The Scion then landed on Moffett, killing him instantly, Schroeder said.

Moffett was not wearing a seat belt. The driver was belted in, Schroeder said, which kept him inside the car even as it hit the barrier and rolled.

Accident stories are usually written using the inverted pyramid form, which organizes facts in the order of newsworthiness. The summary lead reports the most timely information—the arrest of a suspect involved a fatal car accident. It answers most of the questions readers have, including: Who? What? Where? and When? It attributes the story to an official source. The 26-word lead is economical, clear and displays a firm grasp of news judgment.

The second paragraph addresses "how" the accident happened. It draws on eyewitnesses whose accounts are attributed to a named police source. The specific details about the time of the accident, the car's estimated speed and erratic driving enable the reader to visualize the events and locate the scene of the crash. Identifying the year and make of the car may seem like unnecessary product placement, but its inclusion accomplishes the same goal. With the exception of one passive verb in the dependent clause that begins the first sentence, the journalist uses action verbs to dramatize how the accident occurred.

After describing the accident, the story identifies the victim by name and age and his position in the car and describes how he was killed. Journalists must use their news judgment to decide the order of facts. In this case, general information gives way to specific, anticipating audience interest and questions.

Researchers have determined that seat belts reduce the risk of injury and death in motor vehicle accidents, leading to laws in many countries that mandate their usage. Thirty-two states give law enforcement officers the power to ticket a driver or passenger for failing to wear a seat belt. (Critics argue that mandatory seat belt usage lulls drivers into a false sense of security that may encourage reckless driving.) Most official accident reports list seat belt usage. If not, journalists should ask about it and include the information in the story.

The driver was taken to Wesley Medical Center for treatment, then booked into jail. Investigators are waiting on the result of blood tests to see whether the driver was impaired before presenting the case to the Sedgwick County District Attorney's Office, Schroeder said.

Police would like to talk to other motorists who saw the crash or the Scion's path leading up to impact with the wall, Schroeder said. Any witnesses to the crash should call 316-268-4131 or 316-268-4132.

Moffett is the 11th person killed in traffic accidents so far this year in Wichita.

The story now shifts to what happened to the driver after the accident. Since driver impairment is at the root of many car accidents, the journalist includes information about pending blood tests to determine whether the driver was under the influence of drugs and/or alcohol. It also addresses the necessary question What next? The information is attributed to the police official who is the main source for the story. Attribution is critical in stories that involve suspected crimes because the slightest error, even in a news brief, can result in a libel action against the news organization. The story does not identify the driver, although the newspaper is legally protected if it reports an arrest. There's a possibility that the police have not yet released his name. If so, that fact could be made clear as it would addresses an obvious question from readers.

This paragraph makes clear that the official investigation is ongoing. The newspaper provides a public service by publicizing the police request and contact information.

The story could have ended with the previous paragraph, but this ending places the fatal accident in important and relevant context.

SUMMARY

Accident stories must be accurate, clear and concise and contain specific details and descriptions. They should include information that answers the five W's, an H, SW and WN. News organizations almost always use the inverted pyramid to report these stories. Strong news judgment is required to weigh the facts and organize the information in descending order of importance. Accident stories are often posted on news blogs and updated as more information becomes available. In this case, the first post reported the crash. A subsequent story identified the driver and the fact that he was charged with second-degree murder in connection with the accident. (An enterprising reporter might follow-up with a profile of the victim.) While most accidents receive scant attention, a serious case such as this one merits close scrutiny. Reporter Stan Finger demonstrates the professionalism such stories require by producing a story that is accurate, carefully reported and attributed, and clearly written based on the facts available at the time, all in the space of 274 words.

BEATS

Police, Courts, Sports, Business, Education and More

CHAPTER 18

BY THE END OF THIS CHAPTER,

you should be able to...

> Recognize changes in beats over time and learn ways to best cover them

> Translate a beat's jargon into straightforward language

> Develop techniques to turn idle chit-chat with sources into solid story tips

> Recognize that the human side of beat reporting can raise ethical and diversity challenges

> Avoid blurring the line between reporter and source

> Be a better reporter by seeking diverse voices on your beat

IN THE EARLY 1800s, a leading British editor decided that it was a newspaper's job not just to find news, but also to not miss it. Thus, the **beat** was born—it's an assignment to monitor news in places (such as a city, town or suburb) or an institution or a subject (such as police, courts, politics, science or education). Beats are how news organizations stay on top of the news, whether at a professional or college-level publication.

Today, we still name many news beats after the buildings where the sources work: city hall, the cop shop, the White House. But beats aren't buildings—a beat is a series of relationships, and the reporter's job is to identify those ties and explore their effect on society. Covering a beat means getting to know people and their concerns, wishes, complaints, aspirations, challenges and triumphs.

In this chapter, you will learn the importance of beat reporting, the basic beats and specialty assignments, and techniques to help you carry out your responsibilities to best serve your audience.

INGREDIENTS OF SUCCESSFUL BEAT REPORTING

The beat reporter's job is to make sure that all the news in a place or subject area is covered, including breaking news, features and profiles.

❝ Interview everyone who touches your beat. Interview the caterers, interview the photographers. Talk to relatives. . . . Those things can lead to wonderful stories. ❞

—JANE MAYER, STAFF WRITER, *THE NEW YORKER*

Beat reporters bring specialized knowledge to news events. At a 2007 Senate hearing where Ryan Crocker, U.S. ambassador to Iraq and General David Petraeus testified about the future course of the Iraqi War, congressional and defense reporters were on hand to provide insight and background to their stories.

Successful beat reporters generally learn certain things about their beats as soon as possible:

- *Recognize that each beat is a **domain**.* Know the territory, not just geography. Each beat is a sphere of knowledge, skills, rules and language that the reporter must master to translate what's happening for news consumers.
- *Choose sources from all ranks.* Get to know the major players—the mayor, police chief, the coach—but don't ignore those on the sidelines—secretaries, low-level officials, desk sergeants—who know things and may be more willing to share information than sources who work closely with the boss.
- *Get to know all the stakeholders.* Reporters assigned to city hall, the school board and police headquarters should not mistakenly think the boundaries must remain within their "building beat"; they also must venture into the community, developing relationships with those closest to the action, such as activists in neighborhoods petitioning for a new traffic signal at a dangerous intersection.
- *Cultivate your sources.* Become a familiar face. Don't be a stranger who drops in only when a high-profile story breaks. **Cultivating sources** means keeping in touch with them—your chances of getting a tip from a detective or secretary increase when people see you as a constant, credible presence. Remember birthdays. Some would call this opportunism, but others would maintain it simply rewards being a decent human being.
- *Use **digital resources**.* Become familiar with local electronic resources, such as property and court records, yet continue to make people the foundation of your reporting.
- *Learn the laws, policies and procedures of institutions within your beat.* Understand every agency's media policy, system for releasing reports, how and where records are kept and where you can find information about prisoners. Don't be reluctant to file Freedom of Information Act (FOIA) requests if you face a stone wall.
- *Be persistent but professional.* The sources you cultivate should know that you're going to contact them about anything newsworthy that occurs. That doesn't mean they should dread hearing from you. Treat people with respect, and show them you're committed to doing a thorough, fair job of reporting. This is a much better approach than conforming to the "pushy" stereotype of reporters, and will pay off in numerous ways.
- *Translate a beat's jargon and vocabulary.* Prosecutors may say they're going to "nolle prosse" a criminal case; your story should say they chose to drop charges so your readers understand.
- *Be the people's eyes and ears.* Serve as the conscience and the town crier who alerts communities to news they need to know.
- *Don't just round up the usual suspects.* Look beyond traditional sources, story subjects and places to produce stories that better reflect your beat's diversity.
- *Keep a strong ethical compass.* Stay alert to possible conflicts and other ethical challenges.

Diana K. Sugg started her career as an award-winning police reporter and then won a 2003 Pulitzer Prize for beat reporting as a health reporter at the *Baltimore* (MD) *Sun.* She preaches the importance of developing a wide range of sources and immersing oneself in the subject matter of beats.

CONVERGENCE POINT 🌿

Mastering Beat Basics

This free, self-directed course is an ideal starting point for new beat reporters. You'll learn how to determine a beat's key elements, identify key issues and sources for 10 typical beats and develop human and online sources to increase your chances of success.

Find this link on the companion Web site at **www.oup.com/us/ scanlan.**

CHIP'S CORNER

GETTING THEM TO CALL BACK

In recent years, news beats have undergone dramatic transformation in many newsrooms. A century ago, beats included city hall, the coroner's office, shipping offices and hotels. Then, it was news when a ship arrived and a famous person got off the gangplank. Many of these beats still survive: In most newsrooms, someone covers city government, politics, police and other law enforcement issues. But over time the news media expanded their vision of beats in response to community interest. After the urban riots of the '60s, many newspapers assigned reporters to cover race relations. After the Vietnam War, militant veterans prodded news organizations to cover veteran affairs. The recession of the mid-'70s sparked intense interest in consumer affairs; I was a consumer reporter for a newspaper and magazine. But by the time I arrived in Washington in 1989, consumer reporters were mostly a thing of the past.

The best beat reporters I've known are well organized, determined, with a clear sense of mission and a wide range of sources. They are constantly reading about the beat and striving to learn new things. They are well versed in the language, issues and events that matter. They are judged by the breadth of their knowledge and their success at communicating the important stories on their beats.

Beat reporters in the Knight Ridder Washington bureau faced a difficult challenge when I worked there in the early 1990s. We weren't on the top rung of the news gathering ladder. "People here aren't going to answer your calls first," news editor Bob Shaw told me the day I started work. "At the end of the day, there may be a stack of messages from reporters. By the time they've finished calling *The New York Times*, *The Washington Post*, *The Wall Street Journal* and the networks, it's time for them to go home. So how do we get the stories, the information, the access we need?"

Reporters handled it differently, Shaw said. Owen Ullman and Ellen Warren, the White House reporters, did it with persistence by demanding that officials treat them with the same respect as more high-profile competitors. Ricardo Alonzo Zaldivar, Charles Green and David Hess did it in Congress by being everywhere, from committee hearings and bill markups to news conferences, and by talking to as many people as they could. Mark Thompson at the Pentagon and investigative reporter Frank Greve did it by knowing the turf so well that often their sources wanted to talk with them to find out what *they* knew.

Probably the hardest part of being a beat reporter is staying on top of things and dealing with sources you have to return to every day even if you've written a story they don't like. Unlike other journalists, beat reporters every day face the challenge of encountering sources who may not be pleased with their reporting. That experience, although sometimes painful, helps instill the quality of persistence that defines good reporters. That's a lesson *New York Times* reporter George Judson learned early in his career. Judson's first job in newspapers had been in rewrite, turning other people's reporting into stories. Years later, when he went to work as a reporter at *The Hartford Courant* in Connecticut, he saw what he had missed. At the Hartford paper, newcomers were assigned to cover a specific town—everything from police and fire news to zoning commission meetings.

"What they were learning (and that I was not learning as a rewrite man) is that they had to go back to the same people day after day and develop relationships that got beyond the superficial, to find out what was going on that wasn't quite public," Judson recalled in *My First Year as a Journalist*, a collection of insightful memoirs by reporters and editors looking back at the lessons of their first year. "They had to learn to be better reporters than I was required to be." ◢

BASIC BEATS

As a journalist entering the business, it's crucial to be familiar with the characteristics of the most common beats. Prospective employers like to see job candidates who understand what may be expected of them and are prepared to adapt to the needs of the organization. The beats listed here are commonly found at most news outlets.

Police

The police beat is one of the most important beats in the newsroom. Yet for a variety of reasons it is often given to beginners. Novice journalists on this beat need to work with speed, accuracy and clarity, and cope with the emotional stress of **first responders** regularly exposed to crime and accident scenes and the pain of victims and survivors.

QUICK Tips ⏲ COVERING COPS

Stephen Buckley spent 11 months as night police reporter in the District of Columbia for *The Washington Post*. After covering cops, courts and education for three years, he joined the paper's foreign service and served as Nairobi bureau chief from 1995 to 1998. He is dean of The Poynter Institute and offers the following tips for the police beat:

■ *Cops are human, too.* Get to know them. Officers respond to reporters they know. So, if you're on the night cops beat, and things are deadly dull, go down to the police shop and hang out with the detectives. When you meet detectives you like, ask them out for a beer. Tell them a little about yourself. Ask them about their families. And of course, ask them about the work. Steve Aspinall, a detective from the St. Petersburg Police Department, said a reporter once called him in the hospital where he was a patient to see how he was feeling. After that, no matter what he was doing, he always returned that reporter's calls.

■ *When the cops do something good, get it into the paper.* Writing—when it's appropriate—about when the cops do something good is one easy way to build great sources and build lots of good will (that, sooner or later, you'll have to draw on). Even if you think it's just going to be a scrawny six-inch story buried deep in the Metro section, write it up. Police officers feel like they take a lot of criticism but rarely receive praise when they do something good. And they're right. So when they make a key arrest or add some patrol officers somewhere, don't ignore it.

■ *Always go to the scene.* This is where you get the details that the public information officer can't provide. The blood on the sidewalk. The howling, disconsolate mother. The stunned friends. Perhaps the eerie quiet that settles over the neighborhood. And most important, you sometimes find witnesses at the scene. They may be able to tell you only how many shots they heard or how loud the shots sounded, but you can't write great stories without those kinds of details.

■ *Never assume people don't want to talk.* Sometimes, particularly after an especially horrifying crime, victims and their relatives—and a suspect's relatives and friends—don't want to talk. But many, many times, they do talk to reporters. Sometimes, they even talk for hours. The point is: Don't try to guess. Ask. You never know.

■ *Spend time in neighborhoods.* Particularly those known for high

QUICK Tips ⏱ CONTINUED

crime. The temptation is to avoid these communities. The truth is that they often offer rich stories—stories of people trying to save their children; stories of people trying to drive out criminals; stories of people who've seen their beloved communities crumble. Get to know the activists, longtime residents, mothers (mothers talk because their top priority is to save their children; so they're often willing to risk the scorn of neighbors by talking to reporters). The best police stories are almost always in the neighborhood.

■ *Know different sections.* Develop sources around the department. The temptation is to spend most of your time hanging out with the senior detectives, the ones who handle the big cases. Spend time with the folks in the vice squad, the burglary section, the robbery section, and so on. They've got good stories, too.

■ *Look for patterns.* Police departments often have daily logs that they allow reporters to go through. Go through that log. Check to see whether there's been an unusually high amount of crime in a normally quiet neighborhood. Or maybe you'll notice that a normally dangerous community turns quiet for a few weeks. Or maybe you'll see that all the homicides in a neighborhood seem to have the same m.o. (i.e., three cases over a few months in which young professional women are strangled). Don't wait for the cops to put those things together. Be your own detective.

■ *Read police news in out-of-town papers.* Often, crimes move in trends. If you live in Harrisburg, Pennsylvania, and you hear that heroin is making a big comeback in Pittsburgh, ask detectives if they're seeing more heroin on the streets of Harrisburg these days. Crime-fighting strategies also move in waves. If you read that the San

José, California, Police Department has started to employ something called community-oriented policing, make a note of it. Chances are lots of other departments have either started to do the same or are considering taking that route.

■ *Cultivate clerks.* Get clerks and front-desk sergeants on your side. Chat them up when you've got nothing to do. Offer to take them to lunch. Treat them the way you would a homicide detective. You won't win over all, but you'll win over some. Sometimes they'll tip you off to something big happening (like a multiple shooting) or to a major arrest. Sometimes they'll get you a file you've been trying to track down for weeks. Sometimes they'll patch your call through to homicide rather than hang up and tell you that the detectives are busy. As with clerks and lower-level officials everywhere, they respond to people who've shown them respect and courtesy. ▶

"That's what my beat is like: a mixture of the best of the best and the worst of the worst. Heroism and horror. Courage and cowardice," recalled Karin Fischer, who covered cops for the *Charleston* (WV) *Daily Mail*. "My Page 1 story is someone's tragedy."

The police beat is often a feast-or-famine job. It can be boring; keeping one ear tuned to a police scanner, checking with dozens of police departments only to be told, "All's quiet here"—until a story breaks and you're racing to the scene.

Some reporters think that the minute they arrive on the scene of a story, they're entitled to know everything. Professionals recognize that police, fire and rescue personnel have a job to do, without reporters breathing down their necks. Amateurs run up, out of breath, notebook open, demanding information so they can make their deadline.

TABLE 18-1 **Essential Terms for Police Reporters**

Arrest. Apprehension or detention of a person by a law enforcement officer.
Assault. Attempting to kill or cause serious physical injury to another person. The threat of force is called assault, as opposed to *battery*, which is the actual use of force.
Bail. In criminal cases, a sum of money posted by or on behalf of a defendant to guarantee his or her appearance in court after being released from jail. May also be referred to as *bail bond*.
Bail bondsman. A person who posts bail in exchange for a fee, usually 10 percent of the total bail.
Battery. The use of force or violence to inflict an injury on another.
Burglary. Breaking into a building to commit a crime.
Felony. A serious violation of criminal law punishable by a prison sentence of a year or more.
Homicide. The killing of one person by another. Includes first- and second-degree murder and manslaughter.
Juvenile. A young person who has not yet reached the age at which he or she should be treated as an adult for purposes of criminal law. Age varies by state.
Larceny. The illegal taking of another's property.
Manslaughter. The unlawful killing of another without malice or premeditation. It may be either *involuntary*, upon a sudden impulse, or *voluntary*, in the commission of some unlawful act.
Miranda rule. The Supreme Court ruling that confessions cannot be used to prosecute a defendant if the police do not advise the suspect in custody of certain rights before questioning. The rights include: 1. The right to remain silent and to refuse to answer any questions. 2. The right to know that anything the suspect says can and will be used against the suspect in a court of law. 3. The right to consult with an attorney and to have an attorney present during questioning. 4. The right to have counsel appointed at public expense, prior to any questioning, if the suspect cannot afford counsel.
Misdemeanor. A criminal offense, less serious than a felony, that carries a maximum penalty of less than one year in jail or prison.
Murder. The unlawful taking of a human life with malice and premeditation.
Rape. Sexual intercourse without consent.
Robbery. Stealing money or other property from another by force and intimidation.

Sources: AP Style Guide, Ninth Judicial Court of Florida, Utah State Courts, Missouri Press-Bar Association

CONVERGENCE POINT ⚹

Beat Reporting Strategies

NewsLab, dedicated to improving local coverage, offers tip sheets and resources for beats from aviation to water quality.

Find this link on the companion Web site at **www.oup.com/us/ scanlan.**

SEE CLOSE-UP AT WWW.OUP.COM/US/ SCANLAN: PRESS RELEASE TO CRIME STORY

CONVERGENCE POINT ⚹

On the Beat: Covering Cops and Crime

Crime reporting is exciting, but fraught with dangers. Get the facts wrong and you risk a libel suit. Uncooperative sources block your ability to gather news. Understanding police jargon, chains of command and the differences between commonly confused crimes are covered in this free, self-directed course. Learn the best ways to locate valuable resources and tell compelling stories.

Find this link on the companion Web site at **www.oup.com/us/ scanlan.**

You'll get facts faster if you stay cool and wait until there's a lull in the action. Meanwhile, look for those in the crowd who seem most upset; there's a good chance they are victims or survivors who may disappear quickly. Get their stories and phone numbers.

Courts

Covering the legal system can be, well, a trying experience, one newspaper guide tells reporters. Novice journalists usually have little experience with legal issues. Participants, especially prosecutors and investigators, are tight-lipped; interviewing judges is often out of the question.

Even so, the players may open up to a reporter who understands what they're doing. Court systems differ by location. Find out how the court system operates in your area. Court administrators can provide you with background; and many jurisdictions now post this information on the Internet. The legal system, like the actions of law enforcement and the workings of government, is a process, with its own rules and language. Think of it as a collection of territories, each with its own terminology and procedures.

Immersion, the act of deep mental and physical involvement, is the key to effective beat reporting. Understanding a domain is not a one-off, but rather a continuing and time-consuming process. Here are some tips that will help you become a quick study of courts, and every beat:

- *Develop relationships with informed sources unconnected with specific news events to create an expert panel of unofficial guides.* A friendly prosecutor, an impassioned defense attorney, a respected public official, politician and professors at universities are often willing to school a neophyte. It's in the interest of public information officers to educate reporters to ensure stories are accurate and fair. Court and government staffers know the culture, territory and the unspoken rules that govern public actions. They don't want to be identified but are repositories of useful knowledge. Librarians will direct you to vital resources.
- *Read widely.* Professional journals will keep you abreast of current trends. Footnotes teach history and background. Haunt the public affairs section of your local library and bookstores. Authors with deep knowledge and a commitment to communication show you valuable ways to weave in history and expertise that produce compelling stories.
- *Come prepared with specific questions.* Why won't police provide specific details about an investigation rather than generalized ones? How do civil courts operate? Build a contact list of sources that are willing to help on deadline.
- *Keep a running list of terms and situations that mystify you.* Use your sources to teach you, and take careful notes for quick and easy reference. Remember: There are no stupid questions, only journalists afraid to look stupid.
- *Use the Internet, but stay alert to misinformation and hoaxes.* Human and official sources are preferable.
- *Take advantage of the expertise in your newsroom.* Reporters who covered the beat before you are usually happy to share their knowledge. Copy editors pride themselves on knowing terminology and process.

- *Learn more about what's happening on your beat.* No one expects you to become an instant expert, but your credibility depends on your eagerness and commitment to understand how things work on your beat. Making the same mistake repeatedly in your story suggests you don't care.
- *Spend your free time attending court sessions, hearings and other public meetings.* Sources will notice. Soak up the atmosphere. Notice telling details, track the ways people behave and always write down every question you have. Use your expert panel to help you make sense of what you don't understand. Community colleges offer courses in the basics of law enforcement, courts and government. Don't worry about spending your own time. Think of it as an investment in your career. The smarter you are, the more effectively you will serve your audience.

Broadly speaking, the legal system in America is divided into two parts. Think of it as the Law of Twos.

- Two kinds of courts: **federal** and **state**
- Two kinds of laws and legal actions: **criminal** and **civil**
- Two kinds of crimes: **felony** and **misdemeanor**
- Two sides in a legal case: **plaintiff** and **defendant**

If you're a full-time court reporter, you will probably spend most of your time in the courthouse, observing **trials** and **hearings**, studying the **docket**, which lists upcoming proceedings, interviewing lawyers and parties to a case, and checking motions filed in cases. Close inspection of the court docket on his beat led to *Washington Post* reporter Tom Jackman's major discovery that the judge in the 2002 Washington DC sniper cases had illegally investigated facts about the case on his own.

You will need to build up a working relationship with the court clerk, whose office oversees the volumes of paperwork that the legal system produces: **transcripts**, **motions**, **decisions**, **depositions**; generally such records are privileged so you can quote from them without fear of libel or slander.

Court clerks are accessible officials who interact regularly with lawyers and the public. But they're also busy people who have little time for appointments. Regular informal visits off-deadline can make you a familiar face who doesn't surface only when you need something. The same holds true for any beat. Some reporters even make it a practice to show up with doughnuts as they make their beat rounds, a habit that can yield friendships with secretaries, detectives and other staffers. Remembering birthdays and anniversaries shows you're not just a reporter but a human being who can be entrusted with helpful tips and advance word about important developments.

For new beat reporters, especially for journalists who are shy and inexperienced, these bonding approaches can seem unnatural, insincere and even terrifying. Sources recognize that new reporters may not stay on a beat very long and don't want to waste time with them. Others are suspicious, if not downright hostile. It can make for very uncomfortable encounters. But stick with it and your comfort level will increase over time. The key: Make it about them, not you. Genuine interest in people and the role they play in society builds trust. And remember, your goal is to serve the public's right to know, and the steps to develop solid sources, however uncomfortable, help fulfill your responsibility as a beat reporter.

Public records are often elusive but persistence pays off. Student journalist Nathaniel Adams hit a brick wall when looking for court records to help him describe a bloody murder in Jersey City, NJ. He kept asking, and his efforts paid off: He located an audio recording of a trial that convicted one of the suspects and gave him a wealth of detail.

CONVERGENCE POINT ⤓

Beat Reporting Pulitzer Prizes

Study some of the best reporting over the last decade on the site of the Pulitzer Prizes.

Find this link on the companion Web site at **www.oup.com/us/ scanlan.**

SEE CLOSE-UP, P. 419: COURT STORY

TABLE 18-2 **Essential Terms for Court Reporters**

Adversary system. The system of trial practice in the United States and some other countries in which each of the opposing, or adversary, party has the opportunity to present and establish opposing contentions before the court.
Affidavit. A written and sworn statement that may be admitted into evidence.
Arraignment. In a misdemeanor case, the initial appearance before a judge at which the criminal defendant enters a plea; in a felony case, the proceeding after the indictment at which the defendant comes before a judge in district court, is informed of the charges, enters a plea and has a date set for trial or disposition.
Calendar. A court's list of cases for arraignment, hearing, trial or arguments.
Capital crime. An offense that may be punishable by death.
Circumstantial evidence. All evidence of an indirect nature. Testimony not based on actual personal knowledge or observation of the facts in controversy.
Civil case. A lawsuit brought to enforce, redress or protect private rights or to gain payment for a wrong done to a person or party by another person or party. In general, all types of actions other than criminal proceedings.
Class action. A lawsuit filed by a group of plaintiffs on behalf of themselves and numerous other persons in a similar situation.
Complainant. Synonymous with "plaintiff," or, in criminal cases, the "complaining witness."
Concurrent sentence. Sentence imposed for two or more convictions, under which two or more prison or jail terms are served simultaneously, and the prisoner is entitled to discharge when the longest term specified expires (i.e., sentences of 1 to 15 years and 0 to 5 years mean a maximum sentence of 15 years). Differs from a consecutive sentence, in which the sentences are served back to back (1-to-15 and 0-to-5 consecutive sentences could mean up to 20 years).
Continuance. A court order postponing proceedings.
Conviction. In a criminal case, a guilty verdict or finding of guilt resulting from a plea.
Crime. A wrong that violates a statute and injures or endangers the public.
Criminal case. A case brought by the government against a person accused of committing a crime.
Cross-examination. The questioning of a witness by the lawyer for the opposing side. This may be done by asking leading questions: questions that suggest the answer.
Defendant. The accused in a criminal case; the person from whom money or other recovery is sought in a civil case.
Deposition. The taking of testimony of a witness under oath outside of court, usually transcribed in writing by a court stenographer or, less frequently, recorded on videotape.

TABLE 18-2 **Continued**

Discovery. The process through which parties to an action are allowed to obtain relevant information known to other parties or nonparties before trial.

Docket. A brief entry or the book containing such entries of any proceeding in court.

Due process. The guarantee of due process requires that no person be deprived of life, liberty or property without a fair and adequate process. In criminal proceedings this includes the fundamental aspects of a fair trial, including the right to adequate notice in advance of the trial, the right to counsel, the right to confront and cross-examine witnesses, the right to refuse self-incriminating testimony and the right to have all elements of the crime proven beyond a reasonable doubt.

Evidence. Testimony, records, documents, material objects or other things presented at a trial to prove the existence or nonexistence of a fact.

Guilty. The accused plead "guilty" when they confess to the crime with which they are charged, and the jury convicts when the accused is found guilty.

Grand jury. A group of citizens impaneled to hear evidence and decide whether a defendant should be charged with a crime.

Habeas corpus. Latin phrase meaning "you have the body." A proceeding that is used to review the legality of a prisoner's confinement in criminal cases. Also, a writ ordering a law enforcement officer to bring a certain prisoner into court and show legal reasons to keep him or her in custody.

Hung jury. A jury that cannot agree on a final verdict. If a jury is hung, the court declares a mistrial and the case may be retried.

Indictment. The document filed by a prosecuting attorney charging a person with a crime.

Injunction. A writ, or court order, forbidding or requiring a certain action.

Immunity. Legal protection from liability. There are many categories of immunity in civil and criminal law. For example, sovereign immunity protects government agencies from civil liability, and judicial immunity protects judges acting in their official capacities.

Jurisdiction. The legal authority of a court to hear a case or conduct other proceedings; power of the court over persons involved in a case and the subject matter of the case.

Motion. A formal request presented to a court.

Nolo contendere. Legalese for a plea entered by a defendant in a criminal case. Latin for "I do not wish to contend," the plea means the defendant isn't admitting guilt but will offer no defense. Use "no contest" or "no-contest plea." The court can judge the person guilty and give the same punishment that someone would get if convicted or if pleaded guilty. However, the defendant can deny the same charge in another legal proceeding.

Perjury. False swearing of a person under oath. A person inducing another to perjured testimony is equally guilty.

Continued

TABLE 18-2 Continued

Plaintiff. A person who files a lawsuit.
Plea. The defendant's formal response to a criminal charge (guilty, not guilty, nolo contendere, not guilty by reason of insanity, and guilty and mentally ill).
Plea bargaining. A process whereby the prosecutor and defense attorney settle a case without a trial. Under such settlement the accused may be permitted to plead guilty to a lesser offense or plead guilty to one or more charges but have others dismissed, or the prosecuting attorney may agree to recommend a particular sentence. The terms of a negotiated plea must be stated in open court, and it will be effective only if approved by the trial judge. The way most criminal cases are decided.
Presumption of innocence. A cornerstone principle of American criminal justice: Every defendant enters a trial presumed to be innocent. This presumption remains until and unless the state overcomes the presumption by competent evidence of guilt.
Reasonable doubt. A person accused of a crime is entitled to acquittal if, in the minds of the jury or judge, his or her guilt has not been proved beyond a "reasonable doubt," that is, the jurors are not entirely convinced of the person's guilt.
Restitution. Court-ordered payment to restore goods or money to the victim of a crime by the offender.
Search warrant. An order issued by a judge or magistrate commanding a sheriff, constable or other officer to search a specified location for evidence suspected to be related to a crime.
Subpoena. An official order to appear in court (or at a deposition) at a specific time. Failure to obey a subpoena to appear in court is punishable as contempt of court.
Testimony. Evidence given by a competent witness, under oath; as distinguished from evidence derived from writings and other sources.
Venue. The particular county, city or geographical area in which a court with jurisdiction may hear and determine a case.
Verdict. The formal and unanimous decision or finding made by a jury.

Sources: Criminal Justice Journalists, News University

Government

SEE CLOSE-UP AT WWW .OUP.COM/US/SCANLAN: GOVERNMENT STORY

Consider the typical beginning reporter: he or she is young, single, childless; owns no property; has never paid any property tax; may never have voted. These beginners find themselves in towns and cities where institutions decide on taxes, uses of private property and how their children are taught. In other words, government actions are vitally important to the majority of the population, but not so much to novice reporters.

Because of this, government is the beat that most beginners are least prepared to cover and least interested in covering. The key to making it interesting, to you and your readers and viewers, is understanding the way government works—and doesn't work (but might work better)—and communicating that in your stories. Eventually, you will realize that government is one of the most significant beats in journalism.

One of your first stops in a new community should be the town or city hall. Check in with the city manager or town clerk and ask for materials that outline and describe the way the local government operates. Many communities post such information online and alert citizens to upcoming hearings and other actions. Town and city councils, county commissions and boards of supervisors serve as the highest authority within local government in deciding issues of public policy. At open sessions, public officials pass laws, also known as **ordinances**, adopt **resolutions** and lead conversations about how their community will be governed and how to provide services for the citizens' welfare.

Beginning reporters are sometimes afraid to approach local officials and their staff members, especially if they are new to an area. Many sources tend to dismiss beginners who seem naive, prejudiced and ignorant. Rookie reporters can quickly establish credibility with important people by showing that they've already done some homework. You will find generous and sympathetic people. But expect to be treated with condescension and suspicion by some sources. They may dislike the news media, believe public business should be private and be convinced that journalists are biased liberals. Journalists may have burned them in the past by reporting inaccurate or damaging information. Over time, you may be able to earn their trust, but don't expect it from day one. As with any relationship, it takes time.

Sources respect journalists, no matter how inexperienced, who understand and respect the challenges they face and the constraints they work under. But never forget the people's right to know and to expect that public officials work for the public's interest. Be alert to possibilities of corruption.

Communities

Covering a community—a neighborhood, section of a city or area populated by new immigrants—is the way many reporters will begin their careers. The goal is to discover a community by meeting and interviewing people, developing a series of relationships that make it possible to write about news, issues and events that affect them.

But you should go beneath the surface with stories that would be overlooked because they don't generate a press release, or that fall between the cracks of traditional beats. This demands bottom-up sourcing: not just politicians and government officials, but **stakeholders**, people whose lives are affected by decisions made by the more powerful. By reaching out to everyday people, you're giving voice to the voiceless, the poor, minorities, children and the elderly, among others. If you go out and talk to folks instead of just designated leaders, you're painting a more diverse, complete portrait of your community.

Rebecca Catalanello, a student journalist at The Poynter Institute, took a "shoe leather tour," walking neighborhood streets to get acquainted with her community

CONVERGENCE POINT ⚥

On the Beat: Covering Courts

Court reporting poses many challenges. It's important to know the types of courts, legal terms and how to communicate what you hear in court. This free, self-directed course provides an overview of the court system and offers important resources, including an interactive feature that will teach you how to translate legal terms into every day language.

Find this link on the companion Web site at **www.oup.com/us/ scanlan.**

Effective beat reporters don't limit their reporting to official sources but hit the streets to get the views of citizens. A Canadian Broadcasting Corporation radio reporter captures the opinion of a woman at an Oct. 2010 Occupy Nova Scotia protest in Halifax.

beat. Her efforts paid off when she learned about an elderly woman, known as the "fliplady," after the inexpensive sweet ice treats she made in her freezer and sold to neighborhood children who didn't have money to buy store-bought items.

►**EXAMPLE** ST. PETERSBURG — She was a secret only the children knew. (*A blind lead creates suspense.*)

When Gertie Coker's obituary ran in the *St. Petersburg Times* it recounted her life as a highly visible member of St. Petersburg's African American community. She was a retired restaurateur who came to St. Petersburg in 1928. She was the grandmother of Doug Jamerson, Florida's labor secretary. She was an early feminist who kept her maiden name throughout her entire life. She was someone people wanted to be around, even after she retired. (*A full picture, apparently, but the "secret" isn't revealed.*)

But the obit left something out. When she died at 87 on April 22, she left a hole. (*The climax is near, but the writer keeps the reader hanging.*)

To the children of Old Southeast, that hole was "Mama Gert," the neighborhood fliplady. (*Finally, the secret, the WHAT, is revealed, but not the HOW AND WHY. The reader is hooked.*)

Suburbs

For decades, the center of the city has been the source of news coverage. **Suburbs** were dismissed as "bedroom communities," where people lived and shopped but where nothing terribly important happened. That is no longer the case. Suburban communities have grown in size, complexity and sophistication, leading news organizations to devote a substantial percentage of their resources to covering this important component of their readership.

The *Tampa Bay Times* in Florida was a pioneer of suburban reporting. As veteran reporter Bill Coats wrote his editors,

> The nerve center of the community no longer is Main Street or Courthouse Square. The community today is fragmented into many subcultures, each with its own less visible nerve center. We have to prowl around and discover where those communities and nerve centers are. Then we can write stories that touch the lives of thousands of suburbanites. We should broaden our concept of news. We should recognize that nearly all our readers live in suburbs and most of them work there, so many of the most important factors in their lives are there.

Coats drew up a list of story ideas to improve suburban coverage. Here's a sampling:

- *School guidance counselors.* They should be tapped into several communities: a generation of local kids, their parents and their teachers. Potential stories: newest influences, for better or worse, on kids' problems in the classroom; social problems seeping onto campuses; individual cases of achievement, tragedy; the effects, for better or worse, of latest parenting trends.

Sports reporting need not be limited to the major leagues or college athletics. In every community, young people test their skills on the fields of play, like this girl playing softball in St. Pete Beach, FL.

- *High school sports.* Roam the stands during a game. The fan following of a prep sports team can be an eclectic community, crossing many cultural and class lines. Potential stories: the most rabid fan; a family or neighborhood makes a teen athlete its hero; how a community's mood can rise or fall with the fortunes of the team.
- *School and community theater.* Tap into the community of amateur actors and theatergoers. Potential stories: features/advances on the productions; the little crises and triumphs behind the curtains.
- *Churches.* Develop sources among pastors, activists and the community of worshippers. Potential stories: unusual community projects; thriving and dying churches; splits and mergers; multicultural trends, fringe religions; triumphs and tragedies among members.
- *Wildlife rescue agencies.* Develop sources among their staffs. Potential stories: python eats poodle; baby raccoons found in attic; trends in wildlife populations; migration and coping with human encroachment.
- *Flea markets.* Tap into the communities of vendors and regular customers. Potential stories: profiles; the functioning of an offbeat economy (who are the vendors' wholesalers?).

SEE CLOSE-UP AT WWW .OUP.COM/US/SCANLAN: SUBURBAN STORY

CONVERGENCE POINT ⚹

On the Beat: Covering Education

Education reporters face multiple challenges: understanding school budgets, changing curricula, parental concerns and the connections between schools and communities. This self-directed course introduces beginners to the key issues and ways to best cover this vital beat. How to gain access to a classroom, mastering the intricacies of standardized testing and the importance of early childhood education, especially for the poor, are among the important lessons covered.

Find this link on the companion Web site at **www.oup.com/us/ scanlan.**

SPECIALTY BEATS

Many new journalists have their hearts set on beats that reflect their personal interests. But just because you want to cover medicine, entertainment or education doesn't automatically mean the beat is yours. One way to reach your goal is outstanding performance on a basic beat.

Specialty beats are prestigious assignments generally reserved for journalists who've shown outstanding work on basic beats, or those with education or professional practice in the field. People with a law background get the legal beat, those with medical knowledge take on health care, and reporters with economic or financial expertise are assigned to a business beat. If no one in the newsroom has studied or worked in these areas, assignments are given to experienced reporters willing to tackle the challenge of a specialty beat. Specialty and basic beats are, at their core, about people, those doing things and the people affected. Never forget to find human faces and voices to bring stories alive. Strive to find the heart of your beat. Think hard to find the focus of your work

For David Waters, the thinking began even before he wrote his first stories on the religion beat for *The Commercial Appeal* in Memphis:

> I started thinking religion wasn't like any other beat I'd ever had. I'd had government beats and the education beat, the legislative beat, politics. Every other beat I've had had a focal point. There was an agency or a board or a person, someone who seemed to be in charge, where you could go to find the center of that beat. And then I realized God is at the center of this beat. So I decided that my job was to cover God. . . . And in every story I write, whether or not it's set in a church, I look for God. And it seems to work.

Waters learned that thinking is the way writers, whatever the beat, make sense of the material they collect during the reporting. It's the compass that leads the reporter out of the tangled woods of reporting. It's the focusing ring on a camera lens that is turned back and forth until the image is clear.

Here are the major specialty beats, story subjects and required skills:

- *Science/health care.* Ranges from covering local hospitals and noteworthy medical procedures or breakthroughs to whether doctors should accept gifts from vendors. In many news organizations, these beats are combined, and reporters must juggle word of advances in science and medicine reported in journals and try to put a human face on these developments. Requires specialized knowledge. It's not uncommon for doctors or scientists to fill these beats.

  SEE CLOSE-UP AT WWW .OUP.COM/US/SCANLAN: SCIENCE STORY

- *Business.* A business reporter may have a specific beat, such as insurance or the oil industry, or broader subjects such as personal finance, loan practices and housing. Understanding the intricacies of finance and economics is a must.

  SEE CLOSE-UP AT WWW .OUP.COM/US/SCANLAN: BUSINESS STORY

- *Religion.* Focuses on breaking news, such as the ousting of a popular church leader, profiling denominations to help readers understand the differences between them, or localizing national stories, such as the sexual abuse of children by clergy.

- *Education.* Many newsrooms have more than one education reporter. One often covers K–12, writing stories about test scores and dropout rates, while another may focus on higher education. Like the best writers, education reporters connect national trends to local communities and issues on their beat. Knowledge of current issues and trends and understanding how the educational system operates is required.

  SEE CLOSE-UP AT WWW .OUP.COM/US/SCANLAN: EDUCATION STORY

- *Sports.* This coveted beat "is not only fun, but illuminating of the human condition," a panel of judges selecting the best sports writing of the year once observed. Sports writers need to know the games they cover in far greater depth than the average reader, but they also need to approach the task as something more than an educated fan. In addition to keeping their own stats on the fly, sports writers need to prepare their stories as the game progresses, being ready for any contingency yet having a lead in place as soon as possible. Reporting news with social media tools is commonplace.

  SEE CLOSE-UP AT WWW .OUP.COM/US/SCANLAN: SPORTS STORY

- *Politics.* Everything from election coverage and campaign finances to monitoring the events of a legislative session falls within the duties of a political reporter, sometimes known as "legislative correspondent." Political reporters need a solid grounding in how government and elections are conducted. Knowledge of statistics and polls is key.

  SEE CLOSE-UP AT WWW .OUP.COM/US/SCANLAN: POLITICAL STORY

- *Investigative reporting.* Unlike beat reporters, whose portfolio includes breaking news, investigative reporters spend enormous amounts of time and resources to root out wrongdoing, from political corruption to scandalous conditions at public institutions. In 2008, *Washington Post* reporters Anne Hull and Dana Priest and photojournalist Michel du Cille won a Pulitzer Prize for exposing mistreatment of wounded veterans at Walter Reed Hospital, prompting reforms, the kind of outcome investigative reporting often produces. Dogged reporting and familiarity with computer-assisted reporting techniques are required.

  SEE CLOSE-UP AT WWW .OUP.COM/US/SCANLAN: INVESTIGATIVE STORY

Ethical Dilemmas ❗ TO SCOOP OR NOT TO SCOOP

A source on your police beat whose tips have paid off in the past tells you that police are ready to arrest a suspect in a highly publicized murder case that left the community in fear. You and your editors are concerned that the competition has the same information and are ready to publish the story. You can scoop them by posting the information on your Web site. Is it ethical to identify the suspect before an arrest is made given that the report will tarnish the person's reputation? (You could face libel action if the arrest isn't made.) Is competition a valid argument for publishing the story? Should publication await official charges? Is your story accurate and, above all, fair? What purpose would publication serve? How would you justify to your audience your decision to publish? ▼

*SEE CLOSE-UP AT WWW
.OUP.COM/US/SCANLAN:
TECHNOLOGY STORY*

- *Technology.* It's sometimes argued that technology isn't a separate beat because it's less a stand-alone entity than simply a set of tools people use in all walks of life. These days, however, technology is at the heart of multiple cultural phenomena, from entertainment to personal relationships to medicine, all creating the need for extensive coverage. New products and technological innovation. The proliferation of social media. Profiles of industry leaders and software developers. How-to advice pieces. The struggle for market dominance. Those who want to excel at this beat will need to think beyond the obvious. Are there technologies in development that might one day be especially useful to your particular audience? Is someone local using existing technology in an unusual or interesting way?

*SEE CLOSE-UP AT
WWW.OUP.COM/US/
SCANLAN: ARTS AND
ENTERTAINMENT STORY*

- *Arts and entertainment.* News and reviews about cultural events and entertainers. Awards, such as the Oscars, Emmys, Pulitzer Prizes. Trend stories. Profiles. An industry sheltered by spokespersons and public relations experts makes this a challenging beat. Media critics bemoan the dominance of A&E stories in news coverage, but audience interest is strong. As with every beat, the development of solid and diverse sources is crucial.

WHAT A SPECIALTY BEAT REQUIRES

There are several things you should keep in mind to find success in a specialty beat:
- *Knowledge of terms.* A specialty beat requires familiarity with the jargon and terminology associated with the subject. For example, a business reporter needs to know the difference between **revenue** and **income**. Revenue refers to the money received by the business before expenses, such as the cost of raw materials and wages. Income usually means "net" income, which is revenue minus expenses. Every specialty beat, from health care to religion to entertainment, has its own subculture, values and code words that a reporter must understand.

Journalist at Work HOW A VETERAN BEAT REPORTER BECAME A MULTIMEDIA JOURNALIST

Harold Bubil

Among the slides in an audiovisual presentation shown to visitors to the multiplatform newsroom of the *Sarasota (FL) Herald-Tribune* is one with a simple headline: "The Harold Bubil Brand."

Such high billing for Bubil, the paper's soft-spoken real estate editor, reflects his embrace of multimedia journalism to augment traditional reporting, including editing the paper's home and real estate sections, with inexpensive multiplatform tools and delivery methods. He carries a digital camera to take photographs of houses, developments and other items, and a digital audio recorder for interviews in person and by phone.

His online features include:

1. *Blog posts.* In "Real Estate Today," he posts items about real estate that won't support a full story but feed an audience that avidly tracks real estate doings.

2. *Television.* Bubil hosts "Open House," a weekly real estate segment with interviews, on SNN, the *Herald-Tribune*'s cable TV station. These are also available on the paper's Web site.

3. *Podcasts.* Bubil records a weekly podcast about real estate in the newsroom's tiny soundproofed recording studio. As with the TV segments, these are featured on the *Herald-Tribune* Web site.

This veteran journalist sees multimedia journalism as a way to stay relevant and versatile as the industry changes: "Content is king," Bubil says. "The rest is just tools." ▶

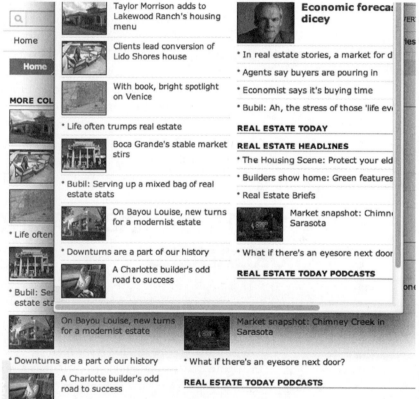

Harold Bubil, real estate editor of the *Sarasota (FL) Herald-Tribune,* has become an online brand by expanding his coverage to photos, video, podcasts and constant updates about the housing market on his Web site.

- *Training.* Investigative reporters often rely on computer-assisted reporting, which requires training in using databases and other software, and expertise in statistics. Political reporters need training to decipher poll results.
- *Reading.* Most beats are supported by associations, from education to science. They provide a wealth of resources, collections of award-winning reporting, FAQs that provide basic information and online resources. Most every field generates numerous journals that contain breaking news; these are required reading.
- *Networking.* Meetings, conferences and conventions are ideal venues where specialty reporters can learn about the latest advances and get to know some of the leading figures.
- *Connecting with audiences.* Specialty reporters sometimes would prefer to be the doctors, scientists and lawyers they cover, and can find it difficult to communicate the complex subjects they understand in ways that the average reader can grasp. Their ability to bridge this gap relies on writing that is clear and often relies on similes, metaphors and other literary devices to connect with their audiences. Amy Ellis Nutt of the *Newark* (NJ) *Star-Ledger* relied on poetic devices for her award-winning series, "The Seekers," which focused on enduring questions about life. In the section on the aging process, she used a simile to convey a challenging concept: "Like money flying out the back of a Brinks truck careening around a corner, these misplaced electrons—now called free radicals—scatter around the insides of cells, bonding indiscriminately with other molecules."

GETTING—AND STAYING—ORGANIZED

Beginning beat reporters often ask, "How do I stay on top of everything?" Here are some useful tips:

- *Use a calendar, either paper or electronic.* You will need to keep track of meetings, hearings and deadlines for reports, upcoming trials and court motions. Keep an address and phone list, whether it's on paper or an electronic device. Develop a "**futures file**" where you can put notes, press releases and other reminders of coming events, deadlines ,and issues that need regular follow-up. Don't leave work at night without making a list of what you need to do the following day.
- *Use the clock as a time management tool.* Divide your day into segments of time and fit the tasks to the time allotted. Take advantage of the alarm feature on a clock, watch or cell phone. (Lawyers, who know that time is money, divide their day into "billable" periods; a journalist's time is just as valuable, especially on deadline.)

The Coaching Way ⁛ⁱ BEATS

- Have you taken a "shoe leather tour" of your beat, introducing yourself and leaving your business cards? Find out the best ways to reach people: phone, email, texting or social media.
- Write a mission statement for your beat, one that explains your goals and what would make it a success. Share it with your supervisor, and find out what is expected of you.

- Draw a map of your beat, identifying where you spend most of your time (include your desk). Include places you've never been to and visit them.
- Check in regularly with your sources, ideally in person, but by phone at least.
- Have you done the reading to learn how your beat works, including jargon and specialized language and how to express terms into ordinary words and phrases?

- Do you keep a calendar for appointments, important events, conferences, sources' birthdays, especially for clerks, secretaries and support staff?
- How do you make it clear to your beat sources that getting information is your job? Are you keeping your relationships with sources on a professional level? Remember: They may be friendly, but they're not your friends. ▼

- *Keep electronic or paper files.* On deadline the last thing a reporter needs is a time-consuming hunt for a fact or quote. These days many reporters keep track of reporting in computer files, while some continue to swear by low-tech manila folders and three-ring binders.
- *Use the Internet.* Smart reporters today subscribe to blogs, Twitter feeds and other news alerts for information about subjects that relate to their beats. The Web can be a great resource, but remember to double-check all information.
- *Keep your eyes and ears open.* It's exciting to cover a beat: A landscape spreads out before you with people and rules and a culture to learn, and as a journalist you get to look at it through a special lens—what people should know to be good citizens and perhaps to improve their lives.

Using these approaches will help you stand out as a beat reporter and outperform the competition. The best of the breed stay on top of the news, breaking exclusive stories, but not neglecting the minutiae—motions, routine follow-ups and regular contact with sources—that distinguish them from lackluster competitors. Information won't always lead to an immediate story, but collecting string (keeping track of reporting that may fit into a future story) enables them to produce important trend stories. The best beat reporters own their beat. They do their homework. They know that beats are a series of relationships and work hard to develop and maintain them. They recognize they are never off duty. They are dogged, unwilling to let a story or a competitor slip past, committed to excellence and the importance of their assignment. They are the lifeblood of every newsroom.

> **❝Participate in discussions on blogs and forums and mailing lists in your beat area. Get on LinkedIn and Facebook and Twitter. It's a form of networking—just like getting out of the office.❞**
>
> —MITCH WAGNER, TECH JOURNALIST, *INFORMATION WEEK*

BEAT REPORTING

Beat reporters are always on duty. Their most important task: cultivating sources who trust them. Their newest challenge: adapting to the Internet. These top the mindset of a good beat reporter, say those who work local and national beats and those who supervise them. The requirements:

- *Own your beat.* From the routine story to the exclusive, be sure you cover it exhaustively.
- *Build trust.* Respect your sources, and they will reward you with tips, access and information.
- *Manage your time.* Beat reporters get swamped without communication and organization skills.

Participants

KEVIN BENZ, news director, News 8, Austin, TX

MICHAEL REGAL, former assigning editor/news, *Erie* (PA) *Times-News*

KARIN FISCHER, reporter, *The Chronicle of Higher Education*

> ### What do you expect from a beat reporter?

Benz: Own it. Find exclusive stories and doggedly pursue them to the end. Have the cell phone number of impeccable, trusted contacts.

Regal: They must become students of their beat. This involves homework and reading extensively about whatever they are covering.

> ### What's the most important lesson you've learned from beat reporting?

Fischer: Treat everyone with respect. I've gotten stories because secretaries put my call through first or because Capitol Police officers let me go down halls that are otherwise off-limits. If you treat people fairly and with respect, it comes back to you.

> ### What advice would you give a new beat reporter?

Regal: Don't just call on people when you're looking for a story. You have to be part salesman. Call up and ask, "Anything going on?" You might be surprised at the response. Attend functions where sources congregate and don't write a story about it. This establishes you as someone who isn't just interested in writing something about them or their organization.

> ### You've covered police in small West Virginia towns; how does that differ from what you're doing in Washington?

Fischer: The reporting skills are, by and large, identical. Be fair, attentive to detail, energetic and aggressive in your reporting.

> *How do the best beat reporters juggle cultivating sources while feeding the daily report?*

Benz: Being a beat reporter is a 24/7 job. It means buying lunch for contacts and working on half a dozen stories at once. You must make being organized a priority.

> *How has the Internet changed your job?*

Fischer: It's changed the fundamental way that I report. I usually have background before I dial a number.

Regal: Print isn't the only game in town. There are a lot of readers on the Internet. That forces us to write differently. Short sentences. Getting the who, what, when, where and why in the first few paragraphs.

SUMMARY GUIDE — BEATS: POLICE, COURTS, SPORTS, BUSINESS, EDUCATION AND MORE

INGREDIENTS OF SUCCESSFUL BEAT REPORTING

Beat reporters are responsible for all news that happens in the place or subject area to which they are assigned.

What to Remember → Every beat represents a field of knowledge, skills, rules and language that must be translated to make news accessible. Good beat reporters develop a range of sources, use public records to bolster their reporting and roam their communities, developing relationships with residents, crime victims and others affected by the news.

BASIC BEATS

Journalists are often assigned to one of five basic beats: police, courts, government, communities and suburbs.

What to Remember → Speed, accuracy and clarity are a must for beat reporters as news organizations rely on social media to deliver news. Beat reporters make daily rounds and take steps to cultivate sources even in the face of suspicion and hostility. They make the effort to link activity on their beats to the community at large and uncover untold stories about groups that rarely receive news coverage.

SPECIALTY BEATS

Specialty beats are prestigious assignments generally reserved for journalists who've shown outstanding work on basic beats, or those with education or professional practice in the field.

What to Remember → Specialty beats include science and health, business, politics, religion, sports, education, investigative reporting, technology and arts and entertainment. As with all beats, juggling breaking news and in-depth specialty coverage is a must.

WHAT A SPECIALTY BEAT REQUIRES

Specialty beats require deep expertise and a commitment to communicate complex subjects in ways that audiences can grasp.

What to Remember → Reporters who specialize usually bring professional education, training and wide-ranging reading of professional and subject-specific publications to their assignments. Their biggest challenge is to use inventive writing skills to communicate the complex subjects and issues they cover.

GETTING—AND STAYING—ORGANIZED

"How can I stay on top of everything on my beat?" is a question that dogs all beat reporters, but there are many ways to overcome the challenge.

What to Remember → Smart beat reporters use a calendar, either paper or electronic, and a clock to stay on top of events, meet deadlines and manage their time. Beat reporters subscribe to blogs, Twitter and news alerts, and remain alert to newsworthy events, follow-ups and trends important to audiences. They recognize that beats are a series of relationship and work hard to cultivate and maintain them.

KEY TERMS

beat, p. 394
civil action, p. 401
criminal action, p. 401
cultivating sources, p. 395
decision, p. 401
defendant, p. 401

deposition, p. 401
digital resources, p. 395
docket, p. 401
domain, p. 395
federal court, p. 401
felony, p. 401

first responders, p. 397
futures file, p. 412
hearing, p. 401
income, p. 410
misdemeanor, p. 401
motion, p. 401

EXERCISES

1. Many law enforcement agencies take journalists on "ride-alongs," allowing them to observe during a shift in a patrol car. Set one up, and take careful notes during the experience. When time permits, interview the officers about their career, why they chose law enforcement, the risks and rewards and the strangest cases they ever handled. Write a 500-word story about your day.

2. Shadow a beat reporter for a day, observing how he or she reports, writes and goes through the editing process, staying alert to the way online duties have expanded beyond their traditional ones. Ask how he or she got into journalism and came to work the beat, and to describe the challenges, risks and rewards. Write a brief profile and answer four questions: What surprised you? What did you learn? and What do you need to learn next? Would you like their beat?

3. Many student journalists are assigned a community beat. Arrange a tour for your classmates. Decide what they need to see and experience to understand your beat community. Lead a guided tour of your beat, and explain your beat. Select one person or group of people who exemplify newsworthiness—a community police officer, nurse or doctor, concerned citizens. Schedule an in-class meeting between your beat representative and your classmates, and lead a discussion about the news they consider worth reporting.

4. Select a beat and report and write a profile, a meeting story, breaking news or story that explores your beat's cultural diversity. Accompany the story with tweets, blog posts and multimedia elements.

5. Create a glossary of indispensable terms needed to understand and report the workings of various beats: courts, law enforcement, sports, local government, business and health care.

READINGS

Gastel, Barbara. *Health Writers Handbook*, **2nd ed.** Oxford, UK: Blackwell Publishing, 2005.
This indispensable guide for anyone writing about health and medical issues covers finding topics and authoritative sources, and blends teaching with best practice examples of reporting and writing. This new edition includes a chapter on medical reporting for the electronic media.

Pulitzer, Lisa Beth, ed. *Crime on Deadline: Police Reporters Tell Their Most Unforgettable Stories.* **New York: Boulevard Press, 1996.**
In 10 short stories, this collection reveals the harsh realities of crime reporting through the accounts of veteran police reporters. It shows how beat reporters filter news through their own experiences and values to write stories that reveal the often-disturbing realities of modern life.

Reinardy, Scott, and Wanta, Wayne. *The Essentials of Sports Reporting and Writing.* **New York: Routledge, 2008.**
This textbook provides a comprehensive treatment of writing about sports from an overview of the profession to the types of sports that encompass this wide-ranging beat, game coverage, profiles, interviews and other story types. It delivers solid reporting and writing tips and techniques, explores the beat's tricky ethical challenges and provides advice on online journalism and blogging.

West, Bernadette M., et al. *The Reporter's Environmental Handbook,* **3rd ed. New Brunswick, NJ: Rutgers University Press, 2003.**
A handy reference book for journalists who cover the environment. With clearly written chapters on air pollution, global climate change and environmental emergencies, the book is an essential tool on deadline for science reporters.

Winkler, Matthew. *The Bloomberg Way: A Guide for Reporters and Editors.* **New York: Bloomberg Press, 2012.**
The ideal handbook for reporters covering business and financials news. In addition to sophisticated discussion of how best to write about companies, economics and the stock market, it offers an impressive collection of advice on reporting, writing and ethics.

COURT STORY

Journalists who cover the courts face daily challenges to communicate legal information in ways audiences can comprehend the reality behind often-arcane proceedings. Working under deadline pressure, court reporters must summarize the news, provide context and pay close attention to details. Accuracy always matters, but errors in a court story can have widespread ramifications. The beat demands understanding of legal procedures, legalese and the various types of actions that accompany any legal case, civil or criminal, as the following story demonstrates.

JUDGE DISMISSES CONSPIRACY COUNT AGAINST MONSIGNOR, PRIEST

By Joseph A. Slobodzian and John P. Martin,
Inquirer **Staff Writers**
Philadelphia Inquirer, **May 18, 2012**

After calling nearly 50 witnesses and presenting close to 1,900 documents over eight weeks, prosecutors rested their case Thursday in the landmark trial involving child sex abuse by Archdiocese of Philadelphia priests.

The team of district attorneys ended by letting jurors handle what they contend is the closest thing to a smoking gun in the case: a tattered gray folder that had been hidden away in a locked safe at archdiocesan offices for more than a decade.

Inside were handwritten and typed records, including a list that Msgr. William J. Lynn drafted in 1994 naming about three dozen priests who had admitted or were accused of sexual misconduct with minors, and other documents suggesting the church was girding against a possible wave of lawsuits.

Lynn and his codefendant, the Rev. James J. Brennan, scored one victory Thursday when Common Pleas Court Judge M. Teresa Sarmina ruled that prosecutors had failed to prove a conspiracy between the two men. She dismissed those counts.

A trial unfolds in installments, a serial narrative that can span several days, weeks or months. The story's lead summarizes the case presented by the prosecution in a child abuse trial involving the Catholic Archdiocese of Philadelphia. The details are specific and concrete: numbers and witnesses, documents offered in evidence, weeks of trial. The use of the word "landmark" signifies the importance of the case and assumes previous reader interest in the ongoing nationwide church scandals over child abuse by priests.

The second paragraph takes the approach of a chronological narrative with a scene including characters, action setting and telling details about a critical piece of evidence. Careful observation is crucial in court reporting. The folder is "tattered gray" and the safe is "locked." The sentence follows subject-verb-object format and uses a colon for punctuation and impact. "Smoking gun" is a cliché, but it is also a clearly understood phrase.

The story steps back to explain the contents of the folder. The paragraph uses specific details and summarizes information that make clear that Msgr. Lynn knew about priests involved—or suspected to be involved—sexually with minors and that the church recognized it faced numerous lawsuits. The sentence is long—47 words—but verbs clearly carry the meaning.

Trials are tedious at times, but there are moments of activity that the reporter must give close attention to or a significant event may slip by. Reporters must also understand and be able to communicate the significance of motions presented to the judge, as this paragraph does. Otherwise, they risk reporting inaccurate and unfair information. This paragraph effectively weaves in the name of a second defendant and the judge, using full names and middle initials to avoid confusion with other people. Identification mistakes in routine stories are responsible for the majority of libel suits against journalists and their news organizations.

But the judge left intact the more substantive charges: that Brennan tried to rape a 14-year-old boy in 1996, and that Lynn endangered children by letting Brennan and another priest, Edward Avery, have active roles in parishes in the 1990s despite knowing or suspecting they would abuse minors. (Avery has pleaded guilty to sexually assaulting a 10-year-old altar boy in 1999.)

In a preview of what could be a closing argument for the commonwealth, Assistant District Attorney Patrick Blessington told the judge that Lynn's actions reflected a broader conspiracy within the church hierarchy.

"It was all about the good of Mother Church," he said, after jurors had been released for the weekend. "They cared about money, they cared about the business of the church, not the flock and not the parishioners."

The gray folder and the list within dominated the prosecution's final week. Lynn had described the list to a grand jury investigating clergy sex abuse in 2004, but said he couldn't find it.

It turned up this year in the archdiocese's center city offices. Along with it, church lawyers turned over another handwritten memo stating that Cardinal Anthony J. Bevilacqua had ordered all copies of the list shredded.

What the documents represent, and who hid them, are central questions the Common Pleas Court jury will be asked to decide.

This paragraph makes clear that the victory described above is a small one. Good court reporters grasp the legal system so they can make the meaning of events clear to their audience. Background information is equally critical in court stories. The reader learns the nature of the charges and in a parenthetical aside the fate of one of the abusive priests. Again, note the use of the colon to set up a long sentence.

The story shifts to future events. Using an inverted pyramid, as this story does, allows journalists to leap across time as they organize their story by facts rather than chronology. The paragraph displays a sophisticated understanding of court procedure. Using careful attribution and context, the paragraph signals the larger context of the case at hand.

Until now, the story has avoided quotes in favor of summary action and one scene. Amid the torrent of words spoken during trials, the best court reporters single out the most dramatic quotes and use them to punctuate observations.

The reporters back up to further describe the significance of the critical piece of evidence, providing a chronological marker in the trial's duration. The paragraph provides additional documentation: testimony before a grand jury. It is illegal to publish grand jury testimony unless it is offered as evidence at trial.

Evidence of a cover-up emerges in a paragraph that provides more information about the "smoking gun." For the first time, the story implicates the highest-ranking church official in Philadelphia, lending support to the use of the word "landmark" in the lead. Faced with an overabundance of information and limited space, court reporters display exceptional news judgment as they must decide what belongs in their stories.

The reporters choose to conclude their story by looking ahead. What may seem like editorializing is in fact an accurate description of the circumstances. Like the rest of the story, the writing is clear, accurate and dispassionate, ruled by strict adherence to what transpired in court.

SUMMARY

Court reporters are skilled, educated observers and analysts of the law and its impact on society. Their stories influence public opinion, which makes accuracy, attention to detail and legal acumen a must. With its close attention to compelling details, crucial background and clear writing, this story demonstrates how the coverage of a pivotal day in an 8-week trial reflects the facts and the drama of a legal proceeding. That reporters Joseph A. Slobodzian and John P. Martin accomplished this in just 380 words is a testament to their reporting and writing skills and expertise, making their story a model worth studying by aspiring court reporters.

Postscript: In June 2012, the *Inquirer* reported, "A jury convicted Msgr. William J. Lynn of child endangerment Friday, finding that as the Archdiocese of Philadelphia secretary for clergy he ignored credible warning signs about a priest who later sexually assaulted a 10-year-old altar boy." The jury deadlocked on a decision to acquit or convict his codefendant. The following month, Lynn was sentenced to 3 to 6 years in prison. The sentencing judge, the *Inquirer* reported, "said he turned a blind eye while 'monsters in clerical garb' sexually abused children, devastating families and shaking the Catholic church across Philadelphia and beyond."

OBITUARIES

423

BY THE END
OF THIS
CHAPTER,

you should be able to...

> Recognize the four basic
  types of obituaries and
  exercise news judgment
  to decide which is most
  appropriate

> Understand differences
  between obituaries
  across media platforms
  and use a process
  approach to meet the
  challenges of each format

> Report and write an
  obituary

> Learn the history of
  obituaries and the ways
  mass disasters and new
  media are changing the
  form

> Confront and respond to
  sensitive issues that may
  surround an obituary

DEATH HAS ALWAYS been news. For centuries, obituaries were the typographical equivalent of a tombstone: a brief outline of a person's life printed in a newspaper. Changes in technology and culture have made them much more than that, often requiring journalists to produce obituaries that accurately sum up a person's life with images, sound and video, as well as words.

Writing an obituary remains a basic and critical assignment—and for some journalists a specialty—that requires the ability to report a death and sum up a life with accuracy, speed and grace. Frequently these will be among novice reporters' first professional tasks. In this chapter, you will learn the importance of the obituary to survivors and society, the changes and challenges of the form and the ethical dilemmas that news of a person's death can pose.

THE OBITUARY: STORIES OF DEATH AND LIFE

An **obituary** (the root of the word is *obit*, the Latin word for "death") is a news report of someone's death, followed by a biographical sketch of the deceased. Think of an obituary as a capsule biography published after a person dies.

"That's what an obit is supposed to be—a picture, a snapshot. It's not a full-length biography," observed Alden Whitman, a legendary obituary writer for *The New York Times*.

66After the first paragraph, an obituary is about life, not death. In ways that few other news stories can, an obituary offers the chance to explore achievement, complexity, success and failure.**99**

—MATT SCHUDEL,
OBITUARY WRITER, *THE
WASHINGTON POST*

FOUR TYPES OF OBITUARIES

Obituaries can be divided into four categories:

1. **News obit**: The report of a death of a community member or one that is considered newsworthy because of the prominence of the individual or his or her place in the community. (The news obit should not be confused with a death notice, usually provided by the family or funeral home, that condenses the person's life and death in laundry list fashion. Some news outlets now charge families to print these boilerplate obituaries, once historically free.)

2. **Feature obit**: The basic news report fleshed out with detailed biographical information, including anecdotes, descriptions, quotes, reminiscences. Although feature obits are usually limited to prominent, influential or famous people, a new form—dubbed the "common man/woman" feature obit—emerged in the 1980s.

3. **Appreciation**: An essay that explores the impact of a person's life—and death—often written by someone familiar with the person or the person's work. This format is often associated with the *Washington Post*'s Style section and its

approach to writing about deceased newsmakers. "I always like to think of the Style Appreciation as the kind of conversation you'd have over drinks after a funeral, after the obit," said Hank Stuever, who has written many appreciations for *The Washington Post*.

4. **Multimedia obit/tribute:** An audio and/or video slide show featuring photos of the deceased, family photos and other artifacts, such as medals or plaques, narrated by a family member of friend.

REPORTING AND WRITING THE OBITUARY: A PROCESS APPROACH

Obituaries have always been a training ground for beginning reporters. They introduce neophytes to the basic form, the inverted pyramid, the demands for accuracy and the painful task of interviewing people at times of stress. As newspapers realized the value of well-written obituaries, they gave the assignments to veteran reporters, but with staff cuts a current reality, you may well get these assignments right off the bat.

Grief lingers long after an obituary appears. Bereaved survivors of the 2003 fire that killed 100 people at The Station nightclub in West Warwick, RI, gather at a grave site.

Idea

Deaths are usually announced by funeral homes, relatives and, in the case of celebrities, by an agent or spokesperson. Word of accidental deaths, motor vehicle accidents and plane crashes may come from police, hospitals or public safety agencies.

Once editors are alerted, they decide on the type of obituary—from a brief news obit to a feature approach. An enterprising reporter could pitch a multimedia obituary, one that focuses on an interesting but little-known person or a cultural icon such as Michael Jackson or the Latina singer Selena.

"The magic word is 'interesting,'" Gayle Ronan Sims, the *Philadelphia Inquirer*'s chief obituary writer, told readers in an online chat. "The person I write about does not have to have been prominent or famous. Sometimes the most ordinary people live the most extraordinary lives."

Focus

Death is the obvious news peg, the topic that makes it newsworthy. But as with any story, the writer must find the focus, or central idea, within the topic. You have to find the theme, the thread that captures a person's essence.

Ask yourself what the person's life story is really about. The answer will help you write an obituary that moves beyond the boilerplate of a death notice.

Matt Schudel, *Washington Post* obituary writer, searched for a focus when he wrote the Feb. 26, 2005, obituary of Robert Kearns, who invented intermittent windshield wipers and ultimately won his battle for credit from the major carmakers that, he believed, stole his idea.

> ❝Some people think the obituaries section is morbid. But in truth, only one line of an obit deals with death. The rest of the article focuses on the amazing lives people lead.❞
>
> —JADE WALKER,
> BLOGGER,
> HTTP://OBITUARYFORUM
> .BLOGSPOT.COM

"I wanted to express something of Kearns' long and lonely crusade against overwhelming odds, as a solitary man fighting against some of the most powerful corporations in the world." Here's how he did it:

▶**EXAMPLE** At long last, Robert Kearns's battles with the world's automotive giants have come to an end. Kearns, who died Feb. 9, devoted decades of his life to fighting Ford Motor Co., Chrysler Corp. and other carmakers in court, trying to gain the credit he thought he deserved as the inventor of the intermittent windshield wiper.

Collect

Obituary writers have to work fast. First stop for most are your news organization's archives and, increasingly, Google and other search engines, and even YouTube.

An obituary contains standard information. Here's a checklist:

- Name of deceased
- Age
- Address
- Occupation
- Cause of death
- Memberships
- Education
- Military, government or community action history
- Survivors
- Names and addresses of family members
- Donation information
- Funeral information

Funeral directors usually obtain answers to these questions, provided by grieving relatives. You have to do additional reporting to flesh out the story and, most important, determine the accuracy of any information you collect. Sometimes closest relatives are too distraught to be of much help. But a co-worker or friend of the deceased can often provide rich details.

Order

News obituaries rely on a formulaic structure, to the dismay of obituary writers who want to move away from the standardized approach. Obituaries are usually written as inverted pyramids with the most important information first followed by details in decreasing order of importance. "More than anything else in the paper, obits groan with boilerplate," complained Margalit Fox, an obituary writer for *The New York Times*. Indeed, most news and feature obituaries shift facts collected and verified to fit this formula:

- *Lead*: Name of deceased, date and place of death, subject's age, address, cause of death.
- *Middle*: Date and place of birth, education, military experience, organizations, marriages, divorces.
- *Ending*: List of surviving spouse, siblings and children, and where they live. Funeral or memorial services and, on occasion, requests for donations to a cause or institution in lieu of flowers.

QUICK Tips 🕐 CHALLENGES AND REWARDS OF WRITING OBITS

- The obit writer must work fast.
- An obit must be short, yet sum up a life with accuracy and grace.
- Obits contribute to society by explaining a life and providing continuity and closure for survivors. ▼

Draft

The reporter uses what's been learned through reporting and follows the traditional structure. The obituary lead includes: name of deceased; a phrase that conveys the person's significance (i.e., "the inventor of the Slinky"); date of death (location, circumstances are optional); age; cause of death.

Here's the standard lead for a news obit:

❯**EXAMPLE** Richard L. Ashton, the city's finance director for more than two decades, has died at 72.

In recent years, obituary writers have been able to add narrative touches to the traditional format, writing storytelling leads. Ken Fuson of the *Des Moines* (IA) *Register* started the obituary of a beloved pediatrician this way: "This one's going to sting."

Even within the traditional structure, talented obituary writers find a way to "telegraph in elegant shorthand what is interesting or innovative about the subject's life," the *Times'* Fox said. Shorthand is an apt description. The obituary writer doesn't get a full paragraph, let alone a full sentence. Instead, "she gets a single, stingy dependent clause, the handful of words between 'who' and 'died,'" Fox said.

But even with those constraints, talented journalists can convey the essence of a person's life between two commas:

❯**EXAMPLE** , a blinded war veteran who, with his wife and mother-in-law, lived a story of great courage and love,

❯**EXAMPLE** , an internationally renowned lexicographer who wrestled the Victorian behemoth known as the Oxford English Dictionary into the era of "wimmin," "sexploitation" and "microwave oven,"

Endings also give the writer a last chance to tell a story. Formulaic requests for charitable donations and an endless list of survivors and where they live robs the writer and reader of a resonant ending.

It's too easy just to wrap it up with the wife and kids, said the *Post's* Schudel. His reporting turned up a fact about inventor Kearns that gave him his ending. Schudel followed the list of survivors with two sentences:

❯**EXAMPLE** In his final years, he drove around in two aging vehicles: a 1978 Ford pickup and a 1965 Chrysler. Neither had intermittent wipers.

The feature obituary is usually reserved for the famous, infamous, and those who made significant contributions to their fields. The writer has space for a detailed biographical section, comprised of anecdotes, physical descriptions, quotes and reminiscences that flesh out the basic obituary. Until the 1980s, with the introduction of

SEE CLOSE-UP, P. 440: NEWS OBIT

WRITING AN APPRECIATION

Appreciations offer the widest latitude in style and content. They draw on the writer's interest and knowledge about the deceased, while giving short shrift to the list of survivors, funeral arrangements and other boilerplate information.

In 2006, legendary writing teacher Donald M. Murray, who was my writing mentor and friend, died at 82. I wrote a 500-word feature obit, then followed up with "The Things He Gave," an appreciation essay that focused on his influence as a proponent of the process approach to writing and coaching writers, and on his impact on me and thousands of journalists, writers and teachers who spread his lessons in newsrooms and classrooms for over 25 years. Here is some of what I wrote:

▶**EXAMPLE** I think I know what it's like to be an apostle.

I don't mean that in a blasphemous way. I make this claim because for the last quarter-century, I have dedicated a big part of my life to spreading a gospel.

I described the first day I met Murray and the unforgettable experience of what he told a gathering of *Providence* (RI) *Journal* reporters and editors.

▶**EXAMPLE** "Writing may be magical," Murray told us, "but it's not magic. It's a process, a rational series of decisions and steps that every writer makes and takes, no matter what the length, the deadline, even the genre. . . ."

The appreciation then shifted to a description of Murray's long career as a Pulitzer Prize–winning journalist, magazine writer and columnist before zeroing in on his impact on thousands of journalists and other writers.

▶**EXAMPLE** Relying on his own experiences and research into how writers work, Murray pulled off the shroud of mystique that snared so many writers. He did so by studying how writers, including himself, worked, just as athletes study films of their performances. By doing so, he made it possible for mere mortals to set off on regular journeys of discovery that led to good stories.

Writing an appreciation demands careful reporting, intimate knowledge, perspective and passion. Its aim: to reveal and celebrate qualities about a person that capture the human condition. ▶

—*Poynter Online, Dec. 31, 2006*

CONVERGENCE POINT ⚹

"They Called Him 'T'"

Check out the video tribute of a local musician in Brooklyn, New York, produced by student journalists Artis Henderson and Alex Hotz.

Find this link on the companion Web site at **www.oup.com/us/ scanlan.**

a new form, dubbed the "common man/woman" feature obit, only the well known or those who made significant contributions to society merited this form.

Newspapers assigned obituary specialists who brought extraordinary skills to the passing of ordinary men and women whose lives were never chronicled in the newspaper. Jim Nicholson of the *Philadelphia Daily News* pioneered the form with stories like the obituary of an ordinary man who hauled ice by horse-drawn wagon and by truck for nearly 40 years. "Bob Clark," he wrote, "said his father had keys to many of the homes; if someone wasn't home he would bring the ice in the house, empty the refrigerator, and then repack the food around the ice."

Revise

Style is important, but accuracy is the top priority in an obituary. Obituaries are often the only time a person's name will appear in the newspaper or online. Often framed or otherwise kept for posterity, obituaries become part of a family's permanent record. Thanks to the Internet, they also become a de facto public record that is available everywhere, potentially forever. Mistakes can add lasting pain to already grieving survivors. Make sure you've got it right.

TIPS FOR PRODUCING OBITUARIES

- Interviews with grieving survivors can be painful. Ask open-ended questions that elicit details: What was his or her greatest accomplishment? When you think of the subject, what makes you smile?
- Remember: An obituary is a story, not only about someone's death but also about his or her life.
- Explore the possibilities of multimedia: Interviews with survivors and family photographs can generate a slide show.
- Employ 21st-century recording tools: A digital camera and audio recorder can capture recollections from family and friends.
- Contact family members for permission to record audio and use photographs. One way is to promise them a DVD recording in return.

DIGITAL OBITUARIES

Once the sole province of newspapers, obituaries went online soon after the World Wide Web spread digital news and information. Digital audio and video provide a new form of remembrance: multimedia obituaries and tributes. Some electronic obituaries link to a funeral home's Web site, which displays a slide show and offer an online guest book. Legacy.com makes it easy to create a tribute page where those who knew the deceased can leave their thoughts.

66 The number one expectation in obit writing is verification and honesty. An error in the story of a person's life is unacceptable. A great deal of time goes into verifying every fact that is written, especially family members, military and work records, notable accomplishments. 99

—GAYLE RONAN SIMS, FORMER CHIEF OBITUARY WRITER, *THE PHILADELPHIA INQUIRER*

SEE CLOSE-UP AT WWW .OUP.COM/US/SCANLAN: FEATURE OBITUARY

Online obituary guest books give family and friends the opportunity to leave their memories about the deceased.

Journalist at Work AN OBITUARY HOAX

An experience involving an obituary taught Greg Toppo, a former reporter for the *Santa Fe New Mexican* who now covers education for *USA Today*, the importance of verification. Here is his account:

This past weekend I was the only reporter on duty at the paper. Saturday afternoon I get a call from a very distraught woman, says she's calling from Washington, D.C.

It seemed a family member, a certain doctor who lived for years in Santa Fe, died Thursday in D.C., and could we run a short obit for him in the Sunday paper? I said sure, just fax us the info, and we'll try to run it, I'm sorry to hear about your loss. She thanks me 100 times over and says she'll try to fax the stuff right away.

A few hours later a three-page handwritten fax comes in, detailing this guy's life. I asked the editor if he wants to run it, he said we've got no room, wait until Sunday to deal with it.

So Sunday rolls around, it's a madhouse. When things calmed down, I go through the pile of stuff on my desk, about 8:30 p.m., and I find the fax. I ask the Sunday editor if she wants to run it. She says sure,

so I typed up six inches on the thing. At the end of the fax, it says that in lieu of flowers, donations should be sent to the New Mexico AIDS Center. Well, I've never heard of the place, so I looked it up in the phone book. No New Mexico AIDS Center. I think, the woman is in D.C., probably doing all of it from memory, she must just have the details wrong. So I look at the fax to see if she's given us a number. No number, no name. She sent it from a Kinkos, but they didn't give their number, either. I gave it to the editor to look at. She said, "I know this guy! I just saw him a month ago! He looked great!" A bell should have gone off, but it didn't. I thought maybe it was a sudden illness. Still, the New Mexico AIDS Center thing was bugging me. I notice that there's a place called NM AIDS Services, but I'm reluctant to type that in, for fear of just plain getting it wrong.

Well, it seems this doctor was married twice and is survived by a longtime companion. The editor, it turns out, knows the longtime companion, leaves a message on her machine, so sorry to hear about it, please give me a call, etc. Meanwhile, she suggests, why don't I try to get the second wife on the phone—she lives in Santa Fe.

I call her, apologize for the inconvenience, but had she heard about the death of etc. and has she ever heard about New Mexico AIDS Center?

She says, "What?!"

Yes, I say, I'm awfully sorry. He died Thursday.

She says, "Well, I just talked to him this morning. His daughter got married today. Who is this?"

The long and short of it is that the second ex-wife tells me that the doctor had a girlfriend in Austin, Texas, with whom he just broke up, plus the longtime companion in Santa Fe: two girlfriends in long-distance relationships for months, and the Texas one just found out about the Santa Fe one. I called Austin info, and sure enough the fax was sent from Austin, not D.C. The jilted girlfriend made up the whole thing. We finally got the Santa Fe girlfriend on the phone. She verified it. The doctor called an hour later and did the same, with great embarrassment. It was then, of course, that I remembered "If your mother says she loves you, check it out." As it turned out, we had no policy on accepting obits from family members, but thanks to this, we will soon. I thank my stars that we made the calls. The editor thanks hers, too. ▶

Scanlan's students at the Columbia University Graduate School of Journalism created audio slide shows that paid tribute to a person's life. *The New York Times* published an online tribute to jazz drummer Squire T. Holman, produced by multimedia journalists Artis Henderson and Alex Hotz.

"We had two and a half minutes to cover a man's life," Henderson said. "Not an easy task. We decided to focus on his music. We both took photographs, interviewed people, and edited the final product."

MAKING TOUGH CHOICES: ETHICS AND OBITUARIES

Obituaries are often controversial, sometimes based on how they're written and sometimes on elements included within or omitted from them. Acceptability of topics has changed over the years in conjunction with social standards. Cancer used to be taboo in obituaries, but now is regularly reported. The appearance of obituaries about black people, which for decades had rarely if ever appeared in newspapers, especially in the South, marked "a softening of the segregationist stance toward the end of the '60s and as the '70s evolved," according to John Hammack, online editor of the *Clarion-Ledger* in Jackson, Mississippi.

Three elements illustrate the form's sensitivities:

- *Disrespecting the dead.* The *Meriden* (CT) *Record Journal* came under fire from subscribers outraged by the obituary of a Wallingford police chief that included the fact that he pleaded guilty to obstruction of justice and resigned his position after he tried to cover up the arrest of a man accused of assaulting one of his own officers. Readers "told us we ought to be ashamed," the paper's editor wrote in a column. "This is one disconnect between the press and the public that is difficult to resolve. There seems to be a feeling that we should not speak ill of the dead," editor James H. Smith wrote. "Mr. Grasser was a high public official in Wallingford and the career of a public official is just that—public. If he had retired with laurels instead of being forced to resign, we would have reported the laurels. But he didn't. Can you imagine leaving out of Richard Nixon's obituary that he resigned from the presidency?"
- *The taboo of disease.* While cancer no longer carries a social stigma, reporting death from AIDS is still considered taboo by some, especially family members who fear the stigma of the disease and don't want it listed as a cause of death. After Herb Ritts, a prominent celebrity photographer died in 2002, many mainstream papers listed the cause of death as "complications from pneumonia." But the *Washington Blade*, a gay and lesbian news magazine, reported Ritts died of AIDS, quoting his publicist. Columnist Michelangelo Signorelli called it "a tragic omission when study after study shows unsafe sex and new infections continuing to rise steeply among younger generations of gay men, often because

CONVERGENCE POINT ☿

Suicide: A Delicate Subject

In "No Perfect Way to Handle This Story," *The (Tacoma, WA) News Tribune* executive editor Susan C. Peterson tells readers how and why the newspaper reported the suicide of a pageant contestant on the eve of the competition. It's a valuable case study in sensitive coverage of a delicate subject.

Find this link on the companion Web site at **www.oup.com/us/ scanlan.**

Gay photographer Herb Ritts succumbs to AIDS

Washington Blade - January 3, 2003
Rhonda Smith

When celebrity photographer Herb Ritts died in 2002, many mainstream newspapers cited the cause as pneumonia. *The Washington Blade*, a gay newspaper, reported the cause as AIDS, highlighting the continuing dangers of the disease.

Ethical Dilemmas DIGGING UP THE PAST

You are preparing the obituary for one of your school's most successful and beloved coaches who died the day before. As you scour the archives for background information, you learn that 15 years earlier the coach was arrested three times for drunk driving, including an incident in which he hit an unoccupied car parked in front of the stadium. You raise the subject with his family. They are irate. After the incidents, they say, the coach sought treatment and had been sober ever since. They insist that this part of his past has no business in the obituary and would unfairly tarnish his reputation. You are torn, but believe the information tells a complete and sympathetic portrait of the man. What do you do? Omit his drunk driving history? Use it but include the comments from his family about his sobriety? What are your ethical responsibilities to the coach, his family, your audience? If you decide to use the information, how would you explain the decision to your audience?▼

CONVERGENCE POINT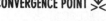

Reporting Suicides

The news media play an important role in their reporting of suicides, but coverage often plays into myths and misperceptions. The Annenberg Public Policy Center at the University of Pennsylvania maintains a Web site of best practices and resources that help journalists report this serious public health issue with accuracy and sensitivity.

Find this link on the companion Web site at **www.oup.com/us/ scanlan.**

the realities of AIDS are abstract to them—enough to allow them to take foolish risks."

Until the mid-1980s, survivors were generally unwilling to list AIDS as the cause of death in their loved ones' obituaries. Following news coverage of the 1985 AIDS-related death of movie star Rock Hudson, "AIDS came out of the shadows," says Allan M. Siegal, former standards editor of *The New York Times*. From then on, the paper, guided by survivors no longer afraid to disclose AIDS as a cause of death, included that fact in obituaries. "AIDS changed from faceless plague to tragic loss of identifiable talent," observed Geneva Overholser, the former ombudsman for *The Washington Post*.

- *The taboo of suicide*. Every year, more than 30,000 Americans kill themselves, many of them young people, according to the Centers for Disease Control and Prevention. Yet suicide as the cause of death rarely appears in an obituary, with exceptions made for newsworthy persons or when the death occurs in a public place. "It would be easy to conclude that suicide is rare, rather than a widespread and ongoing public health problem," says public radio producer Cindi E. Deutschman-Ruiz. "As journalists, we're fond of criticizing ourselves for over-covering homicide. Why do we fail to address our under-coverage of suicide?"

  Bob Steele, a former ethicist at The Poynter Institute, says journalists face three "ethical pressure points" with any suicide: responsibility to the family, deterring copycats and avoiding sensationalism. "Fear of inspiring other suicides, especially among impressionable young people, is a powerful barrier," Steele says. "Copycat suicides are a real problem, but suicide experts generally agree that it's not a question of whether media should cover suicide, but how we do so." Depression and other mental health disorders are commonly linked to suicide deaths and attempts. Before reporting a suicide, consult with experts, such as those at the Centers for Disease Control and Prevention.

PORTRAITS OF GRIEF: A NEW STENCIL

The Sept. 11, 2001, terrorist attacks that left nearly 3,000 dead prompted *The New York Times* to depart from the traditional obituary with "Portraits of Grief," brief essays that melded elements of the feature obituary with the appreciation.

"The portraits were never meant to be obituaries in any traditional sense," said Janny Scott, a *Times* reporter who wrote many of the pieces. "They were brief, informal and impressionistic, often centered on a single story or idiosyncratic detail. They were not intended to recount a person's résumé, but rather to give a snapshot of each victim's personality, of a life lived."

When the *Times'* Sept. 11 coverage won the gold medal Pulitzer Prize for public service, the judges singled out the victims' profiles. As Barbara Stewart, another *Times* reporter, wrote in *Columbia Journalism Review*,

> The portraits are not obituaries or brief biographies. They are something different—impressionistic sketches, or, as one of the metropolitan editors who created them says, "little jewels." Like a quick caricature that captures a likeness, they are intimate tales that give an impression, an image, of a person. Generally, they skip most items required in standard obituaries: survivors, education, jobs held, descriptions of newsworthy accomplishments.

After a nightclub fire in West Warwick, Rhode Island, killed 100 people on Feb. 20, 2003, reporters for the *Providence Journal* produced such portraits of the victims. One 300-word example displays the hallmarks of the form: brevity, a sharp focus, omission of most traditional information and a stylish blending of facts about a person's life.

▶**EXAMPLE** Kevin Anderson was a guy happily stuck in the 1980s.

He collected hundreds of CDs of his favorite bands from that era, including Metallica, Def Leppard and Great White.

"We used to go to the pawn shops and Wal-Mart and buy them," says Dave Penny, one of Kevin's many "best friends."

Kevin, 37, was so into the 1980s that he dressed from that period and wore long hair.

"My kids called him 'Uncle Dude,'" says his sister Sue Sylvia.

"One night a guy came up to him in a club and said, 'You ought to get out of the 80s,'" she says.

Lori Lacques, a former girlfriend, explains Kevin's fascination with the era: "It was his teenage years."

Kevin also loved his Chevrolet Corsica. "You could eat off the inside of that car," his sister says.

As a child, Kevin liked bicycles — "He was always fixing them up."

CONVERGENCE POINT ⚘

Portraits of Grief

Check out a *New York Times* Web page that offers "glimpses of some of the victims of the Sept. 11 attacks." It includes commentary and video interviews featuring reporters and editors discussing their work on the "Portraits of Grief" project.

Find this link on the companion Web site at **www.oup.com/us/ scanlan.**

News outlets sometimes respond to disasters such as the Sept. 11, 2001, terrorist bombings with brief, impressionistic obituaries of the dead. In 2003, the *Providence (RI) Journal* produced a special section commemorating the 100 victims of The Station nightclub fire in West Warwick.

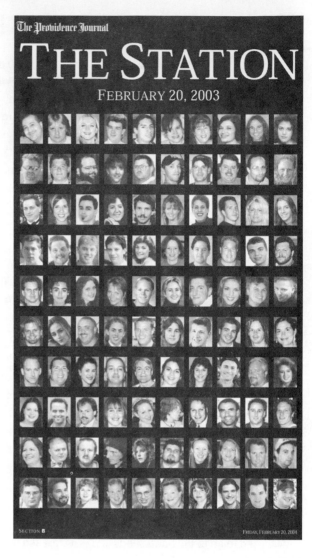

The Coaching Way 👤👤👤 VERIFICATION AND RESPECT

- Double-check every fact, from verifying death to checking the spelling of towns and addresses to correctly naming every survivor.
- Explore the possibilities of multimedia. Interviews with survivors, photographs that can generate an audio slide show, and other types of sounds and images that can help bring the deceased to life.

- Experiment with leads and endings that enhance the story of a person's life rather than relying on the boilerplate forms that funeral homes employ to collect basic facts that are the starting point for the obituary writer.
- Don't insert negative information in an obituary without first consulting your editors. This doesn't mean

censorship; just a close look at the impact such information can have on survivors and how relevant it is to the story.
- Ask about your news organization's policy on reporting AIDS and suicide as a cause of death. Does it differ depending on whether it's a public figure or a private individual? ▸

Kevin was on a crew that cleaned air ducts in restaurants, but he had to leave that work because of a heart ailment. "He got tired because of his heart problem," Dave Penny says.

He and Kevin grew up in Warwick, where they attended Pilgrim High. "I loved the guy like a brother," he says.

Kevin had an 11-year-old son, Kevin Gage. The boy's mother, whom he never married, calls him an "awesome guy."

"We had our differences, but he was my best friend," Melissa Bloomingburgh says. "When I needed a friend to talk to, he was always the one I called."

Just two weeks before the fire, Kevin moved into a new apartment on Pilgrim Drive that he was fixing up so he and his son could get together to listen to music and play video games. That weekend was to be the first time they would be at the apartment together.

—Providence Journal, March 20, 2003

PROFESSIONALS' ROUNDTABLE

SUMMING UP A LIFE

Death is a time of grieving but also an occasion to celebrate a person's life. Obituary writers face many challenges. To meet them, four specialists agree, requires sensitivity, kindness but also being direct about including newsworthy facts that a family might not want publicized. Avoid further pain by being scrupulously accurate.

Participants

MATT SCHUDEL, obituary writer, *The Washington Post*

MARGALIT FOX, obituary writer, *The New York Times*

MACK LUNDSTROM, former obituary writer, *San Jose Mercury News*

ALANA BARANICK, obituary writer, *Life on the Death Beat: A Handbook for Obituary Writers*

> ***How do you decide whose obituary to write?***

Baranick: News value, story power and diversity. I seek out minorities, women, gays, people with disabilities and working class folks, who represent various cultures, religions and occupations.

Lundstrom: If the deceased is a newsmaker and a beat reporter isn't writing the obit for off the obit page, I would look for the number of lives the deceased touched. I would also use a democratizing barometer to make sure that balance over time is achieved in age, sex, race and other characteristics.

> *What do you do when your reporting turns up information the family doesn't want to see in the paper?*

Schudel: I was recently preparing an obituary of a minister when I discovered that he had been convicted of a felony. I told the family I could not publish an obituary without including that fact. The family chose not to have an obituary. In the case of public figures, we include all pertinent facts about a person's life, flattering or not.

Lundstrom: I would carefully try to balance the family's opposition to the deceased's accomplishments. If the deceased has been a public figure and the information tends to taint his résumé, I'd try to find a way to include the information without emphasizing it. I subscribe to the attitude of Alden Whitman: The obit writer's job is to report and write the snapshot of a life, warts and all.

Fox: Many families clearly expect the kind of euphemistic, Victorian obits that one still sees in local papers—the kind in which any information deemed unseemly (cause of death, divorces, acts of public malfeasance) is simply suppressed. We can't do that. It's imperative in purely human terms to treat bereaved families well, but at the same time, one must never lose sight of one's journalistic mandate.

> *What's the most important lesson you've learned writing obituaries?*

Schudel: Grieving families appreciate the chance to offer up the facts and stories of someone's life, prompted by a kind and receptive listener. The purpose of an obituary is to give a full and honest accounting of someone's life. There is a certain honor in being asked to do so.

Fox: An obit is not a eulogy. It must be reported and written as a news story like any other in the paper. This is one of the hardest things to convey to sources when we report our stories.

Lundstrom: Because many surviving spouses aren't experienced in talking to reporters, especially under the circumstances, make absolutely sure that the published story doesn't surprise your sources. Don't let survivors see the story, but read back quotes. Double-check facts and the spelling of names. Avoid errors. Obits are clipped and put in family scrapbooks.

> *How has specializing in writing obituaries affected you?*

Baranick: I've gained knowledge of history, world cultures, anthropology, psychology and philosophy. I've also learned about thousands of people, whom I wish I had met.

> *If you had one piece of advice about obituary writing to share with student journalists, what would it be?*

Lundstrom: Do NOT be afraid to seek the person closest to the deceased as your primary source. The spouse is usually the person who knows the most. Generally speaking that person will welcome the opportunity to talk at length about his or her loved one. Listen; listen intently. Empathize; don't try to hide your own emotions when your sources are crying.

Fox: Obits are correction magnets, and in no other genre does one need to be more careful about fact checking. You're dealing with events that happened 40 or 50 years in the past, families who are exhausted and whose memories may be fuzzy, and a blizzard of names and dates, all of which creates a minefield of potential factual errors. Don't take anything a source tells you at face value; instead, use it as a starting point for your own independent checking.

SUMMARY GUIDE OBITUARIES

THE OBITUARY: STORIES OF DEATH AND LIFE

An obituary is a news report about someone's death, not a full-length biography but a snapshot of a life.

What to Remember → Obituaries offer the opportunity to report achievements, personal challenges, success, failure, the varieties of human experience. A brief biographical sketch and non-negotiable necessities follow the lead, which reports the person's death.

FOUR TYPES OF OBITUARIES

There are four types of obituaries: news, feature, appreciation and multimedia.

What to Remember → A news obit reports the death of a citizen or a newsworthy person. The feature provides fuller treatment of detailed biographical information, including anecdotes, descriptions, quotes and reminiscences. Appreciations explore the impact of a life lost. Multimedia obituaries employ audio, video, photos and other mementoes.

REPORTING AND WRITING THE OBITUARY: A PROCESS APPROACH

Writing a successful obituary requires the same process approach used on all news articles and stories: focusing, reporting, order, drafting and revision.

What to Remember → An obituary demands a sharp focus that answers the question: What is this person's life story really about? It also includes a collection of relevant and accurate information. It is usually written in inverted pyramid form, but an enterprising journalist can suggest alternative story types. Mistakes in an obituary last forever, causing pain to family and friends.

DIGITAL OBITUARIES

Digital audio and video technology has expanded the journalist's ability to convey the impact of a person's life and death.

What to Remember → Multimedia obituaries and tributes use audio, video and photo slide shows. The form requires strong interviewing and new media skills.

MAKING TOUGH CHOICES: ETHICS AND OBITUARIES

> The selection of information and writing of obituaries can often raise ethical dilemmas.

What to Remember →

> Social changes have altered obituary reporting in the areas of illness, such as cancer, and people, such as blacks. Obituary writers should be mindful of three flashpoints: reporting negative but newsworthy information and the lingering taboos of AIDS and suicide.

PORTRAITS OF GRIEF: A NEW STENCIL

> A new obituary form—merging the feature obituary with the appreciation—came into prominence after the Sept. 11, 2011, terrorist attacks presented newspapers with the challenge of reporting thousands of deaths at once.

What to Remember →

> Such stories are brief, impressionistic sketches that omit many traditional facts and often focus on a single revelatory story or detail about the deceased. News organizations now rely on these mini-obits when faced with cases of multiple deaths, such as plane crashes and disasters.

KEY TERMS

appreciation, p. 424
feature obit, p. 424

multimedia obit/tribute, p. 425
news obit, p. 424

obituary, p. 424

EXERCISES

1. Select a living public figure—politician, sports figure, music star, and so on—and conduct extensive research on the Internet and in the library. Write a 750-word advance obituary—excluding date, place and circumstances of death—that captures the person's life and impact.

2. Make an inventory of sources who could be interviewed about the subject. Explain your choices.

3. Imagine that your research turns up evidence of wrongdoing—an arrest, scandal or improper behavior. Do you include the information or not? How do you justify your decision?

4. Find examples of the four types of obituaries—news, feature, appreciation and multimedia. Compare the forms. In 300 words, sum up the differences, pluses and minuses, and explain which is the most effective and compelling way to sum up a life.

5. Imagine someone was producing a multimedia obituary about you. What elements—specific photos, interview subjects, timeline—would be appropriate? What hardware and software would be needed to accomplish the task?

6. Write a 500-word appreciation about one of your favorite people, anyone from your mom or dad, sibling, best friend, or a public figure you admire. For models, search for appreciations on the *Washington Post* Web site.

READINGS

Baranick, Alana, Sheeler, Jim, and Miller, Stephen. *Life on the Death Beat: A Handbook for Obituary Writers.* **Portland, OR: Marion Street Press, 2005.**
An essential guide for obituary specialists and journalists with occasional obituary assignments. It spans the wide variety of contemporary obituaries, illustrated by a wealth of examples, and provides advice on accuracy, deadline writing, research and ways to cope with ethical problems.

Johnson, Marilyn. *The Dead Beat: Lost Souls, Lucky Stiffs, and the Perverse Pleasures of Obituaries.* **New York: Harper Perennial, 2007.**
Johnson is a lover of the obituary who revels in the stories that remember and celebrate the dead, from the famous to the obscure. She quotes from the best examples, but trains her focus on the obituary trade, once the province of rookie reporters or those put out to pasture, but now practiced by specialists and first-class journalists. She looks at the United Kingdom, where obituaries are an art form, and she cites numerous American journalists who bring extraordinary reporting and writing and a passion for celebrating everyday people as skillfully as they do when the subject is famous.

McDonald, William. *The Obits: The New York Times Annual 2012.* **New York: Workman Publishing Co., 2011.**
In this collection, McDonald, the *Times*' obituaries editor, includes nearly 300 of the paper's best obituaries from 2011. They chronicle the lives and deaths of spies, philosophers, artists, inventors and others who influenced society and history. The writers seek out the odd fact, the telling anecdotes and memories that sum up a person's extraordinary life with style, grace and often a dash of humor. An inspiring resource for the occasional obituary writer and the specialist.

Sheeler, Jim. *Obit: Inspiring Stories of Ordinary People Who Led Extraordinary Lives.* **Boulder, CO: Pruett Publishing Co., 2008.**
Sheeler, a Pulitzer Prize–winning journalist from Colorado, writes extraordinary obituaries about ordinary people, bringing strangers to life with creative reporting and a unique writing style that relies on dialogue and telling details that infuse each short story with dignity. This collection, which will inspire journalists, focuses on subjects who are not national or international celebrities or public figures, but individuals—pilots, bartenders, nurses, a carousel caretaker—who made important contributions to local communities and touched those who knew them.

NEWS OBIT

Nearly all obituaries are written in news obituary form. This standardized approach is used to report the death of a community member or one who is considered news-worthy because of his or her prominence or place in the community. It relies on a list of non-negotiable necessities, listed in this chapter, that must be included and a strict inverted pyramid guided by newsworthiness. Journalists must master this form and be able to report and write on deadline with solid reporting, clear writing and, given its importance to survivors, an intense commitment to accuracy. News obituar-ies give journalists a few opportunities to make a person's life and death stand out, but most are reported in boilerplate form, usually based on information provided by funeral homes that interview a surviving relative or friend. But, as the following example shows, an effective journalist can use reporting and background research to create a more complete picture of the deceased.

PLANT EXPERT GIL WHITTON WAS 82

THE GARDENING PUBLIC KNEW HIM FROM NEWSPAPER COLUMNS AND RADIO AND TV SHOWS. HE ALSO DIRECTED THE COUNTY FAIR.

By Craig Basse
© St. Petersburg Times,
published October 31, 2001

Gil Whitton, one of the Suncoast's best-known experts on plants and gardens and former director of the Pinellas County fair, died this week.

Mr. Whitton, director of the Pinellas County Cooperative Extension Service for a quarter century died Tuesday (March 1, 2005) at Roberts Care Center at Hospice of the Lakes, Palatka. He had lung cancer, his family said.

He was 82.

An obituary is a brief biographical sketch: a snapshot, not a portrait. The lead reports the death. Nearly everything that follows is about the deceased's life. The first paragraph contains the name of the deceased, date and death, and a single dependent clause that sums up the person's significance. In the interest of economy, some facts may be presented further on in the story.

Death is the obvious news peg. Journalists have to find the theme, the thread, which captures a person's essence. In this case, the writer has chosen to focus on the deceased's expertise on plant life and his leadership of the county fair, which takes up 18 of the 23 words in the lead. The lead is economical and precise. Note the use of the word "died." Many obituaries use "passed away" instead, which skirts the reality of death. While it may appear to be a euphemism designed to lessen the pain of survivors, be aware that some religions do not believe that the person has died because the soul lives on and has entered a new plane of reality. The choice depends on your news organization's style. The *Associated Press Stylebook* prefers "died" to "passed away."

The specific date and location of death appear in the second paragraph, along with additional information about his occupational background. Most obituaries omit the cause of death, usually at the request of families sensitive about possible stigmas attached to certain diseases. This obituary is notable that it lists the cause of death as lung cancer, once a taboo subject. Age is usually included in the lead. It can be delayed, but no further than the second paragraph.

Mr. Whitton left the extension service post in 1982 but remained a high-profile member of the gardening community as a horticultural consultant and tour guide for gardens abroad.

The gardening public knew him through newsletter and weekly columns in the St. Petersburg Times and the St. Petersburg Evening Independent.

For more than a decade he also had a call-in talk show on radio, WFLA-AM 970, and television, WFLA-Ch. 8, and was the host of In Your Garden on public television

A genial man, he nearly always sported a big grin and a chewed—but unsmoked—cigar.

The cigar "was his trade mark," said Nan Jensen, hired by Mr. Whitton some 30 years ago and now the assistant extension director. "He was a good man and one renowned in the area of horticulture."

Mr. Whitton freely shared his experiences with plants at his former home in Palm Harbor, 2-1/2 acres brightened every spring by hundreds of azaleas growing in woods of pine and oak.

He tried to keep his garden carefree.

"This is what you call a naturalistic garden, nothing formal here," he told a visitor in 1989. "Pine needles fall; I don't mulch."

Since 1996, Mr. Whitton lived in Hawthorne, southeast of Gainesville.

A self-styled farm boy, Gilbert Marshall Whitton Jr. was born in Albany, Mo., and grew up during the Depression. In 1939, he graduated from high school and won a scholarship to Central Business College in Kansas City.

His father gave him $10—"It was all he could spare; in fact, it was more than he could spare," Mr. Whitton once recalled. He got a job paying $1.25 a week plus room, board and tips at a combination dining room-boarding house. After graduation, he worked for Quaker Oats and IBM as a secretary.

When World War II broke out, Mr. Whitton joined the Navy's V-5 program, ending up an electronics technician at air bases in Florida. He later worked as a civilian at the Jacksonville Naval Air Station and for the federal government in Atlanta.

After serving in the Navy during the Korean War, Mr. Whitton studied for a year at the University of Maryland and then enrolled at the University of Florida.

News obituaries are structured around a beginning, middle and end. The circumstances of death and identity of the deceased launch the biography of the deceased. In three paragraphs, the obituary sums up Mr. Whitton's career and his role in the community.

News obits need not be laundry lists of facts. An effective journalist can bring the person to life through description—the unsmoked cigar that was his trademark—testimony from those who knew him well and his own words. The writer provides specific and vivid details about his home that back up the theme—lifelong devotion to plants and sharing that love with others. The last clause is a lyrical description that allows readers to experience this part of the obituary through their senses. The paragraph reflects deep reporting and background information based on the newspaper's archives of previously written stories about the subject. An archive search is a necessary first reporting step for an obituary that is complete, accurate and colorful.

The obituary now reverts to the standard organization and presentation of newsworthy facts. It's important to identify his home since it is outside the circulation area of the newspaper where the obituary appears.

The middle of the story includes date and place of birth, education, military experience, occupational history, organizations and marital history.

But the writer takes the opportunity, drawing on background information in previously published stories, to flesh out the section with anecdotes and quotes.

Military service is always included in an obituary.

Education is another non-negotiable necessity. The section provides more detail than usual about Mr. Whitton's schooling. Note that the family is the source about his doctorate, indicating that the reporter was unable to verify this fact. Grieving relatives, understandably, are often unable to provide complete and accurate information. Journalists must take great pains to verify all information and if unable to do so should not include it in the obituary.

At UF he received a bachelor's degree in horticulture and master's degree in plant pathology. He came within three hours of completing a doctorate in nematology, he said in 1989, but he "couldn't pass German," an overlooked requisite.

Three years ago, however, he finally earned a doctorate, his family said, in philosophy.

He came to Pinellas County in 1957 and joined the Extension Service as an assistant director, beginning a 25-year career.

> The news obit weaves standard information, such as career history, with more detailed descriptions about the person's past, personality and accomplishments.

His gardening columns and broadcasts ultimately landed him in trouble. After about 17 years as extension director, he resigned in 1982 in the midst of an investigation by the county administrator's office that he accepted pay for outside work without approval.

Mr. Whitton said at the time that county officials knew he had outside activities, but they didn't know that he was being paid.

"I never told them," he said. "And certainly they were in violation of county policy. But I guess from the standpoint that I made all the (articles) available (to anyone who wanted to use them), I felt like it was not wrong."

> The obituary sidesteps into a passage about a controversial episode in the life of the deceased. Critics argue that negative information has no place in an obituary because it unfairly tarnishes a person. Journalists counter that when certain information, however negative, is relevant to a complete picture of the deceased it has a rightful place in the obituary. Journalists should take great care in weighing the ethical dimensions of such decisions before they proceed.

He had been a president of the Pinellas County Chapter of the Florida Nurserymen and Growers Association, and a member of the National Garden Writers Association.

> More non-negotiable necessities appear, such as associations, club memberships and church affiliations, as the obituary comes to an end.

Survivors include his wife of 32 years, Dee; two daughters, Lynn Marsh, Clearwater, and Marsha Nagy-Whitton, Moscow, Idaho; two sons, Tom, Melrose, and Todd Chamberlain, Hawthorne; two sisters, Helen Elliott, Tulsa, Okla., and Jean England, Belton, Mo.; eight grandchildren; and a great-grandchild.

> Identifying surviving relatives by name and city is an essential element of the news obituary. Note the use of semicolons to separate the classes of relatives.

Moring Funeral Home, Melrose, is in charge. There will be a memorial service at 4 p.m. March 12 at Sylvan Abbey Funeral Home, 2853 Sunset Point Road, Clearwater.

> Funeral arrangements, and directions for charitable donations when available, remain the default choice for ending news obituaries. Some news organizations try to use an anecdote or a quote as an ending to give the laundry list approach of news obituaries a storytelling flavor.

SUMMARY

The news obit requires strict adherence to presentation of a standard list of facts that provide a brief biographical sketch of the deceased. Most are brief, limited to four to 10 paragraphs. Journalists understand the form's non-negotiable necessities, but effective journalists, such as veteran obituary specialist Craig Basse, stretched the form with anecdotes, descriptions, quotes derived from interviews with surviving relatives and friends and research. A news obit recites the required facts, but, as this example demonstrates, need not be boring. Journalists assigned to produce a news obit must bring extraordinary attention to accuracy, style and ethical decision making. They know that the obituary is a family's last and sometimes the only record of a person's life and death.

CHAPTER 20

EMERGENCIES, DISASTERS AND CONFLICTS

From Weather to War

IN THIS CHAPTER

445

BY THE END OF THIS CHAPTER,

you should be able to...

> Understand the media's role when disaster strikes

> Make preparations that guide your reporting and writing and also keep you safe

> Verify reports to avoid errors that give false hope

> Look for vivid details and scenes

> Take advantage of social networks that can connect you with survivors and experts and spread the news with lightning speed

> Keep in mind that exposure to tragedies will raise ethical dilemmas

> Serve as a watchdog, reporting on wasted resources, rescue delays and bureaucratic missteps

> Acknowledge the physical and psychological effects of exposure to tragedies and your inability to act as a caregiver

KATRINA. COLUMBINE. 9-11. Iraq. Tsunami. Earthquake. Oil spill. Emergencies, unfortunately, provide a steady stream of news. Natural disasters, such as hurricanes, tornadoes, floods and wildfires, top the list. By their nature such stories can be unpredictable, and occur without any known pattern. The same holds true for human-engineered conflicts, such as revolution, terrorist attacks and wars.

This is a particularly difficult area for new reporters because unlike many other types of stories, all the classes or college media experience in the world don't fully prepare you for the challenges that come with covering disasters and conflicts. Nonetheless, in this chapter you will learn the challenges of emergencies, from weather to war, and appropriate ways to report and write about them without taking unnecessary risks.

THE MEDIA'S ROLE

Sometime in your career, an act of nature or man will test your skills, reserves, courage and commitment.

When bad things happen, people want to know how, where, when, why, what and who, so what and what next? Most likely, an emergency, disaster or conflict—a toxic chemical leak, wildfire, flood, hurricane, earthquake, mudslide or, most horrific of all, a terrorist attack or war—will confront you at some point.

Newspaper sales and TV viewership skyrocketed after the terrorist attacks of Sept. 11, 2001, indicating that when the stakes are high, the public feels more compelled to turn to trusted news sources. This phenomenon underscores the importance of professional journalism despite the widespread availability of amateur news reporting via blogs and Twitter.

WHAT'S CHANGED: TECHNOLOGY AND TIMELINESS

Journalists must master a constantly changing variety of tools—hardware and software, social networks—as they develop.

On April 16, 2007, an armed student at Virginia Tech killed 32 students and faculty members, wounded 17 others, and then killed himself. In *The Washington Post* newsroom, reporter José Antonio Vargas saw a brief TV interview with student Trey Perkins, who had been sitting in one of the classrooms targeted by the shooter. Vargas quickly found Perkins on Facebook. Reporter and source "friended" each other. Vargas sent Perkins an instant message. The result: a 25-minute phone interview that provided chilling eyewitness details to coverage that helped the paper win a Pulitzer Prize.

Natural disasters are major news stories. After Hurricane Katrina devastated New Orleans in 2005, the New Orleans *Times Picayune* ran a banner headline pleading for help because federal assistance was slow in coming.

QUICK Tips ⏱ TYPES OF DISASTERS, EMERGENCIES AND WAR

- Airplane crash
- Armed conflict
- Chemical emergency
- Dam failure
- Earthquake
- Epidemic
- Extreme heat

- Fire or wildfire
- Flood
- Hazardous material incident
- Hurricane
- Landslide
- Nuclear power plant emergency
- Terrorism

- Thunderstorm
- Tornado
- Tsunami
- Volcanic eruption
- Wildfire
- Winter storm ▼

Source: Federal Emergency Management Agency

CONVERGENCE POINT ⚡

*Are You Ready
for a Disaster?*

Digital journalist Steve Buttry provides a helpful checklist for disaster reporting based on his experience leading coverage of Midwest floods for the *Cedar Rapids* (IA) *Gazette* in 2008. Among his tips: Use digital tools—interactive maps, live webcams, social media, databases, audio and video—to tell visual stories, and connect displaced victims and volunteers.

Find this link on the companion Web site at **www.oup.com/us/ scanlan.**

As this case illustrates, gone is the era of once-a-day deadlines to put out a daily newspaper or a network news show. "We are always on deadline," is the new reality of online news. But so is the need to get your facts correct because tweets or updates may be published without the safety net of editing. Compounding the problem, says Craig Silverman, who tracks media corrections for Poynter Online, is that "initial, inaccurate information will be retweeted more than any subsequent correction." Verify your facts before you hit send.

WHAT IT TAKES: REPORTING

Depending on newsroom staffing and the scope of the emergency you're covering, you may be the only reporter on the scene, collecting as much information as possible for the story you must write. Your role may be to send in **feeds**—raw data or brief passages—to a reporter in the newsroom who will use them to write the main story. In other cases, you may produce a story on a facet of the event, or be assigned to use Twitter, Facebook and other social networks to post news and information in real time and connect with readers.

At *Newsday* on Long Island, New York, reporters and editors say that a culture that demands an abundance of information—"over-reporting," in their words—is the key to the success of the newspaper's coverage and the richness of the writing in its prize-winning disaster reporting.

Look for examples—details, analysis, anecdotes and scenes. Go the extra mile. Take 95 seconds and the five focusing questions from Chapter 2 and then head out to the scene or pick up the phone.

Collect as much as you can, recognizing that events may shift the story's focus, requiring you to rethink your story. In a fluid event, where it may take time to identify victims or obtain eyewitness accounts, the story can easily turn in another direction. This is critical since the more material you've gathered at the scene, the more prepared you'll be regardless of the outcome.

> ❝ Nothing beats on-the-ground, knock-on-doors reporting. But scouring sites such as YouTube, Facebook and MySpace, where people, especially teenagers and twentysomethings, maintain public diaries, is invaluable when covering a breaking news story. ❞
>
> —JOSÉ ANTONIO VARGAS, REPORTER, *THE WASHINGTON POST*

THINK DIGITAL

Breaking news blogs, message boards, Facebook and Twitter deliver news of disasters online in near real time, and demonstrate the importance of **social networks**. They also enable news organizations to relay information to frantic relatives in other states and counties, and **evacuees** relocated far from home. When vast numbers of your readers have evacuated, many follow developments on the Internet. Collaboration between print and online staffs is essential. Within minutes of reports of a gunman on the Virginia Tech campus, the print and online staffs of *The Washington Post* "began pulling together our **coverage plan**," according to Ju-Don Roberts, managing editor of washingtonpost.com.

QUICK Tips ⏺ MULTIMEDIA IN THE FIELD

New York Times columnist Nicholas Kristof regularly adds multimedia from his travels to hot spots around the world to his Web page on nytimes.com. To do so, he collaborated with multimedia producer Naka Nathaniel. Here's what Nathaniel, who has since left the *Times*, carried in the field:

> Lowe photo backpack
> 15-inch Mac laptop
> Canon digital camera

> Close-up lenses
> Sony Mini DVCam
> Wireless microphone system
> Shotgun microphone
> Batteries
> Tapes
> External hard drive
> Cables of all sizes and shapes
> Notebooks
> RBGAN satellite hookup
> Minidisc recorder with a Sennheiser microphone

> Power strip
> Blank DVDs
> Chargers
> iPod
> Software:
    Audacity
    Final Cut Pro
    Flash
    iPhoto
    iTunes
    Photoshop
    Transmit ▶

"Within the first few hours, we not only had an article explaining the extent of the carnage on the campus, but also a **locator map**, video of the news conferences, audio from faculty and students, images from the scene, a live discussion with the editor of the student newspaper and reactions from washingtonpost.com readers."

VERIFY AND ATTRIBUTE

"If your mother says she loves you," editors have been telling rookie reporters for decades, "check it out." The need to **verify** and **attribute** should be a reporter's mantra, especially when an emergency strikes and rumors, speculation and misinformation fly.

You might sometimes think it's tough to verify information at your desk with a phone and a computer at your disposal, but it's nothing compared to being at a chaotic scene. You'll need to get used to getting facts and figures from hospital officials, fire and rescue personnel, and police and other law enforcement workers. You'll also need to be careful to get names and job titles correct while surrounded by numerous distractions. Attribution can be a major problem if you move too quickly between sources and can't sort out who said what. Keep careful notes. It's important to be organized amid the confusion that reigns in these situations.

When journalists fail to carry out these basic responsibilities, they can cause great pain to survivors and the

On Sept. 12, 2008, a freight train and a Metrolink commuter train collided in Los Angeles, killing 25 people and triggering a massive rescue effort.

Photo of family members rejoicing that all but one of the 13 miners trapped in a 2006 Sago (W. Va) mining disaster were still alive, an unconfirmed report that news organizations spread without verifying the facts.

Devastated relatives after learning that unverified reports were untrue. All but one of the miners had perished.

news media's credibility. That happened during the 2006 Sago coal mine disaster in West Virginia. Initially, word spread after family members and a state official, according to media reports, said rescuers searching for stranded miners had found one dead and 12 survivors. Their families celebrated. With no officials or company spokesperson available to confirm or deny the story, news organizations followed a dangerous maxim: going with what they had. In fact, the opposite was true—12 died and one survived. Frank Langfit, who covered the story for National Public Radio, described what happened: "Cable news shows trumpeted the good (but inaccurate) news; Reporters phoned their newsrooms, editors scrambled to update stories. Some attributed the information to families, others reported it as fact."

Why?

"Most of us suspended disbelief when we should have kept asking the nagging question: How did these guys survive? Maybe we got caught up in the emotions," said Langfit. "Facing the tragedy of 12 dead men—fathers, brothers, sons—we were moved by a miracle, even if it defied logic. And perhaps we were victims of our own humanity. It's a charge you don't hear leveled at reporters very often."

STORY STRUCTURES AND WRITING STRATEGIES

What's the best shape for your story? Breaking news may require a traditional inverted pyramid.

A **chronological narrative**—"**tick-tock**," in newsroom lingo—presents the story as it happened, using a carefully reported timeline of specific days and times and insider accounts that convey suspense and drama. The form is useful to break down complicated developments or unfold dramatic events.

In many cases, you can combine an inverted pyramid with a narrative using the hourglass, allowing you to "sub," or change, the top six to eight paragraphs to report the freshest news, and then switch to a narrative account that introduces characters, anecdotes and details to reveal how the event happened. Make sure you take note of times; that way you can report the calm before the storm, the event and aftermath along with the times reported by eyewitnesses.

In June 2007, a fire at a sofa store in Charleston, South Carolina, killed nine firefighters. "We knew we couldn't go with a straight lead about nine firefighters dying," said reporter Glenn Smith of the *Post and Courier*. "That had been all over our Web site and national television for hours and hours. It would be extremely old news by the following morning. The one thing readers hadn't received at this point was a glimpse inside the fire, a sense of how the events unfolded."

"To take readers into the building," Smith said, the paper chose narrative, combining descriptions from survivors and eyewitnesses as well as snippets from the last radio transmissions of those who died. Writing from feeds, Smith crafted this lead:

❯**EXAMPLE** Two-by-two, Charleston firefighters waded through the belly of the burning furniture store. Swirling black smoke choked the air around them and swallowed all light.

Sofas, chairs and bedding blocked their path at every turn. Darkness and confusion enveloped the men. As the blaze turned deadly, calls for help crackled over the fire department's radios. One man prayed. From another: "Tell my wife I love her."

Their tour of duty had come to an end. Nine lives. Gone.

—*The Charleston (SC) Post and Courier, June 20, 2007*

Details

Details enable readers to envision the story. The key in these situations is to seek specific information. Don't ask witnesses or survivors if they're upset—ask how things looked, smelled or sounded, about normal routines, about actions. Keep your eyes open for information that puts the reader on the scene. Here are two examples from the first *Los Angeles Times* story about a 2008 commercial train crash outside the city that injured 180 and killed 25:

❯**EXAMPLE** Hours after the crash Friday afternoon, Los Angeles City Fire Capt. John Vibrant, his face glistening with sweat . . .

Joelle Ouellette, 38, said she was a few hundred feet away, turning around her horse on a nearby ranch, when the trains collided. "I heard a huge crash," she said. "Then I saw a fireball. I ran over there and there were people lying all over the hill."

—*Los Angeles Times, Sept. 13, 2008*

Careful and sensitive questions elicit the strongest, most evocative details.

RIGHT AND WRONG WAYS TO ASK FOR DETAILS

Wrong	Right
"How did you feel when the earthquake hit? (*trite*)	"What was going through your mind when your house began to shake?"
"Are you upset about what happened?" (*obvious*)	"What upsets you the most about what happened?"
"How does it feel to lose a child?" (*insensitive*)	"What did your son dream of being when he grew up?"
"Do you blame the government for what happened?" (*sensational*)	"How did the authorities react to your emergency?"

Scenes

Be on the lookout for scenes—firsthand observations from witnesses (or yourself), voices of the victims, action, descriptions and details that show characters in action. Like resonant details, scenes bring an event to life.

It may be a woman searching the remains of her house inundated by floodwaters or consumed by wildfires. Or moments normally out of public view.

When three boys were killed in a bombing in Baghdad in 2003, Anthony Shadid, a Pulitzer Prize–winning foreign correspondent for *The Washington Post*, could have written a spot news story that focused on the trio or the impact on the neighborhood. Instead, he decided that those types of stories would simply pile on more "violence and strife and chaos" that deadens readers.

He recalled advice from an editor: "Try to understand the city and people's lives with the war as a backdrop." Shadid chose to follow the ritual of death, from the moment 14-year-old Arkan Daif died until he was buried, including the poignant ritual washing of the body. All it took, Shadid says, "was following in almost the mundane way from step one to step two to step three until his burial."

Timelines

A **timeline** produces of chronology of events. They are especially helpful guides to identify pivotal moments: When was the calm before the storm? When did the battle start? When were survivors found, and how long did it take? Make a habit of recording the time of events, the time eyewitnesses saw it happen. Timelines allow you to weave in actions. For example:

❯EXAMPLE At 3 a.m. Mary Smith woke up to the sound of china shattering. . . .

30 miles away, Jackson Wilson was driving to work when the highway in front of him split in half. He barely had time to stop his car before it disappeared into a crater. . . .

By daybreak, rescue dogs were scouring downtown buildings looking for survivors.

CONVERGENCE POINT ⚹

Interviewing Children Traumatized by Disasters

Tragedies such as the 2012 Newton (CT) school shootings leave children traumatized and in a state of shock. This article presents guidelines for journalists who are faced with the challenge of interviewing children damaged by devastating emergencies. It includes a link to general rules governing legal and ethical behavior by journalists interviewing children for all types of stories.

Find this link on the companion Web site at **www.oup.com/us/ scanlan.**

"When you attach times to events you can put together a chronology of the day, even working under tight deadlines," said Megan Garvey of the *Los Angeles Times*.

Keep track of every date and time in your notebook as you conduct your reporting. Ask witnesses and survivors when things happened. During interviews, slow subjects down and ask them to trace dramatic events: how long they were in a tornado shelter, when did rescuers arrive, when they found a beloved pet. Police, fire and other authorities log times of response, discovery of bodies, search and rescue efforts; ask for them. If these chronological details aren't in your notes, you can't write with clarity, accuracy and precision.

REPORTING PAINFUL TRUTHS

Even as tragic and compelling stories are published, hints of darker truths sometimes emerge. The news media's **watchdog** role often offends some in a community, but good journalists feel "the obligation to detail what happened and let people know how their public safety agencies performed," said Doug Pardue, *The Charleston* (SC) *Post and Courier*'s special assignments editor, describing the dilemma the paper faced when nine firefighters died in the sofa store fire.

While staffers covered every funeral, another team went after "what went wrong," he said. "Six days after the fire, we published our first major look at how the fire department's incident command and firefighting tactics during the fire ran contrary to nationally accepted standards."

Their biggest challenge: revealing that the fire chief, their hometown hero, "arrogantly ignored modern firefighting advances and made critical mistakes in training and command." Despite support from the public and Charleston's mayor, the chief resigned shortly before the one-year anniversary of the fire.

Disasters usually produce horrific damage, and news organizations wrestle with how much to share with their audience. Journalists may find themselves trying to decide which facts or photos should make it into their coverage.

After the space shuttle *Columbia* broke apart on its return to Earth in February 2003, killing all seven astronauts on board and leaving a trail of debris—equipment,

Ethical Dilemmas ❗ SHOULD JOURNALISTS HELP, AS WELL AS WRITE ABOUT, DISASTER VICTIMS?

A tornado has ripped through one of the small towns you cover. At the scene, you interview a single mother struggling to raise three young children. Their home is still habitable but without power or much food in the refrigerator. You're touched by their plight. After you finish the interview, you head for the nearest supermarket, buy $50 worth of groceries and bottled water, and bring it back to the family. It's a generous act, but is it the right thing for a reporter to do? Reporters are supposed to tell stories, not influence them. You are an observer, not a relief worker. When you mention what you did to your editor, she is not happy. How do you defend your decision? Should you tell your audience what you did? ▸

parts, crew remains and astronaut helmets—through Texas, Louisiana and Arkansas, reporters and editors of *The New York Times* grappled with how graphic the stories should be. "We wanted to handle it tastefully because first and foremost, this was a great human tragedy," recalled David Sanger, lead writer, in *Best Newspaper Writing 2004*. "It wasn't until much later in the day for our later editions that we began to hear some of the more gruesome details, mostly the recovery of some of the helmets of the astronauts, and we tried to allude to those without providing great graphic detail."

BREAKING NEWS BLOGS

Coverage of the April 16, 2007, Virginia Tech massacre included a **breaking news blog**, a popular hybrid of new media (the blog) with a traditional standby (the inverted pyramid) written in reverse chronological order to quickly report breaking news. This online form calls on a reporter's news judgment, and ability to quickly sum up news and to tell a story.

Graphics are vital tools when readers want to visualize news events. *The Roanoke (VA) Times* created a timeline and a locator map identifying key spots on the Virginia Tech campus after an armed student at Virginia Tech killed 32 students and faculty members, wounded 17 others, and then killed himself on April 16, 2007.

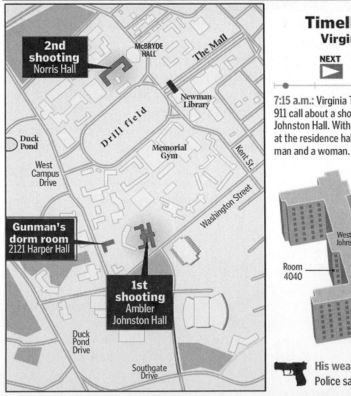

Shooting at Virginia Tech Campus

2nd shooting
Norris Hall

McBRYDE HALL

The Mall

Newman Library

Drill field

Duck Pond

West Campus Drive

Memorial Gym

Kent St.

Washington Street

Gunman's dorm room
2121 Harper Hall

1st shooting
Ambler Johnston Hall

Duck Pond Drive

Southgate Drive

Timeline of events
Virginia Tech Campus

NEXT

7:15 a.m.: Virginia Tech police receive a 911 call about a shooting at West Ambler Johnston Hall. Within minutes, police arrive at the residence hall and find two victims, a man and a woman.

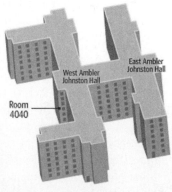

East Ambler Johnston Hall

West Ambler Johnston Hall

Room 4040

His weapons: The types of guns Police say Seung-Hui Cho used

Grant Jedlinsky, Chris Obrion, Rob Lunsford, Hunter Wilson, Reed Williams I The Roanoke Times

At 10:17 a.m., the first blog post appeared on the *Roanoke Times'* Web site, about 30 minutes after reporters near the campus called in:

▶EXAMPLE Multiple shootings have occurred at Virginia Tech this morning involving multiple victims. Police are on the scene and rescue workers have set up a temporary treatment facility. The campus is on lock down. . . .

. . . The university has posted a notice of the incident on its Web site.

Blogs posts are published even if crucial information is missing, counting on reporting to advance the story. Attribution that lends credibility remains a non-negotiable necessity.

By 12:18 p.m., news snippets like this 17-word sentence, topped, but didn't replace, older posts:

▶EXAMPLE Virginia Tech police Chief Wendell Flinchum is saying there are least 20 fatalities in this morning's shootings.

By early afternoon, storytelling posts appeared as eyewitness accounts became available.

Gene Cole . . . was on the second floor of Norris Hall this morning and saw a person lying on a hallway floor. . . .

"Someone stepped out of a classroom and started shooting at me," Cole said. He fled . . . to safety. . . .

"All I saw was blood in the hallways," Cole said.

—*The Roanoke (VA) Times, April 16, 2007*

News blogs can provide readers with a range of information and determine the kind of reporting and writing that is possible even on tight deadlines. They:
- answer the Five W's, H, SW and WN
- acknowledge not all facts are known, with the expectation the facts will emerge later.
- correct errors and comment on differing or inaccurate reports by other news organizations
- offer the chance to write alternate lead types:
  - eyewitness accounts
  - personal accounts from reporters
- set the scene with observations, quotes and dialogue and sensory details; story-telling has a place on news blogs
- identify victims
- add multimedia elements such as audio, video and interactive maps and timelines
- include links to supplementary information from authorities and aid organizations

> **"Keep in mind that in most cases, the person answering questions, despite being shell-shocked, finds these kinds of interviews therapeutic in that they can recall for themselves and others the good qualities of the person they're being asked about."**
>
> —LES GURA, METRO EDITOR, *WINSTON-SALEM* (NC) *JOURNAL*

IN A WAR ZONE: GETTING THE STORY, STAYING SAFE

Colin Nickerson covered armed conflicts in Afghanistan, Angola and Iraq for more than 25 years. "Always frightened," he said, but reported from war zones anyway. "You've got to have a feeling that it's worthwhile journalistically, that the readers are not served just by some guy in the State Department saying he thinks this is what's going on. And the only people really able to go in, scope out what's going on, and communicate what they see are journalists."

Staying safe in a war zone is paramount if you want to live to report the news, says Martha Raddatz, an award-winning correspondent for ABC News who covered the Iraq War. That means talking with experienced reporters to learn the dangers you could face and how to behave in dangerous situations. In her case, she has a "rules that I won't break" list. In Iraq, that meant not riding in an open vehicle, although, she says, she once broke that rule after weighing risk versus importance: She had an important story and no other way to get it.

Raddatz, like most of the hundreds of journalists who covered the Iraq War, traveled with military units as an **embedded journalist** ("embed" for short). The practice continues, but is controversial; it requires journalists to sign a contract that governs when and what they can report. Even so, many editors say the stories that embeds file are worth the restrictions. "From what a blinding sandstorm feels like to reporting how one of our embeds broke his unit's coffee pot, we're giving readers a better sense of the field," said Susan Stevenson, who directed war coverage for the *Atlanta Journal-Constitution*.

Others worry that embedding journalists may distort war coverage. Syracuse University professor Robert Thompson warns, "When you are part of the troops that you're going in with, these are your fellow human beings. You are being potentially shot at together, and I think there is a sense that you become part of that group in a way that a journalist doesn't necessarily want to be."

Countering that argument, *New York Times* reporter Dexter Filkins traveled with the Marines' Bravo Company as they fought street by street in the Iraq city of Fallujah. "It wasn't possible to cover the fighting any other way, as it was in other conflicts, because the insurgents were killing journalists. So it was go with the Marines or not at all."

Even for the most battle-hardened veteran war correspondents, reporting from a war zone is a dangerous business. Marie Colvin, 56, a much-honored American correspondent for the British *Sunday Times*, covered wars in the Middle East, Eastern Europe, Africa and elsewhere for more than 25 years. She lost an eye to a grenade in Sri Lanka in 2001, yet continued to work on the front lines. In February 2012, working without protection from soldiers, she and a French photographer were killed while covering an uprising in Syria. Earlier that month, Anthony Shadid, who had moved from *The Washington Post* to *The New York Times*, died at 43 while covering the same story. Their deaths were a harsh reminder that while covering wars independently allows reporters the freedom that they crave, it also carries great risks.

> **"One can be rightly criticized for covering conflict in Africa at the expense of other kinds of stories. And yet to not cover conflict—and later, its aftermath—would be to ignore an elementary fact. Those places we Americans can barely identify on the map, those places we grow weary of associating with famine and frightful wars— people live there. . . . People who eat and defecate and make love and have dreams. People like us."**
>
> —SOMINI SENGUPTA, REPORTER, *THE NEW YORK TIMES*

Despite the dangers, war correspondents must get close to the action to convey the reality of armed conflicts. Martha Raddatz covered the war in Iraq for ABC News.

CONVERGENCE POINT ⚝

Do Reporters Violate a Cardinal Rule of Journalism if They Buy Food for Starving Sources?

In 2006, touched by the plight of impoverished workers and their families near the capital of Zambia, *New York Times* reporter Michael Wines finished his interviews and then returned with $75 worth of food he purchased for them. In this haunting essay, Wines explores the moral dilemma journalists face when confronted with "the utter destitution of the masses." He describes the rules he follows but leaves it to readers to decide on the ethics of their actions.

Find this link on the companion Web site at **www.oup.com/us/scanlan.**

HUMANIZING THE STORY

One of the major assignments during any emergency, war or natural disaster is to profile the victims. These are usually written under extreme deadline pressure; the clock ticks while you talk to as many people as you can—friends, family, co-workers—and then write a brief story that captures an individual.

Reporters who've faced this challenge focus on describing the essence of a person: how he or she lived, not just how they died. A single detail—a hobby, a character trait, volunteer work—can provide focus for this sketch of a person's life.

RESPONDING TO DISASTER: EASING JOURNALISTS' TRAUMA

"**First responders**" refers to police officers, firefighters, paramedics and other rescuers who immediately descend on disaster scenes, and, in the face of devastation, injuries and death, do what they're trained to do.

Just like other first responders, journalists endure long hours, little sleep and physical hardships. In New Orleans after Katrina struck, Rebecca Catalanello of the *St. Petersburg Times* and her colleagues ran on "adrenaline and Red Bull. . . . When we slept, it felt like a necessary evil—an interruption in what we were really there to do."

SEE CLOSE-UP AT WWW .OUP.COM/US/SCANLAN: TELLING A STORY OF LOSS

Journalists must go to extreme lengths to report on natural disasters. *St. Petersburg* (FL) *Times* reporter Rebecca Catalanello took to a canoe to reach flooded areas in New Orleans after Hurricane Katrina struck the city in August 2005.

CONVERGENCE POINT ⅄

Helping Journalists Cope With Trauma

The Dart Center for Journalism and Trauma is a global network dedicated to improving media coverage of trauma, conflict and tragedy, and its impact on journalists. A "self-care" section discusses the challenges journalists face in extreme situations and offers advice from reporters who have been there.

Find this link on the companion Web site at **www.oup.com/us/ scanlan.**

"Disaster turns reporters into war correspondents—without the training or time to adjust," Margaret Baker of the *Biloxi* (MS) *Sun-Herald*, reflected after Hurricane Katrina devastated their community. She and her colleagues agreed that journalistic first responders need to take care of themselves, too. They advise, if possible, taking a day off "to get out of the disaster zone. Seeing 'normal' helps." This may sound unrealistic, but there's another more powerful reality to consider, the Biloxi journalist added. "If you get mentally or physically sick, you are not doing anyone any good."

Smart news organizations create contingency plans in case of natural disasters and emergencies. Create one for yourself so that if you're called at 4 a.m. one day and told to spend several days at the scene, you've done advance preparation. Pack a survival kit and keep it in your car: protein bars, bottled water, extra clothes, blanket and sleeping bag, weather gear, batteries, flashlight, maps, extra notebooks, pens and pencils. Make sure your digital gear is always charged.

The Coaching Way DISASTERS

- What have you done to prepare yourself to cover a disaster?
- Have you made a gear checklist?
- How faithfully do you record dates and times of events that can become a timeline that's useful for writing a chronological account, or provide to a rewrite person or information graphics artist? Make it a habit on every story so it's second nature when the big story hits.

- How quickly can you tap into online social networks—Twitter, Facebook, Google Plus—to reach students and other young people who communicate that way? Have you already joined these networks?
- Have you asked your supervisor about your organization's policy on providing help to disaster victims? Debate the ethical issues with colleagues.

- How are you going to take care of yourself while covering a disaster?
- Have you studied how other disasters were handled by print, online and broadcast outlets? There's a good chance you'll find coverage on their Web sites. Learn from what they did. Anticipate the scenarios, who they would affect and how and what reporting and writing strategies you'd rely on. ▶

PROFESSIONALS' ROUNDTABLE

WHEN DISASTER STRIKES

No one can predict where disaster will strike, whether it's an earthquake, hurricane or battle. While victims struggle with overwhelming loss and grief, journalists descend on ground zero to tell stories of human suffering and courage, as well as incompetence that compounds the misery. It's a painful assignment, but one you can prepare for, say journalists who've faced destructive forces of nature and man. Their tips:

- There are obvious differences between disasters or battles and a county commission meeting. What remains unchanged: the need to tell stories that connect with audiences.
- Vivid details reveal larger truths and bring readers, viewers and listeners closer to events and those affected by them.
- Take care of yourself. You're no good to anyone if you're sick from overwork or put yourself in harm's way.

Participants

MARTHA RADDATZ, senior foreign affairs correspondent, ABC News, and author, *The Long Road Home: A Story of War and Family*

REBECCA CATALANELLO, former reporter, *St. Petersburg Times*

STEVE BUTTRY, director of community engagement and social media, Digital First Media

---

> *What do reporters need to know when stories break?*

Buttry: Your deadline is now. A single sentence or a few paragraphs are enough to file online. But your standard of accuracy does not change: Don't publish information you have not verified.

> *What's different between disasters and covering city hall or writing a feature?*

Catalanello: There is little comparison. . . . But one thing that is constant is the need to tell a story that the reader can understand, connect with, and hopefully learn something from.

Buttry: You still need to answer the Five W's and How. Verify facts. Use traditional skills such as listening, observation, empathy and hustle and learn new skills such as interactive maps, live blogging, databases, video and social media.

> *Hurricane Katrina struck New Orleans, your hometown. What was covering that story like?*

Catalanello: We tend to do a lot of parachuting in and writing about places we barely know. There's a thrill that comes from being able to write with authority about a place because you know it, you really know it. It's a gift. I don't often have the courage to write with that kind of authority in other communities.

> *How do you prepare yourself for something as horrific as Katrina?*

Catalanello: I don't really think there is any way you CAN prepare for it. You just go.

> *What's the most important lesson you've learned from covering war stories?*

Raddatz: It is easy for journalists to think they will charge into a war zone and find "the truth." It is never that simple. Get as much information as possible to get to the truth.

> *Are there special challenges when you're reporting war for broadcast news?*

Raddatz: It is much harder to blend in, to get people to be themselves or to say what they might say to a print reporter. The most dangerous jobs in broadcast or print are the photographers. You stand out, as do reporters out there trying to do standup.

> *Your stories from New Orleans focused on tiny, but vivid and unforgettable details—the house numbers in a postal worker's notebook, "silver skiffs" transporting nuns. Why?*

Catalanello: A natural disaster begs for these details. A natural disaster is a sensory assignment. You HAVE to tell people what it looks like, feels like, sounds like, the symbols that tell the story.

SUMMARY GUIDE   EMERGENCIES, DISASTERS AND CONFLICTS: FROM WEATHER TO WAR

THE MEDIA'S ROLE

Emergencies, disasters and conflicts test the media's ability to deliver timely and accurate news to audiences hungry for information.

What to Remember → There's a good chance that an emergency, disaster or conflict will someday challenge your skills as a journalist. Despite the proliferation of social media that allows citizens to communicate news, audiences will still turn to professional journalists and trusted news sources.

WHAT'S CHANGED: TECHNOLOGY AND TIMELINESS

In the Internet age, journalists use a variety of hardware, software and social networks to spread timely news when disaster strikes.

What to Remember → Mastery of a range of online and social media skills is a must for reporters covering the wide range of emergencies that make the news. Deadlines may be seconds away, but a commitment to accuracy remains crucial.

WHAT IT TAKES: REPORTING

Whatever your role in disaster coverage, your reporting must be abundant, accurate and fair.

What to Remember → Collect anecdotes, details and quotes to humanize stories. Recognize that your story's focus may rapidly change amid the turmoil of events.

THINK DIGITAL

Collaboration between print, broadcast and online staffs is crucial during emergencies.

What to Remember → Online forms deliver news in near real time and connect information to audiences and those concerned about their loved ones. You will need to be ready and able to work together with many colleagues to provide digital coverage.

VERIFY AND ATTRIBUTE

Rumors, speculation and misinformation abound during emergencies and disasters.

What to Remember → When journalists get the facts wrong, they cause great pain to families and survivors. Always verify and attribute information, and don't rush to publish when in doubt.

STORY STRUCTURES AND WRITING STRATEGIES

Stories about emergencies, disasters and war usually rely on the most basic story form, the inverted pyramid, but others that emphasize storytelling and chronology can communicate suspense and drama.

What to Remember → The inverted pyramid is the story form of choice when disaster strikes. An hourglass or chronological narrative reports the news but also reveals the stories behind events. Carefully reported details from eyewitnesses, scenes and your own observations bring a tragic event to life.

REPORTING PAINFUL TRUTHS

Disaster stories often reveal tragic errors and gruesome images that risk offending audiences with these painful truths.

What to Remember → Journalists must be alert to the possibility of causing unnecessary pain. But the media is society's watchdog and should tell all sides to a story. Strive to balance minimizing harm and maximizing truth telling.

BREAKING NEWS BLOGS

Breaking news blogs combine the strength of social media with the inverted pyramid to report breaking news online.

What to Remember → Blogging, especially under intense pressure, demands solid news judgment, reporting and writing skills. Blogs, tweets and other social media enable news organizations to relay information to frantic relatives in other states and counties, and evacuees relocated far from home.

IN A WAR ZONE: GETTING THE STORY, STAYING SAFE

Journalists who cover wars and other dangerous emergencies bring these stories directly to readers and viewers, but these assignments can be dangerous and sometimes deadly.

What to Remember → Training and learning from experienced reporters can save you from death and injury. Journalists embedded with military units face the added challenge of bonding with those they cover and resisting pressure to report suppressing negative information.

HUMANIZING THE STORY

The plight of human beings should be the focus of most stories about emergencies, disasters and war.

What to Remember → Profiles of victims and survivors require care and sensitive interviewing techniques. The best stories capture the essence of a person's life and death, so seek out relevant and compelling details to focus these mini-biographies.

RESPONDING TO DISASTER: EASING JOURNALISTS' TRAUMA

Journalists covering emergencies face the same challenges as other first responders: long hours, little sleep and physical discomfort.

What to Remember → Journalists are not immune to the physical and emotional stress of emergencies. They need to prepare for these challenges and take care of themselves if they are going to do their job properly.

KEY TERMS

attribute, p. 449
breaking news blog, p. 454
chronological narrative, p. 451
coverage plan, p. 448
embedded journalist, p. 456

evacuees, p. 448
feeds, p. 448
first responders, p. 457
locator map, p. 449
social network, p. 448

tick-tock, p. 451
timeline, p. 452
verify, p. 449
watchdog, p. 453

EXERCISES

1. Study the post–Hurricane Katrina stories by the *New Orleans Times-Picayune* and the *Biloxi* (MS) *Sun Herald* that won the 2006 Pulitzer Prize for Public Service (http://www.pulitzer.org/works/2006 -Public-Service). Identify the various story types used to report breaking news, features and investigations, as well as reporting by photographers and other visual journalists. Pay close attention to the news blogs and other online coverage the newspapers used to maintain contact with readers and allow residents and family members to reach out to one another. In 400 words, describe the most powerful elements of the papers' reporting and explain your choices.

2. Personal experience can bring greater understanding to news reporting. Have you or a friend or family member ever been victimized by a disaster or emergency? If not, interview someone who has been. In 500 words, describe the experience and explore how it might influence the way you report and write such stories.

3. Given the online tools available to journalists, list the various ways you could report news of an emergency or disaster to best communicate breaking news, provide explanations and enable your audience to connect with family and friends.

4. At the scene of a natural disaster, you encounter families and children sorely in need of food and water. Should you stop reporting to help them or not? In 300 words, describe your decision, identify the ethical challenges such a situation raises and justify your actions.

5. Make an inventory of a survival kit that you have ready, should you be dispatched to an emergency.

READINGS

Gastec, Barbara. *Health Writers Handbook*, 2nd ed. Oxford, UK: Blackwell Publishing, 2005.
Health and safety issues follow fast when disaster strikes. This guide provides authoritative information and advice about technical and scientific issues. This knowledge, bolstered by examples of best practice reporting and writing, will make the difference between superficial coverage and news that informs and helps communities struggling to recover from disasters.

West, Bernadette M., et al. *The Reporter's Environmental Handbook*, 3rd ed. New Brunswick, NJ: Rutgers University Press, 2003.
Oil spills and other environmental disasters, hurricanes, tornadoes and other natural emergencies require a firm grasp of the underlying health, environmental and impact issues. This handy reference book includes chapters on environmental and other emergencies, making it an essential resource when disaster strikes.

Terrorism and Other Public Health Emergencies: A Reference Guide for the Media. Washington, DC: U.S. Department of Health and Human Services, 2005.
Developed after the terrorist attacks on Sept. 11, 2001, this is a comprehensive and readable guidebook for journalists reporting on terrorism, ranging from chemical, radiation and biological attacks to other public health emergencies, such as infectious disease outbreaks.

CHAPTER 21

GETTING AND KEEPING A JOB

BY THE END OF THIS CHAPTER,

you should be able to...

> Plan a job search

> Craft a winning résumé in print and online

> Write an effective cover letter

> Build a multimedia portfolio

> Impress potential employers in job interviews

> Enter the industry with a realistic understanding of job prospects, salaries and benefits

> Assess the value of starting at a small operation

> Cultivate professional relationships with editors, sources and colleagues

YOU'VE LEARNED AND practiced the skills needed to succeed as a journalist. The time has come to find a job and translate the lessons you've acquired in the classroom to the newsroom. You'll quickly learn that getting and keeping a journalism job requires the same hard work, accuracy and creativity as do reporting and writing well.

In this chapter you'll learn the process of job hunting, common mistakes that job seekers make and practical ways to avoid them. You'll progress through the job hunt and develop the professional habits that make journalists successful, in their first year and beyond.

GETTING STARTED

The bottom line: To get a job in journalism, you must apply the same creativity, tenacity and accuracy that good reporting and writing demand. There are jobs out there, but they are tougher to find.

Rounds of layoffs have wiped out thousands of jobs at newspapers and radio and TV stations in recent years. Established newspapers such as the *Rocky Mountain News* in Denver and the *Seattle Post-Intelligencer* have gone out of business.

Indeed, the situation is dire at medium to large news organizations. Wall Street demands profitability, and the fastest way to decrease costs is to get rid of experienced journalists with higher salaries and benefits. But that opens the way to newcomers, especially those with digital skills, the most highly prized job qualification.

You may need to ratchet back your dream of walking into a major TV network news show, a major metropolitan newspaper or National Public Radio. Your chances of success increase by starting small, at a local TV or public radio station or community Web site, especially given industry trends that point to a lack of opportunities at major news outlets.

The digital landscape has opened up new opportunities. Jobs can also be found in start-ups and Web sites for established local media organizations. They've become available in hyper-local Web outlets, such as Patch.com, that hire reporters and editors to provide news from communities that mainstream media abandoned in its quest for profitability. The Internet makes it possible to create online outlets without the enormous capital costs that burden news companies that supplement traditional delivery with online sites.

Once it was enough for you to mail a potential employer a cover letter, résumé and samples of your best work. Whether your goal is broadcast, online or print journalism, today you must demonstrate that you also have multimedia skills, including taking and editing photographs and recording and editing video. News organizations want to know you are proficient with editing software and programs that generate data-driven graphics and animations. They expect familiarity with news aggregators and search engines such as Yahoo! and Google. They expect online résumés and portfolios that display your digital skills. They want to see your blogs, tweets, Facebook page and other signs that you use social networks to make connections. Along with all this technological competence, employers still demand solid reporting and writing skills and values that are the foundation of excellent journalism. Here is a step-by-step approach to increase your chances of success.

BEST PRACTICE: GET AN INTERNSHIP

Many college students have heard about **internships** but aren't sure exactly what they are. First impressions may be negative—"Is that where you work for free?"—but there's more to them than first meets the eye.

As a journalism student, you will likely get some valuable writing and reporting experience in classes and in student media (newspaper, magazine, Web site, etc.). You can develop a solid portfolio of work that showcases your strengths based on assignments done for school. The one thing that you're missing at this point, however, is any kind of professional experience. At one time, the journalism industry was thriving to the point that strong classroom clips could get you a job, but those days are gone.

Internships offer college students a chance to prove themselves in the professional ranks. Simply put, news organizations hire college journalists to work inexpensively for set periods (often over the summer), giving the students a little professional experience and the news organizations some cheap help. Many journalism schools require their students to serve at least one internship before graduating, and some students do two or three during their college days. It was commonplace for decades for news organizations to pay interns at least a small stipend—enough to cover the costs of transportation and registering the internship with the student's university. Sadly, many internships today are unpaid due to widespread cost cutting, but paying internships do still exist.

Paid or unpaid, internships provide you with a chance to prove your worth to working professionals who can have beneficial effects on your career. They create networks that you can draw on as you seek work. Smart students seize the opportunity and work their tails off to establish their diligence and their talents among the editors, news directors and reporters with whom they work. Ideally, you can emerge from an internship with several vitally important advantages:

- Professional newsroom experience—knowledge of how professionals handle real-life situations.
- A portfolio of work from a professional news outlet, such as a TV station, online site or newspaper.
- Connections to professional journalists—and in some cases, newsmakers and other sources—that can come in handy later on.
- Solid recommendations from broadcast news directors and top editors who can testify firsthand to the positive impact you've had on a newsroom.
- In the perfect scenario, a job offer.

Even if the organization for which you intern simply has no jobs available, often the connections you make through the internship can give you the break you need to get a first job.

CONVERGENCE POINT ⚡

*Places to Look
for Jobs*

The Poynter Institute Career Center links job seekers with employers. Create a free account, and you can upload a searchable résumé and hunt for available jobs.

You can conduct tailored searches by job types in online, broadcast and print, receive job alerts and locate internships.

TVJobs.com is an "Internet based employment service dedicated to helping you find employment in the highly competitive broadcast marketplace." Its Job Center is free, but the site charges $20–$30 to post résumés.

Find this link on the companion Web site at **www.oup.com/us/ scanlan.**

JOB HUNTING STEP BY STEP

Step 1. Craft a Winning Résumé

A **résumé** is, usually, a one-page summary that gives prospective employers a document that they can scan in a couple of minutes, and in many cases that's all they spend, to find out who you are and whether you are qualified for employment.

Résumés should include journalism experience, such as internships, school news activities, educational achievements, awards or honors. Fluency in second languages, particularly Spanish or Chinese, is a plus. Digital journalism skills are a must, but proficiency in Final Cut Pro won't matter if you lack reporting and writing skills.

A good résumé, like a good story, is clear and direct. Employers want to know who you are, where you've been, what you've done. Don't clutter it up with a job objective up top. That only limits the opportunities a company might see for you.

List your education, work experience and brief details about your assignments. You can include non-journalism jobs as editors look for applicants with real-world experience. Identify the unifying themes behind your experiences and link them to your journalistic ambitions. Special interests and volunteer experiences can be important in demonstrating your success at interacting with the public, leading others and committing yourself to a deadline-based task. Explain gaps; employers spot them and wonder whether you were sailing around the world or just goofing off. For a print résumé, you're safest with good-quality white paper—no pinks or patterns. Save a copy of your updated résumé file on your computer. Ask a journalist friend or professor to critique it. Check and recheck the spelling and style. Include cell phone and fax numbers as well as email addresses. Let employers know the best time and place to reach you. Be easy to find.

QUICK Tips ◔ ANATOMY OF A RÉSUMÉ

- ◼ Your name

- ◼ Address

- ◼ Phone/fax number

- ◼ Email address

- ◼ *Experience*: Include dates of employment (begin with most recent), where you worked, job title and brief description of responsibilities.

- ◼ *Education*: Include the name, city and state of the college or graduate school, major and graduation dates.

- ◼ *Skills*: Include specific competence in foreign languages and digital skills.

- ◼ *Awards and honors*: Reporting and writing awards, scholarships or academic awards.

- ◼ *References*: Include name, title, address and contact information. Be the kind of student that references will quickly remember and be eager to praise. ◤

Don't pad your résumé with trivia. Double-check the accuracy of every fact. Don't inflate your experience, turning an internship into a staff job, for example. Generally, résumés should list two or three references that you can provide prospective employers, along with their contact information. Don't just write "References available on request." Busy editors want that information at their fingertips if your application interests them. Not all recruiters agree, however. They believe references shouldn't be listed unless you are in serious contention for a job. Before you submit your application, check the job advertisement requirements or contact the news outlet directly.

Professional **references**, such as supervisors familiar with your internship performance, are best, followed by journalism teachers. Include each reference's name, title, place of employment, address, phone number and email address. References from friends or relatives are viewed with bias.

Get references' permission. Keep them informed about your progress. Send them stories you're proud of, and alert them when they might be hearing from an editor checking references.

Step 2. Plan Your Search

Sure, you want to be a foreign correspondent for the *Los Angeles Times*, but be realistic. "Face it," says Dan McClintock, creative services director at KJCT TV-8, Grand Junction, Colorado, "unless you are extremely lucky or have a dynamite résumé tape, your first job is going to be with a small-market station or production company in a small city."

Identify four to six news organizations that interest you to begin the search. Tend your list, adding new jobs, updating references, and so on. Include one long shot, but make most of your picks smaller outlets advertising jobs open to newcomers. The Internet has transformed job seeking. Take advantage of online career sites, such as The Poynter Institute's Career Center and JournalismJobs.com, which allow job hunters to post their résumés for free. Post your résumé on LinkedIn, Facebook and other social networks. Craigslist targets writing, editing and online jobs, too, and is available on your mobile phone.

Networking—who you know—has always been a potent force in job searches. Work your internship and alumni connections. Be on the lookout for journalism job fairs and informal meet-ups where online journalists come together in major cities. (Visit http://journalism.meetup.com/ for more information.) If you haven't already, join the Society of Professional Journalists, and, if eligible, minority journalism organizations. Competition for jobs has always been strong, but in a recession any additional and creative steps you can take to stand out can make a difference.

Before you submit an application, always call the news organization to find out where to send it. Aspiring broadcast journalists should consult the *Broadcasting & Cable Yearbook*, which profiles 16,000 radio stations and more than 2,000 television stations in the United States and Canada. Job changes can render directories, even those posted on the company Web site, obsolete. Always call to make sure listings are accurate.

SEE CLOSE-UP AT WWW.OUP.COM/US/ SCANLAN: RÉSUMÉ

CONVERGENCE POINT

Pet Peeves About Job Applications From Broadcast Journalists

News directors and other hiring executives list the things that drive them crazy about job applications for jobs in broadcast journalism. Among them: generic cover letters, implying you are a full-time staffer when you are an intern and applying for a job that calls for 3–5 years' experience when you are just out of school.

Find this link on the companion Web site at **www.oup.com/us/ scanlan.**

Step 3. Select and Package Samples of Your Work

Your work will always be your best résumé. In the newspaper world, they're known as "**clips**," short for "clippings," and that name is still used, even for stories hyperlinked from an online résumé. Broadcast job seekers should send a **résumé tape** or DVD with samples of their radio or television stories. How many clips should you send? No more than six to eight stories with your application; an editor can always ask for more. Remember: The work you produce as a student journalist, an intern, a staffer or contributor to the campus Web site—and even classroom assignments—can demonstrate your range and capabilities.

Effective **portfolios** demonstrate that you can handle standard journalistic tasks: report and write on deadline, cover meetings and generate story ideas.

Include the following story types:

1. One or two stories that you reported and wrote on daily deadline: a meeting, speech or public safety story
2. A story that you wrote on assignment and one that was your idea
3. A feature story about a trend or a profile of a person
4. A multimedia story, such as an audio or video interview
5. A personal essay on a serious or light topic

Sheryl James attracted the attention of editors at the *St. Petersburg* (FL) *Times* with a whimsical piece on pantyhose. Hired in news features, she went on to win a Pulitzer Prize. Pick only your very best work. If you don't have published clips, provide samples of writing for class assignments or freelance projects you have submitted for publication. Keep it simple, and make sure nothing in your package is bigger than 8½ × 11 inches so editors can photocopy the package for others in the newsroom to read. Instead of reducing the print so small an editor needs a magnifying glass, take the time to arrange the story on more than one page. Usually clips that have appeared in print are more visually impressive than online-only material, but don't be shy about including URLs of online work that showcase print, broadcast and multimedia abilities.

If you post your résumé online and link to stories, editors can quickly and easily view your work.

Step 4. Best Foot Forward: Write Your Cover Letter

After you've selected your clips, turn your attention to your **cover letter**, which will be the first item in your application. Keep it short, sincere and to the point.

Select the aspect of your journalism work, personality, background or whatever feature best illustrates who you are and what contributions you can make, and reflect that in your cover letter. Make sure your letter doesn't sound generic—identify specifics from the job announcement that mesh well with your skills. Demonstrate your familiarity with their stories and coverage. Don't think you can wait for the interview to show what you're made of and why you're the best person for the job; you may not get the chance. Express passion in your cover letter to cause an editor to say, "I want to meet this person."

CONVERGENCE POINT ✂

How to Write a Compelling Cover Letter

Veteran recruiter and author of a job-seeking guide Joe Grimm provides solid tips to ensure your cover letter makes an impression. A link takes you to examples of outstanding cover letters and what he calls "non-starters," and an argument that job objectives on a résumé can hurt rather than help your chances.

Find this link on the companion Web site at **www.oup.com/us/ scanlan.**

You can also use the cover letter to briefly comment on your work, or you can attach a separate sheet or notes to individual stories that provide pertinent background, such as the fact that you had just two hours to report and write a breaking story, or liveblogged an event. If you were the only reporter to get an interview with an inmate on death row, or if your essay was published in *Harper's* magazine, don't be shy about it. The last paragraph in your cover letter should be a promise to follow up with the editor in a week.

Step 5. Making Them Want You: The Successful Job Interview and Follow Up

If you're lucky, you'll be called in for a job interview. Here's how to make the most of it:

- *Take special care in your appearance*. Wear professional attire. For women, a suit or pantsuit. For men, a suit or jacket, and tie.
- *Prepare well*. Research the organization and the interviewer; familiarize yourself with the outlet's content and style.
- *Bring a notebook*. Take notes during the interview. You're a journalist; act like one.
- *Let the interviewer talk*. Don't interrupt. At some point, the interviewer will say, "Do you have any questions?" This is not the time to ask about salary, benefits or vacation time; instead ask, "What do you need?" The question can transform a job interview into a collaborative conversation.

After your interview, be sure to write a brief letter or email thanking the person who interviewed you. If you met the top editors or others who play a role in hiring, write them too. It's common courtesy and also a way to keep you in the forefront of their minds. Repeat why you want to join the staff, and refer, if you can, to some aspect of the interview. Mention how you think you can contribute.

THE WORLD WIDE RÉSUMÉ

A cover letter and résumé, photocopies of best stories carefully slipped into a stamped 8½ × 11–inch envelope or a DVD of broadcast work sent to an editor, and a self-addressed, stamped envelope for a reply. That's how journalists carried out job hunts before the advent of the Internet.

Today it's the rare recruiter or hiring editor who doesn't use the Internet to accept résumés and work samples that are a few keystrokes away. Paper résumés aren't dead, but they have increasingly been replaced by online résumés and portfolios. Students at the Columbia University Graduate School of Journalism use WordPress as a blog platform to create personalized Web sites including their résumés, print stories, photographs, audio slide shows, photo galleries and video stories, blog posts, podcasts, videocasts and tweets.

> ❝ The secret to a good cover letter is to seize on the most interesting work you've done or experiences you've had and to tell about them in a brief, but compelling way. ❞
>
> —JOE GRIMM, COLUMNIST, "ASK THE RECRUITER," HTTP://WWW.POYNTER.ORG/CATEGORY/HOW-TOS/CAREER-DEVELOPMENT/ASK-THE-RECRUITER/

CONVERGENCE POINT ⤵

The Worldwide Résumé: Posting Your Clips Online

Online pioneer Jonathan Dube lays out the argument for posting your résumé online, the importance of creating a Web site and practical tips to produce one.

Find this link on the companion Web site at **www.oup.com/us/scanlan.**

Personal Web sites give job candidates, such as Pakistani freelance broadcast journalist Mahawish Rezvi, the opportunity to display their print, online and broadcast samples, making it easy for employers to review their work.

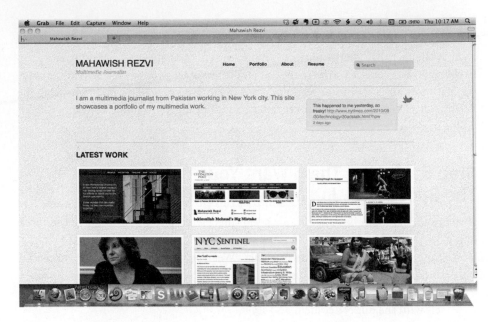

66 I've gotten a number of job offers in the past five years—including the ones at ABCNews.com and MSNBC.com—without ever mailing a single piece of paper. **99**

—JONATHAN DUBE,
GENERAL MANAGER, CBS
FANTASY SPORTS

"Long gone are the days of mailing in résumés," says Mahawish Rezvi, a Pakistani broadcast journalist who earned a master's degree in 2010 from the Graduate School of Journalism at Columbia University. "In this day and age of 'shoot me an email' employers don't open envelopes, they open their inboxes and to get the job your résumé has to be one click away.

"Along with the résumé, as a journalist the best thing that speaks for your talents is your work itself." Rezvi created a Web site featuring stories she reported for television in her native country. "As a multimedia journalist my clips include print, video, audio slideshows, and photographs. One of the fastest and most convenient—and, slowly, the only way—to display your work is by putting it on your own personal Web site."

"An online résumé also has the advantage of demonstrating to an employer that you have multimedia skills," says Jonathan Dube, a new media pioneer who first created a Web site in 1996 that allowed editors to read his résumé and browse through his stories from their computers.

JOB PROSPECTS, SALARIES AND BENEFITS

New journalists face a daunting, but not unattainable, reality as they enter the job market. Competition is fierce, starting salaries are relatively low, and strong skills and experience a must. That has always been the reality, although one worsened in today's economy. But there are signs for optimism.

For more than 20 years, Professor Lee B. Becker and colleagues have surveyed journalism and mass communication graduates to assess the job market for beginning journalists. The group's August 2012 survey of recent graduates found that the news industry was struggling with the same economic woes as the country as a whole. Like the rest of the nation's workforce, today's graduates still face a job market hit hard by the financial crisis of 2008 that contributes to high unemployment rates.

But the employment picture for graduates showed that things were getting a little better than in previous years, especially for candidates with Web skills (see Figure 21-1). While these figures encompassed all journalism, advertising and public relations graduates, the study revealed good news for those focusing on reporting the news.

Among the study's top findings:

- "The job market for graduates of the nation's journalism and mass communication programs showed signs of improvements in 2011 and 2012, continuing the trend from a year earlier."

- "The 2011 graduates were more likely to report having a job upon graduation, more likely to report having a full-time job, and more likely to be working in communication than were graduates a year earlier."

- "The level of bachelor's degree recipients' full-time employment [as of Oct. 31, 2011] was 53.3%, up more than three percentage points from the same date in 2010."

- "Those graduates who had specialized in news-editorial journalism—the traditional print base of journalism and mass communication education—reported a hefty increase in level of full-time employment in 2011 compared with a year earlier . . . The job market –[for broadcast majors improved] in 2011 compared with the year earlier."

- But, the researchers cautioned, "The recovery has quite some distance to go."

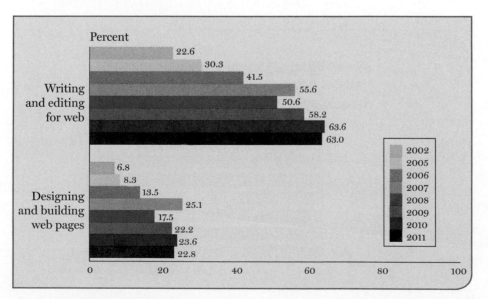

FIGURE 21-1 Web skills improve employment chances, as shown in this 2012 chart, which shows the emergence of a majority of communications graduates doing Web writing and editing between 2004 and 2011. For nearly two-thirds of graduates, Web work is part of their daily workload, a survey by the Grady College of Journalism and Mass Communication at the University of Georgia found.

Says Ross Crystal, a Los Angeles-based broadcast journalist for 25 years: "Throughout my career, every time I would try to get a job, I always heard, 'Oh, the budget is tight. We don't have the budget, it's very tight.' I never heard when it wasn't tight. But there are jobs out there."

Increasingly, they are going to journalists who have the right blend of new and old skills.

As traditional media give way in today's digital landscape, Web skills play a huge role in the workplace. Among all journalism and mass communication graduates, "two-thirds of those who found work in communication in were involved with writing and editing for the web," the University of Georgia survey found. The message is clear: If you didn't learn online skills in college, it's imperative that you take your own steps to get the training you need. It's widely available on the Web, often for free.

Once you find a journalism job, you face a sobering reality—you won't make as much money as graduates in other fields.

Beginning reporters at daily newspapers reported median yearly salaries of $28,000 in 2011, a slight increase and one that beat inflation. Reporters at weekly papers, which vastly outnumber dailies, earn $26,000, on average, up from $24,690 the year before. (A 2012 survey by the National Associate of Colleges and employers pegged the average starting salary for all communication graduates at nearly $41,000, but many journalists objected, arguing that their experience showed otherwise. Veteran hiring editor Joe Grimm said he considered the University of Georgia survey more reliable.) (See Figure 21-2.)

Benefits, the lifeline of health insurance and prescription drug coverage, remained stagnant with about half the journalism and mass communication graduates reporting that their employers paid only part of their basic medical coverage.

Television journalists as a rule make less—about $25,000 a year—than print and online journalists, although their salaries went up for the third year in a row.

FIGURE 21-2 Median salaries for journalism and mass communication bachelor's degree recipients stood at $31,000 in 2011, up from $30,000 the year before, according to the latest annual (2012) survey conducted by the Grady College of Journalism and Mass Communication at the University of Georgia.

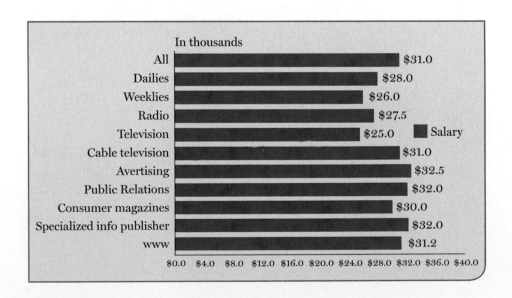

Journalists who find work online bring home the biggest paychecks, according to an informal survey by Will Sullivan, director of Mobile News for Lee Enterprises and an Online News Association board member. Salaries for Web or online producers—"the backbone of most online news Web sites"—range from $30,000 to $40,000 a year, Sullivan found.

Despite these economic challenges, most new journalists—44 percent, the highest figure since 1987—said they were "very satisfied" with their chosen field. "Follow what you genuinely enjoy doing   not the name, not even the salary—but the work itself," a 2010 graduate working for a news wire service told the researchers.

And before you throw your clips into the trash and apply to law school, consider what Eric Crawford, an assistant sports editor at *The Evansville* (IN) *Courier and Press*, had to say about career choice:

> What we do as reporters isn't easy, and yet friends of mine from college in a variety of fields have bolted past me in earnings, benefits, etc. But an experience at a wedding . . . helped put things back into perspective. I was seated at a table with people from a number of high-paying jobs, and while I was envious of what I imagined everybody's salary must be, every guy at that table would've traded a large portion of that salary to do what I do for a living. It is a special profession, and there are rewards beyond the money.

THE CASE FOR STARTING OUT SMALL

News stories ringing the death knell for the newspaper business give a skewed picture of the industry's health. They ignore the well-being of small newspapers—dailies and weeklies with circulation of 50,000 and below.

"Just about all of the research and news reports on the 'struggling' newspaper industry have been based on what's happening at the top 100 major metropolitan newspapers, maybe the top 250," said Brian Steffens, executive director of the National Newspaper Association. "That doesn't tell the story of the remaining 1,200 daily newspapers or 8,000 community weekly papers in America." Better job chances are part of that story. It also doesn't include the opportunities at free newspapers, such as *AM New York* and *tbt* in St. Petersburg, Florida, which emerged in force in the last decade and number more than 3,000 in the United States, according to the Association of Free Community Newspapers. Alternative newsweeklies, which number about 150 nationwide, also provide a valuable training ground.

There are other several other advantages of starting out at small news outlets, according to the late Jim Naughton, who interviewed thousands of reporters and hired hundreds during his 18 years as an editor at *The Philadelphia Inquirer*. They include the following:

- "At a small newspaper you have to do everything, and you make discoveries about your own work and yourself.
- You'll learn what you are good at but hate to do, and what you're not good at but love.

- If you make a mistake, it will probably have lesser consequences in a smaller newsroom.
- Smaller organizations may give the opportunity to take on many different tasks. You'll get to do everything there is to do.
- A smaller organization gives you an opportunity to test yourself in ways that are less threatening."

Journalist at Work LESSONS FROM A FIRST JOB IN JOURNALISM

Karen B. Dunlap is president of The Poynter Institute, where she joined the faculty in 1989. She was a reporter for the *Macon* (GA) *News* and the *Nashville* (TN) *Banner* and staff writer at the *St. Petersburg Times*. She taught journalism at Tennessee State University in Nashville, and at the University of South Florida in Tampa. Dunlap is a graduate of Michigan State University and Tennessee State University, and received her Ph.D. from the University of Tennessee. She has been honored with the Gerald M. Sass Distinguished Service Award from the Association of Schools of Journalism and Mass Communication and the Missouri Honor Medal from the University of Missouri School of Journalism. Here she remembers the lessons of learning, tolerance and cooperation from her first journalism job.

My first journalism job after college was with a small newspaper. A very small newspaper.

I started as editor of the *Warner Robins Enterprise*, a Georgia weekly owned by a real estate tycoon. Not only was I editor, but also I was senior writer, intern reporter, feature writer, food writer, editorial writer and ghostwriter for the publisher's column.

In addition to writing, I was the photographer when the circulation guy wouldn't take pictures. At about 2 a.m. on production night, I became typesetter when the real typesetter's husband called her home.

I learned that I should have paid attention to my college classes in design and headline writing. In school my mind was only on writing, but now I searched my notes and memory for pointers on page makeup and copy editing.

I learned to write quickly and on a range of topics. I covered business openings and city council meetings but also stories of individual success or family distress, as well as the ever-present "Kitchen of the Week."

I learned to respect all jobs in the production process because, at various times, I had to do each job.

I learned to respect all the people I worked with. We were a small group working in a compact office. If dissension broke out and someone stormed out, chances were I would have to finish that job. I was committed to peace and good will by respecting all.

I learned that there is a thin line between editorial and advertising, but sinners can always find redemption with excuses about the bottom line.

I learned to talk past differences. Warner Robins, with nearly an all-white

establishment, awoke to find that the *Enterprise*'s new editor was a 21-year-old black woman with an Angela Davis Afro. I needed their stories. They liked seeing their names in print. We talked.

I learned I needed to know about the community to avoid making errors or just looking silly. The library and conversations with townspeople were my shortcut to learning the history and culture of the place.

I learned that my labor in a small market provided an opening to a larger newspaper. For me, the next step was the *Macon News*.

Most of all I learned to appreciate the small newspaper that gave me a chance to learn and grow while practicing the craft I love.

Years later I taught journalism students who shunned small papers. They expected to start at a leading daily or at least a mid-sized newspaper. Some laughed when they learned of openings with smaller papers. I frowned and told them they would probably end up tossing burgers instead of reporting news. Then I would recall the production night of the *Warner Robins Enterprise*. My students didn't know the experience, the challenges, the fun that they were missing. ▶

ADVICE FOR NEW REPORTERS

Erin Caddell, a Poynter Institute summer reporting and writing fellow, compiled the following list of tips soon after landing his first journalism job. They apply equally for newcomers to broadcast and online journalists.

"My first reporting job was at *The Keene Sentinel*, an afternoon daily in southwestern New Hampshire, with a circulation of about 15,000. In my first few months of beat writing I learned several lessons about one's first reporting job."

- *Build sources or die.* Building sources is a critical part of any reporter's job, but especially a new one. Get past the pat questions and answers to explore the background behind your topic and those you interview. News is about people and relationships. In order to understand the news, you need to know the relationships.

- *Always call back.* Even if it's past deadline, and the story you were working on for that day is done. Just call or stop by to thank that person for getting back to you. Ask a question that can help you with a future story.

- *Take advantage of the "honeymoon period."* Rather than pretending you're somebody you're not, use your ignorance to your advantage. Let everybody know that you're an outsider. When you're starting out on a beat, you have a chance to ask the big questions: What are the biggest challenges facing the police department in the next year? How's morale among city employees? These questions won't be so easy to ask once you're writing difficult stories that may make sources upset and less reluctant to talk to you.

- *Get the little things right.* When you're starting out, you won't know every last little detail of the topics you write about. But you can bet that your readers and your sources do. As a reporter, particularly in a small community, all you have is your reputation. If people know that you will get it right, they will return your calls, drop hints for other stories and won't dismiss your questions. The little things are easy to forget, but they can take the wind out of an otherwise great story. Conversely, if you gain a reputation as someone who misspells names, messes up quotes or makes minor factual errors, you can be branded faster than you think.

- *Manage mistakes.* If a mistake should make it into the paper, and you catch it, try to notify the person or persons affected by the error before they see it, even if you should run a correction the next day. That way they know what's coming and know that you care enough to notify them. It's better than being thought of as just another reporter who doesn't get it right.

- *Surprise your readers, but not your editors.* Everybody wants to make a good impression. But remember that the newspaper didn't start publishing the day you arrived. Your editors can be a great resource to learn the paper's writing style and the way it covers stories. They also can provide context for the issues you're covering and what's already "out there."

- *Know when to say "no."* When you're new and trying to prove yourself you will instinctively try to do all that is asked of you. But know your limits. If you're running out of time, and you don't think you can get all your stories done in a particular week, say so. Your editors may be disappointed, but they'll understand. If they didn't believe in you, they wouldn't have hired you in the first place.

- *Use the clips, but don't be wedded to them.* Everything you write about has a history. When I was assigned stories early on and didn't know much about them, I would look through the clip file and read them pretty thoroughly before I did my own reporting. I'd feel like I wanted to have a sense of the situation before I ventured into uncharted territory and talked to people who had never heard of me. Conversely, you should cover a story differently from anyone who has come before. Use the clips judiciously and your own style will have more of a chance to come through.

- *Follow your instincts.* Your editors may be saying one thing. The reporters from the rival paper or the local TV station covering the same story may be doing something else. But a voice in your head is telling you to do a third thing that is altogether different. Listen to that voice. Do what you have to do to avoid giving your editor fits, and don't try to change things overnight. But don't ignore your instincts. Think about what isn't said at the meeting. Look for what nobody is talking about yet. Following those impulses will distinguish your stories.

- *Be a salesperson.* Early on, you may get assignments from the bottom of an editor's list. But don't think that's where they have to stay. An editor likes nothing more than a brief that turns into a front-page story and will reward the reporter who makes it happen with better assignments next time around.

- *Have fun.* Sometimes it will seem like there is no end to the stories you need to write, the appointments you need to make, the facts you need to check. Take a step back. Go for a walk in the park you've written about but haven't seen. Clip your best stories and send them to your mom or a former teacher. Reporting is a great business. It allows freedom to learn, explore, be creative and have an impact while getting paid.

Ethical Dilemmas ❗ DOING THE RIGHT THING

Over drinks at a bar, a newsroom friend lets slip that he has been hacking into the computers of his colleagues. He says he's just curious about what they're up to. You tell him that it's wrong and he should stop, but he insists that it's just harmless fun. You're horrified, but not sure what to do with the information. You decide to end your friendship, but worry whether that's enough. You consider your options: pretend you don't know anything about it, alert your colleagues or anonymously inform your superiors, knowing that last step will likely cost your friend his job. What do you do, and how do you justify your decision? ▸

The Coaching Way ⲃ GETTING AND KEEPING A JOB

- In one sentence, write down the one thing that you think a potential employer should know about you. Some examples: "I am still learning and anxious to keep the news business alive," "I am the type of reporter who brings the same passion for reporting and writing to a flower show and a breaking news story" and "I'm as comfortable with Flash as I am with Microsoft Word."

- At a job interview, pretend you're interviewing the interviewer for a story about the news organization.

Ask, "What are your needs?" You'll impress the editor or news director with your curiosity. Remember that he or she is looking for journalists. Act like one.

- Develop digital skills news organizations are looking for, or commit to do so today.

- Be honest. Don't call an editor and say you're So-and-So from *The Boston Globe* or CNN if you're just interning there. Don't inflate your qualifications or experience on your résumé. Employers want,

and journalism needs, people with character.

- Join the Society of Professional Journalists (you can visit its Web site at http://www.spj.org/) and/or enroll in a minority journalism group if you qualify. With chapters in most states and many large cities, those groups are especially helpful if you're moving to a new area and are looking for connections or new friends.

- Once you get that job, be the kind of person you'd like to work with. ▸

Journalist at Work ✎ THE RIGHT ATTITUDE

David Maraniss

Attitude is everything.

David Maraniss is a Pulitzer Prize–winning reporter who often devotes months to investigations, series and books at *The Washington Post*, but when news breaks, he's one of the first to pitch in. "Even if I'm doing a series, I say, 'Look, if you guys need me, I'd be happy to do something.'"

In many newsrooms, reporters and editors are natural enemies, who hinder rather than help each other. They cheat themselves of the opportunity to collaborate, to meet halfway, and benefit from the result. Many of these battles end badly, says Maraniss, who has worked as an editor and reporter during his three decades at the *Post*. "So

many reporters keep banging away at their editors and having frustrating confrontations about what they have to do or don't have to do." Yet Maraniss—a veteran, accomplished journalist—brings to his job the attitude of an eager young journalist willing to take on any assignment and make the most of it. "I like newspapers, and I love to write on deadline. And so I volunteer." That approach pays off beyond expectations. "One of the reasons I do that is so that there's a fair exchange, where they know that I'm always around when they need me, and then in return, I get a lot of freedom the rest of the time to do what I want to do." ▸

PROFESSIONALS'

ROUNDTABLE

GETTING A JOB AND KEEPING IT

Journalism jobs exist, recruiters and hiring executives agree, but they're going to journalists who know how to report and write with words, pictures, sound and video. None of these matter, they add, if the applicant can't demonstrate mastery of reporting and writing basics that remain the foundation of good journalism. Their tips:

1. Understand the various ways that audiences consume news and information and care how to meet them.
2. Master digital skills—social networking, blogging, video—along with traditional reporting and writing requirements.
3. Bring passion and preparation for digital journalism to increase your chances of winning jobs.

Participants

JOE GRIMM, "Ask the Recruiter" columnist, and former recruiting and development editor, *Detroit Free Press*

ROB KING, editor-in-chief, ESPN.com

ARLENE MORGAN, former assistant managing editor for readership, hiring and staff, *The Philadelphia Inquirer*

> *What are you looking for in a potential hire?*

King: Solid journalism and writing skills. A deep understanding of what it means to publish in the digital space. Mastery of multiple forms of writing (narrative, blogging, social media updating), and facility with multimedia, particularly in video. Audiences operate in multiple ways, so any hire should be prepared to do so, too. Some experience. Authority is everything in this space.

Morgan: Someone who is pretty selfless about his or her role as a journalist and the social responsibility that involves.

> *What do job hunters do that directs their applications into the trash?*

King: On-air talent résumés for editing jobs, form letters. Queries from newsroom contributors who never took a step into the digital space . . . no blogging, no tweeting, no podcasting, and evidently, no interest.

Morgan: People who want to know what the organization can do for them.

> *What changes have you seen in employer expectations, such as multimedia skills, over the last decade?*

King: Enormous change in the last two years, let alone the last decade. Social media, video and audio podcasting and blogging have exploded not only as necessary skills, but perhaps more importantly, as expectations of audiences. The definition of an ideal candidate is very much a moving target. This means that anyone applying for a job these days must have a much broader range of core competencies. At the same time, the very best candidate must also have at least one area of expertise, whether it's a particular subject or a unique skill.

Morgan: Expectations that the candidate can hit the ground running with little or no feedback or tutoring is much more dominant than it used to be. Every hire is precious and there just is not the leeway to take a chance on someone.

> *Are there jobs out there?*

King: I think so. I see a lot of energy being devoted to serving local audiences better, to reimagining the frequency and depth of reporting, and to identifying ways to tell stories simultaneously across multiple platforms. We're doing it, large networks are doing it, regional sports networks are doing it, professional leagues and teams are doing it, and newspapers are beginning this work. The issue in newspapers, however, is changing internal culture, both in terms of identifying existing staff willing to adopt these new skills or making room for new contributors who are ready to step in and do the work.

Grimm: Today's most passionate journalists will find news operations that let them practice their trade, or they will invent their own ways. The barriers are down and there is nothing to keep them away from journalism, not even when jobs are scarce. They will put themselves to work.

Morgan: There are jobs for those who can think about a story across platforms. And I think there are jobs for young reporters and editors who are not afraid to try new approaches, including using blogs and interactive discussions to connect with readers.

> *What's the best advice you can give someone trying to get and keep their job?*

King: Pay attention to how audiences are changing, and never stop trying to be where they are. Bring solutions and ideas, contribute video or audio, blog, connect with audiences through social media.

Morgan: Be passionate about all the new things that a journalist can do and then do it. Stay out of the office "gloom and doom" politics. Think about the story and you will do okay.

> *The salary at the news organization that wants to hire me is way too low for my needs? What can I do?*

Grimm: As journalists, we can wheedle information out of the balkiest source, but we are very timid about negotiating for our own security. Do this before you go into a negotiation: Look up the CEO's compensation. That will likely give you the temerity to ask for more . . . Ask, ask, ask, even if you expect to be turned down. If you don't ask, you sure won't get.

SUMMARY GUIDE   GETTING AND KEEPING A JOB

GETTING STARTED

Times are very tough in the news business, but there are still jobs out there, and new journalists are continuing to find work in print, broadcast and online news outlets, especially those who bring multimedia skills.

What to Remember → Starting at a smaller news outlet may be your best way to reach your dream of a journalism career. Take creative approaches to job hunting. Never give up.

BEST PRACTICE: GET AN INTERNSHIP

Internships offer college students a chance to prove themselves in the professional ranks.

What to Remember → Paid or unpaid, internships provide you with a chance to prove your worth to working professionals who can have beneficial effects on your career. Smart students seize the opportunity to establish their work ethic and their talents.

JOB HUNTING STEP BY STEP

Job hunting is a process with five steps: crafting a winning résumé, planning your search, selecting and packaging your work, writing a compelling cover letter and preparing for interviews.

What to Remember → Each step demands creativity, attention to accuracy and looking for ways to make employers want you. Your work is your best argument for a job. If you land an interview, dress appropriately, show you've done your homework and demonstrate that you can match an organization's needs.

THE WORLD WIDE RÉSUMÉ

The Internet has transformed the journalistic job search and requires new skills and approaches.

What to Remember → Post your résumé online. Create a personal Web site. Include examples of multimedia experience. Show that you've embraced the world of digital journalism.

JOBS PROSPECTS, SALARIES AND BENEFITS

The recession has hit the news industry hard, with students reporting a weak market and stagnant salaries and benefits, but there are reasons to be optimistic.

What to Remember → A sharp awareness of the changing media landscape requires applicants to bring multimedia and social media skills and to search out nontraditional possibilities. You won't get rich, but journalism offers other rewards—watching history in the making from a front row seat, serving local communities and using your talents.

THE CASE FOR STARTING OUT SMALL

That job at a large newspaper or broadcast station may be out of reach now, but smaller news outlets offer opportunities to start a journalism career.

What to Remember → Small news organizations provide many opportunities to test your skills, try new things and make important contributions that are stepping-stones to bigger opportunities. At any job, a professional attitude is essential.

ADVICE FOR NEW REPORTERS

Beginning reporters face enormous challenges at their first job, but there are many ways to make sure you and your work stand out

What to Remember → Success during your first year in a journalism job depends on cultivating sources, knowing the background of stories you're assigned to, following your instincts, getting the little things right, learning when to say "no," and having fun despite the challenges.

KEY TERMS

clips, p. 470

cover letter, p. 470

internship, p. 467

portfolio, p. 470

references, p. 469

résumé, p. 468

résumé tape, p. 470

EXERCISES

1. Write your résumé and cover letter using the guidelines in this chapter as a model.

2. Produce an online résumé, including your clips and any multimedia stories you developed, and post them to a Web site you've created to display your work.

3. Prepare a résumé tape of your best broadcast work. Upload your work to your Web site.

4. Write three different cover letters, each with a different focus that spells out your qualities and background and why you want to work for a particular news organization.

5. Interview journalists who work for print, broadcast and online news organizations. Ask them why they chose a career that doesn't pay as well as others and if they are happy with their choice. Ask for copies of their résumés, résumé tapes, links to Web sites and cover letters; also ask them to describe successful and unsuccessful job interviews. Solicit their best advice for getting and keeping a job. Map out a job-seeking plan based on what you learned.

6. Prepare a one-page report on a news organization you'd like to work for. List circulation and/or market size, ownership, competition and political affiliation, as well as your analysis of one week's worth of its reporting and writing style and the major news stories covered during that week. Finally, answer the question "Would I want to work here?"

READINGS

Burns, Jennifer Bobrow. *Career Opportunities in Journalism.* New York: Ferguson Publishing Co., 2007.
This guide offers practical advice to students seeking jobs in journalism. It focuses on the need to assess your skills, interests and values; how to analyze your experience; ways to add skills that will make employers want you; and the importance of exploring the jobs market and networking. It also includes materials to help you fine-tune your résumé and write targeted cover letters.

Carroll, Mike. *Breaking Into TV News: How to Get a Job and Excel as a TV Reporter-Photographer.* Charleston, SC: Create Space, 2012.
The author, a veteran TV journalist, offers in-depth interviews with TV news professionals about their job-hunting experiences and news directors who outline what they look for in prospective hires.

Grimm, Joe. *Breaking In: The JobsPage.com Guide to Newspaper Internships.* Canton, MI: David Crumm Media, 2008.
Grimm, a hiring editor with decades of experience advising job candidates and creator of the JobsPage.com Web site, shares his tips and techniques landing a job in journalism. Rich with examples, leavened with humor, it focuses on the job-seeking process and highlights ways to avoid pitfalls that can mean the difference between success and failure.

Swann, Phil, and Achorn, Edward. *How to Land a Job in Journalism.* White Hall, VA: Betterway Publications, 1988.
Although this book is dated, you'll still find good advice on résumés, cover letters and the best ways to handle a job interview. Worst and best practices are revealed through a variety of concrete examples and solid counsel: "Play up your strengths, but don't inflate them" and "Many editors use the cover letter to weed out candidates."

APPENDIX: SOCIETY OF PROFESSIONAL JOURNALISTS CODE OF ETHICS

PREAMBLE

Members of the Society of Professional Journalists believe that public enlightenment is the forerunner of justice and the foundation of democracy. The duty of the journalist is to further those ends by seeking truth and providing a fair and comprehensive account of events and issues. Conscientious journalists from all media and specialties strive to serve the public with thoroughness and honesty. Professional integrity is the cornerstone of a journalist's credibility. Members of the Society share a dedication to ethical behavior and adopt this code to declare the Society's principles and standards of practice.

Seek Truth and Report It

Journalists should be honest, fair and courageous in gathering, reporting and interpreting information.

JOURNALISTS SHOULD:

- Test the accuracy of information from all sources and exercise care to avoid inadvertent error. Deliberate distortion is never permissible.
- Diligently seek out subjects of news stories to give them the opportunity to respond to allegations of wrongdoing.
- Identify sources whenever feasible. The public is entitled to as much information as possible on sources' reliability.
- Always question sources' motives before promising anonymity. Clarify conditions attached to any promise made in exchange for information. Keep promises.
- Make certain that headlines, news teases and promotional material, photos, video, audio, graphics, sound bites and quotations do not misrepresent. They should not oversimplify or highlight incidents out of context.
- Never distort the content of news photos or video Image enhancement for technical clarity is always permissible. Label montages and photo illustrations.

- Avoid misleading re-enactments or staged news events. If re-enactment is necessary to tell a story, label it.
- Avoid undercover or other surreptitious methods of gathering information except when traditional open methods will not yield information vital to the public. Use of such methods should be explained as part of the story.
- Never plagiarize.
- Tell the story of the diversity and magnitude of the human experience boldly, even when it is unpopular to do so.
- Examine their own cultural values and avoid imposing those values on others.
- Avoid stereotyping by race, gender, age, religion, ethnicity, geography, sexual orientation, disability, physical appearance or social status.
- Support the open exchange of views, even views they find repugnant.
- Give voice to the voiceless; official and unofficial sources of information can be equally valid.
- Distinguish between advocacy and news reporting. Analysis and commentary should be labeled and not misrepresent fact or context.
- Distinguish news from advertising and shun hybrids that blur the lines between the two.
- Recognize a special obligation to ensure that the public's business is conducted in the open and that government records are open to inspection.

Minimize Harm

Ethical journalists treat sources, subjects and colleagues as human beings deserving of respect.

JOURNALISTS SHOULD:

- Show compassion for those who may be affected adversely by news coverage. Use special sensitivity when dealing with children and inexperienced sources or subjects.
- Be sensitive when seeking or using interviews or photographs of those affected by tragedy or grief:
- Recognize that gathering and reporting information may cause harm or discomfort. Pursuit of the news is not a license for arrogance.
- Recognize that private people have a greater right to control information about themselves than do public officials and others who seek power, influence or attention. Only an overriding public need can justify intrusion into anyone's privacy.
- Show good taste. Avoid pandering to lurid curiosity.
- Be cautious about identifying juvenile suspects or victims of sex crimes.
- Be judicious about naming criminal suspects before the formal filing of charges.
- Balance a criminal suspect's fair trial rights with the public's right to be informed.

Act Independently

Journalists should be free of obligation to any interest other than the public's right to know.

JOURNALISTS SHOULD:

- Avoid conflicts of interest, real or perceived.
- Remain free of associations and activities that may compromise integrity or damage credibility.
- Refuse gifts, favors, fees, free travel and special treatment, and shun secondary employment, political involvement, public office and service in community organizations if they compromise journalistic integrity.
- Disclose unavoidable conflicts.
- Be vigilant and courageous about holding those with power accountable.
- Deny favored treatment to advertisers and special interests and resist their pressure to influence news coverage.
- Be wary of sources offering information for favors or money; avoid bidding for news.

Be Accountable

Journalists are accountable to their readers, listeners, viewers and each other.

JOURNALISTS SHOULD:

- Clarify and explain news coverage and invite dialogue with the public over journalistic conduct.
- Encourage the public to voice grievances against the news media.
- Admit mistakes and correct them promptly.
- Expose unethical practices of journalists and the news media.
- Abide by the same high standards to which they hold others.

The SPJ Code of Ethics is voluntarily embraced by thousands of journalists, regardless of place or platform, and is widely used in newsrooms and classrooms as a guide for ethical behavior. The code is intended not as a set of "rules" but as a resource for ethical decision-making. It is not—nor can it be under the First Amendment—legally enforceable.

The present version of the code was adopted by the 1996 SPJ National Convention, after months of study and debate among the Society's members. Sigma Delta Chi's first Code of Ethics was borrowed from the American Society of Newspaper Editors in 1926. In 1973, Sigma Delta Chi wrote its own code, which was revised in 1984, 1987 and 1996.

GLOSSARY

abstraction ladder
A graphical device that helps organize reporting and writing with abstract themes appearing on the top rung and concrete steps on the bottom.

accretion
Submitting succeeding portions of a story to an editor as they are written.

active listening
A communication technique that requires the interviewer to respond to a speaker in ways that show they are listening through eye contact, nodding and other body language that indicates interest.

active voice
A grammatical choice that uses the subject-verb-object structure ("The city council passed an ordinance . . .") to make sentences more direct, less awkward and clear.

actual malice
In libel law, publication of a story that a journalist knew was false, or should have known it was false.

actuality
In broadcast news, recorded comments from sources, also known as "sound bites."

ad space
The amount in a newspaper not devoted to editorial content that is allocated for advertising, including classifieds, display advertisements, spots, promotions and preprinted inserts.

adjective
A part of speech that describes a person, place or thing.

advance planning
In broadcast news, finding locations conducive to clear recording vivid imagery and sound, putting subjects at ease, and identifying questions most likely to gather facts for narration and solicit subjective responses.

adverb
A part of speech that modifies verbs, adjectives, clauses and sentences (but not nouns), conveys manner, emotion, or mood and generally ends in "ly."

alternative story forms
News reports broken into small chunks of information and presented in question-and-answer format, graphics, charts and bulleted information, introduced with a small headline or "subhead."

analysis lead
A lead that calls on a journalist's ability to draw conclusions based on reporting, knowledge and confidence to put events, issues and trends in perspective and convey significance.

anchor
A journalist, considered the "face" of the news station, who presents the news, introduces stories and narrates video.

anecdotal lead
A lead with a beginning, middle and end that features characters, dialogue and action.

anonymous sources
Unnamed sources whose identity journalists promise never to reveal.

ANOVA
Stands for analysis of variance. A statistical method to make comparisons that reveal the relationship between variables.

appreciation
An essay that explores the impact of a person's life—and death—often written by someone familiar with the person or the person's work.

article
An organized collection of newsworthy information; should not be confused with stories that convey news and experience to audiences.

assertiveness
Confident behavior that reflects a belief in oneself and the responsibility of journalists to ask questions, request information and approach someone for an interview.

attribute
To identify the source of information.

audience
The core group of readers, listeners or viewers for whom news and information is reported, reflecting their needs and interests.

audience analyst
In online news, employees that monitor site traffic and user habits to maximize advertising and marketing efforts.

audio slideshow
Photo galleries accompanied by narration, natural sound and recorded comments from sources.

average
A way to summarize a set of numbers with a single number.

BBI
Shorthand for "boring but important" information, such as historical background, expert testimony and statistics that make up the fourth box in the "five boxes" story form and bolster the nut graf.

beat
An assignment to monitor news in places, such as a city, town or suburb, or an institution or subject, such as police,

courts, politics, science or education that enable news outlets to stay on top of the news.

bias
A judgment or opinion about a person or group based on a preconception.

blog
Short for Web logs, an online story form that features mostly short entries, appearing in reverse chronological order, featuring informal style and links to online resources.

blurb
In online news, a brief summary that appears below a hyperlinked headline and provides a brief introduction to a compete story.

brainstorming
A technique to conceive many ideas for a story by listing everything that comes to mind without judgment.

breaking news
A current, ongoing and dramatic event, such as a fire, an important vote or a natural disaster. In response, editors dispatch one or more reporters, depending on the story's magnitude.

breaking news blog
A blog, written in reverse chronological order, that usually delivers near real-time news about disasters, major crimes and political events.

bulletin
A brief summary of breaking news.

business manager
Supervises the finances of a news operation.

characters
Fully featured individuals who appear in news stories and narratives.

chief engineer
A broadcast manager in charge of keeping the station on the air and handling other technology issues.

chronological narrative
A narrative that recounts events in chronological order—"tick-tock," in newsroom lingo—using a carefully reported timeline and insider accounts that convey suspense and drama.

chunks
Small blocks of information that are quickly and easily read by users who hopscotch through different Web sites.

citizen journalism
News reported by private individuals as opposed to professional journalists.

civil action
A lawsuit filed to defend a person's civil right or to convince a judge or jury to award monetary damages.

clarify
To make writing clear.

cliché
Overworked phrases, expressions or ideas.

clichés of vision
Stereotypes that rely on hurtful and inaccurate code words or euphemisms.

cliffhanger
A dramatic point that concludes an installment in a serial narrative and that leaves a reader hanging and wanting more.

clips
Examples of news writing.

coaching
An approach to editing based on the idea that the power to recognize a story's problems as well as the means to fix them lies within the person reporting and writing the piece.

code words
A vague word or phrase used instead of an offensive one.

collect
To report information for a news article or story.

colon
A punctuation mark that draws attention to a list, explanation, quotation or additional information.

comma
A punctuation mark that divides parts of sentences and three items in a list.

comma splice
Uses a comma to join two independent clauses when a semicolon or period should be employed to avoid a run-on sentence.

community coverage
Reporting news and information of interest to local communities and neighborhoods.

computer-assisted reporting (CAR)
Using computers to collect and analyze data using spreadsheets, statistical software and mathematics.

conclusions
Judgments based on evidence and critical thinking.

concrete
Writing that draws its strength from words that can be understood with the senses.

conflict
Fighting that pits individuals or groups against each other. In narrative writing, opposition between characters or forces.

conflict-only stories
Journalism that portrays a group only in cases of tension and violence.

conjunction
A part of speech that binds words or groups of words; "but" and "and" are common examples.

consent
Waiver of the right to privacy.

continuous news desk
A team of editors and Web producers that constantly updates a news site.

controller
Supervises the finances of a news operation.

convergence
The sharing of skills, techniques and technology by print, broadcast and online staffs.

copy desk
Trained editors who identify errors before stories are printed or broadcast.

copy editor
An editor who identifies errors and may rewrite stories.

counterphobia
Confronting a feared experience rather than avoiding it.

cover letter
The first item in a job application that introduces the applicant, his or her interest and aptitude for the position.

coverage plan
A detailed approach to covering a news story.

credibility
A news outlet's most important quality: trustworthiness.

criminal action
Prosecution for a criminal offense designed to secure conviction and punishment for a defendant.

critical thinking
Drawing inferences or conclusions from a body of information to make informed news judgments.

criticism
Opinion pieces about the arts, entertainment and popular culture.

cultivating sources
Developing relationships with individuals who contribute news and information.

cultural competence
Understanding the difference between cultures and diverse individuals or groups.

cultural diversity
Recognition of historical and demographic changes that reflect the influx of new and diverse groups into a society.

damages
Money a court awards in a civil action to someone injured because of another person's wrongful action.

dangling modifiers
A word or phrase that connects to a word different from the one the writer apparently meant.

dangling participles
A verb used as an adjective, usually found at the beginning of a sentence, that makes meaning unclear because it appears to modify part of the sentence different than the one it was supposed to modify.

database archives
Computerized collections of information drawn from public records and news organization resources.

database producer
Uses existing content, everything from movie reviews to digitized public records, to create databases that enable users to search for information.

daybook
A journal in which writers can record story ideas, phrases, reading excerpts and other fragments.

decision
A judgment reached by a judge or court after evaluation of the facts and law.

defamation
Publication, broadcast or speech of false statements that injure a person's reputation.

defendant
A person officially accused of a crime or the person against which a civil lawsuit is filed.

dependent clause
A group of words that contains a subject or verb and ends with a comma but is not a sentence.

deposition
The sworn testimony of a witness taken before trial and outside of court.

description
Writing designed to produce a mental picture.

descriptive statistics
Nominal, ordinal and interval measurements.

dialogue
Speech between one or more individuals.

digital audio recorder
A device that records, saves and plays back sound in digital form.

digital literacy
A solid grasp of technology, multimedia and social media and their importance in communicating news, information and experience.

digital resources
Electronic information such as public records, video and audio, programming and social media networks.

direct
Writing that is stripped of irrelevant words and information.

director of content
The top manager of an online news operation, also known as online editor.

director of digital media
The manger of an online news site responsible for all non-news content on the site, including software, content management systems, databases and/or personnel.

director of operations
The online manager directly responsible for hardware and software issues.

diverse communities
Groups of people or places made up of individuals from different ancestries and ethnic groups.

docket
A chronological list of future court proceedings.

document
A public record.

documents state of mind
The assumption that somewhere a record exists.

domain
A sphere of knowledge, skills, rules and language.

draft
The first version of a story.

editorials
Opinion pieces that express the collective view of the publisher and editorial writers who comprise an editorial board.

editor-in-chief
The top news manager who oversees publication of a newspaper and represents the editorial department as a member of the senior management team.

email release
A news release distributed via email.

embedded journalists
Journalists who travel for extended periods with military units.

emblem lead
Uses a single instance or individual to illustrate a larger issue by putting a human face on a social problem or trend.

empathy
The ability to identify with another person's viewpoints and to convey that understanding, "putting yourself in someone else's shoes."

enterprise/investigative projects
Journalism that looks beyond breaking news to heighten audience understanding of people, events and issues; stories that rely on intensive reporting and often computer-assisted reporting to uncover hidden stories of significant public interest.

euphemisms
Generalizations that substitute an inoffensive word or phrase for offensive ones.

evacuees
People displaced by wars, emergencies and natural disasters.

exceptional
An event, issue or person that is out of the ordinary.

executive session
Meeting of a public agency that occurs in private.

exposé
An investigative story or series that reveals startling information the public is not aware of, such as a case of political corruption.

fabrication
Intentionally making up sources, characters, facts or quotes.

false light
In invasion of privacy cases, publishing information about someone that gives a false or negative impression.

feature obit
The basic news report fleshed out with detailed biographical information, including anecdotes, descriptions, quotes, reminiscences.

feature writing
Narrative stories that focus on individuals and their stories.

federal court
Courts of the U.S. government.

feeds
Raw data or brief passages delivered to the reporter writing the main story.

felony
A serious crime that carries a prison sentence of one year or more.

festival and heritage month stories
Diversity reporting limited to ethnic celebrations.

field producer
Coordinates a broadcast story in the field.

findings
In investigative reporting, conclusions reached after intensive reporting.

First Amendment
The First Amendment to the United States Constitution prohibits the making of any law that limits freedom of the press.

first-draft culture
Newswriting that reflects incomplete and unclear writing and leaves little time for crucial editing.

first responders
Police officers, firefighters, paramedics and other rescuers who immediately report to disaster scenes. Journalists may be included in this group.

five boxes
A story form that consists of a lead, a nut graf, a narrative, boring but important information (BBI) and an ending.

flaming
Posting hostile or insulting messages on Web sites, which carries the risk of libel suits.

focus
A theme that guides the journalist through the reporting and writing process and is an essential element of every article or story.

Freedom of Information Act (FOIA)
Federal and state laws that govern access to public meetings and records.

freedom of speech
The constitutionally protected right to express one's opinions and beliefs.

freewriting
Speed, rapid or stream-of-conscious writing.

futures file
A repository of story ideas, news releases and other reminders of coming events, deadlines, and issues.

gallery lead
Assembled anecdotes and examples to demonstrate a trend.

gee whiz stories
Diversity coverage that marvels at the accomplishments of one group or another as if in astonished amazement.

general manager
Responsible for all non-news content on a Web site, including software, content management systems, databases and/or personnel. In broadcast, supervises all station operations and enforces standards.

gold mine source
A willing source with a great memory; court records, a diary, a trunk of letters.

hearing
Meetings of public agencies open to the public.

hourglass
A hybrid story form that combines the news value of the inverted pyramid and the storytelling power of narrative with three parts: a summary lead, or "top"; a transition section, or "turn"; and a narrative that usually unfolds in chronological order.

human interest
Stories that focus on the human condition or appeal to emotions.

idea
The starting point for a news story triggered by an event, persons or issue.

impact
The effect news has on an audience.

importance of reputation
In libel law, the recognition that a person's reputation matters.

incidence
The number or ratio of people in a certain population who are affected by an event, disease or calamity during a certain period of time.

income
Income usually means "net" income, which is revenue minus expenses.

independent clause
A clause, known as a simple sentence that contains a subject and can stand by itself as a statement.

inferential statistics
Measure parallels and correlations between numbers and the real-world conditions that might cause or reflect them.

inflation
An increase in the price of goods and services.

insensitivity
Lacking feeling or sympathy for another person or group.

interjection
A part of speech that reveals emotion and often ends with an exclamation mark or a period.

intern
A student or recent graduate, employed for a limited period of time with or without pay.

international coverage
News about people, events and issues from countries around the globe.

internship
On-the-job training.

interval measurement
Determines by how much things differ from each other, such as time or length.

inverted pyramid
A traditional story form that organizes around facts with the most important information followed by facts ordered by newsworthiness.

jargon
Specialized vocabulary, acronyms, shorthand and code words that professionals and other groups use with each other.

kicker
A resonant quote, image, observation that ends the story and amplifies story's subject and theme.

lead-in
In broadcast writing, a beginning that sums up the story, promises relevant information, provides attribution and concludes by introducing the reporter.

libel
The publication or airing of false statements in writing or pictures that injure a person's reputation by exposing them to ridicule, hatred or contempt in the eyes of the public.

local coverage
Journalism that furnishes audiences with news and information about their community.

locator map
A map that identifies the location of a news scene or describes a news event in detail.

log
In broadcast writing, actualities (quotes) and natsound transcribed verbatim, to create the skeleton of a story.

long-form narratives
Lengthy feature stories, magazine articles written in narrative form.

managing editor
Oversees and coordinates a news outlet's editorial activities working under the editor-in-chief.

manipulation
Electronically altering digital photographs, videos and sound.

mapping
Visual representations of brainstorming.

marketing director
Promotes Web site content through promotions, social media and agreements with other sites.

mashup
A merger of digital information.

mean
The sum of a set of numbers divided by the number of terms in the set, usually the figure that people refer to as "the average."

median
When individual values are put in order by size, the median is equal to the middle value. Also known as the middle number or midpoint.

media sharing network
Connects audiences through social networks and digital communities to share digital information.

microbite
In broadcast writing, a sound bite, or quote, no longer than a few seconds, that completes a sentence or thought.

mindset
The mental habits that govern how journalists respond to challenging situations.

misdemeanor
A crime, less serious than a felony, that carries a maximum penalty of less than one-year imprisonment.

mode
The number that appears most often in a set of numbers.

mojos
Mobile journalists who use digital tools to report from the field.

morbidity
In health statistics, the number or ratio of a disease or all illnesses in a given population.

mortality
In health statistics, the number or ratio of deaths during a certain time in a given population.

motion
A formal request for a decision presented by lawyers to a judge or court.

movie reading
Commentary from a coach that describes reactions to a draft without prescribing action by the writer.

multicultural
A society comprised of many diverse groups.

multiethnic
The presence of diverse ethnic groups.

multimedia
Audio, video, interactivity and other digital content.

multimedia editor
Oversees production of digital packages.

multimedia obit/tribute
An audio and/or video slide show featuring photos of the deceased, family photos and other artifacts, often narrated by a family member or friend.

multimedia producer
Creates and displays original content for Web pages.

multiracial
A society comprised of different racial groups.

narration
In broadcast writing, words spoken by the reporter, anchor or sources whose comments have been prerecorded, often abbreviated VO/SOT, for voiceover/sound on tape.

narrative
A story form with a plot (beginning, middle and end), characters, settings, dialogue, details, a theme, complication, climax and resolution.

narrative arc
A curved line that connects the beginning of the story to the end.

narrative lead
Places central characters in a scene that launches the story with a complication.

national coverage
News about people, events and issues from around the country.

natsound
Environmental sounds recorded by broadcast journalists.

news analyses
Stories that interpret current trends and developments.

news clerk
Usually a beginning journalist performs assorted entry-level tasks.

news director
The top news executive in a broadcast newsroom.

news hole
The portion of a print newspaper not devoted to advertising.

news judgment
A journalist's instinctive ability to know the ideas that make good stories.

news obit
An obituary considered newsworthy because of the prominence of the individual.

news release
A document providing information from a company or other organization interested in getting news coverage.

newscast director
TV news editor who presides over the control room during a live broadcast.

newscast producer
TV journalist who helps assemble raw audio and video into the packages that appear on air.

newsworthy
Possessing characteristics that make for an interesting news story.

nominal measurements
A statistical method that sorts things into categories and expresses them as whole numbers or percentages.

non-negotiable necessities
Facts, details and other information that must be included for a story to be complete and to answer the reader's questions.

not for attribution
Agreement between a reporter and source that information can be used but the source's identity must remain concealed.

note taking
The process of a reporter writing down information for later use in a news story.

noun
A person, place or thing.

nut graf
Can refer to either (a) the second paragraph of an inverted pyramid news story, or (b) a story form that reveals its central information after an anecdotal lead.

obituary
A news report of someone's death, followed by a biographical sketch of the deceased.

observing
Absorbing detailed information at the scene of an event to use later in a news story.

off the record
Agreement between a reporter and source that information cannot be used in a story, even if the source is not identified.

on background
Agreement between a reporter and source that information may be used but not directly quoted.

on the record
Agreement that a reporter can use all information provided by a source and identify that source by name.

online editor
The top editor of the online content team at a news outlet.

online hoax
A fictitious story that spreads far and wide on the Internet.

online presentations editor
Journalist in charge of production of digital packages that blend photos, video, audio and other interactive elements.

online sales manager
Director of advertising for an online media outlet.

open access
Policy allowing citizens unfettered access to government meetings and documents.

open government
Policy allowing citizens the right to follow government action and obtain public records.

open meeting or "sunshine" laws
Statutes requiring public agencies to give notice of all meetings and publish agendas in advance.

ordinal measurements
Measurements that put things in rank orders (first, second, third, etc.).

ordinance
A law, usually created at the local (city or county) level.

organize
Put materials in a sensible order, as with a reporter assembling facts and quotes for a story.

package
TV news term for a story containing audio and video clips and other elements.

paginator
Editor who lays out news pages on a computer and compiles stories, headlines and other elements to create completed pages.

passive voice
Writing in which the subject is acted upon rather than acting.

penetrate
Grab reader's attention in spite of other distractions.

per-capita rate
The rate per person of population.

percent
The rate per 100 of something.

percentage
The rate or amount of a given item in each hundred.

phrase
A group of two or more words.

plagiarism
Taking someone else's words or ideas and passing them off as your own.

plaintiff
A person who files a lawsuit.

podcast
An audio clip posted on a Web site that can be played on demand.

Portable Document Format (PDF)
A computer file format that creates exact electronic copies of documents.

portfolio
A presentation, physical or electronic, of samples of a person's work, used to illustrate his or her capabilities to potential employers.

pre-interview
A broadcast news technique of talking to potential sources before the camera or audio recorder are rolling to identify the best sources, or characters, for the story.

prejudice
Judgments against people based on their race, gender, religion, social class or other traits.

preposition
Word that links nouns, pronouns and phrases to other words in a sentence.

prescription
Telling a writer how to fix a problem with a story.

prevalence
In health reporting, the proportion of persons who have a disease in a given period of time.

privacy
The legal right to be left alone and make personal decisions without interference.

private records
Documentation that people create and keep about their own lives or others'.

process
In journalism, a series of rational steps, actions and decisions that govern and demystify writing.

production manager
In television, usually a supervisor who handles non-news programming and commercials.

project manager
In online news, a supervisor who works with reporters and editors on special projects.

prominence
Being well known to a media audience.

pronoun
General noun that replaces a specific noun ("he" instead of "Tom").

proximity
The degree to which someone or something is physically near or close.

public figure
Someone well known to the general public.

public records
Official information or documents not classified as private.

publication
Communication of information through a mass medium.

publisher
A newspaper or magazine's chief management figure.

racial identifiers
Terms used to classify someone by race.

rate
A ratio, or comparison, of two measurements, usually involving two different units of measure.

reference librarians
Library employees who specialize in finding facts to answer questions.

references
People willing to speak on behalf of an applicant for a job.

regression analysis
Statistical tool that examines the relationship between dependent and independent variables.

relevant
Important to one's day-to-day life.

reporting
Gathering information for a news story.

reporting plan
A reporter's outline of questions that need to be answered in a story and sources that might be useful in answering them.

repurposing
A news outlet using material from its print or broadcast product as the basis for its online product.

research
Studying facts from documents, databases and elsewhere to gather information for a news story.

resolution
An official declaration of the opinion or belief of a government body or institution. In narrative, the outcome of the plot.

résumé
A summary of a job applicant's work history and achievements.

résumé tape
In broadcast news, a video document of a job applicant's best work.

revenue
The money received by a business before expenses are subtracted.

revising
Rewording or reordering a story draft based on reconsideration by the writer or suggestions from an editor.

round-up lead
A story lead that addresses two or more related events.

run-on sentence
A sentence that contains multiple independent clauses and thus runs uncomfortably long.

scene
The area where a news story or action takes place.

search engine optimization (SEO) analyst
Expert at designing Web pages so they draw as much traffic as possible from search engines.

search engines
Web sites that allow users to search for online information by keyword.

segment producer
TV news editor who puts together material for set features within newscasts.

semicolon
A punctuation mark used to join independent clauses rather than separate them into two sentences.

sentence
A grammatical unit composed of a subject and predicate.

SEO
Stands for "search engine optimization," a process for making Web sites draw traffic from search engines.

serial narrative
A storytelling form that breaks stories up into dramatic segments that unfold gradually, usually in installments.

short-short stories
Brief narratives that provide an alternative to inverted pyramid stories.

significant detail lead
A news story lead that uses a detail to tell a larger story about a news event, or introduce tension.

simple sentence
A sentence that contains only a single clause, made up of a subject and predicate.

single-source story
A news story containing material from only one source, thus providing a limited and one-sided point of view of the subject.

slander
Making negative verbal statements about a person.

slideshow
An online arrangement of photos, sometimes containing captions or supporting audio.

social networking site
A Web site that allows people to interact, exchange information and form communities and groups.

sound bite
In broadcast news, a short audio clip taken from a longer interview.

specialty beat
Assignment in which reporters regularly cover an area of specialized interest.

specific
Clearly stated, defined and/or understood.

split page
In TV news, a two-column script format containing both words to be spoken and the graphics, audio and video to run on screen at the same time.

stakeholder
In a news story, a key character with something important at stake.

standard deviation
A mathematical calculation that determines how much numbers vary around the average.

state court
A court with a jurisdiction covering a U.S. state.

status details
In a news story, small elements of an interviewee's behavior, dress, possessions and so on that reveal personal choices and personality traits.

stereotypes
Broad, oversimplified views of different types of people based on race, gender, ethnicity or other factors.

stereotypical stories
News stories that contain stereotypical portrayals of minority groups.

story
A narrative account of news found in a print, broadcast or online media outlet.

stylebook
A reference book containing rules of grammar, spelling, punctuation and other linguistic parameters.

subhead
A secondary headline on a news story, usually appearing near or below the main headline.

subject
The main person or topic discussed in a news story.

subject/verb agreement
In English grammar, this is when the verbs and nouns in a sentence agree in number with each other (singular to singular, plural to plural).

suburb
A residential community outside a city's boundaries.

summary
In online news, a brief introduction to a story.

summary lead
A beginning of a news story that summarizes the story's most important facts.

switchbacks
Surprising reversals of fortune and other plot twists in serial narratives that shock the reader.

tag
In TV news, the end of a story.

tease
In TV news, the beginning of a story that introduces the story and the reporter.

third-person point of view
A story form that presents scenes through the eyes of a particular character.

tick-tock
A news narrative that recounts events in chronological order.

timeline
A news story or illustration that depicts a chronology of events.

tokenism
The practice of assuming a single member of a minority group can represent the entire group.

top
A four-to five-paragraph summary lead that condenses the most newsworthy information in an hourglass story.

traditional story form
One of several common news structures, such as the inverted pyramid, popular for decades.

transcript
A written depiction of what happened in court during a given period.

trend stories
News stories that provide information on popular social developments.

trespassing
Intruding upon people's property or privacy.

trial
Examination of evidence of a crime presented before a judge and/or jury.

truth telling
Honesty and completeness in reporting of news.

t-test
A method of statistical analysis that examines probability distribution.

turn
In an hourglass story, a brief transition paragraph that shifts the narrative from a report to a story.

untold stories
Compelling stories about different communities that often go unnoticed and ignored.

urban legend
An unverified story that is passed around until it is widely known.

verb
Part of speech that shows action or states of being.

verify
To ensure that a piece of information is accurate.

video news release
A video segment created by an organization or individual that is designed to resemble a TV news story.

vital statistics
Data concerning a community's births, deaths, diseases, marriages and other important facts.

voice-over
In TV news, narration behind video footage.

VO/SOT
Stands for voice-over/sound on tape; in TV news, the words spoken by the reporter, anchor or sources whose comments have been prerecorded.

watchdog
A role taken on by reporters in which they seek to expose wrongdoing by government and other institutions.

Web producer
Online news worker who creates and posts multimedia news material.

wiki
Web site where users can add or modify information about a topic.

Wikipedia
The most popular online encyclopedia.

word processing
Using a computer to create, modify or publish written material.

wrap lead
The beginning of a news story that ties together material from multiple related events.

writethrough
A full news story created by assembling successive pieces submitted by a reporter, usually when covering breaking news.

yellow scare
A race-driven panic against Asian Americans that some editors have been accused of trying to create.

zoo stories
News stories that treat members of minority communities with detached condescension, like exotic animals on display.

CREDITS

Chapter 4
Page 77: "Metal to bone" series by Anne Hull. *St. Petersburg Times*, May 3, 1993. Reprinted with permission.
Page 79: "Mom pleads guilty in death," by Michael Kruse. *St. Petersburg Times*, January 14, 2007. Reprinted with permission.
Page 82: Courtesy of *The (Portland) Oregonian*.
Page 85: "Halloween tricks are one thing. But knocking down children to steal their treats may be something else: a felony," by Christine Vendel. *Kansas City Star*, 1995. Reprinted with permission.
Page 86: By Andale Gross. *Kansas City Star*, 1995. Reprinted with permission.
Page 92–7: "A hint of trouble, then tragedy," by Greg Borowski. *The Journal Sentinel*, December 7, 2006. Reprinted with permission.

Chapter 6
Page 124: "Glasses clink for Tiny Tap's owner," by Brady Dennis. *St. Petersburg Times*, March 10, 2004. Reprinted with permission.
Page 129 (top): "For quilt museum proprietor Miss Winnelle, 87, life's not all sewn up yet," by Jeff Klinkenberg. *Tampa Bay Times*, November 27, 2011. Reprinted with permission.
Page 129 (bottom): "Toxic blossoms. Satellite tracking. Anakin Skywalker. Bunnyhuggers. Love sparring. Unlikely friends. Venomous snake room. It's all happening at the zoo," by Thomas French. *St. Petersburg Times*, December 7, 2007. Reprinted with permission.
Page 130: *Biloxi Sun Herald*, August 30, 2005. Reprinted with permission.

Chapter 7
Page 164–7: Excerpts from "Mary Ellen's Will: The Battle for 4949 Swiss," by Lee Hancock. *Dallas Morning News* Special Report, 2006. Reprinted with permission.

Chapter 8
Page 174: *Miami Herald*, November 3, 1995. Reprinted with permission.
Page 175–6: "Virginia's budget: How much will they cut?" by Michael Sluss. *The Roanoke Times*, January 11, 2009. Reprinted with permission.

Chapter 9
Page 213–4: "Kids' arts programs a victim of budget cuts," by Elizabeth Gibson.
The Columbus Dispatch, May 4, 2011. Reprinted with permission.

Chapter 10
Page 225: *McClatchy Newspapers*, May 19, 2012. Reprinted with permission.
Page 226: *The Charlotte Observer*, May 8, 2012. Reprinted with permission.
Page 227: Kathleen Merryman, *The* (Tacoma, WA) *News Tribune*. Reprinted with permission.
Page 228–9: *The Charlotte Observer*, November 10, 2003. Reprinted with permission.
Page 229: *Knight Ridder*. Reprinted with permission.
Page 229: *Arkansas Democrat-Gazette*, December 16, 2003. Reprinted with permission.
Page 229: *The* (Tacoma, WA) *News Tribune*, May 20, 2012. Reprinted with permission.
Page 230 (top): *The Miami Herald*, May 20, 2012. Reprinted with permission.
Page 230 (bottom): *Knight Ridder*. Reprinted with permission.
Page 232: "'Fat Albert' carves out an 891-pound niche," by David Finkel. *St. Petersburg Times*, November 10, 1985. Reprinted with permission.

Chapter 11
Page 245: *McClatchy Newspapers*, May 18, 2012. Reprinted with permission.
Page 259–61: "Hilltop residents share sex-offender concerns with Tacoma council," by Karen Miller and Lewis Kamb. *Tacoma News Tribune*, July 10, 2012. Reprinted with permission.

Chapter 12
Page 269: *The Anniston (Ala.) Star*, August 13, 2008. Reprinted with permission.

Chapter 13
Page 287: "Earch's carbon dioxide levels hit 'troubling milestone' in Arctic." *Anchorage Daily News*, June 1, 2012. Reprinted with permission.

Chapter 14
Page 308–9: "Fourth man accuse din violent mugging of Army sergeant turns himself in," by Marissa Lang, Times Staff Writer. *Tampa Bay Times*, May 30, 2012. Reprinted with permission.

Chapter 17
Page 371: "Celebrating First Engine from Plant, Toyota Chairman, State Delegation Praise Effort to Bring Factory to W.VA,"
by George Hohmann. *Charleston Daily Mail*, December 11, 1998. Reprinted with permission.
Page 390–1: "Police arrest driver in fatal Kellogg crash," by Stan Finger. *The Wichita Eagle*, July 2, 2012. Reprinted with permission.

Chapter 18
Page 419–20: "Judge dismisses conspiracy count against monsignor, priest," by Joseph A. Slobodzian and John P. Martin. *Philadelphia Inquirer*, May 18, 2012. Reprinted with permission.

Chapter 19
Page 440–2: "Plant expert Gil Whitton was 82," by Craig Basse. *St. Petersburg Times*, October 31, 2001. Reprinted with permission.

Chapter 20
Page 455: *The Roanoke* (VA) *Times*, April 16, 2007. Reprinted with permission.

Appendix
Society of Professional Journalists Code of Ethics © Society of Professional Journalists. Reprinted with permission.

Photo and Illustration Credits

Chapter 1
Page 3: Photo courtesy of the Sarasota Herald-Tribune; Page 4: © The Times-Picayune/LANDOV. All rights reserved. Reprinted with permission; Page 6 (left): Artside Economopolous/The Star-Ledger; Page 6 (right): AP Photo/Chris Carlson; Page 13 (left): © 2010 U.S. Latino & Latina World War II Oral History Project/Marc Hamel; Page 13 (center): Photo courtesy of Jan Schaffer; Page 13 (right): Copyright © 2012 The Providence Journal. Reproduced by permission.

Chapter 2:
Page 24: Photo courtesy of The News-Press; Page 39 (left): Photo courtesy of Mark Hamilton; Page 39 (center): Photo by Amanda Punshon; Page 39 (right): Photo courtesy of Kevin McGrath

Chapter 3:
Page 55: © The Milwaukee Business Journal; Page 56: © The Poynter Institute; Page 57: © The Poynter Institute; Page 58: John D. Simmons; Page 61: Drawing © by Gerald Grow, www.longleaf.net; Page 64 (left): © The Poynter Institute; Page 64 (right): © The Poynter Institute

INDEX

Italicized page numbers indicate a photo. Page numbers followed by *f* indicate a figure. Page numbers followed by *t* indicate a table.